ALSO BY JOHN JULIUS NORWICH

Mount Athos (with Reresby Sitwell)

The Normans in the South: 1016–1130
(Published in the United States as *The Other Conquest*)

Sahara

The Kingdom in the Sun: 1130–1194

Christmas Crackers

A History of Venice

A TASTE FOR TRAVEL

A TASTE FOR TRAVEL

an anthology

JOHN JULIUS NORWICH

Alfred A. Knopf NEW YORK *1987*

To Costa
who taught me to travel

THIS IS A BORZOI BOOK
PUBLISHED BY ALFRED A. KNOPF, INC.

Compilation copyright © 1985 by John Julius Norwich

All rights reserved under International and Pan-American Copyright
Conventions. Published in the United States by Alfred A. Knopf, Inc.,
New York, and simultaneously in Canada by Random House of Canada
Limited, Toronto. Distributed by Random House, Inc., New York.
Originally published in Great Britain by Macmillan London
Limited, London.

Library of Congress Cataloging-in-Publication Data

A Taste for travel.

Includes index.
1. Voyages and travels.   I. Norwich, John Julius,
[*date*]
G465.T37   1986   910.4   86-46013
ISBN 0-394-55855-3

Manufactured in the United States of America

FIRST AMERICAN EDITION

Contents

Author's Note

I should like to thank all those authors and holders of copyrights who have kindly allowed me to include so many entries in the pages that follow. Without their willing agreement, this anthology would have been immeasurably the poorer. I am also hugely indebted to all those friends who have not only made many valuable suggestions, but have also brought to my attention any number of books which I might never otherwise have found.

But my most heartfelt thanks of all go to Mollie Philipps. From the very beginning of this enterprise she has worked on it with energy and enthusiasm; she has been talent scout, researcher, indefatigable reader, correlator and copyist. She has encouraged me when encouragement was needed, and stabilised me on those occasions when I was in danger of going overboard. She has had too much to do with this book for it to be possible for me to dedicate it to her; all I can do is to record my gratitude and my love.

Acknowledgements

The author and publishers wish to thank the following who have kindly given permission for the use of copyright materials:

Academy Chicago Publishers for extracts from *Flaubert in Egypt* by Francis Steegmuller.

Curtis Brown Ltd, New York, on behalf of the Estate of W. H. Auden for an extract from *Letters from Iceland* by W. H. Auden and Louis MacNeice.

Curtis Brown Group Ltd on behalf of Wilfred Thesiger for extracts from *Arabian Sands* and *Marsh Arabs*.

Jonathan Cape Ltd on behalf of the Estate of Peter Fleming for extracts from *One's Company*.

Collins Publishers for extracts from *A Short Walk in the Hindu Kush* by Eric Newby; from *Italian Journey* by Goethe, translated by W. H. Auden and Elizabeth Mayer; and from *Companion Guide to Umbria* by Maurice Rowden.

Lady Diana Cooper for extracts from *Trumpets from the Steep* and *The Light of Common Day*.

André Deutsch Ltd for extracts from *As I Walked Out One Midsummer Morning* by Laurie Lee.

E. P. Dutton, division of New American Library, for an extract from *Bitter Lemons* by Lawrence George Durrell, renewed 1985 by Lawrence George Durrell.

Eland Books for extracts from *A Dragon Apparent* and *The Changing Sky* by Norman Lewis and from *Travels with Myself and Another* by Martha Gellhorn.

Michael Haag on behalf of the Estate of Vita Sackville-West for an extract from *Twelve Days*.

Harcourt, Brace, Jovanovich, Inc., for extracts from *The Hill of Devi* by E. M. Forster, from *Venice Observed* by Mary McCarthy, and from *The Letters of Oscar Wilde* edited by Rupert Hart-Davis, copyright 1962 by Vyvyan Holland.

Harper & Row Publishers Inc. for extracts from *The Sudden View: A Mexican Journey* by Sybille Bedford; from *My Journey to Lhasa* by A. David-Neel; and from *Collected Letters* by Sylvia Plath.

David Higham Associates Ltd on behalf of Frank Magro, Literary Executor for the Estate of Osbert Sitwell, for extracts from *Animal Friends;* for an extract from *Hindoo Holiday* by J. R. Ackerley; and for an extract from *Africa Dances* by Geoffrey Gorer.

Hodder & Stoughton Ltd for an extract from *The Gobi Desert* by Mildred Cable.

Houghton Mifflin Company for an extract from *The Great Railway Bazaar* by Paul Theroux, copyright 1975 by Paul Theroux.

John Johnson Ltd, on behalf of Peter Levi for extracts from *The Light Garden of the Angel King*.

Augustus M. Kelley, Publishers, for an extract from *Travels in Asia and Africa* by Ibn Battuta.

Alfred A. Knopf Inc. for an extract from *Halfway Round the World* by Gavin Young.

Mrs Peter Levi for extracts from *The Unquiet Grave* by Cyril Connolly.

Little Brown & Company for an extract from *Jerusalem* by Colin Thubron.

John Murray (Publishers) Ltd. for extracts from *A Winter in Arabia 1937-8, The Southern Gates of Arabia, Letters from Syria 1927-8, Ionia 1952, The Coast of Incense, Beyond Euphrates,* and *Alexander's Path* by Freya Stark; *King Edward the Seventh* by Philip Magnus; *The Alleys of Marrakesh* by Peter Mayne; *Two Middle-Aged Ladies in Andalusia* by Penelope Chetwode; *A Pattern of Islands* by Arthur Grimble; *Gatherings from Spain* by Richard Ford; and *Full Tilt* by Dervla Murphy.

New Directions Publishing Corp. for an extract from *The Colossus of Maroussi* by Henry Miller, copyright 1941 by Henry Miller.

Oxford University Press for extracts from *Wanderings in South America* by Charles Waterton, edited by L. Harrison Matthews (1973), and from *Lichtenberg's Visit to England,* translated by Margaret L. Mare and W. H. Quarrell (1938).

Penguin Books Ltd for an extract from *Geoffrey Chaucer: The Canterbury Tales,* translated by Nevill Coghill.

A. D. Peters & Co. Ltd on behalf of the Estate of Hilaire Belloc for extracts from *The Path to Rome,* published by Thomas Nelson & Sons Ltd, and *The Modern Traveller,* published by Gerald Duckworth & Co. Ltd; on behalf of the Estate of Evelyn Waugh for extracts from *Labels, When the Going Was Good* and *Scoop,* published by Gerald Duckworth & Co. Ltd and Eyre Methuen; on behalf of the Estate of Robert Byron for extracts from *The Station, First Russia then Tibet* and *Road to Oxiana;* and on behalf of Rose Macaulay for an extract from *The Fabled Shore,* published by Hamish Hamilton Ltd.

Random House Inc. for an extract from *Into the Heart of Borneo* by Redmond O'Hanlon.

Anthony Sheil Associates Ltd on behalf of Patrick Leigh Fermor for an extract from *The Traveller's Tree.*

Summit Books, a division of Simon & Schuster Inc. for extracts from *In Patagonia* by Bruce Chatwin and from *Old Glory* and *Arabia* by Jonathan Raban.

Jeremy P. Tarcher Inc. for extracts from *Brazilian Adventures* by Peter Fleming.

Viking Penguin Inc. for extracts from *Reflections on a Marine Venus* by Lawrence Durrell; for extracts from *Journey Without Maps* by Graham Greene, copyright 1936 by Graham Greene; and for extracts from *A Time of Gifts* and *Mani* by Patrick Leigh Fermor.

George Weidenfeld & Nicolson Ltd for an extract from *A Hitch or Two in Afghanistan* by Nigel Ryan.

The publishers have made every effort to trace all the copyright-holders, but if they have inadvertently overlooked any, they will be pleased to make the necessary arrangement at the first opportunity.

Introduction

There's no doubt about it: the easier it becomes to travel, the harder it is to be a traveller. Half a century ago, any young Englishman prepared to venture beyond the shores of Western Europe could lay claim to the title; patience, resourcefulness and robustness of digestion were the only qualities he needed. A year or two later he could return, the pride of his family, the envy of his friends: a trail-blazer, a hero. Alas, those days are over. Everybody goes everywhere – or nearly everywhere – buying their air tickets with their credit cards and being met by airport buses, secure in the knowledge that their hotel reservations have been confirmed, that the rent-a-car firm is expecting them, and that it will be perfectly safe to drink the Coca-Cola.

The man who started the rot, I fear, was that disagreeable old abstainer Thomas Cook, who, already by the middle of the century, had developed the idea of insulating his clients as far as possible from the uncouth conditions all too frequently prevailing in foreign parts by swathing them in a protective cocoon of block bookings, meal vouchers and – most dangerous of all – temperance. He began indeed by offering them even more: on the very first excursion that he ever organised, which took place on Monday, 5 July 1841, the 570 people intrepid enough to venture – at the cost of one shilling – the ten miles from Leicester to Loughborough and back enjoyed the services of a full brass band, to say nothing of tea and buns at Mr Paget's Park. The age of the tourist had arrived.

They travelled, of course, by rail – something which still seemed, to most of their contemporaries, foolhardy to the point of madness. It was barely a decade since the opening, in the presence of the Duke of Wellington, of the Liverpool–Manchester Railway, the first ever to be designed primarily for the carriage of passengers – a ceremony which was actually to prove fatal for one of the most distinguished guests: William Huskisson, Member of Parliament for Liverpool. This tragic, if somewhat ludicrous occurrence – Fanny Kemble's splendid account of which will be found in Chapter Six – hardly increased public confidence in the dawning age of steam; and the general mistrust was further intensified by the countless doctors who gave it as their opinion that this new form of locomotion was injurious to the

1

health, since the lungs would be 'praeternaturally inflated' by the constant rush of air, while the heart could hardly be expected to withstand the strain imposed by the unprecedented velocity. They were supported by other spokesmen, more economically minded, who pointed out that by encouraging the working population to go gadding about the country the railways would rapidly bring industrial life in Britain to a standstill. John Ruskin, perhaps predictably, lent the weight of his own immense reputation to the anti-traction faction: 'No change of pace at a hundred miles an hour', he thundered, 'will make us one whit stronger, happier or wiser. The railways are nothing more than a device for making the world smaller.' People who had nothing to say in the first place, he added, would be unlikely to find anything more to say by getting to places more quickly.

When he wanted to be, Ruskin could be one of the wisest men in England; and even when he was at his most unreasonable there was usually a grain of good sense in what he said and wrote. The railways certainly did make the world smaller, even if they achieved a good many other things as well. Despite their efforts, however, that world remained a pretty big place. It is only now, thanks to the advent of cheap and reliable air travel, that it has become a remarkably small one, diminishing a little more with every year that passes.

This is a fact of life, and there is clearly nothing to be done about it. The question, as it seems to me, is whether we would want to do anything about it even if we could; whether, in fact, it is a good thing. And the answer is far from easy. I began this introduction on a note of regret – that much of the old romance of travel has gone, that the whole thing has become too easy, too run-of-the-mill. That regret is deep and genuine; and it is, I believe, shared by the vast majority of the readers of these pages. On the other hand, I – and, I strongly suspect, they – make regular, frequent and grateful use of aeroplanes whenever possible, complaining bitterly if they are late; and I cannot honestly pretend that I would, in my heart, have the situation any different than it is. (Apart, perhaps, from wishing that the tickets were cheaper.)

We are, in short, trying to have it both ways. We too should love to look on travel as an adventure, just as our grandfathers did. We long for the sinister thrill of the Orient Express, rattling through the Balkans with its inevitable complement of international jewel thieves, slinky Russian countesses and Sir Basil Zaharoff; for the glamour of the *Mauretania*, inching its way out of Southampton Water, with the champagne and the streamers and the *Bon Voyage* telegrams and the band playing on the quay; for the Maughamesque romance of the brave old Pacific schooner, laden with jute and copra, murmuring through the tropic seas on its way to Sumatra, its escort of flying fish playing around the bows. We dream, too, of the excitements that await us after landfall: the sleazy night-clubs of the Kasbah, the

2

yak-skin yurts of the Turkoman tribesmen, the rifle-shots echoing across the Khyber Pass.

On the other hand, we are fully aware that these excitements were never without their disadvantages. The Orient Express must have had distinctly unromantic queues forming up at the ends of the corridors after breakfast; the *Mauretania* passengers doubtless felt somewhat less jaunty the following morning, when they experienced the combined effects of an appalling hangover and a heavy Atlantic swell; while the schooner, if it were to be in any way worthy of its legend, almost certainly had an alcoholic Dutch skipper being copiously sick all over the bridge, and no refrigerator. The Kasbah night-club might well have possessed the latter, but an ice-cube virtually guaranteed dysentery before dawn; the yurts smelt almost as appalling as their inhabitants, whose personal habits were unpleasant and whose conversation stilted; as for the Khyber, it was cold, windy and, more often than not, extremely dangerous – the sooner one carried on up it the better. Besides, as we well know, without dear old British Airways these places would have taken us weeks, if not months, to reach. In all probability, indeed, we should never have got to them at all.

Perhaps, on reflection, we are better off as we are.

The overwhelming majority of the contributors to this volume had no choice in the matter. For them, tourism did not exist: you were a traveller or you were a stay-at-home, and that was that. As to the remainder, they were – or, in some cases, are – travellers because that is what they were determined to be from the start, and they have taught us a vitally important lesson: that we can all still be travellers rather than tourists if we set our minds to it. Moreover, the difference today lies less in the places we go to than in the way in which we go to them: it is perfectly possible to be a traveller in France – or even in England, for that matter – just as it is to be a tourist on the Upper Amazon.

None the less, there are – and always have been – travellers and travellers; and in the summer of 1967, when I was marooned for a somewhat desperate fortnight in Khartoum – which had just been effectively cut off from the outside world by the Arab–Israeli war – and writing the introduction to a book I had just completed about the Sahara, I tried to draw what seemed to me the most important distinction between them:

The world of travel literature divides itself neatly into two regions, the valleys and the heights. On the heights live the nobility – the Burtons and the Doughtys, the Starks and the Thesigers and the Leigh Fermors, those who know and love and respond almost psychically to the lands of which they write, but whose fluency in the languages of their adoption has not dimmed the brilliance with which they wield their own. They are the chosen few, secure in their station. They at least will never lack elbow room.

The valleys, as a residential area, are a good deal less select. They are also growing uncomfortably crowded, for they must accommodate all those who write their travel books, as it were, from the outside, deliberately and unashamedly without specialised knowledge – the innocents abroad.

But they also boast their aristocracy. Kinglake and Mark Twain, Evelyn Waugh and Peter Fleming – to mention only the first names that come into my head – have shown us just how satisfying outsiders' travel books can be; more light-hearted perhaps, more subjective almost certainly, but none the less works of art whose authors have been able to turn their very lack of local expertise to advantage. They have shown too that in travel-writing, more than in any other field of literature, first impressions can be of interest and occasionally of value.

Both kinds of travel writer, then, can be well worth reading; and both will be found plentifully represented in the pages that follow. But they can be classified in other ways too: ways less fundamental, perhaps, but even more revealing of their motivations – not only of why they wrote the way they did, but of why they travelled at all.

Nowadays, I suppose – despite the increasing numbers of grey-faced business men hurtling round the world to company meetings and sales conferences – most of us travel for pleasure; but it was not always so. Up to the end of the Middle Ages, people tended to leave their homes for a very different reason: to save their immortal souls. In the days when every man and woman lived in constant terror of hell-fire, no effort was too great, no earthly risk too formidable, to win salvation; and the surest way of doing so was to set off to some distant shrine as a pilgrim. In this country we are fortunate enough to have one account of a pilgrimage that ranks among the most towering works in all our literature: *The Canterbury Tales*. True, most of Chaucer's company had a relatively short distance to travel; but this should not blind us to the fact that when they reached the tomb of the holy blissful martyr they would be certain to find a throng of fellow-pilgrims from all over Europe. Until the Reformation, Canterbury was one of the chief religious centres of the entire Continent – not quite as important as Rome, admittedly, or as Santiago de Compostela, but certainly on a level with the shrine of the Magi at Cologne or that of the Archangel Michael on Monte Gargano.

The Wife of Bath, incidentally, had not only visited all these places, except possibly the last; she had also been no less than three times to Jerusalem. Moreover – significantly – she was neither noble nor rich; travel in those days was not the prerogative of the upper classes, as it became in later centuries. Having outlived five husbands – 'apart from other company in youth' – and being, Chaucer tells us, a magnificent weaver of cloth, she may have amassed a comfortable nest-egg to help her on her way; but it was by no means rare to find peasants, even serfs, on the pilgrim roads. Living, as most of them did, in windowless hovels at near-starvation level, they had after all little to keep them at home except their feudal obligations, and these were often easy enough to escape. Once they had set out, they would be in no hurry to return – two or three years spent on the journey in each direction was not uncommon – while for food and (more often than not) for lodging they could rely on the great monasteries that lined the route. With company and companionship – for they nearly always travelled in groups – with constant variety, plenty of interest and the certainty of salvation at the end, the pilgrim's calling had a lot to recommend it. No wonder that for many people in those free, uncomplicated days it became virtually a way of life.

Throughout this period, there had always been a few scholars whose travels were undertaken to satisfy a thirst for knowledge. But they were exceptions; in England it was only in the later sixteenth century that travel as such came to be thought of as an essential part of a young gentleman's education. Even then, the new learning of the Renaissance had scarcely begun to penetrate the staunch old intellectual redoubts of Oxford and Cambridge, and Englishmen still felt boorish and unpolished beside their Italian and French counterparts. More and more of them therefore took to sending their sons to foreign universities – above all to those of Bologna and Padua – or to the more sophisticated European courts.

At this time, too, the conduct of affairs between these courts was being revolutionised by an old concept that was rapidly being transformed into a new art: that of diplomacy. Already in Henry VIII's reign a few promising young men had been sent off across the Channel at the King's expense, to familiarise themselves with the languages, laws and customs of countries other than their own; a generation later, in Elizabethan days, the cultivated Englishman was to be found in most of the courts and capitals of Europe, making himself generally agreeable, explaining his Queen's policies to her fellow-princes – and, more likely than not, quietly running a string of secret agents on behalf of the formidable intelligence systems of William Cecil and Sir Francis Walsingham.

Thus the English gradually overcame both their mistrust of foreign countries on the one hand and their feelings of cultural inferiority on the other; and, in doing so, they also discovered the delights of travel for its own sake – delights which they were never again to forget. Once the Wars of Religion were over in 1589, France became by far the most popular European country with Englishmen, but as the seventeenth century continued Italy gradually returned to favour: first the cities of the north, then Florence and Tuscany, and finally Rome – agreeably enlivened, after 1660, by the extravagant carryings-on of Queen Christina of Sweden. Towards the end of the century, Germany too was being revealed as considerably less barbarous than had been generally imagined. By the reign of William and Mary, the wanderings of young Englishmen across Europe in their quest for artistic and intellectual enlightenment – with, in most cases, a good deal of pleasure thrown in – had already acquired a fixed pattern; and for the next hundred years and more that pattern was to remain unchanged, making a deep and ineradicable imprint on cultural life.

What would the upper echelons of English society have been like without the Grand Tour? Every educated man knew his *Odes* and his *Aeneid*, but it was quite another thing to visit Horace's farm or Virgil's tomb, to stroll where Catullus had strolled along the shores of Lake Garda, to cross the Rubicon as Caesar had done or, best of all, to sit amid the ruins in the Roman Forum, thinking elevated thoughts about the transience of greatness. Once returned from the tour, the average Englishman was not only educated – he was cultivated as well. Properly equipped with Palladio's *Four Books of Architecture* – which had been popularised by the grandest of all the Grand Tourists, the great Lord Burlington himself – he was now ready to call in Colen Campbell or William Kent to rebuild his country house in the cool, classical style that had swept away the Baroque of Wren, Hawksmoor and Vanbrugh; or to have his park relandscaped by Capability Brown or Humphry Repton in the style of the Poussins and the Claudes that adorned his walls. Pointing airily to his set of Voltaire, he could tell his friends how he had called on the Sage when passing through Ferney, or how his son had met Goethe while they were both in Rome. The classical columns that he had found and purchased near Lake Trasimene had not yet arrived, but there above the fireplace was his portrait by Pompeo Batoni with the Colosseum in the background. Meanwhile the first four Canalettos were already hanging in the dining room, and Consul Smith in Venice had promised him that the others would not be unreasonably delayed. All these things would be perpetual reminders of what was probably the happiest and almost certainly the most exciting time of his life – a feast of experience for which the loss of his watch to a pickpocket in St Peter's and a mild dose of the pox contracted in Venice was a small price to pay.

Then, suddenly, came the French Revolution, followed almost immediately by the Napoleonic Wars. For a quarter of a century, the greater part of Europe was effectively closed off to the traveller; and when in 1815 the victory of Waterloo finally restored the peace, the world was no longer what it had been before. The old order had changed. Travel had ceased to be the prerogative of the gentry; the roads of the Continent were now thronged with middle-class Englishmen who had made their fortunes in the first wave of the Industrial Revolution and were anxious to show that they too could understand and appreciate all that Europe had to offer. Increased numbers soon resulted in improved facilities: the first cross-Channel steamer was introduced in 1816, a regular service between Dover and Calais was inaugurated in 1821 and five years later there were almost as many crossings as there are today. In France and Germany, Italy and

Switzerland, hotels sprang up like mushrooms along the main routes; the old ferries were replaced by splendid bridges in cast iron; and the road surfaces themselves were improved beyond all recognition – even across the Alps, where regular travellers who remembered the days of mules, pack-sledges and open sedan chairs were astonished to find beautiful new high-ways, their gradients so expertly engineered that they could be negotiated even by a coach-and-four.

Meanwhile, in 1820, another fateful step had been taken when an enter-prising young publisher named John Murray commissioned Mariana Starke, a much-travelled lady with long experience of life on the Continent, to produce a 'handbook'. Such was its success that Murray followed it up with a whole series of detailed guides, covering every European country in turn. By the 1840s 'Murray's Handbooks' were a household name, and no serious traveller would dream of leaving England without one.

There was another difference, too, between this new generation of travellers and its forebears: a passionate appreciation of natural beauty. The eighteenth century, faced with the splendour of the Alps, had averted its languid eye with a polite shudder; as Goethe himself had noted:

When travellers take a delight in climbing mountains, I regard the mania as profane and barbaric. ... These zig-zags and irritating silhouettes and shapeless piles of granite, making the fairest portion of the earth a polar region, cannot be liked by any kindly man.

By the 1780s, thanks largely to the influence of Rousseau, the cult of nature was beginning to spread; what now came to be called 'the pictur-esque' and 'the sublime' were seen to possess a beauty of their own. But it was only with the birth of Romanticism shortly before the end of the cen-tury that the new aesthetic really took hold. Places that no self-respecting early Grand Tourist would have been seen dead in – Chamonix, for example, or the high Apeninnes, or practically anywhere in Switzerland, or the English Lake District – suddenly found themselves inundated with visitors, many of them with sketching-blocks and paint-boxes and wielding a curious kind of mirror called a Claude glass which was thought to enable them to compose their picture more satisfactorily. Throughout the first half of the nineteenth century, most books of Western European travel concen-trate far more on the wonders of nature than on those of art or architecture.

By now, however, people were travelling further afield. In the days of the Grand Tour, only a tiny minority had ventured east of the Adriatic. (Interestingly enough, a number of the most adventurous had been archi-tects, determined to study lesser-known monuments of antiquity – Robert Adam at Spalato, 'Athenian' Stuart and Nicholas Revett in Athens, Robert Wood at Palmyra.) Then, in 1798, Napoleon had launched his great ex-pedition to the East – and suddenly the floodgates had opened. In 1810

Lady Hester Stanhope, Pitt's niece and his erstwhile *maîtresse de maison*, set off for the Levant, where she was to remain until her death twenty-nine years later. In 1812, Burckhardt discovered Petra; and within the next half-century – thanks in a large measure to artists like Edward Lear and David Roberts, RA – Syria and the Lebanon, Palestine and Egypt were furnishing material for whole regiments of travel writers. The age of exploration, too, had arrived. Mungo Park was forging his way through West Africa, Richard Burton – impenetrably disguised – entering Mecca, Charles Waterton studying the flora and (sometimes at alarmingly close hand) the fauna of South America.

And then there was the Empire. India, Burma, Hong Kong, Singapore, even the South Seas witnessed a steady influx of English families, intent on governing, administering and doing business as fast as the P and O and the British India Line could carry them. (Australia and New Zealand had sizeable quotas already.) The world, in short, was open at last. The professional traveller had entered into his own. And so – thanks to Mr Cook – had the professional tourist.

This potted history is, I fear, wildly oversimplified and incomplete. It makes no mention, for example, of the unchanging background against which all these changes of habit and fashion took place: of the merchants, a class of traveller that has existed for as long as travel itself, or of the Christian missionaries, whose record already goes back, for better or for worse, close on 2000 years. It seemed worth attempting, however, for two reasons: to complement the extracts from the earlier writers quoted in the following pages and to provide a setting for the later ones. If an anthology of this kind is to be any fun to read, it must concentrate only on the most interesting and amusing of authors; and the sad but inescapable fact is that such authors are, where the earlier centuries are concerned, in lamentably short supply. Chaucer is, of course, in a class by himself; but after him there is a long gap, and it is only at the end of the sixteenth century, with the meticulous observations of Fynes Moryson and the glorious dottiness of Coryat, that true travel writing in English begins to get off the ground. Even then, progress is slow – though an exciting new discovery for me has been William Lithgow, who (as the passages I have quoted will surely testify) deserves to be far better known than he is. For the rest, if the reader finds that these early centuries are inadequately represented, I can but agree with him – defending myself only on the grounds that in making these selections I have always put readability first, and all other considerations a good way behind.

All the same, the selection has been far from easy. There has been the problem of getting a good geographical spread across the world; you have only to browse for an hour or two in the 'Travel and Topography' section of the London Library to discover, not only that 90 per cent of travel writing is quite paralysingly tedious, but also that countless more really readable books have been written about – for example – the Middle East than about South America. Another worry has been the authors themselves: should as many different names as possible be included, or can a first-class writer be quoted again and again? I agonised a lot about that one, but finally decided on the latter. After all, an anthology is no good unless it reflects the likes and dislikes of the compiler, and if I allow no author more than one or two items, how will the reader ever know who my favourites are, let alone why? As it is, I believe that few readers, laying down this book, will find themselves in any doubt: and confronted with writers of the calibre of Freya Stark, Peter Fleming, Robert Byron and Patrick Leigh Fermor I cannot think that many of them will want to disagree.

The hardest problem of all, however, has been the problem of shape. How *does* one impose any sort of order on several hundred items of such widely differing style and subject matter? The idea of a chronological approach was quickly discarded, for the reasons I have suggested above; so too was that of arranging the extracts on a geographical basis, which would have been a sure-fire recipe for monotony. I finally decided to group them by subject, trusting that so long as the respective headings were vague enough there would be plenty of scope for variety under each. This has inevitably made for a good deal of arbitrary placing, but no matter: such extracts as could legitimately have been allotted to any one of a number of different chapters I have simply dropped in wherever they seemed most comfortable.

In other respects also I am conscious of having adopted a rather cavalier attitude. When I started off, I decided that all fiction should be excluded: travel writing, it seemed to me, should be about journeys that actually happened, not about ones that were made up. I soon discovered, however, that things were not as easy as that. Some fiction – the Prologue to *The Canterbury Tales* for example, or Conrad's superb account of the homecoming of the *Narcissus* that virtually closes the book – is so close to truth as to be not easily distinguishable from it; and had I stuck too rigorously to my self-imposed rule the anthology would, I believe, have suffered. The result is that while extracts from novels and other forms of fiction (like *The Odyssey*) will not very often be come upon in these pages, they have not been eliminated altogether.

The same goes for translations. The range of travel writing in the English language alone is quite big enough as it is, without widening it still further; and translations in any case always lose something of the original. If, on the other hand, one comes upon a really good piece from a foreign source – such as the description of that positive orgy of emotion displayed by the Flaubert family at Gustave's departure on what was, after all, quite a short holiday – why be so doctrinaire as to exclude it? Rules, especially self-made ones, exist to be broken.

I have travelled, in one way or another, all my life. I have loved every moment of it, and fully intend to go on until I drop. There are all too many parts of the world that I have never seen; and although with increasing age I am bound to become less and less of a traveller and more and more of a tourist, I am determined to get to them somehow. But travel, as we all know, is not just a matter of sightseeing, of playing a vast, global game of Happy Families until every country, natural wonder and ancient monument can be ticked off on the list; it carries its own excitement, and its own satisfaction. I have never left this country, by ship, car, train, or even by aeroplane, without experiencing that same thrill of expectancy that I felt when I first crossed the Channel at the age of six; nor have I ever set foot on foreign soil without being conscious of a moment's quickening of the heartbeat – at the realisation that I was, once again, *abroad*.

'Abroad' – the very word, nowadays, seems to have a slightly old-fashioned ring to it; and yet it is this word, more than any other, with all its connotations and its overtones, that I have had in the back of my mind ever since I began putting these extracts together. When George V spoke of 'bloody abroad', he was not entirely wrong; quite a lot of abroad *is* bloody in one way or another, and there is no doubt that a good many of the contributors to the following pages found it so. But that is not the point. For the true traveller, the object of a journey is not pleasure, or comfort, or warmth, or sunshine. He is really travelling – even if he might not quite put it that way himself – in search of excitement, and challenge, and the endless fascination of the unknown; and although I have tried to cater for all tastes and to cast my net as widely as I can, it is of these qualities, above all, that this book is a celebration.

John Julius Norwich
London, April 1985

CHAPTER ONE

Advice to Travellers

Everybody loves giving advice; and it is only sensible for those who are embarking for the first time on a journey to make a few enquiries in advance. These two facts alone are enough to explain the perennial popularity of the guide book, which in one form or another has been in existence almost as long as travel itself. They also account for a good many travel books, most of which – at least nowadays – are written in the assumption that the reader will in all probability be following in the author's footsteps sooner or later. This opening chapter attempts to give a cross-section of all the varied forms of advice that may be given to those about to depart, whether they are determined to travel adventurously for travel's sake or whether they are contemplating nothing more ambitious than a brief holiday on the Continent.

The earliest piece of serious advice that I know was given by Sir Francis Bacon. In his essay 'Of Travel' he writes:

If you will have a young man put his travel into a little room, and in short to gather much, this you must do. First, as was said, he must have some entrance into the language before he goeth. Then he must have such a servant or tutor as knoweth the country, as was likewise said. Let him carry with him also some card or book describing the country where he travelleth; which will be a good key to his inquiry. Let him keep also a diary. Let him not stay long in one city or town; more or less as the place deserveth, but not long; nay, when he stayeth in one city or town, let him change his lodging from one end and part of the town to another; which is a great adamant of acquaintance. Let him sequester himself from the company of his countrymen, and diet in such places where there is good company of the nation where he travelleth. Let him upon his removes from one place to another, procure recommendation to some person of quality residing in the place whither he removeth; that he may use his favour in those things he desireth to see or know. Thus he may abridge his travel with much profit. As for the acquaintance which is to be sought in travel; that which is most of all profitable, is acquaintance with the secretaries and employed men of ambassadors: for so in travelling in one country he shall suck the experience of many. Let him also see and visit eminent persons of all kinds, which are of great name abroad; that he may be able to tell how the life agreeth with the fame. . . . When a traveller returneth home, let him not leave the countries where he hath travelled altogether behind him; but maintain a correspondence by letters with those of his acquaintance which are of most worth. And let his travel appear rather in his discourse than in his apparel or gesture; and in his discourse let him be rather advised in his answers, than forward to tell stories; and let it appear that he doth not change his country manners for those of foreign parts; but only prick in some flowers of that he hath learned abroad into the customs of his own country.[1]

One of the first questions that the intending traveller must put to himself concerns his luggage. Should he travel heavy or light? In *Slowly Down the Ganges*, Eric Newby – the lightest of travellers himself – quotes a list of what he calls 'suggestive articles' from an Indian publication entitled *A Pilgrim's Travel Guide* – a volume that I should dearly love to possess:

Religious	*Cloths*	*Medicines*	*Utensiles*
Japalma	Rugs, Blanket	Amrutanjan	Canvas bucket
Agarbattis	Muffler	Smelling Salt	Cooker
Camphor	Dhavali or Silk	Vaseline bottle	Oven
Dhup Powder	Dhoti	J & J De Chane's	One set of stainless
Kumkuma	Dhoties 2	Medical Service	steel vessels
Sandalwood	Shirts 4	set with its guide	Ladle
Powder	Baniyans 2	book	Spoons – 3
Wicks soaked in	Uppar clothes 3	Homeopathic Box	Fraid pan
ghee and kundi	Towels 3	& a guide Booh	Tiffin Carrier
Asanam	Waterproff cloth	Diarrhoea Pills	Tumbler
Bhagavad Gita or	(2 yards)	Dysentery Pills	Glass
any religious	Rotten cloth	Indigestion Pills	
book for daily	(pieces 4)	Malaria Pills	
use	Coupeens 2	Boric Powder	
Bhajan Songs or	Cloth bag for	Cotton	
Namavali	money to keep	Cloth (Plaster)	
Sri Ramakoti Book	round waist	Bandage cloth	
	Bedding	Aspro Tablets	
	Mosquito Curtain	Purgative	
		chacklets	
		Tooth powder or	
		paste	

Miscellaneous

Looking Glass and comb	Visiting Cards
Soaps for bath and wash	List of departed souls and their Gotras
Nails of all sizes	Hand bags 2
Locks 2	Note book
Cloth bags for food stuffs	White Papers
Pen knife	Fountain pen and pencil
Small gunny bag for coal	Candles
Wrist Watch	Needles and thread
Umbrella	Railway Guide
Hand stick	Pilgrim's Travel Guide

A small hand axe	Haridwar or Gangottari
Good Camera with flash	Rail and Road Maps
Movie (Cene) Camera	Battery light with spare Batteries
Tongue Cleaner	Thermos Flask
Suit case or hand jip bag	Hurricane Lamp
Lock and chain	Match box
Pandari bag to carry things on shoulder	Calendar both Telugu and English
Safety pins	News Papers
Change for Rs. 10–00	Ink bottles
Setuvu from Rameswaram	Postage stamps and cards[2]
Ganges from Allahabad	

The indomitable Mrs Isabella Bird, visiting Japan in the 1870s, prepared a rather different list:

The preparations were finished yesterday, and my outfit weighed 110 lbs., which, with Ito's weight of 90 lbs., is as much as can be carried by an average Japanese horse. My two painted wicker boxes lined with paper and with waterproof covers are convenient for the two sides of a pack-horse. I have a folding-chair – for in a Japanese house there is nothing but the floor to sit upon, and not even a solid wall to lean against – an air-pillow for *kuruma* travelling, an india-rubber bath, sheets, a blanket, and last, and more important than all else, a canvas stretcher on light poles, which can be put together in two minutes; and being 2½ feet high is supposed to be secure from fleas. The 'Food Question' has been solved by a modified rejection of all advice! I have only brought a small supply of Liebig's extract of meat, 4 lbs. of raisins, some chocolate, both for eating and drinking, and some brandy in case of need. I have my own Mexican saddle and bridle, a reasonable quantity of clothes, including a loose wrapper for wearing in the evenings, some candles, Mr. Brunton's large map of Japan, volumes of the Transactions of the English Asiatic Society, and Mr. Satow's Anglo-Japanese Dictionary. My travelling dress is a short costume of dust-coloured striped tweed, with strong laced boots of unblacked leather, and a Japanese hat, shaped like a large inverted bowl, of light bamboo plait, with a white cotton cover, and a very light frame inside, which fits round the brow and leaves a space of 1½ inches between the hat and the head for the free circulation of air. It only weighs 2½ ounces, and is infinitely to be preferred to a heavy pith helmet, and, light as it is, it protects the head so thoroughly, that, though the sun has been unclouded all day and the mercury at 86°, no other protection has been necessary. My money is in bundles of 50 *yen*, and 50, 20, and 10 *sen* notes, besides which I have some rouleaux of copper coins. I have a bag for my passport, which hangs to my waist. All my luggage, with the exception of my saddle, which I use for a footstool, goes into one *kuruma*, and Ito, who is limited to 12 lbs., takes his along with him.[3]

The striped tweed, one would have thought, might have been a bit much when the mercury was at 86°; for Freya Stark, however, the material of one's skirt is less important than its shape:

I wear ordinary woman's dress and find that modesty as to long sleeves, high neck, or skirt are all commented on and appreciated by the ladies among whom I stay.

13

The skirt should be pleated almost like a kilt for convenience in sitting on the floor. It is important to be able to cover up ones feet when sitting cross-legged, as it is insulting to exhibit the sole of the foot and very fatiguing not to do so. A wrap kept near at hand to throw over one's legs is very useful.[4]

Miss Stark, it need hardly be said, has done most of her travelling in hot countries. For those visiting Russia on the other hand, *Murray's Handbook for Northern Europe* of 1849 has some very different advice:

Should, therefore, a traveller visit Russia in the winter, it is evident that he must have a *schooba* (a fur pelisse); and if his route lies through Germany he will make a good speculation by purchasing one at Leipsic, or some other great town on his road – a *schoppen* in Germany will cost only half as much as it will in Russia. A handsome fur pelisse of the yenott or racoon may be purchased at Leipsic for 12*l*. The price of one, even in England, would be much less than in Russia, though perhaps somewhat dearer than in Germany. A seal-skin travelling cap is also essential, the ears not being protected by a hat; and this should be procured at the same time as the schooba. Carpet bags are the most convenient things in which baggage can be conveyed when it is necessary to travel on horseback, the only mode of locomotion in the Crimea: two strapped together by the handles can be thrown across the back of the animal on which the guide will be mounted. An English saddle is also highly desirable, and will save a large portion of cuticle which must inevitably be lost by the use of a Tartar one; the fatigue, too, will be immeasurably less. A schooba will also be indispensable even in the south in winter, and a brown Holland blouse and a straw hat in the summer, for the dust and heat are excessive; there is no climate so parched and dry in Europe as Odessa. A bottle of pure cognac will be found useful everywhere. To those who intend to remain any time in Russia, and mix in Russian society, it will be absolutely necessary that they should bring letters of introduction, speak French fluently, and be able to foot it on the light fantastic; accomplishments highly prized, and likely to be constantly in requisition.

Letters of introduction to persons high in office or rank will indeed be found not only useful but almost absolutely indispensable; many difficulties, otherwise insuperable, will be smoothed away by them, and we strongly recommend the traveller who intends to visit Russia to turn his attention to this point before he leaves England. A long purse, well lined, is also desirable, for considerable expense, not to say extravagance, is unavoidable at St. Petersburgh, particularly if the visitor should desire to take any part in the gaieties and amusements which are unceasing during the winter months; the cost will be half as much again what it would be in Vienna or Rome, and, with good management, the expense *per diem*, with a sledge, will be about twenty-two shillings, not including wine, theatres, and a private servant. Then as to the day of the month, it will be well to remember that the Russians have not yet altered their style, and that they are twelve days behind the rest of Europe, so that if the traveller arrives in Russia on the 1st of June, he will there find it only the 20th of May; it may also be useful to him to recollect that Reaumur is the favourite thermometer on the Continent, and Fahrenheit in his own country, and that each degree of the former is equivalent to 2¼ degrees of the latter. Also that a Russian invariably takes off his hat whenever he enters beneath a roof, be it palace, cottage, or hovel; the reason for which is that in every apartment of every Russian house there hangs in one corner of it, just below the ceiling, a picture of the Virgin. To omit conforming to this usage, and paying respect to the penates of the dwelling, will not be either wise or well-bred, for it may give offence; a man has no business to travel in foreign countries who cannot make up his mind to conform to their customs.[5]

That long and well-lined purse seems, in Russia, to have been a sufficient safeguard for one's valuables. Elsewhere, however, more drastic precautions were advisable. For Francis Galton, whose *Art of Travel* was an indispensable *vade mecum* in Victorian times, one simply couldn't be too careful:

Secreting Jewels. – Before going to a rich but imperfectly civilised country, travellers sometimes buy jewels and bury them in their flesh. They make a gash, put the jewels in, and allow the flesh to grow over them as it would over a bullet. The operation is more sure to succeed if the jewels are put into a silver tube with rounded ends, for silver does not irritate. If the jewels are buried without the tube, they must have no sharp edges. The best place for burying them is in the left arm, at the spot chosen for vaccination. A traveller who was thus provided would always have a small capital to fall back upon, though robbed of everything he wore.[6]

To sum up on the subject of travelling impedimenta, here is another short piece of distilled wisdom from Freya Stark. In *Baghdad Sketches* she writes:

To awaken quite alone in a strange town is one of the pleasant sensations in the world. You are surrounded by adventure. You have no idea of what is in store for you, but you will, if you are wise and know the art of travel, let yourself go on the stream of the unknown and accept whatever comes in the spirit in which the gods may offer it. For this reason your customary thoughts, all except the rarest of your friends, even most of your luggage – everything, in fact, which belongs to your everyday life, is merely a hindrance. The tourist travels in his own atmosphere like a snail in his shell and stands, as it were, on his own perambulating doorstep to look at the continents of the world. But if you discard all this, and sally forth with a leisurely and blank mind, there is no knowing what may not happen to you.[7]

That greatest of all advisers on travel, Dr Karl Baedeker, is similarly in favour of travelling light, though for rather more charitable reasons:

The enormous weight of the large trunks and boxes used by some travellers causes not only great labour but not infrequently serious and even lifelong injury to the railway and hotel porters who have to handle them. Heavy articles should be placed in the smaller packages, and only the lightest articles in the larger trunks.[8]

But there are other things to think about besides baggage. When Redmond O'Hanlon and James Fenton were about to set off into the wilds of Borneo, they took advice from no less an authority than the major in charge of the Training Wing of the SAS.

'You'll find the high spot of your day,' said the Major, 'is cleaning your teeth. The only bit of you you can keep clean. Don't shave in the jungle, because the slightest nick turns septic at once. And don't take more than one change of clothes, because you must keep your Bergen weight well down below sixty pounds. And don't expect your Iban trackers to carry it for you, either, because they have enough to do transporting their own food. So keep one set of dry kit in a sealed bag in your pack. Get into that each night after you've eaten. Powder yourself all over, too, with zinc talc – don't feel sissy about it – you'll halve the rashes and the rot and the skin fungus. Then sleep. Then get up at five thirty and into your wet kit. It's uncomfortable at first, but don't weaken – ever; if you do, there'll be two sets of wet kit in no time, you'll lose sleep and lose strength and then there'll be a disaster. But take as many dry socks as you can. Stuff them into all the crannies in your pack. And, in the morning, soak the pairs you are going to wear in Autan insect repellent, to keep the leeches out of your boots. Stick it on your arms and round your waist and neck and in your hair, too, while you're about it, but not on your forehead because the sweat carries it into your eyes and it stings. Cover yourself at night, too, against the mosquitoes. Take them seriously, because malaria is a terrible thing and it's easy to get, pills or no.

'Get some jungle boots, good thick trousers and strong shirts. You won't want to nancy about in shorts once the first leech has had a go at you, believe me. Acclimatise slowly. The tropics takes people in different ways. Fit young men may pass out top here and then just collapse in Brunei. You'll think it's the end of the world. You can't breathe. You can't move. And then after two weeks you'll be used to it. And once in the jungle proper you'll never want to come out'.[9]

They also consulted another formidable expert on the subject, the twentieth century's answer to Francis Galton and author of *The Tropical Traveller*, John Hatt.

For a man who had been everywhere Hatt seemed far too young, until I realised, with some misgivings on our own account, that the speed and force with which he both talked and Dunlop-green-flashed about the room in his gym shoes was a genuine expression of his genetic make-up; and that a circumnavigation of the globe once a week at the double would probably pose him no particular problem.

'Let me see,' said Hatt, skydiving towards his sofa and collecting a notebook from a table in mid-flight. 'Oh yes – take *lots* of postcards of the Queen, preferably on horseback, and showing all four legs, because they think she's all of a piece. And for the Headmen, packets of salt and aginomoto, sarongs, waterproof digital watches. For yourselves – Hatt's tips for travellers – those sealable transparent document bags, Tubigrip bandage for every part of your anatomy and, as well as your jungle boots, gym shoes. Because in the longhouses you will have to dance every night. It's simply impossible to refuse. Three or four girls will come and pull you up and then you have to do your thing in front of the assembled tribe – just twenty minutes or so. No problem really. And then you must sing, of course. Why not learn a duet? A duet would be splendid, absolutely splendid. The lives of the primitive farmers are pretty monotonous, after all, and isolated and lonely when they are staying out in their huts on the hill-padi fields, so when they are in the

16

longhouse together they snatch any chance to have a party, and you'll provide a good excuse. You're expected to entertain them in any way you can; and you're also expected to get very drunk indeed. Rice-wine, tuak, is deceptively mild, and rice-brandy, arak, is every bit as lethal as it tastes. There's really no escape. Even where you're flat out on the floor, when the bundles of heads in their rattan nets start to jiggle about and wink at you, you're not off the hook. The girls hold your nose; and when you open your mouth to breathe they tip in another glass or two. Then you'll discover just how arak can supercharge an ordinary nightmare. I used to dream that I'd wake up with a palang.'

'A palang?' we asked, uneasily.

'Oh, it's quite a simple little operation, really,' said Hatt, 'although sepsis is always a problem. They clamp the penis in an instrument that looks like a small bow; and then drive a six-inch nail through it, just beneath the glans.'

'Hang on,' said Fenton.

'No – it's perfectly true,' said Hatt, darting at his bookshelves like a kingfisher into the water. 'I can even give you a reference. Here we are. How's that? The *Sarawak Museum Journal* volume VII, December 1956. It's a by-the-way in an article by Tom Harrisson on the Borneo rhinoceros:

'One of the exhibits that excites the most interest in our museum is that of the *palang*. This is the tube or rod of bamboo, bone, hardwood, etc. with which the end of the penis is pierced among many inland people, principally the Indonesian Kenyahs, but also many others – and lately even spreading to the Kelabits in the uplands. In each end of this centre-piece may be attached knobs, points or even blades of suitable material. Some men have two *palang*, at right angles through the penis tip.

'The function of this device is, superficially, to add to the sexual pleasure of the women by stimulating and extending the inner walls of the vagina. It is, in this, in my experience decidedly successful.

'We also have a "natural" *palang*, exhibited alongside. This is the penis of a Borneo rhinoceros. In the natural state this powerful piece of the anatomy has, about four inches behind the tip, a similar sort of cross-bar, projecting nearly two inches out on each side. When tense, this becomes a fairly rigid bar, much like the human *palang* in general implication. The one we have on show in the Museum has had a hardwood rod fixed in it (to keep it rigid). As such, these things were included among the *esoterica* of inland longhouses, along with sacred stones, beads, strange teeth and other charms used mainly in connection with human head and fertility ceremonies.

'Many who have handled this pachyderm device have been unable to credit that it is "genuine". However, in the untouched state it can be even more impressive. The penis of another male (with not full-size horn) in our possession measures over a foot and a half (relaxed), has a longer tip and cross-piece than the Museum's displayed one . . .

'Well,' said Hatt, helpfully, 'if Harrisson can have it done, I don't see why you shouldn't. And I'd be grateful if you could test two other little ideas of mine: could one of you take massive doses of vitamin B1 (thiamine) at about three o'clock every afternoon? And then let me know if it keeps off the mosquitoes?'

'Do we make a comparative count of bites? Or will the first to get malaria decide the issue?'

'Yes, yes – either will do. And could you get your chemist to make this up? It's a possible new repellent.'

Hatt handed Fenton a page of notebook on which was inscribed:

2 – EPHYL – 1 – 3 – HEXANDIOL 846.gr/1
and N,N – DIETHYL – M – TOLUMIDE 95/gr/1

'But Hatt,' said Fenton, 'how do we know that this isn't dynamite?'[10]

Borneo – which I have, alas, never visited – is obviously in a class by itself where tough travelling is concerned; but, even nearer home, journeys can be quite demanding enough. Dr Baedeker had the following advice for those who wished to go walking in Switzerland in 1899:

General Hints. The traveller's ambition often exceeds his powers of endurance, and if his strength be once overtaxed he will sometimes be incapacitated altogether for several days. At the outset, therefore, the walker's performances should be moderate; and even when he is in good training, they should rarely exceed 10 hrs. a day. When a mountain has to be breasted, the pedestrian should avoid 'spurts', and pursue the 'even tenor of his way' at a steady and moderate pace (*'chi va piano va sano; chi va sano va lontano'*). As another golden maxim for his guidance, the traveller should remember that – 'When fatigue begins, enjoyment ceases'. . . .

The traveller is cautioned against sleeping in chalets, unless absolutely necessary. Whatever poetry there may be theoretically in 'a fragrant bed of hay', the cold night-air piercing abundant apertures, the ringing of the cow-bells, the grunting of the pigs, and the undiscarded garments, hardly conduce to refreshing slumber. As a rule, therefore, the night previous to a mountain-expedition should be spent either at an inn or at one of the club-huts which the Swiss, German, and Italian Alpine Clubs have recently erected for the convenience of travellers. . . .

Over all the movements of the pedestrian the weather holds despotic sway. The barometer and weather-wise natives should be consulted when an opportunity offers. The blowing down of the wind from the mountains into the valleys in the evening, the melting away of the clouds, the fall of fresh snow on the mountains, and the ascent of the cattle to the higher parts of their pasture are all signs of fine weather. On the other hand it is a bad sign if the distant mountains are dark blue in colour and very distinct in outline, if the wind blows up the mountains, and if the dust rises in eddies on the roads. West winds also usually bring rain.[11]

Dear Dr Baedeker: he follows his section on walking with one on *cycling* in Switzerland – surely the least suitable country in Europe for that particular pastime. And yet, on the whole, nobody ever gave more or better straight, down-to-earth commonsense advice than he did. When I was living in Beirut in the late 1950s his *Palestine and Syria* of 1906 was seldom out of my hand. The topographical information was as good then as when it was first written, and even if some of the introductory advice did seem a little outdated, it was always well worth reading:

Dress. – The best covering for the head is an ordinary soft felt hat, a cloth cap with a visor, or a pith helmet. In the hottest weather a 'puggery' may be added, i.e. an ample piece of strong white or grey muslin, the ends of which hang down in broad folds at the back as a protection against sunstroke. Some travellers prefer a silk *keffiyeh* [the usual Arab headcloth], which may be tied under or over the hat, falling down behind in a triangular shape. This protects the cheeks and neck admirably. The red fez (Ar. *tarbush*) should be avoided, the hat being nowadays the recognized symbol of the superior dignity of the European.[12]

He is good on money too:

English and French gold (as also Russian) passes everywhere; German gold can be changed without loss only at some German houses. Foreign silver is prohibited all over Turkey [Syria and the Lebanon at this time still formed part of the Ottoman Empire] but francs and shillings are taken at the seaports, and in Jerusalem and Damascus; marks are generally refused. Egyptian money is refused everywhere.[13]

There is a particularly rewarding section entitled 'Intercourse with Orientals'. It begins:

Most Orientals regard the European traveller as a Crœsus, and sometimes as a madman, – so unintelligible to them are the objects and pleasures of travelling. They therefore demand bakhshîsh almost as a right from those who seem so much better supplied with this world's goods. He who gives is a good man (*rijâl taiyib*). In every village the traveller is assailed with crowds of ragged, half-naked children, shouting '*bakhshîsh, bakhshîsh, yâ khawâja!*' The best reply is to complete the rhyme with, '*mâ fish, mâ fish*' (there is nothing). A beggar may be silenced with the words '*Allâh ya'tîk*' (may God give thee!). The custom of scattering small coins for the sake of the amusement furnished by the consequent scramble is an insult to poverty that no right-minded traveller will offer.[14]

Later there comes an equally splendid passage:

Familiarity should always be avoided. True friendship is rare in the East, and disinterestedness hardly exists. . . . Beneath the interminable protestations of friendship with which the traveller is overwhelmed lurks in most cases the demon of cupidity. It is best to pay for every service or civility on the spot, and as far as possible to fix the price of every article beforehand. It will, however, be impossible to avoid extortions or over-charges altogether, and it is better to reconcile oneself to this than to poison one's enjoyment by too much suspicion. Those who understand how to treat the natives will often be struck by their dignity, self-respect, and gracefulness of manner. The stranger should therefore be careful to preserve an equally high standard in his own demeanour, and should do all in his power to sustain the well-established reputation of the '*kilmeh frenjîyeh*', the 'word of a Frank'.[15]

He must, however, be prepared to get tough at times. As early as 1878, Dr Baedeker was warning travellers to Egypt of the sort of behaviour that they might encounter:

The traveller, apart from his ignorance of the language, will find it exceedingly difficult to deal with the class of people with whom he chiefly comes in contact. . . . Even when an express bargain has been made, and more than the stipulated sum paid, they are almost sure to pester the traveller in the way indicated. . . . and if the attacks which ensue are not silenced by an air of calm indifference, the traveller may use the word *râḥ* or *imshi* in an imperative tone, or vigorously brandish his stick at his assailants. Gestures of the latter kind are intelligible everywhere, and when they have produced the desired result the traveller will be inclined to say with the Arabs themselves – 'The stick came from heaven, a blessing from God!' The Egyptians, it must be remembered, occupy a much lower grade in the scale of civilisation than most of the western nations, and cupidity is one of their chief failings; but if the traveller makes due allowance for their shortcomings, and treats the natives with consistent firmness, he will find that they are by no means destitute of fidelity, honesty, and kindliness.[16]

Then there was the problem of language. Arabic was well known to be far beyond the powers of the average European – a fact which was borne out (if such confirmation were necessary) by the publication of J. G. Hava's *Arabic–English Dictionary*, which appeared in Beirut as recently as 1964. Here are just two of the entries:

Jawn: Black. White. Light red. Day. Intensely black (horse).

Khàl: Huge mountain. Big camel. Banner of a prince. Shroud. Fancy. Black stallion. Owner of a th. Self-magnified. Caliphate. Lonely place. Opinion. Suspicion. Bachelor. Good manager. Horse's bit. Liberal man. Weak-bodied, weak-hearted man. Free from suspicion. Imaginative man.[17]

Unfortunately, the more approachable languages of Europe seemed to cause most Englishmen almost as much trouble; and there has long existed a virtually inexhaustible demand for phrase-books of the sort that Noël Coward had in mind when he wrote:

> When the tower of Babel fell
> It caused a lot of unnecessary Hell.
> Personal *rapport*
> Became a complicated bore
> And a lot more difficult than it had been before,
> When the tower of Babel fell.
>
> The Chinks and the Japs
> And the Finns and Lapps
> Were reduced to a helpless stammer,
> And the ancient Greeks
> Took at least six weeks
> To learn their Latin grammar.
> The guttural wheeze

Of the Portuguese
Filled the brains of the Danes
With horror,
And verbs, not lust,
Caused the final bust
In Sodom and Gomorrah.

If it hadn't been for that
Bloody building falling flat
I would not have had to learn Italiano
And keep muttering 'Si, si'
And 'Mi Chiamano Mimi'
Like an ageing Metropolitan soprano!

I should not have had to look
At that ghastly little book
Till my brain becomes as soft as mayonnaise is,
Messrs Hugo and Berlitz
Must have torn themselves to bits
Dreaming up so many useless useful phrases.

Refrain 1 Pray tell me the time,
It is six,
It is seven,
It's half past eleven,
It's twenty to two,
I want thirteen stamps,
Does your child have convulsions?
Please bring me some rhubarb,
I need a shampoo,
How much is that hat?
I desire some red stockings,
My mother is married,
These boots are too small,
My Aunt has a cold,
Shall we go to the opera?
This meat is disgusting,
Is this the town hall?

Refrain 2 My cousin is deaf,
Kindly bring me a hatchet,
Pray pass me the pepper,
What pretty cretonne,
What time is the train?
It is late,
It is early,

It's running on schedule,
It's here,
It has gone.
I have taken my niece
To a symphony concert,
Pray fetch me a horse,
I have need of a groom,
I want *seven* tickets,
For *La Traviata*,
Please show me the way
To Napoleon's tomb.

Refrain 3 The weather is cooler,
The weather is hotter,
Pray fasten my corsets,
Please bring me my cloak,
I've lost my umbrella,
I'm in a great hurry,
I'm going,
I'm staying,
D'you mind if I smoke?
This mutton is tough,
There's a mouse in my bedroom,
This egg is delicious,
This soup is too thick,
Please bring me a trout,
What an excellent pudding,
Pray hand me my gloves,
I'm going to be sick![18]

In fact, many of these phrase-books were a good deal more ambitious, giving free rein to their authors' somewhat whimsical fantasy – at the cost, it must be admitted, of a good deal of their usefulness. The following dialogue is taken from the Modern Polyglot *Conversational Italian*, published by G. Alfano of Naples some time between the wars. (I have omitted the parallel Italian translation.)

– Be quick and put on my wrapper and a white napkin, and strap [*sic*] your razors when you have lathered me.

– Ah! you have put the brush into my mouth.

– It was because you spoke when I did not expect it. The young bride's hair was black, thick, coarse, her forehead broad and square. An ordinary hairdresser would not have been able to hide the sternness of her features; but I have given her head a gentle and languishing expression.

– Truly, I am struck with admiration. But, mister artist, with all your talent you have cut me; I am bleeding. You have been shaving against the grain.

– No, sir; I have only taken off a little pimple. With a bit of courtplaster, it will not be seen.

– Doesn't my hair need to be freshened up a little?

– I will cut a little off behind; but I would not touch the tuft on the forehead nor about the ears.

– Why not?

– Because, sir, you would then appear to have too low a forehead and ears too long. Do you wish me to give you a touch of the curling irons, sir?

– It is unnecessary; my hair curls naturally.

– Shall I put on a little oil or pomatum?

– Put on a little scented oil.

– Please look in the glass.

– It will do very well. I see you are an artist worthy to shave and trim your contemporaries.[19]

Sometimes such phrase-book conversations became positively surrealist – as can be seen in *Hossfeld's New Practical Method for Learning the Spanish Language, by Tomas Enrique Gurrin, revised and enlarged by Fernando de Arteaga, Taylorian Teacher of Spanish in the University of Oxford*:

– Did you not decide to communicate with your friends?
– It would have been useless.

– How so? Would they not have sent you money?
– My friends have no more than enough for their own necessities.

– What does the restorer do with the furniture?
– He cleans them [*sic*] and leaves them like new.

– How many minutes do you give me for consideration?
– I grant you two minutes.

– What was full of paper cuttings?
– The mattress.

– What was the mattress full of?
– Paper cuttings.

– What had these unfortunate people reached?
– The depths of misery.

– In what case would his plan have been realised?
– If they had acted as proposed.

– What was this a proof of?
– That, although he planned well, he executed badly.

– How many means were left?
– Two only were left to them.

– What were they?
– Stealing and begging.

– Which did they choose?
– They chose the second.[20]

In 1903 Mr Hossfeld published a companion volume, designed for students of Russian. The extract that follows is a good deal more comprehensible as far as the general thought-pattern goes; but it seems worth including for the majestic *non sequitur* of the third sentence:

– What did Susanna reply?
– Susanna made no reply, but Eleonora Karpovna suddenly approached and said that Susanna liked music very much and played on the piano most beautifully.
– Then Mr Ratch must have married a widow the first time?
– Probably.
– Did F. also play that evening?
– Yes. I have already said that he played excellently on the zither.
– Do you like this instrument?
– Yes; but I have a horror of the piano since my door-porter's daughter has taken to playing on it.
– You are right. The fact is that one does not know where to take rooms to be out of hearing of the piano; it pursues one everywhere.[21]

Before leaving the subject of language, two more short pieces of advice deserve to be quoted. The first comes from *A Guide to the Native Languages of Africa*, by A Gentleman of Experience. Writing in 1890, he points out that:

In the matter of language it is always best to go to a little more trouble and learn the exact equivalent if possible. 'I am an Englishman and require instant attention to the damage done to my solar topee' is far better than any equivocation that may be meant well but will gain little respect.[22]

Four years later, A Gentleman of Quality – obviously one up on the Gentleman of Experience – remarks helpfully that:

'Why is there no marmalade available?' is better understood in the form '*Quelle marmalade non?*'. 'Bring marmalade' may be simply rendered as '*Marmalade demandez*', always remembering that the z is silent as in 'deman*day*'. The little English joke about jam may be easily translated if one wishes to amuse the proprietor: '*Hier, marmalade; demain, marmalade; mais jamais marmalade de jour.*' Such little pleasantries are often appreciated.[23]

A necessity still more vital to the traveller than that of easy communication with the locals was, however, the preservation of his health. Many of my compatriots, according to Noël Coward, took a somewhat cavalier attitude when in the tropics:

ADVICE TO TRAVELLERS

In tropical climes there are certain times of day
When all the citizens retire
To tear their clothes off and perspire.
It's one of those rules that the greatest fools obey,
Because the sun is much too sultry
And one must avoid its ultry-violet ray. . . .

Mad dogs and Englishmen
Go out in the midday sun,
The Japanese don't care to.
The Chinese wouldn't dare to,
Hindoos and Argentines sleep firmly from twelve to one.
But Englishmen detest a siesta.
In the Philippines
There are lovely screens
To protect you from the glare.
In the Malay States
There are hats like plates
Which the Britishers won't wear.
At twelve noon
The natives swoon
And no further work is done.
But mad dogs and Englishmen
Go out in the midday sun.

It's such a surprise for the Eastern eyes to see
That though the English are effete,
They're quite impervious to heat,
When the white man rides every native hides in glee,
Because the simple creatures hope he
Will impale his solar topee on a tree. . . .

Mad dogs and Englishmen
Go out in the midday sun.
The toughest Burmese bandit
Can never understand it.
In Rangoon the heat of noon
Is just what the natives shun.
They put their Scotch or Rye down
And lie down.
In a jungle town
Where the sun beats down
To the rage of man and beast
The English garb
Of the English sahib
Merely gets a bit more creased.

In Bangkok
At twelve o'clock
They foam at the mouth and run,
But mad dogs and Englishmen
Go out in the midday sun.

Mad dogs and Englishmen
Go out in the midday sun.
The smallest Malay rabbit
Deplores this stupid habit.
In Hongkong
They strike a gong
And fire off a noonday gun
To reprimand each inmate
Who's in late.
In the mangrove swamps
Where the python romps
There is peace from twelve till two.
Even caribous
Lie around and snooze,
For there's nothing else to do.
In Bengal
To move at all
Is seldom, if ever done,
But mad dogs and Englishmen
Go out in the midday sun.[24]

Mr Mansfield Parkyns, on the other hand, whose *Life in Abyssinia* was published by John Murray in 1868, was a good deal more circumspect:

I would also recommend another practice, that of never venturing abroad in a low, unhealthy spot till the sun has risen an hour or more. It is customary to hold the sun in great dread. I do not pretend to say whether my constitution in this respect differs from that of other men; but, for my part, I never retired into the shade to avoid the noonday heat; and for four years I never wore any covering to my head except the rather scanty allowance of hair with which nature has supplied me, with the addition occasionally of a little butter. During the whole of that time I never had a headache.[25]

The practice of buttering one's head would surely have been laughed to scorn by Charles Waterton, that most intrepid of Victorian naturalists who, on his several journeys through the Amazonian jungles, thought nothing of bleeding himself whenever he felt under the weather. As the following passage from his *Wanderings in South America* makes clear, the way of life he recommended was nothing if not Spartan:

Leave behind you your high-seasoned dishes, your wines and your delicacies: carry nothing but what is necessary for your own comfort and the object in view, and depend upon your own skill or that of an Indian for fish and game. A sheet, about twelve feet long, ten wide, painted, and with loop holes on each side, will be of great service; in a few minutes you can suspend it betwixt two trees in the shape of a roof. Under this, in your hammock, you may defy the pelting shower, and sleep heedless of the dews of night. A hat, a shirt, and a light pair of trousers, will be all the raiment you require. Custom will soon teach you to tread lightly and barefoot on the little inequalities of the ground and show you how to pass on, unwounded, amid the mantling briars. ... The youth who incautiously reels into the lobby of Drury Lane, after leaving the table sacred to the god of wine, is exposed to more certain ruin, sickness and decay than he who wanders a whole year in the wilds of Demerara.[26]

Many a nineteenth-century traveller, however, felt really safe only when he could tap his pocket and feel the reassuring shape of the bottle containing that sovereign panacea, Dr J. Collis Browne's Chlorodyne. This superb preparation continued to settle British stomachs with almost unfailing success until quite recent years, when it fell victim to new drug-control legislation; and the leaflet enclosed with every bottle was a treat in itself. Among its testimonials were the following:

From W. VESALIUS PETTIGREW, MD, Hon.FRCS, England:
I have no hesitation in stating, after a fair trial of Chlorodyne, that I have never met with any medicine so efficacious as an Anti-Spasmodic and Sedative. I have used it in Diarrhoea, and other diseases, and am most perfectly satisfied with the results.

EDWARD WHYMPER, Esq., the celebrated Mountaineer, writes on February 16th, 1896: –
I always carry Dr J. Collis Browne's Chlorodyne with me on my travels, and have used it effectively *on others* on Mont Blanc.

From CASSEL'S HISTORY OF THE BOER WAR, page 542: –
'Gaunter and gaunter grew the soldiers of the Queen. Hunger and sickness played havoc with those fine regiments. But somehow the RAMC managed to patch the men up with Chlorodyne and quinine.'[27]

(The italics are my own.) The old travel books are, as one might expect, full of medical advice; as one might also expect, the older the book, the more fanciful are its recommendations. Here is one from William Dampier, whose *New Voyage Round the World* was published in 1697:

Here [off Cape Corrientes, in Central America] I was taken sick of a Fever and Ague that afterwards turned to a Dropsy, which I laboured under a long time after; and many of our Men died of this Distemper, though our Surgeons used their greatest Skill to preserve their Lives. The Dropsy is a general Distemper on this Coast, and the Natives say, that the best Remedy they can find for it, is the Stone or Cod of an Allegator (of which they have four, one near each Leg, within the Flesh) pulverized and drunk in Water: This Receipt we also found mentioned in an

Almanack made at *Mexico*: I would have tried it, but we found no Allegators here, though there are several.[28]

I like Dampier's half-apologetic – though undeniably valid – excuse at the end.

Dampier survived, even without his alligator balls; but there was one disease which, if allowed to run its course, was invariably fatal: starvation. We must return to Francis Galton, for this was clearly a subject to which he had given much thought:

Revolting Food, that may save the Lives of Starving Men. –

Carrion is not noxious to Starving Men. – In reading the accounts of travellers who have suffered severely from want of food, a striking fact is common to all, namely, that, under those circumstances, carrion and garbage of every kind can be eaten without the stomach rejecting it. Life can certainly be maintained on a revolting diet, that would cause a dangerous illness to a man who was not compelled to adopt it by the pangs of hunger. . . .

Skins. – All old hides or skins of any kind that are not tanned are fit and good for food; they improve soup by being mixed with it; or they may be toasted and hammered. Long boiling would make glue or gelatine of them. Many a hungry person has cooked and eaten his sandals or skin clothing.

Bones contain a great deal of nourishment, which is got at by boiling them, pounding their ends between two stones, and sucking them. There is a revolting account in French history, of a besieged garrison of Sancerre, in the time of Charles IX., and again subsequently at Paris, and it may be elsewhere, digging up the graveyards for bones as sustenance. . . .

Flesh from Live Animals. – The truth of Bruce's well-known tale of the Abyssinians and others occasionally slicing out a piece of a live ox for food is sufficiently confirmed. . . .

It is reasonable enough that a small worn-out party should adopt this plan, when they are travelling in a desert where the absence of water makes it impossible to delay, and when they are sinking for want of food. If the ox were killed outright there would be material for one meal only, because a worn-out party would be incapable of carrying a load of flesh. By the Abyssinian plan the wounded beast continues to travel with the party, carrying his carcase that is destined to be turned into butcher's meat for their use at a further stage. Of course the idea is very revolting, for the animal must suffer as much as the average of the tens or hundreds of wounded hares and pheasants that are always left among the bushes after an ordinary English battue. To be sure, the Abyssinian plan should only be adopted to save human life. . . .

Insects. – Most kinds of creeping things are eatable, and are used by the Chinese. Locusts and grasshoppers are not at all bad. To prepare them, pull off the legs and wings and roast them with a little grease in an iron dish, like coffee.[29]

But are we perhaps not concentrating rather too much on the physical aspects of travel? Freya Stark, over a long wandering life, has suffered more than her fair share of sickness in the remoter places of the earth, but she is still able to write the following:

It is, I believe, a fallacy to think of travellers' qualities as physical. If I had to write a decalogue for journeys, eight out of the ten virtues should be moral, and I should put first of all a temper as serene at the end as at the beginning of the day. Then would come the capacity to accept values and to judge by standards other than our own. The rapid judgement of character; and a love of nature which must include human nature also. The power to dissociate oneself from one's own bodily sensations. A knowledge of the local history and language. A leisurely and uncensorious mind. A tolerable constitution and the capacity to eat and sleep at any moment. And lastly, and especially here, a ready quickness in repartee.[30]

And that grandest – if most opaque – of writers on the Middle East, Charles Montagu Doughty, seems to say something of the same kind (though I cannot be altogether sure) in his monumental *Travels in Arabia Deserta*:

Two chiefly are the perils in Arabia, famine and the dreadful-faced harpy of their religion, a third is the rash weapon of every Ishmaelite robber. The traveller must be himself, in men's eyes, a man worthy to live under the bent of God's heaven, and were it without a religion: he is such who has a clean human heart and long-suffering under his bare shirt; it is enough, and though the way be full of harms, he may travel to the ends of the world. Here is a dead land, whence, if he die not, he shall bring home nothing but a perpetual weariness in his bones. The Semites are like to a man sitting in a cloaca to the eyes, and whose brows touch heaven. Of the great antique humanity of the Semitic desert, there is a moment in every adventure, wherein a man may find to make his peace with them, so he know the Arabs. The sour Waháby fanaticism has in these days cruddled the hearts of the nomads, but every Beduin tent is sanctuary in the land of Ishmael (so there be not in it some cursed Jael). If the outlandish person come alone to strange nomad booths, let him approach boldly, and they will receive him. It is much if they heard of thee any good report; and all the Arabs are at the beginning appeased with fair words. The oases villages are more dangerous; Beduin colonies at first, they have corrupted the ancient tradition of the desert; their souls are canker-weed beds of fanaticism. – As for me who write, I pray that nothing be looked for in this book but the seeing of an hungry man and the telling of a most weary man; for the rest the sun made me an Arab, but never warped me to Orientalism.[31]

Let us now consider particular, rather than general, advice to travellers – that advice which relates not to the art of travel itself or to broad areas of the world, but to individual countries and the conditions prevailing therein. There are two principal kinds. The first is official, informing the visitor of the facilities available to him and the formalities that he will be required to undergo on his arrival. This can occasionally prove a source of unexpected pleasure. The best example I know is the official guide to the city of Guadalajara in Mexico, of which I append a few extracts:

WELCOME TO GUADALAJARA

You are now in Guadalajara City, Jalisco State Capital. It is the economic activities focal point, center of the Mexican Republic occidental coast. It is ubicated 1532 meters over sea level and counts with an annual average climate of 22 degrees. . . .

His principal symbol, is his catedral- with its qualities towers and as Pepe Guizar (a mexican musical painter borned here) would say in his famous and popular song called Guadalajara: 'Are his Cathedral towers as backstroke plants'.

Among some attraction places, there is the hospicio cabañas with illustrious mexican artist pictures and frescos. His government palace, where you can still feel history. Over here are murals which are worthy to stop and observe. Its luxurious and traditional Degollado Theater, fun and beautiful expeditions as the Lago-Azul. . . .

There are two important universities considered as some of the Mexico best universities, with almost a countless number of prestigeful schools. . . .

to leave the country

If you have less than 18 years old, you must go with our parents or have a notarized letter permission from your accompanist. If you are traveling alone, you must fill in the Law Article requirement.

You can also import 50 books, sports article or an individual sport equipment which can be hold by one person, set of tools or work instruments portables which must not excced 20 kilos, to 20 cigarrete packets or two pure boxes, 5 playing games for children which must come with therir passangers, three wine liters of liqueur, cosmetics and self cleanliness objects.

important:

To enjoy duty free of those articles they must not be luxurious not even jewelry or precious stones, hunting trophies, weapons and weapons supplies, natural state food or prepared food, can food and other similars, and finally not excessively quantity.

earthly transportation:

For your better comfortable in the Guadalajara International Airport, you will count with earthly transportation, clasified in three kinds with different prices.

emergency medical service:

In the ground floor on the offices section, it has a consultin room and emergency medical service open from 7:00 a.m. to 11:00 p.m. in which they will provide you a unique attention, specially those cases of: traumatism digestives, changes of artery pressure, respiratory, neurotics, gynecology, endocrimology, etc.

baggage calim:

While you are passing through Health and Emigration, the Air Line Company employees (in which you traveled) are unloading you loggage, and they put them on the wide ribbon.[32]

In the second variety, unofficial and literary, the writer assumes that his reader will sooner or later be following in his footsteps and advises him how to get the best out of the city or country concerned. Every guide book must inevitably fall by definition into this category; but I have already quoted enough from guide books. Here, by contrast, is a passage from what is unquestionably a work of literature, and very elegant literature at that. Its title is *Classical Landscape with Figures*; its author is Osbert Lancaster.

In the Romantic Age, when the rule of taste was as yet unchallenged, conscientious travellers went to immense pains to insure that the vista or monument to which they were making pilgrimage should burst upon their properly conditioned gaze at precisely the right angle, in exactly the correct light. A first visit to a really import- ant sight – the Colosseum, the Rhine Falls or Lincoln Cathedral – required a previous preparation and a carefully worked out plan of approach, and in time certain prospects became obligatory. Thus Rome must be surveyed from the Pin- zio, Oxford from Headington Hill, Florence from Fiesole. To-day we have long since abandoned this 'première communion' attitude to sight-seeing much, I fancy, to our impoverishment, for if a thing is worth seeing it is worth seeing well, and one's whole attitude towards, and appreciation of, any monument such as the Parthenon can be as successfully warped and affected by an unfortunate first en- counter as can one's sex-life, or so we are credibly informed by the psychologists, by a fortuitous sight of the housemaid undressing gained at an unduly impression- able age. In the case of the Parthenon such a disaster is all too easily sustained. Thanks to General Metaxas, whose errors of policy have frequently been con- demned with a warmth that would more appropriately have been reserved for his errors of taste, the Acropolis is now formally approached by a neatly macadamised by-pass bordered with newly planted groves of pine and fir. The atmosphere thus happily created is nostalgically Bournemouth and it is with genuine surprise that, having completed the ascent, the English visitor finds himself faced, not with Branksome Chine, but the Propylaea.

The tourist of sensibility should be in no hurry to gain his first view of the Acropolis at close quarters, for more perhaps than any other architectural achieve- ment of a similar order this gains from being seen frequently at a distance. As to which distant prospect is the finest everyone will have his own opinion: I myself favour the view gained from the back road to Vougliameni whence the Parthenon, unexpectedly small, suddenly, but as it were casually, rises above the intervening hills, isolated and remote against the great wall of Parnes with all Athens and its sprawling suburbs lost behind the folds of Hymettus. This is an early morning approach; later in the day few prospects can compare with that to be obtained on the descent from Kaisariani with the great rock floating above the heat-hazed town, its temples and colonnades lit from behind and silhouetted against a burnished sea. In the evening there are just two minutes, if the sky is clear and the traditional transformation scene is going according to plan, when the last rays of the sun having already abandoned the town itself still rest on the Acropolis, and Hymettus forms a rose-red backdrop, richer and more daring in effect than anything conceived by Bakst. This is the hour when Socrates is said to have drained the hemlock. How- ever, to witness the spectacle at its best one must see it from the road coming down from Daphni and this involves one sooner or later in a controversy which still wrecks the peace of senior common-rooms and shatters the harmony (never, be it admitted, very profound) that occasionally prevails in schools of archaeology. For here we are brought face to face with the reconstructed north colonnade of the Parthenon, a feat of archaeological rehabilitation to which many have never become reconciled. Lacking personal knowledge of its former condition it is hard to offer an opinion, but at the risk of appearing a sentimental old ruin-fancier one may perhaps express the hope that the process will not be carried any further as it can only logically end in total reconstruction. Before we know where we are the whole Acropolis, the gigantic statue of Athena and all, will once more be gleaming, if not in purple, then in terracotta, and gold which might quite possibly lead us to revise some of our opinions about fifth-century taste. And in an atomic age our remaining illusions are best hugged tight.

However, the traveller, disregarding these specialized disputes and having absorbed the prospect from one or other, or better still from all three, of these viewpoints, should be at last prepared for his visit and must now select his route with exceptional caution. Avoiding, as though it were a plague-pit, the official approach, he should advance from exactly the opposite, that is to say the northern, direction. In so doing he will climb up through the old streets of the Plaka, and emerge alongside a small Byzantine chapel immediately beneath the Themistoclean wall which at this point, so acute is the angle of vision, completely masks the buildings on the summit. Turning to the right a path follows the contour of the rock, emerging slightly to the north of the Propylaea and opposite Mars Hill where St. Paul, and in recent years several historically minded Anglican Army Chaplains, so eloquently preached. Turning his back sharply on the pine-clad vista of the new by-pass, at this one point unavoidable, he should at once mount the steps of the Propylaea and immediately repair to the Parthenon, firmly resisting all temptation to turn aside to any of the other temples to right or left.

For not only does the Parthenon claim first attention in its right but it also provides a yardstick whereby to form some critical estimate of the Erechtheion and temple of Nike Apteros, and to maintain an attitude of uncritical admiration before the first of these buildings is to sidestep one of the most puzzling questions that arises in the whole history of Greek architecture. How could the Greeks with their clear, logical outlook and their unshakably humanistic standards of taste ever have tolerated, let alone evolved, the caryatid? To them, more than to any other people it would, one would have thought, have been obvious that to employ a naturalistic three-dimensional rendering of the human form as an architectural unit was to invite disaster. When the Baroque architect of the seventeenth century, whose aims were anyhow completely different, flanked a doorway with a pair of groaning Atlases he had an expressionist justification; the over-life-size figures with exaggeratedly bulging muscles do at least emphasize, as they were intended to do, the weight and mass of the architrave or balcony which they supposedly support. But here these elegant flower-maidens simper as unconcernedly as if they had never been called upon to balance two and a half tons of Pentelic marble on their pretty little heads.

The remaining buildings on the Acropolis are likely neither to produce so overwhelming an effect as the Parthenon and the Propylaea nor to pose such awkward questions of taste as the Erechtheion. The little temple of Nike Apteros, re-erected by French archaeologists at the beginning of the last century on its original site which had been used by the Turks for a mortar battery, seldom fails to evoke that enthusiasm which British art-lovers reserve for the very small. Supremely elegant and in perfect taste, there nevertheless clings to it, due perhaps in part to its elevated position, a faint air of Buzzards. Immediately below the rock itself lie the two theatres of Herodes Atticus and Dionysus. The former, built by that celebrated Philhellene Roman millionaire, the Lord Nuffield of the first century, whose gilt-edged spoor we shall come across all over Greece, is a fine dramatic structure that still serves a useful purpose. Acoustically nearly perfect, it provides during the summer months a Piranesi-like setting for the concerts of the admirable, but usually indifferently conducted, Athens State Orchestra. Architecturally, however, it is not much regarded by the *cognoscenti*. Incidentally it is interesting to note how persons who at home will think nothing of dragging one for a six-mile walk across the downs in pouring rain in order to inspect some third-rate fragment of poorly preserved provincial Roman pavement, in Greece will not bother to cross the road to glance at anything, however fine, later than the third-century B.C.

For those with that highly specialized taste for Greek theatres well developed the theatre of Dionysus is scarcely of less interest than Epidauros itself, but the attention of the ordinary visitor is likely to be chiefly focused on the front row of the stalls, on each seat of which is engraved the style and titles of the ecclesiastical dignitary for whom it was reserved. The auditorium in its present form only dates, however, from the third century, so that any Agate-like musing on the vanished glories of Aeschylean first-nights would be misplaced. The stage itself is later still and is chiefly remarkable for a supporting figure of a Triton in whose hirsute features a former generation of Conservative tourists were gratified to detect a striking likeness to the late Marquess of Salisbury.

The remaining classical antiquities of Athens are almost all situated to the north of the Acropolis. Of these the best known is the so-called Theseon, which, although supremely uninteresting in itself, poses a question which could we but answer it satisfactorily might well provide a firm and lasting basis for a rational system of aesthetics. Why should this temple, the best preserved of its date in the world, built within a few years of the Parthenon and embodying all the same principles, remain by comparison so devastatingly boring? True, it lacks the advantages of a noble site, but nevertheless there exists no single fault of proportion or design on which to put a finger. And yet, however receptive one's mood, it produces less effect than many a Doric corn-exchange in an English provincial town.[33]

It could admittedly be argued that in this last passage the admonitory formula is used as little more than a literary device in what is essentially a simple description of the city of Athens; and I should be hard put to refute the argument. Leaving, therefore, all other scenic or monumental descriptions to later chapters of this book, let me conclude this first one with an important piece of genuine advice, tendered by a certain William Kitchiner, MD, whose *Traveller's Oracle, or Maxims for Locomotion*, was published in London in 1827. It is, I think, self-explanatory.

However, as the *Sudden Death* of a Traveller, if intestate, would occasion irremediable distress and disputes in his Family; – if he consult only his own Tranquillity, (and the preservation of *Peace of Mind*, is more preventive of the Disorders and even the decays of our Body, than the most careful precautions against unfavourable Seasons, or unwholesome Diet!) he will certainly make his *Will* before he leaves Home.

From innumerable causes which are beyond human control, there is, in fact, no condition that is not subject to *premature and sudden Death*, even in the very vigour of Life, and under the vigilant exercise of every prudential measure.

'Heav'n from all Creatures hides the Book of Fate,
All but the page prescribed, their present state.'

'As the Lord liveth, and as thy Soul liveth, there is but one step between Thee and *DEATH!*' – nay, not so much; for the strength whereby the Step must be taken, may fail before it is finished; a little change of Weather – a small Cold – a disappointment in Diet, will derange your Health; and a Fall, – a Bruise, – a Tile from a House, – the throwing of a Stone, – the trip of a Foot, – the Scratch of a Nail, – the Wrenching off a bit of Skin, the over-cutting of a Corn, may destroy your Life: – such trifling Accidents have often done as sure Execution, as War, Pestilence, and Famine.

Sickness and Death are always within a Moment's March of us, ready at – GOD's – command to strike the blow. '*Boast not thyself of to-Morrow, for thou knowest not what a day may bring forth;*' therefore, so arrange all your Affairs, that when Sickness and Sorrow come, you may have nothing to do in this World, but to – compose your Soul for that which is to come.

See '*The Pleasure of Making a Will,*' in THE ART OF INVIGORATING LIFE, by the Author of this Work.[34]

CHAPTER TWO

Motivations

A new voice hailed me of an old friend when, first returned from the Peninsula, I paced again in that long street of Damascus which is called Straight; and suddenly taking me wondering by the hand 'Tell me (said he), since thou art here again in the peace and assurance of Ullah, and whilst we walk, as in the former years, toward the new blossoming orchards, full of the sweet spring as the garden of God, what moved thee, or how couldst thou take such journeys into the fanatic Arabia?'[1]

The opening words of *Travels in Arabia Deserta* are so well known – largely, I suspect, because relatively few readers manage to get very much further – that I hesitated for a moment before quoting them here. But the incredulous enquiry made of the author by his friend is one that every traveller has to face sooner or later; and even if Doughty, in those two immense volumes, never quite got round to replying to it himself, there is a good deal to be enjoyed in the explanations of those others who do not find it necessary to write like the Prophet Habakkuk and are perfectly capable of giving a straight answer to a straight question.

Nobody ever wrote less like an Old Testament prophet than Noël Coward; but this question of motivation worried him too:

> Travel they say improves the mind,
> An irritating platitude
> Which frankly, entre nous,
> Is very far from true.
> Personally I've yet to find
> That longitude and latitude
> Can educate those scores
> Of monumental bores
> Who travel in groups and herds and troupes
> Of various breeds and sexes,
> Till the whole world reels
> To shouts and squeals
> And the clicking of Rolliflexes.

> *Refrain 1* Why do the wrong people travel, travel, travel,
> When the right people stay back home?
> What compulsion compels them

And who the hell tells them
To drag their cans to Zanzibar
Instead of staying quietly in Omaha?
The Taj Mahal
And the Grand Canal
And the sunny French Riviera
Would be less oppressed
If the Middle West
Would settle for somewhere rather nearer.
Please do not think that I criticize or cavil
At a genuine urge to roam,
But why oh why do the wrong people travel
When the right people stay back home . . .

Refrain 2 Why do the wrong people travel, travel, travel,
When the right people stay back home?
What explains this mass mania
To leave Pennsylvania
And clack around like flocks of geese,
Demanding dry martinis on the Isles of Greece?
In the smallest street
Where the gourmets meet
They invariably fetch up
And it's hard to make
Them accept a steak
That isn't served rare and smeared with ketchup.
Millions of tourists are churning up the gravel
While they gaze at St Peter's dome,
But why oh why do the wrong people travel
When the right people stay back home . . .

Refrain 3 Why do the wrong people travel, travel, travel,
When the right people stay back home?
What peculiar obsessions
Inspire those processions
Of families from Houston, Tex,
With all those cameras around their necks?
They will take a train
Or an aeroplane
For an hour on the Costa Brava,
And they'll see Pompeii
On the only day
That it's up to its ass in molten lava.
It would take years to unravel – ravel – ravel
Every impulse that makes them roam
But why oh why do the wrong people travel
When the right people stay back home?[2]

36

For many people who have, over the centuries, launched themselves off into foreign lands, the overriding motive has been curiosity pure and simple. That, by his own admission, was what drove Fynes Moryson, Gent., to undertake his journey to the East in the reign of Elizabeth I:

From my tender youth I had a great desire to see forraine Countries, not to get libertie (which I had in Cambridge in such measure, as I could not well desire more), but to enable my understanding, which I thought could not be done so well by contemplation as by experience; nor by the eare or any sence so well, as by the eies. And having once begun this course, I could not see any man without emulation, and a kind of vertuous envy, who had seene more Cities, Kingdomes, and Provinces, or more Courts of Princes, Kings, and Emperours, then my selfe. Therefore having now wandred through the greatest part of Europe, and seene the chiefe Kingdomes thereof, I sighed to my selfe in silence, that the Kingdome of Spaine was shut up from my sight, by the long warre betweene England and Spaine, except I would rashly cast my selfe into danger, which I had already unadvisedly done, when I viewed the Citie and Fort of Naples, and the Citie of Milan. And howsoever now being newly returned home, I thought the going into more remote parts would be of little use to me, yet I had an itching desire to see Jerusalem, the fountaine of Religion, and Constantinople, of old the seate of Christian Emperours, and now the seate of the Turkish Ottoman.[3]

Nearly 200 years later, it was curiosity again – combined on this occasion with an unconcealed longing for adventure – that impelled a twenty-two-year-old Scottish doctor named Mungo Park to apply to the African Association for the first of the two journeys that were to make him famous.

Soon after my return from the East Indies in 1793, having learnt that the noblemen and gentlemen, associated for the purpose of prosecuting discoveries in the interior of Africa, were desirous of engaging a person to explore that continent by the way of the Gambia River, I took occasion, through means of the President of the Royal Society, to whom I had the honour to be known, of offering myself for that service. I had been informed, that a gentleman of the name of Houghton, a captain in the army, and formerly fort-major at Goree, had already sailed to the Gambia, under the direction of the Association, and that there was reason to apprehend he had fallen a sacrifice to the climate, or perished in some contest with the natives; but this intelligence, instead of deterring me from my purpose, animated me to persist in the offer of my services with the greater solicitude. I had a passionate desire to examine into the productions of a country so little known, and to become experimentally acquainted with the modes of life and character of the natives. I knew that I was able to bear fatigue; and I relied on my youth and the strength of my constitution to preserve me from the effects of the climate. The salary which the Committee allowed was sufficiently large, and I made no stipulation for future reward. If I should perish in my journey, I was willing that my hopes and expectations should perish with me; and if I should succeed in rendering the geography of Africa more familiar to my countrymen, and in opening to their ambition and industry new sources of wealth, and new channels of commerce, I knew that I was in the hands of men of honour, who would not fail to bestow that remuneration which my successful services should appear to them to merit. The Committee of the Association, having made such inquiries as they thought necessary, declared themselves satisfied with the qualifications that I possessed, and accepted me for the service; and with that liberality which on all occasions distinguishes their conduct, gave me every encouragement which it was in their power to grant, or which I could with propriety ask.[4]

Thirteen years later, he was dead – the last surviving European of his original party of forty – drowned in the Niger after a mass attack by the natives. His fate, however, in no way deterred Miss Mary Kingsley, who in the centenary year of Park's first trip to Africa set off for the Dark Continent herself. The very first sentence of the preface to her *Travels in West Africa* makes it clear that she was a very different sort of person: where Mungo strikes us, for all his immense toughness and physical courage, as a fairly dour, humorless individual, Mary sparkles:

It was in 1893 that, for the first time in my life, I found myself in possession of five or six months which were not heavily forestalled, and feeling like a boy with a new half-crown, I lay about in my mind, as Mr Bunyan would say, as to what to do with them. 'Go and learn your tropics,' said Science. Where on earth am I to go, I wondered, for tropics are tropics wherever found, so I got down an atlas and saw that either South America or West Africa must be my destination, for the Malayan region was too far off and too expensive. Then I got Wallace's *Geographical Distribution* and after reading that master's article on the Ethiopian region I hardened my heart and closed with West Africa. I did this the more readily because while I knew nothing of the practical condition of it, I knew a good deal both by tradition and report of South East America, and remembered that Yellow Jack was endemic, and that a certain naturalist, my superior physically and mentally, had come very near getting starved to death in the depressing society of an expedition slowly perishing of want and miscellaneous fevers up the Parana.

My ignorance regarding West Africa was soon removed. And although the vast cavity in my mind that it occupied is not even yet half filled up, there is a great deal of very curious information in its place. I use the word curious advisedly, for I think many seemed to translate my request for practical hints and advice into an advertisement that 'Rubbish may be shot here'. This same information is in a state of great confusion still, although I have made heroic efforts to codify it. I find, however, that it can almost all be got in under the following different headings, namely and to wit:

> The dangers of West Africa.
> The disagreeables of West Africa.
> The diseases of West Africa.
> The things you must take to West Africa.
> The things you find most handy in West Africa.
> The worst possible things you can do in West Africa.

I inquired of all my friends as a beginning what they knew of West Africa. The majority knew nothing. A percentage said, 'Oh, you can't possibly go there; that's where Sierra Leone is, the white man's grave, you know'. If these were pressed further, one occasionally found that they had had relations who had gone out there after having been 'sad trials', but, on consideration of their having left not only West Africa, but this world, were now forgiven and forgotten. One lady, however, kindly remembered a case of a gentleman who had resided some few years at Fernando Po, but when he returned an aged wreck of forty he shook so violently with ague as to dislodge a chandelier, thereby destroying a valuable tea-service and flattening the silver teapot in its midst.

No; there was no doubt about it, the place was not healthy, and although I had not been 'a sad trial', yet neither had the chandelier-dislodging Fernando Po gentleman. So I next turned my attention to cross-examining the doctors. 'Deadliest spot on earth', they said cheerfully, and showed me maps of the geographical distribution of disease. Now I do not say that a country looks inviting when it is coloured in Scheele's green or a bilious yellow, but these colours may arise from lack of artistic gift in the cartographer. There is no mistaking what he means by black, however, and black you'll find they colour West Africa from above Sierra Leone to below the Congo. 'I wouldn't go there if I were you,' said my medical friends, 'you'll catch something; but if you must go, and you're as obstinate as a mule, just bring me –' And then followed a list of commissions from here to New York, any one of which – but I only found that out afterwards.

All my informants referred me to the missionaries. 'There were,' they said, in an airy way, 'lots of them down there, and had been for years.' So to missionary literature I addressed myself with great ardour; alas! only to find that these good people wrote their reports not to tell you how the country they resided in was, but how it was getting on towards being what it ought to be, and how necessary it was that their readers should subscribe more freely, and not get any foolishness into their heads about obtaining an inadequate supply of souls for their money. I also found fearful confirmation of my medical friends' statements about its unhealthiness, and various details of the distribution of cotton shirts over which I did not linger.

From the missionaries it was, however, that I got my first idea about the social condition of West Africa. I gathered that there existed there, firstly the native human beings – the raw material, as it were – and that these were led either to good or bad respectively by the missionary and the trader. There were also the Government representatives, whose chief business it was to strengthen and consolidate the missionary's work, a function they carried on but indifferently well. But as for those traders! well, I put them down under the dangers of West Africa at once. Subsequently I came across the good old coast yarn of how, when a trader from that region went thence, it goes without saying where, the Fallen Angel without a moment's hesitation vacated the infernal throne (Milton) in his favour. This, I beg to note, is the marine form of the legend. When it occurs terrestrially the trader becomes a Liverpool mate. But of course no one need believe it either way – it is not a missionary's story.

Naturally, while my higher intelligence was taken up with attending to these statements, my mind got set on going, and I had to go.[5]

Her motivation, like Park's, seems to have been a thirst for adventure, sharpened by a feeling for the romance of 'the tropics'. Like him, too, she paid for it with an early death – nursing Boer prisoners at Simonstown in 1900. She was just thirty-eight.

Freya Stark, more introspective – and, it must be said, vastly more intelligent – than either of them, analysed her own feelings in correspondingly greater depth. In *The Coast of Incense*, published in 1953 when she already had some forty years of travelling behind her, she wrote:

I have often been asked what first turned me towards Arabia, and the explanation usually seems inadequate though I cannot find a better. At the back of the adventure lay a curiosity for things in general which I had even as a child, and a desire, justified I think by the unusually harassing surroundings of my youth, to escape into an emptier, less fretful life. I had leaned towards music and then drawing, and had shown no talent for either: had written something and – encouraged by my godfather, W. P. Ker – sent it to *The Cornhill* to be rejected: the little spark, with no one about to blow it to a flame, went out for the time being. But there was a creative impulse, which is strong as love and deep as life, and if it finds no road available in art will turn to life itself for its shaping. Not wholly consciously, but not quite unconsciously, as far as I can remember, I determined to fashion my future as a sculptor his marble, and there was in it the same mixture of foresight and the unknown. The thing in the mind of the artist takes its way and imposes its form as it wakens under his hand.

And so with life. With my requirements, the answer I found was sure to be remote. It was also bound to include danger, for I remember wishing often to find what might silence fear, and to reach the end of my days free from that mortal weakness. This is no addition of later years, for I have found references to it in notes and diaries, and can remember at the age of fourteen the tranquillity which a first reading of the Phaedon, the death of Socrates, gave me – a widening of the bounds of life which even then I felt to be essential. To turn this widening from a mere concept into a reality remained sometimes consciously, and always, I think, subconsciously, one of my chief desires: and how deep and permanent it was I realized through my joy and relief during the second war, when a rather hopeless operation found me, by some happy coincidences, free from anxiety and ready. My parents were both perfectly gallant in their separate ways, and so was my sister; in all my youth fear seemed to be unrecognized and non-existent except obscurely and ashamed in my own heart: and perhaps, strangely enough but not as unusually as one might imagine, it was this unavowed timidity which made me seek out dangerous things and made me find – even in mountaineering – that the chief delight was *not to be afraid*. Only a person both adventurous and timid can feel this.

With such ingredients, and a love of research for its own sake, a liking for people and language, a habit of travel, and a deep diffidence in social relations which yet I was drawn to – it is not surprising that the adventures came: that they came in Arabia was accident. I wanted space, distance, history and danger, and I was interested in the living world: I think it was some stray conversation with a young man I liked – Gabriel de Bottini – just home from north Africa; the coincidence of a teacher in San Remo; the realization of the wide reach of the Arab lands and the drama of their future, involved in oil: all these things were sufficient to localize those deeper desires which would otherwise have found their outlet equally spontaneously in China or Peru, or anywhere where space, distance, history and danger existed.[6]

For all these last three writers, the urge to travel came first, and what Freya Stark calls the 'localization' of that urge only later. Other travellers, however, have at an early age found their imaginations caught by one particular region or country and have ever afterwards been drawn to it as by some lodestar. Peter Levi, for example:

In Oxford just before Christmas it was dark in the mornings; and on Friday, the day the gardener comes, you could hear him sweeping the lawn in the dark. I was trying to learn Persian (an unsuccessful attempt) and working my way through Tarn's *Greeks in Bactria and India*, a necessary standard book about which everyone complains. The days and the book were full of dark grey gloom and rain, and early in the evening the air became black. I remember the appearance of the pink Christmas lights in St Ebbe's and, passing through Christ Church one night when it was foggy, the long line of isolated gaslights in the quadrangle. There was a performance of John Blow's *Venus and Adonis* at the Playhouse. I went to Eastbourne to see my mother; the air was clearer, but every morning there were seagulls in the garden. The sea was very cold and green-brown and the air had a brownish tinge. Someone sent me a postcard of a Persian painting which I idly propped up on my desk lamp. It began to work on me without my noticing it and, rather without thinking, I jotted down a short paragraph in a notebook as follows:

> In that country it always snows for an hour or two a day; it is a pagan Christmas morning, they don't know there that it's solstice because they have no understanding of the stars. A single star (all they notice) is enough to navigate by. Long-necked gazelles and willow trees as fresh as salad. The people travel on bay mules. The palaces are abandoned and there are storks on the blue minarets, but the gardens are not overgrown. The road towards the White Tower along which caravans pass for one week in every year, and again in autumn for a week, like migrating birds or nomads with their flocks, crossing the whole of Asia at walking pace.

I must evidently have been trying to project an imaginary Afghanistan to see whether it made a coherent model. The reason for recording this strange jotting here is its curious combination of inaccuracies of fact with accuracy of feeling. It is not surprising that a Persian fifteenth-century miniature should be a wonderful tangle of fantasy and accurate observations of Afghanistan, but it does seem remarkable that such a picture, decoded at a distance of centuries and of thousands of miles by someone who has never seen Asia, should still convey (as to me it does) just what Afghanistan is like.[7]

Persia and Afghanistan are admittedly enough to beguile any young man possessing a modicum of wanderlust; Patagonia, on the other hand, seems to most of us distinctly more resistible. That it did not so strike Bruce Chatwin says, I suggest, a good deal more for Mr Chatwin than it does for Patagonia; I can think of no author living or dead who could make so riveting a book out of so grim and desolate a land. None the less, the author's to most of us unaccountable fascination with the place seems to call for some explanation – and, with the opening paragraphs of *In Patagonia*, does in part receive it:

In my grandmother's dining-room there was a glass-fronted cabinet and in the cabinet a piece of skin. It was a small piece only, but thick and leathery, with strands of coarse, reddish hair. It was stuck to a card with a rusty pin. On the card was some writing in faded black ink, but I was too young then to read.

'What's that?'

'A piece of brontosaurus.'

My mother knew the names of two prehistoric animals, the brontosaurus and the mammoth. She knew it was not a mammoth. Mammoths came from Siberia.

The brontosaurus, I learned, was an animal that had drowned in the Flood, being too big for Noah to ship aboard the Ark. I pictured a shaggy lumbering creature with claws and fangs and a malicious green light in its eyes. Sometimes the brontosaurus would crash through the bedroom wall and wake me from my sleep.

This particular brontosaurus had lived in Patagonia, a country in South America, at the far end of the world. Thousands of years before, it had fallen into a glacier, travelled down a mountain in a prison of blue ice, and arrived in perfect condition at the bottom. Here my grandmother's cousin, Charley Milward the Sailor, found it.

Charley Milward was captain of a merchant ship that sank at the entrance to the Strait of Magellan. He survived the wreck and settled nearby, at Punta Arenas, where he ran a ship-repairing yard. The Charley Milward of my imagination was a god among men – tall, silent and strong, with black mutton-chop whiskers and fierce blue eyes. He wore his sailor's cap at an angle and the tops of his sea-boots turned down.

Directly he saw the brontosaurus poking out of the ice, he knew what to do. He had it jointed, salted, packed in barrels, and shipped to the Natural History Museum in South Kensington. I pictured blood and ice, flesh and salt, gangs of Indian workmen and lines of barrels along a shore – a work of giants and all to no purpose; the brontosaurus went rotten on its voyage through the tropics and arrived in London a putrefied mess; which was why you saw brontosaurus bones in the museum, but no skin.

Fortunately cousin Charley had posted a scrap to my grandmother.

My grandmother lived in a red-brick house set behind a screen of yellow-spattered laurels. It had tall chimneys, pointed gables and a garden of blood-coloured roses. Inside it smelled of church.

I do not remember much about my grandmother except her size. I would clamber over her wide bosom or watch, slyly, to see if she'd be able to rise from the chair. Above her hung paintings of Dutch burghers, their fat buttery faces nesting in white ruffs. On the mantelpiece were two Japanese homunculi with red and white ivory eyes that popped out on stalks. I would play with these, or with a German articulated monkey, but always I pestered her: 'Please can I have the piece of brontosaurus.'

Never in my life have I wanted anything as I wanted that piece of skin. My grandmother said I should have it one day, perhaps. And when she died I said: 'Now I *can* have the piece of brontosaurus,' but my mother said: 'Oh, that thing! I'm afraid we threw it away.'

At school they laughed at the story of the brontosaurus. The science master said I'd mixed it up with the Siberian mammoth. He told the class how Russian scientists had dined off deep-frozen mammoth and told me not to tell lies. Besides, he said, brontosauruses were reptiles. They had no hair, but scaly armoured hide. And he showed us an artist's impression of the beast – so different from that of my imagination – grey-green, with a tiny head and a gigantic switchback of vertebrae, placidly eating weed in a lake. I was ashamed of my hairy brontosaurus, but I knew it was not a mammoth.

It took some years to sort the story out. Charley Milward's animal was not a brontosaurus, but the mylodon or Giant Sloth. He never found a whole specimen, or even a whole skeleton, but some skin and bones, preserved by the cold, dryness and salt, in a cave on Last Hope Sound in Chilean Patagonia. He sent the collection to England and sold it to the British Museum. This version was less romantic but had the merit of being true.

My interest in Patagonia survived the loss of the skin; for the Cold War woke in me a passion for geography. In the late 1940s the Cannibal of the Kremlin shadowed our lives; you could mistake his moustaches for teeth. We listened to lectures about the war he was planning. We watched the civil defence lecturer ring the cities of Europe to show the zones of total and partial destruction. We saw the zones bump one against the other leaving no space in between. The instructor wore khaki shorts. His knees were white and knobbly, and we saw it was hopeless. The war was coming and there was nothing we could do.

Next, we read about the cobalt bomb, which was worse than the hydrogen bomb and could smother the planet in an endless chain reaction.

I knew the colour cobalt from my great-aunt's paintbox. She had lived on Capri at the time of Maxim Gorky and painted Capriot boys naked. Later her art became almost entirely religious. She did lots of St Sebastians, always against a cobalt-blue background, always the same beautiful young man, stuck through and through with arrows and still on his feet.

So I pictured the cobalt bomb as a dense blue cloudbank, spitting tongues of flame at the edges. And I saw myself, out alone on a green headland, scanning the horizon for the advance of the cloud.

And yet we hoped to survive the blast. We started an Emigration Committee and made plans to settle in some far corner of the earth. We pored over atlases. We learned the direction of prevailing winds and the likely patterns of fall-out. The war would come in the Northern Hemisphere, so we looked to the Southern. We ruled out Pacific Islands for islands are traps. We ruled out Australia and New Zealand, and we fixed on Patagonia as the safest place on earth.

I pictured a low timber house with a shingled roof, caulked against storms, with blazing log fires inside and the walls lined with the best books, somewhere to live when the rest of the world blew up.

Then Stalin died and we sang hymns of praise in chapel, but I continued to hold Patagonia in reserve.[8]

Sometimes the lodestar is not a region or a country, but a particular landscape or geographical feature: mountains perhaps, or forests, or remote lakes. For Eric Newby it is rivers:

I love rivers. I was born on the banks of the Thames and, like my father before me, I had spent a great deal of time both on it and in it. I enjoy visiting their sources: Thames Head, in a green meadow in the Cotswolds; the river Po coming out from under a heap of boulders among the debris left by picnickers by Monte Viso; the Isonzo bubbling up over clean sand in a deep cleft in the rock in the Julian Alps; the Danube (or one of its sources) emerging in baroque splendour in a palace garden at Donaueschingen. I like exploring them. I like the way in which they grow deeper and wider and dirtier but always, however dirty they become, managing to retain some of the beauty with which they were born.[9]

Of this love was born *Slowly Down the Ganges*, one of the two best river books that I know. (For the other, you will have to wait till the next chapter.)

Surprisingly for many people who have never travelled them, but not at all for most of those who have, the great deserts of the world have always exercised a powerful attraction. The most extraordinary traveller of our time, Wilfred Thesiger, has been drawn to them all his life, and in a memorable passage of *Arabian Sands* he tells us why:

A cloud gathers, the rain falls, men live; the cloud disperses without rain, and men and animals die. In the deserts of southern Arabia there is no rhythm of the seasons, no rise and fall of sap, but empty wastes where only the changing temperature marks the passage of the year. It is a bitter, desiccated land which knows nothing of gentleness or ease. Yet men have lived there since earliest times. Passing generations have left fire-blackened stones at camping sites, a few faint tracks polished on the gravel plains. Elsewhere the winds wipe out their footprints. Men live there because it is the world into which they were born; the life they lead is the life their forefathers led before them; they accept hardships and privations; they know no other way. Lawrence wrote in *Seven Pillars of Wisdom*, 'Bedouin ways were hard, even for those brought up in them and for strangers terrible; a death in life.' No man can live this life and emerge unchanged. He will carry, however faint, the imprint of the desert, the brand which marks the nomad; and he will have within him the yearning to return, weak or insistent according to his nature. For this cruel land can cast a spell which no temperate clime can match.[10]

Yet for Wilfred Thesiger the lure of the desert is not the only force that impels him into the wilderness; later in the same book he reveals that he is pushed as well as pulled:

I could have gone to Bahrain by aeroplane from Sharja but I preferred to go there by dhow. . . .

I was sailing on this dhow because I wanted to have some experience of the Arab as a sailor. Once they had been a great sea-going race, sailing their dhows round the coast of India to the East Indies and perhaps even farther. The Trucial Coast which we had just left had been known and dreaded as the Pirate Coast; in the early nineteenth century Juasimi pirates had fought our frigates on level terms on these very waters. But there was a deeper reason that had prompted me to make this journey. I had done it to escape a little longer from the machines which dominated our world. The experience would last longer than the few days I spent on the journey. All my life I had hated machines. I could remember how bitterly at school I had resented reading the news that someone had flown across the Atlantic or travelled through the Sahara in a car. I had realized even then that the speed and ease of mechanical transport must rob the world of all diversity.

For me, exploration was a personal venture. I did not go to the Arabian desert to collect plants nor to make a map; such things were incidental. At heart I knew that to write or even to talk of my travels was to tarnish the achievement. I went there to find peace in the hardship of desert travel and the company of desert peoples. I set myself a goal on these journeys, and, although the goal itself was unimportant, its attainment had to be worth every effort and sacrifice. Scott had gone to the South Pole in order to stand for a few minutes on one particular and almost inaccessible spot on the earth's surface. He and his companions died on their way back, but even as they were dying he never doubted that the journey had been worth while. Everyone knew that there was nothing to be found on the top of Everest, but even in this materialistic age few people asked, 'What point is there in climbing Everest? What good will it do anyone when they get there?' They recognized that even today there are experiences that do not need to be justified in terms of material profit.

No, it is not the goal but the way there that matters, and the harder the way the more worth while the journey. Who, after all, would dispute that it is more satisfying to climb to the top of a mountain than to go there in a funicular railway? Perhaps this was one reason why I resented modern inventions; they made the road too easy. I felt instinctively that it was better to fail on Everest without oxygen than to attain the summit with its use. If climbers used oxygen, why should they not have their supplies dropped to them from aeroplanes, or landed by helicopter? Yet to refuse mechanical aids as unsporting reduced exploration to the level of a sport, like big-game shooting in Kenya when the hunter is allowed to drive up to within sight of the animal but must get out of the car to shoot it. I would not myself have wished to cross the Empty Quarter in a car. Luckily this was impossible when I did my journeys, for to have done the journey on a camel when I could have done it in a car would have turned the venture into a stunt.[11]

The love of travel, then, is born of many different desires: for knowledge, for adventure, for the realisation of long-held dreams, for self-examination, for escape. All these have impelled men and women to journey to the remotest corners of the earth, and continue still to do so. But there is another motivation which is probably older than any of these: a motivation which, even if it does not normally carry them so far or subject them to so much physical danger, offers – to those who feel it – the greatest rewards of all.

The idea of pilgrimage has existed almost as long as religion itself. Its literature, however – excepting of course *The Canterbury Tales*, where a pilgrimage provides the setting but virtually none of the subject matter – is, to most of us nowadays, largely unreadable. An exception is Hilaire Belloc's *The Path to Rome*:

To every honest reader that may purchase, hire, or receive this book, and to the reviewers also (to whom it is of triple profit), greeting – and whatever else can be had for nothing.

If you should ask how this book came to be written, it was in this way. One day as I was wandering over the world I came upon the valley where I was born, and stopping there a moment to speak with them all – when I had argued politics with the grocer, and played the great lord with the notary-public, and had all but made the carpenter a Christian by force of rhetoric – what should I note (after so many years) but the old tumble-down and gaping church, that I love more than mother-church herself, all scraped, white, rebuilt, noble, and new, as though it had been finished yesterday. Knowing very well that such a change had not come from the skinflint populace, but was the work of some just artist who knew how grand an ornament was this shrine (built there before our people stormed Jerusalem), I entered, and there saw that all within was as new, accurate, and excellent as the outer part; and this pleased me as much as though a fortune had been left to us all; for one's native place is the shell of one's soul, and one's church is the kernel of that nut.

Moreover, saying my prayers there, I noticed behind the high altar a statue of Our Lady, so extraordinary and so different from all I had ever seen before, so much the spirit of my valley, that I was quite taken out of myself and vowed a vow there to go to Rome on Pilgrimage and see all Europe which the Christian Faith has saved; and I said, 'I will start from the place where I served in arms for my sins; I will walk all the way and take advantage of no wheeled thing; I will sleep rough and cover thirty miles a day, and I will hear Mass every morning; and I will be present at high Mass in St Peter's on the Feast of St Peter and St Paul.'

Then I went out of the church still having that Statue in my mind, and I walked again farther into the world, away from my native valley, and so ended some months after in a place whence I could fulfil my vow; and I started as you shall hear.[12]

Admirers – as who could not be? – of Tissot's superb portrait of Colonel Fred Burnaby in the National Portrait Gallery seldom realise that the languid, debonair young officer of the Royal Horse Guards there depicted was, quite apart from being the strongest man in the British Army, the master of half a dozen languages, an intrepid balloonist and a bestselling travel writer. The greatest of his literary successes was *A Ride to Khiva*; and the incentive for this extraordinary journey was wonderfully typical of Burnaby himself. He went because he was told he couldn't. Let him tell the story in his own words:

A low room, with but little furniture, and that of the simplest kind; a few telegraphic instruments scattered about here and there in out-of-the-way corners, and mixed up promiscuously with rifles and wooden boxes, some filled with cartridges, others containing provisions for a journey; two or three bottles, labelled 'Quinine,' on a rickety wooden table; several men of various nationalities all talking at the same time, and a Babel of different languages; – such was the scene around the writer of this work, who was leaning against the window-sill, and glancing from time to time at an old number of an English newspaper.

The host was a German gentleman, now several thousand miles from the Fatherland, which he had been induced to leave by an offer of the post of superintendent and general manager on a long and important line of recently-constructed telegraph. A graceful girl, with large dark eyes and pearl-white teeth, but whose olive complexion and Oriental dress showed that she was in no way akin to the fairer beauties of Europe, was engaged in handing round small cups of coffee to the most excited talkers of the party, an Italian, Arab, and Englishman, the former gesticulating wildly in an endeavour to interpret between his two companions, who were evidently not at all in accord about the subject of conversation. A bright sun, its rays flashing down on a broad stream, nearly the colour of lapis-lazuli, which flowed hard by the dwelling, had raised the temperature of the room to an almost unbearable heat. It was the month of February. In England people were shivering beside their fires or walking in slush or snow; but I was at Khartoum, having just returned from a visit to Colonel Gordon, Sir Samuel Baker's successor, on the White Nile.

It may seem strange thus to commence the narrative of a journey to Central Asia in Central Africa, and yet, had it not been for a remark made by one of the men in the low square room to which I have just referred, in all probability I should never have gone to Khiva. . . .

'I wonder where we shall all be this time next year,' suddenly remarked my companion. 'God knows,' was my answer; 'but I do not think I shall try the White Nile again; if I come to Africa another time I shall select a new line of country.' At that moment my eye fell upon a paragraph in the paper. It was to the effect that the Government at St. Petersburg had given an order that no foreigner was to be allowed to travel in Russian Asia, and that an Englishman who had recently attempted a journey in that direction had been turned back by the authorities. I have, unfortunately for my own interests, from my earliest childhood had what my old nurse used to call a most 'contradictorious' spirit, and it suddenly occurred to me, Why not go to Central Asia? 'Well, I shall try it,' was my remark. 'What, Timbuctoo?' said my friend. 'No, Central Asia;' and I showed him the paragraph.

'You will never get there; they will stop you.' 'They can if they like, but I don't think they will.' And this trifling incident was the first thing which put the idea into my head of again attempting to reach Khiva.[13]

Another bestseller of its day was *A Thousand Miles Up the Nile*, by Mrs Amelia B. Edwards. She lived to be one of this country's leading Egyptologists, and when she died she left to University College, London, a sum of money with which to found the first chair of Egyptology in England. Particularly in view of her later distinction, it is a joy to discover that, as she freely admits, her first visit to Egypt in 1873 was impelled by a single desire: to get away from the rain.

We came from Alexandria, having had a rough passage from Brindisi followed by forty-eight hours of quarantine. We had not dressed for dinner because, having driven on from the station in advance of dragoman and luggage, we were but just in time to take seats with the rest. We intended, of course, to go up the Nile; and had any one ventured to inquire in so many words what brought us to Egypt, we should have replied: – 'Stress of weather.'

For in simple truth we had drifted hither by accident, with no excuse of health, or business, or any serious object whatever; and had just taken refuge in Egypt as one might turn aside into the Burlington Arcade or the Passage des Panoramas – to get out of the rain.

And with good reason. Having left home early in September for a few weeks' sketching in central France, we had been pursued by the wettest of wet weather. Washed out of the hill-country, we fared no better in the plains. At Nismes, it poured for a month without stopping. Debating at last whether it were better to take our wet umbrellas back at once to England, or push on farther still in search of sunshine, the talk fell upon Algiers – Malta – Cairo; and Cairo carried it. Never was distant expedition entered upon with less premeditation. The thing was no sooner decided than we were gone. Nice, Genoa, Bologna, Ancona flitted by, as in a dream; and Bedreddin Hassan when he awoke at the gates of Damascus was scarcely more surprised than the writer of these pages, when she found herself on board the *Simla,* and steaming out of the port of Brindisi.

Here, then, without definite plans, outfit, or any kind of Oriental experience, behold us arrived in Cairo on the 29th of November 1873, literally, and most prosaically, in search of fine weather.[14]

Nearly a quarter of a century after Mrs Edwards had thankfully laid aside her umbrella, three adventurous young men set out from London to do something that nobody had ever done before: to go round the world on their bicycles. By now self-depreciation was the fashion – we had come a long way since the days of Mungo Park – and even if John Foster Fraser's words betray more than a touch of false modesty, they remain fairly typical of that last generation of Victorian England – one that found it hard to take even the British Empire too seriously.

We took this trip round the world on bicycles because we are more or less con-
ceited, like to be talked about, and see our names in the newspapers. We didn't go
into training. We took things easy. We jogged through Europe, had sundry experiences in Asia, and survived the criticisms of our country from the Americans.
For two years we bicycled in strange lands, and came home a great disappointment
to our friends. We were not haggard or worn, or tottering in our gait. We had never
been scalped, or had hooks through our spines; never been tortured, or had our
eyes gouged; never been rescued after living for a fortnight on our shoes. And we
had never killed a man. It was evident we were not real travellers.

Still, away somewhere at the back of our heads, we are rather proud of what we
have done. We have accomplished the longest bicycle ride ever attempted, just
19,237 miles over continuous new ground. We were stoned by the Mohammedans
because they alleged we were Christians, and we were pelted with mud in China
because the Celestials were certain we were devils. We slept in wet clothes, subsis-
ted on eggs, went hungry, and were enforced teetotalers. We had small-pox, fever,
and other ailments. There were less than a dozen fights with Chinese mobs. We
never shaved for five months, and only occasionally washed.

Our adventures therefore were of a humdrum sort. If only one of us had been
killed, or if we had ridden back into London each minus a limb, some excitement
would have been caused. As it was we came home quietly.[15]

Another agreeable motivation – if such it can be called – was that which
took J. R. Ackerley to India and was thus indirectly instrumental in giving
us one of the minor classics of inter-war travel writing, *Hindoo Holiday*.

He wanted some one to love him – His Highness, I mean; that was his real need, I
think. He alleged other reasons, of course – an English private secretary, a tutor for
his son; for he wasn't really a bit like the Roman Emperors, and had to make excuses.

As a matter of fact he had a private secretary already, though an Indian one, and
his son was only two years old; but no doubt he felt that the British Raj, in the
person of the Political Agent who kept an eye on the State expenditure and other
things, would prefer a label – any of the tidy buff labels that the official mind is
trained to recognise and understand – to being told, 'I want some one to love me.'
But that, I believe, was his real reason nevertheless.

He wanted a friend. He wanted understanding, and sympathy, and philosophic
comfort; and he sent to England for them. This will seem strange to many people
who have always understood that Wisdom dwells in the East; but he believed that
it abode in the West – and perhaps I should add that he had never been there. There
are, of course, quite a number of Britishers already living in India; but I don't think
he ever entertained any serious expectation of finding what he wanted among them.
No – the pure, unsullied fountain-head; he must go to that – and that was how it
happened.

Some one who had met him there said to me: 'Why don't *you* go out to him?'
'Are there any qualifications?' I asked.
'Yes, he wants some one like a character named Olaf in *The Wanderer's Necklace*
by Rider Haggard.'
So I went.[16]

49

And so we come to one of the most consistently entertaining travel books ever written, Peter Fleming's *Brazilian Adventure*. Here again, all is self-depreciation and diffidence; this time, however, they are genuine, and the author clearly takes as much pleasure as any of his readers in his description of the total shambles in which the expedition ended. As subsequent extracts will prove – for this hugely enjoyable book will be quoted more than once in the pages that follow – he could also write like an angel.

It began with an advertisement in the Agony Column of *The Times*.

I always read the Agony Column first, and the news (if there is time) afterwards. This is a practice which most people will deplore, saying that it argues, not only disrespect to a great journal, but an almost impudent lack of curiosity with regard to what are called World Events.

I suppose they are right. But this is a dull life, and the only excuse for the existence of newspapers is that they should make it less dull. It is popularly supposed to be a good thing to know what happened in the world yesterday; but for my part I find it at least equally important to know what may be happening in the world to-day. I fail to see how anyone who has the industry to acquire, and the fortitude to assimilate without panic, a working knowledge of the morning's news can find life any easier to face for the assurance that there is deadlock at Geneva, vacillation at Westminster, foot-and-mouth in Leicestershire, sabotage in Poland, and a slump in Kaffirs. I, on the other hand, without burdening my memory with a lot of facts of uncertain value and ephemeral validity – without even opening the paper – can start the day equipped with several agreeable and stimulating subjects for speculation. What strange kind of a creature can it be whose wolf-hound – now lost in Battersea Park – answers to the name of Effie? How will the Jolly Winter Sports Party ('only sahibs need apply') be finally constituted? Why is Bingo heart-broken? And what possible use can Box A have for a horned toad?

It will be objected that these are frivolous and unprofitable topics for thought: that in these distressful times one ought to be concentrating on graver matters – on War Debts, and on finding fresh excuses for Japan. Theoretically, I know, there is a great deal in this. But at heart I am impenitent. At heart I prefer – and I am afraid I always shall prefer – the world of the Agony Column to that great stage of fools to which the editorial pages of *The Times* so faithfully hold up a mirror. The world of the Agony Column is a world of romance, across which sundered lovers are for ever hurrying to familiar rendezvous ('same time, same place'): a world in which jewellery is constantly being left in taxi-cabs with destinations which must surely be compromising: a world of faded and rather desperate gentility, peopled largely by Old Etonians and ladies of title: a world of the most tremendous enterprise, in which Oxford B.A.s, though equipped only with five European languages, medium height and the ability to drive a car, are ready to 'go anywhere, do anything': a world of sudden and heroic sacrifices ('owner going abroad'): a world in which every object has a sentimental value, every young man a good appearance, and only the highest references are exchanged: an anxious, urgent, cryptic world: a world in which anything may happen. . . .

'Exploring and sporting expedition, under experienced guidance, leaving

England June, to explore rivers Central Brazil, if possible ascertain fate Colonel Fawcett; abundance game, big and small; exceptional fishing; ROOM TWO MORE GUNS; highest references expected and given. – Write Box X, *The Times*, E.C.4.'

This is my favourite sort of advertisement. It had the right improbable ring to it. As I gazed, with all possible detachment, at a map of South America, I seemed to hear the glib and rapid voice of Munchausen, the clink of gold bricks. I had a curiously distinct vision (I don't know why) of two men with red faces deciding, in the bar of the Royal Automobile Club, that what they wanted was a couple of suckers to put up a thou. So wisdom prevailed; and for ten days, though I thought quite often about the interior of Brazil, I did nothing to increase my chances of exploring it.

But on the tenth day, or thereabouts, I found myself reading a long article on the middle page of *The Times* which was clearly about this expedition. Its plans were outlined, its itinerary indicated, and the latest theories about Colonel Fawcett's fate were discussed with that almost medieval disregard for the geographical facts involved of which I was shortly to become a leading exponent. So the thing really existed. The project was genuine. There was an expedition leaving England in June. And *The Times* took it seriously.

This was altogether too much for me. I was still careful to pretend to myself that it would be out of the question for me to go to Brazil. It would cost too much and take too long; and it would be the act of a madman to throw up the literary editorship of the most august of weekly journals in favour of a wild-goose chase. All the same, I argued, it will do no harm to find out a little more about it. . . .

So I wrote to Box X asking for particulars, and presently got an answer from which it appeared that neither the time nor the money involved were as far beyond my means as I had expected. From that moment I gave up struggling with the inevitable. I wrote back and applied for an option on one of the vacancies in the expedition, which, I explained, I would not be in a position to take up definitely for another fortnight or so. In this letter I had meant to rehearse at considerable length my qualifications to take part in an enterprise of this sort, but when the time came these proved curiously indefinable. So I only put down my age (which was 24) and where I had been educated. As a regular reader of the Agony Column, I knew that this latter piece of information, though seemingly irrelevant, might well prove of the first importance; for by Agony Column standards an Old Boy is worth two young men.

This verbal economy I have always believed was good policy. Surfeited with the self-portraiture of applicants who appeared, almost to a man, to be as strong as a horse, as brave as a lion, and to have some knowledge of commercial Spanish, Box X was instantly attracted by my laconic method of approach. More letters were exchanged, a meeting took place, and before long I found myself committed – in the capacity of special correspondent to *The Times* – to a venture for which Rider Haggard might have written the plot and Conrad designed the scenery.[17]

There are countless other reasons why people travel which have not even been touched on in this chapter: health, sport, sex, sight-seeing, art galleries and museums – the list is endless. But sometimes it seems to me that one sets off for no other reason than the joy of travel itself; and I know of no prose writer who has expressed this joy as fully as a poet – Rudyard Kipling.

The Long Trail

There's a whisper down the field where the year has shot her yield,
 And the ricks stand grey to the sun,
Singing: 'Over then, come over, for the bee has quit the clover,
 'And your English summer's done.'

  You have heard the beat of the off-shore wind,
  And the thresh of the deep-sea rain;
  You have heard the song – how long? how long?
  Pull out on the trail again!
Ha' done with the Tents of Shem, dear lass,
 We've seen the seasons through,
And it's time to turn on the old trail, our own trail, the out trail,
Pull out, pull out, on the Long Trail – the trail that is always new!

It's North you may run to the rime-ringed sun
 Or South to the blind Horn's hate;
Or East all the way into Mississippi Bay,
 Or West to the Golden Gate –
  Where the blindest bluffs hold good, dear lass,
  And the wildest tales are true,
  And the men bulk big on the old trail, our own trail, the out trail,
  And life runs large on the Long Trail – the trail that is always new.

The days are sick and cold, and the skies are grey and old,
 And the twice-breathed airs blow damp;
And I'd sell my tired soul for the bucking beam-sea roll
 Of a black Bilbao tramp,
  With her load-line over her hatch, dear lass,
  And a drunken Dago crew,
  And her nose held down on the old trail, our own trail, the out trail
  From Cadiz south on the Long Trail – the trail that is always new.

There be triple ways to take, of the eagle or the snake,
 Or the way of a man with a maid;
But the sweetest way to me is a ship's upon the sea
 In the heel of the North-East Trade.
  Can you hear the crash on her bows, dear lass,
  And the drum of the racing screw,
  As she ships it green on the old trail, our own trail, the out trail,
  As she lifts and 'scends on the Long Trail – the trail that is always new?

MOTIVATIONS

See the shaking funnels roar, with the Peter at the fore,
  And the fenders grind and heave,
And the derricks clack and grate, as the tackle hooks the crate,
  And the fall-rope whines through the sheave;
      It's 'Gang-plank up and in,' dear lass,
      It's 'Hawsers warp her through!'
      And it's 'All clear aft' on the old trail, our own trail, the out trail,
      We're backing down on the Long Trail – the trail that is always new.

O the mutter overside, when the port-fog holds us tied,
  And the sirens hoot their dread,
When foot by foot we creep o'er the hueless, viewless deep
  To the sob of the questing lead!
      It's down by the Lower Hope, dear lass,
      With the Gunfleet Sands in view,
      Till the Mouse swings green on the old trail, our own trail, the out trail,
      And the Gull Light lifts on the Long Trail – the trail that is always new.

O the blazing tropic night, when the wake's a welt of light
  That holds the hot sky tame,
And the steady fore-foot snores through the planet-powdered floors
  Where the scared whale flukes in flame!
      Her plates are flaked by the sun, dear lass,
      And her ropes are taut with the dew,
      For we're booming down on the old trail, our own trail, the out trail,
      We're sagging south on the Long Trail – the trail that is always new.

Then home, get her home, where the drunken rollers comb,
  And the shouting seas drive by,
And the engines stamp and ring, and the wet bows reel and swing,
  And the Southern Cross rides high!
      Yes, the old lost stars wheel back, dear lass,
      That blaze in the velvet blue.
      They're all old friends on the old trail, our own trail, the out trail,
      They're God's own guides on the Long Trail – the trail that is always new.

Fly forward, O my heart, from the Foreland to the Start –
  We're steaming all too slow,
And it's twenty thousand mile to our little lazy isle
  Where the trumpet-orchids blow!
      You have heard the call of the off-shore wind
      And the voice of the deep-sea rain;
      You have heard the song – how long? – how long?
      Pull out on the trail again!

The Lord knows what we may find, dear lass,
And The Deuce knows what we may do –
But we're back once more on the old trail, our own trail, the out trail,
We're down, hull-down, on the Long Trail – the trail that is always new![18]

CHAPTER THREE

Beginnings

There is only one true beginning to any book: its title. There are, however, two sorts of titles. The first, illustrating the no-nonsense approach, is what might be called the Title Direct; of this, James (now Jan) Morris's *Venice* is the ultimate example, though others almost as succinct, such as Charles Dickens's *American Notes* or Frederick Burnaby's *A Ride to Khiva* – both quoted below – would also qualify. The second is the Title Poetic, which sounds lovely but means, more often than not, remarkably little. Titles Poetic are wonderfully easy to find – a random opening of the *Oxford Book of English Verse* will yield *Season of Mists, Mellow Fruitfulness, Close-Bosom Friend, The Maturing Sun* in a single couplet – and work very well for novels; for travel books, on the other hand, they have always seemed to me inappropriate. Readers of these, whether or not they are contemplating a journey of their own, have a right to know exactly what parts of the world are to be described and discussed; and titles such as *Through Bulgaria with Butterfly-net and Beetle-box* or *Three Weeks Awheel in Tuscany* must surely be preferable to *The Plaintive Anthem* or *Neither Do They Spin*. Fortunately, most travel writers seem to agree; and one can only regret the way the modern fashion for brevity has put an end to those leisurely, rambling titles beloved of former centuries which, at the very outset, laid the author's cards fairly and squarely on the table. Here is my favourite, published in London in 1770; one can only wonder how much more virulent it might have been some forty years later. The author is thought to have been a certain Philip Plastowe, who was commissioned lieutenant in 1757, but since the book was anonymous nobody seems quite sure.

The Gentleman's Guide in his Tour through France; Wrote by an Officer who lately Travelled on a Principle which he most Sincerely Recommends to his Countrymen, viz., not to spend more Money in the Country of our Natural Enemy than is Required to support with Decency the Character of an English-man.[1]

After the title comes the dedication; and here I unhesitatingly award my palm to Colonel Angus Buchanan – who is, so far as I am aware, the only author in the English (or, come to that, any other) language to have dedicated a book to a camel. He does so in the following words:

To
FERI N'GASHI

only a camel,
but steel-true
and great of heart.[2]

Later in that same work – which he entitled, with a laudable predilection for the Title Direct, simply *Sahara* – Colonel Buchanan attempted an even more peculiar literary feat; for the full horror of that, however, the reader must wait until he reaches Chapter Fifteen.

Next we come to the prologue (if there is one). The very word immediately evokes *The Canterbury Tales* – which, for all its digressions, is indisputably an account of a journey and therefore qualifies for a place here. The modern English translation used below is by Nevill Coghill.

When in April the sweet showers fall
And pierce the drought of March to the root, and all
The veins are bathed in liquor of such power
As will bring on the engendering of the flower,
When also Zephyrus with his sweet breath
Exhales an air in every grove and heath
Upon the tender shoots, and the young sun
His half-course in the sign of the *Ram* has run,
And the small fowl are making melody,
That sleep away the night with open eye
(So nature pricks them and their heart engages),
Then people long to go on pilgrimages,
And palmers long to seek the stranger strands
Of far-off saints, hallowed in sundry lands,
And specially, from every shire's end
In England, down to Canterbury they wend
To seek the holy blissful martyr, quick
In giving help to them when they were sick.
    It happened in that season that one day
In Southwark, at *The Tabard*, as I lay
Ready to go on pilgrimage and start
For Canterbury, most devout at heart,
At night there came into that hostelry
Some nine and twenty in a company
Of sundry folk happening then to fall
In fellowship, and they were pilgrims all
That towards Canterbury meant to ride.

The rooms and stables of the inn were wide;
They made us easy, all was of the best.
And shortly, when the sun had gone to rest,
By speaking to them all upon the trip
I soon was one of them in fellowship,
And promised to rise early and take the way
To Canterbury, as you heard me say.[3]

But already a century before Chaucer there was written – or, more accurately, dictated – another prologue: very different in its tone from the one just quoted, and as quintessentially Italian as the other is English. It introduces Marco Polo's account of his travels, and rings like a trumpet call.

Emperors and kings, dukes and marquises, counts, knights, and townsfolk, and all people who wish to know the various races of men and the peculiarities of the various regions of the world, take this book and have it read to you. Here you will find all the great wonders and curiosities of Greater Armenia and Persia, of the Tartars and of India, and of many other territories. Our book will relate them to you plainly in due order, as they were related by Messer Marco Polo, a wise and noble citizen of Venice, who has seen them with his own eyes. There is also much here that he has not seen but has heard from men of credit and veracity. We will set down things seen as seen, things heard as heard, so that our book may be an accurate record, free from any sort of fabrication. And all who read the book or hear it may do so with full confidence, because it contains nothing but the truth. For I would have you know that from the time when our Lord God formed Adam our first parent with His hands down to this day there has been no man, Christian or Pagan, Tartar or Indian, or of any race whatsoever, who has known or explored so many of the various parts of the world and of its great wonders as this same Messer Marco Polo. For this reason he made up his mind that it would be a great pity if he did not have a written record made of all the things he had seen and had heard by true report, so that others who have not seen and do not know them may learn them from this book.

Let me tell you, then, that to gain this knowledge he stayed in these various countries and territories fully twenty-six years. Afterwards, in the year of the Nativity of Our Lord Jesus Christ 1298, while he was in prison in Genoa, wishing to occupy his leisure as well as to afford entertainment to readers, he caused all these things to be recorded by Messer Rustichello of Pisa, who was in the same prison. But what he told was only what little he was able to remember.[4]

And so at last the preliminaries are over and the book itself gets under way. If the author has not revealed himself already – which he probably has – he must certainly do so now. How strange it is, after the extrovert confidence of the last two passages, to come upon the sensitive, almost tentative, writing of Victoria Sackville-West, here beginning *Twelve Days* – what sort of title is that, I wonder? – the account of her journey in 1928 with Harold Nicolson across the Bakhtiari Mountains of south-west Persia:

For a long time I believed that it would be impossible to make a book out of these experiences; I could see no shape in them, no pleasing curve; nothing but a series of anti-climaxes, and too much repetition of what I had done, and written down, before. Yet I was loath to let the whole thing go unrecorded. Was it for this that I had gone footsore, cold, hot, wet, hungry? climbed up, and scrambled down? covered all those miles? looked at all those goats? Surely not. There must be a possible book in it somewhere. The book was always in my mind, teasing at me, and little by little, as time receded, it began to take shape, a meaning began to rise up out of the welter, a few definite conclusions which really had some bearing on half-formulated ideas; besides, the fingers which have once grown accustomed to a pen soon itch to hold one again: it is necessary to write, if the days are not to slip emptily by. How else, indeed, to clap the net over the butterfly of the moment? for the moment passes, it is forgotten; the mood is gone; life itself is gone. That is where the writer scores over his fellows: he catches the changes of his mind on the hop. Growth is exciting; growth is dynamic and alarming. Growth of the soul, growth of the mind; how the observation of last year seems childish, superficial; how this year, – even this week, – even with this new phrase, – it seems to us that we have grown to a new maturity. It may be a fallacious persuasion, but at least it is stimulating, and so long as it persists, one does not stagnate.

I look back as through a telescope, and see, in the little bright circle of the glass, moving flocks and ruined cities.[5]

At this point there is an important distinction to be drawn: the distinction between those travel writers who, like Miss Sackville-West, set out to tell the story of a single journey, and those whose object is to combine their knowledge of a given country or city with their memories of perhaps a dozen visits and so to produce not a narrative but a portrait. Of the portraitists, the most dazzling by far writing today remains Jan Morris – one of those rare authors who, while being naturally extrovert (I know of few travel writers who keep themselves so resolutely in the background), yet cannot help constantly reminding her readers of her presence, if only by the sparkling brilliance of her style. The opening paragraphs of *The Presence of Spain* betray not the faintest hint of the first person; at the same time, hardly a sentence in them could have been written by anyone else:

Spain is almost an island – a fragment crudely soldered, so the poet Auden thought, to the shape of Europe. Whichever way you enter her, from Portugal, France, Gibraltar, or the open sea, instantly you feel a sense of separateness – a geographical fact exaggerated by historical circumstance. The first of the invading Moors actually thought Spain was an island, and it was the Phoenicians, already sensing this seclusion or withdrawal, who called the country *Spania* – a word which some dullard philologists believe to mean The Land of Rabbits, but which all proper amateurs of Spain accept in its alternative interpretation, The Hidden Land.

The best entrance of all is the pass of Roncesvalles, the most heroic of the ten defiles that pierce the Pyrenees. It is a high demanding route, resonant with romance. Here, a thousand years ago, the knight-errant Roland blew his enchanted horn so deafeningly that the birds fell dead about him, and here the savage Basques, hurling themselves upon Charlemagne's rear guard, slaughtered half his men-at-arms. Through the pass of Roncesvalles, throughout the Middle Ages, caravans of pilgrims plodded southwards to the shrine of St. James at Santiago de Compostela, carrying forests of palm-crosses and singing brave hymns. Potentates of every era have passed this way into Spain, spies and ambassadors, merchants and marriage brokers, princesses destined for Spanish thrones and holy men on their way to sainthood. Here Marshal Soult fought a running battle with the British, as they chased the French out of the peninsula in 1813, and along this road thousands of wretched refugees stumbled into France during the Spanish Civil War. Roncesvalles is one of the classic passes of Europe, and a properly sombre gateway into Spain.

Winter is the time to make the journey. Then, as you approach the pass, the Pyrenean ramparts of Spain are at their most suggestive: brown, purple, and forbidding, with blushes of pink along their high snow-ridges, and wild white clouds eddying down their valleys. Beyond them, you feel, floodlights are perpetually blazing upon the stage of Spain, and you approach them with all the excitement of a visit to the theatre. There is a fanfare to the very name of Spain, and no nation offers an image more vivid. She seems to follow no fashion, obey no norm. She has generally stood aloof from the events of the recent past, from the Second World War to the nuclear race, and while to some her allure is only the spell of bathing beach and cheap wine, to others she stands apart because she does not yet feel reconciled to the twentieth century – has not quite succumbed to those pressures of materialism which we, like so many dim Frankensteins, half regret having devised.

Spain is one of the absolutes. Most States nowadays are willy-nilly passive, subject always to successive alien forces. Spain still declines in the active mood. She is not a Great Power, but in her minor way she is one of the prime movers still – still a nation that sets its own standards. To us poor ciphers of the computer culture, us cosmopolitan, humanist, cynical serfs of the machine, nothing is more compelling than the drama, at once dark and dazzling, of that theatre over the hills – the vast splendour of the Spanish landscape, the intensity of Spain's pride and misery, the adventurous glory of a history that set its seal upon half the world, the sadness of a decline that edged so inexorably from triumph to tragedy, through so many centuries of rot. All this, distilled in blazing heat and venomous cold, dusted by the sand of Africa, guarded by that mountain barricade above you – all this seems to await your arrival, beyond the pass of Roncesvalles.

Presently it all comes true. Skidding upwards through the windy sleet, soon you reach the head of the pass, and stand at the gate of Spain. All is deserted and forlorn up there. An old snow-plough lies tilted beside the road, a line of army huts lies derelict among the firs. Between the trees there broods the gaunt Augustinian monastery of Roncesvalles, with roofs that look like corrugated iron, and a great wet empty courtyard. A woman looks out of a door as you pass through its sullen hamlet. Two hooded policemen, huddled against the wind, respond numbly to your wave. Your first moments of Spain, if theatrical enough, hardly make you tingle.

But then you turn a corner out of the woodland, and suddenly there before you, below the level of the mist, there unfolds the great plain of the Ebro, with the foothills sweeping down towards the river. Space immeasurable seems to lie down there. All is brown but magnificent monotony – monotony of the desert kind, that has something mystic and exciting to it. In the middle distance a group of gypsies hastens with caravans, donkeys, and skinny dogs along the road, and beyond them all Spain seems to be expecting you – Spain of the shrines, Spain of the knights-errant, Spain of the guitars, the bull-rings, and the troglodytes. That evening you will sleep in Pamplona, where they let the young bulls loose in the streets on the feast of St. Fermín, where legend says they once killed ten thousand Jews to celebrate a prince's wedding, where the church bells sound like the clashing of coal shovels in the small hours, and the hotel pillows feel as though they are stuffed with mule-hair.[6]

Among those writers who describe particular journeys, there are still a few who start off with an impressionistic pen picture of their subject. Such a one is Jonathan Raban, whose book *Old Glory* consists of a compulsively readable account of his descent, alone and in a very small boat, of the Mississippi from St Louis to the delta.

It is as big and depthless as the sky itself. You can see the curve of the earth on its surface as it stretches away for miles to the far shore. Sunset has turned the water to the colour of unripe peaches. There's no wind. Sandbars and wooded islands stand on their exact reflections. The only signs of movement on the water are the lightly-scratched lines which run in parallel across it like the scores of a diamond on a windowpane. In the middle distance, the river smokes with toppling pillars of mist which soften the light so that one can almost reach out and take in handfuls of that thickened air.

A fish jumps. The river shatters for a moment, then glazes over. The forest which rims it is a long, looping smudge of charcoal. You could make it by running your thumb along the top edge of the water, smearing in the black pines and bog oaks, breaking briefly to leave a pale little town of painted clapboard houses tumbling from the side of a hill. Somewhere in the picture there is the scissored silhouette of a fisherman from the town, afloat between the islands in his wooden pirogue, a perfectly solitary figure casting into what is left of the sun.[7]

More often, however, the travel narrative begins as it means to go on – with a heavy emphasis on the personal. Here is Charles Dickens, embark-ing for America:

I shall never forget the one-fourth serious and three-fourths comical astonishment, with which, on the morning of the third of January eighteen-hundred-and-forty-two, I opened the door of, and put my head into, a 'state-room' on board the Britannia steam-packet, twelve hundred tons burthen per register, bound for Halifax and Boston, and carrying Her Majesty's mails.

That this state-room had been specially engaged for 'Charles Dickens, Esquire, and Lady,' was rendered sufficiently clear even to my scared intellect by a very small manuscript, announcing the fact, which was pinned on a very flat quilt, covering a very thin mattress, spread like a surgical plaster on a most inaccessible shelf. But that this was the state-room concerning which Charles Dickens, Esquire, and Lady, had held daily and nightly conferences for at least four months preceding: that this could by any possibility be that small snug chamber of the imagination, which Charles Dickens, Esquire, with the spirit of prophecy strong upon him, had always foretold would contain at least one little sofa, and which his lady, with a modest yet most magnificent sense of its limited dimensions, had from the first opined would not hold more than two enormous portmanteaus in some odd corner out of sight (portmanteaus which could now no more be got in at the door, not to say stowed away, than a giraffe could be persuaded or forced into a flower-pot): that this utterly impracticable, thoroughly hopeless, and profoundly preposterous box, had the remotest reference to, or connection with, those chaste and pretty, not to say gorgeous little bowers, sketched by a masterly hand, in the highly varnished lithographic plan hanging up in the agent's counting-house in the city of London: that this room of state, in short, could be anything but a pleasant fiction and cheerful jest of the captain's, invented and put in practice for the better relish and enjoyment of the real state-room presently to be disclosed: – these were truths which I really could not, for the moment, bring my mind at all to bear upon or comprehend. And I sat down upon a kind of horsehair slab, or perch, of which there were two within; and looked, without any expression of countenance whatever, at some friends who had come on board with us, and who were crushing their faces into all manner of shapes by endeavouring to squeeze them through the small doorway.

We had experienced a pretty smart shock before coming below, which, but that we were the most sanguine people living, might have prepared us for the worst. The imaginative artist to whom I have already made allusion, has depicted in the same great work, a chamber of almost interminable perspective, furnished, as Mr. Robins would say, in a style of more than Eastern splendour, and filled (but not inconveniently so) with groups of ladies and gentlemen, in the very highest state of enjoyment and vivacity. Before descending into the bowels of the ship, we had passed from the deck into a long narrow apartment, not unlike a gigantic hearse with windows in the sides; having at the upper end a melancholy stove, at which three or four chilly stewards were warming their hands; while on either side, extending down its whole dreary length, was a long, long table, over each of which a rack, fixed to the low roof, and stuck full of drinking-glasses and cruet-stands, hinted dismally at rolling seas and heavy weather. I had not at that time seen the ideal presentment of this chamber which has since gratified me so much, but I observed that one of our friends who had made the arrangements for our voyage, turned pale on entering, retreated on the friend behind him, smote his forehead involuntarily, and said below his breath, 'Impossible! it cannot be!' or words to that effect. He recovered himself however by a great effort, and after a preparatory cough or two, cried, with a ghastly smile which is still before me, looking at the same time round the walls, 'Ha! the breakfast-room, steward – eh?' We all foresaw what the answer must be: we knew the agony he suffered. He had often spoken of *the saloon*; had taken in and lived upon the pictorial idea; had usually given us to understand, at home, that to form a just conception of it, it would be necessary to multiply the size and furniture of an ordinary drawing-room by seven, and then fall short of the reality. When the man in reply avowed the truth; the blunt, remorseless, naked truth; 'This is the saloon, sir' – he actually reeled beneath the blow.[8]

There is plenty of humour here, but not much subtlety. Personally, I prefer the gentler approach of Sybille Bedford; in *A Visit to Don Otavio* – one of my favourite books – she effortlessly combines the two techniques, beginning with impressionism and then, almost imperceptibly, threading in a quiet personal strand.

Wide French windows opened from the domed, white-washed room on to a sun-splashed loggia above a garden white and red with the blooms of camellia, jasmine and oleander and the fruits of pomegranate, against a shaped luxuriance of dense, dark, waxed, leaves; and below the garden lay the lake, dull silver at that hour. At the end of a balustrade, the extravagant stone figure of St. Peter, fleeced with moss, raised a broken arm towards the waters. Another figure sprawled ensnared among the creepers where it had fallen a decade or two ago, and from an Italian urn grew a crimson flower like a banner. Three tall, tall, tapering palms swayed lightly on the shore. The air was sweet with tuberose and lime, and dancing like a pointilliste canvas with brilliant specks, bee and moth, humming-bird and dragonfly. Birds everywhere: slender birds with pointed scarlet tails, plump birds with yellow breasts and coral beaks, smooth birds with smarmed blue wings; darting birds and soft birds and birds stuck all over with crests and plumes and quills; tight-fitted birds and birds that wore their feathers like a Lully flourish, and striped birds as fantastically got up as cinquecento gondoliers; ibis and heron, dove and quail, egret and wild duck, swallows and cardinals, afloat, in the trees, on the lawn, dipping and skimming, in and out, out and in of a dozen open windows. A white cockatoo shrieked hideously from a shrub and was answered by the house parrot in Spanish. Bead curtains clicked from the kitchen quarters; and below, under the shade of a papaya-tree I could see Anthony reclining on a bamboo chaise-longue engaged in reading the works of Mr. Somerset Maugham.

The room behind me was all space and order and that aired and ample, hard white cleanness of the South that has the quality of lucidity substantiated and forms the limpid element in which the mind and body move at ease. An almost abstract room, rejecting the clutter of personality – a ceiling vaulted by an Indian whose father was taught by a Spaniard taught by a Moor; walls that were walls, and windows that were windows; a red-tiled floor; two or three pieces of Mexican Louis Seize beautifully waxed, a bed designed in another century and built in this one, a rug of shampooed angora goat and a pair of easy-chairs, perennial local products of pig-skin and bamboo.

The house was built in the eighteenth century for a family that would spend three months a year, and added on to later without a visible break in style. It is a two-storeyed Hacienda, washed apricot, with wings enclosing quadrangles and a long south-western front facing the lake. The ground plan is native, the statuary was brought from Italy; the garden is believed to be English. All is tempered by alternate periods of prosperity and care, absence and neglect.

Presently we shall bathe. E. will call to me, or I shall call to Anthony; we will walk to the end of the garden and slide into the lake without a shock, and with one leaping stroke coolly out of depth splash upon the mild and level water. The lake is immense, an inland-sea with bays set deep into three provinces, freshened by many rivers. A hundred miles of shore, undisgraced by rail or concrete, curve eastward toward Michoacán; and opposite our inlet one can see the outline of green hills upon another coast. Trees dip their branches over the calm water-front, a donkey drinks stiff-legged and two Indian women stand waist-deep washing each other's hair, while we lie under the palms on coarse sand and crackling birch-bleached weed, Anthony in full repose like an animal that has run, E. and I more restless, teasing a complacent fowl with pebbles and a rhyme in the manner of Edward Lear.

'The fish's come in.' Without lifting head from arms, Anthony has sensed the boat. Now the *comida* will be ready at the house; we shall eat under the thick shade of a west pergola, with the quick, straight, insouciant appetite of these altitudes: rice stewed with vegetables, fried eggs, *blanco*, a kind of small fat sole, very firm, brought up from the cold centre of the lake, avocados and fruit; attended by runners, two stocky Indian boys, Andreas and Domingo, swarthy, eager, tireless and headstrong like a pair of young mules. Something retrieves the meal from chaos:

> 'this eternal spring,
> Which here enamels every thing,
> And sends the fowls to us in care,
> On daily visits through the air; . . .'

The household and Anthony, who is reverting to some planter ancestry, will sleep the afternoon away. I, enlivened rather by these days of peace, have the choice of many shades to take my book. E. will pace the loggia swinging a small stick, the single upright figure during the slow hours, east west, west east, composing step by step, clause by clause the periods of an exegesis of one of the more incomprehensible personages of seventeenth-century France.[9]

Miss Bedford, to be sure, is not really writing about a journey; her book is primarily concerned with her stay in Mexico, rather than with how she actually got there. If we are looking for the beginnings of an adventure, she is not for us. We must then turn elsewhere – to Gavin Maxwell, for example, whose journey to the marshes of southern Iraq with Wilfred Thesiger was sparked off by his chance reading of an article by the latter in the *Journal* of the Royal Geographical Society. In *A Reed Shaken by the Wind* he gives what has always struck me as a quite hilarious account of the two men's first meeting:

When I read this article I had been searching for somewhere to go, somewhere that was not already suburbanised and where there was still something left to see that had not already been seen and described by hundreds or thousands of my kind before me. The margins of the atlas were closing in; the journeys I had dreamed in years before were blocked by the spreading stains of new political empires and impenetrable frontiers behind which, if propaganda is to be believed, the suburbanising process progressed but the faster.

I wrote to Thesiger, who was in London for the autumn and early winter, and we arranged to meet. He was very unlike the preconceived theories I had held about his appearance. The knowledge of his years of primitive living in the Sudan, Ethiopia, and Arabia, of ordeals and hardships past, had led me, perhaps, to expect someone a little indifferent to his personal appearance, someone with a contempt for conformity to the conventions of a European social group. The bowler hat, the hard collar and black shoes, the never-opened umbrella, all these were a surprise to me.

He was willing enough that I should accompany him when he returned to his marshes in January, but doubtful of my ability to stand the discomfort of the life.

'You seem to have led a fairly rough life,' he said, 'but this would be a bit different from anything you've had before. Can you sleep on the hard ground all right? – because you won't see a mattress in the marshes.'

I told him that I was well accustomed to it.

'And insect bites. The fleas there can be really quite something. They don't happen to bite me, but sometimes they keep me awake by sheer weight of numbers, and the Arabs themselves are often driven half crazy by them.'

Any flea within a mile's radius finds me and falls on me as though famished; they walk about me munching as they go, leaving red mountains with long connecting ridges between them. I thought it better not to mention this for the moment.

'And then there's diseases. The marsh people have every disease you can think of and lots that you can't – practically all infectious. It's my hobby; I'm not a trained doctor, but one acquires knowledge through experience and necessity. One tries to do something for them, and you'll find that we spend a lot of time doctoring. I've built up a certain immunity, but I don't know how you'd get on. They've all got dysentery, you know, and as the water level round their houses fluctuates the drinking supply and the public lavatory become one and the same thing. I took one Englishman into the marshes and he was carried out after ten days two stone lighter than he came in. He'd have died if I hadn't sent him back.'

I was determined to let nothing stand between me and this opportunity, and I professed complete indifference to all diseases. He had one more try. 'I wonder how long you can sit cross-legged. I'm always on the move, rarely spend two nights in the same place, and we travel in a canoe. So a great deal of every day is spent sitting cross-legged in the bottom of it. And you'll find that when you are ashore you spend a lot more time cross-legged on the floor of a marshman's hut. Can you sit cross-legged?'

I said I could try.

'Well,' said Thesiger, 'if you're so determined to come I'll be glad to have you with me.' And so it was arranged.[10]

I like, too, the young Evelyn Waugh's account of the preparations for his first journey to Ethiopia – or Abyssinia, as he still insisted on calling it. The book in which this account first appeared, *Waugh in Abyssinia* (a title which Waugh himself blamed on his publisher), is now very rare indeed; fortunately the best bits were included in an omnibus volume, published many years later and called *When the Going Was Good*. By then they had also provided valuable material for two of Waugh's funniest novels, *Black Mischief* and *Scoop*.

In the summer of 1935 the *Evening Standard* published a cartoon representing the Throne of Justice occupied by three apes who squatted in the traditional attitude, each with his hands covering his eyes, ears or mouth; beneath was the legend, '*See no Abyssinia; hear no Abyssinia; speak no Abyssinia*'.

This may have expressed the atmosphere of Geneva; it was wildly unlike London. There the editorial and managerial chairs of newspaper and publishing offices seemed to be peopled exclusively by a race of anthropoids who saw, heard and spoke no other subject.

Abyssinia was News. Everyone with any claims to African experience was cashing in. Travel books whose first editions had long since been remaindered were being reissued in startling wrappers. Literary agents were busy peddling the second serial rights of long-forgotten articles. Files were being searched for photographs of any inhospitable-looking people – Patagonian Indians, Borneo head-hunters, Australian aborigines – which could be reproduced to illustrate Abyssinian culture. In the circumstances anyone who had actually spent a few weeks in Abyssinia itself, and had read the dozen or so books which constituted the entire English bibliography of the subject, might claim to be an expert, and in this unfamiliar but not uncongenial disguise I secured employment with the only London newspaper which seemed to be taking a sane view of the situtation, as a 'war correspondent'.

There followed ten inebriating days of preparation, lived in an attitude of subdued heroism before friends, of knowledgeable discrimination at the tropical outfitters. There was a heat wave at the time. I trod miasmic pavements between cartographers and consulates. In the hall of my club a growing pile of packing cases, branded for Djibouti, began to constitute a serious inconvenience to the other members. There are few pleasures more complete, or to me more rare, than that of shopping extravagantly at someone else's expense. I thought I had treated myself with reasonable generosity until I saw the luggage of my professional competitors – their rifles and telescopes and ant-proof trunks, medicine chests, gas-masks, pack saddles, and vast wardrobes of costume suitable for every conceivable social or climatic emergency. Then I had an inkling of what later became abundantly clear to all, that I did not know the first thing about being a war correspondent.[11]

I have left the best till last. It is an extract from the long letter to Xan Fielding that forms the introduction to Patrick Leigh Fermor's *A Time of Gifts*. At the time of which he is writing, the author was eighteen years old.

About lamplighting time at the end of a wet November day, I was peering morosely at the dog-eared pages on my writing table and then through the panes at the streaming reflections of Shepherd Market, thinking, as *Night and Day* succeeded *Stormy Weather* on the gramophone in the room below, that *Lazybones* couldn't be far behind; when, almost with the abruptness of Herbert's lines . . . inspiration came. A plan unfolded with the speed and the completeness of a Japanese paper flower in a tumbler.

To change scenery; abandon London and England and set out across Europe like a tramp – or, as I characteristically phrased it to myself, like a pilgrim or a palmer, an errant scholar, a broken knight or the hero of *The Cloister and the Hearth*! All of a sudden, this was not merely the obvious, but the only thing to do. I would travel on foot, sleep in hayricks in summer, shelter in barns when it was raining or snowing and only consort with peasants and tramps. If I lived on bread and cheese and apples, jogging along on fifty pounds a year like Lord Durham with a few noughts knocked off, there would even be some cash left over for paper and pencils and an occasional mug of beer. A new life! Freedom! Something to write about!

Even before I looked at a map, two great rivers had already plotted the itinerary in my mind's eye: the Rhine uncoiled across it, the Alps rose up and then the wolf-harbouring Carpathian watersheds and the cordilleras of the Balkans; and there, at the end of the windings of the Danube, the Black Sea was beginning to spread its mysterious and lopsided shape; and my chief destination was never in a moment's doubt. The levitating skyline of Constantinople pricked its sheaves of thin cylinders and its hemispheres out of the sea-mist; beyond it Mount Athos hovered; and the Greek archipelago was already scattering a paper-chase of islands across the Aegean. (These certainties sprang from reading the books of Robert Byron; dragon-green Byzantium loomed serpent-haunted and gong-tormented; I had even met the author for a moment in a blurred and saxophone-haunted night club as dark as Tartarus.)

I wondered during the first few days whether to enlist a companion; but I knew that the enterprise had to be solitary and the break complete. I wanted to think, write, stay or move on at my own speed and unencumbered, to gaze at things with a changed eye and listen to new tongues that were untainted by a single familiar word. With any luck the humble circumstances of the journey would offer no scope for English or French. Flights of unknown syllables would soon be rushing into purged and attentive ears.

The idea met obstruction at first: why not wait till spring? (London by now was shuddering under veils of December rain.) But when they understood that all was decided, most of the objectors became allies. Warming to the scheme after initial demur, Mr. Prideaux [his tutor at a London crammer] undertook to write to India [where his father lived] putting my démarche in a favourable light; I determined to announce the *fait accompli* by letter when I was safely on the way, perhaps from Cologne ... Then we planned the despatch of those weekly pounds – each time, if possible, after they had risen to a monthly total of four – by registered letter to suitably spaced-out *postes restantes*. (Munich would be the first; then I would write and suggest a second.) I next borrowed fifteen pounds off the father of a school friend, partly to buy equipment and partly to have something in hand when I set out. I telephoned to my sister Vanessa, back from India again a few years before, and married and settled in Gloucestershire. My mother was filled with apprehension to begin with; we pored over the atlas, and, bit by bit as we pored, the comic possibilities began to unfold in absurd imaginary scenes until we were falling about with laughter; and by the time I caught the train to London next morning, she was infected with my excitement.

During the last days, my outfit assembled fast. Most of it came from Millet's army surplus store in The Strand: an old Army greatcoat, different layers of jersey, grey flannel shirts, a couple of white linen ones for best, a soft leather windbreaker, puttees, nailed boots, a sleeping bag (to be lost within a month and neither missed nor replaced); notebooks and drawing blocks, rubbers, an aluminium cylinder full of Venus and Golden Sovereign pencils; an old *Oxford Book of English Verse*. (Lost likewise, and, to my surprise – it had been a sort of Bible – not missed much more than the sleeping bag.) The other half of my very conventional travelling library was the Loeb *Horace*, Vol. I, which my mother, after asking what I wanted, had bought and posted in Guildford. (She had written the translation of a short poem by Petronius on the flyleaf, chanced on and copied out, she told me later, from another volume on the same shelf: 'Leave thy home, O youth, and seek out alien shores . . . Yield not to misfortune: the far-off Danube shall know thee, the cold North-wind and the untroubled kingdom of Canopus and the men who gaze on the new birth of Phoebus or upon his setting . . .' She was an enormous reader, but Petronius was not in her usual line of country and he had only recently entered mine. I was impressed and touched.) Finally I bought a ticket on a small Dutch steamer sailing from Tower Bridge to the Hook of Holland. All this had taken a shark's bite out of my borrowed cash, but there was still a wad of notes left over.

At last, with a touch of headache from an eve-of-departure party, I got out of bed on the great day, put on my new kit and tramped south-west under a lowering sky. I felt preternaturally light, as though I were already away and floating like a djinn escaped from its flask through the dazzling middle air while Europe unfolded. But the grating hobnails took me no farther than Cliveden Place, where I picked up a rucksack left for me there by Mark Ogilvie-Grant. Inspecting my stuff, he had glanced with pity at the one I had bought. (His – a superior Bergen affair resting on a lumbar semicircle of metal and supported by a triangular frame, had accompanied him – usually, he admitted, slung on a mule – all round Athos with Robert Byron and David Talbot-Rice when *The Station* was being written. Weathered and faded by Macedonian suns, it was rife with *mana*.) Then I bought for ninepence a well-balanced ashplant at the tobacconist's next to the corner of Sloane Square and headed for Victoria Street and Petty France to pick up my new passport. Filling in the form the day before – born in London, 11 February 1915; height 5′ 9¾″; eyes, brown; hair, brown; distinguishing marks, none – I had left the top space empty, not knowing what to write. Profession? 'Well, what shall we say?' the Passport Official had asked, pointing to the void. My mind remained empty. A few years earlier, an American hobo song called *Hallelujah I'm a bum!* had been on many lips; during the last days it had been haunting me like a private *leitmotif* and without realizing I must have been humming the tune as I pondered, for the Official laughed 'You can't very well put *that*', he said. After a moment he added: 'I should just write "student"'; so I did. With the stiff new document in my pocket, stamped '8 December 1933', I struck north over the Green Park under a dark massing of cloud. As I crossed Piccadilly and entered the crooked chasm of White Horse Street, there were a few random splashes and, glistening at the end of it, Shepherd Market was prickly with falling drops. I would be just in time for a goodbye luncheon with Miss Stewart and three friends – two fellow-lodgers and a girl: then, away. The rain was settling in.[12]

CHAPTER FOUR

Departures

Are the horses come?
Yes, sir.
Have them put to directly, for we wish to set off immediately.
They are to already.
Is the trunk well fastened?
Yes, sir; it is well secured.
Have you not put the chain round it?
Yes, sir; that was the first thing we did.
I should not like the trunk to be stolen on the road.
There is no danger.
Look into all the rooms, that nothing may be forgotten.
I have looked everywhere, nothing is forgotten.
Come, let us go down, gentlemen; it is time to set off.
Take these two hats, and put them in the net.
Put this cane and umbrella into the case; and these shoes and boots into the boot.
But, my dear sir, what must we do with these books?
We will carry them down ourselves, and put them in the pockets.
Postilion, mind you go slowly when the road is bad, and when you make a turn;
    we do not wish either to be jolted or overturned.
I shall obey your orders, sir.
Go on the side of the road as much as you can, to avoid jolting, and then drive
    quick.
Yes, sir.
Where there are ruts or stones, drive on the pavement.
I shall try to please you.
John, open the door, and let down the step.
Good bye.
I wish you a good journey, gentlemen.[1]

This conversation, from Dr Baedeker's *Traveller's Manual* of 1886, seems to me to give a quite extraordinarily vivid picture of a departure by coach as it must have been not only in the nineteenth, but also in the eighteenth and even the seventeenth centuries. What it does not describe, however, is the amount of preparation that must have been necessary in former times before any major journey could be undertaken at all. Captain Fred

Burnaby, for example, making himself ready for his great ride to Khiva, had to have not only his travelling clothes but even his sleeping bag – of which then quite recent invention this is, I suspect, the first mention in English literature – specially made for him:

The time was wearing on, November was drawing to a close, my leave of absence would begin on the first of the following month. On that day I must commence my travels. Preparations were rapidly made. Under the advice of Captain Allen Young, of Arctic fame, I ordered a huge waterproof, and, consequently, air-proof, bag of prepared sail-cloth. The bag was seven feet and a half long, and ten feet round. A large aperture was left on one side, and the traveller could thus take up his quarters inside, and sleep well protected from the cold winds. The bag would also be useful in many other ways, and I found it of great convenience for every purpose save the one for which it was originally intended. The manufacturer, not calculating on the enormous dimensions an individual assumes when enveloped in furs, had not made the aperture large enough. The consequence was that the difficulties, when I attempted to take a header into the recess of my sleeping apartment, were almost insurmountable. Only on one occasion, and when somewhat lighter clad than usual, I succeeded in effecting an entrance. Four pairs of the thickest Scotch fishing stockings were also ordered; and jerseys and flannel shirts of a texture to which people in this country are but little accustomed. Then came a suit of clothes, made by Messrs. Kino, of Regent Street, and in which they assured me it would be impossible to feel cold. The clothes, I must admit, were exceptionally well made, and well suited to be worn under a sheepskin attire, but I cannot wish my worst enemy a greater punishment than forcing him to sleep out on the steppes in winter time with mere cloth attire, no matter how thick. Fur or skins of some kind must be worn, or without this precaution the traveller, should he once close his eyes, will undergo a great risk of never opening them again. Two pairs of boots lined with fur were also taken; and for physic – with which it is as well to be supplied when travelling in out-of-the-way places – some quinine, and Cockle's pills, the latter a most invaluable medicine, and one which I have used on the natives of Central Africa with the greatest possible success. In fact, the marvellous effects produced upon the mind and body of an Arab Sheik, who was impervious to all native medicines, when I administered to him five Cockle's pills, will never fade from my memory; and a friend of mine, who passed through the same district many months afterwards, informed me that my fame as a 'medicine man' had not died out, but that the marvellous cure was even then a theme of conversation in the bazaar.[2]

By Evelyn Waugh's day virtually everything required for travel to distant parts of the earth was obtainable over the counter, if you knew which counter to go to. One suspects that William Boot, the hero of *Scoop*, was sent by his paper to the Army and Navy Stores:

The Foreign Contacts Adviser of *The Beast* telephoned the emporium where William was to get his kit and warned them of his arrival; accordingly it was General Cruttwell, F.R.G.S., himself who was waiting at the top of the lift shaft.

An imposing man: Cruttwell Glacier in Spitzbergen, Cruttwell Falls in Venezuela, Mount Cruttwell in the Pamirs, Cruttwell's Leap in Cumberland marked his travels; Cruttwell's Folly, a waterless and indefensible camp near Salonika, was notorious to all who served with him in the war. The shop paid him six hundred a year and commission, out of which, by contract, he had to find his annual subscription to the R.G.S. and the electric treatment which maintained the leathery tan of his complexion.

Before either had spoken the General sized William up; in any other department he would have been recognized as a sucker; here, amid the trappings of high adventure he was, more gallantly, a greenhorn.

'Your first visit to Ishmaelia, eh? Then perhaps I can be some help to you. As no doubt you know I was there in '97 with poor "Sprat" Larkin . . .'

'I want some cleft sticks, please,' said William firmly.

The General's manner changed abruptly. His leg had been pulled before, often. Only last week there had been an idiotic young fellow dressed up as a missionary . . . 'What the devil for?' he asked tartly.

'Oh, just for my despatches you know.'

It was with exactly such an expression of simplicity that the joker had asked for a tiffin gun, a set of chota pegs and a chota mallet. 'Miss Barton will see to you,' he said, and turning on his heel he began to inspect a newly-arrived consignment of rhinoceros hide whips in a menacing way.

Miss Barton was easier to deal with. 'We can have some cloven for you,' she said brightly. 'If you will make your selection I will send them down to our cleaver.'

William, hesitating between polo sticks and hockey sticks, chose six of each; they were removed to the work-shop. Then Miss Barton led him through the departments of the enormous store. By the time she had finished with him, William had acquired a well-, perhaps rather over-, furnished tent, three months' rations, a collapsible canoe, a jointed flagstaff and Union Jack, a hand-pump and sterilizing plant, an astrolabe, six suits of tropical linen and a sou'-wester, a camp operating table and set of surgical instruments, a portable humidor, guaranteed to preserve cigars in condition in the Red Sea, and a Christmas hamper complete with Santa Claus costume and a tripod mistletoe stand, and a cane for whacking snakes. Only anxiety about time brought an end to his marketing. At the last moment he added a coil of rope and a sheet of tin; then he left under the baleful stare of General Cruttwell.[3]

A comparison of this passage with the corresponding one from *Waugh in Abyssinia*, quoted in the previous chapter, shows how brilliantly the author could construct a comic scene out of his own personal experience. (The character of the general, incidentally, is a typical Waughlike dig at C.R.M.F. Cruttwell, Dean of Hertford College, Oxford, during his university days, of whom he was many years later to write: 'He was tall, almost loutish, with the face of a petulant baby. He smoked a pipe which was usually attached to his blubber-lips by a thread of slime.' The same name is given to a minor character, either ridiculous or repugnant, in each of his first five novels.)

But all this concerns more the preliminaries to departure than the departure itself. For the real thing, here is Captain Joshua Slocum, setting out at the age of fifty-one on the first ever single-handed circumnavigation of the globe:

But at last the time arrived to weigh anchor and get to sea in earnest. I had resolved on a voyage around the world, and as the wind on the morning of April 24, 1895, was fair, at noon I weighed anchor, set sail, and filled away from Boston, where the *Spray* had been moored snugly all winter. The twelve-o'clock whistles were blowing just as the sloop shot ahead under full sail. A short board was made up the harbour on the port tack, then coming about she stood seaward, with her boom well off to port, and swung past the ferries with lively heels. A photographer on the outer pier at East Boston got a picture of her as she swept by, her flag at the peak throwing its folds clear. A thrilling pulse beat high in me. My step was light on deck in the crisp air. I felt that there could be no turning back, and that I was engaging in an adventure the meaning of which I thoroughly understood. I had taken little advice from any one, for I had a right to my own opinions in matters pertaining to the sea. That the best of sailors might do worse than even I alone was borne in upon me not a league from Boston docks, where a great steamship, fully manned, officered, and piloted, lay stranded and broken. This was the *Venetian*. She was broken completely in two over a ledge. So in the first hour of my lone voyage I had proof that the *Spray* could at least do better than this full-handed steamship, for I was already farther on my voyage than she. 'Take warning, *Spray*, and have a care,' I uttered aloud to my bark, passing fairylike silently down the bay.

The wind freshened, and the *Spray* rounded Deer Island light at the rate of seven knots.

Passing it, she squared away direct for Gloucester to procure there some fishermen's stores. Waves dancing joyously across Massachusetts Bay met her coming out of the harbour to dash them into myriads of sparkling gems that hung about her at every surge. The day was perfect, the sunlight clear and strong. Every particle of water thrown into the air became a gem, and the *Spray*, bounding ahead, snatched necklace after necklace from the sea, and as often threw them away. We have all seen miniature rainbows about a ship's prow, but the *Spray* flung out a bow of her own that day, such as I had never seen before. Her good angel had embarked on the voyage; I so read it in the sea.[4]

Reading that last paragraph, we can almost share Slocum's own exhilaration. Alas, not all departures are quite like that, as Peter Fleming knew only too well. In *One's Company* he writes:

Whenever people tell me how passionately they desire to Get Away From It All, I think I know what is in their mind's eye. They see themselves riding off into the sunset, or paddling a canoe down the silver wake of the moon, or very slowly (but ecstatically) stretching their arms on the edge of a huge precipice; they see themselves, in fact, in terms of the silent film. They imagine some vast solitude with a healthy climate, where no telephones ring and no maids give notice, where there are no income-tax returns and incidentally no insects: where the Simple Life is possible.

Such an Arden, though it may exist, would not, I fear, be as they like it. But where they make their gravest error is in supposing, as dramatists and film-directors have licence to suppose, that the process of Getting Away From It All has a climax, that there comes a sharp, sweet moment when the escaper consciously relishes the full flavour of escape. In my experience no such moment exists. We do not, to-day, cut loose. We wriggle out of one complicated existence like a snake sloughing its skin, and by the time we have wriggled into the next it has become complicated too. The raptures, the first flush of flight, wither unfelt as we say our farewells, and catch our train and then our boat, and wire back some instructions that we forgot to leave behind, and find that we have lost our certificate of vac-cination. The old life overlaps what should have been the most exhilarating moments of the new; the first stage on the golden road to Samarkand has no enchantment for the man who is doubtful whether they packed his evening shoes.[5]

Nevertheless, he is a world-weary man indeed who does not feel some thrill at the thought that in a few hours he will be on his way to some distant and as yet unfamiliar land. Even the last-minute hitches have been known to add to the excitement. Every major departure must have its moments of anxiety, even of panic; but once the train has been caught, the ship boarded – once, I might even dare to suggest, the aeroplane has left the ground – then, sooner or later, a mild euphoria steals quietly over the traveller. He is on his way. Listen to Robert Byron, setting off for Mount Athos:

The sun, admitted at eight o'clock, struck the doors of the cupboard opposite with a meaning that sent a tremor through the nerves and a ball of air into the pit of the body. Over the bed the fringes danced response to a quickened heartbeat. For the day of departure had dawned; day, in another sense, of return.

That afternoon I proceeded to London, and arose next morning to shop. The manager of that imperial institution, Fortnum and Mason's, improvised poems on the contents of the saddle-bags. Six pound tins of chocolate, two of chutney, a syphon brooding like a hen over its sparklets in a wooden box, pills, toilet requisites and stationery gradually accrued, together with the ink in a tin case from which these magic words pour. But to devise chemical armour against the insects which await with hideous patience the infrequent tenants of those musty guest-rooms, defied the ingenuity of every pharmacist from W.2 to E.C.4. I am fortunate, however, in possessing some revolting physical attribute, which prevents me, though not impervious to tickling, from being bitten.

At 10.51 on Friday, August 12th, I left Victoria, surrounded by suit-case, kit-bag, saddle-bags, hat-box (harbouring, besides a panama, towels and pillow-cases), syphon-box, and a smug despatch-case that contained a lesser known Edgar Wal-lace and credentials to every grade of foreign dignitary, from the Customs to the higher clergy. Only as the train started did I discover the loss of the keys to these receptacles. Fortunately the carpenter of the Channel boat was able to provide substitutes for all but the suit-case. Meanwhile, troubles fell away as the pages of perhaps the greatest master of English fiction disclosed the appalling mis-demeanours of Harry Alford, 18th Earl of Chelford. These were tempered with the

items of the *Central European Observer*, a periodical new to my journalistic appetite, whose title had peeped like a succulent strawberry from a cabbage-bed of
Liberal weeklies and Conservative quarterlies.

The Channel was rough; but with the undoing of the luggage, the plying of the
carpenter with beer, and the delightful spectacle of an arrogant humanity draped
about the seats in green and helpless confusion, the passage passed unnoticed.
Happiness untrammelled was restored at the sight of the rotund coaches of the
Train Bleu. For itinerant comfort, the palm must ever remain with this serpentine
palace. Curled against the garter-blue velvet of a single compartment, the French
afternoon whirred past me in comatose delight. At length came Paris, the clumped
ova of the Sacré Cœur standing high and white against copper storm-clouds. Slowly
we shunted round the *ceinture* amid those intimacies of slum-life presented by the
main line traverse of any great city: hopeless figures gazing in immobile despon-
dency through the importance of the train at their own troubles; children roving
the open spaces on tenement balconies; garments sexless, patched, one inevitably
Tartan, listless on their lines; healthy plants and flowers rendered pathetic by
environment; the whole gamut of man's misery, so it seems to the looker. At the
Gare de Lyons the train doubled itself, gathered up its passengers, and started for
the south.

Dinner was epic. Sleep cradled in the clouds. Morning broke with Avignon. And
the sun rose over a barber's chair at Marseilles.[6]

It must be admitted, however, that Robert Byron was not always so
lucky. A few years later, in 1933, he attempted another departure, this time
from Teheran to Meshed:

Teheran, November 11th. – Saturday. Still here.

I decided to leave on Tuesday. On Monday I found a Morris car for sale at £30.
This seemed a bargain. In fact I actually supposed it would enable me to leave next
day.

The sequence, which then began, of getting possession of the car, getting a
licence to drive it with, getting a permit to stay in Persia at all, getting a permit to
go to Meshed, getting a letter to the Governor of Meshed, and getting other letters
to the governors en route, obliterated four days. I was said to be 'recalcitrant de la
loi' for having no identity card. To obtain one, I furnished the state archives with
the secret of my mother's birthplace, in triplicate. Meanwhile, the owner of the car
had left Teheran, confiding his power of attorney to a very old lawyer in a pink
tweed frock-coat. A bargain was struck; signatures were officially witnessed; but
the police refused to register the transaction because, although the lawyer's power
of attorney extended to all his employer's worldly goods, a Morris car was not
mentioned in the list of those goods. This decision was reversed, on appeal to a
higher police official, who telephoned the fact to his subordinate. But when we
returned to the other department, 300 yards away, they knew nothing of it. Neighbouring departments were asked if they had had the message. At last someone
remembered that the person who must have answered the telephone had gone out.
Heaven favoured us; we met him in the street, and followed him to his desk. This

annoyed him. He would do nothing, he said, without a copy of the power of attorney. Till it was ready, perhaps we would be good enough to leave him in peace. The lawyer hobbled off to buy a clean sheet of paper. We, the owner's son, the garage proprietor and myself, sought asylum on the pavement of the main square, squatting round the crabbed old scribe while his spectacles fell off his nose, and his pen harpooned the paper till it looked like a stencil. A sentence was not finished before the police moved us on; another scarcely begun, before they did so again. Like a colony of disturbed toads, we scuttled round and round the square, jabbing down a word here and there, while dusk deepened into night. When the copy was presented, it had again to be copied, in the office. The square had been better than this; for the office electricity had failed, and matches had to be struck in such quantities that our fingers were burned to the quick. I laughed; the others laughed; the police laughed like madmen; but suddenly becoming serious, said the certificate of ownership could not after all be ready for three days. An hour's argument evoked a promise of next morning. Next morning I went in search of it; again they said three days. But now, being alone, I had the advantage, speaking enough Persian to say what I wanted, but not enough to understand a refusal. Once more we trooped off to the officer across the street. Men rushed from room to room. The telephone spluttered. The document was born. And all this, let me add, was only a tithe, a mere sample, of my fate during these last four days.

The date of the car is 1926, and its engine has needed some attention. After testing it yesterday, I proposed to start at six this morning. But by the end of the test, the battery had failed. I shall leave at midday and hope to make Amiriya tonight, where the worst of the passes but one will be over. . . .

Ayn Varzan (c. 5000 ft.), later 7.30 p.m. – The back axle has broken, sixty miles from Teheran.

'To Khorasan! To Khorasan!' shouted the policeman at the city gate. I felt a wonderful exhilaration as we chugged through the Elburz defiles. Up or down, the engine was always in bottom gear; only this could save us from being precipitated, backwards or forwards as the case might be, over the last or next hairpin bend.

Seven chanting peasants pushed the car uphill to a shed in this village. It is a total loss. But I won't go back to Teheran.[7]

One of the most wholly enjoyable travel books ever written is *Eothen*, the narrative by Alexander Kinglake of his journey to the East in 1834. In Chapter Eleven you will find a hilarious account of his conversation with the Turkish Pasha at Belgrade, then the frontier town of the Ottoman Empire; soon afterwards, in the company of his friend Lord Pollington (referred to here as Methley after his country seat), he departs:

In two or three hours our party was ready; the servants, the Tatar, the mounted Suridgees, and the baggage-horses altogether made up a strong cavalcade. The accomplished Mysseri, of whom you have heard me speak so often, and who served me so faithfully throughout my Oriental journeys, acted as our interpreter, and was, in fact, the brain of our corps. The Tatar, you know, is a government courier properly employed in carrying despatches, but also sent with travellers to speed them on their way and answer with his head for their safety. The man whose head was thus pledged for our precious lives was a glorious looking fellow, with that regular and handsome cast of countenance which is now characteristic of the Otto-man race.* His features displayed a good deal of serene pride, self-respect, forti-tude, a kind of ingenuous sensuality, and something of instinctive wisdom, without any sharpness of intellect. He had been a Janissary (as I afterwards found), and he still kept up the old praetorian strut which used to affright the Christians in former times – a strut so comically pompous, that any close imitation of it, even in the broadest farce, would be looked upon as a very rough over-acting of the character. It is occasioned in part by dress and accoutrements. The weighty bundle of weapons carried upon the chest throws back the body so as to give it a wonderful portliness, and, moreover, the immense masses of clothes that swathe his limbs force the wearer in walking to swing himself heavily round from left to right, and from right to left. In truth, this great edifice of woollen, and cotton, and silk, and silver, and brass, and steel, is not at all fitted for moving on foot; it cannot even walk without frightfully discomposing its fair proportions; and as to running – our Tatar ran *once* (it was in order to pick up a partridge that Methley had winged with a pistol-shot), and the attempt was one of the funniest misdirections of human energy that wondering man ever saw. But put him in his stirrups, and then is the Tatar himself again: there he lives at his pleasure, reposing in the tranquillity of that true home (the home of his ancestors), which the saddle seems to afford him, and drawing from his pipe the calm pleasures of his 'own fireside'; or else dashing sudden over the earth, as though for a moment he felt the mouth of a Turcoman steed, and saw his own Scythian plains lying boundless and open before him.

It was not till his subordinates had nearly completed their preparations for the march that our Tatar, 'commanding the forces', arrived; he came sleek and fresh from the bath (for so is the custom of the Ottomans when they start upon a journey), and was carefully accoutred at every point. From his thigh to his throat he was laden with arms and other implements of a campaigning life. There is no scarcity of water along the whole road from Belgrade to Stamboul, but the habits of our Tatar were formed by his ancestors, and not by himself, so he took good care to see that his leathern water-flask was amply charged and properly strapped to the saddle along with his blessed tchibouque. And now, at last, he has cursed the Suridgees, in all proper figures of speech, and is ready for a ride of a thousand miles; but before he comforts his soul in the marble baths of Stamboul he will be another and a lesser man – his sense of responsibility, his too strict abstemiousness, and his restless energy, disdainful of sleep, will have worn him down to a fraction of the sleek Moostapha who now leads out our party from the gates of Belgrade.

The Suridgees are the men employed to lead the baggage-horses. They are most of them Gipsies. Their lot is a sad one: they are the last of the human race, and all the sins of their superiors (including the horses) can safely be visited on them. But the wretched look often more picturesque than their betters; and though all the world despise these poor Suridgees, their tawny skins and their grisly beards will

---

* The continual marriages of these people with the chosen beauties of Georgia and Circassia have overpowered the original ugliness of their Tatar ancestors.

gain them honourable standing in the foreground of a landscape. We had a couple of these fellows with us, each leading a baggage-horse, to the tail of which last another baggage-horse was attached. There was a world of trouble in pursuading the stiff angular portmanteaus of Europe to adapt themselves to their new condition, and sit quietly on pack-saddles, but all was right at last, and it gladdened my eyes to see our little troop file off through the winding lanes of the city, and show down brightly in the plain beneath: the one of our party most out of keeping with the rest of the scene was Methley's Yorkshire servant, who always rode doggedly on in his pantry jacket, looking out for 'gentlemen's seats'.[8]

Eothen carries no dedication; it is, however, prefaced by a letter 'addressed by the Author to One of his Friends' – in fact a certain Eliot Warburton, who had been a contemporary of Kinglake's at Eton and whose searching enquiries after the latter's return had encouraged him to write the book. A year or two afterwards Warburton himself set out on his travels. His humour is more ponderous than that of his friend, and he is already infected with that arch sentimentality which was to become the inescapable scourge of the generation following his own; but he writes well none the less, and produces a wonderfully evocative picture of what must always be the most romantic of all departures – by ship to the East.

We took leave of Old England and the Old Year together. New Year's daylight found us standing on Southampton Pier, while the town itself lay buried beneath an avalanche of snowy mist, through which a few spires scarcely struggled into sight. The Oriental steam-ship lay about a gun-shot from the shore, sucking in a mingled mass of passengers and luggage through a cavernous mouth in her cliff-like side; boatload after boatload was swallowed like mere spoonfuls, until it seemed marvellous how even her aldermanic bulk could 'find stomach for them all.' I had the Polyphemian boon of being devoured last, and was thus a mere observer of the partings and departings of the 'Outward bound.'

On mounting the ship's side, I found the lower deck one vast pile of luggage, vainly endeavouring to be identified by its distracted owners. No one seemed to find anything they wanted; cyclopean portmanteaus, 'to be opened at Calcutta,' presented themselves freely; saddlery and bullock-trunks were quite obtrusive; but little 'indispensables for the voyage' were nowhere to be found – night garments were invisible, and remedies for sea-sickness reserved themselves for the overland journey. Search and suspense, however, were soon terminated by the sinking of the whole chaotic mass into the yawning depths of the hold, and the tomb-like hatches closed over our 'loved and lost.' After this bereavement, we all assembled on the upper-deck, in involuntary and unconscious muster, each inspecting and inspected by his fellow-travellers.

With the exception of two or three families, every one seemed to be a stranger to every one, and each walked the deck in a solitude of his own. There were old men, with complexions as yellow as the gold for which they had sold their youth, returning to India in search of the health which their native country, longed for through a life, denied them. There were young cadets, all eagerness and hope, though these, their predecessors, stood before them, mementos, – like the mummies at Egyptian banquets, – of the end of their young life's festival. There were missionary clergymen with Ruth-like wives; merchants, with invoices apparently as fondly prized; young widows, with eyes black as their mourning, and sparkling as their useless marriage-ring; and one or two fair girls – Heaven knows what sorrow sent them there! – straying from their English homes of peace and purity, over the ocean and the desert, to encounter the worst dangers of Indian society. Then there were little cadets, in whom the pride of new-born independence and uniform contended with fond and melancholy thoughts of home: there were sailors, with the blunt manly bearing, and free open speech of their profession: and, lastly, there were two or three vague wanderers, like myself, who were only leaving Europe, as men leave a crowded room, to breathe awhile freely in the open East.

All these, in various groups, were scattered over the spacious upper deck, on which there was no stain, nor any interruption to the lady's walk or the sailor's rush; it was smooth, flush, and level, except for the graceful and almost imperceptible swell and rise towards the bows.

Below, the busy, bustling scene was very different. Miss Mitford herself might recognise the lower deck as a complete village. It was a street of cabins, over whose doors you read the addresses of the doctor, the baker, the butcher, the confectioner, the carpenter, and many others; besides the 'quality at the west end,' in the shape of officers quarters. This street terminated in a rural scene, where the smell of new-mown hay, the lowing of cattle, the bleating of sheep, and the crowing of cocks, produced quite a pastoral effect. Among these signs of peace and plenty, four carronades frowned rather gloomily; and beneath the farm-yard throbbed the iron heart of the gigantic engine.

About noon, the last boat shoved off, the gangway curled itself up, a voice from the paddle-boxes said quietly – 'Go on!' – and the vast vessel glided away as smoothly as a gondola.

The first day of our voyage passed very silently away: many of my comrades were sea-sick, and more were sick at heart; but in the evening there was a startling eruption of writing-desks, and a perfect flutter of pens preparing for the Falmouth post-bag. I think I see those eager scribes before me now: men of business, with their swift and steady quill; women, gracefully bending over their twice-crossed notes (not the more legible, lady! for that tear –); and lonely little boys, biting their bran-new pen-holders, and looking up to the ceiling in search of pleasant things to say to some bereaved mother. Her only comfort, perhaps, was to be that little scrawl, till her self-sacrificing heart was at rest for ever, or success had gilded her child's far-distant career.[9]

Even then, however, some sailings – like some writers – were more romantic than others. Edward Lear's departure from the South of France for Corsica seems not to have been romantic in the least, but then nor was Lear himself; he never learnt to take himself seriously enough, for one thing.

APRIL 8, 1868 It seems a pity to leave Cannes just as the most pleasant and beautiful season is beginning; but if a sketching tour is to be made in Corsica, this is the right and perhaps the only time to choose, at least if all parts of the island are to be visited; earlier, the snow would have made the higher districts unavailable to the landscape painter; later, the heat would prevent work being easy or possible. So I close my rooms in M. Guichard's house, and say good-bye for the present to the cheerful town and its quiet bay, with the beautiful Esterelles on the horizon.

Off by rail to Nice, whence every week a steamer starts for Corsica, going alternately to Ajaccio on the west coast, and to Bastia on the east. This week Ajaccio is the point, and the *Insulaire* is to leave the port at 8 p.m., a roomy and well-appointed steamboat, fares thirty-one and twenty-one francs for first- and second-class places. I go from the pier at seven, and on reaching the boat meet with a pleasant surprise in finding my friend J.A.S., [John Adington Symonds] with Mrs. J.S. and the little Janet [for whom Lear was to write *The Owl and the Pussycat*] already on board.

Meanwhile clouds cover the sky – so bright and clear all day – the wind rises before we are fairly off at eight-thirty, and instead of the smooth sea, full moonlight, and other delicacies of a night voyage fondly hoped for, the most ugly forebodings are heard concerning a rough passage, whereby the landscape painter, always a miserable sailor, begins to repent of his decision to draw all Corsica, and, were it possible, would fain return to land. But it is too late; and the only alternative is to cultivate sulkiness and retreat instantly to bed; the cabin will be at least a tolerably quiet one, for of passengers there are but few. Neither on deck is any living being left but two fat and perpetually backwards-and-forward trotting poodles.

APRIL 9   The night voyage, though far from pleasant, has not been as bad as might have been anticipated. He is fortunate, who, after ten hours of sea passage, can reckon up no worse memories than those of a passive condition of suffering – of that dislocation of mind and body, or inability to think straightforward, so to speak, when the outer man is twisted, and rolled, and jerked, and the movements of thought seem more or less to correspond with those of the body. Wearily go by

> The slow sad hours that bring us all things ill

and vain is the effort to enliven them as every fresh lurch of the vessel tangles practical or pictorial suggestions with untimely scraps of poetry, indistinct regrets and predictions, couplets for a new *Book of Nonsense* and all kinds of inconsequent imbecilities – after this sort –

Would it not have been better to have remained at Cannes, where I had not yet visited Theoule, the Saut de Loup, and other places?

Had I not said, scores of times, such and such a voyage was the last I would make?

Tomorrow, when 'morn broadens on the borders of the dark', shall I see Corsica's 'snowy mountain tops fringing the (Eastern) sky'?

Did the sentinels of lordly Volaterra see, as Lord Macaulay says they did, 'Sardinia's snowy mountain-tops', and not rather these same Corsican tops, 'fringing the southern sky'?

Did they see any tops at all, or if any, which tops?

Will the daybreak ever happen?

Will two o'clock ever arrive?

Will the two poodles above stairs ever cease to run about the deck?

Is it not disagreeable to look forward to two or three months of travelling quite alone?

Would it not be delightful to travel, as J.A.S. is about to do, in company with a wife and child?

Does it not, as years advance, become clearer that it is very odious to be alone?

Have not many very distinguished persons, Œnone among others, arrived at this conclusion?

Did she not say, with evident displeasure –

> And from that time to this I am alone,
> And I shall be alone until I die? –

Will those poodles ever cease from trotting up and down the deck?

Is it not unpleasant, at fifty-six years of age, to feel that it is increasingly probable that a man can never hope to be otherwise than alone, never, no, never more?

Did not Edgar Poe's raven distinctly say 'Nevermore'?

Will those poodles be quiet? 'Quoth the raven, nevermore.'

Will there be anything worth seeing in Corsica?

Is there any romance left in that island? Is there any sublimity or beauty in its scenery?

Have I taken too much baggage?

Have I not rather taken too little?

Am I not an idiot for coming at all? –

Thus, and in such a groove, did the machinery of thought go on, gradually refusing to move otherwise than by jerky spasms, after the fashion of mechanical Ollendorff exercises, or verb-catechisms of familiar phrases –

Are there not Banditti?

Had there not been Vendetta?

Were there not Corsican brothers?

Should I not carry clothes for all sorts of weather?

Must *thou* not have taken a dress coat?

Had *he* not many letters of introduction?

Might *we* not have taken extra pairs of spectacles?

Could *you* not have provided numerous walking boots?

Should *they* not have forgotten boxes of quinine pills?

Shall *we* possess flea-powder?

Could *you* not procure copper money?

May *they* not find cream cheeses?

Should there not be innumerable moufflons?

Ought not the cabin lamps and glasses to cease jingling?

Might not those poodles stop worrying? –

thus and thus, till by reason of long hours of monotonous rolling and shaking, a sort of comatose insensibility, miscalled sleep, takes the place of all thought, and so the night passes.[10]

The least romantic form of departure must surely be by bicycle – even if one *is* proposing to ride round the world. Here once again is John Foster Fraser, spokesman for those three cheerful young men whom we met in Chapter Two:

Friday morning, July 17th, 1896, and the dingy gilt hands on the clock face of St. Pancras Church pointed to half-past five. Rain had been falling heavily, and the roads were slushy and greasy; the sky was murky and scowling, and London generally looked disagreeable. Maybe London was sorry we were leaving.

Half a dozen courageous fellows dragged themselves out of bed at the abnormal hour of five a.m., and came along, unwashed and uncombed, to bid us farewell.

'Good-bye, old chap,' said one. 'Take care of yourself,' said another. 'Don't break your neck while breaking records,' said a third.

The handshakes were soon over. The three of us jumped upon our bicycles. We turned in our saddles and gave a wave of the hand to the chaps we were leaving behind. And so we were off.

Our wheels were good, sturdy roadsters, painted black. In the diamond frames were leathern bags stuffed with repairing materials. Over the rear wheels had been fixed luggage carriers, and to these were strapped bags containing underclothing. We were clad in brown woollen garb, guaranteed by the tailor to wear for ever and a fortnight, and we each wore big, bell-shaped helmets.

There must have been something of a daring-African-traveller look about us. The early workman, slouching to his work, stood still and looked at us. We were strange wild-fowl to go spinning through the City at that early hour.

'Hey! mateys, where are you off to?' shouted one old fellow.

'Them's the bloomin' blokes what's goin' ter ride rhan the bloomin' hearth,' roared a man in Holborn.

'What's brought the military hout?' asked a sallow cynic by a coffee-stall.

We had no time for repartee. Along Cheapside we whizzed. There was not a hansom, or a 'bus, or a silk hat to be seen. Away down the Mile End Road we rushed, already noisy with the morning traffic; we bumped over the uncomfortable cobbles; we were glad to reach villadom and spurt along macadam roads.

The milkman was tinkling his way from house to house; servant girls yawned sleepily over the scrubbing of the front doorsteps; little shopkeepers paused in the taking down of the shutters, and gazed in our direction curiously.

The morning cleared from grey to sunshiny. The roads were fairly good. For two hours we rode without a halt. Then breakfast, then a brisk spin to Colchester, where there was lunch; then away to Harwich, and the kicking of our heels for several hours around the dismal Parkeston Quay.

That last day's ride in England was to linger long in my thoughts. We were going to strange lands. We had been told we were rash and foolish and mad, and we were hastening to our deaths. We didn't believe it.[11]

My own particular *penchant* has always been for travelling by train – the further the better. In my youth I longed to cross the American continent; but now, after reading Robert Louis Stevenson's account of his departure from New York for San Francisco, I am not so sure:

Monday. – It was, if I remember rightly, five o'clock when we were all signalled to be present at the Ferry Depot of the railroad. An emigrant ship had arrived at New York on the Saturday night, another on the Sunday morning, our own on Sunday afternoon, a fourth early on Monday; and as there is no emigrant train on

Sunday, a great part of the passengers from these four ships was concentrated on the train by which I was to travel. There was a Babel of bewildered men, women, and children. The wretched little booking-office, and the baggage-room, which was not much larger, were crowded thick with emigrants, and were heavy and rank with the atmosphere of dripping clothes. Open carts full of bedding stood by the half-hour in the rain. The officials loaded each other with recriminations. A bearded, mildewed little man, whom I take to have been an emigrant agent, was all over the place, his mouth full of brimstone, blustering and interfering. It was plain that the whole system, if system there was, had utterly broken down under the strain of so many passengers.

My own ticket was given me at once, and an oldish man, who preserved his head in the midst of this turmoil, got my baggage registered, and counselled me to stay quietly where I was till he should give me the word to move. I had taken along with me a small valise, a knapsack, which I carried on my shoulders, and in the bag of my railway rug the whole of Bancroft's *History of the United States*, in six fat volumes. It was as much as I could carry with convenience even for short distances, but it ensured me plenty of clothing, and the valise was at that moment, and often after, useful for a stool. I am sure I sat for an hour in the baggage-room, and wretched enough it was; yet, when at last the word was passed to me and I picked up my bundles and got under way, it was only to exchange discomfort for downright misery and danger.

I followed the porters into a long shed reaching downhill from West Street to the river. It was dark, the wind blew clean through it from end to end; and here I found a great block of passengers and baggage, hundreds of one and tons of the other. I feel I shall have a difficulty to make myself believed; and certainly the scene must have been exceptional, for it was too dangerous for daily repetition. It was a tight jam; there was no fair way through the mingled mass of brute and living obstruction. Into the upper skirts of the crowd, porters, infuriated by hurry and overwork, clove their way with shouts. I may say that we stood like sheep, and that the porters charged among us like so many maddened sheep-dogs; and I believe these men were no longer answerable for their acts. It mattered not what they were carrying, they drove straight into the press, and when they could get no farther, blindly discharged their barrowful. With my own hand, for instance, I saved the life of a child as it sat upon its mother's knee, she sitting on a box; and since I heard of no accident, I must suppose that there were many similar interpositions in the course of the evening. It will give some idea of the state of mind to which we were reduced if I tell you that neither the porter nor the mother of the child paid the least attention to my act. It was not till some time after that I understood what I had done myself, for to ward off heavy boxes seemed at the moment a natural incident of human life. Cold, wet, clamour, dead opposition to progress, such as one encounters in an evil dream, had utterly daunted the spirits. We had accepted this purgatory as a child accepts the conditions of the world. For my part, I shivered a little, and my back ached wearily; but I believe I had neither a hope nor a fear, and all the activities of my nature had become tributary to one massive sensation of discomfort.

At length, and after how long an interval I hesitate to guess, the crowd began to move, heavily straining through itself. About the same time some lamps were lighted, and threw a sudden flare over the shed. We were being filtered out into the river boat for Jersey City. You may imagine how slowly this filtering proceeded, through the dense, choking crush, every one overladen with packages or children, and yet under the necessity of fishing out his ticket by the way; but it ended at length for me, and I found myself on deck under a flimsy awning and with a trifle of elbow-room to stretch and breathe in. This was on the starboard; for the bulk of the emigrants stuck hopelessly on the port side, by which we had entered. In vain the seamen shouted to them to move on, and threatened them with shipwreck. These poor people were under a spell of stupor, and did not stir a foot. It rained as heavily as ever, but the wind now came in sudden claps and capfuls, not without danger to a boat so badly ballasted as ours; and we crept over the river in the darkness, trailing one paddle in the water like a wounded duck, and passed ever and again by huge, illuminated steamers running many knots, and heralding their approach by strains of music. The contrast between these pleasure embarkations and our own grim vessel, with her list to port and her freight of wet and silent emigrants, was of that glaring description which we count too obvious for the purposes of art.

The landing at Jersey was done in a stampede. I had a fixed sense of calamity, and to judge by conduct, the same persuasion was common to us all. A panic selfishness, like that produced by fear, presided over the disorder of our landing. People pushed, and elbowed, and ran, their families following how they could. Children fell, and were picked up to be rewarded by a blow. One child, who had lost her parents, screamed steadily and with increasing shrillness, as though verging towards a fit; an official kept her by him, but no one else seemed so much as to remark her distress; and I am ashamed to say that I ran among the rest. I was so weary that I had twice to make a halt and set down my bundles in the hundred yards or so between the pier and the railway station, so that I was quite wet by the time that I got under cover. There was no waiting-room, no refreshment-room; the cars were locked; and for at least another hour, or so it seemed, we had to camp upon the draughty, gas-lit platform. I sat on my valise, too crushed to observe my neighbours; but as they were all cold, and wet, and weary, and driven stupidly crazy by the mismanagement to which we had been subjected, I believe they can have been no happier than myself. I bought half a dozen oranges from a boy, for oranges and nuts were the only refection to be had. As only two of them had even a pretence of juice, I threw the other four under the cars, and beheld, as in a dream, grown people and children groping on the track after my leavings.

At last we were admitted into the cars, utterly dejected, and far from dry. For my own part, I got out a clothes-brush, and brushed my trousers as hard as I could till I had dried them and warmed my blood into the bargain; but no one else, except my next neighbour to whom I lent the brush, appeared to take the least precaution. As they were, they composed themselves to sleep. I had seen the lights of Philadelphia, and been twice ordered to change carriages and twice countermanded, before I allowed myself to follow their example.[12]

All the departing travellers whom I have so far quoted have been conspicuously dry-eyed; indeed, as well-brought-up young Englishmen, what else could they have been? It is all the more surprising when one comes across a writer (a Continental, *cela va sans dire*) who not only milked his departure for every drop of emotion that he could wring out of it, but then carefully captured the drops to savour in subsequent tranquillity. The writer in question is Gustave Flaubert, no less; reading his account of the start of his journey to Egypt, it is hard to believe that he was going to be away only a few weeks:

I left Croisset on Monday, 22 October 1849. Of those of the household who bade me goodbye only Bossière, the gardener, seemed to me to be really moved. For me the moment of emotion had come two days before, on Saturday, when I put away my pens and papers. The weather was neither good nor bad. At the [Rouen] station, my sister-in-law and her daughter; also Bouilhet. . . . The next day we had dinner [in Paris] with Monsieur Cloquet. My mother was doleful throughout the meal. . . . Wednesday at four o'clock we left for Nogent. My uncle Parain kept us waiting a long time and I was afraid we might miss the train, which would have seemed a bad omen.

. . . The next day, Thursday – atrocious day, the worst I have ever spent. I was not supposed to leave [for Paris, en route to Marseilles] until the day after the next, but I decided to go at once; it was unbearable. Endless strolls with my mother in the little garden. I set my departure for five; the clock seemed to stand still. I put my hat in the living-room and sent my trunk on ahead to the station; it would take me only a minute to get there. As for local callers, I remember Mme Dainez, the postmistress. Also M. Morin, in charge of the mail coach, who as he left shook hands with me over the gate, saying: 'You're going to see a great country, a great religion, a great people,' etc., and much more such palaver.

Finally I got away. My mother was sitting in an armchair beside the fire, and in the midst of caressing her and talking with her I suddenly kissed her on the forehead, rushed from the room, seized my hat, and ran out of the house. How she screamed when I closed the door of the living-room behind me! It reminded me of her scream just after the death of my father, when she took his hand.

My eyes were dry; I felt a kind of constriction around my heart, but little emotion except nervousness and even a kind of anger; my face must have looked set. I lit a cigar, and Bonenfant [my cousin] ran out and joined me. He spoke to me of the necessity, the advisability, of making a will, and of leaving a power-of-attorney because some disaster might overtake my mother in my absence, etc. I have never experienced such a feeling of hatred towards anyone as towards him at that moment. God has probably forgiven him for the wrong he did me, but the memory of it will always remain. He nearly drove me mad, and yet I stopped him politely!

At the station entrance, a priest and four nuns: bad omen! All afternoon a dog in the neighborhood had been howling dismally. I envy strong-minded men who don't notice such things at those moments.

My uncle Parain said nothing to me at all – a proof of his big heart. I shall always be more grateful to him for his silence than for any great service he could do me.

In the waiting-room there was a gentleman (a business acquaintance of Bonenfant's) who was deploring the fate of dogs in trains. 'They are with unknown dogs who give them fleas; the small dogs are trampled on by the big ones; one would rather pay a little more,' etc. Suddenly Eugénie appeared, in tears: 'Monsieur Parain! Madame wants you, she is having hysterics!' And they went off.

From Nogent to Paris. What a ride! I closed the windows (I was alone in the compartment), held my handkerchief to my mouth, and wept. After a time the sound of my own voice (which reminded me of Dorval two or three times) brought me to myself, then the sobs began again. At one point my head was spinning so that I was afraid. 'Calm down! Calm down!' I opened the window; the moon, surrounded by a halo of mist, was shining in puddles; it was cold. I thought of my mother, her face all contracted from weeping, the droop at the corners of her mouth. . . .

At Montereau I went into the station restaurant and drank three or four glasses of rum, not to try to forget things, but just to do something, anything.

Then my misery took another form: I thought of returning. (At every station I was on the point of getting off; only the fear of being a coward prevented me.) I imagined the voice of Eugénie, crying: 'Madame! It's Monsieur Gustave!' I could give my mother this tremendous joy at once; it was up to me entirely. I lulled myself with this idea; I was exhausted, and it relaxed me.

Arrival in Paris: interminable wait for my baggage. I cross the city, via the Marais and the Place Royale. I had to make up my mind before arriving at Maxime's. He was out. Aimée lets me in, tries to stir up the fire. Maxime returns at midnight. I was exhausted and completely undecided. He left it up to me, and finally I decided not to return to Nogent. At one in the morning, after hours of sobbing and anguish such as no other separation ever caused me, I wrote a letter. I have it now: I have just re-read it and am holding it in my hand, quite without emotion; its paper gives no hint that it is different from any other piece of paper, and the letters are like any other letters in any other sentences. Between my self of that night and my self of tonight [when he was copying and expanding his notes, two years later] there is the difference between the cadaver and the surgeon doing the autopsy.

The next two days I lived lavishly – huge dinners, quantities of wine, whores. The senses are not far removed from the emotions, and my poor tortured nerves needed a little relaxation.[13]

Nearly thirty years ago now, we awarded the Duff Cooper Memorial Prize to Lawrence Durrell, for a brilliant book about Cyprus called *Bitter Lemons*. It opens with a description of his departure by ship from Venice.

Journeys, like artists, are born and not made. A thousand differing circumstances contribute to them, few of them willed or determined by the will – whatever we may think. They flower spontaneously out of the demands of our natures – and the best of them lead us not only outwards in space, but inwards as well. Travel can be one of the most rewarding forms of introspection. . . .

These thoughts belong to Venice at dawn, seen from the deck of the ship which is to carry me down through the islands to Cyprus; a Venice wobbling in a thousand fresh-water reflections, cool as a jelly. It was as if some great master, stricken by dementia, had burst his whole colour-box against the sky to deaden the inner eye of the world. Cloud and water mixed into each other, dripping with colours, merging, overlapping, liquefying, with steeples and balconies and roofs floating in space, like the fragments of some stained-glass window seen through a dozen veils of rice-paper. Fragments of history touched with the colours of wine, tar, ochre, blood, fire-opal and ripening grain. The whole at the same time being rinsed softly back at the edges into a dawn sky as softly as circumspectly blue as a pigeon's egg.

Mentally I held it all, softly as an abstract painting, cradling it in my thoughts – the whole encampment of cathedrals and palaces, against the sharply-focused face of Stendhal as he sits forever upon a stiff-backed chair at Florian's sipping wine: or on that of a Corvo, flitting like some huge fruit-bat down these light-bewitched alleys. . . .

The pigeons swarm the belfries. I can hear their wings across the water like the beating of fans in a great summer ballroom. The *vaporetto* on the Grand Canal beats too, softly as a human pulse, faltering and renewing itself after every hesitation which marks a landing-stage. The glass palaces of the Doges are being pounded in a crystal mortar, strained through a prism. Venice will never be far from me in Cyprus – for the lion of Saint Mark still rides the humid airs of Famagusta, of Kyrenia.

It is an appropriate point of departure for the traveller to the eastern Levant.[14]

And how could I possibly omit Laurie Lee's lovely account of what happened *As I Walked Out One Midsummer Morning*?

The stooping figure of my mother, waist-deep in the grass and caught there like a piece of sheep's wool, was the last I saw of my country home as I left it to discover the world. She stood old and bent at the top of the bank, silently watching me go, one gnarled red hand raised in farewell and blessing, not questioning why I went. At the bend of the road I looked back again and saw the gold light die behind her; then I turned the corner, passed the village school, and closed that part of my life for ever.

It was a bright Sunday morning in early June, the right time to be leaving home. My three sisters and a brother had already gone before me; two other brothers had yet to make up their minds. They were still sleeping that morning, but my mother had got up early and cooked me a heavy breakfast, had stood silently while I ate it, her hand on my chair, and had then helped me pack up my few belongings. There had been no fuss, no appeals, no attempts at advice or persuasion, only a long and searching look. Then with my bags on my back I'd gone out into the early sunshine and climbed through the long wet grass to the road.

I was nineteen years old, still soft at the edges, but with a confident belief in good fortune. I carried a small rolled-up tent, a violin in a blanket, a change of clothes and a tin of treacle biscuits. I was excited, vain-glorious, knowing I had far to go; but not, as yet, how far. As I left home that morning and walked away from the sleeping village, it never occurred to me that others had done this before me.

I was propelled, of course, by the traditional forces that had sent many genera-tions along this road – by the small tight valley closing in around one, stifling the breath with its mossy mouth, the cottage walls narrowing like the arms of an iron maiden, the local girls whispering. 'Marry, and settle down.' Months of restless unease, leading to this inevitable moment, had been spent wandering about the hills, mournfully whistling, and watching the high open fields stepping away eastwards under gigantic clouds . . .

And now I was on my journey, in a pair of thick boots and with a hazel stick in my hand.[15]

Let us finish off with a piece of theatre: the finale to James Elroy Flecker's verse play *Hassan*, the last scene of which – set 'At the Gate of the Moon, Bagdad' in 'blazing moonlight' – consists exclusively of the famous song, sung as the great caravan makes ready to depart.

THE MERCHANTS
(*Together*)
    Away, for we are ready to a man!
      Our camels sniff the evening and are glad.
    Lead on, O Master of the Caravan,
      Lead on the Merchant-Princes of Bagdad.

THE CHIEF DRAPER
Have we not Indian carpets dark as wine,
    Turbans and sashes, gowns and bows and veils,
And broideries of intricate design,
    And printed hangings in enormous bales?

THE CHIEF GROCER
We have rose-candy, we have spikenard,
    Mastic and terebinth and oil and spice,
And such sweet jams meticulously jarred
    As God's Own Prophet eats in Paradise.

THE PRINCIPAL JEWS
And we have manuscripts in peacock styles
    By Ali of Damascus: we have swords
Engraved with storks and apes and crocodiles,
    And heavy beaten necklaces for lords. . . .

ISHAK
We are the Pilgrims, master; we shall go
    Always a little further: it may be
Beyond that last blue mountain barred with snow
    Across that angry or that glimmering sea.

White on a throne or guarded in a cave
    There lives a prophet who can understand
Why men were born: but surely we are brave,
    Who take the Golden Road to Samarkand. . . .

HASSAN

Sweet to ride forth at evening from the wells,
    When shadows pass gigantic on the sand,
And softly through the silence beat the bells
    Along the Golden Road to Samarkand.

ISHAK

We travel not for trafficking alone;
    By hotter winds our fiery hearts are fanned:
For lust of knowing what should not be known,
    We take the Golden Road to Samarkand.

MASTER OF THE CARAVAN

Open the gate, O watchman of the night!

THE WATCHMAN

Ho, travellers, I open. For what land
Leave you the dim-moon city of delight?

MERCHANTS

(*With a shout*)
    We take the Golden Road to Samarkand!
        (*The Caravan passes through the gate.*)

WATCHMAN

(*Consoling the women*)
    What would ye, ladies? It was ever thus.
    Men are unwise and curiously planned.

A WOMAN

They have their dreams, and do not think of us.
        (*The* WATCHMAN *closes the gate.*)

VOICES OF THE CARAVAN

(*In the distance singing*)
    We take the Golden Road to Samarkand.

CURTAIN[16]

Flecker in fact wrote another verse, which he gave to another character in the play, the Chief Humanist. It was subsequently omitted, one suspects at the request of the Lord Chamberlain; but it can still be seen, crossed out, in the original manuscript at the Fitzwilliam Museum, Cambridge. It runs:

And we have boys and girls of special kinds,
    White, brown and black, fragile or fair or strong;
Their bosoms shame the roses: their behinds
    Awake the astonished nightingales to song.[17]

CHAPTER FIVE

First Impressions

When, discussing travel writers in the Introduction, I drew a distinction between the aristocrats of their profession and the Innocents Abroad, I defended the latter by pointing out that first impressions could be 'of interest and occasionally of value'. As I look back on those words – first written nearly twenty years ago – they strike me as being more than a little patronising, though that was by no means their intention at the time; I can only hope that the authors of the passages quoted below – or their shades – will forgive me.

The phrase seems peculiarly inadequate when applied to so majestic a figure as Henry James; so let me, as it were, make amends by starting this chapter with him, as he steps ashore at Liverpool and begins his life-long love affair with this country:

There is a certain evening that I count as virtually a first impression – the end of a wet, black Sunday, twenty years ago, about the first of March. There had been an earlier vision, but it had turned to gray, like faded ink, and the occasion I speak of was a fresh beginning. No doubt I had mystic prescience of how fond of the murky modern Babylon I was one day to become; certain it is that as I look back I find every small circumstance of those hours of approach and arrival still as vivid as if the solemnity of an opening era had breathed upon it. The sense of approach was already almost intolerably strong at Liverpool, where, as I remember, the perception of the English character of everything was as acute as a surprise, though it could only be a surprise without a shock. It was expectation exquisitely gratified, superabundantly confirmed. There was a kind of wonder, indeed, that England should be as English as, for my entertainment, she took the trouble to be; but the wonder would have been greater, and all the pleasure absent, if the sensation had not been violent. It seems to sit there again like a visiting presence, as it sat opposite to me at breakfast at a small table in a window of the old coffee-room of the Adelphi Hotel – the unextended (as it then was), the unimproved, the unblushingly local Adelphi. Liverpool is not a romantic city, but that smoky Saturday returns to me as a supreme success, measured by its association with the kind of emotion in the hope of which, for the most part, we betake ourselves to far countries.

It assumed this character at an early hour – or rather, indeed, twenty-four hours before – with the sight, as one looked across the wintry ocean, of the strange, dark, lonely freshness of the coast of Ireland. Better still, before we could come up to the city, were the black steamers knocking about in the yellow Mersey, under a sky so low that they seemed to touch it with their funnels, and in the thickest, windiest light. Spring was already in the air, in the town; there was no rain, but there was still less sun – one wondered what had become, on this side of the world, of the big white splotch in the heavens; and the gray mildness, shading away into black at every pretext, appeared in itself a promise. This was how it hung about me, between the window and the fire, in the coffee-room of the hotel – late in the morning for breakfast, as we had been long disembarking. The other passengers had dispersed, knowingly catching trains for London (we had only been a handful); I had the place to myself, and I felt as if I had an exclusive property in the impression. I prolonged it, I sacrificed to it, and it is perfectly recoverable now, with the very taste of the national muffin, the creak of the waiter's shoes as he came and went (could anything be so English as his intensely professional back? it revealed a country of tradition), and the rustle of the newspaper I was too excited to read.[1]

James was, it need hardly be said, already a sophisticated man of the world – could there ever have been a moment when he wasn't? – at the time he is describing. By way of contrast, therefore, here is part of a letter from Catherine Wilmot, twenty-eight years old but still all wide-eyed excitement, accompanying an Irish nobleman and his wife on what was to be a two-year visit to Europe and waking up in Calais on the first morning after their arrival:

Monday 30th Novr [1801] – On waking at a very early hour with the confusion incident to that State, you will laugh at me when I confess to you the flash of transport I experienced in saying to myself 'I absolutely then am in France,' and in drawing aside the Curtain of my Bed to prove it to myself, by contemplating the Painted ceiling, the white marble Tables, the looking-glass panels, the polish'd oak floor, and all the little circumstances of difference in the Apartment; without exception I never remember, in all my Life a moment of such unfeign'd extacy! Instinctively I fancied some metamorphoses was taking place in me, and putting up my hand, to try if my Nightcap at least was not turning into a 'Cap of Liberty' (still leaning out of Bed) I lost my balance – and down I flump'd upon the floor, to the utter destruction of all my glorious visions and abhorring those prodigious looking glasses, which multiplied my downfall without mercy, in every direction and wherever I turned my eyes. Getting into bed again in due humiliation I hid my head under the cloaths, ruminating on my disgrace when the door open'd and Lady Mount Cashell, in her white dressing gown appear'd before my eyes. She neither, cou'd compose her senses to rest, so animated were they by the cause which had been so fatal to me and therefore fully countenancing one another in every sanguine anticipation of pleasure, we agreed to sally forth in quest of adventures.[2]

The wonders of nature can almost invariably be trusted to awaken strong feelings in persons of sensibility when beheld for the first time. Hilaire Belloc, in *The Path to Rome*, describes one such reaction:

The wood went up darkly and the path branched here and there so that I was soon uncertain of my way, but I followed generally what seemed to me the most southerly course, and so came at last up steeply through a dip or ravine that ended high on the crest of the ridge.

Just as I came to the end of the rise, after perhaps an hour, perhaps two, of that great curtain of forest which had held the mountain side, the trees fell away to brushwood, there was a gate, and then the path was lost upon a fine open sward which was the very top of the Jura and the coping of that multiple wall which defends the Swiss Plain. I had crossed it straight from edge to edge, never turning out of my way.

It was too marshy to lie down on it, so I stood a moment to breathe and look about me.

It was evident that nothing higher remained, for though a new line of wood – firs and beeches – stood before me, yet nothing appeared above them, and I knew that they must be the fringe of the descent. I approached this edge of wood, and saw that it had a rough fence of post and rails bounding it, and as I was looking for the entry of a path (for my original path was lost, as such tracks are, in the damp grass of the little down) there came to me one of those great revelations which betray to us suddenly the higher things and stand afterwards firm in our minds.

There, on this upper meadow, where so far I had felt nothing but the ordinary gladness of The Summit, I had a vision.

What was it I saw? If you think I saw this or that, and if you think I am inventing the words, you know nothing of men.

I saw between the branches of the trees in front of me a sight in the sky that made me stop breathing, just as great danger at sea, or great surprise in love, or a great deliverance will make a man stop breathing. I saw something I had known in the West as a boy, something I had never seen so grandly discovered as was this. In between the branches of the trees was a great promise of unexpected lights beyond.

I pushed left and right along that edge of the forest and along the fence that bound it, until I found a place where the pine-trees stopped, leaving a gap, and where on the right, beyond the gap, was a tree whose leaves had failed; there the ground broke away steeply below me, and the beeches fell, one below the other, like a vast cascade, towards the limestone cliffs that dipped down still further, beyond my sight. I looked through this framing hollow and praised God. For there below me, thousands of feet below me, was what seemed an illimitable plain; at the end of that world was an horizon, and the dim bluish sky that overhangs an horizon.

There was brume in it and thickness. One saw the sky beyond the edge of the world getting purer as the vault rose. But right up – a belt in that empyrean – ran peak and field and needle of intense ice, remote, remote from the world. Sky beneath them and sky above them, a steadfast legion, they glittered as though with the armour of the immovable armies of Heaven. Two days' march, three days' march away, they stood up like the walls of Eden. I say it again, they stopped my breath. I had seen them.

So little are we, we men: so much are we immersed in our muddy and immediate interests that we think, by numbers and recitals, to comprehend distance or time, or any of our limiting infinities. Here were these magnificent creatures of God, I mean the Alps, which now for the first time I saw from the height of the Jura; and because they were fifty or sixty miles away, and because they were a mile or two high, they were become something different from us others, and could strike one motionless with the awe of supernatural things. Up there in the sky, to which only clouds belong and birds and the last trembling colours of pure light, they stood fast and hard; not moving as do the things of the sky. They were as distant as the little upper clouds of summer, as fine and tenuous; but in their reflection and in their quality as it were of weapons (like spears and shields of an unknown array) they occupied the sky with a sublime invasion: and the things proper to the sky were forgotten by me in their presence as I gazed.

To what emotion shall I compare this astonishment? So, in first love one finds that *this* can belong to *me*.[3]

Evelyn Waugh, in *Labels*, records another:

I do not think I shall ever forget the sight of Etna at sunset; the mountain almost invisible in a blur of pastel grey, glowing on the top and then repeating its shape, as though reflected, in a wisp of grey smoke, with the whole horizon behind radiant with pink light, fading gently into a grey pastel sky. Nothing I have ever seen in Art or Nature was quite so revolting.[4]

Mrs Sarah Siddons, the celebrated actress, was less explicit. Her companion Miss Patty Wilkinson, writing in her diary of their Welsh tour of May 1802, records:

We left Conway next morning and ere long crossed Penman Maur, where, like other travellers, we alighted from our carriages to look from a bridge that commands the fullest view of the sublime landscape, with all its rocks and water. A lady within hearing of us was in such ecstasies, that she exclaimed, 'This awful scenery makes me feel as if I were only a worm, or a grain of dust, on the face of the earth.' Mrs Siddons turned round, and said, 'I feel very differently.'[5]

Charles Dickens, with that infallible eye of his for the telling detail, was a superb recorder of his first impressions. In *Pictures from Italy* he gives us an unforgettable picture of Albaro, in his day a suburb of Genoa:

The Villa Bagnerello (or the Pink Jail, a far more expressive name for the mansion) is in one of the most splendid situations imaginable. The noble bay of Genoa, with the deep blue Mediterranean, lies stretched out near at hand; monstrous old desolate houses and palaces are dotted all about; lofty hills, with their tops often hidden in the clouds, and with strong forts perched high up on their craggy sides, are close upon the left; and in front, stretching from the walls of the house, down to a ruined chapel which stands upon the bold and picturesque rocks on the sea-shore, are green vineyards, where you may wander all day long in partial shade, through interminable vistas of grapes, trained on a rough trellis-work across the narrow paths.

This sequestered spot is approached by lanes so very narrow, that when we arrived at the Custom-house, we found the people here had *taken the measure* of the narrowest among them, and were waiting to apply it to the carriage; which ceremony was gravely performed in the street, while we all stood by in breathless suspense. It was found to be a very tight fit, but just a possibility, and no more – as I am reminded every day, by the sight of various large holes which it punched in the walls on either side as it came along. We are more fortunate, I am told, than an old lady, who took a house in these parts not long ago, and who stuck fast in *her* carriage in a lane; and as it was impossible to open one of the doors, she was obliged to submit to the indignity of being hauled through one of the little front windows, like a harlequin.

When you have got through these narrow lanes, you come to an archway, imperfectly stopped up by a rusty old gate – my gate. The rusty old gate has a bell to correspond, which you ring as long as you like, and which nobody answers, as it has no connection whatever with the house. But there is a rusty old knocker, too – very loose, so that it slides round when you touch it – and if you learn the trick of it, and knock long enough, somebody comes. The brave Courier comes, and gives you admittance. You walk into a seedy little garden, all wild and weedy, from which the vineyard opens; cross it, enter a square hall like a cellar, walk up a cracked marble staircase, and pass into a most enormous room with a vaulted roof and whitewashed walls: not unlike a great Methodist chapel. This is the *sala*. It has five windows and five doors, and is decorated with pictures which would gladden the heart of one of those picture-cleaners in London who hang up, as a sign, a picture divided, like death and the lady, at the top of the old ballad: which always leaves you in a state of uncertainty whether the ingenious professor has cleaned one half, or dirtied the other. The furniture of this *sala* is a sort of red brocade. All the chairs are immovable, and the sofa weighs several tons.

On the same floor, and opening out of this same chamber, are dining-room, drawing-room, and divers bed-rooms: each with a multiplicity of doors and windows. Up-stairs are divers other gaunt chambers, and a kitchen; and down-stairs is another kitchen, which, with all sorts of strange contrivances for burning charcoal, looks like an alchemical laboratory. There are also some half-dozen small sitting-rooms, where the servants in this hot July, may escape from the heat of the fire, and where the brave Courier plays all sorts of musical instruments of his own manufacture, all the evening long. A mighty old, wandering, ghostly, echoing, grim, bare house it is, as ever I beheld or thought of.

There is a little vine-covered terrace, opening from the drawing-room; and under this terrace, and forming one side of the little garden, is what used to be the stable. It is now a cow-house, and has three cows in it, so that we get new milk by the bucketfull. There is no pasturage near, and they never go out, but are constantly lying down, and surfeiting themselves with vine-leaves – perfect Italian cows enjoying the *dolce far' niente* all day long. They are presided over, and slept with, by an old man named Antonio, and his son; two burnt-sienna natives with naked legs and feet, who wear, each, a shirt, a pair of trousers, and a red sash, with a relic, or some sacred charm like the bonbon off a twelfth-cake, hanging round the neck. The old man is very anxious to convert me to the Catholic faith, and exhorts me frequently. We sit upon a stone by the door, sometimes in the evening, like Robinson Crusoe and Friday reversed; and he generally relates, towards my conversion, an abridgment of the History of Saint Peter – chiefly, I believe, from the unspeakable delight he has in his imitation of the cock.

The view, as I have said, is charming; but in the day you must keep the lattice-blinds close shut, or the sun would drive you mad; and when the sun goes down you must shut up all the windows, or the mosquitoes would tempt you to commit suicide. So at this time of the year, you don't see much of the prospect within doors. As for the flies, you don't mind them. Nor the fleas, whose size is prodigious, and whose name is Legion, and who populate the coach-house to that extent that I daily expect to see the carriage going off bodily, drawn by myriads of industrious fleas in harness. The rats are kept away, quite comfortable, by scores of lean cats, who roam about the garden for that purpose. The lizards, of course, nobody cares for; they play in the sun, and don't bite. The little scorpions are merely curious. The beetles are rather late, and have not appeared yet. The frogs are company. There is a preserve of them in the grounds of the next villa; and after nightfall, one would think that scores upon scores of women in pattens were going up and down a wet stone pavement without a moment's cessation. That is exactly the noise they make.[6]

Rome, by contrast, was initially something of a disappointment:

As soon as we were out of the pig-sty [Ronciglione], we entered on the Campagna Romana; an undulating flat (as you know), where few people can live; and where, for miles and miles, there is nothing to relieve the terrible monotony and gloom. Of all kinds of country that could, by possibility, lie outside the gates of Rome, this is the aptest and fittest burial-ground for the Dead City. So sad, so quiet, so sullen; so secret in its covering up of great masses of ruin, and hiding them; so like the waste places into which the men possessed with devils used to go and howl, and rend themselves, in the old days of Jerusalem. We had to traverse thirty miles of this Campagna; and for two-and-twenty we went on and on, seeing nothing but now and then a lonely house, or a villainous-looking shepherd: with matted hair all over his face, and himself wrapped to the chin in a frowsy brown mantle, tending his sheep. At the end of that distance, we stopped to refresh the horses, and to get some lunch, in a common malaria-shaken, despondent little public-house, whose every inch of wall and beam, inside, was (according to custom) painted and decorated in a way so miserable that every room looked like the wrong side of another room, and, with its wretched imitation of drapery, and lop-sided little daubs of lyres, seemed to have been plundered from behind the scenes of some travelling circus.

When we were fairly going off again, we began, in a perfect fever, to strain our eyes for Rome; and when, after another mile or two, the Eternal City appeared, at length, in the distance; it looked like – I am half afraid to write the word – like LONDON!!! There it lay, under a thick cloud, with innumerable towers, and steeples, and roofs of houses, rising up into the sky, and high above them all, one Dome. I swear, that keenly as I felt the seeming absurdity of the comparison, it was so like London, at that distance, that if you could have shown it me, in a glass, I should have taken it for nothing else.[7]

It is quite a usual reaction, on an initial encounter with an unknown city or landscape, to be struck by its similarity with somewhere one knows; my mother, I remember, gazing for the first time on the celebrated skyline of Istanbul, was ineluctably reminded of Liverpool. In the absence of any resemblance at all, one can always fall back on a comparison: the following little poem comes from a work entitled *Nothing To Do: A Tilt at Our Best Society*, published in Boston in 1857.

A Fashionable New Yorker Abroad

And so we reached Athens – a sizable place,
   Some three or four miles from the Gulf of Aegina;
It contains a cathedral not equal to Grace
   Church in New York, which I think is much finer.
Went up to the top of the famous Acropolis,
   Which is visited daily by hundreds of people,
But can't say I think that the view from the top o' this
   Is equal to that from our Trinity steeple.
The houses are mostly unsightly and small;
   In Minerva and Hermes' street noticed a few
Which will do very well, but are nothing at all
   Compared with our mansion in Fifth-Avenue.
The piles of old ruins one sees here and there
   I consider a perfect disgrace to the town;
If they had an efficient and competent Mayor,
   Like our Mayor Wood, he would soon have them down.[8]

Americans have always been particularly good at first impressions of Europe; the breadth of the Atlantic seems to give them an objectivity that the British, distanced only by the Channel, seem all too often to lack. Here is Mark Twain – who after all *invented* the Innocent Abroad – in Baden-Baden:

Baden-Baden sits in the lap of the hills, and the natural and artificial beauties of the surroundings are combined effectively and charmingly. The level strip of ground which stretches through and beyond the town is laid out in handsome pleasure grounds, shaded by noble trees and adorned at intervals with lofty and sparkling fountain-jets. Thrice a day a fine band makes music in the public promenade before the Conversation-House, and in the afternoons and evenings that locality is populous with fashionably dressed people of both sexes, who march back and forth past the great music-stand and look very much bored, though they make a show of feeling otherwise. It seems like a rather aimless and stupid existence. A good many of these people are there for a real purpose, however; they are racked with rheumatism, and they are there to stew it out in the hot baths. These invalids looked melancholy enough, limping about on their canes and crutches, and apparently brooding over all sorts of cheerless things. People say that Germany, with her damp stone houses, is the home of rheumatism. If that is so, Providence must have foreseen that it would be so, and therefore filled the land with these healing baths. Perhaps no other country is so generously supplied with medicinal springs as

Germany. Some of these baths are good for one ailment, some for another; and again, peculiar ailments are conquered by combining the individual virtues of several different baths. For instance, for some forms of disease the patient drinks the native hot water of Baden-Baden, with a spoonful of salt from the Carlsbad springs dissolved in it. That is not a dose to be forgotten right away.

They don't *sell* this hot water; no, you go into the great Trinkhalle, and stand around, first on one foot and then on the other, while two or three young girls sit pottering at some sort of ladylike sewing-work in your neighbourhood and can't seem to see you – polite as three-dollar clerks in government offices.

By and by one of these rises painfully and 'stretches'; – stretches fists and body heavenwards till she raises her heels from the floor, at the same time refreshing herself with a yawn of such comprehensiveness that the bulk of her face disappears behind her upper lip, and one is able to see how she is constructed inside – then she slowly closes her cavern, brings down her fists and her heels, comes languidly forward, contemplates you contemptuously, draws you a glass of hot water and sets it down where you can get it by reaching for it. You take it and say:

'How much?' – and she returns you, with elaborate indifference, a beggar's answer:

'*Nach Beliebe* (what you please).'

This thing of using the common beggar's trick and the common beggar's shibboleth to put you on your liberality when you were expecting a simple, straightforward, commercial transaction, adds a little to your prospering sense of irritation. You ignore her reply, and ask again:

'How much?'

And she calmly, indifferently, repeats:

'*Nach Beliebe.*'

You are getting angry, but you are trying not to show it; you resolve to keep on asking your question till she changes her answer, or at least her annoyingly indifferent manner. Therefore, if your case be like mine, you two fools stand there, and without perceptible emotion of any kind, or any emphasis on any syllable, you look blandly into each other's eyes, and hold the following idiotic conversation:

'How much?'

'Nach Beliebe.'

'How much?'

'Nach Beliebe.'

'How much?'

'Nach Beliebe.'

'How much?'

'Nach Beliebe.'

'How much?'

'Nach Beliebe.'

I do not know what another person would have done, but at this point I gave it up; that cast-iron indifference, that tranquil contemptuousness, conquered me, and I struck my colours. Now I knew she was used to receiving about a penny from manly people who care nothing about the opinions of scullery-maids, and about tuppence from moral cowards; but I laid a silver twenty-five-cent piece within her reach and tried to shrivel her up with this sarcastic speech:

'If it isn't enough, will you stoop sufficiently from your official dignity to say so?'

She did not shrivel. Without deigning to look at me at all, she languidly lifted the coin and bit it! – to see if it was good. Then she turned her back and placidly waddled to her former roost again, tossing the money into an open till as she went along. She was victor to the last, you see.

I have enlarged upon the ways of this girl because they are typical; her manners are the manners of a goodly number of the Baden-Baden shopkeepers. The shop-keeper there swindles you if he can, and insults you whether he succeeds in swindling you or not. The keepers of baths also take great and patient pains to insult you. The frowsy woman who sat at the desk in the lobby of the great Friederichsbad and sold bath tickets, not only insulted me twice every day, with rigid fidelity to her great trust, but she took trouble enough to cheat me out of a shilling, one day, to have fairly entitled her to ten. Baden-Baden's splendid gamblers are gone, only her microscopic knaves remain.[9]

So much for Europe; now for Africa, and two perfect little thumb-nail sketches of two very dissimilar West African towns. First, Dakar. The book is *Journey Without Maps*: the author, Graham Greene.

It must have been two days later that I woke to the grating of iron against stone, and there was the Coast. The word was already over-familiar. People said, 'Eld-ridge. Of course, he's an old Coaster,' and Eldridge, the middle-aged shipping agent, at the beginning of every meal would say, 'Chop, as we call it on the Coast,' or handing a plate of onions, 'Violets, we say on the Coast.' One's pink gin was called a Coaster. There was no other Coast but the West Coast and this was it.

On the quay the Senegalese strolled up and down, long white and blue robes sweeping up the dust blown from the ridge of monkey-nuts twenty-five feet high. The men walked hand-in-hand, laughing sleepily together under the blinding verti-cal glare. Sometimes they put their arms round each other's necks; they seemed to like to touch each other, as if it made them feel good to know the other man was there. It wasn't love; it didn't mean anything we could understand. Two of them went about all day without loosing hold; they were there when the boat slid in beside the monkey-nuts; they were there in the evening when the loading was finished and the labourers washed their hands and faces in the hot water flowing from the ship's side; they hadn't done a stroke of work themselves, only walked up and down touching hands and laughing at their own jokes; but it wasn't love; it wasn't anything we could understand. They gave to the blinding day, to the first sight of Africa, a sense of warm and sleepy beauty, of enjoyment divorced from activity and the weariness of willing.

> Là, tout n'est qu'ordre et beauté,
> Luxe, calme et volupté.

One found it hard to believe at Dakar that Baudelaire had never been to Africa, that the nearest he had come to it was the body of Jeanne Duval, the mulatto tart from Le Théâtre du Panthéon, for Dakar was the Baudelaire of *L'Invitation au Voyage*, when it was not the René Clair of *Le Million*.

It was René Clair in its happy lyrical absurdity; the two stately Mohammedans asleep on the gravel path in the public gardens beside a black iron kettle; the tiny Syrian children going to school in white topees; the men's sewing parties on the pavements; the old pock-marked driver who stopped his horses and disappeared into the bushes to tell his beads; the men laden with sacks moving rhythmically up and down a ladder of sacks, building higher the monkey-nut hill, like the tin toy figures sold in Holborn at Christmas-time; in the lovely features of the women in the market, young and old, lovely less from sexual attractiveness than from a sharp differentiated pictorial quality. In the restaurant, a little drunk on iced Sauterne, one didn't trouble about the Dakar one had heard about, the Dakar of endemic plague and an unwieldy bureaucracy, the most unhealthy town on the Coast. Mr Gorer in his *Africa Dances* tells how in Dakar the young negroes simply die, not of tuberculosis, plague, yellow fever, but of inanition, of hopelessness. He stayed too long, I suppose, and saw too much; that sudden sense of happiness which came to one in Dakar doesn't last, which came to one in *Le Million*, a happiness that tingles behind the eyes, beautiful and insecure, a wish fulfilment.[10]

Second, Freetown:

Freetown, the capital of Sierra Leone, at first was just an impression of heat and damp; the mist streamed along the lower streets and lay over the roofs like smoke. Nature, conventionally grand, rising in tree-covered hills above the sea and the town, a dull uninteresting green, was powerless to carry off the shabby town. One could see the Anglican cathedral, laterite bricks and tin with a square tower, a Norman church built in the nineteenth century, sticking up out of the early morning fog. There was no doubt at all that one was back in home waters. Among the swarm of Kru boats round the ship the *Princess Marina* with its freshly painted name was prominent. '*Princess Marina*,' the half-naked owner kept on calling. 'Sweetest boat on the Coast.'

Tin roofs and peeling posters and broken windows in the public library and wooden stores, Freetown had a Bret Harte air without the excitement, the saloons, the revolver shots or the horses. There was only one horse in the whole city, and it was pointed out to me by the proprietor of the Grand Hotel, a thin piebald beast pulled down the main street like a mule. There had been other horses from time to time, but they had all died. Where there wasn't a tin shed there were huge hoardings covered with last year's Poppy Day posters (the date was January the fifteenth). On the roofs the vultures sat nuzzling under their wings with horrible tiny undeveloped heads; they squatted in the gardens like turkeys; I could count seven out of my bedroom window. When they moved from one perch to another they gave no sensation of anything so aerial as flight; they seemed to hop across the street, borne up just high enough by the flap-flap of their dusty wings.

This was an English capital city; England had planted this town, the tin shacks and the Remembrance Day posters, and had then withdrawn up the hillside to smart bungalows, with wide windows and electric fans and perfect service. Every call one paid on a white man cost ten shillings in taxi fares, for the railway to Hill Station no longer ran. They had planted their seedy civilisation and then escaped from it as far as they could. Everything ugly in Freetown was European: the stores, the churches, the Government offices, the two hotels; if there was anything beautiful in the place it was native: the little stalls of the fruit-sellers which went up after dark at the street corners, lit by candles; the native women rolling home magnificently from church on a Sunday morning, the cheap European cottons, the deep coral or green flounces, the wide straw hats, dignified by the native bearing, the lovely roll of the thighs, the swing of the great shoulders. They were dressed for a garden party and they carried off cheap bright grandeur in the small back-yards among the vultures as nature couldn't carry off Freetown.[11]

There have probably been more travel books written about Egypt than about the rest of Africa put together. Not surprisingly – at least among earlier authors – first impressions of the country tend to be centred on Alexandria. They are not invariably favourable. One of the best descriptions is by Eliot Warburton:

All that is now visible within the shrunken and mouldering walls is a piebald town – one-half European, with its regular houses, tall, and white, and stiff; the other half, Oriental, with its mud-coloured buildings and terraced roofs, varied with fat mosques and lean minarets. The suburbs are encrusted with the wretched hovels of the Arab poor; and immense mounds and tracts of rubbish occupy the wide space between the city and its walls: all beyond is a dreary waste. Yet this is the site Alexander selected from his wide dominions, and which Napoleon pronounced to be unrivalled in importance. Here luxury and literature, the Epicurean and the Christian, philosophy and commerce, once dwelt together. Here stood the great library of antiquity, 'the assembled souls of all that men held wise.' Here the Hebrew Scriptures expanded into Greek under the hands of the Septuagint. Here Cleopatra, 'vainqueur des vainqueurs du monde,' revelled with her Roman conquerors. Here St. Mark preached the truth upon which Origen attempted to refine, and here Athanasius held warlike controversy. Here Amru conquered, and here Abercrombie fell. Looking now along the shore, beneath me lies the harbour in the form of a crescent – the right horn occupied by the palace of the Pasha, his hareem, and a battery; the left, a long, low sweep of land, alive with windmills; in the centre is the city: to the westward, the flat, sandy shore stretches monotonously away to the horizon; to the eastward, the coast merges into Aboukir Bay.

Having taken this general view of our first Egyptian city, let us enter it in a regular manner to view it in detail. The bay is crowded with merchant vessels of every nation, among which tower some very imposing-looking three-deckers, gigantic, but dismantled; the red flag with the star and crescent flying from the peak. Men-of-war barges shoot past you with crews dressed in what look like red nightcaps and white petticoats. They rise to their feet at every stroke of the oar, and pull all out of time. Here, an 'ocean patriarch' (as the Arabs call Noah), with white turban and flowing beard, is steering a very little ark filled with unclean-looking animals of every description; and there, a crew of swarthy Egyptians, naked from the waist upward, are pulling some pale-faced strangers to a vessel with loosened top-sails, and blue-peter flying.

At length, amid a deafening din of voices, and a pestilential effluvia from dead fish and living Arabs, you fight your way ashore; and if you had just awakened from a sleep of ages, you could scarcely open your eyes upon a scene more different from those you have lately left. The crumbling quays are piled with bales of eastern merchandize, islanded in a sea of white turbans wreathed over dark, melancholy faces. Vivid eyes glitter strangely upon solemn-looking and bearded countenances. High above the variegated crowd peer the long necks of hopeless-looking camels. Wriggling and struggling amidst all this mass were picturesquely ragged little boys, dragging after them shaven donkeys with carpet saddles, upon one of which you suddenly find yourself seated with scarcely a volition of your own; and are soon galloping along filthy lanes, with blank, white, windowless and doorless walls on either side, and begin to wonder when you are to arrive at the Arab city. You have already passed through it, and are emerging into the Frank quarter, a handsome square of tall white houses, over which the flags of every nation in Europe denote the residences of the various consuls. In this square is an endless variety of races and costumes, most picturesquely grouped together, and lighted brilliantly by a glowing sun in a cloudless sky. In one place, a drove of camels are kneeling down, with jet black slaves in white turbans, or crimson caps, arranging their burdens; in another, a procession of women waddles along, wrapped in large shroud-like veils from head to foot, with a long black bag, like an elephant's trunk, suspended from their noses, and permitting only their kohl-stained eyes to appear. In another, a group of Turks in long flowing drapery are seated in a circle smoking their chibouques in silence, and enjoying society after the fashion of other gregarious animals; grooms in petticoat trousers are leading horses with crimson velvet saddles richly embroidered; a detachment of sad-looking soldiers in white cotton uniform is marching by to very wild music; and here and there a Frank with long moustaches is lounging about, contemplating these unconscious tableaux as if they had been got up simply for his amusement.[12]

Sir Richard Burton travelled from Alexandria to Cairo by way of the Mahmoudiyeh Canal, connecting the port with the mainstream of the Nile. He too was unimpressed:

I saw the canal at its worst, when the water was low; and I have not one syllable to say in its favour. Instead of thirty hours, we took three mortal days and nights to reach Cairo, and we grounded with painful regularity four or five times between sunrise and sunset. In the scenery on the banks sketchers and describers have left you nought to see. From Pompey's Pillar to the Maison Carrée, Kariom and its potteries, Al-Birkah of the night birds, Bastarah with the alleys of trees, even unto Atfah, all things are perfectly familiar to us, and have been so years before the traveller actually sees them. The Níl al-Mubárak itself – the Blessed Nile, – as notably fails too at this season to arouse enthusiasm. You see nothing but muddy waters, dusty banks, a sand mist, a milky sky, and a glaring sun: you feel nought but a breeze like the blast from a potter's furnace. . . . You are nearly wrecked, as a matter of course, at the Barrage; and you are certainly dumbfoundered by the sight of its ugly little Gothic crenelles. The Pyramids of Khufa and Kháfrá (Cheops and Cephren) 'rearing their majestic heads above the margin of the Desert,' only suggest of remark that they have been remarkably well-sketched; and thus you proceed till with a real feeling of satisfaction you moor alongside of the tumble-down old suburb 'Bulak.'

To me there was double dulness in the scenery: it seemed to be Sind over again – the same morning mist and noon-tide glare; the same hot wind and heat clouds, and fiery sunset, and evening glow; the same pillars of dust and 'devils' of sand sweeping like giants over the plain; the same turbid waters of a broad, shallow stream studded with sand-banks and silt-isles, with crashing earth slips and ruins nodding over a kind of cliff, whose base the stream gnaws with noisy tooth. On the banks, saline ground sparkled and glittered like hoar-frost in the sun; and here and there mud villages, solitary huts, pigeon-towers, or watch turrets, whence little brown boys shouted and slung stones at the birds, peeped out from among bright green patches of palm-tree, tamarisk, and mimosa, of maize, tobacco, and sugar-cane. Beyond the narrow tongue of land on the river banks lay the glaring, yellow Desert, with its low hills and sand slopes, bounded by innumerable pyramids of Nature's architecture. The boats, with their sharp bows, preposterous sterns, and lateen sails, might have belonged to the Indus. So might the chocolate-skinned, blue-robed peasantry; the women carrying progeny on their hips, with the eternal waterpot on their heads; and the men sleeping in the shade or following the plough, to which probably Osiris first put hand. The lower animals, like the higher, were the same; gaunt, mange-stained camels, muddy buffaloes, scurvied donkeys, sneaking jackals, and fox-like dogs. Even the feathered creatures were perfectly familiar to my eye – paddy birds, pelicans, giant cranes, kites and wild water-fowl.

I had taken a third-class or deck-passage, whereby the evils of the journey were exasperated. A roasting sun pierced the canvas awning like hot water through a gauze veil, and by night the cold dews fell raw and thick as a Scotch mist. The cooking was abominable, and the dignity of Darwaysh-hood did not allow me to sit at meat with Infidels or to eat the food which they had polluted. So the Pilgrim squatted apart, smoking perpetually, with occasional interruptions to say his prayers and to tell his beads upon the mighty rosary; and he drank the muddy water of the canal out of a leathern bucket, and he munched his bread and garlic with a desperate sanctimoniousness.[13]

As for Harriet Martineau, visiting the Pyramids in February 1847, she seems to have been uncertain quite what to think:

I was surprised to find myself disappointed in the Pyramids now, when it had been precisely the reverse at a distance. Instead of their growing larger as we approached, they became less and less wonderful, till at last they exactly met one's preconception, except in being rougher, and of a brighter tint. The platform on which the largest stands is higher than our reading had given us to suppose; and the Second Pyramid, which at a distance looks as large as the other, here sinks surprisingly. This was to me the strongest evidence of the magnitude of the Great Pyramid. Though I have spoken of disappointment on a near approach, these mighty objects were perfectly absorbing, as a little incident presently proved. One of our party said, on our arrival, 'When we were passing the Sphinx –' 'O! the Sphinx!' cried I.

'You don't mean that you have seen the Sphinx!' – To be sure they had: and they insisted on it that I had too; – that I must have seen it – could not have missed it. I was utterly bewildered. It was strange enough to have forgotten it: but not to have seen it was inexplicable. However, on visiting it, later in the day, I found I had seen it. Being intent on the Pyramid before me, I had taken the Sphinx for a capriciously-formed rock, like so many that we had passed – forgetting that I should not meet with limestone at Geezeh. I rather doubt whether any traveller would take the Sphinx for anything but a rock unless he was looking for it, or had his eye caught by some casual light. – One other anecdote, otherwise too personal for print, will show how engrossing is the interest of the Pyramid on the spot. – The most precious articles of property I had with me abroad were two ear-trumpets, because, in case of accident happening to them, I could not supply the loss. I was unwilling to carry my trumpet up the Pyramid – knocking against the stones while I wanted my hands for climbing. So I left it below, in the hands of a trusty Arab. When I joined my party at the top, I never remembered my trumpet: nor did they: and we talked as usual, during the forty minutes we were there, without my ever missing it. When I came down, I never thought of it: and I explored the inside, came out and lunched, and still never thought of my trumpet, till, at the end of three hours and a half from my parting with it, I saw it in the hands of the Arab, and was reminded of the astonishing fact that I had heard as well without it as with it, all that time. Such a thing never happened before, and probably never will again: and a stronger proof could not be offered of the engrossing interest of a visit to the Pyramid.[14]

Freya Stark, on the other hand, on her first impact with the desert, had no doubts at all. In *Letters from Syria, 1927–8*, she wrote:

Camels appeared on our left hand: first a few here and there, then more and more till the whole herd came browsing along, five hundred or more. I got out and went among them to photograph. The two beduin leaders, dressed gorgeously, perched high up and swinging slowly with the movement of their beasts, shouted out to me, but the beduin Arabic is beyond me. I can't tell you what a wonderful sight it was: as if one were suddenly in the very morning of the world among the people of Abraham or Jacob. The great gentle creatures came browsing and moving and pausing, rolling gently over the landscape like a brown wave just a little browner than the desert that carried it. Their huge legs rose up all round me like columns; the foals were frisking about: the herdsmen rode here and there. I stood in a kind of ecstasy among them. It seemed as if they were not so much moving as flowing along, with something indescribably fresh and peaceful and free about it all, as if the struggle of all these thousands of years had never been, since first they started wandering. I never imagined that my first sight of the desert would come with such a shock of beauty and enslave me right away.[15]

Reactions are more difficult when they are prompted not only by a visual scene, but also by spiritual considerations. There was, alas, no traveller's handbook to advise the Hon. Robert Curzon how properly to comport himself at his first sight of Jerusalem:

As our train of horses surmounted each succeeding eminence, every one was eager to be the first who should catch a glimpse of the Holy City. Again and again we were disappointed; another rocky valley yawned beneath us, and another barren stony hill rose up beyond. There seemed to be no end to the intervening hills and dales; they appeared to multiply beneath our feet. At last, when we had almost given up the point, and had ceased to contend for the first view by galloping ahead, as we ascended another rocky brow we saw the towers of what seemed to be a Gothic castle; then, as we approached nearer, a long line of walls and battlements appeared crowning a ridge of rock which rose from a narrow valley to the right. This was the valley of the pools of Gihon, where Solomon was crowned, and the battlements which rose above it were the long-looked-for walls of Jerusalem. With one accord our whole party drew their bridles, and stood still to gaze for the first time upon this renowned and sacred city.

It is not easy to describe the sensations which fill the breast of a Christian when, after a long and toilsome journey, he first beholds this, the most interesting and venerated spot upon the whole surface of the globe – the chosen city of the Lord, the place in which it pleased Him to dwell. Every one was silent for a while, absorbed in the deepest contemplation. The object of our pilgrimage was accomplished, and I do not think that anything we saw afterwards during our stay in Jerusalem made a more profound impression on our minds than this first distant view.

It was curious to observe the different effect which our approach to Jerusalem had upon the various persons who composed our party. A Christian pilgrim, who had joined us on the road, fell down upon his knees and kissed the holy ground; two others embraced each other, and congratulated themselves that they had lived to see Jerusalem. As for us Franks, we sat bolt upright upon our horses, and stared and said nothing; whilst around us the more natural children of the East wept for joy, and, as in the army of the Crusaders, the word Jerusalem! Jerusalem! was repeated from mouth to mouth; but we, who consider ourselves civilised and superior beings, repressed our emotions; we were above showing that we participated in the feelings of our barbarous companions. As for myself, I would have got off my horse and walked barefooted towards the gate, as some did, if I had dared; but I was in fear of being laughed at for my absurdity, and therefore sat fast in my saddle. At last I blew my nose, and, pressing the sharp edges of my Arab stirrups on the lank sides of my poor weary jade, I rode on slowly towards the Bethlehem gate.[16]

Such problems would not, I think, have troubled Robert Byron, passing over much the same route a century later as his noble namesake. But Byron was nevertheless capable of even more excitement and enthusiasm when he came upon some monument that really caught his imagination; and he travelled a good deal further than Curzon ever did. In what is perhaps his best book, *The Road to Oxiana*, he describes his reactions to Herat in Afghanistan:

On approaching Herat, the road from Persia keeps close under the mountains till it meets the road from Kushk, when it turns downhill towards the town. We arrived on a dark but starlit night. This kind of night is always mysterious; in an unknown country, after a sight of the wild frontier guards, it produced an excitement such as I have seldom felt. Suddenly the road entered a grove of giant chimneys, whose black outlines regrouped themselves against the stars as we passed. For a second, I was dumbfounded – expecting anything on earth, but not a factory; until, dwarfed by these vast trunks, appeared the silhouette of a broken dome, curiously ribbed, like a melon. There is only one dome in the world like that, I thought, that anyone knows of: the Tomb of Tamerlane at Samarcand. The chimneys therefore must be minarets. I went to bed like a child on Christmas Eve, scarcely able to wait for the morning.

Morning comes. Stepping out on to a roof adjoining the hotel, I see seven sky-blue pillars rise out of the bare fields against the delicate heather-coloured mountains. Down each the dawn casts a highlight of pale gold. In their midst shines a blue melon-dome with the top bitten off. Their beauty is more than scenic, depending on light or landscape. On closer view, every tile, every flower, every petal of mosaic contributes its genius to the whole. Even in ruin, such architecture tells of a golden age. Has history forgotten it?[17]

A passage in *First Russia Then Tibet*, however, makes it clear that not all his responses were equally whole-hearted:

Suddenly, round a corner, the snowy back of Kanchenjunga leapt into the sky, a stupendous horizon of glittering vertebrae, packed with cotton-wool clouds, and encroaching on three-quarters of the heavens. Below, a profundity of spurs and valleys, darkly feathered in pines, was lost in shadow like the bottom of a well. The heart beat; the breath came quickly. Until, round another corner, appeared Darjeeling, and all relapsed into hate and misery.

Imagine Margate, Filey, and Bognor Regis wholly roofed in red corrugated iron; distorted into a phantasmagoria of chalets and châteaux, such as even they have yet to achieve; vomited into the tittups of an Italian hill-town; and then lifted bodily on to a long spur, a promontory rising from a sea of depths that seem to pierce the very core of the world; overseen by the white throne of God, a continent on end, trees, cliffs, and shores of snow five miles high, as the eye travels up them to the blue vault above; and still preserving all the inevitable accessories of our national life: the exclusive clubs, the Anglican, Scottish, and Roman Catholic churches, the Tudor hotel, the seaside milliners, and the polo-ground in the bottom of a tea-cup; streets without motors, but municipally railed; rickshaws pulled and pushed by crowds of ragged Mongols; tiny ponies with saddles like high-chairs for children who can scarcely walk; all the races of the Himalayas: Nepali women with their huge necklaces of gold beads and red flannel, like Lord Mayors' chains; the elfin Lepchas and Sikkimese; emigrant Tibetans, mottled lumps of turquoise in the men's ears, the women's chests hung with enormous rhomboid charm-boxes, silver and jewelled; the clouds, as the morning advances, closing in, arriving mysteriously from both above and below, till the last glimpse of Kanchenjunga is obscured behind a wall of mist, the valleys themselves are lost, and at last, thank God, even Darjeeling is invisible but for the two nearest villas and their front-gardens; such is the conflict of joy and horror at the first sight of Anglo-Himalaya.[18]

India: Robert Byron was blasé by then, but to most young Englishmen and Englishwomen arriving on the subcontinent for the first time – and for many of them, in the nineteenth century, it was their initiation to all foreign travel – the impact of the East must have been overwhelming. Here is an extract from a letter written from Shahpur in 1889 by Anne, Lady Wilson (who married a member of the Indian Civil Service in 1888 and accompanied him on his return to India in 1889):

Five weeks have passed since we landed, and they have seemed like five years. So many novel experiences have been crowded into the time. First of all, there was the journey from Bombay, which occupied four days, – think of it, you who consider twelve hours in the train to London an undertaking! It must be granted that the trial is mitigated as far as may be; the seats are arranged, for instance, like a waggonette, so that no one sits with his back to the engine. The compartments are broad and comfortable, and only four people occupy them at night, upper berths being let down to complete the four beds. Each carriage has a dressing-room, and the windows have outer wooden venetian shutters to keep out dust and sun if possible. Still, the four days and four nights, never hasting, never resting, were to me interminable.

The immensity of everything struck one like the statistics that might be given by an American fond of 'tall' stories. One saw miles upon miles of flat land, and knew that thousands of miles lay behind them, and such masses of people swarmed everywhere. Every station platform was densely crowded by them, and it seemed to me that the later it grew, the livelier and younger the people became! In the small hours of the night women rushed about, with babies in their arms and crying children at their heels; men ran helter-skelter, as you never see able-bodied men running, from sheer excitement and the love of screaming to their friends, at a railway station, at any rate in Scotland! And water-carriers and sweetmeat-vendors shouted above the pitch of their voices, as if there were no such thing as night and sleep in their programme. From which you may judge that there was practically very little sleep in mine. Once, about four o'clock in the morning, Jim roused me to 'look at a glorious sunrise.' I explained to him very quietly that I hoped it was the last, as it was the first, I had seen in India, and I do not think this will occur on a railway journey again!

I honestly confess that the overwhelming crowds of people frightened me. It was a very foolish feeling, as I have since been told; still there it was. What were we in the land, I thought, but a handful of Europeans at the best, and what was there to prevent these myriads from falling upon and obliterating us, as if we had never existed? There are many things to prevent it, independently of their being, as everybody tells me, the most law-abiding and loyal people in the world. But even yet my scepticism and fears get the better of my reason or my faith.

If anything could have reassured one, it would have been the reception Jim received on his return after six months' absence. At the first station we reached on the outskirts of his district were a crowd of Indian officials and notables, who travelled along with us, their ranks swelling at each succeeding station. Finally, when we reached Khushab and looked out of the carriage window, behold the moon shining down on the dusky faces and white robes of several hundreds, waiting to welcome us! Triumphal arches had been raised in our honour, and as we walked through the crowd bowing in answer to their salaams, it was naturally 'one of the proudest moments of my life.' I felt as if I were the Princess of Wales at least, without any of the responsibility. After an excellent champagne dinner, which good Mr O'D. had ready for us in the rest-house, we sat out of doors and enjoyed the fireworks and illuminations displayed in our honour.

Next day about fifty of the Indian 'squires' rode behind us as we drove to our home. At one point in the road an old veteran, in military gear and covered with medals, was drawn up with his retainers to fire a salute as we passed. He and his men had fought on our side in the Mutiny, and like the rest of the Punjaub, had been true to us throughout. Jim assures me that just such a kindly welcome as we have received would be given by the people of every district in the Punjaub, to any Civilian they had known before. . . .

Every room looks as high as a country church, the ceilings are of unplastered rafters, the doors are folding-doors, bolted in the middle. If you wish them shut, you must bolt them. If you wish to keep them open, you have to fix a wooden block in behind the hinges. At present a white cotton-sheet-like curtain hangs from a wooden rod before each. The fireplaces, in which only wood is burnt, are low brick slabs innocent of grating. Every bedroom has a bathroom attached, with a low wall in one corner surrounding the place where the big bath is. The bath is emptied on to the floor when one has done with it, the water running off through a hole in the wall.

There is no home-like pantry, with dresser and endless shelves, press, and hot and cold water arrangement. There is no kitchen with plate-rack, scullery and larder. The kitchen is a little dark room, with a board on the mud floor to hold the meat, two tumble-down brick 'ranges' in one corner, a stone receptacle in another into which the water is thrown, to run out through its hole in the wall into a sunk tub. There are two shelves on which are an array of pots, a hatchet, drainer, one or two tin spoons, and some pudding and pâté shapes. . . .

Servants differ greatly in different parts of the country, and their employers' opinions of them as a class vary as widely, ranging from enthusiasm to despair. Take them as a whole, I think I find them as yet distinctly trying, not so much from what they do, as from what they leave undone, and I constantly recall the advice of the old Scotch lady I met when I landed, who, in answer to my question as to how I could help missions in India, said: 'The best way you can do that, my dear, is to keep your temper with your servants, and stick to your husband in the heat!'

It amuses me to notice the way the Indians reverse the order in which we do things. For instance, at home men take off their hats when they come into a house; Indians keep on their turbans, but take off their shoes. We beckon with the palms of our hands turned inwards; they beckon with them turned out. My ayah lays my slippers in a row with the toes pointing towards me. The cook begins to read his Hindustani book of recipes from the last page backwards, and writes his accounts from right to left. When the carpenter uses native screws, he screws them in from right to left, and saws *inwards*, which makes one nervous! And when they play cards, they deal from the undermost card in the pack, and send them round by their right. They think it rude to laugh, but they never hesitate to yawn![19]

One of my favourite books as a child was *Japanese Fairy Tales* by Lafcadio Hearn. It was really five separate books in a slip-case held together by little ivory wedges; they were marvellously illustrated, printed on crinkly rice-paper, and they smelt perfectly delicious. They were totally unlike any other book that I had ever seen, far less possessed. I was therefore particularly interested when several of Hearn's were published in King's *Writings from Japan* in 1984. Until then I knew nothing about him; I have since learnt that he was born in 1850 in Lefkas in the Ionian Islands—hence his adopted first name—that he emigrated to America at the age of nineteen and that in 1891 he was sent by *Harper's Weekly* to Japan, where he married a Japanese girl, became a Japanese subject and remained the rest of his life.

'Do not fail to write down your first impressions as soon as possible,' said a kind English professor whom I had the pleasure of meeting soon after my arrival in Japan: 'they are evanescent, you know; they will never come to you again, once they have faded out; and yet of all the strange sensations you may receive in this country you will feel none so charming as these.' I am trying now to reproduce them from the hasty notes of the time, and find that they were even more fugitive than charming; something has evaporated from all my recollections of them – something impossible to recall. I neglected the friendly advice, in spite of all resolves to obey it: I could not, in those first weeks, resign myself to remain indoors and write, while there was yet so much to see and hear and feel in the sun-steeped ways of the wonderful Japanese city. Still, even could I revive all the lost sensations of those first experiences, I doubt if I could express and fix them in words. The first charm of Japan is intangible and volatile as a perfume.

It began for me with my first kuruma-ride out of the European quarter of Yokohama into the Japanese town; and so much as I can recall of it is hereafter set down.

It is with the delicious surprise of the first journey through Japanese streets – unable to make one's kuruma-runner understand anything but gestures, frantic gestures to roll on anywhere, everywhere, since all is unspeakably pleasurable and new – that one first receives the real sensation of being in the Orient, in this Far East so much read of, so long dreamed of, yet, as the eyes bear witness, heretofore all unknown. There is a romance even in the first full consciousness of this rather commonplace fact; but for me this consciousness is transfigured inexpressibly by the divine beauty of the day. There is some charm unutterable in the morning air, cool with the coolness of Japanese spring and wind-waves from the snowy cone of Fuji; a charm perhaps due rather to softest lucidity than to any positive tone – an atmospheric limpidity, extraordinary, with only a suggestion of blue in it, through which the most distant objects appear focused with amazing sharpness. The sun is only pleasantly warm; the jinrikisha, or kuruma, is the most cosy little vehicle imaginable; and the street-vistas, as seen above the dancing white mushroom-shaped hat of my sandaled runner, have an allurement of which I fancy that I could never weary.

Elfish everything seems; for everything as well as everybody is small, and queer, and mysterious: the little houses under their blue roofs, the little shop-fronts hung with blue, and the smiling little people in their blue costumes. The illusion is only broken by the occasional passing of a tall foreigner, and by divers shop-signs bearing announcements in absurd attempts at English. Nevertheless, such discords only serve to emphasize reality; they never materially lessen the fascination of the funny little streets.

'Tis at first a delightfully odd confusion only, as you look down one of them, through an interminable flutter of flags and swaying of dark blue drapery, all made beautiful and mysterious with Japanese or Chinese lettering. For there are no immediately discernible laws of construction or decoration: each building seems to have a fantastic prettiness of its own; nothing is exactly like anything else, and all is bewilderingly novel. But gradually, after an hour passed in the quarter, the eye begins to recognize in a vague way some general plan in the construction of these low, light, queerly gabled wooden houses, mostly unpainted, with their first stories all open to the street, and thin strips of roofing sloping above each shop-front, like awnings, back to the miniature balconies of paper-screened second stories. You begin to understand the common plan of the tiny shops, with their matted floors well raised above the street level, and the general perpendicular arrangement of sign-lettering, whether undulating on drapery or glimmering on gilded and lac-quered sign-boards. You observe that the same rich dark blue which dominates in popular costume rules also in shop draperies, though there is a sprinkling of other tints – bright blue and white and red (no greens or yellows). And then you note also that the dresses of the laborers are lettered with the same wonderful lettering as the shop draperies. No arabesques could produce such an effect. As modified for decorative purposes, these ideographs have a speaking symmetry which no design without a meaning could possess. As they appear on the back of a workman's frock – pure white on dark blue – and large enough to be easily read at a great distance (indicating some guild or company of which the wearer is a member or employee), they give to the poor cheap garment a factitious appearance of splendor.

And finally, while you are still puzzling over the mystery of things, there will come to you like a revelation the knowledge that most of the amazing pictur-esqueness of these streets is simply due to the profusion of Chinese and Japanese characters in white, black, blue or gold, decorating everything – even surfaces of doorposts and paper screens. Perhaps, then, for one moment, you will imagine the effect of English lettering substituted for those magical characters; and the mere idea will give to whatever aesthetic sentiment you may possess a brutal shock, and you will become, as I have become, an enemy of the Romaji-Kwai – that society founded for the ugly utilitarian purpose of introducing the use of English letters in writing Japanese.[20]

But if the impact of the East was overwhelming, so too was that of the West. On 8 November 1519, 400-odd Spaniards under the leadership of Hernán Cortés reached the top of a 12 000-foot pass and gazed down – the first white men ever to do so – on to the valley of Mexico and the vast lake from which rose the Aztec capital, Tenochtitlán, and the towns and villages surrounding it. Among those Spaniards was Bernal Díaz del Castillo, whose *History of the Conquest of New Spain* is nothing less than a master-piece – a first-hand, eye-witness account of an achievement so astonishing that to this day one can hardly believe it true.

And when we saw all those cities and villages built in the water, and other great towns on dry land, and that straight and level causeway leading to Mexico, we were astounded. These great towns and buildings rising from the water, all made of stone, seemed like an enchanted vision from the tale of Amadis. Indeed, some of our soldiers asked whether it was not all a dream. It is not surprising therefore that I should write in this vein. It was all so wonderful that I do not know how to describe this first glimpse of things never heard of, seen or dreamed of before.

When we arrived near Iztapalapa we beheld the splendour of the other *Caciques* who came out to meet us, the lord of that city whose name was Cuitlahuac, and the lord of Culuacan, both of them close relations of Montezuma. And when we entered the city of Iztapalapa, the sight of the palaces in which they lodged us! They were very spacious and well built, of magnificent stone, cedar wood, and the wood of other sweet-smelling trees, with great rooms and courts, which were a wonderful sight, and all covered with awnings of woven cotton.

When we had taken a good look at all this, we went to the orchard and garden, which was a marvellous place both to see and walk in. I was never tired of noticing the diversity of trees and the various scents given off by each, and the paths choked with roses and other flowers, and the many local fruit-trees and rose-bushes, and the pond of fresh water. Another remarkable thing was that large canoes could come into the garden from the lake, through a channel they had cut, and their crews did not have to disembark. Everything was shining with lime and decorated with different kinds of stonework and paintings which were a marvel to gaze on. Then there were birds of many breeds and varieties which came to the pond. I say again that I stood looking at it, and thought that no land like it would ever be discovered in the whole world. . . . But today all that I then saw is overthrown and destroyed; nothing is left standing.[21]

Let me end the chapter, once again, with a poem. It is called 'Air Travel in Arabia' and its author is my old friend Sir Charles Johnston. He used to be our ambassador in Jordan, so he ought to know.

> Then Petra flashed by in a wink.
> It looked like Eaton Square – but pink.[22]

CHAPTER SIX

Modes of Travel

In the literature of travel, almost all descriptions of the means by which the authors actually proceeded from one place to another are unfavourable – so much so that one sometimes finds oneself wondering how they ever managed to face the journey at all. The heat was suffocating, the cold was appalling, the jolting dislocated every bone in their bodies, the engines failed, the motion made them violently sick, the driver was drunk – so the grim list goes on, frequently with suggestions of acute physical danger into the bargain. This chapter then, if it does nothing else, may at least cheer the reader with a sense of quiet complacency that he is – at this particular moment, anyway – a good deal more comfortable than they were.

Let us start close to home – with the young German Carl Philip Moritz, the first English translation of whose *Travels, Chiefly on Foot, Through Several Parts of England in 1782, Described in Letters to a Friend* was published in 1795. His account of a journey by stage coach from Leicester to Northampton is more than enough to explain words two to four of his title:

Towards evening I arrived in Leicester through a pleasant meadow by way of a footpath; lying lengthways before me Leicester looked well, and bigger than it really is.

I walked down a long street until I came to the inn from which the coaches start. Here I learned that another stage-coach for London would leave that evening, but all the inside seats were booked. But there was still room on the outside. Time was short, however, if I was to reach London in time to keep my appointment with the Hamburg sea-captain who had agreed to take me to Germany. I therefore booked a place on the outside of the coach as far as Northampton.

That journey from Leicester to Northampton I shall remember as long as I live.

The coach started from the courtyard of the inn. The inside passengers got in there, but the roof of the archway leading from the courtyard to the street was too low to permit passengers to be on the top of the coach without danger to their heads, so we 'outsiders' had to clamber up in the street.

My travelling companions on top of the coach were a farmer, a young man quite decently dressed, and a young Negro. Climbing up was in itself at the risk of life and when I got on top I made straight for a corner where I could sit and take hold of a little handle on the side of the coach. I sat over the wheel and imagined I saw certain death before my eyes as soon as we set off. All I could do was to take a firmer grip of the handle and keep my balance.

The coach rolled along the stony street at great speed and every now and then we were tossed into the air; it was a near wonder that I always landed back on the coach. This sort of thing happened whenever we went through a village or down a hill.

Being continually in fear of my life finally became intolerable. I waited until we were going comparatively slowly and then crept from the top of the coach into the luggage-basket behind.

'In the basket you will be shaken to death!' exclaimed the Negro.

And I took it for a mere figure of speech!

Going uphill everything was comfortable and I nearly went to sleep between the travelling-boxes and the parcels, but as soon as we started to go downhill all the heavy luggage began to jump about. Everything came alive! I got so many hard knocks from them at every moment that I thought my end had come. Now I knew that the Negro had uttered no mere figure of speech. My cries for help were of no avail. I had to suffer this buffeting for nearly an hour until we began to go uphill again and, badly bruised and shaken, I crept back on to the roof of the coach and took up my former position.

'Didn't I tell you you would be shaken to death?' asked the Negro as I crawled back. I kept silent.

I am writing this as a warning to anyone who should unwittingly think of riding on the outside of an English stage-coach – or even in the basket!

We arrived about midnight in Market Harborough, where I was able to rest a little before being driven at full speed through many villages to arrive some time before dawn in Northampton, thirty-three miles from Leicester.

I had an equally fearful ride from Market Harborough to Northampton. It rained nearly all the time, and so we who were on the outside of the coach and had already been covered with dust, were now drenched as well. My neighbour, the young man, who sat with me in the middle, slept occasionally and in doing so fell against me with the full weight of his body, so that I feared he would push me right off my seat.

At last we came to Northampton where I went straight to bed and have slept nearly until noon.[1]

After the coming of the railways, things obviously got a lot better; though even they got off to a shaky start. I have already referred, in the Introduction, to the tragedy which befell Mr William Huskisson, Member for Liverpool, at the opening of the Liverpool – Manchester Railway on 15 September 1830; among the eye-witnesses – a distinguished gathering which also included the Duke of Wellington – was Fanny Kemble, who subsequently described it in a letter:

We started on Wednesday last, to the number of about eight hundred people. . . . The most intense curiosity and excitement prevailed, and, though the weather was uncertain, enormous masses of densely packed people lined the road, shouting and waving hats and handkerchiefs as we flew by them. What with the sight and sound of these cheering multitudes and the tremendous velocity with which we were borne past them, my spirits rose to the true champagne height, and I never enjoyed anything so much as the first hour of our progress. I had been unluckily separated from my mother in the first distribution of places, but by an exchange of seats which she was enabled to make she rejoined me when I was at the height of my ecstasy, which was considerably damped by finding that she was frightened to death, and intent upon nothing but devising means of escaping from a situation which appeared to her to threaten with instant annihilation herself and all her travelling companions. While I was chewing the cud of this disappointment, which was rather bitter, as I had expected her to be as delighted as myself with our excursion, a man flew by us, calling out through a speaking-trumpet to stop the engine, for that somebody in the directors' carriage had sustained an injury. We were all stopped accordingly, and presently a hundred voices were heard exclaiming that Mr. Huskisson was killed; the confusion that ensued is indescribable: the calling out from carriage to carriage to ascertain the truth, the contrary reports which were sent back to us, the hundred questions eagerly uttered at once, and the repeated and urgent demands for surgical assistance, created a sudden turmoil that was quite sickening. At last we distinctly ascertained that the unfortunate man's thigh was broken. From Lady W—, who was in the duke's carriage, and within three yards of the spot where the accident happened, I had the following details, the horror of witnessing which we were spared through our situation behind the great carriage. The engine had stopped to take in a supply of water, and several of the gentlemen in the directors' carriage had jumped out to look about them. Lord W—, Count Batthyany, Count Matuscenitz, and Mr. Huskisson among the rest were standing talking in the middle of the road, when an engine on the other line, which was parading up and down merely to show its speed, was seen coming down upon them like lightning. The most active of those in peril sprang back into their seats: Lord W— saved his life only by rushing behind the duke's carriage, and Count Matuscenitz had but just leaped into it, with the engine all but touching his heels as he did so; while poor Mr. Huskisson, less active from the effects of age and ill health, bewildered, too, by the frantic cries of 'Stop the engine! Clear the track!' that resounded on all sides, completely lost his head, looked helplessly to the right and left, and was instantaneously prostrated by the fatal machine, which dashed down like a thunderbolt upon him, and passed over his leg, smashing and mangling it in the most horrible way. (Lady W— said she distinctly heard the crushing of the bone.) So terrible was the effect of the appalling accident that, except that ghastly 'crushing' and poor Mrs. Huskisson's piercing shriek, not a sound was heard or a word uttered among the immediate spectators of the catastrophe.[2]

Before long, the railways had managed to redeem their reputation; it was some time, however, before they came to see themselves as providers of a universal public service for all classes. The following passage is taken from a book entitled *Nineteenth Century Railway Carriages*, by Hamilton Ellis:

The attitude of many companies was that summed up in the amiable pronounce- ment made by Charles Saunders, secretary of the Great Western, before a

Parliamentary Committee in July 1839, that perhaps the Company would arrange later on to convey the very lowest order of passengers, once a day at very low speed in carriages of an inferior description, at a very low price, perhaps at night.[3]

A similar philosophy seems to have been applied to the Emigrant Trains, designed to carry would-be settlers to the West in the second half of the nineteenth century. Robert Louis Stevenson took one (to San Francisco) in 1879:

It was about two in the afternoon of Friday that I found myself in front of the Emigrant House, with more than a hundred others, to be sorted and boxed for the journey. A white-haired official, with a stick under one arm, and a list in the other hand, stood apart in front of us, and called name after name in the tone of a command. At each name you would see a family gather up its brats and bundles and run for the hindmost of the three cars that stood awaiting us, and I soon concluded that this was to be set apart for the women and children. The second or central car, it turned out, was devoted to men travelling alone, and the third to the Chinese. . . .

The families once housed, we men carried the second car without ceremony by simultaneous assault. I suppose the reader has some notion of an American railroad-car, that long, narrow wooden box, like a flat-roofed Noah's ark, with a stove and a convenience, one at either end, a passage down the middle, and transverse benches upon either hand. Those destined for emigrants on the Union Pacific are only remarkable for their extreme plainness, nothing but wood entering in any part into their constitution, and for the usual inefficacy of the lamps, which often went out and shed but a dying glimmer even while they burned. The benches are too short for anything but a young child. Where there is scarce elbow-room for two to sit, there will not be space enough for one to lie. Hence the company, or rather, as it appears from certain bills about the Transfer Station, the company's servants, have conceived a plan for the better accommodation of travellers. They prevail on every two to chum together. To each of the chums they sell a board and three square cushions stuffed with straw, and covered with thin cotton. The benches can be made to face each other in pairs, for the backs are reversible. On the approach of night the boards are laid from bench to bench, making a couch wide enough for two, and long enough for a man of the middle height; and the chums lie down side by side upon the cushions with the head to the conductor's van and the feet to the engine. When the train is full, of course this plan is impossible, for there must not be more than one to every bench, neither can it be carried out unless the chums agree. It was to bring about this last condition that our white-haired official now bestirred himself. He made a most active master of ceremonies, introducing likely couples, and even guaranteeing the amiability and honesty of each. The greater number of happy couples the better for his pocket, for it was he who sold the raw material of the beds. . . .

The match-maker had a difficulty with me; perhaps, like some ladies, I showed myself too eager for union at any price; but certainly the first who was picked out to be my bedfellow declined the honour without thanks. He was an old, heavy, slow-spoken man, I think from Yankeeland, looked me all over with great timidity, and then began to excuse himself in broken phrases. He didn't know the young man, he said. The young man might be very honest, but how was he to know that? There was another young man whom he had met already in the train; he guessed *he* was honest, and would prefer to chum with *him* upon the whole. All this without any sort of excuse, as though I had been inanimate or absent. I began to tremble lest every one should refuse my company, and I be left rejected. But the next in turn was a tall, strapping, long-limbed, small-headed, curly-haired Pennsylvania Dutchman, with a soldierly smartness in his manner. To be exact, he had acquired it in the navy. But that was all one; he had at least been trained to desperate resolves, so he accepted the match, and the white-haired swindler pronounced the connubial benediction, and pocketed his fees.

. . . The class to which I belonged was of course far the largest, and we ran over, so to speak, to both sides; so that there were some Caucasians among the Chinamen, and some bachelors among the families. But our own car was pure from admixture, save for one little boy of eight or nine, who had the whooping-cough. At last, about six, the long train crawled out of the Transfer Station and across the wide Missouri river to Omaha, westward bound.

It was a troubled uncomfortable evening in the cars. There was thunder in the air, which helped to keep us restless. A man played many airs upon the cornet, and none of them were much attended to, until he came to 'Home, sweet Home.' It was truly strange to note how the talk ceased at that, and the faces began to lengthen. . . . An elderly, hard-looking man, with a goatee beard and about as much appearance of sentiment as you would expect from a retired slaver, turned with a start and bade the performer stop that 'damned thing.' 'I've heard about enough of that,' he added; 'give us something about the good country we're going to.' A murmur of adhesion ran round the car; the performer took the instrument from his lips, laughed and nodded, and then struck into a dancing measure; and, like a new Timotheus, stilled immediately the emotion he had raised.

The day faded; the lamps were lit; a party of wild young men, who got off next evening at North Platte, stood together on the stern platform, singing 'The Sweet By-and-by' with very tuneful voices; the chums began to put up their beds; and it seemed as if the business of the day were at an end. But it was not so; for, the train stopping at some station, the cars were instantly thronged with the natives, wives and fathers, young men and maidens, some of them in little more than nightgear, some with stable lanterns, and all offering beds for sale. Their charge began with twenty-five cents a cushion, but fell, before the train went on again, to fifteen, with the bed-board gratis, or less than one-fifth of what I had paid for mine at the Transfer. This is my contribution to the economy of future emigrants.[4]

Personally, I love trains; and I have always longed to travel on the Trans-Siberian Railway. Peter Fleming did so in 1933, and described the journey in *One's Company*:

You wake up in the morning. Your watch says it is eight o'clock; but you are travelling east, and you know that it is really nine, though you might be hard put to it to explain why this is so. Your berth is comfortable. There is no need to get up, and no incentive either. You have nothing to look forward to, nothing to avoid. No assets, no liabilities.

If you were on a ship, there would be any number of both. A whacking great breakfast, sunny decks, the swimming bath, that brilliant short story you are going to write, the dazzling creature whose intuitive admiration for your writings you would be the last to undermine – these are among the assets. Liabilities include the ante-final of the deck quoits, the man who once landed on Easter Island, the ship's concert, dressing for dinner, and boat-drill.

At first the balance sheet strikes you as sound. But gradually, as the tedious days become interminable weeks, the traitorous assets insensibly change sides and swell the ranks of the liabilities. A time comes when there is nothing to look forward to, everything to avoid. That brilliant short story, still-born, weighs upon your con-science, a succession of whacking great breakfasts upon your digestion; the sunny decks are now uncomfortably so, and even the swimming bath has been rendered for practical purposes inaccessible by that dazzling creature whose intuitive ad-miration for your writings you have been the first to undermine. At sea there is always a catch somewhere, as Columbus bitterly remarked on sighting America.

But on the Trans-Siberian Railway there are neither ups nor downs. You are a prisoner, narrowly confined. At sea you are a prisoner too, but a prisoner with just enough rope to strangle at birth the impulses of restlessness or inspiration. The prisoner sits down to write, then thinks it would be more pleasant on deck. On deck there is a wind; his papers are unmanageable. With a sigh he takes up a book, a heavy book, a book which it will do him good to read. After four pages there comes an invitation to deck-tennis. He cannot refuse. He goes below to change, comes up again, and desultorily plays. There follows conversation and a bath. The morning is over.

The morning is over. His typewriter is in the smoking-room, his book is on B deck, his coat is on A deck, and he has lost his pipe and broken a finger-nail. In everything he has attempted he has failed. All this peace and leisure has been sterile without being enjoyable. The afternoon will be the same.

Most men, though not the best men, are happiest when the question 'What shall I do?' is supererogatory. (Hence the common and usually just contention that 'My schooldays were the happiest days of my life'.) That is why I like the Trans-Siberian Railway. You lie in your berth, justifiably inert. Past the window plains crawl and forests flicker. The sun shines weakly on an empty land. The piles of birch logs by the permanent way – silver on the outside, black where the damp butts show – give the anomalous illusion that there has been a frost. There is always a magpie in sight.

You have nothing to look at, but no reason to stop looking. You are living in a vacuum, and at last you have to invent some absurdly artificial necessity for getting up: 'fifteen magpies from now', or 'next time the engine whistles'. For you are inwardly afraid that without some self-discipline to give it a pattern this long period of suspended animation will permanently affect your character for the worse.

So in the end you get up, washing perfunctorily in the little dark confessional which you share with the next compartment, and in the basin for which the ex-perienced traveller brings his own plug, because the Russians, for some reason connected – strangely enough – with religion, omit to furnish these indispensable adjuncts to a careful toilet.

Then, grasping your private pot of marmalade, you lurch along to the dining-car.

It is now eleven o'clock, and the dining-car is empty. You order tea and bread, and make without appetite a breakfast which is more than sufficient for your needs. The dining-car is almost certainly stuffy, but you have ceased to notice this. The windows are always shut, either because the weather is cold, or because it is warm and dry and therefore dusty. (Not, of course, that the shutting of them excludes the dust. Far from it. But it is at least a gesture; it is the best that can be done.)

After that you wander back to your compartment. The *provodnik* has transformed your bed into a seat, and perhaps you hold with him some foolish conversation, in which the rudiments of three languages are prostituted in an endeavour to compliment each other on their simultaneous mastery. Then you sit down and read. You read and read and read. There are no distractions, no interruptions, no temptations to get up and do something else; there is nothing else to do. You read as you have never read before.

And so the day passes. If you are wise you shun the regulation meal at three o'clock, which consists of five courses not easily to be identified, and during which the car is crowded and the windows blurred with steam. I had brought with me from London biscuits and potted meat and cheese; and he is a fool who does not take at least some victuals of his own. But as a matter of fact, what with the airless atmosphere and the lack of exercise, you don't feel hungry on the Trans-Siberian Railway. A pleasant lassitude, a sense almost of disembodiment, descends on you, and the food in the dining-car, which, though seldom really bad, is never appetizing and sometimes scarce, hardly attracts that vigorous criticism which it would on a shorter journey.

At the more westerly stations – there are perhaps three stops of twenty minutes every day – you pace the platforms vigorously, in a conscientious British way. But gradually this practice is abandoned. As you are drawn further into Asia, old fetishes lose their power. It becomes harder and harder to persuade yourself that you feel a craving for exercise, and indeed you almost forget that you ought to feel this craving. At first you are alarmed, for this is the East, the notorious East, where white men go to pieces; you fear that you are losing your grip, that you are going native. But you do nothing about it, and soon your conscience ceases to prick and it seems quite natural to stand limply in the sunlight, owlish, frowsty, and immobile, like everybody else.

At last evening comes. The sun is setting somewhere far back along the road that you have travelled. A slanting light always lends intimacy to a landscape, and this Siberia, flecked darkly by the tapering shadows of trees, seems a place at once more friendly and more mysterious than the naked non-committal flats of noon. Your eyes are tired, and you put down your book. Against the grey and creeping distances outside memory and imagination stage in their turn the struggles of the past and of the future. For the first time loneliness descends, and you sit examining its implications until you find Siberia vanished and the grimy window offering nothing save your own face, foolish, indistinct, and as likely as not unshaved. You adjourn to the dining-car, for eggs.[5]

We have already met the intrepid Captain Fred Burnaby. When he was in Russia he found that the only way he could travel the eighty-five miles from Sizeran to Samara was by sleigh – a mode of conveyance not always as agreeable as it sounds:

'You had better put on plenty of clothes,' was the friendly caution I received from my companion as I entered the dressing-room. 'The thermometer marks 20 degrees below zero (Reaumur), and there is a wind.' People in this country who have never experienced a Russian winter have little idea of the difference even a slight breeze makes when the mercury stands low in the thermometer, for the wind then cuts through you, furs and all, and penetrates to the very bones. Determining to be on my guard against the frost, I dressed myself, as I thought, as warmly as possible, and so as to be utterly impervious to the elements.

First came three pairs of the thickest stockings, drawn up high above the knee. Over them a pair of fur-lined low shoes, which in their turn were inserted into leather goloshes, my limbs being finally deposited in a pair of enormous cloth boots, the latter reaching up to the thigh. Previously I had put on some extra thick drawers and a pair of trousers, the astonishment of the foreman of Messrs. Kino's establishment, 'Lord love you, sir!' being his remark, when I tried them on, 'no cold can get through them trousers anyhow.' I must confess that I rather chuckled as my legs assumed herculean proportions, and I thought that I should have a good laugh at the wind, no matter how cutting it might be: but Æolus had the laugh on his side before the journey was over. A heavy flannel under-shirt, and shirt covered by a thick wadded waist-coat and coat, encased my body, which was further enveloped in a huge shuba, or fur pelisse, reaching to the heels. My head was protected with a fur cap and bashlik, a sort of cloth headpiece of a conical shape made to cover the cap, and having two long ends which tie round the throat.

Being thus accoutred in all my armour, I sallied forth to join my companion, who, an enormous man naturally, now seemed a very Colossus of Rhodes in his own winter attire. How people would have laughed if they could have seen us in Piccadilly in our costumes! 'I think you will do,' said my friend, scanning me well over; 'but you will find your feet get very cold for all that. It takes a day or so to get used to this sleigh travelling, and though I am only going a little beyond Samara I shall be uncommonly glad when my journey is over.'

He was buckling on his revolver; and as we were informed that there were a great many wolves in the neighbourhood, I tried to do the same. This was an impossibility, the man who made the belt had never foreseen the gigantic proportions my waist would assume when clad in this Russian garb. I was obliged to give it up in despair, and contented myself by strapping the weapon outside my saddle bags.

For provisions for possibly a thirty-six hours' journey, and as nothing could be bought to eat on the road, I provided myself with some cutlets and chicken, which fitted capitally into the mess tins. My companion agreed to furnish the tea and bread, the former an article without which no true Russian will ever travel. He had not much baggage with him, and my own had been reduced to as little as possible; but we soon discovered that it was impossible to stow away the luggage in the first sleigh that had been brought for our inspection. When my railway bag, saddle bags, cartridge box, gun, and sleeping sack had been put inside, and were well covered with straw, I essayed to sit upon them, but found that there was too little distance from the improvised seat to the roof. My back was nearly bent double in consequence.

'Bring out another sleigh,' said my friend. 'How the wind cuts; does it not?' he continued, as the breeze whistling against our bodies made itself felt in spite of all the precautions we had taken. The vehicle now brought was broader and more commodious than the previous one, which, somewhat in the shape of a coffin, seemed especially designed so as to torture the occupants, particularly if, like my companion and self, they should happen to be endowed by Nature with that curse during a sleigh journey – however desirable appendages they may be when in a crowd – long legs.[6]

One of the only consolations, in fact, of travelling in Russia must have been the reflection that at least one was not doing so in Finland. *Murray's Handbook for Northern Europe* of 1849 explains why:

Carrioles, similar to those used in Norway and Sweden, are the carriages most generally in use in Finland, and by far the best adapted for speed, particularly where the road is sandy, which is the case, more or less, nearly all the way from Åbo to Helsingforss, and also along the shore of the Gulf of Bothnia to Bjornsberg, and they far excel vehicles of any other construction for whirling down hill at full gallop, – the only plan of descending the sharp pitches in the road with which the Finnish horses appear to be acquainted. Besides the carriole there is another species of vehicle, called a *kibitka*, a long narrow cart without springs, and covered with a kind of leather hood, extending over about one-half of the carriage. The bottom of the *kibitka* is usually provided with a feather bed, or a thick covering of hay or straw, and on this the traveller reclines at full length. As to repose, it is doubtful whether any will be obtained in such a vehicle; in addition to which, you see nothing whatever of the country through which you pass. This *kibitka* is an introduction from Russia; the really national carriage of the Fin is a machine called a *bondkara*, and the traveller should reflect seriously before he submits his body to the indescribable agonies created by the cart so called, unless, indeed, it is his intention to travel in the *telega* when he reaches Russia; in this case it will be well for him to accustom his bones and muscles to the dislocations which he will be subjected to in the *bondkara*, for though these two vehicles are equally rough, the roads in Finland are far superior to the no roads in Russia. This machine, which has no springs, is nothing more than an oblong kind of box without a back, placed on an axle-tree and two wheels, and a board is nailed or tied to the sides like the seat of a taxed cart; on this bench the traveller and the postillion are seated, and there is no slight difficulty in keeping an equilibrium, while on bad parts of the road one is sometimes obliged to cling firmly to it with both hands. Scarcely, too, has the tourist got a little accustomed to the sway and play of this horrid cart, than he finds himself at a post station, where he is obliged to turn out and get into another *bondkara*, the bench of which is perhaps tied at a different angle from the last.[7]

Descending a steep hill at the gallop in a carriole cannot be a pleasant experience; but it would have been child's play to the Abbé Huc, one of two Lazarist missionaries who in 1844, when the Pope established a Vicariate of Mongolia, were sent to find out more about the new diocese. One of the by-products of the Abbé's journey – he actually reached Lhasa before being deported – was a book entitled *Travels in Tartary, Thibet and China*, from which the following extract is taken:

'Here we are, at the glacier of the Mountain of Spirits,' said Ly-Kouo-Ngan [their Mandarin companion]. 'We shall have a bit of a laugh now.' We regarded with amazement the Pacificator of Kingdoms. 'Yes, here is the glacier; look here.' We proceeded to the spot he indicated, bent over the edge of the plateau, and saw beneath us an immense glacier jutting out very much, and bordered with frightful precipices. We could distinguish, under the light coating of snow, the greenish hue of the ice. We took a stone from the Buddhic monument, and threw it down the glacier. A loud noise was heard, and the stone gliding down rapidly, left after it a broad green line. The place was clearly a glacier, and we now comprehended partly Ly-Kouo-Ngan's remark, but we saw nothing at all laughable in being obliged to travel over such a road. Ly-Kouo-Ngan, however, was right in every point, as we now found by experience.

They made the animals go first, the oxen, and then the horses. A magnificent long-haired ox opened the march; he advanced gravely to the edge of the plateau; then, after stretching out his neck, smelling for a moment at the ice, and blowing through his large nostrils some thick clouds of vapour, he manfully put his two front feet on the glacier, and whizzed off as if he had been discharged from a cannon. He went down the glacier with his legs extended, but as stiff and motionless as if they had been made of marble. Arrived at the bottom, he turned over, and then ran on, bounding and bellowing over the snow. All the animals, in turn, afforded us the same spectacle, which was really full of interest. The horses, for the most part, exhibited, before they started off, somewhat more hesitation than the oxen; but it was easy to see that all of them had been long accustomed to this kind of exercise.

The men, in their turn, embarked with no less intrepidity and success than the animals, although in an altogether different manner. We seated ourselves carefully on the edge of the glacier, we stuck our heels close together on the ice, as firmly as possible, then using the handles of our whips by way of helm, we sailed over these frozen waters with the velocity of a locomotive. A sailor would have pronounced us to be going at least twelve knots an hour. In our many travels, we had never before experienced a mode of conveyance at once so commodious, so expeditious, and, above all, so refreshing.[8]

It certainly sounds a lot more fun than crossing the Alps in the eighteenth century. One of the best short descriptions of this is by Horace Walpole, who wrote to his friend Richard West from Turin on 11 November 1739:

So, as the song says, we are in fair Italy! I wonder we are; for on the very highest precipice of Mount Cenis, the devil of discord, in the similitude of sour wine, had got amongst our Alpine savages, and set them a-fighting with Gray and me in the chairs: they rushed him by me on a crag, where there was scarce room for a cloven foot. The least slip had tumbled us into such a fog, and such an eternity, as we should never have found our way out of again. We were eight days in coming hither from Lyons; the four last in crossing the Alps. Such uncouth rocks, and such uncomely inhabitants! My dear West, I hope I shall never see them again! At the foot of Mount Cenis we were obliged to quit our chaise, which was taken all to pieces and loaded on mules; and we were carried in low arm-chairs on poles, swathed in beaver bonnets, beaver gloves, beaver stockings, muffs, and bear-skins. When we came to the top, behold the snows fallen! and such quantities, and conducted by such heavy clouds that hung glouting, that I thought we could never have waded through them. The descent is two leagues, but steep and rough as O's father's face, over which, you know, the devil walked with hobnails in his shoes. But the dexterity and nimbleness of the mountaineers are inconceivable: they run with you down steeps and frozen precipices, where no man, as men are now, could possibly walk. We had twelve men and nine mules to carry us, our servants, and baggage, and were above five hours in this agreeable jaunt![9]

A similar sort of litter was used, though in somewhat different conditions, by Mrs Eliza Fay in 1779, when she and her husband were travelling overland from Alexandria to Suez to join the ship that was to take them to India. On 15 September she wrote to her sister from Mocha:

My Dear Sister,

I resume my pen in order to give you some account of our passing the Desert, which being done by a method of travelling totally different from any thing in England, may afford amusement, and even without the charm of novelty could not fail to interest you, as the narrative of one so nearly and dearly connected.

When a Caravan is about to depart, large tents are pitched on the skirts of the City, whither all who propose joining it repair: there they are drawn up in order, by the persons who undertake to convey them. Strong bodies of Arabian soldiers guard the van and rear; others flank the sides –; so that the female passengers, and the merchandise, are completely surrounded –, and, as one would hope, defended in case of attack. Each gentleman of our party had a horse, and it is common to hire a camel between two, with panniers to carry their provisions &c. – : across the panniers, which are of wicker, a kind of mattress is thrown, whereon they take it by turns to lie, and court repose, during their journey. Females who can afford the expence, are more comfortably accommodated – ; these travel in a kind of litter, called a Tataravan; with two poles fastened between two camels, one behind, the other before. The litter has a top and is surmounted by shabby, ill contrived Venetian blinds, which in the day, increase the suffocating heat, but are of use during the nights which are cold and piercing. – Every camel carries skins of water, but before you have been many hours on the Desert, it becomes of the colour of coffee. I was warned of this, and recommended to provide small guglets of porous earth, which after filling with *purified* water, I slung to the top of my *Tataravan*; and these with water melons, and *hard* eggs, proved the best refreshments I could have taken. The water by this means was tolerably preserved; but the motion of the camels and the uncouth manner in which the vehicle is fastened to them, made such a constant rumbling sound among my provisions, as to be exceedingly annoying. Once I was saluted by a parcel of hard eggs breaking loose from their net, and pelting me completely: it was fortunate that *they were* boiled, or I should have been in a pretty trim; to this may be added the frequent violent jerks, occasioned by one or other of the poles slipping out of its wretched fastening, so as to bring one end of the litter to the ground; and you may judge how pleasing this mode of travelling must be.[10]

Mrs Amelia Edwards, a century later, would have scorned such a contrivance. While fully aware – even in Egypt, there were no flies on Mrs Edwards – that the camel ride from Aswan to Philae figured as 'the crowning achievement of every Cook's tourist' she mounted her steed none the less and drew the usual conclusions:

The camel has his virtues – so much at least must be admitted; but they do not lie upon the surface. My Buffon tells me, for instance, that he carries a fresh-water cistern in his stomach; which is meritorious. But the cistern ameliorates neither his gait nor his temper – which are abominable. Irreproachable as a beast of burden, he is open to many objections as a steed. It is unpleasant, in the first place, to ride an animal which not only objects to being ridden, but cherishes a strong personal antipathy to his rider. Such, however, is his amiable peculiarity. You know that he hates you, from the moment you first walk round him, wondering where and how to begin the ascent of his hump. He does not, in fact, hesitate to tell you so in the roundest terms. He swears freely while you are taking your seat; snarls if you but move in the saddle; and stares you angrily in the face, if you attempt to turn his head in any direction save that which he himself prefers. Should you persevere, he tries to bite your feet. If biting your feet does not answer, he lies down.

Now the lying-down and getting-up of a camel are performances designed for the express purpose of inflicting grievous bodily harm upon his rider. Thrown twice forward and twice backward, punched in his 'wind' and damaged in his spine, the luckless novice receives four distinct shocks, each more violent and unexpected than the last. For this 'execrable hunchback' is fearfully and wonderfully made. He has a superfluous joint somewhere in his legs, and uses it to revenge himself upon mankind.

His paces, however, are more complicated than his joints and more trying than his temper. He has four: – a short walk, like the rolling of a small boat in a chopping sea; a long walk which dislocates every bone in your body; a trot that reduces you to imbecility; and a gallop that is sudden death. One tries in vain to imagine a crime for which the *peine forte et dure* of sixteen hours on camel-back would not be a full and sufficient expiation. It is a punishment to which one would not willingly be the means of condemning any human being – not even a reviewer.[11]

Alexander Kinglake was inclined to take a more charitable view of the camel than did most of his compatriots. He saw it, however, with the eyes of a traveller rather than those of a tourist; for him, it was not an excuse for a joy-ride so much as a necessity of life.

In a couple of days I was ready to start. The way of providing for the passage of the desert is this: there is an agent in the town who keeps himself in communication with some of the desert Arabs that are hovering within a day's journey of the place; a party of these, upon being guaranteed against seizure or other ill treatment at the hands of the governor, come into the town, bringing with them the number of camels which you require, and then they stipulate for a certain sum to take you to the place of your destination in a given time. The agreement thus made by them includes a safe-conduct through their country, as well as the hire of the camels. According to the contract made with me, I was to reach Cairo within ten days from the commencement of the journey. I had four camels, one for my baggage, one for each of my servants, and one for myself. Four Arabs, the owners of the camels, came with me on foot. My stores were a small soldier's tent, two bags of dried bread brought from the convent at Jerusalem, and a couple of bottles of wine from the same source, two goatskins filled with water, tea, sugar, a cold tongue, and (of all things in the world) a jar of Irish butter which Mysseri had purchased from some merchant. There was also a small sack of charcoal, for the greater part of the desert through which we were to pass is void of fuel.

The camel kneels to receive her load, and for a while she will allow the packing to go on with silent resignation, but when she begins to suspect that her master is putting more than a just burthen upon her poor hump, she turns round her supple neck, and looks sadly upon the increasing load, and then gently remonstrates against the wrong with the sigh of a patient wife. If sighs will not move you, she can weep. You soon learn to pity, and soon to love her for the sake of her gentle and womanish ways.

You cannot, of course, put an English or any other riding saddle upon the back of the camel, but your quilt or carpet, or whatever you carry for the purpose of lying on at night, is folded and fastened on to the pack-saddle upon the top of the hump, and on this you ride, or rather sit. You sit as a man sits on a chair when he sits astride. I made an improvement on this plan: I had my English stirrups strapped on to the cross bars of the pack-saddle; and thus, by gaining rest for my dangling legs, and gaining, too, the power of varying my position more easily than I could otherwise have done, I added very much to my comfort.

The camel, like the elephant, is one of the old-fashioned sort of animals that still walk along upon the (now nearly exploded) plan of the ancient beasts that lived before the flood; she moves forward both her near legs at the same time, and then awkwardly swings round her off-shoulder and haunch, so as to repeat the manœuvre on that side; her pace therefore is an odd, disjointed, and disjoining sort of movement that is rather disagreeable at first, but you soon grow reconciled to it. The height to which you are raised is of great advantage to you in passing the burning sands of the desert, for the air at such a distance from the ground is much cooler and more lively than that which circulates beneath.[12]

While it is admittedly difficult to feel much emotional *rapport* with a camel – though not impossible, as Colonel Angus Buchanan proves twice in this book – most people feel a good deal friendlier towards the elephant. An exception was Mrs Isabella Bird, who entrusted herself to one for a journey into the interior of the Malay Peninsula in 1879, and did *not* enjoy the experience:

The elephant at last came up and was brought below the porch. They are truly hideous beasts, with their gray, wrinkled, hairless hides, the huge ragged 'flappers' which cover their ears, and with which they fan themselves ceaselessly, the small mean eyes, the hideous proboscis which coils itself snakishly round everything; the formless legs, so like trunks of trees; the piggish back, with the steep slope down to the mean, bare tail, and the general unlikeness to all familiar and friendly beasts. . . .

Before I came I dreamt of howdahs and cloth of gold trappings, but my elephant had neither. In fact there was nothing grand about him but his ugliness. His back was covered with a piece of raw hide, over which were several mats, and on either side of the ridgy backbone a shallow basket, filled with fresh leaves and twigs, and held in place by ropes of rattan. I dropped into one of these baskets from the porch, a young Malay lad into the other, and my bag was tied on behind with rattan. A noose of the same with a stirrup served for the driver to mount. He was a Malay, wearing only a handkerchief and *sarong*, a gossiping careless fellow, who jumped off whenever he had a chance of a talk, and left us to ourselves. He drove with a stick with a curved spike at the end of it, which, when the elephant was bad, was hooked into the membranous 'flapper,' always evoking the uprearing and bran- dishing of the proboscis, and a sound of ungentle expostulation, which could be heard a mile off. He sat on the head of the beast, sometimes cross-legged, and sometimes with his legs behind the huge ear covers. . . .

This mode of riding is not comfortable. One sits facing forwards with the feet dangling over the edge of the basket. This edge soon produces a sharp ache or cramp, and when one tries to get relief by leaning back on anything, the awkward, rolling motion is so painful, that one reverts to the former position till it again becomes intolerable. Then the elephant had not been loaded 'with brains,' and his pack was as troublesome as the straw shoes of the Japanese horses. It was always slipping forwards or backwards, and as I was heavier than the Malay lad, I was always slipping down and trying to wriggle myself up on the great ridge which was the creature's backbone, and always failing, and the mahout was always stopping and pulling the rattan ropes which bound the whole arrangement together, but never succeeding in improving it.

Before we had travelled two hours, the great bulk of the elephant without any warning gently subsided behind, and then as gently in front, the huge, ugly legs being extended in front of him, and the man signed to me to get off, which I did by getting on his head and letting myself down by a rattan rope upon the driver, who made a step of his back, for even when 'kneeling,' as this queer attitude is called, a good ladder is needed for comfortable getting off and on. While the whole arrangement of baskets was being re-rigged, I clambered into a Malay dwelling of the poorer class, and was courteously received and regaled with bananas and buffalo milk. . . .

When the pack was adjusted the mahout jumped on the back, and giving me his hands hauled me up over the head, after which the creature rose gently from the ground, and we went on our journey.

But the ride was 'a fearful joy,' *if* a joy at all! Soon the driver jumped off for a gossip and a smoke, leaving the elephant to 'gang his ain gates' for a mile or more, and he turned into the jungle, where he began to rend and tear the trees, and then going to a mud-hole he drew all the water out of it, squirted it with a loud noise over himself and his riders, soaking my clothes with it, and when he turned back to the road again, he several times stopped and seemed to stand on his head by stiffening his proboscis and leaning upon it, and when I hit him with my umbrella he uttered the loudest roar I ever heard. My Malay fellow-rider jumped off and ran back for the driver, on which the panniers came altogether down on my side, and I hung on with difficulty, wondering what other possible contingencies could occur, always expecting that the beast, which was flourishing his proboscis, would lift me off with it and deposit me in a mud-hole.

On the driver's return I had to dismount again, and this time the elephant was allowed to go and take a proper bath in a river. He threw quantities of water over himself, and took up plenty more with which to cool his sides as he went along. Thick as the wrinkled hide of an elephant looks, a very small insect can draw blood from it, and when left to himself he sagaciously plasters himself with mud to protect himself like the water buffalo. Mounting again, I rode for another two hours, but he crawled about a mile an hour, and seemed to have a steady purpose to lie down. He roared whenever he was asked to go faster, sometimes with a roar of rage, sometimes in angry and sometimes in plaintive remonstrance. The driver got off and walked behind him, and then he stopped altogether. Then the man tried to pull him along by putting a hooked stick in his huge 'flapper,' but this produced no other effect than a series of howls; then he got on his head again, after which the brute made a succession of huge stumbles, each one of which threatened to be a fall, and then the driver with a look of despair got off again. Then I made signs that I would get off, but the elephant refused to lie down, and I let myself down his unshapely shoulder by a rattan rope till I could use the mahout's shoulders as steps. The baskets were taken off and left at a house, the elephant was turned loose in the jungle; I walked the remaining miles to Kwala Kangsa, and the driver carried my portmanteau! Such was the comical end of my first elephant ride.[13]

After such exotics, it seems rather a come-down to turn our attention to the poor old internal-combustion engine. But as every traveller knows, motor transport in distant lands can prove just as bloody-minded as the most recalcitrant of quadrupeds. Freya Stark encountered a typical example when she was trying to get from Malayir (in Persia) to Hamadan in 1931:

The next lorry has been my home for a day and two nights and is now laboriously getting under way for the next bit, as it goes south while I hope for another and better to Hamadan. You wouldn't believe so many different things would be wrong with one car. The first breakdown always occurs just outside the town and is a sort of indispensable beginning to a Persian journey. Then we had a more alarming trouble: the screw which kept the back wheel on, whether lost or only unsafe I don't know, but we went on, looking back at intervals to see if the wheel was still there. Then the clutch had to be changed – and so on. About midnight we stopped and I was given a bed made of two benches with quilts and was tucked in among all the sleeping passengers in the long room of the *chaikhana* by the *chaikhana* keeper, and very glad of the warmth. He pulled down one of his curtains to cover me.

In the morning early they all woke up and said their prayers: mostly pilgrims returning from Meshed, a patient and pleasant lot of people with a number of querulous veiled females whom one only heard vaguely asking for water to drink at intervals inside their cage, and hushing a little indiscriminate heap of babies. The passenger here is not a privileged being to be looked after: he has taken a share for the time being in the lorry or car and it is all one concern where everyone takes the good or bad as it comes: walks up the hills when the lorry is tired, and takes it as a matter of Fate when it breaks down. The driver was also the owner, a young Assyrian with a pleasant face but so much taken up with a young lady who said she was his wife that he was useless for anything else. We took a day more than even the local average over this bit of journey. It was an interesting landscape for an hour or two – the waste salt lands with their domed villages at long intervals, built like the old Sassanian palaces, with little decorations in the mud that showed the trace of old beautiful brick models some time in the past. But I soon got tired of landscape of any description. We spent the morning mending the clutch: then five hours at the town of 'Iraq in a house where women walked about with very little on and where our driver's lady seemed much at home. They were kind and gave me a bed to sleep on and food to eat, but it was impossible to get the driver away until the afternoon: and two more breakdowns and a puncture, besides walking up the steep hill to save the lorry, made it night before we reached Malayir, where I still am in hopes of a car. It was annoying as there is an American doctor here, and if I had got in in time I would have gone and got at least a good bath and supper.

During the last puncture the lady and the Assyrian had a quarrel: the lady was pretty in a fierce and gipsy fashion: she had friends in Teheran she said: the driver tried to put his arm round her, and then being repulsed, sang Assyrian songs in a loud voice while the lady sat beside me in tears. They made it up however and decided to stay here the night instead of taking their passengers on to their destination. I found another bed like the night before and was unfortunately given a lamp, which is always a mistake because of bugs. However, I was much too tired to set up my own things and further demoralized by discovering that my soap had been stolen. The landlord was distressed because I slept alone in the building. This was not really a worry to me and I slept like a log in spite of the dreary surroundings. But I *do* want a wash.

I came down into the yard and sucked a pomegranate on a carpet by the gate while my fellow travellers were getting into the car and the chauffeur was patching up a new puncture. 'May you arrive to-night if it please God,' said I, which pleased them, as it is supposed to be only an hour's journey away. The lorry is a Chevrolet and only a year old, so they told me: so that one wonders how it can pay them at a maximum of 1*d*. a mile per passenger.[14]

Sometimes, it seems, even a road can have a mind of its own. Peter Fleming certainly thought so. Here is another extract from *Brazilian Adventure*.

The last gun-case was wedged into the lorry's mountainous load. The drivers of the two decrepit cars raced their engines and hooted. The crowd raised a faint derisive cheer. The expedition was under weigh again.

The cadets of the Military Academy, who were present in force, withdrew to the pavement. Self-important little girls picked up infants from the middle of the road and deposited them in the gutter. On the steps of the hotel our landlady smiled inscrutably into her moustache. The dentist, with streaming eyes – the result not so much of emotion as of a cold caught in his ambush under the fruit trees – wished us good hunting. Once more the Dutchman implored us to accept the gift of a fantastically inaccurate map of the Araguaya which he himself had made. A middle-aged lieutenant, who lived in the hotel, appeared with five of his beastly little children to bid us farewell; for the last time I remarked the contrast between his placid and dignified bearing and his costume, which, combining as it did spurs with a pyjama jacket, powerfully suggested the exigencies of a night alarm. Craning with precarious nonchalance out of windows all down the street, the beauties of Goyaz risked their necks and their dignity to see us go. We began to move forward, bumping slowly over the cobbles. The crowd cheered again, with kindly scorn. We left Goyaz.

It is about 130 miles from Goyaz to Leopoldina, which was to be our point of embarkation for the journey down the Araguaya and our last contact with civiliz-ation for some time to come. There had been stretches of road on the way up to Goyaz which had seemed pretty bad at the time. Not often, we had supposed, are cars, even in Brazil, called upon to negotiate going as rough as this; and if worse roads do indeed exist, they can hardly be accounted passable. But the road to Leopoldina proved this supposition to be gravely at fault. It was not like other bad roads, which incommode you with continuous and petty malice. 'Look how far we can go,' they seem to say, as you crawl painfully along them, 'and yet still be called a road.' You hate them the more bitterly for the knowledge that they will keep within certain bounds. They will madden you with minor obstacles, but in the end they will let you through. They dare do all that will become a road; who dares do more is none. However gross the indignities that they heap upon you, they will yet deny you the hollow revenge of calling them impassable. You know that they will observe the letter, though not the spirit, of their contract with your wheels.

But with the road to Leopoldina it was not like this. It had no quarrel with us. It took no count of us at all. It did not fight a sly delaying action, raising our hopes only to dash them, but always keeping them alive. It did not set out to tantalize or gall us. It seemed, rather, preoccupied with its own troubles. It had never wished to be a road, and now it cursed itself for not refusing its function before it was too late. It lashed itself into a fury of self-reproach. It writhed in anguish. It was clearly a tormented thing. At any moment, we felt, it might decide to End It All.

But it didn't. It stuck it out. It saw it through. It mastered its distress and got us to Leopoldina.

That was a stormy passage. Of the scenery, though I believe it to have been savage and beautiful, I can remember little. For in its agony the road plunged so frequently into the jungle (going there, I suppose, like the people in novels, To Forget) that we spent most of the journey gazing steadfastly into the lining of our hats, held up in front of us to protect our faces. On their crowns the little branches drummed a spiteful tattoo. The driver was reluctant to slow down, however for-midable the obstacles in his path, so that our sweating bodies were hurled either sideways against each other or upwards at the roof with a tiresome regularity. The driver, as always in Brazil, was an impetuous fellow.

It was a very hot day. We had a breakdown: it was one of those breakdowns (I know so little about cars that I cannot classify even this commonest type of mishap) which everyone believes will be remedied if only the car is pushed along the road for a certain distance. We tried this remedy, several times; but no one – certainly not the car – was any the better for it. We resorted to hanky-panky with a spanner and to grovelling, in the *Punch* tradition, underneath the vehicle: and in the end this was successful. The car started with a triumphant roar. A quarter of a mile further on we had a puncture.[15]

I wonder how many readers of this book have ever travelled by *net*. It used to be the regular way of ascending to certain of the monasteries of Meteora in Greece, as Robert Curzon explains:

On the tops of these rocks in different directions there remain seven monasteries out of twenty-four which once crowned their airy heights. How anything except a bird was to arrive at one which we saw in the distance on a pinnacle of rock was more than we could divine; but the mystery was soon solved. Winding our way upwards, among a labyrinth of smaller rocks and cliffs, by a romantic path which afforded us from time to time beautiful views of the green vale below us, we at length found ourselves on an elevated platform of rock, which I may compare to the flat roof of a church; while the monastery of Barlaam stood perpendicularly above us, on the top of a much higher rock, like the tower of this church. Here we fired off a gun, which was intended to answer the same purpose as knocking at the door in more civilized places; and we all strained our necks in looking up at the monastery to see whether any answer would be made to our call. Presently we were hailed by some one in the sky, whose voice came down to us like the cry of a bird; and we saw the face and grey beard of an old monk some hundred feet above us peering out of a kind of window or door. He asked us who we were, and what we wanted, and so forth; to which we replied, that we were travellers, harmless people, who wished to be admitted into the monastery to stay the night; that we had come all the way from Corfu to see the wonders of Meteora, and, as it was now getting late, we appealed to his feelings of hospitality and Christian benevolence.

'Who are those with you?' said he.

'Oh! most respectable people,' we answered; 'gentlemen of our acquaintance, who have come with us across the mountains from Mezzovo.'

The appearance of our escort did not please the monk, and we feared that he would not admit us into the monastery; but at length he let down a thin cord, to which I attached a letter of introduction which I had brought from Corfu; and after some delay a much larger rope was seen descending with a hook at the end, to which a strong net was attached. On its reaching the rock on which we stood the net was spread open: my two servants sat down upon it; and the four corners being attached to the hook, a signal was made, and they began slowly ascending into the air, twisting round and round like a leg of mutton hanging to a bottle-jack. The rope was old and mended, and the height from the ground to the door above us was, we afterwards learned, 37 fathoms, or 222 feet. When they reached the top I saw two stout monks reach their arms out of the door and pull in the two servants by main force, as there was no contrivance like a turning-crane for bringing them nearer to the landing-place. The whole process appeared so dangerous that I determined to go up by climbing a series of ladders which were suspended by large wooden pegs on the face of the precipice, and which reached the top of the rock in another direction, round a corner to the right. The lowest ladder was approached by a pathway leading to a rickety wooden platform which overhung a deep gorge. From this point the ladders hung perpendicularly upon the bare rock, and I climbed up three or four of them very soon; but coming to one, the lower end of which had swung away from the top of the one below, I had some difficulty in stretching across from the one to the other; and here unluckily I looked down, and found that I had turned a sort of angle in the precipice, and that I was not over the rocky platform where I had left the horses, but that the precipice went sheer down to so tremendous a depth that my head turned when I surveyed the distant valley over which I was hanging in the air like a fly on a wall. The monks in the monastery saw me hesitate, and called out to me to take courage and hold on; and, making an effort, I overcame my dizziness, and clambered up to a small iron door, through which I crept into a court of the monastery, where I was welcomed by the monks and the two servants who had been hauled up by the rope. The rest of my party were not admitted; but they bivouacked at the foot of the rocks in a sheltered place, and were perfectly contented with the coffee and provisions which we lowered down to them.[16]

The next morning, when the time came for Curzon's departure:

The monks and the abbot had now assembled in the room where the capstan stood. Ten or twelve of them arranged themselves in order at the bars, the net was spread upon the floor, and having sat down upon it crosslegged, the four corners were gathered up over my head, and attached to the hook at the end of the rope. All being ready, the monks at the capstan took a few steps round, the effect of which was to lift me off the floor and to launch me out of the door right into the sky, with an impetus which kept me swinging backwards and forwards at a fearful rate; when the oscillation had in some measure ceased the abbot and another monk, leaning out of the door, steadied me with their hands, and I was let down slowly and gently to the ground.[17]

That was in 1834. Sir Henry Layard, paying a similar visit just a few years later, found the experience still more alarming:

There were two ways of reaching the summit: either to climb the rock by ladders attached, or rather suspended, to its face, which required a steady head, and was a somewhat perilous proceeding; or to be drawn up in a net attached to a rope, which was lowered and raised by a rude windlass. I chose the latter method. The net having been spread out at the foot of the rock, I seated myself upon it with my Greek servant. When the signal that we were ready was given, the four corners were raised, and we shortly found ourselves, like two fish in a landing-net, suspended in mid-air. My companion, when he saw that he was leaving the solid earth and was powerless, became greatly alarmed and plunged violently, struggling with his arms and legs, and inflicting blows upon me with both. He continued to do so, roaring out with fear, until we had reached the summit, and found ourselves before an archway, in which were two monks. When the net with its contents was on a level with them, they gave it a violent push outwards, and when it had swung back over the platform on which they stood, suddenly loosened the rope, and sent us rolling on the floor. This primitive mode of ascent was neither pleasant nor safe. I was black and blue from the blows and kicks of my companion, and the windlass and the rope which sustained the net appeared to be old and in a very rotten condition. I spent a night in the convent, and then descended to the valley below in the same fashion that I had ascended from it, except that I took care to be alone in the net.[18]

So far, it will be noticed, I have confined this chapter to terrestrial transportation. I have, however, one account of an air journey that must be included. It is by Martha Gellhorn; the other principal character, whom she refers to as 'U.C.' – Unwilling Companion – is in fact her former husband, Ernest Hemingway. The date is early 1941, and they are returning from a nightmare visit to China – of which two further brief vignettes will be found in Chapters Fifteen and Nineteen – where she had been reporting on the Chinese army in action against the Japanese:

Farewell forever to awful China. U.C. was prepared for the flight with half a bottle of gin and his Lily Cup. Where and how U.C. acquired his Lily Cup, I never knew. He carried it, folded in the breast pocket of his jacket; he was inseparable from it; he guarded it jealously; he shared it with no one, it was his dearest private property.

The plane was almost full of Chinese passengers, very jolly to be leaving. For a brief spell they remained sprightly, but the plane was soon behaving like a butterfly in a hurricane, tipping from wing to wing and floating in large zig-zags over the scenery. That quieted the passengers. Then we hit the up and down draughts over the Burma Road. Instead of moving ahead we seemed to be in an express elevator. The passengers began to wail loudly. U.C. and I, not subject to airsickness, admired the pilot. We were well strapped in and U.C. had just carefully filled his Lily Cup when the plane was seized by a colossal current and hurled upwards like a rocket. Despite strapping we rose in our seats. Screams of fear rent the air, mixed with sobs and the sound of violent vomiting. Having soared into outer space, the plane now dropped, like a descending rocket.

Folk wisdom claims (by what proof I'd like to know) that a drowning person sees his whole life in a flash before the final fatal swallow. I can testify that in however many seconds of that descent, I did a lot of thinking. I knew the wings had to fall off. Possibly we would crash before the wings ripped away but, in any case, survival was impossible. I wanted to tell U.C. that I regretted bitterly having nagged him into this horror journey and would never forgive myself for causing his death, cut off in his prime, his work unfinished, his children fatherless; my heart was breaking with sorrow for U.C. and racked by guilt. U.C., in a strange rigid position, held his Lily Cup with both hands, his eyes fixed on the cabin ceiling. Except for the Lily Cup, he might have been praying. In the tumult of passenger shrieks, I laid my oozing gloved hand on his sleeve and said. 'I'm sorry, I'm sorry', as I had no time to make a speech. U.C. did not hear or notice. I closed my eyes, because I thought I'd rather not actually see a wing take leave of the fuselage.

The plane, close to ground level, slowly rose complete with wings. We regained whatever normal flying height was, though nothing was normal on a CNAC flight, and the plane advanced in butterfly style. U.C. smiled happily.

'I didn't lose a drop,' he said. 'The gin shot out of my Lily Cup and I watched it and caught it after it hit the roof. Not a single drop.'

'Thank God,' I said, breathless at still having breath.

'You know, M.,' U.C. said, 'for someone who doesn't believe in Him, you've sure as hell been in close contact with the Lord since you came to China.'[19]

My next offering refuses to be put in any category at all – land, sea or air. Indeed, I know of only one example of this particular form of travel – by *telescope* – in the literature of the world. And here it is – an extract from Mark Twain's *A Tramp Abroad*:

After breakfast, that next morning in Chamonix, we went out in the yard and watched the gangs of excursionizing tourists arriving and departing with their mules and guides and porters; then we took a look through the telescope at the snowy hump of Mont Blanc. It was brilliant with sunshine, and the vast smooth bulge seemed hardly five hundred yards away. With the naked eye we could dimly make out the house at the Pierre Pointue, which is located by the side of the great glacier, and is more than 3,000 feet above the level of the valley, but with the telescope we could see all its details. While I looked, a woman rode by the house on a mule, and I saw her with sharp distinctness; I could have described her dress. I saw her nod to the people of the house, and rein up her mule, and put her hand up to shield her eyes from the sun. I was not used to telescopes; in fact, I never had looked through a good one before; it seemed incredible to me that this woman could be so far away. I was satisfied that I could see all these details with my naked eye; but when I tried it, that mule and those vivid people had wholly vanished, and the house itself had become small and vague. I tried the telescope again, and again everything was vivid. The strong black shadows of the mule and the woman were flung against the side of the house, and I saw the mule's silhouette wave its ears.

The telescopulist – or the telescopulariat – I do not know which is right – said a party were making the grand ascent, and would come in sight on the remote upper heights, presently; so we waited to observe this performance.

Presently I had a superb idea. I wanted to stand with a party on the summit of Mont Blanc, merely to be able to say I had done it, and I believed the telescope could set me within seven feet of the uppermost man. The telescoper assured me that it could. I then asked him how much I owed him for as far as I had got? He said, one franc. I asked him how much it would cost me to make the entire ascent? Three francs. I at once determined to make the entire ascent. But first I inquired if there was any danger? He said no – not by telescope; said he had taken a great many parties to the summit, and never lost a man. I asked what he would charge to let my agent go with me, together with such guides and porters as might be necessary? He said he would let Harris go for two francs; and that unless we were unusually timid, he should consider guides and porters unnecessary, it was not customary to take them when going by telescope, for they were rather an incumbrance than a help. He said that the party now on the mountain were approaching the most difficult part, and if we hurried we should overtake them within ten minutes, and could then join them and have the benefit of their guides and porters without their knowledge, and without expense to us.

I then said we would start immediately. I believe I said it calmly, though I was conscious of a shudder and of a paling cheek, in view of the nature of the exploit I was so unreflectingly engaging in. But the old dare-devil spirit was upon me, and I said that as I had committed myself, I would not back down; I would ascend Mont Blanc if it cost me my life. I told the man to slant his machine in the proper direction, and let us be off.

Harris was afraid and did not want to go, but I heartened him up and said I would hold his hand all the way; so he gave his consent, though he trembled a little at first. I took a last pathetic look upon the pleasant summer scene about me, then boldly put my eye to the glass and prepared to mount among the grim glaciers and the everlasting snows.

We took our way carefully and cautiously across the great Glacier des Bossons, over yawning and terrific crevasses and amongst imposing crags and buttresses of ice, which were fringed with icicles of gigantic proportions. The desert of ice that stretched far and wide about us was wild and desolate beyond description, and the perils which beset us were so great that at times I was minded to turn back. But I pulled my pluck together and pushed on.

We passed the glacier safely and began to mount the steeps beyond, with great celerity. When we were seven minutes out from the starting-point, we reached an altitude where the scene took a new aspect; an apparently limitless continent of gleaming snow was tilted heavenward before our faces. As my eye followed that awful acclivity far away up into the remote skies, it seemed to me that all I had ever seen before of sublimity and magnitude was small and insignificant compared with this.

We rested a moment, and then began to mount with speed. Within three minutes we caught sight of the party ahead of us, and stopped to observe them. They were toiling up a long, slanting ridge of snow – twelve persons, roped together some fifteen feet apart, marching in single file, and strongly marked against the clear blue sky. One was a woman. We could see them lift their feet and put them down; we saw them swing their alpenstocks forward in unison, like so many pendulums, and then bear their weight upon them; we saw the lady wave her handkerchief. They dragged themselves upwards in a worn and weary way, for they had been climbing steadily from the Grands Mulets, on the Glacier des Bossons, since three in the morning, and it was eleven now. We saw them sink down in the snow and rest, and drink something from a bottle. After a while they moved on, and as they approached the final short dash of the home stretch we closed up on them and joined them.

Presently we all stood together on the summit! What a view was spread out below! Away off under the north-western horizon rolled the silent billows of the Farnese Oberland, their snowy crests glinting softly in the subdued lights of distance; in the north rose the giant form of the Wobblehorn, draped from peak to shoulder in sable thunder-clouds; beyond him, to the right, stretched the grand processional summits of the Cisalpine Cordillera, drowned in a sensuous haze; to the east loomed the colossal masses of the Yodelhorn, the Fuddlehorn, and the Dinnerhorn, their cloudless summits flashing white and cold in the sun; beyond them shimmered the faint far line of the Ghauts of Jubbulpore and the Aiguilles des Alleghenies; in the south towered the smoking peak of Popocatapetl and the unapproachable altitudes of the peerless Scrabblehorn; in the west-south-west the stately range of the Himalayas lay dreaming in a purple gloom; and thence all around the curving horizon the eye roved over a troubled sea of sun-kissed Alps, and noted here and there the noble proportions and soaring domes of the Bottlehorn, and the Saddlehorn, and the Shovelhorn, and the Powderhorn, all bathed in the glory of noon, and mottled with softly-gliding blots, the shadows flung from drifting clouds.

Overcome by the scene, we all raised a triumphant, tremendous shout, in unison. A startled man at my elbow said:

'Confound you, what do you yell like that for, right here in the street?'

That brought me down to Chamonix like a flirt. I gave that man some spiritual advice and disposed of him, and then paid the telescope man his full fee, and said that we were charmed with the trip, and would remain down, and not re-ascend and require him to fetch us down by telescope. This pleased him very much, for of course we could have stepped back to the summit and put him to the trouble of bringing us home if we had wanted to.[20]

As for the sea, I cannot do better than to commend a perfectly splendid book by Gavin Young, with its self-explanatory title *Slow Boats to China*. In 1979–80 he took no less than twenty-three ships of various sizes and degrees of seaworthiness to travel from Piraeus to Canton; the journey took him seven months. We pick him up here in Colombo:

My rough ride to the Maldives sticks in my mind as the 'Tale of Two Bird Men'. I shall never really know how close I was to being drowned. On the other hand, I now know how to open a coconut with a spanner.

There was a good bird man and a bad one. The bad one sat in an office in Chatham Street, cold, white-haired and hunched over like a vindictive sea eagle. He represented the owners of the small Maldivian launch, a mere twenty-five tons, that would accommodate me for three days and three nights across that quite wide stretch of water. He took obvious delight in keeping customers seated on hard chairs while, with excruciating deliberation, he busied himself with other matters without so much as a glance, much less a 'good morning'. There was no offer of tea here, nor even a minimum of Sri Lankan warmth. The only good thing about Sea Eagle was that he finally arranged my passage, and this was all that really mattered. . . .

It was a filthy night when I reported to the harbour for sailing. Rain was bouncing off the docks, but it would have been difficult in any weather to spot the launch, the smallest of all the vessels I sailed in during my odyssey: twenty-five tons, forty feet long, powered by a Thorneycroft 125-h.p. engine making six knots – with luck. I found her at last, crouched like a frightened pygmy between two metal giants, a Sri Lankan freighter and a ship from Canton. The comparatively huge hawsers of these two towering neighbours somehow added a puny absurdity to the launch's littleness, so that she looked more like a dinghy. I stood in the rain and thought, Is this what we're going to cross more than four hundred miles of water in? Three days or more in *this*? . . .

The launch had two bunks, no mattresses and no awnings. Space in the tiny hutchlike cabin area, apparently constructed out of a handful of nails and a hundredweight of driftwood, was further diminished by the metal trunks of the crew, a spare outboard motor, and the exhaust pipe of the engine that thrust up through the middle of the cabin to the upper air. This exhaust was a serious continual danger to the unwary because in rough weather it was exceedingly well placed to serve as a natural handhold, and yet was almost red-hot. As a result, by the time we reached Malé, I lacked skin on three fingers of my right hand. . . .

We moved out of the harbour at last, past the friendly light at the end of the breakwater, and felt the light lift and fall of the open sea. Lightning flashes silhouetted mountainous cloud formations.

I moved back to the stern of the launch – it wasn't far to scramble over the roof of the cabin with its protruding funnel – and found the captain, a thin young man with big teeth, and a helmsman, an even younger Maldivian, standing in a small raised, roofed area, an even tinier hutch than the cabin and engine housing. The launch had no wheel; the helmsman steered standing up by straddling a long thick, rounded wooden spar attached to the rudder, pushing it or restraining its movements with the muscles of his thighs. It looked agonizing. The spar was heavy, and in a high sea I imagined that it would slam back and forth almost uncontrollably.

The helmsman was having no trouble now. He stood in a red undershirt and bathing trunks, peering at the compass on the ledge formed by the roof of the engine housing in front of him, the helm spar protruding between his upper thighs like a giant phallus, each vibration of the rudder travelling up the spar and shaking his leg muscles like jelly. He looked at me, grinned and wrapped a tiny, inadequate towel around his hips. If this was modesty, it was misjudged; the great spar thrusting through the towel only increased the effect. . . .

The launch's crew spoke very few words of English, and that included the Starling Cook, although when I think of him I recall that somehow we communicated quite effectively. I call him the Starling Cook because of his looks. He was more or less the colour of a starling, very dark in blue shorts and shirt. He was short and fat-bodied, and his skinny bowlegs protruded out of his shorts like a black wishbone. He had long bare feet and very little neck; his shoulders were hunched, his arms long, and his nose was a beak that curved thinly between large expressive eyes. I suppose he was in his forties or fifties. Some seamen, I have noticed, quietly observe the pitch and toss of a deck and time their moves across it like a computer, perhaps quite unaware of their calculation. The Starling Cook was not like that; he scuttled crablike over the deck, hardly laying a hand on any support.

The first morning, the wind rose and the broken water swayed and rocked us quite a bit – a foretaste of things to come. The launch was so small that anything affected its stability. I could hear the fresh water sloshing in the two tanks of the foredeck. The sea looked very big. . . .

I watched the Starling Cook for hours as he moved about his restricted kingdom. I saw, for example, how he opened a coconut with a spanner, holding it in one hand, the spanner in the other, and tapping it with many small, firm strokes around its middle until it fell apart in two neat halves. He scraped each half against the upturned sharp metal prong of what looked like a shoehorn, which he clamped between his knees; then he wrapped the gratings in a porous cloth, and dunked them into a wide pan of water and rice. He scooped up seawater to cook the rice in, and always cleaned his pots and pans in seawater too. On vessels like this, no one dreams of using fresh water for anything but drinking. His implements were few but sufficient; a huge soot-black kettle and two deep cooking pans were the basic containers. There was also a wide, open tray onto which he poured uncooked rice before he and a wild-haired assistant of dishevelled aspect picked out the bad grains. Just inside the cabin door were arranged his little sacks of cabbages, beans, leaves, chillies (green and red), cardamom, small cumin seeds, coriander, black peppers, cinnamon and garlic. . . .

The weather was unfriendly. The sea was black and ominous like the sky, and soon seemed to grow bigger. Although it retained its oily smoothness, I felt as if under the surface something very big and unpleasant were waiting to burst up and horrify us. . . .

When the Starling Cook had finished swilling out his pots and pans with sea-water, the waves started to grow larger, and a big and mounting swell from the star-board began to push the launch over to an angle of thirty degrees. The sky was quite bright, not at all like the sky in my nightmare, and a full moon was rising behind us, coming up over Sri Lanka, which by now was well out of sight. The moonlight turned the agitated water into heaving sheets of wet mackintosh. I thought of the immense depths below us. 'No bottom at the depth of 200 fathoms.' . . .

I paid a hazardous visit to the captain in the stern, who gave me all his white teeth in an ugly grin and said, 'Storm. Moon make big sea. Big sea storm.' I staggered back to the bows and lay down tensely on my towel in the hard little bunk. . . . I tried to wedge myself by pushing one foot against the ceiling and the other against the bulkhead, grasping with one hand the window frame over my head. The strain on my legs and arms soon became too great. Hauling myself out on deck, I saw that clouds now covered the stars and that the moon was only an area of bright haze in the sky. The wind took one's breath away.

My notes become sea-stained here:

We are nearly on our beam ends once every minute and a half. The planks shuffle back and forth on the deck as the waves strike us, and the grinding and creaking parts of the old launch drown the noise of the engine, pistons, prop shaft, wind and sea. The chimney seems to be red-hot, and acts like a stove in the already overheated, confined space of the cabin. Boxes slide and fall; metal trunks shift. A heavy case – it must weigh a lot because it was the last thing to be loaded, and the whole crew had to struggle to manhandle it aboard – has begun to crash into and buckle the only lifeboat, which in any case is a poor light metal thing buried under a small mountain of pineapples, bamboo furniture and ceramic lavatory bowls.

One of the fresh-water tanks is leaking. The crew ladles the water from it to the other tank, which requires much rushing up and slithering down sodden decks in semi-darkness, with sarongs hitched up, slipping down or falling open. (Sarongs, it seems, are fair-weather garments.)

The sight of Hassan Ali in the wheelhouse window alarms me. He is clutching for dear life two vertical beams on either side of the compass. His face is fixed in an expression of agony or terror, teeth gritted, eyes staring. He looks terrified to dementia: a man facing a watery death? But I remember what I cannot see. His lower half is straining to control that heavy rudder handle, which must be vibrating and jerking about like a bucking bronco, battering his thighs. Hassan is grimacing with effort, not fear.

The seas are very big; they are breaking over us. The moon has gone behind two banks of cloud: one grim, thick and unmoving, the other low and scudding. From my 'porthole' I can see the black and grey strips of cloud streaming past back and forth according to the roll and dip of the launch. The corkscrew motion is exhausting. Two of the Maldivian passengers have already been very sick; they huddle together, green and horrified. I have offered them my ledge and seasickness pills, but they have refused both.

Now the Starling Cook joins the drama. Facing me, he is smiling and gibbering unintelligibly. Suddenly his eyes switch from my face to something over my shoulder – something, to judge by the horror on his face, too appalling to imagine. His eyes stretch open to an amazing size, and he opens his wide mouth and screams, '*Eeeeeeeeeee————aaaaaa————aaayyyyyyyyyyy.*'

The sound was shattering, rising like the mixed sound of a whistling kettle and an air-raid siren above the racket of creaks and thuds of shifting cargo, wind, and crashing of the sea against the old wooden hull. Even if the whale of my dreams had surfaced behind us, I would have had to follow his pointing finger, turn and look. There was no whale; instead, I saw a low black cliff, visible because it was darker than the grey-black of the clouds. Higher than our stubby mast, it was about eighty yards away and advancing.

Thanks to the Starling Cook's scream, I had time to wedge myself into the cabin doorway, bracing myself with feet and elbows. The Starling Cook himself leaped with astounding agility for the mast and clung to it, wrapping his arms and wishbone legs around it like a koala bear on a eucalyptus trunk. The impact of the wave was awesome. The launch heeled over – ninety degrees? God knows. Solid slabs of black water toppled over the gunwales, and everything on deck or in the cabin seemed to go adrift. Water filled my clothes, eyes and ears. Water cascaded from the legs of the Starling Cook's shorts. He squawked like a wet hen and gestured at me, pointing once more at the moon with one hand and at the waves with the other. . . .

Again and again, the clifflike waves came at us and every few minutes the eyes of the Starling Cook forewarned me of impending disaster. Sometimes he tugged at my shirt before releasing his awful cry – '*Eeeeeeeeeee————aaaaaa————aaaaayyyyyy*' – and again we would cling: I in my doorway, he like a monkey to the mast. There was nothing else to do but hope – although once or twice I did ask myself what I was doing there at all.

During the night I saw the lights of three or four big ships going north or south. They were small comfort; we could have capsized quite near them and they would have been none the wiser, for we had neither radio nor rockets.[21]

For those of us who are less adventurously inclined than Mr Young but have none the less some experience of ocean travel, the following phrase-book conversation, appearing in Dr Baedeker's *Traveller's Manual* of 1886, may jog a few memories. It seems to me to say it all:

On embarking, and of what happens at sea.
The wind increases. See that great wave which is coming to break against our vessel. I fear we shall have a storm: the sky is very dark towards the west.
So far the wind is favourable, and the ship sails well.
But the sea is very rough; the waves are very high; the rolling of the vessel makes me sick; I have got a headache.
My head is very bad.
The smell of the tar affects me.
Smell some *eau de Cologne*, it will do you good.
I am very much inclined to be sick.
Drink some Hollands; it will strengthen your stomach, and you will feel relieved.
I am very weak; I must lie down in my hammock.
Yes, lie down, that will do you good.
I am better again, the rest has refreshed me.
The wind has fallen too, and the sea is smoother.[22]

By now the message of this chapter should be patently obvious to the most dim-witted reader: that, for most of us, physical discomfort in vary-ing degrees of acuteness is part and parcel of foreign travel, and that this discomfort increases as the countries visited become more exotic or remote. But there are exceptions. I can conceive of no better ending to this chapter than the account, in the admirable biography of King Edward VII by Philip Magnus, of the visit to Egypt of the Prince and Princess of Wales in 1869:

On 6th February the Prince's party started up the Nile in six blue and gold steamers, each towing a barge filled with luxuries and necessities including four riding horses, and a milk-white donkey for the Princess; 3,000 bottles of cham-pagne and 4,000 of claret; four French chefs and a laundry. No expense had been spared by the generous Khedive, and although the panelled décor of the steamers, on the theme of Anthony and Cleopatra, was garish, the double pile carpets and solid English furniture had been chosen personally on the Khedive's behalf by Sir Samuel Baker, who 'has really', the Prince informed his mother, 'taken a great deal of trouble to make all the necessary arrangements for our comfort, in which he has most thoroughly succeeded. ... I cannot say how glad I am to have asked him to accompany us.'
Throughout that thousand-mile voyage to Wadi Halfa and back, the Prince took

the services and read the lessons on Sundays, and the captain and sailors turned towards Mecca at six o'clock every evening and touched the decks with their foreheads. Famous monuments and ruins were explored, and the Prince, who killed his first crocodile – a female, nine feet long, containing eighty eggs – with an expanding bullet on 28 February, failed to shoot a hyena, but killed quantities of cormorants, cranes, doves, flamingoes, hawk-owls, herons, hoopoes, mallards, merlins and spoonbills.

The Prince and Princess returned to Cairo on 16 March with 32 mummy cases, an immense sarcophagus, and a 10-year-old chocolate-coloured orphan boy, Ali Achmet, who was loathed by the English servants and who was despatched, in consequence, with a mass of other trophies to Sandringham, where he served coffee in native dress.[23]

CHAPTER SEVEN

Journeys

This will be a short chapter, containing as it does only five items – even though two of them are admittedly a little longer than usual. It is concerned with moving from place to place rather than with one individual spot, with the aggregate of impressions rather than with any single reaction on the part of the traveller. But one example is, as always, worth pages of explanation; so here is a lightning impressionist – almost *pointilliste* – sketch, from *The Unquiet Grave* by Palinurus (alias Cyril Connolly), of a drive with a loved one through France:

Leaving Bellac after crossing for two days the plains of the sandy Loire, we enter the Bocage Limousin, traverse a country of tall tree-hedges blueing into the pale spring sky and reach the first hills, the Blond mountains, forest beginnings of the Châtaigneraie. A new strip of maps and the sun always warmer; mountain nights in stone buildings, melted snow in the running water, darker wine in the inns, deeper beds. Rivers tumbling through towns; rain-drenched chestnuts green in the swinging lights of Tulle; Mauriac, Sainte-Flour, Saint-Chély-d'Apcher; snow-driven moorlands of the Margeride, pine-forests of Velay and Vivarais; cloud-shadows over the Gerbier de Jonc. There on the edge of the tableland stands the haunted Auberge de Peyrebeilhe (where once so few come out who went in).* But now the low room with blackened ceiling has grown less dangerous to lovers than the almond-blossom airs of the warm Ardèche, than the limestone chasm leading down to civilization where the Furies are awaiting Ennoia and happiness is thrown away. . . .

Peeling off the kilometres to the tune of 'Blue Skies', sizzling down the long black liquid reaches of Nationale Sept, the plane trees going sha-sha-sha through the open window, the windscreen yellowing with crushed midges, she with the Michelin beside me, a handkerchief binding her hair. . . .

Early morning on the Mediterranean: bright air resinous with Aleppo pine, water spraying over the gleaming tarmac of the Route Nationale and darkly reflecting the spring-summer green of the planes; swifts wheeling round the oleander, waiters unpiling the wicker chairs and scrubbing the café tables; armfuls of carnations on the flower-stall, pyramids of lemon and aubergine, *rascasses* on the fishmonger's

---

* The innkeeper and his coloured wife used to murder their guests.

slab goggling among the wine-dark urchins; smell of brioches from the bakers, sound of reed curtains jingling in the barber's shop, clang of the tin kiosk opening for *Le Petit Var*. Our rope-soles warm up on the cobbles by the harbour where the *Jean d'Agrève* prepares for a trip to the Islands and the Annamese boy scrubs her brass. Now cooks from many yachts step ashore with their market-baskets, one-eyed cats scrounge among the fish-heads, while the hot sun refracts the dancing sea-glitter on the café awning, until the sea becomes a green gin-fizz of stillness in whose depth a quiver of sprats charges and counter-charges in the pleasure of fishes.[1]

The next author whom I feel I must quote is my mother, Lady Diana Cooper, writing to her friend Conrad Russell an account of a cruise on which she and my father had been invited by King Edward VIII in June 1936, the only summer of his reign. They had met the *Nahlin* in Venice, and remained on board as far as Athens. What follows has been reluctantly, but mercilessly, cut: the fuller account will be found in the second volume of my mother's autobiography, *The Light of Common Day*.

17 June There's no traffic in Ragusa [Dubrovnik] and there are baroque and gothic churches and palaces and monasteries. The people were mostly in national dress and on this occasion they were all out in orderly rows, both sides of the streets that the Consul had mapped out for our tour of the sights. They were cheering their lungs out with looks of ecstasy on their faces.

The King walks a little ahead talking to the Consul or Mayor, and we follow adoring it. He waves his hand half-saluting. He is utterly himself and unselfconscious. That I think is the reason why he does some things (that he likes) superlatively well. He does not *act*. In the middle of the procession he stopped for a good two minutes to tie up his shoe. There was a knot and it took time. We were all left staring at his behind. You or I would have risen above the lace, wouldn't we, until the procession was over? But it did not occur to him to wait, and so the people said: 'Isn't he human! Isn't he natural! He stopped to do up his shoe like any of us!' . . .

19 June Another night on deck with a 7 a.m. waking. After sour milk and foaming coffee ashore Duff and I hired a rather Heath Robinson motorcar driven by a 'middy' of the Jugoslav Navy. We told him to drive to an old patrician villa twenty miles away. It took an hour to get to, and was a drive of the greatest beauty and the greatest danger – narrow hairpinned road, thick layers of loose shingle as a skidding-surface, and unparapetted. It was worth the pain. The little old owner of eighty-four received us in brown boots, good tussore trousers and a pyjama-top. The property has been in their possession since 1200 and he is the last of the line and thankful for it. He thinks the new world so abominable. He spoke only unintelligible French but managed to make me cry with a story of the Emperor Maximilian of Mexico and his wife Carlotta. They were having a meal under a great tree in his garden, and they took the knives from the table and carved their names and hearts on the tree. She threw her arms around him and said: 'O *Maximilian*, O *Maximilian, nous allons toujours être heureux comme aujourd'hui.*' . . .

At five-ish we turned into the Bocche di Cattaro [Kotor], the fiord of the Adriatic, very beautiful sinister country, the wall of the mountain so high that the light is depressing. We went ashore with the usual arrangements of Mayors. It's a very small town of only 2500 souls, very poor-looking, no shops, hotels or bars, Venetian influence strongly marked and a great deal of treasure owned by the Churches, both Catholic and Greek – silver tables, many silver arms and legs enclosing fragments of shins and funnybones of various saints. The party wanted to be off again at 7, but there were pathetic Japanese lanterns with single candles hung up and little pyramids of Greek Fire along the quayside, so thank God we settled to wait for such illumination as there was. And was it not lucky! You have never seen so sensational a display. Every mountain-peak was set afire, every house and every mountain-path lit with living (not electric) lights. Guns from the forts booming and echoing through the ravines. The same was done all along the fifteen miles of gorge. So magnificent was it that we determined to say 'Thank you' by sending up some excellent S.O.S. rockets ourselves, and our Nannies gave a search-light display, and in return for their serenading Mr Fletcher, the King's piper, gave them 'Over the sea to Skye,' walking round and round the deck, the King shouting explanations of bagpipes to the crowd.

20 June . . . At 4 Wallis [later Duchess of Windsor], the King, Duff and I went off in the launch to see the famous villa built by the Empress Elizabeth and bought by the Kaiser. We landed on the pompous broken quay and found to our horror that the gates of the demesne were heavily chained. The King began climbing, but there was barbed wire. A lot of peasants and fishermen were watching us when Mr Evans, the detective, and an Adonis dressed in the same clothes as the King, started fiddling with the chains, broke them, took pliers to the wire and opened it all up! I thought it a funny gate-crash for a King, but no one commented on it.

Then came a forty-minute climb of beauty – one endless flight of steps bordered by symmetrical cypresses culminating in a charming 1890 statue of the Empress Elizabeth in marble skirt and collar of modish cut. The top when reached (dead with fatigue) showed a tremendous view and a colossal figure of Achilles erected by the Kaiser, and a house the size of Chatsworth of such hideosity that it takes seeing to believe. Pompeian in style. The electric light is installed with great fancy – baskets full of electric-light flowers, groups of plaster cherubs blowing electric-light bubbles. An amusing piece of furniture is the Kaiser's own writing-table. It consists of a high clerk's desk, painted white and gold, and another little platform from which rises a pole crowned with a stirrupless saddle that revolves. . . .

Back fatigued to dress for the King of Greece's dinner. Everybody making a great groan about it, but I thinking that 'it will make a change.' I wore the grey organdie, but I was too tired to look as spry as necessary for that material. A couple of cocktails before starting at 8.45 did no good. We piled into the slow launch called *Queen Victoria* and chugged across a very wide bay, an even slower Greek launch piloting us. Of course we were a good hour late for 9.30 dinner and found the King of Greece twiddling his thumbs on the quay. He packed us into two open cars, himself at one of the wheels, and we hairpinned up a steep cypress-lined road and came to a magnificent villa rented for the summer. We sat out to dinner on a lordly terrace and the dinner was A.1. I sat next to the Greek King. I never got going at all, but I observed everything and watched our King turn to Mrs Jones next him (an exceedingly good-looking Englishwoman, whose soldier husband has just divorced her, or been divorced by her) and turn the charm on full force. Meanwhile Wallis, on the King of Greece's other side, was doing splendidly, the wisecracks following in quick succession, the King clearly very admiring and amused. It went on until 1.30. I was nearly crying by this time. I suppose that I had done too much in too great heat: anyway the journey home made me almost unconscious.

I woke on the 22nd no better, in fact rather worse than the night before. . . .

At 5 I forced myself to bathe and felt a little better. The King was in high spirits. He took a walk to the top of a hill in the early afternoon, then later appeared suddenly with an old shrimping-net on his shoulder, looking like a child of eight. He ordered out a dinghy and set about catching jelly-fish, while we all leant over the ship's side shrieking 'There's a big one, Sir.' At meals he gets served last, with the result that there is never anything left for him. The fool stewards don't realise it and go on passing sauces and extras to his meatless plate, so that every day he has to say at least once: 'Yes, but I do want something to eat.' . . .

Cephalonia

23 June Woke up with new-spangled ore. The nights on deck are almost the loveliest part of the twenty-four hours. One is cool, breeze-blown, the stars are clear and one wakes up to new surprises every morning. Duff and I went ashore at 9, struggling to get a car to take us a drive round the island. The village was very primitive, so we were lucky to get the crazy vehicle we did get. We always forget what tortures of terror and vertigo we are taking on ourselves when we set forth on these expeditions. A man with a few words of English offered us a police escort. We refused in true British style, but under pressure we took a uniformed young gentleman along. It was a magnificent drive and took four hours. At one moment we had to get out and walk, for terror of the sheer precipice.

Duff is really worse than me. These goat-paths, no wider than a car's axle, with crumbling precipitous edges and a surface of shifting shingle, give him acute vertigo. I get only abject terror. He can shut his eyes at least, while I have to drive the car with hands and feet and eyes, but I can carry away a picture of the heights and cliffs and wine-dark sea. Poor Duff has only his lids to remember. We were well rewarded for our enterprise by hearing first a jangle of the most beautiful bells miles and miles away. They came from a strange Greek church with open belfry attached, of great architectural value. It seemed that anyone could run up and have a bang at the bells, and the result was a pleasant discord. The village was *mouvementé* to a degree. Even a few so-called cars were parked outside the church, and a lot of saddle-donkeys. We looked round the church which was empty and from there we heard the noise of a mourning crowd. We passed out through the opposite door, and there to our delight was Reinhardt's *Miracle* (Orthodox style) and all the props, banners, crucifixes, reliquaries, candles, staves, choirboys, clergy, a tremendous bearded Archimandrite with a bulbous oriental gold crown on his head, an ornamental silver coffin with a visible Saint carried in a standing position, cripples and old chronics laid on the ground, moaning, praying, but alas! no miracle that we could see. Were we not lucky, though, to hit off the Saint's feast, and the actual hour of his procession? We arrived back with something accomplished before the height of the mid-day sun, to find the others just coming out into it from their airless cabins.

After lunch a siesta, well earned by us but the others have only just got up, so aren't as keen about it. They wander about trying to find a cool place on deck, while the mad-dog English King rows for an hour or two or takes a strapping walk.

Delphi

There was a sudden movement last evening amongst the few that we had better go and consult the Oracle on our own or we might easily miss it. So the three (Duff, me and Godfrey Thomas) went ashore at 9 and hired a car and a guide, and buzzed up the parapetless road, preceded by eight soldiers jammed into a Ford car and followed by the same. What made the whole thing funny, as usual, was our clothes and the fact that nothing would persuade the natives that one of us was not the King. The guide said that it was no good. The more explanation given them, the surer they were that it was an incognito stunt. Even though we signed the book, our names were shown to another batch of our party who went to Delphi as the King's signature. . . .

Athens

Because of a general muddle of plans, Duff and I got the Acropolis to ourselves, also the full attention of the Head of the Fine Arts, who took us round and showed us the most beautiful of the seven wonders of the world. It isn't only the proportions and the marble's warm tone and the wonder of it – it's the sky and the air and the arrangement of mountains and sea together with the human inspiration of the temple that give you a catch in the throat, and that strange restless sensation one had so often as a child (and very rarely now) that something must be done about it. Mere looking does not seem enough. . . .

27 June Our last day and I planned an expedition. It was a complete success but it gave me anxious moments. The yacht was to sail at 7 a.m. and take us to the island of Ægina. . . .

The island when we got there looked quite insubstantial – *Tempest*-like and crowned with a solemn temple, improved by ruin. We landed and then a bad moment came to torment me. Twenty donkeys were waiting to take us up. The crowd fell on us, all of them natives who did not know about him being a King but thought that by grabbing physically they would be certain of a client for their donkey. So they shouted: '*Aristo, Aristo!*' and grabbed and pulled us about. They were old clean crones and young shepherd boys, and it was funny to see Duff being led off by two crabbed Fates. He looked under arrest and went quietly. But others didn't like being manhandled and panicked a bit. There was no means of getting onto a donkey for being pulled towards another. As we walked the gay pack jostled around us. I had had exactly the same experience six months ago in Morocco and enjoyed it no end, but this company is different. However it ended as bad moments do, and the donkeys got picked and the rest didn't follow and we rode (Wallis, Mrs Rogers, Duff and I), the others walking, to the temple, up a steep difficult path through pine-trees and views of sea and mountain. . . . A romantic bay with translucent water and cavefuls of sirens called to us, and there we bathed. I got over-keen and fell on the rock, covering myself with blood, but I behaved splendidly. So, when it ended, as good things must, it was proclaimed the best thing we had done, and as scheduled we were back on board for lunch and steaming home to Phaleron Bay.[2]

In August 1984 I went for the second time to Iceland, and found myself even more captivated by it than I had been on my first visit ten years before. It was only then, too, that I discovered that William Morris had travelled widely over the country in the 1870s, and written most enjoyably about it in a book called, very sensibly, *Journals of Travel in Iceland*. Here is a sample:

Wednesday, August 16th. In camp in the home-stead of Staðastaðr.
. . . Eyvindr brought us coffee at six instead of seven by mistake; but our early rising didn't avail us much, as one of our horses had run away in the night, and Gisli had to mount and go after him. Meantime we had to breakfast, and C.J.F. and Evans busied themselves with rearranging the boxes, while I sauntered toward the sea, and going down a sort of rough stairs, came to a little bit of strand, smooth and dipping into a smooth sea, between two walls of rock one of which is continued out to sea by masses of pillared rocks which give the place its name (Stapi, Staff). Close down by the sea, and not all troubling themselves about my presence, are five ravens stuffing themselves with fish-guts, and all the near sea is alive with eider-duck, sanderlings, gulls and cormorants: there is no ripple on the water, and the sun shines bright on the mountains that fence in the wide bay: the said bay is Broadwick (Breiðavík) which names Biorn, the Broadwick champion of Eyrbyggia, him who was found in America in the last chapter of the saga. Just opposite me is a long range of cliff down the face of which tumbles fifty feet of grey glacier stream right into the sea. So back to the camp where I notice that the little stream running round our meadow which was quite clear last night has gone all turbid now, I can't think why. Gisli had just come back with the missing horse when I got back to the tents, and we were off in a few minutes, and riding out from our ness-meadows, came on to a high plateau under the mountains that ends in the cliffs (the same I saw from the beach), close to whose edge we had to ride presently. Many streams running down from the mountains fell from the cliffs' edge besides the big grey one above mentioned: some of them had cut a passage through a rock, but the more part fell right over the bare edge; it is strange riding through these to see the sea below over their waters. As we rode over these cliffs an eagle flew to meet us, and sailing quite close to our heads, pitched down on the cliff's edge not twenty yards from where I rode. . . . One of the horses fell clean into a hole, and we had to pull him out with ropes; I wonder he didn't break his neck, but Icelandic ponies fall soft, and he was only a little bit scratched about the nose and legs. After a while the lava gets sprinkled with sand, which soon partly covers the rocks and then is grown over with wild oats, and then we come out on to sand and grass alone and are at the station of Búðir where are several neat houses and a church, on the top of whose cross sits

a raven gravely watching our arrival. Here we had to swim our horses over the creek and have our luggage flitted over in a boat, so having seen this done and the horses all happy in the fields beyond, we went into the merchant's house, who would fain have had us stay the night with him, which was impossible; so we had to put up with chocolate and biscuits for entertainment, and afterwards went into his store to see what we could buy, for he boasted he had every thing up to live falcons. We bought some blue-fox skins there, and presently afterward crossed the river and went our ways over flats near the sea, with a wall of mountains always on our left: it was bright still at about three in the afternoon, and I thought it pretty, as we rode along apace, to see all the hoofs glittering in the sun.

We rode on what seemed a longish way at last till Magnússon, beginning to have doubts about the road, turned off to a little stead, and finding an old woman there, asked the way and thus reported to me the dialogue that followed.

She: What men are you?
He: Four travellers and two followers.
She: Where do you come from?
He: London.
She: What is your name?
He: I am called Eiríkr, and am Magnússon.
She: Where are you going to?
He: Staðastaðr: is it a long way hence?
She: Yes, long.
He: How far?
She: I don't know.
He: Do you know the road?
She: No.

Nevertheless about twenty minutes afterwards we turned round by some big pools, and saw the church and stead of Staðastaðr lying on a low mound a furlong off, and were soon in the tún of it, the day now, at about seven o'clock, getting spoilt, grey clouds covering the hills and spreading downwards as it seemed. The priest seemed glad to see us and offered to kill us a lamb which we accepted, and then I went off with Faulkner and Evans to help pitch the tents, and coming back presently saw a sorry sight, for the lamb was killed, and the poor old ewe was bleating and rubbing her nose against the skin in a way to make you forswear flesh-meat for ever; happily however the ending relieved one somewhat, for one of the sheep-dogs sniffing about, came rather too near the ewe, who suddenly charged him, hit him in the ribs and bowled him over howling.

To dinner in the stove, and soon after to bed in our tents, the rain coming down a little.[3]

Now, another rather extended – though also much abridged – series of extracts, this time from the war diaries of Sir Ronald Storrs (who became Governor of Cyprus in 1926 and of Northern Rhodesia 1932–4). At the time of which he writes, he was visiting Mesopotamia (as it then was) on behalf of the Anglo-French Military Mission to the Egyptian Expeditionary Force.

May 8th, 1917. We left Azīzīē about 6 and swirled along an uneventful day past gradually rising banks, and leaving the Diala Canal on our right just before tea. Soon afterwards the arch of Ctesiphon hove in sight, not very impressive in the distance. Though we had wasted the best part of an hour in pulling a Political's pinnace off a shoal we were well up to time, and had the amazing good fortune to be gliding into Baghdad about the setting of the sun. The river broadens out and enhances the dignity and nobility of the entry. To the E. a broken discontinuous façade of Stambūli houses with crooked verandas and deep recesses: the red light splashed about like blood on the uneven glass. An effect of repose on the W. bank, where for some distance there are lush fields and no buildings at all. Everywhere God's plenty of palm trees. Gradually as we rounded the last corner the larger houses, greater minarets and gleaming domes shone out against the powdered gold sky: and amid a mass of shipping, next to *Tarantula* and *Grey Fly*, opposite paddle-boats and heavy barges, hard by an ancient Babylonian wicker *guffa*,* exactly one month since the train took me out of Cairo Station, I came to rest and found myself at my goal. Very soon Lieut.-Col. The Hon. Sir Percy Zachariah Cox, K.C.S.I., K.C.I.E. (once for all), Chief Political Officer and future High Commissioner, stood by with Gertrude Bell, very welcoming, and took me off in a launch to his house, ex-Deutsche Orient Bank, whose middle balcony, with an ultra-Venetian sensation, projects far over the flood. Cox is a longer Duke of Wellington, *bella testa* and friendly of aspect. He pumped me for an hour on the balcony, and G. B. repeated the process at dinner; after which we walked her home to her Persian garden with a room in each corner, and returned amid the baying of 1000 dogs. . . .

  May 9th, 1917. Work with Cox and Gertrude Bell, whose *maîtrise* of Arab tribe details is amazing, all the morning: and shortly after two with her in car to the Marjanīa Mosque, the most notable features of which are the inscriptions, in Kufic, and flowing, cut into stone and brick. The Boches stole 60 tiles from the Mosque, which we shall try to restore. Up to a little room on the lower roof, and conversed with the Shaikh Alūsi, a *sympathique* and cultivated Arab of the old school, who with his companions sat kneeling back, like figures in a Persian miniature, throughout the interview. Cox tells me he aspires to the position of Shaikh al-Islam, which I think he could very well occupy. The mosque dirty and in very bad repair, stucco swelling off from damp and great structural fissures across the walls, domes and vaults. People very friendly, and no bakshish or doffing of shoes demanded. The Imam even carried civility so far as to whisper to an elderly worshipper to hurry up with his prayers and get out of the light. Walking across the road we came upon one of the most noble and convincing buildings I have ever seen, the Khan Ortma, also of the fourteenth century. It resembles the inverted hull of a ship, with giant brown brick ribs meeting in a great Gothic span of unusual width. Never have I had more pleasure from structure visibly working as such, and my regret is that Gilbert Scott cannot borrow from it for the Cairo Cathedral.† Thence in and round the bazaars, of infinite length, all vaulted according to a still living tradition. The vaulting is varied by an occasional wooden pitched roof as in Basra. Shops and atmosphere more or less as in Cairo, but less sophisticated save only in the matter

---

* Deep round hide coracles.
† Then under consideration: on a large piece of land presented by the Egyptian Government.

of prices, where they have little to learn. But only one request for bakshish, which died away on the speaker's lips when he saw my expression. . . .

Streaks of white mist steal up the Tigris after sunset, enhancing the wealth of palms as in Hiroshige's *Tokaido*. As for the dogs, their din, indescribably ferocious even from across the river, made sustained conversation almost impossible. . . .

May 11th, 1917. . . . Round the Suq, where I found Salman, who took me to an ineffective and ruinous Armenian. No rugs, some very expensive Greek coins and a few Babylonian bricks and cylinders – the local industry: a Turk, arrested about a year ago for being in possession of antiquities, cleared himself by proving that they were his own manufacture. . . .

May 15th, 1917. . . . About 5.30 took the launch with Gertrude Bell and walked with her, at a pace attainable by few women, out to the tomb of the Lady Zubaida,* a construction in the Gunter Buzzard hymeneal manner, reputed of the ninth but really of the fourteenth century. The sausage-shaped dome, mammillated like Diana of the Ephesians, is hideous in itself and bears no sort of relation to the clumsy and obviously restored octagon which supports it. The door was closed, so we missed the less ridiculous interior, and walked back past the tiled dome and minaret of Shaikh Maarūf in a brown fog of dust. . . .

At dinner Cox related to me some of the grosser gaffes of the Intelligence, as shown forth in their *Iraq Personalities*, where allusion is made to the Engineer of the Hindyia *Garage*; and under the letter I: Issimo – General: Commander-in-Chief of the Turkish forces. . . .

May 17th, 1917. Away by 6.30 with a train of eight Ford motors, some of them box cars. Our having to carry a Gurkha escort and petrol for 150 miles reduces the available room by about half. Started with Goldsmith and the *Nawwāb* (in charge of a great box containing 29,000 rupees). Picked up Garbett with a most elaborate canteen, bedding, etc., which it was the devil to fit in. Over the Bridge we had to pick up the two Shaikhs representing the tribes through whom we pass, for a fortnight ago travellers were being held up by brigands. The unfortunate military drivers had been 100 miles yesterday, and had not returned till seven, when they learnt their fate for the morrow. Very old tyres, and no spare parts. Road along the dyke made a little over five times longer owing to the floods caused by Arabs, who broke through a bund to water their lands. Three or four long breakdowns from various members of our octave, during which I learned a little of the management of the latest prismatic compass, lent me by Gertrude Bell; an operation simpler and less esoteric than I had supposed. The heat grew intense, and punctures and engine 'trouble' more and more frequent, the road hardly ever appearing through the hillocks, ditches and ploughed fields. Yet I was glad to have pushed on, sure that, even without reaching Karbalā, we gain a day. Throughout my journey there is a tendency for all to say 'Take your time – why rush it?' etc. as if one were on a honeymoon. It is only by going a little faster than everybody wants that I succeed in moving at all. Two miles away from Khan Iskandarīa a gigantic yellow curtain began to pace us and draw nearer to us. It reached some 400 feet high, and discovered brown and black chasms. We began to hope to outstrip it, and might

---

* Queen of Harūn al-Rashīd. Zubaida, diminutive of *Zibda* = Little Cream, so named by her grandfather the Caliph Mansūr from her fresh sleekness.

possibly have done so, if we had not heard the (hundredth) sharp bleat of a box car in distress. With a wealth of expletive we turned, and almost at once were caught. It grew quite dark. For about half an hour the thing roared past us, far too loud for any talk or word, then with a few hard raindrops gradually cleared, allowing us to rattle in to Khan Iskandarīa, where luncheon was served by Garbett's Indian servant, with the assistance of a Badawi local policeman with four long and beautifully braided pigtails. . . .

May 18th, 1917. A cold wind came up with the dawn, chilling me through my single sheet: started 10. Said had to sit outside a lorry, on the luggage, and complained of the sun, wind, bumping, etc., till I stole for him an Indian's umbrella, under which he lurched the remainder of the journey in grotesque contentment. By the little blue tiled dome of Aun our half-way halt, we had done 10 miles in nearly two hours, a rate I have lived to think very respectable. At Aun a local Arab notable insisted on giving us tea and wonderfully good and strong coffee in a Damascene tent, whilst some forty of his hangers-on watched each drop anxiously down our throats. After about an hour the immense palms of Karbalā grew in sight, and outside the town we found the notables drawn up to escort us in. We alighted to salute these; and then on, followed and preceded by them in carriages and on horses (one elder galloping very martially under an old umbrella), and with an escort of some forty prancing Arabs. Later the two groups amalgamated; and surrounded by an appalling dust which almost hid from us the green gardens the palms the vines and the oleanders; with bystanders cheering women thrilling and trilling, some of the procession drawing swords and others umbrellas; all shouting like the King's champion loud defiances to non-existent foes, the first motor in history, gravely punctured in its near hind Stepney, struggled rattling into Karbalā. Then we went through a wooden door in the wall, down a few steps, into what I have not seen since August three years ago – green upon green under green. A Persian garden with long vine trellises and pergolas, and narrow paths,

> 'Annihilating all that's made
> To a green thought in a green shade.'

We followed the brother of our host, Muhammad Ali Kamūna, through alleys of oleanders, palms, roses, apricots and greengages, to a little pavilion – 'a cottage in a garden of cucumbers' – for our private use, with a larger one a short distance away for Receptions. I walked round and saw how

> 'The nectarine and curious peach
> Into my hand themselves did reach',

and under the trellised grapes was complete shelter from the sun. In England, less perhaps than nothing – for hardly a flower; but in Chaldaea after the long waste of the East, those voyages, and the bang and crash of the kettly Fords, generally in bottom gear, the contrast was astonishing. At about 1.30 we were called for luncheon, which was spread, all the dishes at once, on a table in the garden. Several sorts of Turkish dishes including *Bāmia* which I ate with pleasure for the first time – a sort of salt rhubarb. About a melon each besides *mishmish** and *barqūq†*.

---

* Apricot. † Plum.

But an excess of their black coffee gave me a feeling of weakness for the rest of the day. We were served by a Persian servant of great dignity and charm, who subsequently smoked a cigarette in a great amber mouthpiece like those that are sold in Cairo as umbrella handles. A merchant brought us round unbelievably poor carpets, brass, rubies, turquoise and emeralds, and it is my belief that the place has been scientifically gutted by German Baghdad. The entire staff having vanished to the *hammām* we were left to our own resources till 4.30 when the *Nawwāb*, returning in a lilac and white silk *aba*, conducted us round the bazaars and general sights of the town. Arab policemen with slung rifles and canes in their hands preceded us, and went through the form of technically thrashing the boys out of the way. Tall, narrow and well-roofed bazaars; but Karbalā produces nothing of its own, so of little interest. At a photographer's I found, and had removed, conspicuously hung chromolithographs of Franz Josef, Wilhelm, Ferdinand and Muhammad V; the *geste* richly approved by the throng. The *Nawwāb* has but little idea of planning our time. . . . He had made no sort of arrangement for getting us even a distant view of the golden shrines, and it was not until we had seen the Municipality that I had to insist upon a roof climb, for which the house of Yázdi was selected. The tread of the stairs, almost 16 inches, is drastic, but the golden dome, golden minarets and golden clock-tower with great storks walking slowly round their summits, and the brilliantly tiled courtyard whose walls are like gardens, is an addition to visual experience; not but what the tiles are in themselves poor in design and colour suffused with that pink which is the sure and fatal sign of contact with the West. The people thronging our path greeted us with an indifferent friendliness; their faces bore an expression, if so it may be called, of dull depravity. . . .

May 19, 1917. Aetat 35½. Up at 6 and after breakfast to a round of visits. The first of these to Husain Mazandarāni, easily the most important *Mujtahid* of Karbalā. An old man of charming manners (up stairs of appalling severity), sitting in a small library of I should say 400 books, chiefly manuscripts, which fit easily into the arcade of shallow recessed arches, a feature in all these houses. H. M. is a rare example of the vanishing sage. Equally, and, for the visitor, bafflingly at home in Arabic, Persian and Hindustani, he is (alas) prepared upon the lightest pretext to reopen the question of the comparative merits of Plato and Aristotle. Seeing my interest in his books he sent for the key of another library of about the same size and showed it to me with pride. I asked if we might photograph him and he said 'after your fortunate return from Nájaf', rightly interpreting which as an evasion, and using the privilege of the Arab Guest, I called to the servants in a terrible voice, 'Go, some of you and bring the picture of our master', and in about ten minutes one returned with an admirable portrait which H. M. sealed for me himself. Neither in his house nor in any other, did I see a chair, and in all the sons in a row knelt inclining backwards against the wall. The other *Mujtahids* were equally interested in and approving of the Sharífial movement. These visits were repaid us, even by Mazandarāni (who cried 'Allah!'* some eight times before he faced the stairs), in the house of the *Nawwāb's* cousin, where there went up a *parfum impérissable*, which only could not be the drains themselves, because there are

---

* To warn the ladies.

none; and in spite of the charm of the storks flying slowly round and round high over the courtyard, I left the house almost fainting. We visited the Persian school, a model of ideal and decorative pedagogy. The plan is roughly Shakespeare's Theatre. The pupils are the groundlings, and the professors sit on Juliet's balcony or pace Crookback's Tower roof. A gallery runs round this first floor, and gives into a score of little rooms, each with its round arched door. Decorative system, tiles on the floor, alcoves with returned white plaster arches. A few Persian maps hung against these; no other implements of science visible. The pupils 'ran' from 4 to 10 years. Several wore the green turban of the Sayyid; many, great silver-bossed belts, and only one poor devil a ready-made European suit, complete with black Kalpak and huge black boots. I implored and persuaded the Headmaster to make Persian costume obligatory down to the smallest detail. Heard a rather pathetic song, in unison, commemorating the glories of Irān. Photographed the entire establishment and back to luncheon in the garden, after which we left Karbalā with lively regret soon after one. Outside to the West appear three or four perfect glowing turquoises, which are the blue-tiled domes of the saints. . . . The road to Nájaf is fairly easy, divided into four by three *Khans*, which we made on an average in about an hour apiece. Far away on the western bank of the Euphrates, Birs Nimrūd, the Tower of Babel, is visible for many miles round. Good going on the whole, though we had to get out and shove through the heavy sand several times, in great heat. Soon after half-way a diamond point of light became a glittering topaz, deepened to an inverted golden bowl and finally revealed the dome of the shrine of Our Master the Martyr Ali. Sand-grouse in small coveys walked or fluttered within 20 yards of us and many curious creatures that we imagined were armadillos galloped about still closer and disappeared into their burrows. We reached the walled town of Nájaf before 5.30, which, unlike Karbalā in its cup of land, stands up to view; thousands coming to greet us, and the bazaars being (tiresomely) closed in honour of our advent, which happens to coincide with the feast of the Prophet Muhammad's *Mab'ath* – Election, Calling or Mission. Walked through the tall narrow well-roofed bazaars; the end of one of which, as by a hanging of gorgeous silk, is barred by the great tiled gate of the Holy Precinct. An enormous crowd was waiting for us at the house of the *Kiliddar*, a triple edifice with kitchen and harem of three stories, including, as everywhere in Mesopotamia, immense *sardabs*, built deep in the ground of solid vaulted masonry (supported on short fat Norman columns) which kept a temperature of at least 10 degrees lower than any other room in the building. Tea was given us in a long grey-green oddly Venetian room, with ceiling-panels of glass so bad as to be almost successful; on to the central court is a continuous row of small arched windows, and below a number of rather attractive children, some with short hair and turbans, others bareheaded with flowing locks, hung about, got in the way, were furiously cursed and, as throughout the East, moved away each time a few feet to return after five minutes, when *da capo*. The din was infernal; we were spent with the banging car, and heartily relieved when invited to visit the great flat roof which gives, within 50 yards, on to the golden dome, minarets and clock-tower, of Sayyidna Ali. There I photographed in the setting sun, and then sat watching the gleam fail until the sun went down, and the clock chimed 12,* with all four quarters, taking me back to

---

* Sunset, the end of the Moslem day.

Cambridge, or Big Ben – a better man than the lot of them. There is not a foot of green in all Nájaf, and as we supped on the still, gloomy roof with our agreeable but eructating host, we sharply regretted not being able to plan another evening in the garden of Karbalā. . . .

May 20th, 1917. Rose about 6, intending to visit Kūfa at 8, but having to see various persons first, waited till after 10. G. told me I made a speech in Arabic in my sleep. He snores. I called for carpet and silk merchants, and sent for the astrologer most in repute. My shaving was watched throughout by one of the children very much in the attitude of a Sistine cherub, and my bath compassed about with a cloud of witnesses, to the *pudeur* of Garbett, whose home is not, like mine, broke these six years to the Nude.

My horoscope was then cast by the astrologer, without, however, any reference to my own dates or to the Celestial Bodies. The henna-bearded sage, who is also a schoolmaster, after scratching a number of Morse dots and dashes on the writing paper, told me to ask any questions I might wish resolved, as he had no remarks to offer himself. By this I perceived him to be no true Mage, and contented myself with the information that I should return to my country but after a long time, and by sea. This, if it comes true, is certainly worth ten rupees. . . . We left Kūfa, which is little more than a village, stopping to see and photograph the shrine (again under a turquoise dome), commemorating the spot where Ali was slain. I had read somewhere that it contained an ancient granite pillar, with the curious property of deciding whether or no a person was legitimate, by allowing or not allowing his arms to encircle it; and asked if this were so. The Sayyid Abbās and all present replied with enthusiasm that it was, but that we could not see it as it was within the hallowed precinct. I was disappointed, but agreed nevertheless that this discriminating and potentially tactless column is far better left in Kūfa where it is. . . .

May 22nd, 1917. . . . The Euphrates banks are wonderfully picturesque, and almost as varied and beautiful as an English river: palms, pomegranates, apricots and un-Egyptian grass. But the hours dragged on, and we did not reach Hilla until 2.30, or 7¾ hours' journey. The town is pretty, and will be of great importance when it has recovered from the late Turkish visitation, in which many of the people were shot, every single notable, to the number of 170, hanged, and many of the women abducted. (Said thinks the Euphrates is a continuation of the Nile, and resolutely refuses to be impressed by anything except the Turkish atrocities. . . . It is a good thing for Egyptians to see such things with their own eyes.) Goldsmith at present in Menahem's clean and pleasant house: he tells me that the Venerable offered to provide him also with a lady companion. Business till three when I suggested a visit to Babylon. Every one estimated its distance differently, varying between 2 and 4 hours: also, the road being considered unsafe, we had to wait till four for mounted police. Walking at nearly five miles an hour, the time from Menahem Daniel's house to the temple of Mardak is 1½ hours, and very hard work at that. This most famous city of remoter antiquity is still impressive in the melancholy vastness and abandon of its mounds. The excavation, though immense, cannot represent one-thousandth of the real area. All brick, save for the colossal stone lion that tramples on a headless man. The animals in relief beautifully executed, and equal, in my opinion, to the best Egyptian work. We could not spend much more than an hour there, and passed on to the German Archaeological Mission's house, in a palm-grove, well and solidly built. The keeper, a villainous-looking ruffian, was in great terror of us, and I am sure has been far more guiltily engaged even than in bombing boats, which he is known to have done to extract toll. We warned him to be terribly careful what he did, and went over the house, which has not been visibly pillaged. I will confess to a lively sympathy with those Boches, whose work remains stacked, packed, numbered, ticketed and catalogued in the best German tradition of con-scientious exactitude. But Oh, to find in the library, as first specimen, *Der Telemak von Fénelon*: yet they say the English take their pleasures sadly. Much Scott, in English, and of course Science. In the study one or two picture postcards of Female Loveliness struck a lighter but not more agreeable note. We rode back on police horses of which I requisitioned one for Said, as 'the renowned Ālem of Egypt', a title which his turban carries off better than his sheepish grin. . . .

May 23rd, 1917. Rose soon after 5, and away by car to Birs Nimrūd, the Tower of Babel. Our four-seater being under repair, I was driven in a lorry by a Blackpool dentist from Burton-on-Trent, who told me the story of his life. Road across the plains very bad, so much so that we had to get to work several times with the spade, and on one occasion lift the car over a difficult chasm. This famous mound is visible far across the plain, and is surmounted by a square brick tower, riven right through by lightning. Everywhere traces of an ancient conflagration. We reached it at 9.40 and stayed till 10. All around, remains in beautiful dull red brick, and about a quarter of a mile away the Tomb, or rather *Maqām*, of Abraham, a little dome over a square mud-brick wall. I asked our armed police: 'What is this place called?' '*Qaṣr* or *Birs Nimrūd*.' 'And who was Nimrūd?' '*Málik-y-Dúnya*' – 'King of the World.' Our four drivers delighted, 'honoured', to stand on the Tower of Babel – which after all has as good a title to authenticity as most very ancient monuments; for what could be more natural than that vassal labour collected by kingly ambition from widely diverse countries, none understanding the other, should lead to rows? Or that the all-dreaded thunderstone should be ascribed by strikers' union-leaders to the Wrath of Heaven. . . . afterwards saw in the bazaar the exquisite tile-fronted *Maqām*, where the last Mahdi Imam was last seen. . . . Domed, of course, and the interior octagon pendentives finely utilized for decorative script. Blue- and yellow-tiled floors and wall wainscoting. The stairs of the Municipality of Hilla are built almost exclusively of inscribed Babylonian bricks, and I urged Garbett to have them replaced and deciphered. The whole town is constructed out of ancient Babylon, though of course not all inscribed cuneiform. We left at 12.40 and reached Baghdad with little mishap at 6.15, beyond our wildest hopes. The second bridge having disappeared we took oars, and reached our houses, deeply caked in sand, about 6.30. Long talks with Cox and Gertrude Bell.[4]

And finally, a letter from Oscar Wilde. He wrote it from 'c/o Thomas Cook & Son, Piazza di Spagna, Rome' on 16 April 1900, to his friend Robert Ross:

Well, all passed over very successfully. Palermo, where we stayed eight days, was lovely. The most beautifully situated town in the world, it dreams away its life in the Conca d'Oro, the exquisite valley that lies between two seas. The lemon-groves and the orange-gardens were so entirely perfect that I became again a Pre-Raphaelite, and loathed the ordinary Impressionists, whose muddy souls and blurred intelligences would have rendered but by mud and blur those 'golden lamps hung in a green night' that filled me with such joy. The elaborate and exquisite detail of the true Pre-Raphaelites is the compensation they offer us for the absence of motion; Literature and Music being the only arts that are not immobile.

Then nowhere, not even at Ravenna, have I seen such mosaics. In the Cappella Palatina, which from pavement to domed ceilings is all gold, one really feels as if one was sitting in the heart of a great honeycomb *looking* at angels singing; and looking at angels, or indeed at people singing, is much nicer than listening to them. For this reason the great artists always give to their angels lutes without strings, pipes without vent-holes, and reeds through which no wind can wander or make whistlings.

Monreale you have heard of, with its cloisters and cathedral. We often drove there, the *cocchieri* most dainty finely-carved boys. In them, not in the Sicilian horses, is race seen. The most favoured were Manuele, Francesco, and Salvatore. I loved them all, but only remember Manuele.

I also made great friends with a young Seminarist who lived *in* the Cathedral of Palermo, he and eleven others in little rooms beneath the roof, like birds.

Every day he showed me all over the Cathedral, and I really knelt before the huge porphyry sarcophagus in which Frederick the Second lies. It is a sublime bare monstrous thing, blood-coloured, and held up by lions, who have caught some of the rage of the great Emperor's restless soul. At first, my young friend, Giuseppe Loverde by name, gave *me* information: but on the third day I gave information to him, and re-wrote History as usual, and told him all about the Supreme King and his Court of Poets, and the terrible book that he never wrote.* Giuseppe was fifteen, and most sweet. His reason for entering the Church was singularly mediaeval. I asked him why he thought of becoming a *clerico*: and how.

He answered 'My father is a cook, and most poor, and we are many at home, so it seemed to me a good thing that there should be in so small a house as ours one mouth less to feed, for, though I am slim, I eat much: too much, alas! I fear.'

I told him to be comforted, because God used poverty often as a means of bringing people to Him, and used riches never, or but rarely. So Giuseppe was comforted, and I gave him a little book of devotion, very pretty, and with far more pictures than prayers in it; so of great service to Giuseppe, whose eyes are beautiful. I also gave him many *lire*, and prophesied for him a Cardinal's hat, if he remained very good, and never forgot me. He said he never would: and indeed I don't think he will, for every day I kissed him behind the high altar.

At Naples we stopped three days. Most of my friends are, as you know, in prison, but I met some of nice memory, and fell in love with a Sea-God, who for some extraordinary reason is at the Regia Marina School, instead of being with Triton.

* Frederick II (1194–1250), Roman Emperor, King of Sicily and Jerusalem, popularly known as *Stupor Mundi*. Italian poetry, according to Dante, was born at his court, and he was suspected by the Papal party of writing a book called *De Tribus Impostoribus* (the three impostors – Moses, Jesus and Mahomet).

We came to Rome on Holy Thursday. H. M. left on Saturday for Gland, and yesterday, to the terror of Grissell and all the Papal Court, I appeared in the front rank of the pilgrims in the Vatican, and got the blessing of the Holy Father – a blessing they would have denied me.

He was wonderful as he was carried past me on his throne, not of flesh and blood, but a white soul robed in white, and an artist as well as a saint – the only instance in History, if the newspapers are to be believed.

I have seen nothing like the extraordinary grace of his gesture, as he rose, from moment to moment, to bless – possibly the pilgrims, but certainly me. Tree should see him. It is his only chance.

I was deeply impressed, and my walking-stick showed signs of budding; would have budded indeed, only at the door of the chapel it was taken from me by the Knave of Spades. This strange prohibition is, of course, in honour of Tannhäuser.

How did I get the ticket? By a miracle of course. I thought it was hopeless, and made no effort of any kind. On Saturday afternoon at five o'clock Harold and I went to have tea at the Hôtel de l'Europe. Suddenly, as I was eating buttered toast, a man, or what seemed to be one, dressed like a hotel porter, entered and asked me would I like to see the Pope on Easter Day. I bowed my head humbly and said 'Non sum dignus,' or words to that effect. He at once produced a ticket!

When I tell you that his countenance was of supernatural ugliness, and that the price of the ticket was thirty pieces of silver, I need say no more.[5]

153

CHAPTER EIGHT

Architecture

Until some thirty or forty years ago, anyone travelling to foreign parts for pleasure was impelled, more likely than not, by an urge to See the Sights; and although a few of those sights – Niagara Falls, the Grand Canyon or Mount Etna, for example – ranked as natural rather than artificial wonders, the vast majority of them were buildings of brick or stone. Nowadays, with the pleasure-traveller easily outnumbering every other kind, the lure of the bucket and spade has proved – fortunately for us sightseers – a good deal more powerful; the sad fact remains, however, that many of the great monuments of the world have received more visitors in the past ten years than in the whole of their previous existence, and the remorseless flood shows no sign of abating. One can only envy Celia Fiennes who, travelling round England at the very end of the seventeenth century, must have had every one of the great country houses that she visited virtually to herself. Here she is at Chatsworth:

We go from Chesterffield to the Duke of Devonshires house and ascend a high hill at least two to three miles long . . . the same long steep hill we had to descend which comes to Chattsworth; the Duke's house lyes just at the foote of this steepe hill which is like a precipice just at the last, notwithstanding the Dukes house stands on a little riseing ground from the River Derwent which runs all along the front of the house and by a little fall made in the water which makes a pretty murmurring noise; before the gate there is a large Parke and severall fine Gardens one without another with gravell walkes and squairs of grass with stone statues in them and in the middle of each Garden is a large fountaine full of images Sea Gods and Dolphins and Sea Horses which are full of pipes which spout out water in the bason and spouts all about the gardens; 3 Gardens just round the house; some have gravell walks and square like the other with Statues and Images in the bason, there is one bason in the middle of one Garden thats very large and by sluces besides the Images severall pipes plays out the water, about 30 large and small pipes altogether, some flush it up that it frothes like snow; there is one Garden full of stone and brass statues; so the Gardens lyes one above another which makes the prospect very fine; above these gardens is an ascent of 5 or 6 stepps up to a wilderness and close arbours and shady walks, on each end of one walke stands two piramidies full of pipes spouting water that runns down one of them, runs on brass hollow work which looks like rocks and hollow stones; the other is all flatts stands one above another like salvers so the water rebounds one from another, 5 or 6 one above the other; there is another green walke and about the middle of it by the Grove stands a fine Willow tree, the leaves barke and all looks very naturall, the roote is full of rubbish or great stones to appearance, and all on a sudden by turning a sluce it raines from each leafe and from the branches like a shower, it being made of brass and pipes to each leafe but in appearance is exactly like any Willow; beyond this is a bason in which are the branches of two Hartichocks Leaves which weeps at the end of each leafe into the bason which is placed at the foote of lead steps 30 in number; on a little banck stands blew balls 10 on a side, and between each ball are 4 pipes which by a sluce spouts out water across the stepps to each other like an arbour or arch; while you are thus amused suddenly there runs down a torrent of water out of 2 pitchers in the hands of two large Nimphs cut in stone that lyes in the upper step, which makes a pleaseing prospect, this is designed to be enlarged and steps made up to the top of the hill which is a vast ascent, but from the top of it now they are supply'd with water for all their pipes so it will be the easyer to have such a fall of water even from the top which will add to the Curiositye.[1]

My next offering comes from a minor classic of travel literature which, though it has long been celebrated in America where it first appeared in 1908, was published in this country only a year or two ago. It is the result of several journeys in Mexico by one Charles Macomb Flandrau, whose brother was a coffee-planter there, and it is called simply *Viva Mexico!*

One December morning, while I was aimlessly strolling in the white, dry sunlight of Puebla, I wandered into the cathedral. The semireligious, semiculinary festival known as Christmas had come and gone for me in Jalapa, but as soon as I went into the church and walked beyond the choir, the awkward situation of which in Spanish cathedrals shows on the part of catholics an unusual indifference to general impressiveness, it was apparent – gorgeously, overwhelmingly apparent – that here Christmas still lingered. This cathedral is always gorgeous and always somewhat overpowering, for, unlike any other I can recall, that which, perhaps, was the original scheme of decoration looks as if it had been completed a few moments before one's arrival. We have learned to expect in these places worn surfaces, tarnished gilt, a sense of invisible dust and tones instead of colors. So few of them look as they were intended to look that, just as we prefer Greek statues unpainted, we prefer the decorations of cathedrals to be in the nature of exquisite effacement. In the great church of Puebla, however, little is exquisite and certainly nothing is effaced. On entering, one is at first only surprised that an edifice so respectably old can be so jauntily new. But when, during mass, one passes slightly before the choir, and is confronted by the first possible view of any amplitude, it is something more than rhetoric to say that for a moment the cathedral of Puebla is overpowering.

The use of gold leaf in decoration is like money. A little is pleasant, merely too much is vulgar; but a positively staggering amount of it seems to justify itself. My own income is not vulgar; neither is Mr. Rockefeller's. The ordinary white and gold drawing-room done by the local upholsterer is atrociously vulgar, but the cathedral of Puebla is not. Gold – polished, glittering, shameless gold – blazes down and up and across at one; from the stone rosettes in the vaulting overhead, from the grilles in front of the chapels, from the railings between which the priests walk to altar and choir, from the onyx pulpit and the barricade of gigantic candle-sticks in front of the altar, from the altar itself – one of those carefully insane eighteenth-century affairs, in which a frankly pagan tiempolito and great lumps of Christian symbolism have become gloriously muddled for all time. Gold flashes in the long straight sun shafts overhead, twinkles in the candle flames, glitters from the censers and the chains of the censers. The back of the priest at the altar is incrusted with gold, and to-day – for Christmas lingers – all the pillars from capital to base are swathed in the finest of crimson velvet, fringed with gold. It isn't vulgar, it isn't even gaudy. It has surpassed all that and has entered into the realm of the bewildering – the flabbergastric.

As I sank upon one of the sparsely occupied benches 'para los señores,' there was exhaled from the organ, somewhere behind and above me, a dozen or more bars of Chopin. During the many sartorial interims of the mass the organ coquetted frequently with Chopin as well as with Saint-Saëns, Massenet, and Gounod in some of his less popular but as successfully cloying moments – and never anywhere have I seen so much incense. As a rule, unless one sits well forward in churches, the incense only tantalizes. Swing and jerk as the little boys may, it persists in clinging to the altar and the priests, in being sucked into the draught of the candle flames and then floating up to the sunlight of the dome. It rarely reaches the populace until it has become cool and thin. At Puebla they may be more prodigal of it, or they may use a different kind. It at any rate belches out at one in fat, satiating clouds of pearl-gray and sea-blue, and what with Chopin and all the little gasping flames, the rich, deliberate, incrusted group about the altar, the forest of crimson pillars and the surfeit of gold, I experienced one of those agreeable, harmless, ecclesiastical debauches that in Mexico, where the apparatus of worship does not often rise above the tawdry, and the music is almost always execrable, are perforce rare.[2]

Flandrau was a good writer; our next author, John Ruskin, was a great one. No man, even in the nineteenth century, was capable of so sustained a flow of imaginative prose-poetry. For many readers today he is too flowery, too fragrant; but not for me. If, as I suspect, his celebrated description of St Mark's in Venice has been anthologised countless times already, so much the better – here it is again:

A yard or two farther, we pass the hostelry of the Black Eagle, and glancing as we pass through the square door of marble, deeply moulded, in the outer wall, we see the shadows of its pergola of vines resting on an ancient well, with a pointed shield carved on its side; and so presently emerge on the bridge and Campo San Moisè, whence to the entrance into St. Mark's Place, called the Bocca di Piazza (mouth of the square), the Venetian character is nearly destroyed, first by the frightful façade of San Moisè and then by the modernising of the shops as they near the piazza, and the mingling with the lower Venetian populace of lounging groups of English and Austrians. We will push fast through them into the shadow of the pillars at the end of the 'Bocca di Piazza,' and then we forget them all; for between those pillars there opens a great light, and, in the midst of it, as we advance slowly, the vast tower of

St. Mark seems to lift itself visibly forth from the level field of chequered stones; and, on each side, the countless arches prolong themselves into ranged symmetry, as if the rugged and irregular houses that pressed together above us in the dark alley had been struck back into sudden obedience and lovely order, and all their rude casements and broken walls had been transformed into arches charged with goodly sculpture, and fluted shafts of delicate stone.

And well may they fall back, for beyond those troops of ordered arches there rises a vision out of the earth, and all the great square seems to have opened from it in a kind of awe, that we may see it far away; – a multitude of pillars and white domes, clustered into a long low pyramid of coloured light; a treasure-heap, it seems, partly of gold, and partly of opal and mother-of-pearl, hollowed beneath into five great vaulted porches, ceiled with fair mosaic, and beset with sculpture of alabaster, clear as amber and delicate as ivory, – sculpture fantastic and involved, of palm leaves and lilies, and grapes and pomegranates, and birds clinging and fluttering among the branches, all twined together into an endless network of buds and plumes; and in the midst of it, the solemn forms of angels, sceptred, and robed to the feet, and leaning to each other across the gates, their figures indistinct among the gleaming of the golden ground through the leaves beside them, interrupted and dim, like the morning light as it faded back among the branches of Eden, when first its gates were angel-guarded long ago. And round the walls of the porches there are set pillars of variegated stones, jasper and porphyry, and deep-green serpentine spotted with flakes of snow, and marbles, that half refuse and half yield to the sunshine, Cleopatra-like, 'their bluest veins to kiss' – the shadow, as it steals back from them, revealing line after line of azure undulation, as a receding tide leaves the waved sand; their capitals rich with interwoven tracery, rooted knots of herbage, and drifting leaves of acanthus and vine, and mystical signs, all beginning and ending in the Cross; and above them, in the broad archivolts, a continuous chain of language and of life – angels, and the signs of heaven, and the labours of men, each in its appointed season upon the earth; and above these, another range of glittering pinnacles, mixed with white arches edged with scarlet flowers, – a confusion of delight, amidst which the breasts of the Greek horses are seen blazing in their breadth of golden strength, and the St. Mark's lion, lifted on a blue field covered with stars, until at last, as if in ecstasy, the crests of the arches break into a marble foam, and toss themselves far into the blue sky in flashes and wreaths of sculptured spray, as if the breakers on the Lido shore had been frost-bound before they fell, and the sea-nymphs had inlaid them with coral and amethyst.[3]

It is not only great architecture, however, that can inspire dazzling writing. Versailles, for example, except in the matter of its size, could not conceivably be so described. But see what fun Horace Walpole has with it – writing from Paris to his friend Richard West in 1739:

Stand by, clear the way, make room for the pompous appearance of Versailles le Grand! – But no: it fell so short of my idea of it, mine, that I have resigned to Gray the office of writing its panegyric. He likes it. They say I am to like it better next Sunday; when the sun is to shine, the king is to be fine, the water-works are to play, and the new knights of the Holy Ghost are to be installed! Ever since Wednesday, the day we were there, we have done nothing but dispute about it. They say, we did not see it to advantage, that we ran through the apartments, saw the garden *en passant*, and slubbered over Trianon. I say, we saw nothing. However, we had time to see that the great front is a lumber of littleness, composed of black brick, stuck full of bad old busts, and fringed with gold rails. The rooms are all small, except the great gallery, which is noble, but totally wainscoted with looking-glass. The garden is littered with statues and fountains, each of which has its tutelary deity. In particular, the elementary god of fire solaces himself in one. In another, Enceladus, in lieu of a mountain, is overwhelmed with many waters. There are avenues of water-pots, who disport themselves much in squirting up cascadelins. In short, 'tis a garden for a great child. Such was Louis Quatorze, who is here seen in his proper colours, where he commanded in person, unassisted by his armies and generals, and left to the pursuit of his own puerile ideas of glory.[4]

How sad, I have often thought, that Walpole saw so little of Italy. He spent over a year in Florence on his Grand Tour with Thomas Gray, and from there once paid a flying visit to Rome; but he never went to Padua or Bologna, Naples or Venice. What marvellous letters we should have had from there! Nor, indeed, did he ever visit Sicily: he would have been a good deal more amused by the astonishing Villa Palagonia at Bagheria than was Goethe, who visited it in 1787 and described it in his *Italian Journey* (the translation here quoted is by W. H. Auden and Elizabeth Mayer):

April 9

Our entire day has been taken up with the madness of the Prince of Pallagonia [*sic*]. His follies turned out to be quite different from anything I had imagined after hearing and reading about them. . . .

On entering the great hall on the boundary of the estate, we found ourselves in an octagon, very high in proportion to its width. Four colossal giants in modern gaiters support the cornice, over which, facing the gate, hovers the Holy Trinity. The drive to the house is unusually broad, and each wall has been transformed into an uninterrupted socle on which excellent pedestals sustain strange groups interspersed with vases. The repulsive appearance of these deformities, botched by inferior stonecutters, is reinforced by the crumbly shell-tufa of which they are made, but a better material would, no doubt, have made the worthlessness of the form still more conspicuous. I called them groups, but the word is inappropriate, for they are not the products of calculation or even of caprice; they are merely accidental jumbles.

The following list may give you a better idea of what Prince Pallogonia has perpetrated in his madness.

Human beings

Beggars of both sexes, men and women of Spain, Moors, Turks, hunchbacks, deformed persons of every kind, dwarfs, musicians, Pulcinellas, soldiers in antique uniforms, gods and goddesses, persons dressed in French fashions of long ago, soldiers with ammunition pouches and leggings, mythological figures with grotesque accessories; for instance: Achilles and Chiron with Pulcinella.

Animals
Only parts of them; a horse with human hands, the head of a horse on a human body, deformed monkeys, many dragons and snakes, every kind of paw attached to every kind of body, double heads and exchanged heads.

Vases
Every kind of monster and scroll, emerging from their bellies or their bases.

Now imagine similar figures multiplied *ad infinitum*, designed without rhyme or reason, combined without discrimination or point, pedestals and monstrosities in one unending row, and the painful feelings they must inspire, and you will sympathize with anyone who has to run the gauntlet of this lunacy. . . .

In the house, the fever of the Prince rises to a delirium. The legs of the chairs have been unequally sawn off, so that no one can sit on them, and we were warned by the castellan himself not to use the normal chairs, for they have spikes hidden under their velvet-cushioned seats. In corners stood candelabra of Chinese porcelain, which turned out, on closer inspection, to be made up of single bowls, cups and saucers, all glued together. Some whimsical object stares out at you from every corner. . . .

A description of the chapel alone would fill a book. Here lies the clue to the whole madness. Only in the brain of a religious fanatic could it have grown to such rampant proportions. I must leave you to imagine how many caricatures of a perverted piety have been assembled here, and only mention the most conspicuous one.

A carved crucifix of considerable size, painted in realistic colours and varnished and gilded in places, is fixed flat to the ceiling. Into the navel of the Crucified a hook has been screwed from which hangs a chain. The end of this chain is made fast to the head of a man, kneeling in prayer and painted and varnished like everything else. He hangs suspended in the air as a symbol of the ceaseless devotions of the present owner. . . .

It was the first time I had seen Kniep lose patience. His feelings as an artist were outraged by this madhouse, and when I tried to study the details of these misbegotten horrors, he hustled me away. But, good-natured fellow that he is, he finally drew one of the groups, the only one that at least made some sort of picture. A woman with a horse's head is seated in a chair playing cards with her vis-à-vis, a cavalier in old-fashioned clothes. He has a griffin's head, dressed in a full-bottomed wig with a crown perched on top of it. Which reminds me: the coat-of-arms of the House of Pallagonia is a satyr holding up a mirror to a woman with a horse's head. Even after having seen the other absurdities, this seems to me the most peculiar of all.[5]

Three days later Goethe actually saw the perpetrator of the absurdities:

April 12
This evening another of my wishes was fulfilled and in a surprising fashion. I was standing in the main street, joking with my old shopkeeper friend, when I was

suddenly accosted by a tall, well-dressed runner who thrust a silver salver at me, on which lay several copper coins and a few pieces of silver. Since I had no idea what he wanted, I shrugged my shoulders and ducked my head, the usual gesture for showing that one has not understood or does not wish to. He left as quickly as he had come, and then I saw another runner on the opposite side of the street, occupied in the same fashion.

I asked the shopkeeper what all this was about, and he pointed with a meaningful, almost furtive gesture to a tall, thin gentleman, dressed in the height of fashion, who was walking down the middle of the street through all the dung and dirt with an air of imperturbable dignity. In a freshly curled and powdered wig, carrying his hat under his arm and wearing a silk coat, a sword and neat shoes with jewelled buckles, the elderly gentleman walked solemnly on, ignoring all the eyes that were turned in his direction.

'That is Prince Pallagonia,' said the shopkeeper. 'From time to time he walks through the city collecting ransom money for the slaves who have been captured by Barbary pirates. The collection never amounts to much, but people are reminded of their plight, and those who never contribute during their lifetime often leave a considerable legacy to this cause. The Prince has been president of this charity for many years now, and has done a great deal of good.'

'If,' I said, 'instead of spending vast sums on follies for his villa, he had used them for this cause, no prince in the world would have accomplished more.' My shopkeeper disagreed: 'Aren't we all like that? We pay gladly for our follies but we expect others to pay for our virtues.'[6]

A very different sort of building was the one found by Patrick Leigh Fermor in Antigua:

At the end of this broad street, which sloped slightly as it receded, from the shallow harbour, an Anglican but extremely baroque-looking cathedral stood among the trees. The twin towers that flanked the classical façade were topped by polygonal bronze cupolas and everything in the treatment of the massive stone fabric led one to believe that it had been built in the late seventeenth or the eighteenth century. Accustomed as we were becoming to surprises of this kind, we were taken aback by the information that it was built – on the exact lines, though, of its predecessor, which an earthquake had destroyed – in 1847. There was nothing inside to impair the illusion. The spacious and airy proportions, the Corinthian pillars, the panelling, the gilding, and the lettering of the Ten Commandments all belonged to the Augustan age of English architecture. And the presiding Godhead, one felt (as one feels in all the churches built between Wren and the Gothic revival) is also a denizen of that prolonged and opulent afternoon. He is not the mysterious Presence of the Middle Ages, nor is He the avenging Thunderer of the Puritans, nor the top-hatted Puseyite of later times, nor yet the stoled and white-overalled Scientist of today. Gazing through the thin, drained atmosphere at the fluted columns and the acanthus leaves, the cornucopias and the formal flutter of the ribbons of wood that secure the carved festoons, our island Deity of the reigns of Queen Anne and the Georges slowly begins, like an emerging portrait by Kneller or Gainsborough or Raeburn, to take shape. The placid features assemble and the misty grey eyes with their compound expression of humour and severity; the heavy judicial curls of the wig, the amaranthine volume of the robes, and the soft blue of the Garter are unfolded in mid-air. A forefinger marks the place in a pocket edition of Voltaire; on a marble table, the tea-time sunlight rests on the vellum-bound Pentateuch and the Odes of Horace, and gently glows on the scales, the marshal's baton and the metal strawberry-leaves. A heavy curtain is looped back, and beyond, with the sweep of soft shadow and faded gold of a gentleman's deer-park, lie the mild prospects of Paradise, the pillared rotunda reflected in the lake, the dreaming swans, and at last, the celestial mansion built by Vanbrugh, rearing, against the sky of Sèvres blue and the whipped-cream clouds, its colonnaded entablature, its marble Graces and its urns. ... This Elysian fancy paled all at once at the sight, on the cushion of one of the pews in the chancel, of the black pom-pom of a biretta. The Hanoverian vision grew vaporous and confused with anachronistic draughts from Oxford and Rome; and vanished.[7]

Robert Byron, whose perception of the subtleties of Islamic architecture was a good deal more acute than that of most people, even managed to discern an Augustan flavour in Isfahan:

The Mosque of Sheikh Lutfullah is Persian in the fabulous sense: the Omar Khayam brigade, to whom rational form is as much anathema as rational action, can wallow in it to their hearts' content. ... Colour and pattern are a commonplace in Persian architecture. But here they have a quality which must astonish the European, not because they infringe what he thought was his own monopoly, but because he can previously have had no idea that abstract pattern was capable of so profound a splendour.

As though to announce these principles as soon as possible, the outside of the mosque is careless of symmetry to a grotesque degree. Only the dome and portal are seen from the front. But owing to the discrepancy between the axis of the mosque and that of the Ali Gapu opposite, the portal, instead of being immediately under the dome, is set slightly to one side of it. Yet such is the character of the dome, so unlike is it to any other dome in Persia or elsewhere, that this deformity is hardly noticeable. Round a flattened hemisphere made of tiny bricks and covered with prawn-coloured wash runs a bold branching rose-tree inlaid in black and white. Seen from close to, the design has a hint of William Morris, particularly in its thorns; but as a whole it is more formal than pre-raphaelite, more comparable to the design of a Genoese brocade immensely magnified. Here and there, at the junction of the branches or in the depths of the foliage, ornaments of ochre and dark blue mitigate the harshness of the black and white tracery, and bring it into harmony with the soft golden pink of the background: a process which is continued by a pervading under-foliage of faint light blue. But the genius of the effect is in the play of surfaces. The inlay is glazed. The stucco wash is not. Thus the sun strikes the dome with a *broken* highlight whose intermittent flash, moving with the time of day, adds a third texture to the pattern, mobile and unforeseen.

If the outside is lyric, the inside is Augustan. Here a still shallower dome, about seventy feet in diameter, swims above a ring of sixteen windows. From the floor to the base of the windows rise eight main arches, four enclosing right-angles, four flat wall-space, so that the boundaries of the floor form a square. The space between the tops of the arches is occupied by eight pendentives divided into planes like a bat's-wing.

The dome is inset with a network of lemon-shaped compartments, which increase in size as they descend from a formalised peacock at the apex and are surrounded by plain bricks; each is filled with a foliage pattern inlaid on plain stucco. The walls, bordered by broad white inscriptions on dark blue, are similarly inlaid with twirling arabesques or baroque squares on deep ochre stucco. The colours of all this inlay are dark blue, light greenish blue, and a tint of indefinite wealth like wine. Each arch is framed in turquoise corkscrews. The mihrab in the west wall is enamelled with tiny flowers on a deep blue meadow.

Each part of the design, each plane, each repetition, each separate branch or blossom has its own sombre beauty. But the beauty of the whole comes as you move. Again, the highlights are broken by the play of glazed and unglazed surfaces; so that with every step they rearrange themselves in countless shining patterns; while even the pattern of light through the thick window traceries is inconstant, owing to outer traceries which are several feet away and double the variety of each varying silhouette.

I have never encountered splendour of this kind before. Other interiors came into my mind as I stood there, to compare it with: Versailles, or the porcelain rooms at Schönbrunn, or the Doge's Palace, or St. Peter's. All are rich; but none so rich. Their richness is three-dimensional; it is attended by all the effort of shadow. In the Mosque of Sheikh Lutfullah, it is a richness of light and surface, of pattern and colour only. The architectural form is unimportant. It is not smothered, as in rococo; it is simply the instrument of a spectacle, as earth is the instrument of a garden. And then I suddenly thought of that unfortunate species, modern interior decorators, who imagine they can make a restaurant, or a cinema, or a plutocrat's drawing-room look rich if given money enough for gold leaf and looking-glass. They little know what amateurs they are. Nor, alas, do their clients.[8]

Now for a guide book – *The Companion Guide to Umbria* by Maurice Rowdon, who here describes what happens when, in the little town of Montefalco, we visit:

the church of *S. Chiara* – the St Clare of Montefalco, an Augustinian nun (1268–1308). It came into being during the thirteenth century but manifestly underwent complete overhauling in the seventeenth century to make the present sad brick mausoleum. Inside, at the right of the chancel, we find a door with a bell: we ring this and a nun answers, to show us the saint's body. She speaks to us from behind a hidden grille, and goes away for a little time. There is suddenly a frightening crash in the right transept, and little doors are flung open, revealing a glass case in which the 'uncorrupted' Saint lies. The nun will tell us, hidden still, that St Clare was a great enthusiast for the image and meaning of the Cross: legend says that she met Christ in a dream and he told her that he had always been looking for someone to take the cross from his shoulders, and she replied, 'I shall carry it in my heart.' So when she died the nuns, in the frightened and pagan state of mind that festered in these convents, cut out her heart to see if this was the case. And it was. There was a little cross made up of muscular tissue, which the nun will show us if we step to the right, by flinging open, after an unnerving silence and another crash, a second door. There we see the heart, in a tiny glass case, together with a container of her congealed blood, the knife and scissors she was cut open with, and – presumably – the cross she was blessed with. We look closely at the heart but cannot find the cross in it. And in fact we have made a mistake: the cross itself comes after a third crash: for this we have to step over to the left and a third cupboard is flung open (we are in quite a state by now) and we see another little glass case containing the actual tissue in a cross shape; the little stones at the arms and top of the cross were taken from the Saint's liver of all places, and these, the nun will tell us, are miraculous. She then explains why: one of these tiny stones weighs the same as two, two of them the same as three, and three the same as one again. That is the miracle. You ask her to repeat this and she does: one weighs the same as two, two as three, and three as one. It has been tried again and again through the centuries, she goes on, and never failed: it is the miracle of the Trinity, and you can take it or leave it. This little show is played out perhaps a dozen times a day in the summer, with the greatest warmth and care.

Then we ask her to conduct us to the Chapel of S. Croce: and the frescoes there reassure us. They were done in 1333 (restored 1932): we must ask the nun for the strong light to be switched on. Above in the ceiling are the *evangelists* with the symbolic heads of beasts: in the wall behind the altar, *Calvary*, and on the side wall *scenes from the lives of St Clare, St Catherine and S. Biagio*: and next to them again *St Catherine*. On the right wall, middle, *Jesus is helped by St Clare*, and on the left of the arch we see Clare's sister, the Blessed Giovanna, with St Clare on the right as a child, in the company of the child Jesus; underneath, she brings food to S. Biagio (he is the saint of the throat, by the way). This was the work of a local artist, rather heavy, rustic and slow, an Umbrian working in the post-Giotto idiom but with the old really Byzantine consciousness, where observation did not count. The nun will also take us behind the Enclosure, if we ask her, to the closed cloister of the fifteenth century, and then to the nuns' private chapel, where, on the right of the entrance, we see a very Giottoesque *St Lucy* and the first coffin of the saint, painted, and a tall wooden crucifix in the Byzantine manner. We shall be shown into the little garden too, after we have been modestly offered little trinkets – key-holders, rosaries. This garden has a tree planted by the saint, which botanical authorities say does not exist anywhere else in Europe: but we have stopped believing these sweet, hesitant, kindly nuns by now.[9]

To end this chapter, another little adventure of my mother's, while she and my father were on a visit to Burma in October 1941:

In Rangoon there is a very famous temple-pagoda called the Shwe Dagôn. It rises gold to the sky. Luncheon conversation was about it. To my surprise no one had ever been inside it. 'Footwear' was the explanation, 'You have to enter barefoot. An Englishman can't do that. People do everything there.' 'Full of lepers,' 'the stink of the place' – out rolled the excuses. I said one's feet were washable, one did much worse with one's hands, leprosy wasn't thus caught, a temple *vaut bien* a whiff. They looked exaggeratedly shocked. I've got mixed. It was tea, of course, when this conversation took place, and when it was over we drove in closed cars to have a look round. When we came to the temple door I said 'I'm going in.' There was a bit of a scene. Captain Richmond looked revolted and Pilate-ish. Duff shook his cheeks at me, but I am 'blind and deaf when I list' and in a flash I had my shoes and stockings off and was following the votaries into the great dark doorway. It was one of the most repaying sights I have ever seen. I was quite breathless with excitement. In this high dark corridor that is always ascending are congregated sleepers, vendors, priests, water-carriers, every caste, every age, every race. Everything sold is beautiful – fantastically-made miniature white pagoda-umbrellas to offer to Buddha, bunches of ginger-flowers, lotus and jasmine, cocks and hens like Chinese ornaments, shining gold Buddhas inset with jewels. On and on you mount, the stairs are very steep, faint with the smell of exotic flowers. Burma girls smoking always their 'whacking white cheroot and (actually) wasting Christian kisses on an 'eathen idol's foot,' their hair agate-smooth, though like the White Queen they carry a comb in it (so handy!). They wear a flower in it too, and a clean muslin shirt (always clean) above their bright, tight sarong. At last you come out on to an open circular court, in the centre of which rises the cloud-high gold-leaf pagoda, surrounded by hundreds of Buddha shrines. The devotees vary from nakedish men who walk round and round, falling whistling-bomb flat between every two steps (progress is slow), and the pretty little maidens, smoking and playing with their babies under Buddha's nose. Orange and saffron priests lounge around, and little oil-saucers with floating wicks were everywhere being lit. I wished I could have stayed until dark to see the flickering, but Duff and Captain Richmond were weighing a ton on my conscience, so I hurried round. Even without pausing it took me over an hour. When I came out the atmosphere had improved a bit. My excited, radiant expression I think subdued Duff's irritation, but the Captain still looked nauseated and sulked.

I liked nothing else of the drive round except the buying of a priest's umbrella for practical use. It only differs from an ordinary oiled Chinese one in that it has a five-foot-long handle and a pagoda-ish other end. These peculiarities make packing and even getting into a car more difficult, so it wasn't a popular buy. . . .

Next day

We had a dreadful dinner-party of ten white men and one Burman, the acting Prime Minister, complete in sarong, black buttoned boots, native black jacket, bright pink head-kerchief, white European shirt with gold collar-stud but no collar (*de rigueur*). My going into the pagoda was talked about with bated horror. It may apparently lose us Burma.[10]

CHAPTER NINE

Nature

But the road, West, the road! winding round a prodigious mountain, and surround-ed with others, all shagged with hanging woods, obscured with pines, or lost in clouds! Below, a torrent breaking through cliffs, and tumbling through fragments of rocks! Sheets of cascades forcing their silver speed down channelled precipices, and hasting into the roughened river at the bottom! Now and then an old foot-bridge, with a broken rail, a leaning cross, a cottage, or the ruin of an hermitage! This sounds too bombast and too romantic to one that has not seen it, too cold for one that has. If I could send you my letter post between two lovely tempests that echoed each other's wrath you might have some idea of this noble roaring scene, as you were reading it. Almost on the summit, upon a fine verdure, but without any prospect, stands the Chartreuse. We staid there two hours, rode back through this charming picture, wished for a painter, wished to be poets! Need I tell you we wished for you? Good night![1]

So wrote – I need hardly say – Horace Walpole to his friend Richard West, from Aix-les-Bains on 30 September 1739. It was only quite recently that people had come to appreciate the beauties of what was then known as 'the sublime'; but Walpole was, as always, in the forefront of fashion and he was doubtless to remember those Alpine splendours when he came to write *The Castle of Otranto* a quarter of a century later.

Mountains, as the most prodigious of all geographical phenomena, have inspired any amount of fine writing. Listen, for example, to Lafcadio Hearn, having just arrived at Yokohama on his first day in Japan:

I turn a moment to look back through the glorious light. Sea and sky mingle in the same beautiful pale clear blue. Below me the billowing of bluish roofs reaches to the verge of the unruffled bay on the right, and to the feet of the green wooded hills flanking the city on two sides. Beyond that semicircle of green hills rises a lofty range of serrated mountains, indigo silhouettes. And enormously high above the line of them towers an apparition indescribably lovely – one solitary snowy cone, so filmily exquisite, so spiritually white, that but for its immemorially familiar outline one would surely deem it a shape of cloud. Invisible its base remains, being the same delicious tint as the sky: only above the eternal snow-line its dreamy cone appears, seeming to hang, the ghost of a peak, between the luminous land and the luminous heaven – the sacred and matchless mountain, Fujiyama.[2]

And there is not only the view *of* mountains to be wondered at: there is also the view *from* them. Thus did Robert Byron describe, in *The Station*, what he saw from the summit of Mount Athos:

Reared a mile and a quarter off the globe, we might, had we wished, have put out a hand to pluck the sky, have palmed away a cup of blue. For that broad illimitable space was now reality, possessing an interesting and unsuspected texture. Its scope had shrunk. All around the horizon of land and sea had risen to three-quarters up the range of vision, and in so doing, assumed new character, as when a face, seen only in profile, is turned to the front. To the east, whence we had climbed, tiny contours uttered Lemnos and the Asia Minor coast: the plains of Troy, whence Tozer saw this platform of ours 'towering up from the horizon, like a vast spirit of the waters, when the rest of the peninsula is concealed below.' In the north, all the coastline of Thrace, Cavalla, and Dedeagatch wound away to the junction of the Dardanelles, with Turkey's remnant hovering in soft uncertainty. In the west, battling for definition athwart the cadent sun, the other two fingers of Chalcidice, Longos and Cassandra lay one above the other in the sea; and over them Olympus and the line of Greece. While, farther south, another transient shape proclaimed Eubœa and the satellite Sciathos, which means, in Greek, 'Shadow of Athos.' Thither, in the morning, the shadow stretches. Had it been the dawn we witnessed, instead of hazy sunset, we should also have seen, as all the Orthodox world knows, Constantinople, the great capital. We looked; but the flat dome of St. Sophia rose only in the mind. Christ saw the town, no doubt, the old Byzantium. For the Orthodox world knows, too, that it was here the devil led him.

Below the church, distance galloped down the gilded crags to peaks beneath, where tattered breaths of cloud hung forgotten to their spurs. Until, infinitely far, the tree-clad spine of the peninsula began, twisting its serpentine course up the vertical panorama; land meeting water with cape and cleft, a warm glow to each face; the monasteries clinging pale and diminutive to their sides. As the forty miles stretch out, only a shadow in the haze remains, outlined in the silver gleams of the farther sea; spreading then to a farther shadow – the mainland.[3]

Finally, there is the very process of climbing them. In *Pictures from Italy*, Charles Dickens tells of his intrepid ascent of Vesuvius:

At four o'clock in the afternoon, there is a terrible uproar in the little stable-yard of Signior Salvatore, the recognised head-guide, with the gold band round his cap; and thirty under-guides who are all scuffling and screaming at once, are preparing half-a-dozen saddled ponies, three litters, and some stout staves, for the journey. Every one of the thirty, quarrels with the other twenty-nine, and frightens the six ponies; and as much of the village as can possibly squeeze itself into the little stable-yard, participates in the tumult, and gets trodden on by the cattle.

After much violent skirmishing, and more noise than would suffice for the storming of Naples, the procession starts. The head-guide, who is liberally paid for all the attendants, rides a little in advance of the party; the other thirty guides proceed on foot. Eight go forward with the litters that are to be used by-and-by; and the remaining two-and-twenty beg.

We ascend, gradually, by stony lanes like rough broad flights of stairs, for some time. At length, we leave these, and the vineyards on either side of them, and emerge upon a bleak bare region where the lava lies confusedly, in enormous rusty masses: as if the earth had been ploughed up by burning thunderbolts. And now, we halt to see the sun set. The change that falls upon the dreary region, and on the whole mountain, as its red light fades, and the night comes on – and the unutterable solemnity and dreariness that reign around, who that has witnessed it, can ever forget!

It is dark, when after winding, for some time, over the broken ground, we arrive at the foot of the cone: which is extremely steep, and seems to rise, almost perpendicularly, from the spot where we dismount. The only light is reflected from the snow, deep, hard, and white, with which the cone is covered. It is now intensely cold, and the air is piercing. The thirty-one have brought no torches, knowing that the moon will rise before we reach the top. Two of the litters are devoted to the two ladies; the third, to a rather heavy gentleman from Naples, whose hospitality and good-nature have attached him to the expedition, and determined him to assist in doing the honours of the mountain. The rather heavy gentleman is carried by fifteen men; each of the ladies by half-a-dozen. We who walk, make the best use of our staves; and so the whole party begin to labour upward over the snow, – as if they were toiling to the summit of an antediluvian Twelfth-cake.

We are a long time toiling up; and the head-guide looks oddly about him when one of the company . . . suggests that, as it is freezing hard, and the usual footing of ashes is covered by the snow and ice, it will surely be difficult to descend. But the sight of the litters above, tilting up and down, and jerking from this side to that, as the bearers continually slip and tumble, diverts our attention; more especially as the whole length of the rather heavy gentleman is, at that moment, presented to us alarmingly foreshortened, with his head downwards.

The rising of the moon soon afterwards, revives the flagging spirits of the bearers. Stimulating each other with their usual watchword, 'Courage, friend! It is to eat maccaroni!' they press on, gallantly, for the summit.

From tingeing the top of the snow above us, with a band of light, and pouring it in a stream through the valley below, while we have been ascending in the dark, the moon soon lights the whole white mountain-side, and the broad sea down below, and tiny Naples in the distance, and every village in the country round. The whole prospect is in this lovely state, when we come upon the platform on the mountain-top – the region of Fire – an exhausted crater formed of great masses of gigantic cinders, like blocks of stone from some tremendous waterfall, burnt up; from every chink and crevice of which, hot, sulphurous smoke is pouring out: while, from another conical-shaped hill, the present crater, rising abruptly from this platform at the end, great sheets of fire are streaming forth: reddening the night with flame, blackening it with smoke, and spotting it with red-hot stones and cinders, that fly up into the air like feathers, and fall down like lead. What words can paint the gloom and grandeur of this scene!

The broken ground; the smoke; the sense of suffocation from the sulphur; the fear of falling down through the crevices in the yawning ground; the stopping, every now and then, for somebody who is missing in the dark (for the dense smoke now obscures the moon); the intolerable noise of the thirty; and the hoarse roaring of the mountain; make it a scene of such confusion, at the same time, that we reel again. But, dragging the ladies through it, and across another exhausted crater to the foot of the present Volcano, we approach close to it on the windy side, and then sit down among the hot ashes at its foot, and look up in silence: faintly estimating the action that is going on within, from its being full a hundred feet higher, at this minute, than it was six weeks ago.

There is something in the fire and roar, that generates an irresistible desire to get nearer to it. We cannot rest long, without starting off, two of us, on our hands and knees, accompanied by the head-guide, to climb to the brim of the flaming crater, and try to look in. Meanwhile, the thirty yell, as with one voice, that it is a dangerous proceeding, and call to us to come back; frightening the rest of the party out of their wits.

What with their noise, and what with the trembling of the thin crust of ground, that seems about to open underneath our feet and plunge us in the burning gulf below (which is the real danger, if there be any); and what with the flashing of the fire in our faces, and the shower of red-hot ashes that is raining down, and the choking smoke and sulphur; we may well feel giddy and irrational, like drunken men. But, we contrive to climb up to the brim, and look down, for a moment, into the Hell of boiling fire below. Then, we all three come rolling down; blackened, and singed, and scorched, and hot, and giddy: and each with his dress alight in half-a-dozen places.[4]

For a combination of the natural with human artifice, the most astonishing place I know in the world is Petra. Charles Johnston's first impression of it has already been quoted: here is Edward Lear, arriving for the first time (and entering from the north, instead of the east as is normal):

Two small boys tending some ten or twelve goats had been descried far on in the valley as we came down into it; but these brown-striped-vested youths did not await our arrival, and were no more seen. My tents were pitched low down on one of the terraces near the river, about half-way between the east and west cliffs. Taking with me Giorgio and the black Feragh (that jewel among swine) I wandered on eastward through the valley, of which the spaciousness seemed to me more impressive at each step, and the mighty accumulation of ruin more extraordinary. Wonderful is the effect of the east cliff as we approach it with its colours and carved architecture, the tint of the stone being brilliant and gay beyond my anticipation. 'Oh master,' said Giorgio (who is prone to culinary similes), 'we have come into a world where everything is made of chocolate, ham, curry powder, and salmon;' and the comparison was not far from an apt one. More wonderful yet is the open space, a portion of it cut out into the great theatre, from which you approach to the ravine of the Sik. Colour and detail are gorgeous and amazing beyond imagination. At length we reached the mouth of the Sik, the narrowing space between the loftier walls of rock becoming more overgrown with oleander and broom, and the ravine itself, into which you enter by a sharp turn on your right, seeming to close appallingly above your head. Not far from the entrance I turned round to see the effect of the far-famed Khasmé [sic] or rock-fane which is opposite this end of the ravine, a rose-coloured temple cut out in the side of the mountain, its lower part half hidden in scarlet blossom, and the whole fabric gleaming with intense splendour within the narrow cleft of the dark gorge, from four to seven hundred feet in height, and ten or twelve broad. I did not penetrate farther into the Sik, supposing I should have ample time in the several days I had arranged to spend at Petra, and wishing as soon as possible to obtain a general view of the valley. Retracing my steps I sat down at noon to draw, and did so uninterruptedly until it grew too dark to see the marks of my pencil or the colours I was using. First promising to call the anxious Feragh if I strayed out of sight of the tents, I worked on the whole view of the valley looking eastward to the great cliff, then in the bed of the stream among its flowering shrubs, then on one of the higher terraces where a mass of fallen columns lies in profuse confusion, not unlike the ruins of the Sicilian Selinunti [*sic*], and gathered scraps and coloured effects of the whole scene from various points. And lastly at sunset I turned to draw the downward stream running to the dark jaws of the western cliff, all awful in deep shadow which threw a ghastly horror over their tomb-crowded sides, above which rose the jagged summit of Mount Hor against the clear golden sky. As the sun went down, the great eastern cliff became one solid wall of fiery-red stone, rose-coloured piles of cloud resting on it and on the higher hills beyond like a new poem-world betwixt earth and heaven. Purple and darkling the shadows lengthened among the overthrown buildings and over the orange, red, and chocolate rocks of the foreground, over the deep green shrubs and on the livid ashiness of the white watercourse. Silent and ghostly-terrible rose darker and darker the western cliffs and the heights of Aaron's burial-place, till the dim pale lights fading away from the myriad crags around left this strange tomb-world to death-like quiet and the gray gloom of night. Slowly I went to my tent, happy that, even if I could carry little with me as a correct remembrance of this wonderful place, I had at least seen the valley and ruins of the rock-city of Edom.[5]

Rupert Brooke is nowadays remembered – when he is remembered at all – for his poetry; his single travel book, *Letters from America*, which was posthumously published in 1916 with a preface by Henry James, is almost forgotten. The letters are, for the most part, quite funny and light-hearted: A. C. Benson wrote in his diary that 'after all H.J.'s pontification, dim with incense-smoke, stately, mysterious, R.B.'s robust letters are almost a shock. It is as if one went up to receive a sacrament in a great, dark church, and were greeted by shouts of laughter and a shower of chocolate creams.' But there are occasional passages of beautiful writing, like this one:

It is that feeling of fresh loneliness that impresses itself before any detail of the wild. The soul – or the personality – seems to have indefinite room to expand. There is no one else within reach, there never has been anyone; no one else is *thinking* of the lakes and hills you see before you. They have no tradition, no names even; they are only pools of water and lumps of earth, some day, perhaps, to be clothed with loves and memories and the comings and goings of men, but now dumbly waiting their Wordsworth or their Acropolis to give them individuality, and a soul. In such country as this there is a rarefied clean sweetness. The air is unbreathed, and the earth untrodden. All things share this childlike loveliness, the grey whispering reeds, the pure blue of the sky, the birches and thin fir-trees that make up these forests, even the brisk touch of the clear water as you dive.

That last sensation, indeed, and none of sight or hearing, has impressed itself as the token of Canada, the land. Every swimmer knows it. It is not languorous, like bathing in a warm Southern sea; nor grateful, like a river in a hot climate; nor strange, as the ocean always is; nor startling, like very cold water. But it touches the body continually with freshness, and it seems to be charged with a subtle and unexhausted energy. It is colourless, faintly stinging, hard and grey, like the rocks around, full of vitality, and sweet. It has the tint and sensation of a pale dawn before the sun is up. Such is the wild of Canada. . . .

There are only the wrinkled, grey-blue lake, sliding ever sideways, and the grey rocks, and the cliffs and hills, covered with birch-trees, and the fresh wind among the birches, and quiet, and that unseizable virginity. Dawn is always a lost pearly glow in the ashen skies, and sunset a multitude of softly-tinted mists sliding before a remotely golden West. They follow one another with an infinite loneliness. And there is a far and solitary beach of dark, golden sand, close by a deserted Indian camp, where, if you drift quietly round the corner in a canoe, you may see a bear stumbling along, or a great caribou, or a little red deer coming down to the water to drink, treading the wild edge of lake and forest with a light, secret, and melancholy grace.[6]

We have already met the young Irish girl Catherine Wilmot in Chapter Five – waking up in Calais on her first morning 'abroad'. Two years later, in 1803, she visited Russia, where she stayed on the country estate of Troitskoe:

I told you I believe that Troitskoe was circumstanc'd like a sprig of Lily of the Valley, that is the white stucco'd House is shaded with a dark spreading Forest of seven miles breadth. Into this we regularly penetrate on our sledges drawn by three Horses abreast full speed surging us through the snow like a Boat breaking through the waves, and sending up a sparkling spray which makes us move in an atmosphere of Diamonds. The opening of the Forest is like the Charnel House of Nature! Every Tree rattles like a bleach'd Skeleton, moaning, hollow, gaunt, and menacing, till we lose the Apparition by bursting our way through towering Firs whose Pyramidical shafts swell into Columns of snow & flit in thousands of marble Pillars before our watry Eyes which, as the bitter effect of the atmosphere, gives perhaps an illusive medium to reality. The Underwood, feather'd like a Swansdown on the wirey branches, trembles under the weight of Snowy Tufts, so precisely resembling Guilda Roses that in their instance Winter outvies the Garlands of the brightest Summer. Nor is the gilding of the setting Sun less diversifying, for so surely as a horizontal beam strikes upon the snow it seems to awaken all the treasures of Golconda, and the ground blazes in Sapphires, Emeralds, Amethysts, Opals and Brilliants. The Solitude of this Forest, which in the Night is broken sometimes by the marauding of the Wolves, is seldom interrupted in *our* course, excepting by Wood cutters who look like Satyrs rather than human beings & whose endless Beards, clogg'd in snow and lengthen'd by icicles, crackle in responsive measure to their Hatchets' strokes. The appearance of the Ladies of the Castle however – like Magic – suspends all labour, and till the Traineau is out of sight a circle of these Shaggy Satyrs clothed in the skins of Beasts with Fur nightcaps in their paws assemble to shew their devotion & reverence by bowing repeatedly their *bear* heads to the ground. There is no possibility hardly of distinguishing the Women from the Men excepting for the Headdress. It differs in every Government, even in every village sometimes, and here it is precisely like a pair of budding Horns subdued by bandages which nevertheless are gaudily decorated with gold & spangles & a deep fringe of little beads upon their Pole in place of hair. *That* never is seen by human Eye after the Ceremony of Marriage takes place.[7]

Now for another piece of virtuoso description – this time of the river Rhône at Geneva. Only one man could have written it – John Ruskin: it comes from his last book, *Praeterita*.

For all other rivers there is a surface, and an underneath, and a vaguely displeasing idea of the bottom. But the Rhône flows like one lambent jewel; its surface is nowhere, its ethereal self is everywhere, the iridescent rush and translucent strength of it blue to the shore, and radiant to the depth. . . .

Waves of clear sea are, indeed, lovely to watch, but they are always coming or gone, never in any taken shape to be seen for a second. But here was one mighty wave that was always itself, and every fluted swirl of it, constant as the wreathing of a shell. No wasting away of the fallen foam, no pause for gathering of power, no helpless ebb of discouraged recoil; but alike through bright day and lulling night, the never-pausing plunge, and never-fading flash, and never-hushing whisper, and, while the sun was up, the ever-answering glow of unearthly aquamarine, ultramarine, violet-blue, gentian-blue, peacock blue, river-of-paradise blue, glass of a painted window melted in the sun, and the witch of the Alps flinging the spun tresses of it for ever from her snow.

The innocent way, too, in which the river used to stop to look into every little corner. Great torrents always seem angry, and great rivers too often sullen; but there is no anger, no disdain, in the Rhône. It seemed as if the mountain stream was in mere bliss at recovering itself again out of the lake-sleep, and raced because it rejoiced in racing, fain yet to return and stay. There were pieces of wave that danced all day as if Perdita were looking on to learn; there were little streams that skipped like lambs and leaped like chamois; there were pools that shook the sunshine all through them, and were rippled in layers of overlaid ripples, like crystal sand; there were currents that twisted the light into golden braids, and inlaid the threads with turquoise enamel; there were strips of stream that had certainly above the lake been millstreams, and were looking busily for mills to turn again; there were shoots of stream that had once shot fearfully into the air, and now sprang up again laughing that they had only fallen a foot or two; – and in the midst of all the gay glittering and eddied lingering, the noble bearing by of the midmost depth, so mighty, yet so terrorless and harmless, with its swallows skimming instead of petrels, and the dear old decrepit town as safe in the embracing sweep of it as if it were set in a brooch of sapphire.[8]

In May 1850, the twenty-nine-year-old Gustave Flaubert crossed the Egyptian desert on camel-back from Qena, just north of Luxor, to Quseir on the Red Sea. The journey took three days. Here is an extract from his travel notes:

Saturday, 18 May. We rise at dawn; drawn up on the beach are four slave-traders' boats. The slaves come ashore and walk in groups of fifteen to twenty, each led by two men. When I am on my camel, Hadji-Ismael runs up to give me a handshake. The man on the ground raising his arm to shake the hand of a man mounted on his camel, or to give him something, is one of the most beautiful gestures of the Orient; especially at the moment of departure there is something solemn and sad about it. The inhabitants of Kena are not yet up; the almehs, decked with golden piastres, are sweeping their doorways with palm branches and smoking their morning chibouk. The sun is dim, veiled by the *khamsin*. On the left, the cliff-like Arabian hills; ahead, the grayish desert; on the right, green plains. We follow the desert's edge, gradually leave the cultivated plain behind: it drops away to the right, and we plunge into the desert. . . .

The terrain is rolling and stony, the trail arid, we are in full desert, our camel-drivers sing, and their song ends with a half-whistling, half-guttural modulation meant to excite the dromedaries. Visible on the sand are several tracks that wind parallel: these are caravan trails – each track was made by a camel. Sometimes there are fifteen to twenty such tracks; the wider the trail, the more numerous they are. Here and there, about every two or three leagues (but irregularly spaced), large plaques of yellow sand that look as if they were varnished with *terre-de-Sienne* – colored laqueur; these are the places where the camels stop to piss. It is hot; on the right a *khamsin* dust-cloud is moving our way from the direction of the Nile (of which all that we can faintly see now is a few of the palms that line the bank). The dust-cloud grows and comes straight at us – it is like an immense vertical cloud that before enveloping us is already high above us for some time, while its base, to the right, is still distant. It is reddish brown and pale red; now we are in the midst of it. A caravan passes us coming the other way; the men, swathed in *kufiyehs* [head-cloths] (the women are thickly veiled) lean forward on the necks of their dromedaries; they pass very close to us, no one speaks; it is like a meeting of ghosts amid clouds. I feel something like terror and furious admiration creep along my spine; I laugh nervously; I must have been very pale, and my enjoyment of the moment was intense. As the caravan passed, it seemed to me that the camels were not touching the ground, that they were breasting ahead with a ship-like move-ment, that inside the dust-cloud they were raised high above the ground, as though they were wading belly-deep in clouds.

From time to time we meet other caravans. One first sees them as a long horizontal line on the horizon, barely distinguishable from the horizon itself; then that dark line rises above the other, and on it one begins to make out small dots; the small dots themselves rise up – they are the heads of camels walking abreast, swaying regularly along the entire line. Seen foreshortened, they look like the heads of ostriches.

The hot wind comes from the south; the sun looks like a tarnished silver plate;

a second dust-spout comes on us. This one advances like the smoke from a conflagration, suet-colored, with jet-black tones at the base: it comes ... and comes
... and the curtain is on us, bulging out in volutes below, with deep black fringes.
We are enveloped by it: the force of the wind is such that we have to clutch our
saddles to stay on. When the worst of the storm has passed, there comes a hail of
small pebbles carried by the wind: the camels turn their tails to it, stop, and lie
down. We resume our way.[9]

Mary Kingsley, when describing the scenery of West Africa, wrote a
good deal more light-heartedly; indeed, one has the feeling – probably
correctly – that nothing ever got her down:

There is an uniformity in the habits of West Coast rivers, from the Volta to the
Coanza, which is, when you get used to it, very taking. Excepting the Congo, the
really great river comes out to sea with as much mystery as possible; lounging lazily
along among its mangrove swamps in a what's-it-matter-when-one-comes-out and
where's-the-hurry style, through quantities of channels inter-communicating with
each other. Each channel, at first sight as like the other as peas in a pod, is bordered
on either side by green-black walls of mangroves, which Captain Lugard graphic-
ally described as seeming 'as if they had lost all count of the vegetable proprieties,
and were standing on stilts with their branches tucked up out of the wet, leaving
their gaunt roots exposed in mid-air'. High-tide or low-tide, there is little difference in the water; the river, be it broad or narrow, deep or shallow, looks like a
pathway of polished metal; for it is as heavy weighted with stinking mud as water
e'er can be, ebb or flow, year out and year in. But the difference in the banks,
though an unending alternation between two appearances, is weird.
  At high-water you do not see the mangroves displaying their ankles in the way
that shocked Captain Lugard. They look most respectable, their foliage rising
densely in a wall irregularly striped here and there by the white line of an aërial root,
coming straight down into the water from some upper branch as straight as a
plummet, in the strange, knowing way an aërial root of a mangrove does, keeping
the hard straight line until it gets some two feet above water-level, and then spreading out into blunt fingers with which to dip into the water and grasp the mud. Banks
indeed at high water can hardly be said to exist, the water stretching away into the
mangrove swamps for miles and miles, and you can then go, in a suitable small
canoe, away among these swamps as far as you please.
  This is a fascinating pursuit. For people who like that sort of thing it is just the
sort of thing they like, as the art critic of a provincial town wisely observed anent
an impressionist picture recently acquired for the municipal gallery. But it is a
pleasure to be indulged in with caution; for one thing, you are certain to come
across crocodiles. Now a crocodile drifting down in deep water, or lying asleep
with its jaws open on a sand-bank in the sun, is a picturesque adornment to the
landscape when you are on the deck of a steamer, and you can write home about
it and frighten your relations on your behalf; but when you are away among the
swamps in a small dug-out canoe, and that crocodile and his relations are awake –
a thing he makes a point of being at flood tide because of fish coming along – and
when he has got his foot upon his native heath – that is to say, his tail within holding

reach of his native mud – he is highly interesting, and you may not be able to write home about him.[10]

I have left till last an extraordinary passage by Mildred Cable – a missionary who, with her two friends Eva and Francesca French, crossed the Gobi Desert five times between 1926 and 1938 – the first Western women ever to do so and the first Christians since the sixth century. Her book, *The Gobi Desert* – written with Francesca – was first published in 1943. Apart from a short epilogue, this is how it ends – on a wonderful note of stillness and peace:

I sat for long hours in my sand-chair by the Crescent Lake [near Chuguchak (T'ach'ang) on Chinese–Soviet border] and reflected on the teaching of those desert experiences, the illusive mirage, the tormenting bitter water, the sweet water of the *karez* channel and the invigorating water of the living spring. Then slowly the lovely lake at my feet recaptured my attention, seeming to say, 'Now consider what lies before your eyes.' So I dismissed all thought of desert rigours and yielded myself to the charm of the moment.

The whole scene, from the brilliant glazed-tiled roofs, the light loggia, the golden sand, the silver trees, the fringe of green sedge, and the delicate hues of wheeling pigeons, was reflected in the still water as sharply as in a mirror. An acolyte came to the water's edge, stooped, filled a bucket with lake water and turned back toward the temple. The scene had an unreal quality which held me motionless as though a movement on my part might shatter the spell and disperse its beauty like a dream. Overhead the great dunes towered threateningly. 'Why,' I asked, 'why was this lake not long since buried by these encroaching sands? Why does its fragile beauty last when the whole configuration of the landscape is changed by obliterating sandstorms? Towns and villages have vanished in a wilderness of death and desiccation, yet this lake remains and no one has ever seen its water margin low. What is the secret of its permanence and of the unseen source from which it draws such plentiful supplies that drought has no effect on it?'

At that moment I saw one of my comrades walking over the crest of the hill, ploughing a deep furrow in the sands as she went. From the summit she slid down the face of the dune, and as she did so I heard the sands sing, then she walked to the guest-house and passed through the door, leaving the whole line of her path, from the top of the hill to the lip of the lake, profoundly disturbed. The sands which, before, had not shown one wrinkle were now furrowed with deep ridges, but, as I watched, I saw their surface slowly but surely smoothed out again till, gradually, every mark was obliterated. The ceaseless winds of God were at work and, as always, they blew off the lake and upward toward the crest of the hill. By some mystery of orientation the lake was so placed that every breath which stirred the encircling sand-mounds blew upward and lifted the drift away from the water. I picked up a handful of sand and threw it downward, but the breeze caught it and blew it back in my face. This, then, was the secret of this exquisite lake's permanence – its exposure to the upward-wafting winds of God, and its deep unfailing source of supply.

'Do you understand this picture of one who has attained what you seek and reached the goal of your desire?' something within me said. 'In the midst of threatening danger this lake lifts its face heavenward, reflecting as in a mirror the glory of the sky. It is not withdrawn from the terrible sand which constantly threatens to engulf it, its position is always perilous and it lives dangerously, but every time the sand threatens, the winds of God are there to protect it, and no harm touches it. This is why its peace, its purity and its serenity can never be destroyed. Surely the parable is clear – it is the pure in heart who see God.'

The sight of a red-robed lama walking in my direction called me back to the immediate, and I rose, greeting him, then sat down and talked with him, first of his long pilgrimage and later of the search for God which urged him to such an arduous undertaking. Walking back together toward the guest-house we met the guardian of the temple, who appeared strangely agitated. 'Look,' he said, 'did you ever see anything like that?' He pointed to a curious triple halo in the sky. The three rims of light spread a diffused radiance, and we all stood and watched the strange atmospheric effect. 'This is a terrible omen,' said the priest, 'a sign of awful happenings, and of trouble coming such as the world has never known. Alas, alas for this world!' Too profoundly disturbed to say more, the old man turned off to the temple shrine to burn incense and seek to pacify the anger of the gods.

Next morning the lama, carrying his little bundle, passed on his way toward Tibet. With my companions I walked once more round the lovely lake, gazing till every detail of its beauty was impressed on my memory. Then we said goodbye to the priest, walked to the foot of the great sand-hills, stood there for a moment and gave one last backward look, then waved a long farewell to the lovely lake, and rode away.[11]

CHAPTER TEN

Towns, Islands and Other Places

Let us begin with one of the earliest of true travel writers – Fynes Moryson, Gent., who left England in 1591 at the age of twenty-five and spent the better part of the next six years wandering through Europe and the Near East. His *Itinerary* was published in 1617; here he is in Jerusalem – at that time part of the Turkish Empire:

All the Citizens are either Tailors, Shoomakers, Cookes, or Smiths (which Smiths make their keyes and lockes not of Iron, but of wood), and in generall poore rascall people, mingled of the scumme of divers Nations, partly Arabians, partly Moores, partly the basest inhabitants of neighbour Countries, by which kind of people all the adjoyning Territorie is likewise inhabited. The Jewes in Turky are distinguished from others by red hats, and being practicall, doe live for the most part upon the sea-coasts, and few or none of them come to this Citie, inhabited by Christians that hate them, and which should have no traffique, if the Christian Monasteries were taken away. Finally, the Inhabitants of Jerusalem at this day are as wicked as they were when they crucified our Lord, gladly taking all occasions to use Christians despitefully. They esteemed us Princes, because wee wore gloves, and brought with us shirts, and like necessaries, though otherwise we were most poorely appareled, yet when we went to see the monuments, they sent out their boyes to scorne us, who leaped upon our backes from the higher parts of the streete, we passing in the lower part, and snatched from us our hats and other things, while their fathers were no lesse ready to doe us all injuries, which we were forced to beare silently and with incredible patience. Hence it was that Robert Duke of Normandy, being sicke, and carried into Jerusalem upon the backs of like rascalls, when he met by the way a friend, who then was returning into Europe, desiring to know what hee would command him to his friends, hee earnestly intreated him to tell them, that he saw Duke Robert caried into heaven upon the backs of Divels.[1]

Some time later, having sailed up the Dalmatian Coast, Moryson found himself in Rovingo, now the Yugoslav town of Rovinj:

I did not a little wonder, when I observed each second or third person of this City to halt and be lame of one foot, which made me remember the Citizens of Islebe in Germany, and in the Province of Saxony, where almost all the men have wry neckes; whereof I knew the cause, namely because they used daily to dig in mines, with their neckes leaning on one side: but of this common lamenes of the Inhabitants in Rovingo, I could not learne any probable cause, except it were the foule disease of lust, raigning in those parts, which I rather thought likely, because the lamenesse was common to weomen as men.[2]

Fynes Moryson's example was followed a few years later by Thomas Coryat, a curious combination of scholar and buffoon who, according to Thomas Fuller, 'carried folly (which the charitable called merriment) in his very face. The shape of his head had no promising form, being like a sugarloaf inverted, with the little end before, as composed of fancy and memory, without any common-sense.' After a few years as hanger-on at the court of James I, Coryat left England in May 1608; he returned a little less than five months later, having travelled – mostly on foot – nearly 2000 miles to Venice and back, and having visited forty-five cities on his way. Four years later he was off again, travelling first to Constantinople and thence to Greece, Asia Minor, Egypt, Palestine, the Lebanon, Mesopotamia, Persia, and finally to India – where he arrived in October 1616 at Agra and where, at the age of forty, he died in the following year. In this passage he describes the baths of 'Hinderhove' at Baden-Baden:

Most of the private bathes are but little, but very delicate and pleasant places, being divided asunder by certaine convenient partitions wherein are contrived divers windowes, to the end that those in the bathes may have recourse to each other, and mutually drinke together. For they reach out their drinking glasses one to another through the windowes. The roomes over head are lodgings for the strangers. Here I have observed the people in the bathes feede together upon a table that hath swimmed upon the superficies of the water. Also I have noted another strange thing amongst them that I have not a little wondred at. Men and women bathing themselves together naked from the middle upward in one bathe: whereof some of the women were wives (as I was told) and the men partly bachelers, and partly married men, but not the husbands of the same women. Yet their husbands have bene at that time at Hinderhove, and some of them in the very place standing hard by the bathe in their cloathes, and beholding their wives not onely talking and familiarly discoursing with other men, but also sporting after a very pleasant and merry manner. Yea sometimes they sing merily together but especially that sweet & most amorous song of solus cum solâ; I meane another mans wife, & another man naked upward (as I have aforesaid) in one bath. Yet all this while the husband may not be jelous though he be at the bathes, and seeth too much occasion of many women. ... And so finally I end this discourse of the Helveticall bathes of Hinderhove with that elegant Elogium of Poggius the Florentine in praise of the same, even that it is a second Paradise, the seate of the Graces, the bosome of Love, and the Theater of pleasure.[3]

There is no indication that Coryat, on his wanderings through Asia Minor, ever found himself at what I have always thought to be one of the

loveliest classical sites anywhere, the ancient Greek city of Priene. But
Freya Stark did, and these are the thoughts that it inspired in her:

What remains of Priene lies high up in the sun. The entry to the theatre is so
unobtrusive that one scarcely notices it. Without preparation, it is there. One steps
suddenly between the seats and the proscenium, into the orchestra, a small grassy
space light with daisies, enclosed in a semicircle where six stone arm-chairs for the
most important people are evenly spaced with an altar among them. The seats
behind rise in their tiers; the narrow shallow steps of gangways cut them at intervals; and I felt that I was interrupting – that actors and audience, like a flight of shy
birds, had fled in the very instant of my stepping across their threshold with my feet
still shod in Time. I lingered in the little theatre as if I were a person in the legend,
who is given one glimpse of a world which appears to last for seconds only, though
all the expanses of time are packed there.

The whole city was built in the flower of the Hellenistic age, and to that its rich
austerity belonged.

What was the secret? *Respect* perhaps, so closely tied to love? Respect for what
gives itself, and is therefore vulnerable, whether it be a human being or a piece of
stone? A gratitude that inspires fastidiousness, a longing to keep intact in its own
dignity the object or the being that has helped one to create and to become?

That so subtle a scruple can transmute itself into stone and stay there, is magic;
and no conscious effort of the craftsman, nothing but the feeling itself, can leave
that mark. Where it exists, it is definite, and every true artist will recognize it across
any bridge of time. Without it there is neither sincerity nor greatness. It is a sharing
partnership, both giving and taking – a marriage in terms of human life – a tender
thankfulness for a benefit received and a forgetfulness of self in the interest of
another; and it reaches through the depths of being to that which Heraclitus
thought of as Fire and we think of as Love.[4]

A very different place, and a good deal less salubrious, is Algiers. I have
long treasured Evelyn Waugh's account, in his early travel book *Labels*, of
what happened to his fellow-passengers on his Mediterranean cruise ship
when they disembarked to see the town:

There was very little begging or street hawking except the inevitable swarm of boot-
cleaners, and no native dragomans. Except on the harbour front one could walk
about unmolested; there, however, one had to run the gauntlet of a great number
of guides – nasty, jaunty young men for the most part, dressed in European suits
and straw hats, bow ties, and Charlie Chaplin moustaches; they spoke French and
some English, and were, I imagine, of vaguely European extraction. Their particular trade was organizing parties to see native dances – *fêtes Mauresques* – and
an intolerable nuisance they were over it. Many of the passengers from the *Stella*
went off with them and came back with very different reports of the entertainment.
Some appeared to have seen decorous and perfectly genuine performances in the
courtyards of one or other of the medieval Moorish houses; they described a native
band with drums and wind instruments and a troupe of veiled dancing girls who
went through the figures of various traditional tribal dances; they said it was a little

monotonous, but they seemed quite satisfied with their evening. Another party, including two Englishwomen, were led to the top floor of a house of ill-fame, where they were sat round the walls of a tiny room. Here they waited for some time in the light of a small oil lamp, becoming more and more uneasy, until the curtains of the door were suddenly thrust aside and a very large, elderly Jewess pranced in among them, quite naked except for a little cheap jewellery, and proceeded to perform a *danse de ventre* on the few yards of the floor that separated them. The verdict of one of the Englishwomen on this experience was: 'Well, I am quite glad in a way to have seen it, but I should certainly never wish to go again.' Her companion refused to discuss the subject at all, from any angle, with anyone, and for the rest of the voyage entirely avoided the company of the gentlemen who had escorted her that evening.

But there was one party who had a still sadder time of it. They were five Scots people in early middle age, three women and two men, inter-related in some way that I never had occasion to define. These were caught by a very shady guide who took them up to the Kasbar in a taxi-cab. He charged them 200 francs for this drive, which they politely paid without question. He then took them to a house in a blind alley, knocked on the door three times, and excited their uneasiness by saying, 'This is very dangerous. You are safe as long as you are with me, but on no account get separated or I cannot answer for the consequences.' They were admitted one at a time and charged a 100 francs each. The door was shut behind them and they were led down to a cellar. The guide explained to them that they must order coffee, which they did at the cost of 20 francs a head. Before they had tasted it a revolver shot sounded just outside the door.

'Run for your lives,' said the guide.

They scampered out and found their taxi, which, by apparent good fortune, was waiting for them.

'No doubt the ladies are feeling unsettled by their experience. Would they like a little cognac?'

He then directed the car, which cost another 200 francs, to one of the ordinary cafés of the town and gave them each a tot of *eau-de-vie*. He settled the bill for them and explained that it had come to 25 francs a head and 10 francs for the tip.

'That is the advantage of coming with me,' he explained. 'I do the tips for you and you are not put upon. There are many cheats in this town who would take advantage of your inexperience if you were alone.'

He then saw them back to the ship, reminding them discreetly that the fees for his evening's services were 100 francs or whatever they liked to make it. They were still so bewildered and agitated that they gave him a hundred and fifty, thanking him very much and congratulating themselves on the narrow escape they had had. Only later, talking it over among themselves, did the suspicion arise that perhaps the charges had been unduly heavy, and that the house from which they had made their escape might, in fact, be the guide's own home, and that his wife or small son or a kindly neighbour had fired the pistol for them.

I think it did them great credit that they did not conceal this dismal story, but told it to everyone on board, half resentfully but half humorously.

'I'd like to go back and have a few words with that merchant,' remarked the men of the party, but, alas, by that time we had left Algiers.[5]

I like, too, Peter Fleming's comment (in *One's Company*) on Harbin, in Manchuria:

Harbin has been called the Paris of the Far East, but not, I think, by anyone who has stayed there for any length of time.[6]

Harbin may not indeed be up to much; but it is almost certainly a considerable improvement on Turfan in Sinkiang, of which Mildred Cable – the missionary whom we met in the last chapter – has this to say:

During the long summer Turfan is undoubtedly one of the hottest places on the face of the earth, and the thermometer registers around 130° Fahr. in the shade, but it is not hot all the year round and in winter the temperature falls to zero Fahr. The heat is accounted for by its geographical location, which is in a depression watered by no river of any size, and lying below sea-level. Between May and August the inhabitants retire underground, for the mud or brick houses, even though they have deep verandahs and spacious airy rooms, are intolerable by day. In each courtyard there is an opening which leads by a flight of steps to a deep dug-out or under-ground apartment. Here are comfortable rooms and a *kang* spread with cool-surfaced reed matting and grass-woven pillows which help the people to endure the breathless stagnation of the midday hours; they eat and sleep underground and only emerge at sunset. The shops, which have been closed during the hot hours, are opened by lamplight, and all necessary business is done then, but people avoid the living and sleeping rooms of their houses because they are infested with vermin. There are large and virulent scorpions which creep under sleeping-mats, drop on to the unconscious sleeper from the beams or hide themselves in his shoes. One jumping spider with long legs and a hairy body as large as a pigeon's egg leaps on its prey and makes a crunching noise with its jaws. Another burrows holes in the ground, and its bite is as painful as that of a scorpion. Turfan cockroaches are over two inches in length, with long feelers and red eyes which make them a repulsive sight. All these creatures know how to conceal themselves in sleeping-bags and rolls of clothing, so that man is handicapped in dealing with them. Apart from these virulent monsters, the inns provide every variety of smaller vermin such as lice, bugs and fleas, and each is of an order well able to withstand all the patent nostrums guaranteed to destroy them. On account of these pests the people of Turfan sleep on wooden beds in the courtyards, but the constant watering of the ground results in swarms of mosquitoes, which torment the sleeper almost beyond endurance. The underground conditions of life are not healthy, and the sudden chill of a dug-out striking on a perspiring body results in all kinds of rheumatic troubles; more-over, the cellars are badly ventilated and one phthisical or leprous patient may infect the whole family with the disease.[7]

After that, it is something of a relief to return to Western Europe. There is a charming book by Henry James, recently reissued, but first published in 1884 as *A Little Tour in France*. This is what he writes about the city of Tours:

I am ashamed to begin with saying that Touraine is the garden of France; that remark has long ago lost its bloom. The town of Tours, however, has something sweet and bright, which suggests that it is surrounded by a land of fruits. It is a very agreeable little city; few towns of its size are more ripe, more complete, or, I should suppose, in better humour with themselves and less disposed to envy the responsibilities of bigger places. It is truly the capital of its smiling province; a region of easy abundance, of good living, of genial, comfortable, optimistic, rather indolent opinions. Balzac says in one of his tales that the real Tourangeau will not make an effort, or displace himself even, to go in search of a pleasure; and it is not difficult to understand the sources of this amiable cynicism. He must have a vague conviction that he can only lose by almost any change. Fortune has been kind to him: he lives in a temperate, reasonable, sociable climate, on the banks of a river which, it is true, sometimes floods the country around it, but of which the ravages appear to be so easily repaired that its aggressions may perhaps be regarded (in a region where so many good things are certain) merely as an occasion for healthy suspense. He is surrounded by fine old traditions, religious, social, architectural, culinary; and he may have the satisfaction of feeling that he is French to the core. No part of his admirable country is more characteristically national. Normandy is Normandy, Burgundy is Burgundy, Provence is Provence; but Touraine is essentially France. It is the land of Rabelais, of Descartes, of Balzac, of good books and good company, as well as good dinners and good houses. George Sand has somewhere a charming passage about the mildness, the convenient quality, of the physical conditions of central France – 'son climat souple et chaud, ses pluies abondantes et courtes'. In the autumn of 1882 the rains perhaps were less short than abundant; but when the days were fine it was impossible that anything in the way of weather could be more charming. The vineyards and orchards looked rich in the fresh, gay light; cultivation was everywhere, but everywhere it seemed to be easy. There was no visible poverty; thrift and success presented themselves as matters of good taste. The white caps of the women glittered in the sunshine, and their well-made sabots clicked cheerfully on the hard, clean roads. Touraine is a land of old châteaux, – a gallery of architectural specimens and of large hereditary properties. The peasantry have less of the luxury of ownership than in most other parts of France, though they have enough of it to give them quite their share of that shrewdly conservative look which, in the little chaffering *place* of the market-town, the stranger observes so often in the wrinkled brown masks that surmount the agricultural blouse. This is, moreover, the heart of the old French monarchy; and as that monarchy was splendid and picturesque, a reflection of the splendour still glitters in the current of the Loire. Some of the most striking events of French history have occurred on the banks of that river, and the soil it waters bloomed for a while with the flowering of the Renaissance. The Loire gives a great 'style' to a landscape of which the features are not, as the phrase is, prominent, and carries the eye to distances even more poetic than the green horizons of Touraine. It is a very fitful stream, and is sometimes observed to run thin and expose all the crudities of its channel – a great defect certainly in a river which is so much depended upon to give an air to the places it waters. But I speak of it as I saw it last; full, tranquil, powerful, bending in large slow curves and sending back half the light of the sky. Nothing can be finer than the view of its course which you get from the battlements and terraces of Amboise. As I looked down on it from the elevation one lovely Sunday morning, through a mild glitter of autumn sunshine, it seemed the very model of a generous, beneficent stream. The most charming part of Tours is naturally the shaded quay that overlooks it, and looks across too at the friendly faubourg of Saint Symphorien and at the terraced heights which rise above this. Indeed, throughout Touraine it is half the charm of the Loire that you can travel beside it. The great dyke which protects it, or protects the country from it, from Blois to Angers, is an admirable road; and on the other side as well the highway constantly keeps it company. A wide river, as you follow a wide road, is excellent company; it brightens and shortens the way.

The inns at Tours are in another quarter, and one of them, which is midway between the town and the station, is very good. It is worth mentioning for the fact that everyone belonging to it is extraordinarily polite – so unnaturally polite as at first to excite your suspicion that the hotel has some hidden vice, so that the waiters and chambermaids are trying to pacify you in advance. There was one waiter in especial who was the most accomplished social being I have ever encountered; from morning till night he kept up an inarticulate murmur of urbanity, like the hum of a spinning-top. I may add that I discovered no dark secrets at the Hôtel de l'Univers; for it is not a secret to any traveller today that the obligation to partake of a lukewarm dinner in an overheated room is as imperative as it is detestable.[8]

And so to Venice. Here, of course, the choice is impossible. How much easier it would be to compile a complete anthology of Venice alone – something that I have every intention of doing one of these days. Inevitably, the city has made occasional appearances in previous chapters, just as it will make a few more in later ones; here, however, I will confine myself to just one short passage. It is by Mary McCarthy, and comes from a book that is almost as dazzling as the place itself, *Venice Observed*:

But why should it be beautiful at all? Why should Venice, aside from its situation, be a place of enchantment? One appears to be confronted with a paradox. A commercial people who lived solely for gain – how could they create a city of fantasy, lovely as a dream or a fairy tale? This is the central puzzle of Venice, the stumbling-block that one keeps coming up against if one tries to *think* about her history, to put the facts of her history together with the visual fact that is there before one's eyes. It cannot be that Venice is a happy accident or a trick of light. I have thought about this a long time, but now it occurs to me that, as with most puzzles, the clue to the answer lies in the way the question is framed. 'Lovely as a dream or a fairy tale . . .' There is no contradiction, once you stop to think what images of beauty arise from fairy tales. They are images of money. Gold, caskets of gold, caskets of silver, the miller's daughter spinning gold all night long, thanks to Rumpelstiltskin, the cave of Ali Baba stored with stolen gold and silver, the underground garden in which Aladdin found jewels growing on trees, so that he could gather them in his hands, rubies and diamonds and emeralds, the Queen's lovely daughter whose hair is black as ebony and lips are red as rubies, treasure buried in the forest, treasure guarded by dogs with eyes as big as carbuncles, treasure guarded by a Beast – this is the spirit of the enchantment under which Venice lies, pearly and roseate, like the Sleeping Beauty, changeless throughout the centuries, arrested, while the concrete forest of the modern world grows up around her.

A wholly materialist city is nothing but a dream incarnate. Venice is the world's unconscious: a miser's glittering hoard, guarded by a Beast whose eyes are made of white agate, and by a saint who is really a prince who has just slain a dragon.[9]

Still, there is a limit to self-denial; even if I am to have no more pieces on the city, I don't see why I should altogether ignore its neighbouring island, Torcello. Here, then, is Ruskin once again, with another famous passage from *The Stones of Venice*:

Seven miles to the north of Venice, the banks of sand, which near the city rise little above low-water mark, attain by degrees a higher level, and knit themselves at last into fields of salt morass, raised here and there into shapeless mounds, and intercepted by narrow creeks of sea. One of the feeblest of these inlets, after winding for some time among buried fragments of masonry, and knots of sunburnt weeds whitened with webs of fucus, stays itself in an utterly stagnant pool beside a plot of greener grass covered with ground ivy and violets. On this mound is built a rude brick campanile, of the commonest Lombardic type, which if we ascend towards evening (and there are none to hinder us, the door of its ruinous staircase swinging idly on its hinges), we may command from it one of the most notable scenes in this wide world of ours. Far as the eye can reach, a waste of wild sea moor, of a lurid ashen grey; not like our northern moors with their jet-black pools and purple heath, but lifeless, the colour of sackcloth, with the corrupted sea-water soaking through the roots of its acrid weeds, and gleaming hither and thither through its snaky channels. No gathering of fantastic mists, nor coursing of clouds across it; but melancholy clearness of space in the warm sunset, oppressive, reaching to the horizon of its level gloom. To the very horizon, on the north-east; but, to the north and west, there is a blue line of higher land along the border of it, and above this, but farther back, a misty band of mountains, touched with snow. To the east, the paleness and roar of the Adriatic, louder at momentary intervals as the surf breaks on the bars of sand; to the south, the widening branches of the calm lagoon, alternately purple and pale green, as they reflect the evening clouds or twilight sky; and almost beneath our feet, on the same field which sustains the tower we gaze from, a group of four buildings, two of them little larger than cottages (though built of stone, and one adorned by a quaint belfry), the third an octagonal chapel, of which we can see but little more than the flat red roof with its rayed tiling, the fourth, a considerable church with nave and aisles, but of which, in like manner, we can see little but the long central ridge and lateral slopes of roof, which the sunlight separates in one glowing mass from the green field beneath and grey moor beyond. There are no living creatures near the buildings, nor any vestige of village or city round about them. They lie like a little company of ships becalmed on a far-away sea.

Then look farther to the south. Beyond the widening branches of the lagoon, and rising out of the bright lake into which they gather, there are a multitude of towers, dark, and scattered among square-set shapes of clustered palaces, a long and irregular line fretting the southern sky.

Mother and daughter, you behold them both in their widowhood, – TORCELLO, and VENICE.

Let us go down into that little space of meadow land. The inlet which runs nearest to the base of the campanile is not that by which Torcello is commonly approached. Another, somewhat broader, and overhung by alder copse, winds out of the main channel of the lagoon up to the very edge of the little meadow which was once the Piazza of the city, and there, stayed by a few grey stones which present some semblance of a quay, forms its boundary at one extremity. Hardly larger than an ordinary English farmyard, and roughly enclosed on each side by broken palings and hedges of honeysuckle and briar, the narrow field retires from the water's edge, traversed by a scarcely traceable footpath, for some forty or fifty paces, and then expanding into the form of a small square, with buildings on three sides of it, the fourth being that which opens to the water. Two of these, that on our left and that in front of us as we approach from the canal, are so small that they might well be taken for the outhouses of the farm, though the first is a conventual building, and the other aspires to the title of the 'Palazzo publico,' both dating as far back as the beginning of the fourteenth century; the third, the octagonal church of Santa Fosca, is far more ancient than either, yet hardly on a larger scale. Though the pillars of the portico which surrounds it are of pure Greek marble, and their capitals are enriched with delicate sculpture, they, and the arches they sustain, together only raise the roof to the height of a cattle-shed; and the first strong impression which the spectator receives from the whole scene is, that whatever sin it may have been which has on this spot been visited with so utter a desolation, it could not at least have been ambition. Nor will this impression be diminished as we approach, or enter, the larger church, to which the whole group of building is subordinate. It has evidently been built by men in flight and distress, who sought in the hurried erection of their island church such a shelter for their earnest and sorrowful worship as, on the one hand, could not attract the eyes of their enemies by its splendour, and yet, on the other, might not awaken too bitter feelings by its contrast with the churches which they had seen destroyed. The exterior is absolutely devoid of decoration, with the exception only of the western entrance and the lateral door, of which the former has carved side posts and architrave, and the latter, crosses of rich sculpture; while the massy stone shutters of the windows, turning on huge rings of stone, which answer the double purpose of stanchions and brackets, cause the whole building rather to resemble a refuge from Alpine storm than the cathedral of a populous city; and, internally, the two solemn mosaics of the eastern and western extremities, – one representing the Last Judgment, the other the Madonna, her tears falling as her hands are raised to bless, – and the noble range of pillars which enclose the space between, terminated by the high throne for the pastor and the semicircular raised seats for the superior clergy, are expressive at once of the deep sorrow and the sacred courage of men who had no home left them upon earth, but who looked for one to come, of men 'persecuted but not forsaken, cast down but not destroyed.'[10]

And, talking of islands, what of the Isles of Greece? I shall not quote burning Sappho, or even Byron himself, finding as I do *Don Juan* and *Childe Harold* equally unreadable; but it still seems hard to resist including two quick sketches by Lawrence Durrell, in *Reflections on a Marine Venus*, of Kalymnos and Cos respectively:

In Kalymnos the infant's paint-box has been at work again on the milky slopes of the mountain. Carefully, laboriously it has squared in a churchyard, a monastery, and lower down repeated the motif: a church, a monastery, a town; then, simply for the sake of appropriateness, a harbour with a shelf of bright craft at anchor, and the most brilliant, the most devastatingly brilliant houses. Never has one seen anything like it – the harbour revolving slowly round one as one comes in. Plane after stiff cubistic plane of pure colour. The mind runs up and down the web of vocabulary looking for a word which will do justice to it. In vain. Under the church the half-finished caieques stand upon a slip – huge coops of raw wood looking for all the world like the skeletons of dismembered whales.

Three little girls in crimson dresses stand arm in arm and watch us. The harbour liquefies under the keel as we throttle down and move towards the port, our engines now puffy and subdued, yet quickened like our heartbeats as we sit and watch the island. The echo of our passage – the hard *plam-plam-plam* of the exhaust – bounces gravely off the rusted iron hull of a steamer which lies on its side in the shallows, its funnels sticking up like nostrils, but all the rest of it submerged in water as clear as the purest white gin. This is Kalymnos. High up, under the walls of the Church of the Golden Hand a woman is singing, slowly, emphatically, while from the wharves across the way a man in a blue overall is hammering at a coffin. Uncanny isolation of sound and object, each dissimilar, each entire to itself. Detached from the temporal frame. A song and a hammering which exist together but never mix or muddle the hard outlines of each other.

Cos is the spoiled child of the group. You know it at once, without even going ashore. It is green, luxuriant and a little dishevelled. An island that does not bother to comb its hair. Hard by the port the famous tree of Hippocrates (to which Mills has promised himself a sentimental pilgrimage) stands, in a little arbour of greenery, like some Nubian woman stricken with elephantiasis. Whole trees have burst out of it in all directions, and with no reference whatsoever to gravity or proportion. The kindly worshippers have propped, here an arm, there a thigh, with votive pillars of bricks or stone. Somehow the whole improbable structure still stands – indeed its luxuriant foliage covers a whole courtyard like a tent. The children play wonderful games among the branches. 'A stranger,' they cry, 'a stranger.' I must be the first foreign civilian they have seen for some time. We exchange oranges against sweets and discuss life in Cos.[11]

There is a lovely description of Poros, too, by Henry Miller in *The Colossus of Maroussi*:

I don't know which affected me more deeply – the story of the lemon groves just opposite us or the sight of Poros itself when suddenly I realized that we were sailing through the streets. If there is one dream which I like above all others it is that of sailing on land. Coming into Poros gives the illusion of the deep dream. Suddenly the land converges on all sides and the boat is squeezed into a narrow strait from which there seems to be no egress. The men and women of Poros are hanging out of the windows, just above your head. You pull in right under their friendly nostrils, as though for a shave and haircut en route. The loungers on the quay are walking with the same speed as the boat; they can walk faster than the boat if they choose to quicken their pace. The island revolves in cubistic planes, one of walls and windows, one of rocks and goats, one of stiff-blown trees and shrubs, and so on. Yonder, where the mainland curves like a whip, lie the wild lemon groves and there in the Spring young and old go mad from the fragrance of sap and blossom. You enter the harbour of Poros swaying and swirling, a gentle idiot tossed about amidst masts and nets in a world which only the painter knows and which he has made live again because, like you, when he first saw this world, he was drunk and happy and care-free. To sail slowly through the streets of Poros is to recapture the joy of passing through the neck of the womb. It is a joy too deep almost to be remembered. It is a kind of numb idiot's delight which produces legends such as that of the birth of an island out of a foundering ship. The ship, the passage, the revolving walls, the gentle undulating tremor under the belly of the boat, the dazzling light, the green snake-like curve of the shore, the beards hanging down over your scalp from the inhabitants suspended above you, all these and the pal-pitant breath of friendship, sympathy, guidance, envelop and entrance you until you are blown out like a star fulfilled and your heart with its molten smithereens is scattered far and wide.[12]

A little further east still brings us to Smyrna – the modern Izmir. Mark Twain was there in the 1860s, and in *The Innocents Abroad* he calls our attention to a strange enigma:

The ascent of the hill of the citadel is very steep, and we proceeded rather slowly. But there were matters of interest about us. In one place, five hundred feet above the sea, the perpendicular bank on the upper side of the road was ten or fifteen feet high, and the cut exposed three veins of oyster shells, just as we have seen quartz veins exposed in the cutting of a road in Nevada or Montana. The veins were about eighteen inches thick and two or three feet apart, and they slanted along downward for a distance of thirty feet or more and then disappeared where the cut joined the road. Heaven only knows how far a man might trace them by 'stripping'. They were clean, nice oyster shells, large, and just like any other oyster shells. They were thickly massed together, and none were scattered above or below the veins. Each one was a welldefined lead by itself, and without a spur. My first instinct was to set up the usual

NOTICE:
We, the undersigned, claim five claims of two hundred feet each (and one for discovery) on this ledge or lode of oyster shells, with all its dips, spurs, angles, variations, and sinuosities, and fifty feet on each side of the same, to work it, etc., etc., according to the mining laws of Smyrna.

They were such perfectly natural-looking leads that I could hardly keep from 'taking them up'. Among the oyster shells were mixed many fragments of ancient, broken crockeryware. Now how did those masses of oyster shells get there? Broken crockery and oyster shells are suggestive of restaurants – but then they could have had no such places away up there on that mountainside in our time, because nobody has lived up there. A restaurant would not pay in such a stony, forbidding, desolate place. And besides, there were no champagne corks among the shells. If there ever was a restaurant there, it must have been in Smyrna's palmy days, when the hills were covered with palaces. I could believe in one restaurant on those terms, but then how about the three? Did they have restaurants there at three different periods of the world? Because there are two or three feet of solid earth between the oyster leads. Evidently the restaurant solution will not answer.

The hill might have been the bottom of the sea once, and been lifted up, with its oyster beds, by an earthquake – but, then, how about the crockery? And moreover, how about *three* oyster beds, one above another, and thick strata of good honest earth between.

That theory will not do. It is just possible that this hill is Mount Ararat, and that Noah's Ark rested here, and he ate oysters and threw the shells overboard. But that will not do, either. There are the three layers again and the solid earth between – and besides, there were only eight in Noah's family, and they could not have eaten all these oysters in the two or three months they stayed on top of that mountain. The beasts – however, it is simply absurd to suppose he did not know any more than to feed the beasts on oyster suppers.

It is painful – it is even humiliating – but I am reduced at last to one slender theory: that the oysters climbed up there of their own accord. But what object could they have had in view? What did they want up there? What could any oyster want to climb a hill for? To climb a hill must necessarily be fatiguing and annoying exercise for an oyster. The most natural conclusion would be that the oysters climbed up there to look at the scenery. Yet when one comes to reflect upon the nature of an oyster, it seems plain that he does not care for scenery. An oyster has no taste for such things; he cares nothing for the beautiful. An oyster is of a retiring disposition and not lively – not even cheerful above the average and never enterprising. But above all, an oyster does not take any interest in scenery –, he scorns it. What have I arrived at now? Simply at the point I started from, namely, *those oyster shells are there*, in regular layers, five hundred feet above the sea, and no man knows how they got there. I have hunted up the guidebooks, and the gist of what they say is this: 'They are there, but how they got there is a mystery.'[13]

I have already quoted Peter Fleming once in this chapter; but as it was only two lines, perhaps it doesn't really count. So here he is again, at the very top of his form, with his description – from *Brazilian Adventure* – of the public statuary in Rio de Janeiro:

Victory has got a half-Nelson on Liberty from behind. Liberty is giving away about half a ton, and also carrying weight in the shape of a dying President and a brace of cherubs. (One of the cherubs is doing a cartwheel on the dying President's head, while the other, scarcely less considerate, attempts to pull his trousers off.)

Meanwhile an unclothed male figure, probably symbolical, unquestionably winged, and carrying in one hand a model railway, is in the very act of delivering a running kick at the two struggling ladies, from whose drapery on the opposite side an eagle is escaping, apparently unnoticed. Around the feet of these gigantic principals all is bustle and confusion. Cavalry are charging, aboriginals are being emancipated and liners launched. Farmers, liberators, nuns, firemen and a poet pick their way with benign insouciance over a subsoil thickly carpeted with corpses, cannonballs and scrolls. So vehement a confusion of thought, so arbitrary an alliance of ideas, takes the reason captive and paralyses criticism.[14]

We will close with London – the London not, as it has so often been described, of Dickens's day, but of the late eighteenth century. At that time, in the early 1770s, the city was twice visited by a hunchbacked German physicist named Georg Christoph Lichtenberg. He grew to know it well, and described it brilliantly in his letters and diaries – translations of which were published in 1938 under the title *Lichtenberg's Visits to England*. He seems to be, in a way, the literary counterpart of Hogarth, who had died only a few years before his arrival: there is the same energy, the same darting, all-seeing eye, the same fascination with low life. London, one realises, must have been filthy and overcrowded, dissolute and disease-ridden; but it can never have been dull. Here is a sample – of London and Lichtenberg together:

I will make you a hasty sketch of an evening in the streets of London; I will not merely paint it for you in words, but fill in my picture with some groups, which one does not care to paint with such a lasting pigment as ink. For this purpose I will take Cheapside and Fleet Street, as I saw them last week, when I was going from Mr. Boydell's house to my lodging in the evening rather before 8 o'clock. Imagine a street about as wide as the Weender in Göttingen, but, taking it altogether, about six times as long. On both sides tall houses with plate-glass windows. The lower floors consist of shops and seem to be made entirely of glass; many thousand candles light up silverware, engravings, books, clocks, glass, pewter, paintings, women's finery, modish and otherwise, gold, precious stones, steel-work, and endless coffee-rooms and lottery offices. The street looks as though it were illuminated for some festivity: the apothecaries and druggists display glasses filled with gay-coloured spirits, in which Dieterich's lackey could bathe; they suffuse many a wide space with a purple, yellow, verdigris-green, or azure light. The confectioners dazzle your eyes with their candelabra and tickle your nose with their wares, for no more trouble and expense than that of taking both into their establishments. In these hang festoons of Spanish grapes, alternating with pineapples, and pyramids of apples and oranges, among which hover attendant white-armed nymphs with silk caps and little silk trains, who are often (here's the devil to pay) too little attended. Their masters wisely associate them with the cakes and tarts, to make the mouth of even the most replete water, and to strip the poor purse of its last shilling but one; for to entice the hungry and rich, the cakes and their brilliant surroundings would suffice. All this appears like an enchantment to the unaccustomed eye; there is therefore all the more need for circumspection in viewing all discreetly; for scarcely do you stop than, crash! a porter runs you down, crying 'By your leave', when you are lying on the ground. In the middle of the street roll chaises, carriages, and drays in an unending stream. Above this din and the hum and clatter of thousands of tongues and feet one hears the chimes from church towers, the bells of the postmen, the organs, fiddles, hurdy-gurdies, and tambourines of English mountebanks, and the cries of those who sell hot and cold viands in the open at the street corners. Then you will see a bonfire of shavings flaring up as high as the upper floors of the houses in a circle of merrily shouting beggar-boys, sailors, and rogues. Suddenly a man whose handkerchief has been stolen will cry: 'Stop thief', and every one will begin running and pushing and shoving – many of them not with any desire of catching the thief, but of prigging for themselves, perhaps, a watch or purse. Before you know where you are, a pretty, nicely dressed miss will take you by the hand: 'Come, my Lord, come along, let us drink a glass together', or 'I'll go with you if you please'. Then there is an accident forty paces from you; 'God bless me', cries one, 'Poor creature', another. Then one stops and must put one's hand into one's pocket, for all appear to sympathize with the misfortunes of the wretched creature: but all of a sudden they are laughing again, because some one has lain down by mistake in the gutter; 'Look there, damn me', says a third, and then the procession moves on. Suddenly you will, perhaps, hear a shout from a hundred throats, as if a fire had broken out, a house fallen down, or a patriot were looking out of the window. In Göttingen one hastens thither and can see from at least forty yards off what has happened; here a man is fortunate (especially by night and in this part of the town – the City) if he can weather the storm unharmed in a side street. Where it widens out, all hasten along, no one looking as though he were going for a walk or observing anything, but all appearing to be called to a deathbed. That is Cheapside and Fleet Street on a December evening.[15]

CHAPTER ELEVEN

Characters and Social Intercourse

If, as Alexander Pope so pithily maintained, the proper study of mankind is man, it follows that any self-respecting traveller should, by rights, be more interested in the natives of the country in which he travels than in the country itself. In my experience, he very seldom is. There are exceptions, of course: Freya Stark, Wilfred Thesiger and C. M. Doughty immediately spring to mind, with several others hot on their heels. But the sad fact is that, for most of us in most places, getting to know the locals is uphill work. First there is the language barrier, then the culture gap; and even if these formidable obstacles can be overcome the problems are not over, for where there are no mutual acquaintances, topical issues, local scandals, books, films or television programmes to be discussed, subjects for satisfactory conversation may well be in short supply. It is not altogether surprising that, unless we know the country well, have friends there, and can at least muddle through in the language, we tend all too often to take the line of least resistance and concentrate on less demanding aspects – like natural scenery, architecture or animals.

Fortunately, there is no such thing as a complete cocoon. Excepting only if we happen to be Muslim ladies travelling in the most impenetrable purdah we are bound, whether we like it or not, to find ourselves rubbing shoulders with a large number of the local people; and it is they who are the subject of this chapter. They may not, however, be natives in the strictest sense of the word; and, even if they are, they may belong to settler families who have never allowed themselves to become entirely integrated. An excellent example of this phenomenon is given by Charles Macomb Flandrau in *Viva Mexico!*:

Trawnbeigh's place was seven miles from the main road, and as I happened to be near the parting of the ways when the off hind leg of Catalina began to limp, I decided to leave her with my mozo at an Indian village until a pack train should pass by (there is always some one in a pack train who can remove a bad shoe), while I proceeded on the mozo's mule to the Trawnbeighs'. . . . Time and again I had been told of Trawnbeigh's early adventures, and I felt sure he could 'put me up' (as he would have said himself) for the night. He 'put me up' not only that night, but as my mozo didn't appear until late the next afternoon, a second night as well. And when I at last rode away, it was with the feeling of having learned from the Trawnbeighs a great lesson.

In the first place they couldn't have expected me; they couldn't possibly have expected anyone. And it was a hot afternoon. But as it was the hour at which people at 'home' dropped in for tea, Mrs. Trawnbeigh and her three plain, heavy looking daughters were perfectly prepared to dispense hospitality to any number of mythical friends. They had on hideous but distinctly 'dressy' dresses of amazingly stamped materials known, I believe, as 'summer silks,' and they were all four tightly laced. Current fashion in Paris, London, and New York by no means insisted on small, smooth, round waists, but the Trawnbeigh women had them because (as it gradually dawned on me) to have had any other kind would have been a concession to anatomy and the weather. To anything so compressible as one's anatomy, or as vulgarly impartial as the weather, the Trawnbeighs simply did not concede. I never could get over the feeling that they all secretly regarded weather in general as a kind of popular institution, of vital importance only to the middle class. Cyril, an extremely beautiful young person of twenty-two, who had been playing tennis (by himself) on the asoleadero, was in 'flannels,' and Trawnbeigh admirably looked the part in gray, middle-aged riding things, although, as I discovered before leaving, their stable at the time consisted of one senile burro with ingrowing hoofs. . . .

Of course we had tea in the garden. There wasn't any garden, but we nevertheless had tea in it. The house would have been cooler, less glaring, and free from the venomous little rodadoras that stung the backs of my hands full of microscopic polka dots; but we all strolled out to a spot some fifty yards away where a bench, half a dozen shaky, homemade chairs, and a rustic table were most imperfectly shaded by three tattered banana trees.

'We love to drink tea in the dingle dangle,' Mrs. Trawnbeigh explained. How the tea tray itself got to the 'dingle dangle,' I have only a general suspicion, for when we arrived it was already there, equipped with caddy, cozy, a plate of buttered toast, a pot of strawberry jam, and all the rest of it. But try as I might, I simply could not rid myself of the feeling that at least two footmen had arranged it all and then discreetly retired; a feeling that also sought to account for the tray's subsequent removal, which took place while Trawnbeigh, Cyril, Edwina, and I walked over to inspect the asoleadero and washing tanks. I wanted to look back; but something (the fear, perhaps, of being turned into a pillar of salt) restrained me.

With most English-speaking persons in that part of the world, conversation has to do with coffee, coffee and – coffee. The Trawnbeighs, however, scarcely touched on the insistent topic. While we sat on the low wall of the dilapidated little asoleadero we discussed pheasant shooting and the 'best places' for haberdashery and 'Gladstone bags.' Cyril, as if it were but a matter of inclination, said he thought he might go over for the shooting that year; a cousin had asked him 'to make a seventh.' I never found out what this meant and didn't have the nerve to ask.

'Bertie shoots the twelfth, doesn't he?' Edwina here inquired.

To which her brother replied, as if she had shown a distressing ignorance of some fundamental date in history, like 1066 or 1215, 'Bertie *always* shoots the twelfth.'

The best place for haberdashery in Mr. Trawnbeigh's opinion was 'the Stores.' But Cyril preferred a small shop in Bond Street, maintaining firmly, but with good humor, that it was not merely, as 'the pater' insisted, because the fellow charged more, but because one didn't 'run the risk of seeing some beastly bounder in a cravat uncommonly like one's own.' Trawnbeigh, as a sedate parent bordering on middle age, felt obliged to stand up for the more economical 'Stores,' but it was evident that he really admired Cyril's exclusive principles and approved of them. Edwina cut short the argument with an abrupt question.

'I say,' she inquired anxiously, 'has the dressing bell gone yet?' The dressing bell hadn't gone, but it soon went. For Mr. Trawnbeigh, after looking at his watch, bustled off to the house and rang it himself. Then we withdrew to our respective apartments to dress for dinner.

'I've put you in the north wing, old man; there's always a breeze in the wing,' my host declared as he ushered me into a bamboo shed they used apparently for storing corn and iron implements of an agricultural nature. But there was also in the room a recently made-up cot with real sheets, a tin bath tub, hot and cold water in two earthenware jars, and an empty packing case upholstered in oil-cloth. When Trawnbeigh spoke of this last as a 'wash-hand-stand,' I knew I had indeed strayed from life into the realms of mid-Victorian romance.

The breeze Trawnbeigh had referred to developed in the violent Mexican way, while I was enjoying the bath tub, into an unmistakable norther. Water fell on the roof like so much lead and then sprang off (some of it did) in thick, round streams from the tin spouts; the wind screamed in and out of the tiles overhead, and through the 'north wing's' blurred windows the writhing banana trees of the 'dingle dangle' looked like strange things one sees in an aquarium. As soon as I could get into my clothes again – a bath was as far as I was able to live up to the Trawnbeigh ideal – I went into the sala where the dinner table was already set with a really heartrending attempt at splendor. ... While I was standing there wondering how the Trawn-beighs had been able all those years to keep it up, a window in the next room blew open with a bang. I ran in to shut it; but before I reached it, I stopped short and, as hastily and quietly as I could, tiptoed back to the 'wing.' For the next room was the kitchen and at one end of it Trawnbeigh, in a shabby but perfectly fitting dress-coat, his trousers rolled up halfway to his knees, was patiently holding an umbrella over his wife's sacred dinner gown, while she – bebangled, becameoed, beplumed, and stripped to the buff – masterfully cooked our dinner on the brasero.[1]

And Bruce Chatwin found another in Patagonia:

I left Río Pico and came to a Scottish sheep-station. The notice on the gate read 'Estancia Lochinver – 1.444 kilometres'. The gate was in excellent trim. On the post was a painted topknot in the form of a thistle.

I walked the 1.444 kilometres and reached a house of corrugated iron, with twin gables and a high pitched roof, built in a style more suitable for granite. The Scotsman stood on the steps, a big, gristly man with white hair and black eyebrows. He had been rounding up sheep all day. Three thousand animals grazed in his paddock. He was expecting the shearers in the morning.

'But ye can't trust 'em to come when they say. Ye can't even talk to people in this country. Ye can't tell 'em they did a bad job or they'll pack and leave. Ye tell 'em anything's wrong and they'll cut the beasts to ribbons. Aye, it's a butchery, not a shearing that they do.'

His father had been a crofter on the island of Lewis and came out when the big sheep companies were opening up. The family did well, bought land, learned a little Spanish, and kept Scotland in their hearts.

He wore the kilt and piped at Caledonian Balls. He had one set of pipes sent from Scotland and another he made himself in the long Patagonian winter. In the house there were views of Scotland, photographs of the British Royal Family, and Karsh's picture of Winston Churchill.

'And ye know who he was, don't ye?'

A tin of Mackintosh's toffees was placed reverently under the Queen.

His wife had been stone deaf since her car collided with a train. She had not learned to lip-read and you had to scribble questions on a pad. He was her second husband and they had been married twenty years. She liked the refinements of English life. She liked using a silver toast-rack. She liked nice linen and fresh chintzes and polished brass. She did not like Patagonia. She hated the winter and missed having flowers.

'I've a terrible time getting things to grow. Lupins do well, but my carnations never survive the cold, and mostly I make do with annuals – godetias, clarkias, larkspurs and marigolds – but you can never tell how they're going to do. This year the sweet peas are a disaster, and I do so love them for vases. Flowers do improve the home, I think.'

'Aagh!' he muttered. 'I care none for her damn flowers.'

'What's that you said, dear? He's overworked, you know. Bad heart! He shouldn't be riding round the camp all day. *I'm* the one who should be rounding up sheep. He *hates* horses. When I lived in Buenos Aires I always loved to ride.'

'Bah! She knows bugger all about it. She rides round some fancy estancia and she thinks she can round up sheep.'

'What are you saying, dear?'

'She's right in one thing, though. I never liked the horse. But ye can't get anyone to ride for ye now. This was a fine country once. Ye paid 'em and they worked. Now I've got the boy and he'll be off any minute, and I've got the old peon, but he's eighty-three and I have to strap him to his horse.'

The Scotsman had lived forty years in the valley. He had the reputation of being very tight-fisted. One year, when the price of wool was up, he and his wife went to Scotland. They stayed in first-class hotels and were a week on Lewis. There he became familiar with the things his mother spoke of – gulls, herring boats, heather, peat – and he had felt the call.

Now he wanted to leave Patagonia and retire to Lewis. She wanted to leave, but not necessarily to Lewis. She was in better health than he. He did not know how to get out. The price of wool was falling and the Perónistas were after the land.

Next morning we stood outside the house and looked along the line of telegraph poles, watching for the shearers' truck. In place of a lawn was a flat expanse of packed dirt, and, in the middle, a wire-netting cage.

'And what do you keep in there?' I asked.

'Aagh! The bugger died on me.'

Curled in the bottom of the cage lay the dried-up skeleton of a thistle.[2]

And then of course there were the missionaries. In *One's Company*, Peter Fleming tells of how he stayed with some in Jehol, Manchuria:

We sat down four to breakfast: Mr. and Mrs. Panter, young Mr. Titherton, and myself. They were American missionaries.

Mr. Panter was a very tall, very doleful man. His voice was the voice of Doom, slow and terrible; it seemed to come from a very long way away. He never smiled. He had an aloof and absent-minded manner. For thirty years he had struggled in a remote place to convert heathens to Christianity and (harder still) to make the converts Christians in something more than name; you had the feeling that this had bred in him a bitterness of soul which once it had been difficult to suppress. Now he had the mastery of it; but the inner superadded to the outer conflicts had left him worn out. He had no longer any interest or energy left for anything outside the duties which he so indomitably carried out. He was more nearly a ghost than anyone I have ever met.

His wife had, and needed to have, both feet on the earth. Her manner was not nearly so sepulchral as Mr. Panter's. Though almost ostentatiously narrow in her sympathies, she was a person of great kindliness. She was accessible. She reflected her husband's austerity and his controlled fanaticism, but she remained nevertheless an ordinary human being, capable of laughter and willing to admit vulnerability.

Young Mr. Titherton was the most interesting of the three. He was out there, I gathered, on probation; he was a kind of apprentice missionary. Although he had lived with the Panters for a year, and although for hundreds of miles round there were not more than half a dozen other white people, he was still addressed as 'Mr. Titherton'. He was not, I think, entirely approved of. He was about twenty-five. His bland, slightly unctuous face became, when he was amused, all of a sudden facetious in a curiously disreputable way; you would almost have said that he leered. He quite often was amused. He had a natural leaning towards controversy, and at meal times would gratuitously stir up trouble for himself by defending the use of the word 'damn' in moments of ungovernable annoyance, or by putting in a word for Confucianism, or by partially condoning the less respectable aspects of Chinese life. Mr. Panter, reproving him with a vehemence which he clearly found it difficult to curb, would become for a moment almost human.

However sternly reproved, Mr. Titherton was irrepressible. A supremely tactless man, he would both make and withdraw his heretical statements in such a way as to give the maximum of offence. 'Well, well,' he would chirp, when enfiladed by a withering fire of orthodoxy from either end of the table, 'I dare say you know best. Let's say no more about it.' Then he would wink at me in a very sophisticated way. This put me in a false and embarrassing position.

Breakfast was at 7.30. We sat down, and then Mr. Panter said a grace. But he never said it quite soon enough for me. Try as I would, I could *not* remember about that grace. The opening words always caught me with a spoon or a sugar-bowl poised guiltily over my porridge, while the others all had their hands folded devoutly on their laps. This made me appear both greedy and irreligious.

After breakfast, prayers.

Mr. Titherton distributes little red books entitled, 'Redemption Songs: for Choir, Solo, or The Home'. Mrs. Panter seats herself at an instrument distantly related to the harmonium and strikes a wheezy chord.

'No. 275!' announces Mr. Panter in an awful voice.

Mrs. Panter rolls up the sleeves of her dress. We are off . . .

The Redemption Songs do not seem to me very good songs. Their composer often expresses himself in so turgid and involved a style as to be practically incomprehensible. His syntax is occasionally weak, and even at its strongest is over-richly encrusted with allusions and invocations ('Oh Tsidkenu!' is a favourite one) which mean nothing to me. Nor is Mrs. Panter, at the harmonium, particularly adept at glossing over his frequent metrical inconsistencies; her lively but straightforward attack is based on the assumption – too often unjustifiable – that both lines in a couplet will contain roughly the same number of syllables.

However, save for some daring experiments in the third verse, this morning's Song is fairly plain sailing. Each verse ends with the lilting refrain 'Wonderful Man of Calvaree-ee!' and we usually manage that bit rather well.

On the whole, though, the singing is ragged. Mr. Panter's voice, though not lacking in vigour, ploughs a lonely furrow just where we most needed co-operation. Mr. Titherton flutes away modestly and, as far as I can judge, in tune; but he stands no chance against Mr. Panter, who produces a consistently formidable volume of sound and makes a point of shouting all the holier words at the top of his voice. In all this uproar I myself am a mere cipher, for I well know that I cannot sing and it is better that I should not try. I go nevertheless through the motions, opening and shutting my mouth with a rapt air, and occasionally emitting a little sort of mew.

At last the Song is over.

A passage from the Bible is now read aloud, either by Mr. Panter or Mr. Titherton, and afterwards extracts from a commentary upon it. This is an extraordinary compilation, thunderously phrased but somewhat bigoted in conception. Yesterday the commentator launched a furious attack upon witches. It was ridiculous, he warned us, to assert that these creatures were either harmless or non-existent. On the contrary, they represented a very real peril to Church and State alike, and when encountered should be severely dealt with.

To-day he is in milder mood. Sternly, but in temperate terms, he animadverts on the folly of attaching undue importance to some popular prejudice or superstition.

He must have been a remarkable man.

After that we pray for fellow-missionaries belonging to the Panters' denomination. A little pamphlet is produced – the Army List, as it were, of the Church Militant – and all the names and addresses on one page are read out as being those to which on this day we especially wish to call Divine attention. Yesterday they were all in Spain, and Mr. Panter, who is not too good at foreign words and when reading the commentary gets terribly tied up over Latin phrases like *vox populi, vox dei*, had considerable difficulty with the Spanish place-names.

But to-day it is Mr. Titherton's turn, and Mr. Titherton is much more nimble-tongued. Also he has the pleasing custom of annotating the list, wherever possible, from personal knowledge of the people whose names are on it. His manner towards the Deity is friendly and informal. He reads out something like this:

'ADDIS ABABA – Reverend Macintyre. ... MEDINA – Miss Tackle, Miss P. Flint (*I know those two ladies, Our Father. Please look on them to-day. They're two of the very best, I can tell you*). ... ALEPPO – Reverend and Mrs. Gow. ... MOSUL – Miss Gondering, Miss J. Gondering. (*Now that printing press they've rigged up, Our Father! That's a splendid bit of work. I do hope you'll help them to make a success of it, Our Father.*)...DAMASCUS—Reverend Pretty, Reverend Polking-horne, Miss O'Brien...'and so on, ending up with a swift and delightful transition from the Near Eastern deserts to 'ICELAND—Reverend Gook'.

Now we kneel down, and either Mr. Panter or Mr. Titherton embarks on a long impromptu prayer. Here again I prefer Mr. Titherton's technique. Mr. Panter is apt to be stilted and ponderous; he thanks God for 'the bright weather which obtains'. Mr. Titherton is very different. Nothing stilted about him. He has a straight talk to God. He is confidential, almost racy. 'Stop me if you've heard this one, Our Father', you expect to hear him say at any moment.

I much admire his ingenuity – far greater than Mr. Panter's – in finding things to give thanks for. Mr. Panter has to rack his brains to recall a blessing; his struggles are indeed a sad comment on human felicity. But Mr. Titherton is never at a loss. It rained yesterday. Mr. Panter would have thanked God for the rain and left it at that. But Mr. Titherton examines every aspect of the shower. Its timeliness: its cooling propensities: its value to both the flora and fauna of the district: the damage it inflicted on the graceless poppy-fields: and last of all, just when it seemed that Mr. Titherton must have exhausted all the potential cues for thanksgiving, its effectiveness, in falling on good and evil alike, as a reminder of God's impartiality. Mr. Titherton's pious courtesy is Oriental in more than its setting.

After this there are more prayers, of a general nature: at the end of which I am suddenly shaken out of a stupor by the discovery that I myself am being prayed for. The experience, however salutary, is embarrassing. The prayee – his mind flashing back to the ritual of after-dinner toasts – has an uncomfortable feeling that he ought to stand up, or at any rate adopt some posture other than the kneeling. There is also the haunting fear that he may have to – and certainly ought to – reply.

Mr. Titherton's position, however, is almost equally awkward. Aware, like the rest of that tiny congregation, that my prime desire is to leave Jehol with the mini-mum of delay, he leads off with a request for Divine intervention to accelerate my departure. Then something – perhaps a cough from Mrs. Panter – tells him that this was not the happiest of beginnings, and in the end the difficulty of reconciling the purpose of his prayer with the laws of hospitality is overcome only by a great deal of circumlocution, qualification, and parenthesis. His voice becomes halting and apologetic. For the first time uncertainty has reared its ugly head in that comical but gallant little community.

In several ways, Prayers were rather a strain.[3]

I myself had a curious experience, which I recounted in a book I wrote about the Sahara. Even now I should find it not entirely easy to believe, if I did not have a photograph in the book to prove it:

Our first stage on this homeward journey was the oasis of In Amenas, where the French continue to run a small meteorological research station. With half an hour to wait before taking off again, we had just got out to stretch our legs and see what the chances were of finding a glass of beer when suddenly we were brought up short. Sitting motionless on a camp stool in the full sun twenty yards away was a latter-day Simple Simon – a youngish, plumpish Frenchman, wearing nothing but a pair of swimming trunks and a little round sailor hat, fishing with rod and line in a plastic bucket. Incredulous, we altered course to take us past him. There was no mistake; the bucket was half full of water, the line ended in a hook, on which was attached something that looked like bait. Neither in the bucket or anywhere near it was there any sign of a fish. The man did not even look up as we passed, and none of his colleagues around the airstrip took the slightest notice of him.

We felt a little alarmed. Could Saharitis go further? Had this man better not be taken in hand and given proper attention, before worse befell? Gratefully we noticed a sign saying BAR, and made for it. Several other Frenchmen, similarly clothed, were sitting around. Did they not, we asked, think their colleague's behaviour a little odd? They shrugged. No, they said, there was nothing wrong with him; it was just his way. He loved fishing; at home in France he always went fishing on Sundays, and he apparently saw no reason why the Sahara should force him to give up the habit of a lifetime. Today was Sunday, and so there he was. He had been there since soon after dawn, but he would probably be stopping shortly; four hours were usually enough for him. Yes, look – he was coming in now.

With a stentorian 'Bonjour, la Compagnie!' he strode up to the bar, ordered beer, and beamed at us. 'Any luck?' I asked him. No, he said, not a nibble all morning. The fish were very unco-operative at this time of year. My initial overture having clearly gone down rather well, I grew braver. What was he fishing for, salmon? Good heavens no, he said, whoever heard of anyone fishing for salmon in the middle of the Sahara? I must be crazy. Trout, that was what he was after – he was not interested in anything else. They weren't easy, those trout, but he'd get them in the end.

Back on board the aeroplane we discussed the case. Was he really mad? Could this fishing thing be a genuine delusion, an isolated Achilles' heel in what seemed otherwise to be a perfectly normal psychological make-up? We did not think so. My own guess was that he was as sane as any of us, that this was simply a piece of harmless make-believe that amused him and appealed to his sense of humour. Was it really any worse, after all, than lying on one's bunk and staring at the ceiling? But my friends thought I was being too charitable. They suspected that the whole performance was a stunt, put on regularly for the benefit of transit passengers like ourselves. Well, perhaps it was; and if so, why not? The man had intrigued us, amused us, given us something to think and talk about. He had done no one any harm, and he had made In Amenas a place to remember. In his way he had per-formed a public service, and if he performed it regularly, so much the better. It showed initiative and imagination which deserved to be recognised; and I should like to think that one day there may be held on that airfield a little ceremony, at the conclusion of which the mayor – if such there be – of In Amenas may unveil, not perhaps a statue, but a little plaque let into the wall. It will carry no inscription –

merely a representation, in suitably light relief, of a man sitting in front of a pail, fishing. Thus our friend will be quietly commemorated and, as successive plane-loads of passengers depart, baffled as we had been, on the next stage of their journey, the great work which he began will be continued down the years.[4]

My friend Colin Thubron, who not only writes superb travel books but also possesses an astonishing degree of what can only be described as social serendipity, tells of a short but strangely moving encounter in his book *Jerusalem*:

I found a White Russian general living nearby, a handsome, fine-mannered man whose white hair flowed down to a military beard. Aide-de-camp once to Czar Nicholas II, he had brought the remnant of the Imperial Cossack Guard into Yugo-slavia when the war was lost, and there they had worked on the railways for a while before disbanding for ever. A liturgical reader now, he chanted in the church with the nuns, and looked after his delicate wife with masculine gentleness.

'The past is finished,' he said, smiling. 'Why dwell on these things? They are fifty years away, and all our lives have happened in between. In heaven I will not say "I was a general to the Czar of all the Russias"; I will tell them that I was a reader here in the church of St Mary Magdalene.'

He bent near to catch my answer, for he was almost deaf, and I shouted approval.

'To tell the truth,' he said, 'I am not much proud of my youth. But luckily one forgets. Now we are just two old people ending our lives. We are content and we look to God.' He smiled at his wife, as if their happiness were a secret. 'So you are a writer? Have you heard our Christmas services? They, at least, are worth writing of. But don't speak of our past: nobody is interested in that any more. Only say, if you like, that you heard an old man singing in the Russian church at Gethsemane.'

If he should read this, I hope he will forgive me.[5]

Religious houses of one kind or another are always a fertile field for those in search of memorable characters. Robert Byron, in *The Station*, gives a marvellous portrait of Father Aristarchus, of the monastery of Vatopedi on Mount Athos:

... a thickly built, athletic young man with a curly brown beard. He suggested, as there was an idle day in front of us, that I should accompany him up to the vineyards.

I fetched my cigarettes. He donned a white linen sandboy's hat, and was joined by a friend wearing a broad straw, which, surmounting as it did, a tied bunch of chestnut hair reaching to his waist and a tight-fitting cassock, produced the effect of a Victorian schoolgirl in a crocodile. Each carried a basket and a miniature sickle; I suggested I might do likewise, but, being the honoured visitor, was not allowed. ...

Continuing up shady paths, we came within sound and then sight of the har-vesters. .... I sat down on a bank, while Aristarchus disappeared into a small stone house. From this he bore ceremoniously upon a plate *ouzo* and a glass of water.

'A drink, sir,' he said, in those actual words. He then proceeded to outline his life. From this and subsequent conversations resulted a tale of the modern Levant from the unexpected viewpoint of the practical man.

English he had learnt as a sailor, in which capacity he had sojourned some weeks in Cardiff. But, in a land where many people speak American, it was the manner, not the language, that counted. This he had acquired on a yacht belonging to an English colonel resident in Constantinople.

'Good morning, sir,' was now his daily greeting to us, with a touch of his holy black hat. He knew, too, that no Englishman could begin the day without breakfast, and a table fully laid with napkins, knives, forks, slices of bread, and that precious preserve jam, was always set ready to greet our demure sardines. Nor, when some early appointment demanded, would he allow us to forgo the meal. It happened late, on return from the vineyards, that David was discovered to have set off to Caryes for letters.

'Well, sir,' said Father Aristarchus, 'I'm sure I don't know what Mr. Rice is going to do about his lunch.'

Aristarchus' manners were, without exception, the most impressive monument to British civilisation that I have met.[6]

When I myself was last on Athos in 1963, an elderly monk approached me one evening after supper and asked me if I could help him. I said that I would be happy to try, whereat, with his finger to his lips and several other signs of what seemed to me to be somewhat unnecessary stealth, he led me to his cell, ferreted under the bed, brought out a small portable tape-recorder and asked me if I could interpret the English instructions about how he should hook it up to his transistor radio. Now all radios, recorders and such were, as I was well aware, forbidden on the Holy Mountain; and it was then that I realised how, just sometimes, its inhabitants might fail to adjust altogether to the demands of monastic life and might yearn, touchingly, for an occasional breath of the outside world. I was reminded of this incident when I read the following story in *Letters from the East* by John Carne, who visited St Catherine's monastery on Mount Sinai in the early years of the last century:

A venerable monk, above ninety years of age, the oldest in the convent, paid us a visit in our apartments: he had resided here seventy years; and we asked him in what manner his life had passed during this best part of a century's confinement within the convent and garden-walls. One day, he said, had passed away like another; he had seen only the precipices, the sky, and the desert; and he strove now to fix all his thoughts on another world, and waited calmly the hour of his departure. He then dwelt much on the vanity of human pleasures and the nearness of eternity, and ended by asking me, very earnestly, for a bottle of rum. We had but one left for our future journey, but gave it, however, to gratify the old father, who requested that my servant, when he brought it to his cell, would conceal it beneath his cloak, lest his brethren should catch a glimpse of it.[7]

Monks, however, like foreign settlers, are a race apart. We now pass on to the natives proper – beginning with Hilaire Belloc's magnificent character in 'The Modern Traveller' (Sin and Blood are companions on the expedition):

In getting up our Caravan
We met a most obliging man,
The Lord Chief Justice of Liberia,
And Minister of the Interior;
Cain Abolition Beecher Boz,
Worked like a Nigger – which he was –
   And in a single day
Procured us Porters, Guides, and kit,
And would not take a sou for it
   Until we went away.*
We wondered how this fellow made
Himself so readily obeyed,
And why the natives were so meek;
Until by chance we heard him speak,
And then we clearly understood
How great a Power for Social Good
   The African can be.
He said with a determined air:
'You are not what your fathers were;
Liberians, you are Free!
Of course, if you refuse to go –'
And here he made a gesture.
He also gave us good advice
Concerning Labour and its Price.
'In dealing wid de Native Scum,
Yo' cannot pick an' choose;
Yo' hab to promise um a sum
Ob wages, paid in Cloth and Rum.
But, Lordy! that's a ruse!
Yo' get yo' well on de Adventure,
And change de wages to Indenture.'

We did the thing that he projected,
The Caravan grew disaffected,
   And Sin and I consulted;
Blood understood the Native mind.
He said: 'We must be firm but kind.'
   A Mutiny resulted.
I never shall forget the way
That Blood upon this awful day
Preserved us all from death.

* But when we went away, we found
  A deficit of several pound.

He stood upon a little mound,
Cast his lethargic eyes around,
And said beneath his breath:
'Whatever happens we have got
The Maxim Gun, and they have not.'[8]

But Mr Boz is not, of course, typical. To redress the balance, here is Mildred Cable, telling us of a blind beggar in the Gobi Desert:

Presently I noticed a young boy approach, leading a strange-looking man by means of a short stick, of which each held one end. The man's clothes were ragged, and he had every appearance of extreme poverty. I saw at once that he was blind, yet his face bore the expression of one whose inner being is supplied with some constant and secret delight. His body was broad and well developed, but his bare feet and ankles were the smallest I ever saw attached to so powerful a frame, and he walked with a delicate, mincing tread, as though stepping to the rhythm of a tune that he alone heard.

He sat down on the ground and with a quiet, absorbed air said very simply: 'This is the male eagle's call.' Then followed a perfect bird-call reproducing the sound so familiar to us in wild mountain ranges. 'Now listen,' he went on, 'the female pitches this note and the little ones in the nest call out thus for their food.' Then followed the various cries, each with a subtle change of intonation. He then gave in rapid succession the different notes of the wild pigeon, the pheasant, the magpie, the kingfisher, the water-wagtail and the hoopoe. With complete accuracy he reproduced the travel-call of the wild geese when the birds cleave the air, taking their way to the south marshes. For a full half-hour this beautiful concert continued. The liquid notes, the delicate trills and warbling sounds filled the grimy courtyard with such melody as is only associated with shady woods and babbling streams.

I asked him how he came by so much bird-lore and he replied: 'I just listen.'

'When did you lose your sight?' I asked him.

'I was born blind,' was his reply.

'He lives alone with his mother and she too is blind,' the small boy explained. 'They are very poor, and when visitors come to the inn I bring him here and so he earns enough to feed them both, but when there are no travellers he and his mother go hungry.'

I placed a loaf of bread in his basket and a little string of copper coins, which sent him away delighted at so generous a reward, although it represented merely the value of a few pence in my own country. Darkness was coming on and his young guide took him by the hand to lead him away. Day and night were but a change of word to him, and as he trod his way daintily through the filth of the inn-court his face still gleamed with the delight of artistic achievement.[9]

Lady Mary Wortley Montagu, in Constantinople in 1717, did not invariably approve of everything that she saw; one visit, however, she never forgot:

The Greek lady, with me, earnestly solicited me to visit the Kahya's lady, saying, he was the second officer in the Empire, and ought indeed to be looked upon as the first, the Grand Vizier having only the name, while he exercised the authority. I had found so little diversion in the Vizier's Haram, that I had no mind to go into another. But her importunity prevailed with me, and I am extremely glad I was so complaisant. All things here were with quite another air than at the Grand Vizier's; and the very house confessed the difference between an old devotee, and a young beauty. It was nicely clean and magnificent. I was met at the door by two black Eunuchs, who led me through a long gallery, between two ranks of beautiful young girls, with their hair finely plaited, almost hanging to their feet, and dressed in fine light damasks, brocaded with silver. I was sorry that decency did not permit me to stop to consider them nearer. But that thought was lost upon my entrance into a large room, or rather pavillion, built round with gilded sashes, which were most of them thrown up, and the trees planted near them gave an agreeable shade, which hindered the sun from being troublesome. The jessamines and honey-suckles that twisted round their trunks, shed a soft perfume, increased by a white marble fountain playing sweet water in the lower part of the room, which fell into three or four basons, with a pleasing sound. The roof was painted with all sorts of flowers, falling out of gilded baskets, that seemed tumbling down. On a sofa, raised three steps and covered with fine Persian carpets, sat the Kahya's lady, leaning on cushions of white sattin embroidered; and at her feet sat two young girls about twelve years old, lovely as angels, dressed perfectly rich, and almost covered with jewels. But they were hardly seen near the fair Fatima, (for that is her name) so much her beauty effaced every thing I have seen, nay, all that has been called lovely, either in England or Germany. I must own, that I never saw any thing so gloriously beautiful, nor can I recollect a face that would have been taken notice of near her's. She stood up to receive me, saluting me, after their fashion, putting her hand to her heart with a sweetness full of majesty, that no court breeding could ever give. She ordered cushions to be given me, and took care to place me in the corner, which is the place of honour. I confess, though the Greek lady had before given me a great opinion of her beauty, I was so struck with admiration, that I could not, for some time, speak to her, being wholly taken up in gazing. That surprizing harmony of features! That charming result of the whole! That exact proportion of body! That lovely bloom of complexion unsullied by art! The unutterable enchantment of her smile; – But her eyes! – – Large and black, with all the soft languishment of the blue! every turn of her face discovering some new grace.

After my first surprize was over, I endeavoured, by nicely examining her face, to find out some imperfection, without any fruit of my search, but my being clearly convinced of the error of that vulgar notion, that a face exactly proportioned, and perfectly beautiful, would not be agreeable; nature having done for her, with more success, what Apelles is said to have essayed by a collection of the most exact features to form a perfect face. Add to all this a behaviour so full of grace and sweetness, such easy motions with an air so majestic, yet free from stiffness or affectation, that I am persuaded could she be suddenly transported upon the most polite throne of Europe, no body would think her other than born and bred to be a Queen, though educated in a country we call barbarous. To say all in a word, our most celebrated English beauties would vanish near her.

She was dressed in a Caftan of gold brocade, flowered with silver, very well fitted to her shape, and shewing to admiration the beauty of her bosom, only shaded by the thin gauze of her shift. Her drawers were pale pink, her waistcoat green and silver, her slippers white sattin, finely embroidered; her lovely arms adorned with bracelets of diamonds, and her broad girdle set round with diamonds; upon her head a rich Turkish handkerchief of pink and silver, her own fine black hair hanging a great length, in various tresses, and on one side of her head some bodkins of jewels. I am afraid you will accuse me of extravagance in this description. I think I have read some where, that women always speak in rapture, when they speak of beauty, and I cannot imagine why they should not be allowed to do so. I rather think it a virtue to be able to admire without any mixture of desire or envy. The gravest writers have spoke with great warmth of some celebrated pictures and statues. The workmanship of heaven certainly excels all our weak imitations, and, I think, has a much better claim to our praise. For my part, I am not ashamed to own, I took more pleasure in looking on the beauteous Fatima, than the finest piece of sculpture could have given me. She told me the two girls at her feet were her daughters, though she appeared too young to be their mother. Here fair maids were ranged below the Sofa, to the number of twenty, and put me in mind of the pictures of the antient nymphs. I did not think all nature could have furnished such a scene of beauty. She made them a sign to play and dance. Four of them immediately began to play some soft airs on instruments between a lute and a guitar, which they accompanied with their voices, while the others danced by turns. This dance was very different from what I had seen before. Nothing could be more artful, or more proper to raise *certain ideas*. The tunes so soft; – The motions so languishing! – Accompanied with pauses and dying eyes! – half falling back, and then recovering themselves in so artful a manner, that I am very positive, the coldest and most rigid prude upon earth, could not have looked upon them without thinking of 'something not to be spoke of.' – I suppose you may have read that the Turks have no music, but what is shocking to the ears; but this account is from those who never heard any but what is played in the streets, and is just as reasonable, as if a foreigner should take his ideas of English music from the bladder and string, or the marrowbones and cleavers. I can assure you, that the music is extremely pathetic; 'tis true I am inclined to prefer the Italian, but perhaps I am partial. I am acquainted with a Greek lady, who sings better than Mrs. Robinson; and is very well skilled, in both, who gives the preference to the Turkish. 'Tis certain they have very fine natural voices, these were very agreeable. When the dance was over, four fair slaves came into the room, with silver censors in their hands, and perfumed the air with amber, aloes-wood, and other scents. After this, they served me coffee upon their knees, in the finest Japan china, with *soucoups* of silver gilt. The lovely Fatima entertained me all this while in the most polite agreeable manner, calling me often *Uzelle Sultanam*, or the beautiful Sultana, and desiring my friendship with the best grace in the world, lamenting that she could not entertain me in my own language.

When I took my leave, two maids brought in a fine silver basket of embroidered handkerchiefs; she begg'd I would wear the richest for her sake, and gave the others to my woman and interpretess. – I retired, through the same ceremonies as before, and could not help thinking I had been some time in Mahomet's paradise, so much was I charmed with what I had seen.[10]

Lucie Duff Gordon, writing from the Cape in 1862, tells of another historic encounter:

But first I must tell what struck me most. I asked one of the Herrenhut brethren whether there were any *real* Hottentots, and he said, 'Yes, one;' and next morning, as I sat waiting for early prayers under the big oak-trees in the Plaats (square), he came up, followed by a tiny old man hobbling along with a long stick to support him. 'Here,' said he, 'is the *last* Hottentot; he is a hundred and seven years old, and lives all alone.' I looked on the little, wizened, yellow face, and was shocked that he should be dragged up like a wild beast to be stared at. A feeling of pity which felt like remorse fell upon me, and my eyes filled as I rose and stood before him, so tall and like a tyrant and oppressor, while he uncovered his poor little old snow-white head, and peered up in my face. I led him to the seat, and helped him to sit down, and said in Dutch, 'Father, I hope you are not tired; you are old.' He saw and heard as well as ever, and spoke *good* Dutch in a firm voice. 'Yes, I am above a hundred years old, and alone – quite alone.' I sat beside him, and he put his head on one side, and looked curiously up at me with his faded, but still piercing little wild eyes. Perhaps he had a perception of what I felt – yet I hardly think so; perhaps he thought I was in trouble, for he crept close up to me, and put one tiny brown paw into my hand, which he stroked with the other, and asked (like most coloured people) if I had children. I said, 'Yes, at home in England;' and he patted my hand again, and said, 'God bless them!' It was a relief to feel that he was pleased, for I should have felt like a murderer if my curiosity had added a moment's pain to so tragic a fate.

This may sound like sentimentalism; but you cannot conceive the effect of looking on the last of a race once the owners of all this land, and now utterly gone. His look was not quite human, physically speaking; – a good head, small wild-beast eyes, piercing and restless; cheek-bones strangely high and prominent, nose *quite* flat, mouth rather wide; thin shapeless lips, and an indescribably small, long, pointed chin, with just a very little soft white woolly beard; his head covered with extremely short close white wool, which ended round the poll in little ringlets. Hands and feet like an English child of seven or eight, and person about the size of a child of eleven. He had all his teeth, and though shrunk to nothing, was very little wrinkled in the face, and not at all in the hands, which were dark brown, while his face was yellow. His manner, and way of speaking were like those of an old peasant in England, only his voice was clearer and stronger, and his perceptions not blunted by age. He had travelled with one of the missionaries in the year 1790, or thereabouts, and remained with them ever since.[11]

Lady Duff Gordon was fortunate enough to speak Dutch – which gave her a basis for conversation with her Hottentot; and those of us who find ourselves in a foreign country for any length of time will normally have a stab at the language – although, unless we are very young or praeternaturally gifted, we shall seldom progress quite as rapidly as we somehow thought we would. Much, it needs hardly be said, depends on the teacher.

The best one that I ever knew taught me Serbo-Croat in 1954; the worst was a starving White Russian lady in Paris in 1945, to whom my mother made the disastrous mistake of offering tea *during* my lesson rather than after it. She ate so ravenously throughout – imperiously demanding more sticky cakes when she had finished the first lot – that to this day the rudiments of the Russian language are associated in my mind with a relentless chomping noise and, after certain consonants, a deluge of crumbs. In *A Year in Marrakesh*, Peter Mayne describes his Arabic teacher:

I hate the primer from which El-Meknasi is trying to teach me Arabic. It must be intended for children – but do French children learn Arabic? Not as a rule, I am sure. Perhaps even an adult learning a language is expected to be content with the sort of vocabulary and phrase that these early lessons provide. Subject–verb–object. Very well. I agree. And tomorrow an adjective to brighten the image. But: "Aysha (*nom de jeune fille*) has a *jolie* headscarf (*sibnīya*, fem.),' or, 'The slave-woman (*khadem*, fem.) works well.' I grow sick of everything being so *joli* and sweet and dutiful. I want to get on with life as we live it.

El-Meknasi makes me take notes on what I learn and when he leaves me his primer goes with him (he has other pupils, but only one primer, I suppose), so that I have no means of secretly dashing ahead to something more earthy. I have therefore bought myself a dictionary *Français–Arabe* and a new era has dawned for me. It is invaluable, this dictionary, full of examples to show how the various words are used, and of idiomatic phrases, adult and outspoken. So now with its help I write out sentences of my own composition and these I present to El-Meknasi when he comes to visit me. Today I had written:

'The lady in the green *djellaba* squeaks when she is pinched. She says she will complain to the Pasha, but the gentleman is unafraid.'

El-Meknasi read so far with a disapproving dead-pan face and then explained that 'squeak' is reserved for animals, and that the passive voice is best avoided. He also said that '*rājel*' (man) would be more appropriate to the context than '*sidi*' (which I had used for gentleman), all of which may be useful to know, but it is clear that he has missed the nuances. He continued reading.

'. . . "Mother of whores!" the gentleman remarked. . . .'

but he would read no further. A pity, because I had something nice waiting for him a line or two below.

I don't believe that he will ever teach me the language properly. . . .

My determination to surprise and affront El-Meknasi has cost me hours of preparation and some minutes of acute embarrassment. Last night I applied myself to compiling a suitable text – with the dictionary, of course. Today, when the porter arrived in a woolly cloud of *djellabas*, kicked off his shoes and slumped himself down on the window-sill, I went into the attack immediately. I am recording the conversation in English, though it took place in Arabic (a triumph in itself), and that is why it may appear a little stilted. I do not come out of it very well, but then neither does the porter.

'Listen, O Bouchaib,' I began, before he had time to complete even his greetings and get on with the news of the day. 'What do they say, the one to the other, when they desire to speak about Love?'

'Love?' He repeated the word I had used. It is one of two words given in my dictionary. The second, unhappily, begins with the letter *"ain'* which is still beyond my powers.

'Yes. Love,' I repeated.

He shook his head slowly. I had anticipated a barrier of this sort and went on to my second prepared sentence. 'If, in the alleyway or upon the Djema'a el-Fna, you should see a person who is pleasing to you, and you should desire to make the acquaintance of that person, then how . . . ?'

To my disgust he was not even listening. I believe he had been worrying over the word for 'love'. He suddenly interrupted me:

'Ah-h-h-h! . . .' he exclaimed, wriggling with pleasure. *'L-Hwāya, yak?'*

This was neither of the two words for love to which I have referred, though, as it happens, I have stumbled upon it under a different heading in wandering idly through my dictionary. It is not, in fact, a word that would be printable in English. 'Yes,' I admitted sternly, 'but in what words will we make this improper suggestion?'

He burst out laughing, a terrible conniving laugh. Then he leaned forward and with a new familiarity pinched me in the side. I could not be certain whether this pinch was the method he would employ or whether he merely wished to show his appreciation of a joke. He saw that I was puzzled, so he got to his feet and drew me to my feet too.

'Stand!' he commanded, placing me in the middle of the room. Then he pointed at me with a thick forefinger. 'You! You are that person!'

'Let us pretend so,' I said in French, rather primly I dare say. I had no sentence ready for this emergency.

He withdrew to the far end of the room. *'I,'* he cried, 'see . . .' – his finger went to his eye which flashed tigerishly – 'YOU!' He pointed straight at me.

I stood my ground as he came surging forward down the room, a shambling James Thurber figure. He stared first into my face, his own contorted with winks, and then at my ankles, and as he passed, he delivered a vicious blow with his elbow. I was left gasping as he turned.

'Understand?' he cried with a triumphant smile.

'But what do you say . . . ?' I began plaintively.

'Say? Say? Is not *l-hwāya* for *doing* then, in your country?'

'Of course, but . . .'

'Wakhkha!' he remarked, struggling to get out of the first of his *djellabas.* 'How much you give? You give me nice *favor?'*

I am afraid that the whole character of my relationship with the porter, hitherto so satisfactory, has been ruined by this incident. Of course I had to tell him to go at once. But I could not put things right for exactly the same reason as they went wrong – lack of vocabulary and the power to use it. He didn't understand, but he went, shaking his head like a poor bewildered ox, looking at the 100-franc note I had given him for today's lesson and tomorrow's in lieu of notice. It is a great pity, because he was proving an excellent conversation man and I must now search for another.[12]

Once you have given up the language as a bad job, you can fall back with relief on an interpreter; the only problem is that, especially in the East, the interpreter prefers to interpret what he thinks you ought to have said rather than what you actually did. The results of this tendency in practice are best illustrated by Alexander Kinglake; we find him once again at Belgrade on the Ottoman frontier, this time paying his courtesy call on the local Pasha:

The Pasha received us with the smooth, kind, gentle manner that belongs to well-bred Osmalees. . . .
Yet unless you can contrive to learn a little of the language, you will be rather bored by your visits of ceremony; the intervention of the interpreter, or Dragoman as he is called, is fatal to the spirit of conversation. I think I should mislead you, if I were to attempt to give the substance of any particular conversation with Orientals. A traveller may write and say that, 'the Pasha of So-and-So was particularly interested in the vast progress which has been made in the application of steam, and appeared to understand the structure of our machinery – that he remarked upon the gigantic results of our manufacturing industry – shewed that he possessed considerable knowledge of our Indian affairs, and of the constitution of the Company, and expressed a lively admiration of the many sterling qualities for which the people of England are distinguished.' But the heap of common-places thus quietly attributed to the Pasha, will have been founded perhaps on some such talking as this: –
Pasha. – The Englishman is welcome; most blessed among hours is this, the hour of his coming.
Dragoman (to the Traveller.) – The Pasha pays you his compliments.
Traveller. – Give him my best compliments in return, and say I'm delighted to have the honour of seeing him.
Dragoman (to the Pasha.) – His Lordship, this Englishman, Lord of London, Scorner of Ireland, Suppressor of France, has quitted his governments, and left his enemies to breathe for a moment, and has crossed the broad waters in strict disguise, with a small but eternally faithful retinue of followers, in order that he might look upon the bright countenance of the Pasha among Pashas – the Pasha of the everlasting Pashalik of Karagholookoldour.
Traveller (to his Dragoman.) – What on earth have you been saying about London? The Pasha will be taking me for a mere cockney. Have not I told you *always* to say, that I am from a branch of the family of Mudcombe Park, and that I am to be a magistrate for the county of Bedfordshire, only I've not qualified, and that I should have been a Deputy-Lieutenant, if it had not been for the extraordinary conduct of Lord Mountpromise, and that I was a candidate for Goldborough at the last election, and that I should have won easy, if my committee had not been bought. I wish to heaven that if you *do* say any thing about me, you'd tell the simple truth.
Dragoman – [is silent.]

Pasha. – What says the friendly Lord of London? is there aught that I can grant him within the Pashalik of Karagholookoldour?

Dragoman (growing sulky and literal.) – This friendly Englishman – this branch of Mudcombe – this head-purveyor of Goldborough – this possible policeman of Bedfordshire is recounting his achievements, and the number of his titles.

Pasha. – The end of his honours is more distant than the ends of the Earth, and the catalogue of his glorious deeds is brighter than the firmament of Heaven!

Dragoman (to the Traveller). – The Pasha congratulates your Excellency.

Traveller. – About Goldborough? The deuce he does! – but I want to get at his views, in relation to the present state of the Ottoman Empire; tell him the Houses of Parliament have met, and that there has been a Speech from the throne, pledging England to preserve the integrity of the Sultan's dominions.

Dragoman (to the Pasha). – This branch of Mudcombe, this possible policeman of Bedfordshire, informs your Highness that in England the talking houses have met, and that the integrity of the Sultan's dominions has been assured for ever and ever, by a speech from the velvet chair.

Pasha. – Wonderful chair! Wonderful houses! – whirr! whirr! all by wheels! – whiz! whiz! all by steam! – wonderful chair! wonderful houses! wonderful people! – whirr! whirr! all by wheels! – whiz! whiz! all by steam!

Traveller (to the Dragoman). – What does the Pasha mean by that whizzing? he does not mean to say, does he, that our Government will ever abandon their pledges to the Sultan?

Dragoman. – No, your Excellency, but he says the English talk by wheels, and by steam.

Traveller. – That's an exaggeration; but say that the English really have carried machinery to great perfection; tell the Pasha (he'll be struck with that), that whenever we have any disturbances to put down, even at two or three hundred miles from London, we can send troops by the thousand, to the scene of action, in a few hours.

Dragoman (recovering his temper and freedom of speech). – His Excellency, this Lord of Mudcombe, observes to your Highness, that whenever the Irish, or the French, or the Indians rebel against the English, whole armies of soldiers, and brigades of artillery, are dropped into a mighty chasm called Euston Square, and in the biting of a cartridge they arise up again in Manchester, or Dublin, or Paris, or Delhi, and utterly exterminate the enemies of England from the face of the earth.

Pasha. – I know it – I know all – the particulars have been faithfully related to me, and my mind comprehends locomotives. The armies of the English ride upon the vapours of boiling cauldrons, and their horses are flaming coals! – whirr! whirr! all by wheels! – whiz! whiz! all by steam!

Traveller (to his Dragoman). – I wish to have the opinion of an unprejudiced Ottoman gentleman, as to the prospects of our English commerce and manufactures; just ask the Pasha to give me his views on the subject.

Pasha (after having received the communication of the Dragoman). – The ships of the English swarm like flies; their printed calicoes cover the whole earth, and by the side of their swords the blades of Damascus are blades of grass. All India is but an item in the Ledger-books of the Merchants, whose lumber-rooms are filled with ancient thrones! – whirr! whirr! all by wheels! – whiz! whiz! all by steam!

Dragoman. – The Pasha compliments the cutlery of England, and also the East India Company.

Traveller. – The Pasha's right about the cutlery, (I tried my scimitar with the common officers' swords belonging to our fellows at Malta, and they cut it like the leaf of a Novel). Well, (to the Dragoman), tell the Pasha I am exceedingly gratified to find that he entertains such a high opinion of our manufacturing energy, but I should like him to know, though, that we have got something in England besides that. These foreigners are always fancying that we have nothing but ships, and railways, and East India Companies; do just tell the Pasha, that our rural districts deserve his attention, and that even within the last two hundred years, there has been an evident improvement in the culture of the turnip, and if he does not take any interest about that, at all events, you can explain that we have our virtues in the country – that the British yeoman is still, thank God! the British yeoman: – Oh! and by the by, whilst you are about it, you may as well say that we are a truth-telling people, and, like the Osmanlees, are faithful in the performance of our promises.

Pasha (after hearing the Dragoman). – It is true, it is true: – through all Feringhistan the English are foremost, and best; for the Russians are drilled swine, and the Germans are sleeping babes, and the Italians are the servants of Songs, and the French are the sons of Newspapers, and the Greeks they are weavers of lies, but the English, and the Osmanlees are brothers together in righteousness; for the Osmanlees believe in one only God, and cleave to the Koran, and destroy idols, so do the English worship one God, and abominate graven images, and tell the truth, and believe in a book, and though they drink the juice of the grape, yet to say that they worship their prophet as God, or to say that they are eaters of pork, these are lies, – lies born of Greeks, and nursed by Jews!

Dragoman. – The Pasha compliments the English.

Traveller (rising). – Well, I've had enough of this. Tell the Pasha, I am greatly obliged to him for his hospitality, and still more for his kindness in furnishing me with horses, and say that now I must be off.

Pasha (after hearing the Dragoman, and standing up on his Divan). – Proud are the sires, and blessed are the dams of the horses that shall carry his Excellency to the end of his prosperous journey. – May the saddle beneath him glide down to the gates of the happy city, like a boat swimming on the third river of Paradise. – May he sleep the sleep of a child, when his friends are around him, and the while that his enemies are abroad, may his eyes flame red through the darkness – more red than the eyes of ten tigers! – farewell!

Dragoman. – The Pasha wishes your Excellency a pleasant journey. So ends the visit.[13]

But even Kinglake was luckier with his interpreter than he might have been. Norman Lewis, in *A Dragon Apparent*, remembers a nightmare conversation when he tried to hire a boat to take him from Vientiane to Luang Prabang:

N. L. Is that the owner of the boat?
INTERPRETER. Yes.
N. L. Tell him I want to go to Luang Prabang.

INTERPRETER (*to* BOATMAN). Him content go Luang Prabang.

BOATMAN (*in French*). Yes.

INTERPRETER. Him say yes.

N. L. Ask him when he expects to start.

INTERPRETER. Yes, possible you go. Him say.

N. L. I know, but when?

INTERPRETER. When? Ha! Today, tomorrow. Maybe you content to go. All right.

N. L. Do you mind asking him?

INTERPRETER (*determined not to lose face by speaking a word of Chinese, puts this into a long incomprehensible rigmarole of pidgin.* BOATMAN *replies similarly.*)

INTERPRETER. Him say engine no good. Sick. Soon he cure.

N. L. When?

INTERPRETER. Today, tomorrow, maybe. You content go – you go.

N. L. (*converted to pidgin*). How long trip take?

BOATMAN (*in French*). Ten nights.

INTERPRETER. Fifteen nights.

N. L. Why you say fifteen? Him no know?

INTERPRETER. Ten nights runnings maybe. Stoppings too.

(*Another Chinese arrives and does his best to spread confusion. He describes himself as a Hong Kong Englishman.*)

H. E. (*in English*). This boat good. First top-rate class. You come back tomorrow, after yesterday gone. How?

N. L. Why come back tomorrow?

INTERPRETER (*suddenly falling into line with* H. E., *and pointing to* BOATMAN). Him no say go. Him brother say.

N. L. Him brother where?

INTERPRETER and H. E. Him brother gone.

N. L. When him come?

BOATMAN. Today, tomorrow, approximately.

INTERPRETER. Approximately.[14]

CHAPTER TWELVE

Travelling Companions

The greatest travellers travel alone. They may hire guides, porters or camel-drivers; they may join caravans or other groups of local people, either for safety, or for greater economy or to keep them company along the way; but they bring no fellow-countryman with them, believing – rightly – that such a companion would come between themselves and the land through which they are passing, cushioning them from its impact and, as it were, desensitising their antennae.

On the other hand, we are not all the greatest travellers. Some of us, perhaps, may like a little cushioning; in any case, we may well find it agreeable to have an old friend with us – someone with whom to share our enjoyment, to compare our impressions, and with whom we need not always be on our best behaviour. Others of us, with no old friend available, deliberately join a party, knowing that there is in travel some curious alchemy which accelerates the growth of a friendship, and that the new friends that we are sure to make will somehow have become old friends by the time the journey is over.

Perhaps the most celebrated party of travelling companions in all literature is that of Chaucer's Canterbury pilgrims. I have already said a little bit about them in the Introduction, and there is no point in repeating myself here; but it does seem worth including portraits of three of them – the Knight, the Squire and the Wife of Bath – not simply for their own sake, but also as an indication of how astonishingly widely people travelled in the fourteenth century:

> There was a *Knight*, a most distinguished man,
> Who from the day on which he first began
> To ride abroad had followed chivalry,
> Truth, honour, generousness and courtesy.
> He had done nobly in his sovereign's war
> And ridden into battle, no man more,
> As well in christian as in heathen places,
> And ever honoured for his noble graces.
>   When we took Alexandria, he was there.
> He often sat at table in the chair

Of honour, above all nations, when in Prussia.
In Lithuania he had ridden, and Russia,
No christian man so often, of his rank.
When, in Granada, Algeciras sank
Under assault, he had been there, and in
North Africa, raiding Benamarin;
In Anatolia he had been as well
And fought when Ayas and Attalia fell,
For all along the Mediterranean coast
He had embarked with many a noble host.
In fifteen mortal battles he had been
And jousted for our faith at Tramissene
Thrice in the lists, and always killed his man.
This same distinguished knight had led the van
Once with the Bey of Balat, doing work
For him against another heathen Turk;
He was of sovereign value in all eyes.
And though so much distinguished, he was wise
And in his bearing modest as a maid.
He never yet a boorish thing had said
In all his life to any, come what might;
He was a true, a perfect gentle-knight.
   Speaking of his equipment, he possessed
Fine horses, but he was not gaily dressed.
He wore a fustian tunic stained and dark
With smudges where his armour had left mark;
Just home from service, he had joined our ranks
To do his pilgrimage and render thanks.
   He had his son with him, a fine young *Squire*,
A lover and cadet, a lad of fire
With locks as curly as if they had been pressed.
He was some twenty years of age, I guessed.
In stature he was of a moderate length,
With wonderful agility and strength.
He'd seen some service with the cavalry
In Flanders and Artois and Picardy
And had done valiantly in little space
Of time, in hope to win his lady's grace.
He was embroidered like a meadow bright
And full of freshest flowers, red and white.
Singing he was, or fluting all the day;
He was as fresh as is the month of May.
Short was his gown, the sleeves were long and wide;
He knew the way to sit a horse and ride.
He could make songs and poems and recite,
Knew how to joust and dance, to draw and write.

He loved so hotly that till dawn grew pale
He slept as little as a nightingale. ....
   A worthy *woman* from beside *Bath* city
Was with us, somewhat deaf, which was a pity.
In making cloth she showed so great a bent
She bettered those of Ypres and of Ghent.
In all the parish not a dame dared stir
Towards the altar steps in front of her,
And if indeed they did, so wrath was she
As to be quite put out of charity.
Her kerchiefs were of finely woven ground;
I dared have sworn they weighed a good ten pound,
The ones she wore on Sunday, on her head.
Her hose were of the finest scarlet red
And gartered tight; her shoes were soft and new.
Bold was her face, handsome, and red in hue.
A worthy woman all her life, what's more
She'd had five husbands, all at the church door,
Apart from other company in youth;
No need just now to speak of that, forsooth.
And she had thrice been to Jerusalem,
Seen many strange rivers and passed over them;
She'd been to Rome and also to Boulogne,
St. James of Compostella and Cologne,
And she was skilled in wandering by the way.
She had gap-teeth, set widely, truth to say.
Easily on an ambling horse she sat
Well wimpled up, and on her head a hat
As broad as is a buckler or a shield;
She had a flowing mantle that concealed
Large hips, her heels spurred sharply under that.
In company she liked to laugh and chat
And knew the remedies for love's mischances,
An art in which she knew the oldest dances.[1]

Our next author is a Scotsman, William Lithgow, whose *Rare Adventures and Painfull Peregrinations*, first published in 1632, is one of the most wholly enjoyable early travel books that I know. The villain of the following extract is admittedly more of a chance acquaintance than a true travelling companion, but we cannot lose a good story on that account. The scene is Constantinople:

The forme, or situation of this Citty, is like unto a Triangle. It is in compasse about the walles, esteemed to be eighteene miles: in one of these triangled points, being the South-east part, and at the joyning of Bosphorus and Marmora, standeth the Pallace of the Great Turke, called Seraglio, and the Forrest wherein he hunteth; which is two miles in length.

The speciall object of Antiquity, I saw within this Citty, was the incomparable Church of Saint Sophia, now consecrate to Mahomet, after a diabolicall manner. ...

I have seene men and women as usually sold here in Markets, as Horses and other beasts are with us: The most part of which are Hungarians, Transylvanians, Carinthians, Istrians, and Dalmatian Captives, and of other places besides, which they can overcome. Whom, if no compassionable Christian will buy, or relieve; then must they either turne Turke, or be addicted to perpetuall slavery. Here I remember of a charitable deede, done for a sinfull end, and thus it was; A Ship of Marseilles, called the great Dolphin, lying here forty dayes at the Galata, the Maister Gunner, named Monsieur Nerack, and I falling in familiar acquaintance, upon a time he told me secretly that he would gladly for Conscience and Merits sake, redeeme some poore Christian slave from Turkish Captivity. To the which, I applauded his advice, and told him the next Friday following I would assist him to so worthy an action: Friday comes, and he and I went for Constantinople, where the Market of the slaves being ready, we spent two houres in viewing, and reviewing five hundreth Males and Females. At last I pointed him to have bought an old man or woman, but his minde was contrary set, shewing me that he would buy some virgin, or young widdow, to save their bodies undefloured with Infidels. The price of a virgin was too deare for him, being a hundred Duckets, and widdows were farre under, and at an easier rate: When we did visite and search them that we were mindfull to buy, they were strip'd starke naked before our eyes, where the sweetest face, the youngest age, and whitest skin was in greatest value and request: The Jewes sold them, for they had bought them from the Turkes: At last we fell upon a Dalmatian widdow, whose pittifull lookes, and sprinkling teares, stroke my soule almost to the death for compassion: whereupon I grew earnest for her relief, and he yeelding to my advice, she is bought and delivered unto him, the man being 60. yeares of age, and her price 36. Duckets. We leave the market and came over again to Galata, where he and I tooke a Chamber for her, and leaving them there, the next morning I returned earely, suspecting greatly the dissembling devotion of the Gunner to be nought but luxurious lust, and so it proved: I knocked at the Chamber doore, that he had newly locked, and taken the key with him to the ship, for he had tarried with her all that night; and she answering me with teares, told me all the manner of his usage, wishing her selfe to be againe in her former captivity: whereupon I went a shipboord to him, & in my griefe I swore, that if he abused her any more after that manner, and not returned to her distresse, her Christian liberty; I would first make it knowne to his Maister the Captaine of the ship, and then to the French Ambassadour: for he was mindfull also, his lust being satisfied to have sold her over againe to some other: At which threatning the old Pallyard became so fearefull, that he entred in a reasonable condition with me, and the ship departing thence six dayes thereafter, he freely resigned to me her life, her liberty and freedome: which being done, and he gone, under my hand before divers Greekes, I subscribed her libertie.[2]

In every group of travellers there seems to be one who fails to fit in, and who arouses increasing dislike as the journey progresses. Sometimes, indeed, there are more than one; Mrs Eliza Fay, travelling out to India on the *Nathalia* in October 1779, found hardly a good word to say about anyone on board. One cannot help wondering, however, what her fellow-travellers thought about *her*.

We have now been six weeks at sea, and in the course of a few days hope to reach Calicut. Our passage across the Indian Ocean, we found very pleasant. . . . You will now expect me to say some thing of those with whom we are cooped up, but my account will not be very satisfactory, although sufficiently interesting to us – to begin then.

The woman, of whom I entertained some suspicion from the first, is I am now credibly informed, one of the very lowest creatures taken off the streets in London; she is so *perfectly* depraved in disposition, that her supreme delight consists in rendering everybody around her, miserable. – It would be doing her too much honour to stain my paper with a detail of the various artifices she daily practices to that end. – Her pretended husband having been in India before, and giving himself many airs, is looked upon as a person of mighty consequence, whom nobody chooses to offend; therefore Madam has full scope to exercise her mischievous talents, wherein he never controuls her – not but that he perfectly understands how to make himself feared; coercive measures are *some times* resorted to; it is a common expression of the lady. 'Lord bless you, if I did such, or such a thing, Tulloh would make no more to do, but knock me down like an ox.' I frequently amuse myself with examining their countenances, where ill nature has fixed her Empire so firmly, that I scarcely believe either of them ever smiled unless maliciously. Miss Howe's description of Solmes, in Clarissa Harlowe, recurs to me as admirably suiting this *amiable* pair – to that I refer you.

Chenu, the Captain, is a mere 'Jack in office;' being unexpectedly raised to that post from second mate, by the death of poor Capt. Vanderfield and his chief officer on the *fatal* Desert, is become from this circumstance so insolent and overbearing, that every one detests him. Instead of being ready to accommodate every person with the few necessaries left by the plundering Arabs, he constantly appropriates them to himself. 'Where's the Captain's silver spoon? God bless my soul. Sir, you have got my chair, must you be seated before the captain? What have you done with the Captain's glass?' and a great deal more of the same kind; but this may serve as a specimen. And altho' the wretch half starves us, he frequently makes comparisons between *his* table, and that of an Indiaman, which we dare not contradict while in his power; tell me now, should you not doat on three such companions for a long voyage? – but I have a fourth who at least, merits to be added to the triumvirate; his name John Hare, Esqr., Barrister at Law, a man of the very first fashion I assure you, and who would faint at the thought of any thing Plebeian. Taylor was one day shewing him a very handsome silver hilted sword, which he greatly admired, till chancing to cast his eye on the scabbard he read 'Royal Exchange.' 'Take your sword' said he, 'its surprizing a man of your sense should commit such an error; for fifty guineas I would not have a City name on any article of *my* dress; now St. James's or Bond street, has a *delicious* sound, don't you think so my dear friend?' – Now would any one suppose this fine gentleman's father was in trade, and he himself brought up in that very City, he effects to despise? very true nevertheless – Quadrille he would not be thought to know; it is only played by the wives and daughters of Tradesmen, in country towns: I want to make you see him; figure to yourself a little mortal, his body constantly bent in a rhetorical attitude, as if addressing the Court, and his face covered with scorbutic blotches. Happily from an affectation of singularity, he always wears spectacles. I say happily, as they serve to conceal the most odious pair of little white eyes mine ever beheld. What Butler says of Hudibras – that

'he could not ope
His mouth, but out there flew a trope,'

may literally be applied to this Heaven-born Orator, who certainly outdoes all I ever heard, in the use of overstrained compliments and far-fetched allusions. But with all those oddities, were he only a good-natured harmless simpleton, one might pity him. At first he took so much pains to ingratiate himself with us, that he became a sort of favorite; – so many confessions of superior abilities in Mr. Fay – such intreaties to spare him, when they should practise in the Courts together, – a studied attention to me in the *minutest* article – effectually shielded him from suspicion, till his end was answered, of raising a party against us, by means of that vile woman, who was anxious to triumph over me; especially as I have been repeatedly compelled (for the Honour of the Sex) to censure her swearing, and indecent behaviour. I have therefore little comfort to look forward to, for the remainder of the voyage. ...

I had almost forgotten to mention Pierot, the purser of the ship – a lively, well informed little Frenchman, – full of anecdotes and always prepared with a repartée; in short, the *soul* of the party. He sings an excellent song, and has as many tricks as a monkey. I cannot help smiling at his sallies, though they are frequently levelled at me; for he is one of my most virulent persecutors. Indeed, such is our general line of conduct; for, having early discovered the confederacy, prudence determined us to go mildly on, seemingly blind to what it was beyond our power to remedy. Never intermeddling in their disputes, all endeavours to draw us into quarrels are vainly exerted –: indeed I despise them too much to be angry.

During the first fortnight of our voyage my foolish complaisance stood in my way at table; but I soon learnt our genteel maxim was 'catch as catch can,' – the longest arm fared best; and you cannot imagine what a good scrambler I am become, – a dish once seized, it is my care, to make use of my good fortune: and now provisions running very short, we are grown quite savages; two or three of us perhaps fighting for a bone; for there is no respect of persons. The wretch of a captain wanting our passage money for nothing, refused to lay in a sufficient quantity of stock; and if we do not soon reach our Port, what must be the consequence, Heaven knows.[3]

On board ship it is usually possible, at least up to a point, to keep oneself to oneself; on a train this is a good deal harder, the lack of space and consequent enforced proximity making, on a journey of any length, some degree of *camaraderie* almost unavoidable. For anyone, therefore, keen to make new travelling companions, the train is the thing. One of the most surprising reports of rail travel that I know of occurs in the diary of the Reverend Francis Kilvert; the date is Wednesday, 18 May 1870:

Went down to the Bath Flower Show in Sydney College Gardens. Sam walked with me towards the station beyond the bottom of Huntsman's Hill. Found the first train going down was an Excursion train and took a ticket for it. The carriage was nearly full. In the Box tunnel as there was no lamp, the people began to strike foul brimstone matches and hand them to each other all down the carriage. All the time we were in the tunnel these lighted matches were travelling from hand to hand in the darkness. Each match lasted the length of the carriage and the red ember was thrown out of the opposite window, by which time another lighted match was seen travelling down the carriage. The carriage was chock full of brimstone fumes, the windows both nearly shut, and by the time we got out of the tunnel I was almost suffocated. Then a gentleman tore a lady's pocket handkerchief in two, seized one fragment, blew his nose with it, and put the rag in his pocket. She then seized his hat from his head, while another lady said that the dogs of Wootton Bassett were much more sociable than the people.[4]

In May 1904, Maurice Baring travelled in a rather more exotic train: the Trans-Siberian, from Moscow to Harbin. He describes it in *What I Saw in Russia*:

The next day I gradually made the acquaintance of all the occupants of the compartment. They divided the day into what they called 'occupation' and 'relaxation.' Occupation consisted of busying oneself with something, that is, reading, constructing a musical instrument – one of the soldiers was making a violin – reading aloud, or making a 'composition.'
'Relaxation' consisted of playing cards, doing card tricks, telling stories, or singing songs. My fellow-travellers played a game of cards which baffled my understanding. Two people play, and the cards are equally divided on the table. A hand of five cards is chosen and the game begins. When the five cards are played five more are chosen indiscriminately from the visible pack, so that all bother of thinking what might be in one's adversary's hand is avoided. The soldiers had two meals a day – dinner and tea – their rations consisting of three pounds of black bread, half a pound of meat, and cabbage soup. Sometimes they read aloud from some volumes of Gogol and Pushkin I had with me. They began anywhere in the book and stopped anywhere, and always thought it interesting. One of them pointed out to another the famous letter in Pushkin's *Evgenie Oniegin* and said that it was very good. I asked him to read a poem called *Besg*, which is about the little demons that lead the sledge-driver astray in a snowstorm. He said it was good because one could sing it.
The soldiers had not read much. They have no time; but the book I found that they had nearly all of them read was Milton's *Paradise Lost*. When two years ago a schoolmaster in the Tambov Government told me that *Paradise Lost* was the most popular book in the village library I was astonished, and thought it an isolated instance. At a fair at Moscow, during Passion Week last year, I noticed that there

were five or six different editions of translations of Milton's poem, with illustrations, ranging in price from 12 roubles to 30 kopecks, and while I was looking at one of them a *muzhik* came up to me and advised me to buy it. 'It's very interesting,' he said. 'It makes one laugh and cry.' I now understand why Milton is to the Russian peasantry what Shakespeare is to the German nation. They like the narrative of supernatural events which combine the fantasy of a fairy tale and the authority of the Scriptures – the schoolmaster in Tambov also told me that the peasants refused to read historical novels or stories because they said they were mere '*Vydumki*' (inventions) – some of it makes them laugh, and the elevated language gives them the same pleasure as being in church. It is possible to purchase *Paradise Lost* at almost any village booth. I bought an illustrated edition at a small side station between Harbin and Baikal. Another English author who is universally popular, not among the soldiers but with the officers, the professional and upper and middle classes, is Jerome K. Jerome. He has for the present generation become a popular classic in the same way as Dickens did for the preceding generation. It was possible to buy a cheap edition of his works at every railway station where there was a bookstall between Moscow and Harbin.

Conan Doyle's books were also universally popular. I never came across an officer who had not heard of Sherlock Holmes. The officers used to take in a great quantity of magazines. These magazines consisted largely of translations from the English; from the works of Jerome, Wells, Kipling, Conan Doyle, Marie Corelli, and Mrs. Humphrey Ward. Officers used often to ask me who was the most popular English author. I used to answer that I thought it was Rudyard Kipling. This used to astonish them as they considered him rather childish. But then his stories lost their salt in translation. Mrs. Humphrey Ward, they used to say, was a really *serious* author. Translations of Wells and Conan Doyle used to be running as serials in several magazines at a time.

Far the most cultivated of the men in the train was the sailor; he had read Gogol, Tolstoy, Turgenev, and Pushkin. . . .

The journey to Harbin passed off without any incident. Some excitement was caused by the announcement that a band of *Hun-hu-zes* had been seen, and that they might very likely attack the train. This, however, did not occur; but a whole crowd of Chinese officers boarded the train at one station and filled up the spare seats, especially the top-seats, from whence they spat, without ceasing, on the occupants of the lower seats, much to the annoyance of a French lady, who remarked: '*les chinois sont impossibles.*'[5]

Among modern travel writers, however, the acknowledged king of the long-distance train is Paul Theroux. Here, from *The Great Railway Bazaar*, is a typical vignette – part of a journey on the Grand Trunk Express:

The lumbering express that bisects India, a 1400-mile slash from Delhi south to Madras, gets its name from the route. It might easily have derived it from the kind of luggage the porters were heaving on board. There were grand trunks all over the platform. I had never seen such heaps of belongings in my life, or so many laden people: they were like evacuees who had been given time to pack, lazily fleeing an ambiguous catastrophe. In the best of times there is nothing simple about an Indian boarding a train, but these people climbing into the Grand Trunk Express looked as if they were setting up house – they had the air, and the merchandise, of people moving in. Within minutes the compartments were colonized, the trunks were emptied, the hampers, food baskets, water bottles, bedrolls, and Gladstones put in place; and before the train started up its character changed, for while we were still standing at Delhi Station the men stripped off their baggy trousers and twill jackets and got into traditional South Indian dress: the sleeveless gym-class undershirt and the sarong they call a *lungi*. These were scored with packing creases. It was as if, at once – in expectation of the train whistle – they all dropped the disguise they had adopted for Delhi, the Madras-bound express allowing them to assume their true identity. The train was Tamil; and they had moved in so completely, I felt like a stranger among residents, which was odd, since I had arrived earlier than anyone else.

Tamils are black and bony; they have thick straight hair and their teeth are prominent and glisten from repeated scrubbings with peeled green twigs. Watch a Tamil going over his teeth with an eight-inch twig and you begin to wonder if he isn't trying to yank a branch out of his stomach. One of the attractions of the Grand Trunk Express is that its route takes in the forests of Madhya Pradesh, where the best toothbrush twigs are found; they are sold in bundles, bound like cheroots, at the stations in the province. Tamils are also modest. Before they change their clothes each makes a toga of his bedsheet, and, hopping up and down and working his elbows, he kicks his shoes and trousers off, all the while babbling in that rippling speech that resembles the spluttering of a man singing in the shower. Tamils seem to talk constantly – only tooth-brushing silences them. Pleasure for a Tamil is discussing a large matter (life, truth, beauty, 'walues') over a large meal (very wet vegetables studded with chillies and capsicums, and served with damp *puris* and two mounds of glutinous rice). The Tamils were happy on the Grand Trunk Express: their language was spoken; their food was served; their belongings were dumped helter-skelter, giving the train the customary clutter of a Tamil home.

I started out with three Tamils in my compartment. After they changed, un-strapped their suitcases, unbuckled bedrolls, and had a meal (one gently scoffed at my spoon: 'Food taken with hand tastes different from food taken with spoon – sort of metal taste') they spent an immense amount of time introducing themselves to each other. In bursts of Tamil speech were English words like 'reposting', 'casual leave', 'annual audit'. As soon as I joined the conversation they began, with what I thought was a high degree of tact and courage, to speak to one another in English. They were in agreement on one point: Delhi was barbarous.

'I am staying at Lodi Hotel. I am booked months ahead. Everyone in Trich tells me it is a good hotel. Hah! I cannot use telephone. You have used telephone?'

'I cannot use telephone at all.'

'It is not Lodi Hotel,' said the third Tamil. 'It is Delhi.'

'Yes, my friend, you are right,' said the second.

'I say to receptionist, "Kindly stop speaking to me in Hindi. Does no one speak English around this place? Speak to me in English if you please!" '

'It is really atrocious situation.'

'Hindi, Hindi, Hindi. *Tcha!*'[6]

Indian trains, as everyone knows, are the most enjoyable trains of all – at least in retrospect. And, as an additional bonus, the stations can be no whit less rewarding than the trains themselves. For proof, you have only to turn to Eric Newby's *Slowly Down the Ganges*. He is travelling with his wife Wanda who, at this point in their journey, has a temperature of 103:

That evening we took the train to Bareilly in grey rain with Wanda wrapped in a blanket, like Lazarus newly-risen from the grave. Her fever had gone down a little, however, and she insisted that she was fit to continue, which was obviously untrue.

At Bareilly all was wet confusion. The bridge over the tracks was jammed with people half of whom were endeavouring to catch the train we had just left, the other half leaving it – both parties were accompanied by porters carrying huge tin trunks – and all became immovably locked together like a Roman testudo. In this mêlée we lost Wanda and it took some time to find her because of her red sweater which rendered her indistinguishable from the porters, but finally she was discovered propped against a pillar, not caring whether she lived or died.

'I have been twenty-five times,' she announced proudly. She told me that there was a train to Kachhla Bridge on the Ganges that left the following morning. I said that it would be madness to attempt to take it. 'I'd rather die on the Ganges than on a railway station,' she said.

At the waiting-rooms we separated. Wanda went to the ladies' department where I made up her bed for her under the frightened gaze of a number of Hindu ladies who were already in bed, closely watched by the attendant, a dissolute old crone, who agreed to supply her with tea and lemon; G. and I went off to the men's waiting-room.

We had tried, unsuccessfully, to get one of the rest-rooms which had real beds with sheets; but they were all occupied by Indian sahibs who were already tucked up with their kit neatly stacked around them, placidly reading. It was a cosy scene and although the regulations, which were prominently displayed, stated that these rooms were only to be occupied by bona-fide travellers, there was every sign that they had been there for some time. Station rest-rooms in India are favourite haunts of Members of Parliament and officials who use them as base camps from which they carry on their activities. Things were little better in the men's waiting-room where all the cane sofas, except one, were already occupied; as G. was still not feeling well, I suggested that he should make use of it.

The room was at least twenty-five feet high with small windows at the top which could be opened and shut by hauling on long cords, the sort that invariably break when you pull them. On the wall there was a framed inventory of everything in the waiting-room, both movable and immovable, and a printed tariff of the refreshments which were available in the restaurant together with the weights and measures of each dish and beverage which were listed with meticulous accuracy:

Tea in cup (Readymade 200 cc)	035nP
Tea in pot 285 cc with separate milk and sugar	035nP
1 Dal, 2 Vegetables and Curd, 8 Chapatis (225 gms) or 4 Chapatis (115 gms) plus Rice (225 gms when cooked) or Rice (450 gms when cooked) 1 Papad, Chutney or Pickle or Salad	1 Rs. 15nP

Sandwitches (Eggs 3 pieces) per plate	065nP
Fish if served with Chips or Whaffers	2 Rs. 50nP
Fruit Tipsy Pudding	05nP
Iced Water per glass	0.30nP
Ice per 454 gms	0.09nP
(quantity of less than 454 gms will not be sold)	

Under the list of table d'hôte meals there was a warning notice:

N.B. The above charges are Per Person and Persons found sharing more than one will be charged full rates according to the number of persons partaking.

By the time I had made up my bed on the floor I felt tired and dirty. There was a shower-bath in the washroom and I decided to have one.

It was unfortunate that whoever had painted the towel-rack a strong shade of burnt umber had omitted to put up a wet-paint sign when he had completed his labours. As a result, when I put on the complete change of clothing that I had been happily anticipating for some days, I looked like part of a zebra. Unfortunate though it was, this mishap did have the effect of cheering up the other occupants of the waiting-room, all of whom except myself were already in bed, and there was a lot of deep-throated 'ho-ho-hoing'. I, too, decided to follow their example and go to bed, partly because of my extraordinary striped appearance and partly because I was reluctant to dine alone in the gloom of the refreshment room on Whaffers and Fruit Tipsy Pudding.

The only reading matter that I had which was easily accessible was an Indian Railway Timetable in which the following notice was prominently displayed:

I WOULD ADVISE THE RAILWAY MANAGEMENT TO TELL THE PUBLIC THAT UNLESS THEY PURCHASED TICKETS TRAINS WOULD BE STOPPED AND THEY WOULD RESUME JOURNEY ONLY IF THE PASSENGERS WILLINGLY PAID THE FARES DUE
MAHATMA GANDHI

It was interesting to speculate on what would have happened if the management had taken the Mahatma's advice, or even been given it. The wording of the pronouncement left it in some doubt as to whether he had actually tendered the advice or was merely threatening to do so. If the management had taken it seriously the entire railway system would have been permanently paralysed.

But I was soon to have access to more interesting literature.

Lying on their couches, facing me where I lay on the floor, snugly tucked up in their bedding rolls, were two Hindu gentlemen of about my own age. Both were reading paper-backed books; occasionally the fatter of the two would utter a chuckle. Finally he could contain himself no longer.

'Excuse me, you are knowing Miss Keeler?'

'No, I don't actually know her I'm afraid,' I said.

'But you are knowing Doctor Ward, of course?'

'No; besides, he's dead.'

'It is strange that you were not knowing him. It seems that all people were knowing him. Listen to this.'

The entire waiting-room was listening happily with the exception of his companion, who was deep in a huge pink paper-back.

'Dukes, Princes and Lords sometimes got their limps impacted or depressed in games or sports and they were all cured by that vateran osteopath. Tender, slim and delicate ladies were relieved of their pains if they suffered from sprain, strain or ruptured muscles. He painted for Royal Family and people crowded to him for their photographs and nude paintings.'

'It sounds funny to me,' I said. 'Besides I'm not a Lord.'

'You are not believing this book? It is called true love story.'

'Ho-ho-ho! Very funny!' said the man in the next bed apparently to himself.

'Do not take any notice of what he says,' said my new acquaintance. 'He is very dirty fellow. He is my friend,' he added parenthetically. 'You have only to see what he is laughing at to know that he is dirty fellow. He is reading book *120 days of Sodom*, in this book there are six hundred perversions.'

'How do you know there are six hundred perversions?'

'Because it is my book. I am counting them and now I am lending it to him. He is my friend. But he is dirty chap.'

'Ho-ho-ho!' came from the dirty chap in the next bed.

'But now I am showing you this other book. It is serious worrk.'

The 'worrk' was rather wonkily printed. With rare candour the authors had written on the fly-leaf:

'The whole of the story, which is a wonderful chapter and addition in the political and religious history of ENGLAND, is based on the facts and figures that have been reported in the newspapers and journals of the world. And most of them are fictitious and imaginary and make a good piece of fiction.'

'Read it,' he said. 'Read it aloud.' You could have heard a pin drop in the waiting room.

'No,' I said firmly. It would have been just like reading to a lot of schoolboys in the 'dorm'. 'You'll be too excited to sleep.'

Before attempting to go to sleep myself, I asked my new acquaintance whose job it was to carry out the audit at various bookstalls, if I could obtain this particular book from the one on the station.

'Certainly you cannot obtain this book on station,' he said severely. 'It is indecent book. It is not suitable book for general public.'

I asked him where he had got his copy from.

'I am procuring it from Manager of one bookstall,' he said. 'He is kindly man. He also is my friend.'

The rest of the night resembled an awful dream. It was more like being on a quayside than in a station waiting-room. The whistles of the locomotives when they blasted off were as loud as ships' sirens, and as the trains came in porters carrying goods and chattels marched over me, where I lay on the floor, planting their great feet on my shins as they went. All through the night something, probably a rat – but I was too frightened to look – rustled and writhed under the head of my bedding roll. At about half-past two bathing and clearing of throats began in the wash-house, and from time to time a disgruntled figure would emerge with his dhoti covered with nice fresh paint; even the departure of a singularly beautiful girl wrapped in a sari of blue and gold tissue who for some unexplained reason had spent the night in the men's waiting-room was spoiled by her breaking wind as she went through the door. At six-thirty rain began to fall with such violence that it seemed as if it was filling with water. It was a night both to remember and forget.[7]

From India to Kenya – where, as Martha Gellhorn wrote in *Travels with Myself and Another*, 'I knew exactly what I wanted: hire or buy a second-hand Landrover, pick up a driver to share the work and act as interpreter, and set forth alone to explore East Africa.' The idea sounded fine; the only problem was the driver:

Joshua presented himself in the cocktail lounge of the New Stanley with a chit from the Honorary Consul, guaranteeing that Joshua was 'reliable'. In local code, this meant that Joshua would not rape and/or rob me. Neither of those possibilities have ever seemed worth fretting over. Instinct, which I regularly ignore, told me that Joshua was not the man for the job.

Joshua was small, cordoba brown in colour, delicate to fragile, neat and clean. We sat on a bench by the wall while Joshua extolled his virtues. He was, first and foremost, 'eddicated', that implied higher pay than for an average driver. He had driven a Government Landrover throughout the Emergency (Mau Mau time) and lately had been driving a large American car for a tourist company in the city. I was not enthusiastic about Joshua; there was something finicky in him which I felt would not wear well, and I would have preferred a sturdier type. But I was scratchy with impatience to leave, three whole days in Nairobi were enough. Nairobi was bliss but it wasn't Africa either. I was still searching for the Africa that I had come this weary way to find.

So I hired Joshua, despite the loud alarm bells of instinct, and told him we would leave at eight in the morning. My equipment for the journey was a large thermos filled with cold water, a flashlight, new khaki trousers and shirts, comfortable safari boots, the old straw hat, a fresh stock of paperback thrillers and goofy confidence.

Joshua arrived in black imitation Italian silk pipestem trousers, white shirt, black pointed shoes, black sunglasses in ornate red frames, holding a cardboard suitcase. The lobby of the New Stanley and the Thorn Tree café outside teemed with people going on or returning from safaris, or pretending to do so. The correct outfit was a deep sunburn, well-cut, much-worn, faded starched khaki trousers, long or short, a short-sleeved khaki bush jacket or shirt with ample pockets, old safari boots: new clothes betrayed the tenderfoot tourist. The tone was easy machismo; everyone had been eyeball to eyeball with a lion. African safari servants also wore khaki though rumpled and baggy, not Bwana standard. Departures were impressive and rather theatrical, especially if celebrities were about to venture into the bush. Mr Kirk Douglas and Mr Robert Ruark were leaving glamorously at this time. Joshua looked a comic cut; I looked sheepish. Only the dusty, beat-up, dented, patched Landrover looked right.

I expected Joshua to take the wheel and steer us out of Nairobi to the main Nairobi–Kampala road; gently but firmly, Joshua declined the honour. He could direct me better if I drove. . . .

223

'You drive this morning, Joshua.'

'Better later, Memsaab,' Joshua said and nipped smartly into the passenger seat.

The mornings were always easier no matter what the road because the daylight-distance phobia hadn't engulfed me. We made the forty-four miles to Nakuru in two hours, quick work, and I stopped for petrol. Petrol stations were infrequent. Whenever I saw one, I behaved as if I had come on an oasis in the desert and drew in to replenish the tank and check the oil and water and tyre pressure, though we carried two jerry cans of petrol and one of water. Joshua sat and watched while I jumped out to make sure the air gauge was properly read, the oil gauge properly wiped and inserted and inspected, the petrol actually filling the tank.

'Really, Joshua,' I said crossly, 'You could take care of this.'

'Better you, Memsaab. These boys obey you more.'

The African Ranger at the gate of Lake Nakuru Park warned me about water-logged side tracks. It would be wiser to leave the Landrover on the main track and walk to the shore. After driving far enough to feel alone in darkest Africa and therefore ecstatic, I parked the Landrover on a reliable piece of stubble-covered ground, got my kit together, sandwiches, thermos of cold tea, *Field Guide to the National Parks*, binoculars and said, 'Ready, Joshua?'

Joshua stared at the squashy track and wrinkled his nose. 'Very bad mud.'

'Are you coming or not?'

'Memsaab, they got lions?'

'No,' I said with authority, having read the *Field Guide* which stated that lions were rare hereabouts.

'I watch the car. Some man could come stealing your clothes.'

I much preferred to be by myself but thought it would be an awful bind if we had to circle East Africa without getting Joshua's fancy footwear dirty. . . .

The Landrover was turned so that the passenger seat faced the track. Joshua sat therein, with the door open, his knees crossed, one foot swinging languidly outside. He held a miniature teacup and saucer in his left hand and as I stared, transfixed, he lifted the cup, his little finger curled, and sipped daintily. It struck me with the force of revelation: a Kikuyu Presbyterian pansy. Joshua turned and said graciously, 'Jambo, Memsaab, you have good time?'

'Jambo, Joshua, very good.' I busied myself looking up the small antelopes in the guide book while Joshua stowed the remains of our picnics and his china ware: Thomson's gazelles. But how could I have guessed, I didn't even know African pansies existed. When you thought of all the clamour about black men lusting for white women and white women lusting for black men due to their massive virility, it was even funnier. What I could absolutely not do was have a fit of giggles.

'Want to drive now, Joshua?'

'I dunno this road, Memsaab.'

'Have you ever heard about the blind leading the blind?'

'No, how can that be? If somebody is blind now how can he be leading another fellow as well he is blind too?'

'We are going to find out, Joshua, day by day. Get your sweater now, it will be cold later.' And thought that before we were through no doubt I would bring him morning tea and tuck him in at night. . . .

A month after I got home to London, where I spent my time mourning for Africa, a letter arrived from Joshua. It was written in purple ink on green notepaper with a daisy stamped at the top right-hand corner. Joshua must have bought this fine paper especially for the occasion. He said that he would never forget our safari, he had never been so happy in his life, and I was his mother and father.[8]

Captain Philip Thicknesse, travelling on the Continent in 1775–6, had much more satisfactory companions. Apart from Mrs Thicknesse and their two daughters, there was the horse, Callee ('a little touched in the wind'), a spaniel, a pet parakeet (uncaged) and a monkey, Jocko:

My Monkey, with a pair of French jack boots, and his hair *en queue*, rode postillion upon my sturdy horse some hours every day; such a sight, you may be sure, brought forth old and young, sick and lame, to look at him and his master. *Jocko* put whole towns in motion, but never brought any affront on his master; they came to look and to laugh, but not to deride or insult. The post-boys, it is true, did not like to see their fraternity *taken off*, in my *little Theatre;* but they seldom discovered it, but by a grave salutation; and sometimes a good humoured fellow called him comrade, and made *Jocko* a bow; they could not laugh at his bad seat, for not one of them rode with more ease, or had a handsomer laced jacket. Mr. *Buffon* says, the Monkey or *Maggot*, (and mine is the latter, for he has no tail) make their grimace or chattering equally to shew their anger or to make known their appetite. With all due deference to this great naturalist, I must beg leave to say, that his observation is not quite just; there is as much difference between the grimace of my *Jocko*, when he is angry or hungry, and when he grins to shew delight, as there is in a man, when he gnashes his teeth in wrath, or laughs from mirth.

Between *Avignon* and this town I met a dancing bear, mounted by a *Maggot*: as it was upon the high road, I desired leave to present *Jocko* to his grandfather, for so he appeared both in age and size; the interview, though they were both males, was very affecting; never did a father receive a long-lost child with more seeming affection than the *old gentleman* did my *Jocko;* he embraced him with every degree of tenderness imaginable, while the *young gentleman* (like other young gentlemen of the present age) betrayed a perfect indifference.[9]

To conclude, here is Eric Newby again, in his early classic *A Short Walk in the Hindu Kush*. With his friend Hugh Carless, he is just returning to Kabul from Nuristan:

We crossed the river by a bridge, went up through the village of Shāhnaiz and downhill towards the Lower Panjshir.

'Look,' said Hugh, 'it must be Thesiger.'

Coming towards us out of the great gorge where the river thundered was a small caravan like our own. He named an English explorer, a remarkable throwback to the Victorian era, a fluent speaker of Arabic, a very brave man, who has twice crossed the Empty Quarter and, apart from a few weeks every year, has passed his entire life among primitive peoples.

We had been on the march for a month. We were all rather jaded; the horses were galled because the drivers were careless of them, and their ribs stood out because they had been in places only fit for mules and forded innumerable torrents filled with slippery rocks as big as footballs; the drivers had run out of tobacco and were pining for their wives; there was no more sugar to put in the tea, no more jam, no more cigarettes and I was reading *The Hound of the Baskervilles* for the third time; all of us suffered from a persistent dysentery. The ecstatic sensations we had experienced at a higher altitude were beginning to wear off. It was not a particularly gay party.

Thesiger's caravan was abreast of us now, his horses lurching to a standstill on the execrable track. They were deep-loaded with great wooden presses, marked 'British Museum', and black tin trunks (like the ones my solicitors have, marked 'Not Russel-Jones' or 'All Bishop of Chichester').

The party consisted of two villainous-looking tribesmen dressed like royal mourners in long overcoats reaching to the ankles; a shivering Tajik cook, to whom some strange mutation had given bright red hair, unsuitably dressed for Central Asia in crippling pointed brown shoes and natty socks supported by suspenders, but no trousers; the interpreter, a gloomy-looking middle-class Afghan in a coma of fatigue, wearing dark glasses, a double-breasted lounge suit and an American hat with stitching all over it; and Thesiger himself, a great, long-striding crag of a man, with an outcrop for a nose and bushy eyebrows, forty-five years old and as hard as nails, in an old tweed jacket of the sort worn by Eton boys, a pair of thin grey cotton trousers, rope-soled Persian slippers and a woollen cap comforter.

'Turn round,' he said, 'you'll stay the night with us. We're going to kill some chickens.'

We tried to explain that we had to get to Kabul, that we wanted our mail, but our men, who professed to understand no English but were reluctant to pass through the gorges at night, had already turned the horses and were making for the collection of miserable hovels that was the nearest village.

Soon we were sitting on a carpet under some mulberry trees, surrounded by the entire population, with all Thesiger's belongings piled up behind us.

'Can't speak a word of the language,' he said cheerfully. 'Know a lot of the Koran by heart but not a word of Persian. Still, it's not really necessary. Here, you,' he shouted at the cook, who had only entered his service the day before and had never seen another Englishman. 'Make some green tea and a lot of chicken and rice – three chickens.'

'No good bothering the interpreter,' he went on, 'the poor fellow's got a sty, that's why we only did seventeen miles today. It's no good doing too much at first, especially as he's not feeling well.'

The chickens were produced. They were very old; in the half-light they looked like pterodactyls.

'Are they expensive?'

'The Power of Britain never grows less,' said the headman, lying superbly.

'That means they are very expensive,' said the interpreter, rousing himself.

Soon the cook was back, semaphoring desperately.

'Speak up, can't understand a thing. You want sugar? Why don't you say so?' He produced a large bunch of keys, like a housekeeper in some stately home. All that evening he was opening and shutting boxes so that I had tantalizing glimpses of the contents of an explorer's luggage – a telescope, a string vest, the *Charterhouse of Parma, Du Côté de Chez Swann*, some fish-hooks and the 1/1000000 map of Afghanistan – not like mine, a sodden pulp, but neatly dissected, mounted between marbled boards.

'That cook's going to die,' said Thesiger; 'hasn't got a coat and look at his feet. We're nine thousand feet if we're an inch here. How high's the Chamar Pass?' We told him 16,000 feet. 'Get yourself a coat and boots, do you hear?' he shouted in the direction of the camp fire.

After two hours the chickens arrived; they were like elastic, only the rice and gravy were delicious. Famished, we wrestled with the bones in the darkness.

'England's going to pot,' said Thesiger, as Hugh and I lay smoking the inter-preter's King Size cigarettes, the first for a fortnight. 'Look at this shirt, I've only had it three years, now it's splitting. Same with tailors; Gull and Croke made me a pair of whipcord trousers to go to the Atlas Mountains. Sixteen guineas – wore a hole in them in a fortnight. Bought half a dozen shotguns to give to my headmen, well-known make, twenty guineas apiece, absolute rubbish.'

He began to tell me about his Arabs.

'I give them powders for worms and that sort of thing.' I asked him about surgery. 'I take off fingers and there's a lot of surgery to be done; they're frightened of their own doctors because they're not clean.'

'Do you do it? Cutting off fingers?'

'Hundreds of them,' he said dreamily, for it was very late. 'Lord, yes. Why, the other day I took out an eye. I enjoyed that.

'Let's turn in,' he said.

The ground was like iron with sharp rocks sticking up out of it. We started to blow up our air-beds. 'God, you must be a couple of pansies,' said Thesiger.[10]

CHAPTER THIRTEEN

Hardships

Leaving Ahansal behind us, and entring the Countrey of the Agaroes, we found the best inhabitants halfe cled, the Vulgars naked, the Countrey voyd of Villages, Rivers, or Cultivage: but the soyle rich in Bestiall, abounding in Sheep, Goates, Camels, Dromidores, and passing good horses: Having an Emeere of their owne, being subject to none, but to his owne passions, and them to the disposition of his scelerate nature; yet hee, and they had a bastard show of Mahometanicall Religion. . . . In our six dayes toyle, traversing this Countrey, we had many troubles and snarlings from these Savages, who sometimes over-laboured us with Bastinadoes, and were still inquirous what I was, and whether I went; yea, and enough for the Dragoman to save my life and liberty.

Having past the perverstnesse of this calamity, upon the seaventh day, wee rancountred with another soyle, and worser tribe of the Hagans or Yamnites, most part whereof were white Moores, a people more uglye then the Nigroes, yet some of the better sort had their members covered, but of condition farre more wicked then the former.

. . . wee were involved in a dis-inhabited Country, being Desartuous and dangerous for Wilde beasts, and full of Mountaynes. Pitching our Tent neare to a Rocke, we burnt all that night shrubs of Tara, to affright the Beasts of all kinds, and so did we every night of that wofull wandring, which flaming light their nature cannot abide. Day come, and our comfort yet fresh, we sought further in, thinking to finde people and Tents to relieve us with Victuales, and informe us of the Countrey, but we found none, neither seven daies thereafter. The matter growing hard, and our victuals and water done, we were forced to relye upon Tobacco, and to drinke our owne wayning pisse, for the time aforesayd.

The Soyle we daily traced, was covered with hard and soft Sands, and them full of Serpents, being interlarded with Rockey heights, faced with Caves and Dens: the very habitacle of Wilde beasts, whose hollow cryes, as we heard in the night, so we too often sighted their bodies in the day, especially Jackals, Beares, and Boares, and sometimes Cymbers, Tygers, and Leopards, agaynst whom in the day time if they approached us, we eyther shot off a Harquebuse, or else flashed some powder in the Ayre; the smell whereof, no ravenous beast can abide.[1]

So wrote William Lithgow of his wanderings in the western Sahara in the first quarter of the seventeenth century. He was, it may be thought, piling it on a bit; but hardship has always been part and parcel of foreign travel, and few indeed are the writers who soft-pedal the subject. At much the same time as Lithgow was suffering in Africa, Thomas Coryat was having a rather unfortunate time in, of all places, Bergamo:

This City yeelded me the worst lodging for one night that I found in all my travels out of England. For all the Innes were so extreme full of people by reason of the faire, that I could not get a convenient lodging though I would have given two or three duckats for it. So that I was faine to lye upon straw in one of their stables at the horse feete, according to a picture that I have made of it in the frontispice of my booke. Where (notwithstanding my repose upon so uncouth a pallate) I slept in utramque aurem, even as securely as upon a bedde of downe, because of my long journey the day before. And it was long before I could obtayne this favour, which was at last granted me by the meanes of an honest Italian Priest who had beene a traveller. Unto whom I was not a litle beholding for some curtesies that I received at his hands in Bergomo. He promised to revisit me the next morning, to the end to shew me the antiquities of the City. But he was prevented to my great griefe by the villany of a certaine bloud-thirsty Italian, who for an old grudge he bare to him, shot him through the body in his lodging with a pewternell.[2]

But neither Lithgow's nor Coryat's sufferings were anything in comparison with those endured by Captain John Stedman and his fellow-members of the expedition to Surinam (Dutch Guiana) in 1772:

I have already mentioned the prickly heat, ring-worm, dry gripes, putrid fevers, biles, consaca, and bloody flux, to which human nature is exposed in this climate; also the mosquitoes, Patat and Scrapat lice, chigoes, cockroaches, ants, horse-flies, wild-bees, and bats, besides the thorns and briars, and the alligators and peree in the rivers; to which if we add the howling of the tigers, the hissing of serpents, and the growling of Fourgeoud, the dry sandy savannahs, unfordable marshes, burning hot days, cold and damp nights, heavy rains, and short allowance, the reader may be astonished how any person was able to survive the trial. Notwithstanding this black catalogue, I solemnly declare I have omitted many other calamities that we suffered, as I wish to avoid prolixity, though perhaps I have been already too often guilty of it.[3]

For all his fear of prolixity, let us allow poor Captain Stedman to enlarge a little on just two of these plagues:

Having advanced rather a less distance than we did the day before, we were ordered early to sling our hammocks and to sleep without any covering to prevent the enemy from hearing the sound of cutting the trees; nor were any fires allowed to be lighted nor a word to be spoken, while a strict watch was kept round the camp. These, in fact, were all very necessary precautions; but if we were not discovered by the enemy, we were almost devoured by the clouds of gnats or mosquitoes which arose from a neighbouring marsh. For my own part I suffered more here than I had even done on board the fatal barges in the upper Cottica, as we could make no smoke to drive them away. In this situation I saw the poor mén dig holes with their bayonets in the earth, into which they thrust their heads, stopping the entry and covering their necks with their hammocks, while they lay with their bellies on the ground. To sleep in any other position was absolutely impossible. . . .

This was the principal distress of the night, while during the day, we had frequently been attacked by whole armies of small emmets, called here *fire-ants*, from their painful biting. These insects are black, and very diminutive, but live in such amazing multitudes together, that their hillocks have sometimes obstructed our passage by their size, over which, if one chances to pass, the feet and legs are instantly covered with innumerable of these creatures, which seize the skin with such violence in their pincers, that they will sooner suffer the head to be parted from their body, than let go their hold. I can aver that I have seen them make a whole company hop about, as if they had been scalded with boiling water.[4]

Insects may not be the worst of the dangers that the intrepid traveller has to face, but they are surely the greatest irritation; many is the cynic who has emerged from a night of misery believing, for the first time in his life, in the existence of the Devil. As Alexander Kinglake discovered, not even the Holy Land could offer any protection:

Except at Jerusalem, never think of attempting to sleep in a 'holy city'. Old Jews from all parts of the world go to lay their bones upon the sacred soil; and since these people never return to their homes, it follows that any domestic vermin they may bring with them are likely to become permanently resident, so that the population is continually increasing. No recent census had been taken when I was at Tiberias; but I know that the congregation of fleas which attended at my church alone must have been something enormous. It was a carnal, self-seeking congregation, wholly inattentive to the service which was going on, and devoted to the one object of having my blood. The fleas of all nations were there. The smug, steady, importunate flea from Holywell Street – the pert, jumping 'puce' from hungry France – the wary, watchful 'pulce' with his poisoned stiletto – the vengeful 'pulga' of Castile with his ugly knife – the German 'floh' with his knife and fork, insatiate, not rising from table – whole swarms from all the Russias, and Asiatic hordes unnumbered – all these were there, and all rejoiced in one great international feast. I could no more defend myself against my enemies, than if I had been 'pain à discrétion' in the hands of a French communist. After passing a night like this, you are glad to gather up the remains of your body long, long before morning dawns. Your skin is scorched – your temples throb – your lips feel withered and dried – your burning eye-balls are screwed inwards against the brain. You have no hope but only in the saddle, and the freshness of the morning air.[5]

Nor did the Hon. Robert Curzon have a much better time of it on the island of Lemnos:

After dinner I made inquiries of my host what he had in the way of bed. His answer was specific. There was no bed, no mattress, no divan: sheets were unknown things, and the wool he did not recommend. But at last I was told of a mattress which an old woman next door was possessed of, and which she sometimes let out to strangers; and in an evil hour I sent for it. That treacherous bed and its clean white coverlet will never be forgotten by me. I lay down upon it and in one minute was fast asleep – the next I started up a perfect Marsyas. Never until that day had I any idea of what fleas could do. So simultaneous and well-conducted was their attack, that I was bitten all over from top to toe at the first assault. They evidently were delighted at the unexpected change of diet from a grim, skinny old woman to a well-fed traveller fresh from the table of the embassy. I examined the white coverlet – it was actually brown with fleas. I threw away my clothes, and taking desperate measures to get rid of some myriads of my assailants, I ran out of the room and put on a dressing-gown in the outer hall, at the window of which I sat down to cool the fever of my blood. I half-expected to see the fleas open the door and march in after me, as the rats did after Bishop Hatto on his island in the Rhine; but fortunately the villains did not venture so far from home. The mattress was, I am inclined to believe, entirely stuffed with fleas. How so large a party could be provided with regular meals it is difficult to conjecture: they could not have had board as well as lodging in the old lady's house, or she would have been eaten up long ago; whatever their diet usually was, the sharpness of their appetites proved that they were in excellent health. There I sat, fanning myself in the night air and bathing my face and limbs in water till the sun rose, when with a doleful countenance I asked my way to a bath. I found one, and went into the hot inner room with nothing on but a towel round my waist and one on my head, as the custom is. There was no one else there, and when the bath-man came in he started back with horror, for he thought I had got that most deadly kind of plague which breaks out in an eruption and carries off the patient in a few hours. When it was explained to him how I had fallen into the clutches of these Lemnian fleas, he proceeded to rub me and soap me according to the Turkish fashion, and wonderfully soothing and comforting it was.[6]

But there are other things as well as insect life that can sorely disturb the traveller's rest. The ubiquitous Mrs Isabella Bird describes, in *Unbeaten Tracks in Japan*, a most disagreeable night in Tochigi in 1878:

The *yadoya* was a very large one, and, as sixty guests had arrived before me, there was no choice of accommodation, and I had to be contented with a room enclosed on all sides not by *fusuma* but *shôji*, and with barely room for my bed, bath, and chair, under a fusty green mosquito net which was a perfect nest of fleas. One side of the room was against a much-frequented passage, and another opened on a small yard upon which three opposite rooms also opened, crowded with some not very sober or decorous travellers. The *shôji* were full of holes, and often at each hole I saw a human eye. Privacy was a luxury not even to be recalled. Besides the constant application of eyes to the *shôji*, the servants, who were very noisy and rough, looked into my room constantly without any pretext; the host, a bright, pleasant-looking man, did the same; jugglers, musicians, blind shampooers, and singing girls, all pushed the screens aside; and I began to think that Mr. Campbell was right, and that a lady should not travel alone in Japan. Ito, who had the room next to mine, suggested that robbery was quite likely, and asked to be allowed to take charge of my money, but did not decamp with it during the night! I lay down on my precarious stretcher before eight, but as the night advanced the din of the house increased till it became truly diabolical, and never ceased till after one. Drums, tom-toms, and cymbals were beaten; *kotos* and *samisens* screeched and twanged; *geishas* (professional women with the accomplishments of dancing, singing, and playing) danced, accompanied by songs whose jerking discords were most laughable; story-tellers recited tales in a high key, and the running about and splashing close to my room never ceased. Late at night my precarious *shôji* were accidentally thrown down, revealing a scene of great hilarity, in which a number of people were bathing and throwing water over each other.[7]

Yet all these are, in a way, minor hardships compared with what some travellers have had to face. Take Mungo Park, for example, battling his way through West Africa – not for nothing known as the White Man's Grave – on his second journey of 1805–6:

July 4th. – Agreed with the canoe people to carry over our baggage and cattle for sixty bars. There being but one canoe, it was near noon before all the bundles were carried over. The transporting of the asses was very difficult. The river being shallow and rocky, whenever their feet touched the bottom they generally stood still. Our guide, Isaaco, was very active in pushing the asses into the water, and shoving along the canoe; but as he was afraid that we could not have them all carried over in the course of the day, he attempted to drive six of the asses across the river farther down where the water was shallower. When he had reached the middle of the river, a crocodile rose close to him, and instantly seizing him by the left thigh, pulled him under water. With wonderful presence of mind he felt the head of the animal, and thrust his finger into its eye; on which it quitted its hold, and Isaaco attempted to reach the farther shore, calling out for a knife. But the crocodile returned and seized him by the other thigh, and again pulled him under water; he had recourse to the same expedient, and thrust his fingers into its eyes with such violence that it again quitted him; and when it rose, flounced about on the surface of the water as if stupid, and then swam down the middle of the river. Isaaco proceeded to the other side, bleeding very much. As soon as the canoe returned I went over, and found him very much lacerated. The wound on the left thigh was four inches in length; that on the right not quite so large, but very deep; besides several single teeth wounds on his back. Drew the lips of the wounds together with slips of adhesive plaster secured with a roller; and as we were not far from a village, he thought it best for him to go forwards before his wounds had become very painful. He accordingly rode forwards to the village of Boolinkoomboo on one of our horses. Found myself very sick, and unable to stand erect without feeling a tendency to faint; the people so sickly that it was with some difficulty we got the loads put into the tents, though it threatened rain. To my great astonishment, Ashton, the sailor whom I had left in the woods the evening before, came up quite naked, having been stripped of his clothes by three of the natives during the night. Found his fever much abated.

July 5th. – With great difficulty got the asses loaded, but had not a sufficient number of spare asses for the sick. Set one of them on my horse, and walked, feeling a remission of the fever, though still very giddy and unwell. We soon reached Boolinkoomboo, it being only two miles from the landing-place. This village is sometimes called Moiaharra: it does not contain above one hundred people. On collecting the asses, found that three were missing, besides a sickly one, which was too weak to cross the river, and was eaten by the people of Fonilla. All this diminished our means of carrying forward the sick.

I now found my situation very perplexing. To go forward without Isaaco to Keminoom, I knew, would involve us in difficulties; as Keminoom's sons are reckoned the greatest thieves and blackguards on the whole route. To stop till Isaaco recovered (an event which seemed very doubtful), would throw us into the violence of the rains. There was no other person that I could trust; and, what was worst of all, we had only *two days' rice*, and a great scarcity prevailed in the country. I determined to wait three days, to see how Isaaco's wounds looked, and in the meantime sent two of his people away to Serracorra with an ass and three strings of No. 5 amber to purchase rice.

July 6th. – All the people either sick, or in a state of great debility, except one. Bought all the milk I could find, and boiled a camp kettle full of strong decoction of barks every day.

July 7th. – Dressed Isaaco's wounds: they looked remarkably well.[8]

Park seldom mentions the heat; he seems to have taken it for granted. Besides, he had more important things to worry about. In West Africa, in any case, the humidity – unhealthy and uncomfortable as it may be – must greatly reduce the risk of serious dehydration. It is in the desert places of the world that the sun is at its most deadly. Dervla Murphy, cycling to India in the 1960s, here describes in *Full Tilt* what she suffered one June day in Pakistan; the 'we' in the narrative refers to herself and Roz, her bicycle:

Chilas, 17 June ...
We left Goner at 5.30 a.m. and arrived here at 4.30 p.m., having only covered twenty-eight miles, yet I came into the shade of this nullah in a state of total collapse, so decidedly at the end of my tether that I don't believe I could have kept going *one* more mile. The Tahsildar here told me that when I arrived the temperature was 114° – he didn't really have to say it! I had to walk all the way as the first twenty miles were through very deep sand, up and down very steep hills, and after that I was too dizzy from the heat to balance on Roz, even where the track was level. By 7 a.m. the sun was so hot that I was saturated through with sweat and as we only came to one nullah for wetting, cooling and refilling the waterbottle, dehydration became my fear. I found shade once, under a rock, and slept very soundly from 1.40 to 2.50 p.m., although lying on sharp flints. After that the real trouble began and by 3 p.m. I was seriously worried: I had stopped sweating, which is a danger signal, and my mouth was so dry that my tongue felt like an immovable bit of stiff leather. By 3.30 I was shivering with cold, though the heat was so intense that I did not dare touch any metal part of Roz. After that I just kept going but don't remember one bit of the road – only that the green trees of Chilas were visible in the distance. I had just enough sense left, on getting to the nullah, not to drink gallons, but to lie under a willow and take mouthfuls at a time until gradually I began to sweat again and get warm. Then I rolled into the water and lay there for

a few minutes with it rushing deliciously over me, after which I was able to walk another half-mile to the Tahsildar's house, where I drank gallons of buttermilk and salt followed by cups and cups of hot tea; but I couldn't look at food this evening.

Chilas is only 3,000 feet above sea level and is hellishly hot even amidst all the running brooks and dense green trees and shrubs – because it's completely encircled by naked rock-mountains which relentlessly throw back that intolerable sun. The Tahsildar (a minor local government official) says that I must stay here tomorrow for a day's rest before going over the Babusar and I couldn't agree more! Not that the pass will be difficult after the last three days; once I get eight miles up (and I'll start at 3.30 a.m.) it will be cool, and it's heat, not gradients, that finish me off.

The horror of today's trek really was extreme with heat visibly flowing towards me in malevolent waves off the mountainsides and the dreadful desert stench of burning sand – which still persists here – nauseating me; the terrifying dehydration of mouth and nostrils and eyes until my eyelids could barely move and a sort of staring blindness came on, with the ghastly sensation of scorching air filling my lungs, and the overpowering drug-like effect of the wild thyme and sage, that grow thickly over the last few miles, being 'distilled' by the sun; and above all the despair of coming round corners and over hilltops time and time again, hoping always to see water – and never seeing it. I have often thought that death by thirst must be grimmer than most deaths and now my surmise has been confirmed. The irony of it all was that all day the vast, swirling Indus flowed beside me, inaccessible.[9]

There is another fearsome description of desert heat, combined this time with utter physical exhaustion, in Wilfred Thesiger's *Arabian Sands*. Remembering his legendary, almost superhuman toughness and powers of endurance, one finds oneself wondering whether in such conditions any other European could have survived at all:

Al Auf woke us again while it was still dark. As usual bin Kabina made coffee, and the sharp-tasting drops which he poured out stimulated but did not warm. The morning star had risen above the dunes. Formless things regained their shape in the first dim light of dawn. The grunting camels heaved themselves erect. We lingered for a moment more beside the fire; then al Auf said 'Come', and we moved forward. Beneath my feet the gritty sand was cold as frozen snow.

We were faced by a range as high as, perhaps even higher than, the range we had crossed the day before, but here the peaks were steeper and more pronounced, rising in many cases to great pinnacles, down which the flowing ridges swept like draperies. These sands, paler coloured than those we had crossed, were very soft, cascading round our feet as the camels struggled up the slopes. Remembering how little warning of imminent collapse the dying camels had given me twelve years before in the Danakil country, I wondered how much more these camels would stand, for they were trembling violently whenever they halted. When one refused to go on we heaved on her head-rope, pushed her from behind, and lifted the loads on either side as we manhandled the roaring animal upward. Sometimes one of them lay down and refused to rise, and then we had to unload her, and carry the water-skins and the saddle-bags ourselves. Not that the loads were heavy. We had only a few gallons of water left and some handfuls of flour.

We led the trembling, hesitating animals upward along great sweeping ridges where the knife-edged crests crumbled beneath our feet. Although it was killing work, my companions were always gentle and infinitely patient. The sun was scorching hot and I felt empty, sick, and dizzy. As I struggled up the slope, knee-deep in shifting sand, my heart thumped wildly and my thirst grew worse. I found it difficult to swallow; even my ears felt blocked, and yet I knew that it would be many intolerable hours before I could drink. I would stop to rest, dropping down on the scorching sand, and immediately it seemed I would hear the others shouting, 'Umbarak, Umbarak'; their voices sounded strained and hoarse.

It took us three hours to cross this range.

On the summit were no gently undulating downs such as we had met the day before. Instead, three smaller dune-chains rode upon its back, and beyond them the sand fell away to a salt-flat in another great empty trough between the mountains. The range on the far side seemed even higher than the one on which we stood, and behind it were others. I looked round, seeking instinctively for some escape. There was no limit to my vision. Somewhere in the ultimate distance the sands merged into the sky, but in that infinity of space I could see no living thing, not even a withered plant to give me hope. 'There is nowhere to go', I thought. 'We cannot go back and our camels will never get up another of these awful dunes. We really are finished.' The silence flowed over me, drowning the voices of my companions and the fidgeting of their camels.

We went down into the valley, and somehow – and I shall never know how the camels did it – we got up the other side. There, utterly exhausted, we collapsed. Al Auf gave us each a little water, enough to wet our mouths. He said, 'We need this if we are to go on.' The midday sun had drained the colour from the sands. Scattered banks of cumulus cloud threw shadows across the dunes and salt-flats, and added an illusion that we were high among Alpine peaks, with frozen lakes of blue and green in the valley, far below. Half asleep, I turned over, but the sand burnt through my shirt and woke me from my dreams.[10]

Captain Fred Burnaby, between Orenburg and Orsk on his *Ride to Khiva*, suffered from the opposite extreme:

After waiting for several hours I was informed that some horses had been procured. The snowstorm had somewhat lulled, but the wind was almost as high as ever, and the cold more intense than anything hitherto experienced. On leaving the station I had forgotten to put on my thick gloves, and took my seat in the sleigh, with each hand folded in the sleeve of its fellow, the fur pelisse in this way forming a sort of muff, and protecting my hands from the cold. The road was less jolty than usual, and the sleigh glided along, comparatively speaking, smoothly. The change of motion before long produced an effect; leaning back in the vehicle, I fell fast asleep.

In the course of my slumber my hands slipped from the warm fur covering in which they were inserted, resting themselves on the side of the sleigh, unprotected by any thick gloves, and exposed to the full power of the biting east wind. This, if impossible to withstand when stationary or on foot, was now doubly dangerous owing to the movement of the sleigh, which, going in an opposite direction, added considerably to the force with which the wind blew.

In a few minutes I awoke, a feeling of intense pain had seized my extremities; it seemed as if they had been plunged into some corrosive acid which was gradually eating the flesh from the bones.

I looked at my finger-nails; they were blue, the fingers and back part of my hands were of the same colour, whilst my wrists and the lower part of the arm were of a waxen hue. There was no doubt about it, I was frostbitten, and that in no slight degree; so calling to my servant, I made him rub the skin with some snow in hopes of restoring the vitality. This he did for several minutes, but all this time the same pain previously described was gradually ascending up my arms, whilst the lower portions of the limbs were lost to all sensation, dead to pain – dead to every sense of feeling – hanging quite listlessly by my side, Nazar in vain using all his energies so as to restore circulation.

'It is no good,' he said, looking sorrowfully at me; 'we must get on as fast as possible to the station. How far off is it?' he inquired of the driver. 'Seven miles,' was the answer.

'Go as fast as you can,' I cried.

The pain, which by that time had ascended to the glands under my arms, had become more acute than anything I had hitherto experienced. Apparently, extreme cold acts in two ways on the nervous system: sometimes, and more mercifully, by bringing on a slumber from which the victim never awakes, and at others by consuming him, as it were, over a slow fire, and limb by limb.

All this time the perspiration was pouring down my forehead, my body itself being as if on fire, the pain gradually ascending the parts attacked.

There are moments in a man's life when death itself would be a relief; it was about the day that an unfortunate criminal would have to undergo the last dread sentence of the law, and I remember distinctly the thought occurring to my mind, as to whether the physical pain I was then undergoing was less than the mental agony of the poor wretch on the drop.

Would the distance that separated us from the station ever be traversed? Each mile seemed to me a league, and each league a day's journey. At last we arrived. Hurrying to the waiting-room, I met three Cossacks to whom I showed my hands. The soldiers led me into an outer room, and having taken off my coat and bared my arms, they plunged them up to the shoulder in a tub of ice and water. However, there was now no sensation whatever, and the limbs, which were of a blue colour, floated painlessly in the water.

The elder of the Cossacks shook his head and said – 'Brother, it is a bad job, you will lose your hands.'

'They will drop off,' remarked another, 'if we cannot get back the circulation.'

'Have you any spirit with you?' added a third.

Nazar on hearing this ran out and brought in a tin bottle containing naphtha for cooking purposes, upon which the Cossacks, taking my arms out of the icy water, proceeded to rub them with the strong spirit.

Rub, rub, rub, the skin peeled under their horny hands, and the spirit irritated the membrane below. At last a faint sensation like tickling pervaded the elbow-joints, and I slightly flinched.

'Does it hurt?' asked the elder of the Cossacks.

'A little.'

'Capital, brothers,' he continued, 'rub as hard as you can;' and after going on with the friction until the flesh was almost flayed, they suddenly plunged my arms again into the ice and water. I had not felt anything before, but this time, the pain was very acute.

'Good,' said the Cossacks. 'The more it hurts the better chance you have of saving your hands.' And after a short time they let me take them out of the tub.

'You are fortunate, little father,' said the elder of the Cossacks. 'If it had not been for the spirit your hands would have dropped off, if you had not lost your arms as well.'

Rough, kind-hearted fellows were these poor soldiers; and when I forced on the elder of them a present for himself and comrades, the old soldier simply added, 'Are we not all brothers when in misfortune? Would you not have helped me if I had been in a like predicament?'

I shook his hand heartily, and went to the waiting-room to rest on the sofa, as the physical shock just undergone had for the moment thoroughly prostrated me. My arms also were sore and inflamed, the spirit having in some places penetrated the raw flesh; and it was several weeks before I thoroughly recovered from the effects of my carelessness.[11]

Hunger is another torment about which many travellers have written. Of all the hardships described so far in this chapter, it is the only one from which I personally have never suffered – not, at least, beyond the stage of mild (and mercifully short-lived) discomfort. Probably for that reason, I used to think that it might be marginally less agonising to endure than the others; since reading *Arabian Sands*, however, I am not so sure:

Next morning Hamad, Jadid, and bin Kabina went to the settlements in Liwa to buy food. They took three camels with them, and I told bin Kabina to buy flour, sugar, tea, coffee, butter, dates, and rice if he could get any, and above all to bring back a goat. Our flour was finished, but that evening Musallim produced from his saddle-bags a few handfuls of maize, which we roasted and ate. It was to be the last food we had until the others returned from Liwa three days later. They were three interminable nights and days.

I had almost persuaded myself that I was conditioned to starvation, indifferent to it. After all, I had been hungry for weeks, and even when we had had flour I had had little inclination to eat the charred or sodden lumps which Musallim had cooked. I used to swallow my portion with even less satisfaction than that with which I eventually avoided it. Certainly I thought and talked incessantly of food, but as a prisoner talks of freedom, for I realized that the joints of meat, the piles of rice, and the bowls of steaming gravy which tantalized me could have no reality outside my mind. I had never thought then that I should dream of the crusts which I was rejecting.

For the first day my hunger was only a more insistent feeling of familiar emptiness; something which, like a toothache, I could partly overcome by an effort of will. I woke in the grey dawn craving for food, but by lying on my stomach and pressing down I could achieve a semblance of relief. At least I was warm. Later, as the sun rose, the heat forced me out of my sleeping-bag. I threw my cloak over a bush and lay in the shade and tried to sleep again. I dozed and dreamt of food; I woke and thought of food. I tried to read, but it was difficult to concentrate. A moment's slackness and I was thinking once more of food. I filled myself with water, and the bitter water, which I did not want, made me feel sick. Eventually it was evening and we gathered round the fire, repeating, 'Tomorrow they will be back'; and thought of the supplies of food which bin Kabina would bring with him, and of the goat which we should eat. But the next day dragged out till sunset, and they did not come.

I faced another night, and the nights were worse than the days. Now I was cold and could not even sleep, except in snatches. I watched the stars; some of them – Orion, the Pleiades, and the Bear – I knew by name, others only by sight. Slowly they swung overhead and dipped down towards the west, while the bitter wind keened among the dunes. I remembered how I had once awakened with hunger during my first term at school and cried, remembering some chocolate cake which I had been too gorged to eat when my mother had taken me out to tea two days before. Now I was maddened by the thought of the crusts which I had given away in the Uruq al Shaiba. Why had I been such a fool? I could picture the colour and texture, even the shape, of the fragments which I had left.

In the morning I watched Mabkhaut turn the camels out to graze, and as they shuffled off, spared for a while from the toil which we imposed upon them, I found that I could only think of them as food. I was glad when they were out of sight. Al Auf came over and lay down near me, covering himself with his cloak; I don't think we spoke. I lay with my eyes shut, insisting to myself, 'If I were in London I would give anything to be here.' Then I thought of the jeeps and lorries with which the Locust Officers in the Najd were equipped. So vivid were my thoughts that I could hear the engines, smell the stink of petrol fumes. No, I would rather be here starving as I was than sitting in a chair, replete with food, listening to the wireless, and dependent upon cars to take me through Arabia. I clung desperately to this conviction. It seemed infinitely important. Even to doubt it was to admit defeat, to forswear everything to which I held.

I dozed and heard a camel roaring. I jerked awake, thinking, 'They have come at last', but it was only Mabkhaut moving our camels. The shadows lengthened among the sand-hills; the sun had set and we had given up hope when they returned. I saw at once that they had no goat with them. My dream of a large hot stew vanished. We exchanged the formal greetings and asked the formal questions about the news. Then we helped them with the only camel which was loaded. Bin Kabina said wearily, 'We got nothing. There is nothing to be had in Liwa. We have two packages of bad dates and a little wheat. They would not take our *riyals* – they wanted rupees. At last they took them at the same valuation as rupees. God's curse on them!' He had run a long palm-splinter into his foot and was limping. I tried to get it out but it was already too dark to see.

We opened a package of dates and ate. They were of poor quality and coated with sand, but there were plenty of them. Later we made porridge from the wheat, squeezing some dates into it to give it a flavour. After we had fed, al Auf said, 'If this is all we are going to have we shall soon be too weak to get on our camels.' We were a depressed and ill-tempered party that evening.[12]

There is another memorable story of hunger in *A Hitch or Two in Afghanistan* by my friend Nigel Ryan, in the field with the Afghan guerilla fighters during the summer of 1982:

Almost as an afterthought, I had brought half a dozen packets of soup with me. We chose a camping place beside the river and, seeking kindling by torchlight, found only dung. Somehow we got a wretched fire going, and began to heat water in a pan. Ghul Bas had disappeared. As we were about to share two cups of watery soup between ourselves, half a dozen more *mujahideen* appeared from the darkness and squatted beside us. Damnable though it was, we knew we had to share our rations, as they would have done in our place. There was scarcely enough for two sips each.

That night I felt the zest ebb from my limbs, as much from weakness through lack of food as from a sense of helplessness in chaos. I lay awake on the bare rock, my stomach even less tutored than my head in the ways of fatalism, too hungry to sleep.

After about half an hour we heard someone approaching: it was Ghul Bas and on his face was his magician's smile, while in his arms was a steaming bowl of boiled goat.

Greedily as beggars we gathered round. There were ten of us, and enough meat for four. Even before the bowl was set down each eater had measured his share with an eye quickened by hunger, then dipped a right hand in, taking not too much to reveal the ravenous beast within, but enough to be sure of not being cheated.

An ugly little incident marred the meal. It was over in a moment but it was to linger in my memory like a splinter.

I drew a bone with some of the grey unsalted meat on it; another bone, with more, clung to it. As I raised it to my lips, Charles, sitting next to me, stretched out a hand to take the second bone from my grasp.

I took the whole portion and set it down before him, a counter-challenge to his challenge.

'Oh no. I didn't mean it like that,' he said, in a voice of distress. 'Not like that.'

And perhaps he didn't. As quickly as lightning it had come to us and gone again, the moment of naked aggression; but for a pinprick in time the beast was let loose, then barred and caged again. Thinking back on that instant I found the story of Captain Oates the more extraordinary. When survival is at risk survival is all that comes into the mind: honour and shame come a poor second. Perhaps hope brings out the worst in us all, including a mean streak in the will to survive; and it is only when hope has gone that there is room for the noble deeds that distinguish men from animals. Or perhaps Captain Oates and the Astor who gave up his place in the *Titanic*'s lifeboat were not noble after all, but only afraid to live with the shame of surviving at another man's expense.

But our meagre supper that night provided no uplifting insights: only the lesson that hunger is a diminishing experience. We ate like hungry rats.[13]

Finally, a nasty little vignette by Robert Byron in *The Road to Oxiana*. He is writing from Beirut on 14 September 1933:

September 14th. – To come here, we took two seats in a car. Beside us, at the back, sat an Arab gentleman of vast proportions, who was dressed like a wasp in a gown of black and yellow stripes and held between his knees a basket of vegetables. In front was an Arab widow, accompanied by another basket of vegetables and a small son. Every twenty minutes she was sick out of the window. Sometimes we stopped; when we did not, her vomit flew back into the car by the other window. It was not a pleasant three hours.[14]

CHAPTER FOURTEEN

Health and Hygiene

Let us begin with Queen Victoria. She is seldom thought of as a great traveller; but in *Leaves from the Journal of Our Life in the Highlands* she proudly describes what she calls 'The First Great Expedition'. Starting from Balmoral, this took not one but two whole days, and necessitated doing something that Her Majesty had done seldom, if ever, before – staying the night in a hotel. The establishment in question was the Grant Arms Hotel and Posting House, Grantown, and it is only fair to say that in the old sepia photograph reproduced in my copy (signed, I am proud to say, by the Author) it looks pretty grim. The royal couple travelled incognito, but not alas very successfully; it was their passion for hygiene at all costs that gave them away. Throughout the Queen's account, it will be noted that cleanliness looms large:

We went up a small staircase, and were shown to our bedroom at the top of it – very small, but clean – with a large four-post bed which filled the whole room. Opposite was the drawing and dining-room in one – very tidy and well sized. Then the room where Albert dressed was the same in which our two maids had to sleep, and the two beds made the room very small. . . . Made ourselves clean and tidy, and then sat down to our dinner. . . . The dinner was very fair, and all very clean. Soup, 'hodge-podge,' mutton-broth with vegetables, which I did not much relish, fowl with white sauce, good roast lamb, very good potatoes, besides one or two other dishes which I did not eat, finishing with a good tart of cranberries. After dinner, tried to write part of this account, (but the talking round me confused me,) while Albert played at 'patience.' Then went away, to begin undressing, and it was about half-past eleven when we got to bed – a very hard bed, but quite clean. We had taken the precaution of having our own sheets, which, however, told *tales* the next day, from the mark of the crown and V. R. on them.[1]

That was in September 1860; let us now go back a century or so, and turn our attention from Scotland to France and Italy, through which Tobias Smollett was travelling from 1763–5. He has got no further than Boulogne before the complaints begin:

There is no such thing as a carpet to be seen, and the floors are in a very dirty condition. They have not even the implements of cleanliness in this country. . . .

241

Everything shows a deficiency in the mechanic arts. There is not a door, nor a window, that shuts close. The hinges, locks, and latches are of iron, coarsely made, and ill contrived. The very chimneys are built so open, that they admit both rain and sun, and all of them smoke intolerably. If there is no cleanliness among these people, much less shall we find delicacy, which is the cleanliness of the mind. Indeed, they are utter strangers to what we call common decency; and I could give you some high-flavoured instances, at which even a native of Edinburgh would stop his nose. There are certain mortifying views of human nature, which undoubtedly ought to be concealed as much as possible, in order to prevent giving offence; and nothing can be more absurd, than to plead the difference of custom in different countries, in defence of those usages which cannot fail giving disgust to the organs and senses of all mankind. Will custom exempt from the imputation of gross indecency a French lady, who shifts her frousy smock in presence of a male visitant, and talks to him of her *lavement*, her *medicine*, and her *bidet*? An Italian *signora* makes no scruple of telling you, she is such a day to begin a course of physic for the *pox*. The celebrated reformer of the Italian comedy introduces a child befouling itself on the stage. . . . I have known a lady handed to the house of office by her admirer, who stood at the door, and entertained her with *bons mots* all the time she was within. But I should be glad to know whether it is possible for a fine lady to speak and act in this manner, without exciting ideas to her own disadvantage in the mind of every man who has any imagination left, and enjoys the entire use of his senses, howsoever she may be authorized by the customs of her country? There is nothing so vile or repugnant to nature, but you may plead prescription for it in the customs of some nation or other. A Parisian likes mortified flesh; a native of Legiboli will not taste his fish till it is quite putrefied; the civilized inhabitants of Kamschatka get drunk with the urine of their guests, whom they have already intoxicated; the Nova Zemblans make merry on train-oil; the Greenlanders eat in the same dish with their dogs; the Caffres, at the Cape of Good Hope, piss upon those whom they delight to honour, and feast upon a sheep's intestines with their contents, as the greatest dainty that can be presented. A true-bred Frenchman dips his fingers, imbrowned with snuff, into his plate filled with ragout; between every three mouthfuls, he produces his snuff-box, and takes a fresh pinch, with the most graceful gesticulations; then he displays his handkerchief, which may be termed the *flag of abomination*, and, in the use of both, scatters his favours among those who have the happiness to sit near him. It must be owned, however, that a Frenchman will not drink out of a tankard in which, perhaps, a dozen of filthy mouths have slabbered, as is the custom in England. Here every individual has his own goblet, which stands before him, and he helps himself occasionally with wine, or water, or both, which likewise stand upon the table. But I know no custom more beastly than that of using water-glasses, in which polite company spirt, and squirt, and spue the filthy scourings of their gums under the eyes of each other. I knew a lover cured of his passion, by seeing this nasty cascade discharged from the mouth of his mistress. I don't doubt but I shall live to see the day when the hospitable custom of the ancient Egyptians will be revived; then a conveniency will be placed behind every chair in company, with a proper provision of waste paper, that individuals may make themselves easy without parting company. I insist upon it, that this practice would not be more indelicate than that which is now in use.[2]

A hundred years later, however, many a traveller must have regretted those free and easy ways of personal hygiene as he found himself faced with that nightmare of nineteenth-century health legislation, the Quarantine. *Murray's Handbook* of 1847 recommends travellers proceeding from Egypt to continental Europe to stop at Malta, 'where the quarantine is less irksome than in most places'. It seems, nevertheless, to have been quite irksome enough – particularly as one had to stay there nineteen days. ('When the plague is at Alexandria this is increased to 22 and upwards.')

Shortly after the steamer is anchored in the quarantine harbour, an officer comes alongside to inquire about the number of the passengers, in order to prepare for their accommodation in the lazaretto, and fix upon the part they are to occupy. They then go ashore to choose their rooms, leaving their baggage, properly packed up, to follow after them. The traveller must make up his mind to be detained some time before each person is satisfied, and he will be fortunate if the passengers are few. When numerous, there is often a scramble for rooms, and two persons are put into the same bedroom. A sitting-room is not given except as a favour, or when there are few passengers; but it is not refused to a party of five or six persons who intend to dine together. If without a servant, the first thing after securing rooms is to take one, who may be engaged beforehand by writing to a friend at Malta, or may be found at the door of the lazaretto; where many come to offer their services, with letters of recommendation from former masters, which may be read *but not touched*. When engaged, they come into quarantine and perform the same number of days as their master. They are paid 1*s*. 8*d*. a day wages, and 7*d*. a day for living. Two or three persons may employ one servant between them. The necessity of a servant is very evident, when it is remembered that no guardian is allowed to render the stranger any services beyond those demanded by lazaretto duties, and there is no one to bring him a drop of water. Nor can the porters who carry his luggage from the boat on hand-trucks touch any thing, as they are in *pratique*, and all must be put on and taken off by the person himself, or his servant.[3]

Two years later still, in 1849, *Murray's Handbook for Northern Europe* warned its readers that anyone who planned to go from Constantinople up the Bosphorus to Odessa might find the regulations actively embarrassing:

Besides a well furnished purse, a large stock of patience and temper is needful, more especially if the empire of the Tzar be entered by the Black Sea. In this case the traveller should, when at Constantinople, write to his banker in Odessa, and request him to send some one to meet him on his arrival at the Lazaret with a pair of shoes, (his measure can be sent in the letter,) socks or stockings, trowsers, shirt, waistcoat and coat or dressing-gown; this is supposing the infected man arrives in the summer; if he is unfortunate enough to land in the winter, a *schooba* will be highly necessary. Unless this precaution is taken the traveller will be confined one day more in quarantine by being obliged to remain on board the steamer until a suit of his own wardrobe has been fumigated, for the clothes that he arrives in must be thrown off, and in a state of nature must he show himself to the medical officers of the establishment before he is allowed to go into another room to clothe himself in fresh garments – ladies and children, not even excepting the most minute baby, are not exempt from this shedding of plumage. If, on the other hand, the new arrival is content to wear the habiliments let out for the occasion by the restaurateur of the Lazaret, he need not write to his banker, but he must be prepared to look very grotesque, and probably to find his stockings too small, his shoes too large, or the tail of his coat, if a small man, touching the ground.[4]

Ironically enough, it was precisely in Turkey that there had been invented the process which, had it only been universally applied, would have made many of these regulations unnecessary. On 1 April 1717 Lady Mary Wortley Montagu – no fool she – writes from Adrianople:

A-propos of distempers, I am going to tell you a thing, that will make you wish yourself here. The small pox, so fatal, and so general amongst us, is here intirely harmless, by the invention of engrafting, which is the term they give it. There is a set of old women, who make it their business to perform the operation, every autumn, in the month of September, when the great heat is abated. People send to one another to know if any of their family has a mind to have the small-pox; they make parties for this purpose, and when they are met (commonly fifteen or sixteen together) the old woman comes with a nut-shell full of the matter of the best sort of small-pox, and asks what vein you please to have opened. She immediately rips open that, you offer to her, with a large needle, (which gives you no more pain than a common scratch) and puts into the vein as much matter as can lie upon the head of her needle, and after that, binds up the little wound with a hollow bit of shell, and in this manner opens four or five veins. The Grecians have commonly the superstition of opening one in the middle of the forehead, one in each arm, and one on the breast, to mark the sign of the cross; but this has a very ill effect, all these wounds leaving little scars, and is not done by those that are not superstitious, who chuse to have them in the legs, or that part of the arm that is concealed. The children or young patients play together all the rest of the day, and are in perfect health to the eighth. Then the fever begins to seize them, and they keep their beds two days, very seldom three. They have very rarely above twenty or thirty in their faces, which never mark, and in eight days time they are as well as before their illness. Where they are wounded, there remains running sores during the distemper, which I don't doubt is a great relief to it. Every year thousands undergo this operation, and the French Ambassador says pleasantly, that they take the small-pox here by way of diversion, as they take the waters in other countries. There is no example of any one that has died in it, and you may believe I am well satisfied of the safety of this experiment, since I intend to try it on my dear little son. I am patriot enough to take pains to bring this useful invention into fashion in England, and I should not fail to write to some of our doctors very particularly about it, if I knew any one of them that I thought had virtue enough to destroy such a considerable branch of their revenue, for the good of mankind.[5]

Lady Mary meant what she said: her son Edward was the first English child ever to be vaccinated against the small-pox, and she herself was indeed to do everything in her power to popularise the practice in England, a quarter of a century before the birth of Edward Jenner.

But disease of one kind or another continued to be a constant threat to travellers, in Europe as well as further afield, and few indeed were those who managed to escape it altogether. To quote once again Hilaire Belloc's 'The Modern Traveller':

> Thus, greatly to our ease of mind,
> Our foreign foes we left behind;
> But dangers even greater
> Were menacing our path instead.
> In every book I ever read
> Of travels on the Equator,
> A plague, mysterious and dread,
> Imperils the narrator.[6]

Freya Stark never, thank God, succumbed to the plague. She did, however, suffer a severe attack of measles in the Hadhramaut, while in the fortress of Masna'a. In *The Southern Gates of Arabia* she tells us about it:

For three nights I was actually delirious, pursuing in broken and miserable dreams a search for some vague thing, undulating and alive, which had been given me and on whose recovery my happiness depended; it was, I thought, the secret of happiness, an object simple but elusive, as one might have expected, and I only wish I could remember exactly what: for I used to come upon it in the early dawn, when the fever dropped, and then slept peacefully, until Nur, with my breakfast in her hand, dressed in black and gold, rustling with bracelets, her lovely eyes brilliant with kohl under the oiled and plastered triangle of hair, appeared to my awakening sight as some strange continuation of the nightly dreams.

'Qumī,' she used to say: 'get up,' regardless of my condition: and when I told her that I had a fever: 'We all have that,' she would answer cheerfully, and gave me her pulse to feel, which, as a matter of fact, was racing along. She, too, coughed, as did nearly everyone: the healthiness of patriarchal town-life I soon came to regard as a myth, for I never saw so many sick. But no one lay down unless actually incapable of rising. The ladies trooped in to me, surprised to find that I had crept to bed again after breakfast on the floor.

'Ma shī sharr,' they would say; which means, in other words, that all is going as well as possible. But there is nothing so irritating as the optimism of other people at one's own expense, and I finally was driven to retaliate and to say that all diseases come from Allah, when they asked for impossible cures. And then I would be put to shame, for all they would answer was: 'Praise be to God,' in meek, unquestioning acceptance: and they would repeat this even when telling me of the deaths of their children, submissive to a destiny over which they have so little control. 'A fearful lot of work is left for God to do,' I find written in my diary.

They told me that disease comes with the hot wind which blows from the sea. It beat the shutters to and fro and rushed in the organ pipes of the valley, and I looked out, wondering to hear its noise and to see only the motionless cliffs, their pure and sharp outline and the shadow that falls and rises on their sides with the steps of the sun, like a bucket in a well, measuring out the days. A sense of prison overshadowed me between those perpendicular buttresses; they seemed as unescapable as the delirium of the night.

In the daytime, however, there was plenty to occupy my thoughts.

For one thing, there was the question of food. Milk, as the Bents had found before me, and vegetables or fruit, were almost unobtainable: everyone was anxious to give me all I could desire, and they would send round for all the goats and wring from their droughty udders a small and earthy tumbler-full, which I gladly welcomed at breakfast. Raw carrots they sometimes ate, and Nur cooked some of these: and they would bring meat which I was too ill to bite; and would never believe that with a lacerated throat I really liked my rice pepperless and fat-less. I felt too ill even to touch the flat bread cooked in oil and soaked in honey, and lived on eggs and soup, on tablets of Horlick's milk which I had with me, and – one day – on the luxury of a water-melon and apples sent as a present to the Governor from the coast, and hospitably shared: the harim would not have had a bite in the ordinary way; but my being there procured a fat red slice for the child who sat beside me, her little face framed in an orange satin hood stiff with grease and tinsel.

The babies were the playthings of the harim, and suffered, I thought, from over-wrought nerves due to the constant avalanche of caresses to which they were subjected as they were handed from one lady to the other among the coffee cups. The older children ran in and out and brought the latest news from one house to the next. They came freely into my room, and so did anybody else – slaves and mistresses, beduin girls round-faced and healthier than the towns-women, and old men and women in need of medicines. A friendly democracy accepted all: the grubbiest could sit there on the carpet, using it as a handkerchief, or lifting the edge now and then to spit carefully underneath. It was the life of the medieval castle in all its details; a life so much lived in common that privacy and cleanliness are almost unobtainable luxuries. Saintliness on the other hand, is made not only possible, but frequently essential.

All sorts of things happened around me as I lay in bed. Old peddling 'dallalas' came to sell bracelets, their goods tied up in a kerchief full of coral, amber, silver girdles, and embroideries: they would go from town to town in the valley, and brought us gossip.

A pretty woman came, 'Atiya, from the village below: her husband, newly married, had just left her to go to Somaliland. She suffered from some pain so that she could hardly stand, and came for medicine: but I was asleep at the moment, and Mahmud the doorkeeper took her to an upper room, and there branded the soles of her feet with a hot iron: when I woke up, she came down to me, apparently perfectly restored and cheerful. She sang, shyly, a qasida, to wish her young husband a safe return: his aunt had made up the words, and his bride sang it in a light sweet voice, innocent and moving – five shorts, a long, and a short – three times, and five shorts and a long to close, when the voice lowered and dropped into a depth of longing.

'Return. Thy uncle's daughter is alone at the fall of night.'

The girls laughed as they sat round. 'Atiya put out her little grubby hands, blushing with soft eyes.

'Is it not right?' she said. 'Is he not my husband? Must I not wish for him to come?'

'And how long will he stay away?'

'Ah, who knows? Perhaps ten years. The Will of God.'

They all sighed, for this is the sorrow of all in these valleys, and all, no doubt, were thinking of their husbands, married to others, far away. 'The life of the world is hard for women,' said Nur.

They were anxious to try a hot iron on me at the back of my neck, which they say is a good remedy for measles. I avoided this, but I was not so lucky with an old witch of a woman who came in one day from Hajarain, dressed in the black gown of that northern region, all decorated with little coloured patches, and with her elderly horsey face still painted yellow. She gave herself airs of holiness. Her husband had (very sensibly) divorced her, and her absence of youth, beauty, or human kindness were now devoted to God. When she saw me lying helpless, she pounced upon me: she uttered invocations, and whirled her indigo fingers and skinny arms like windmills about my head. With every invocation she tied and untied a knot in her shawl (a practice of sorcery already deplored in the Quran), and then she suddenly bent over me and spat. It was meant kindly.[7]

In one of the most moving passages of early travel writing that I know, Fynes Moryson records how he took the road in 1596 from Aleppo to Iskenderun (which he calls Scanderona, though it would later be better known in the West as Alexandretta) with his brother, already seriously ill with dysentery:

Being now to enter this journey, we hired for seventy one piastri, a Camell to carry our victuals, an ambling Mule for my brother, and a horse for my selfe, and so much we presently gave into the hands of our Muccaro, with covenant that he should pay for the meat of the beasts. Moreover we presently laid out one hundred and twenty piastri for divers necessaries, namely, two long chaires, like cradles covered with red cloth, to hang on the two sides of our Camell, (which chaires the Turkes use to ride in, and to sleepe upon Camels backes, but we bought them to carry victuals), for bisket, and a tent wherein we might sleepe, and for like provisions. But behold, when all this mony was laid out, and the very evening before the day in which we were to begin our journey, my brother Henry fell sicke of a flux. Being amased with this sudden chance, we stood doubtfull for a time what to do, til the consideration of the great summes of money we had laied out, and of the difficulty to get more, made us resolve to take this fatall journey, yet with this purpose, when we came to Scanderona, some foure daies journy distant, to goe no further, except in that time he recovered his health, propounding this comfort to our miserable estate, that there we might have commodity of convenient lodging with an Englishman, there abiding factor for our Merchants.

247

Upon Thursday the last of . . . June we went out of Haleppo, passing over stony hils, and by the Village Havaden, where the Jewes say the Prophet Jeremy was buried. Then riding forward all that night, at last we sate downe at eight of the clocke in the morning, and pitched our Tents neere a Village, where I did see a pillar erected to Pompey, and here we rested and refreshed our selves the heat of the day. This kind of journying was strange to us, and contrary to our health: for we beganne our journey at foure in the afternoone, to shun the heat of the day past, and rode all night, so as we not used to this watching, were so sleepy towards the Sunne rise, as we could not abstaine from nodding, and were many times like to fall from our horses. To which mischiefe we could find no other remedy, then to ride swiftly to the head of the Caravan, and there dismounting, to lie downe and slumber, with our horses bridle tied to our legges, one of us by course walking by us, to keepe us from injuries, and to awaken us when the last Camel passed by, lest we should there be left a pray to theeves. And we having some two hundred Camels in our Caravan, did in this sort passe the sleepy houres in the morning, till seven or eight of the clocke, at which time we used to pitch our tents, and rest. Moreover this greatly afflicted us, that spending the morning till ten or eleven of the clocke in pitching our Tent, preparing meat, and eating, we had no time to rest, but the extreme heat of the noone day, which so pierced our tents, that we could no more sleepe, then if in England upon a Summers day we had lien neere a hot sea-cole fire. And howsoever wee lessened this heate, by flinging our gownes over our Tent, betweene the sunne and us, yet for my part I was so afflicted with want of sleepe, and with this immoderate heate, as I feared to fall into a Lunacy, what then should a man think would become of my sickly brother in this case?

Upon Friday the first of July, towards evening, wee tooke up our Tents, supping while our Muccaro loaded our beasts, then we rode over Mountaines all night, and the next morning againe pitched our Tents neere a poore Village. And our Muccaro bought us some fresh victuals in the Village, according to the manner of Turky, where the very Cities yeeld no Innes. Upon Saturday [2 July] towards evening, wee set forward, and rode that night over a large Plaine, and next day after Sunne-rise wee came to Antioch, a citie of Asia, famous for the Patriarchate, and by Histories sacred and prophane. . . . Here first wretched I perceived the imminent danger of my most deare brothers death, which I never suspected til this day, much lesse had any just cause to feare it. A Turke in this Caravan troubled with the same disease of a Flux, went to the ground more then twentie times each nights journey, and yet lived; whereas my brother only three or foure times descended from his Mule to that purpose, which filled us with good hope. But here first I learned by miserable experience, that nothing is worse for one troubled with the Flux, then to stop or much restraine the course therof. For my brother stopping this naturall purge, by taking Red wine and Marmelat, experienced men did attribute (all too late) his death to no other thing. I could not hire a horse-litter by any endevour of our Muccaro, nor for any price, though I offered an incredible summe for that, or like commoditie to carrie him, and we thought it very dangerous to stay here among the Turkes, after our Caravan departed, especially since Scanderona was but five and twenty miles distant, where wee should have the commoditie to lodge with an Englishman, and so to get all necessaries for his recoverie. Therefore upon Sunday in the evening, wee put all our provisions in one of the foresaid covered chaires or cradles, caried by the Camell, and made my brother a bed in the other cradle, where (as we thought) he might commodiously rest. And I promised the Muccaro halfe a piastro for every time my brother should descend from the Camell to ease himselfe, for wee were to ride before with the horsemen, and hee was now to come behind with the Camels. So we set forward, and my selfe twice in the night, and once towards morning, left the horsemen, and rode back to my brother, to know how he fared, and when hee gave mee no answere, I returned to the horsemen, thinking that he slept. Then towards morning I was so afflicted with my wonted desire of sleepe, as I thought an howers rest worth a Kings ransome. Therefore my selfe and Master Jasper Tyant our loving consort, rode a good pace to the Village Byland, where we were to pitch our Tents, that we might make all things ready to receive him.

But within short space our Muccaro running to our Tent, and telling me, that hee had left my brother ready to give up his last breth in the first house of the Village, seemed to say to me, Goe quickly and hang thy selfe. With all possible speede I ran to this house, imbraced my dying brother, and confounded with sorrow, understood from his mouth, how farre the events of our nights journey had been contrary to our hope. For whereas my selfe advised him to leave his Mule, and lie in the chaire upon the Camels backe, he told me that he was shaken in pieces with the hard pace of the Camell. And whereas I had offered the Muccaro halfe a piastro, for each time hee should light to ease himselfe, he told mee that he had often asked this favour of the Muccaro, but could never obtaine it, he excusing himselfe by feare to be left behind the Caravan, for a prey to theeves. And whereas the Camels hinder parts being higher then the fore parts, I had laied my brothers head towards the hinder parts, and raised it as high as I could with pillowes and clothes, for his better ease, it happened (which I being ignorant of the way could not foresee) that we all the night ascending mountaines, his feet were farre higher then his head; whereupon he told me, that most part of the night he had lien in a trance, which was the cause that he could not answer me, at such times as I came to inquire of his health. Thus mischiefe lighted upon mischiefe, to make my wretched state most miserable: Why should I use many words in a case, from the remembrance whereof my mind abhorreth. Therefore I will say in a word; My most deere brother Henry upon Munday the fourth of July, (after the old stile), the yeere of our Lord 1596, and of his age the seven and twentieth, died in my armes, after many loving speeches, and the expressing of great comfort in his Divine meditations.[8]

Dysentery, or the flux, is nowadays mercifully rare; and we can be grateful, too, that even the minor upheavals which beset us all from time to time will usually respond to modern treatment within a few days. Even these, however, can have embarrassing results: in his *Wanderings in South America*, that most eccentric of naturalists Charles Waterton tells – somewhat archly – of an unfortunate Scotsman with whom he chanced to find himself when staying in a planter's house on the river Paumaron. The very next night after a disagreeable encounter with a vampire bat – an experience much envied by Waterton, who habitually left his feet sticking out of his hammock to attract them, but always in vain –

he was doomed to undergo a kind of ordeal unknown in Europe. There is a species of large red ant in Guiana, sometimes called Ranger, sometimes Coushie. These ants march in millions through the country, in compact order, like a regiment of soldiers; they eat up every insect in their march; and if a house obstruct their route, they do not turn out of the way, but go quite through it. Though they sting cruelly when molested, the planter is not sorry to see them in his house; for it is but a passing visit, and they destroy every kind of insect vermin that has taken shelter under his roof.

Now, in the British plantations of Guiana, as well as in Europe, there is always a little temple dedicated to the goddess Cloacina. Our dinner had chiefly consisted of crabs, dressed in rich and different ways. Paumaron is famous for crabs, and strangers who go thither consider them the greatest luxury. The Scotch gentleman made a very capital dinner on crabs; but this change of diet was productive of unpleasant circumstances: he awoke in the night in that state in which Virgil describes Cæleno to have been, viz. 'fædissima ventris proluvies.' Up he got, to verify the remark,

'Serius aut citius, sedem properamus ad unam.'

Now, unluckily for himself, and the nocturnal tranquillity of the planter's house, just at that unfortunate hour, the Coushie Ants were passing across the seat of Cloacina's temple; he had never dreamed of this; and so, turning his face to the door, he placed himself in the usual situation which the votaries of the goddess generally take. Had a lighted match dropped upon a pound of gunpowder, as he afterwards remarked, it could not have caused a greater recoil. Up he jumped, and forced his way out, roaring for help and for a light, for he was worried alive by ten thousand devils. The fact is, he had sat down upon an intervening body of coushie ants. Many of those which escaped being crushed to death, turned again, and, in revenge, stung the unintentional intruder most severely. The watchman had fallen asleep, and it was some time before a light could be procured, the fire having gone out; in the mean time, the poor gentleman was suffering an indescribable martyr-dom, and would have found himself more at home in the Augean stable than in the planter's house.[9]

Even when one is in perfect health, the body's natural functions can cause problems enough. Freya Stark encountered some when travelling to Aden in an Arab dhow in 1937; in *A Winter in Arabia* she explains:

It must be indelicate to eat in public. When the moment comes, a sail is brought and arranged like a curtain around me. But there are other moments for which no provision is made. The only sanitation are two small wooden cages, tied with rope to the outside of the dhow; here at intervals travellers stay meditating, their lower halves decently hidden, but the rest all exposed to the general view. This publicity I could not face and at last put the problem to the Nakhuda, who looked as if he had been a family man many times over. He saw my point and sent for three oars and a sail; these were draped like a tent, and there I could retire precariously over an ocean that rushed with great speed below, and with some reluctance, since, as I could not monopolize one-half of the sanitation altogether, the tent had to be erected afresh every time. There are inherent difficulties in the situation of a solitary female on a boat.[10]

Two Middle-Aged Ladies in Andalusia is the title of a book by Penelope Chetwode – Mrs John Betjeman. The ladies concerned are herself and her mare, Marquesa. Marquesa, one imagines, had no problems of this kind; they do not seem to have weighed very heavily with Penelope either:

The *posada* often has the advantage over the *fonda* in that it possesses only stable sanitation. When the water variety is attempted it is always a dismal failure, partly because there is never any water laid on. You simply ladle it into the pan from a large stone jar, and the stink from the drains is overpowering. The Spaniards possess a great variety of talents but plumbing is not one of them.

The technique of using stable sanitation successfully and without undue strain on the nerves is as follows: when you want to enter the stable to attend to your horse, you open the door with a smile on your face, switch on the light and advance towards the animal, welcoming any help from your landlord or fellow-guest which may be offered. When, however, you wish to enter it for the other purpose you go towards the door with a look of grim determination upon your face, do not turn on the light, and slam the door hard behind you. Should you hear a giant pee-ing close by it is almost certain to be a mule or donkey: and when your eyes, growing used to the dim light, discern the figure of your landlady squatting in a corner, the custom is for both of you to roar with laughter as if this clandestine meeting were the most natural thing in the world, which indeed it is.[11]

Mary Kingsley, answering the calls of hygiene on a journey through the Fan country in West Africa, found herself confronted not just by problems but by physical dangers as well:

I was left in peace at about 11.30 p.m., and clearing off the clothes from the bench threw myself down and tried to get some sleep, for we were to start, the Fans said, before dawn. Sleep impossible – mosquitoes! lice!! – so at 12.40 I got up and slid aside my bark door. I found Pagan asleep under his mosquito bar outside, across the doorway, but managed to get past him without rousing him from his dreams of palaver which he was still talking aloud, and reconnoitred the town. The inhabitants seemed to have talked themselves quite out and were sleeping heavily. I went down then to our canoe and found it safe, high up among the Fan canoes on the stones, and then I slid a small Fan canoe off, and taking a paddle from a cluster stuck in the sand, paddled out on to the dark lake.

It was a wonderfully lovely quiet night with no light save that from the stars. One immense planet shone pre-eminent in the purple sky, throwing a golden path down on to the still waters. Quantities of big fish sprung out of the water, their glistening silver-white scales flashing so that they look like slashing swords. Some bird was making a long, low boom-booming sound away on the forest shore. I paddled leisurely across the lake to the shore on the right, and seeing crawling on the ground some large glow-worms, drove the canoe on to the bank among some hippo grass, and got out to get them.

While engaged on this hunt I felt the earth quiver under my feet, and heard a soft big soughing sound, and looking round saw I had dropped in on a hippo banquet. I made out five of the immense brutes round me, so I softly returned to the canoe and shoved off, stealing along the bank, paddling under water, until I deemed it safe to run out across the lake for my island. I reached the other end of it to that on which the village is situated; and finding a miniature rocky bay with a soft patch of sand and no hippo grass, the incidents of the Fan hut suggested the advisability of a bath. Moreover, there was no china collection in that hut, and it would be a long time before I got another chance, so I go ashore again, and, carefully investigating the neighbourhood to make certain there was no human habitation near, I then indulged in a wash in peace. Drying one's self on one's cummerbund is not pure joy, but it can be done when you put your mind to it.[12]

For those travelling through the Ottoman dominions, the abysmal level of sanitary standards was largely made up for by the joys, for male and female alike, of the Turkish bath or *hammam*. In another letter, Lady Mary Wortley Montagu tells of one that she visited in Sofia:

I went to the Bagnio about ten o'clock. It was already full of women. It is built of stone, in the shape of a dome, with no windows but in the roof, which gives light enough. There were five of these domes joining together, the outmost being less than the rest, and serving only as a hall, where the portress stood at the door. Ladies of quality generally give this woman a crown or ten shillings, and I did not forget that ceremony. The next room is a very large one, paved with marble, and all round it are two raised Sofas of marble, one above another. There were four fountains of cold water in this room, falling first into marble basons, and then running on the floor in little channels made for that purpose, which carried the streams into the next room, something less than this, with the same sort of marble sofas, but so hot with steams of sulphur, proceeding from the baths joining to it, 'twas impossible to stay there with one's clothes on. The two other domes were the hot baths, one of which had cocks of cold water turning into it, to temper it to what degree of warmth the bathers pleased to have.

I was in my travelling habit, which is a riding dress, and certainly appeared very extraordinary to them. Yet there was not one of them that shewed the least surprise or impertinent curiosity, but received me with all the obliging civility possible. I know no European court, where the ladies would have behaved themselves in so polite a manner to such a stranger. I believe, upon the whole, there were two hundred women, and yet none of those disdainful smiles, and satirical whispers, that never fail in our assemblies, when any body appears that is not dressed exactly in the fashion. They repeated over and over to me: 'UZELLE, PEK UZELLE,' which is nothing but 'charming, very charming.' – The first sofas were covered with cushions and rich carpets, on which sat the ladies; and on the second, their slaves behind them, but without any distinction of rank by their dress, all being in the state of nature, that is, in plain English, stark naked, without any beauty or defect concealed. Yet there was not the least wanton smile or immodest gesture among them. They walked and moved with the same majestic grace, which Milton describes our General Mother with. There were many amongst them, as exactly proportioned as ever any goddess was drawn by the pencil of a Guido or Titian, – and most of their skins shiningly white, only adorned by their beautiful hair, divided into many tresses, hanging on their shoulders, braided either with pearl or ribbon, perfectly representing the figures of the graces.

I was here convinced of the truth of a reflection I have often made, that if it were the fashion to go naked, the face would be hardly observed. I perceived that the ladies of the most delicate skins and finest shapes, had the greatest share of my admiration, though their faces were sometimes less beautiful than those of their companions. To tell you the truth, I had wickedness enough to wish secretly, that Mr. Gervais could have been there invisible. I fancy it would have very much improved his art, to see so many fine women naked in different postures, some in conversation, some working, others drinking coffee or sherbert, and many negligently lying on their cushions, while their slaves (generally pretty girls of seventeen or eighteen) were employed in braiding their hair in several pretty fancies. In short, 'tis the woman's coffee-house, where all the news of the town is told, scandal invented, &c. – They generally take this diversion once a week, and stay there at least four or five hours, without getting cold by immediate coming out of the hot-bath into the cold room, which was very surprising to me. The lady that seemed the most considerable among them, entreated me to sit by her, and would fain have undressed me for the bath. I excused myself with some difficulty. They being, however, all so earnest in persuading me, I was at last forced to open my shirt, and shew them my stays, which satisfied them very well; for, I saw, they believed I was locked up in that machine, and that it was not in my own power to open it, which contrivance they attributed to my husband.[13]

Over a century later, Eliot Warburton describes in *The Crescent and the Cross* another *hammam*, even more luxurious, in the Palace of Beit-ed-Din, which still stands among the mountains of the Lebanon:

Having examined the Palace, we were ready for the bath, and found the magnificent suite of rooms appropriated to that purpose ready to receive us. We were first conducted into a beautiful pavilion of pale-coloured marble, in the centre of which crystal streams leaped into an alabaster basin from four fountains. Vases of fresh flowers were tastefully arranged round the carved edges of the basin; a ceiling of soft green and purple porcelain reflected the only light that fell upon this pleasant place.

A Turkish bath is a very complicated business, but, as it is one of the greatest luxuries of the East, and indeed almost a necessary of life, it is fit to give some description of it: – this will apply equally to all, from Cairo to Constantinople. As soon as we laid aside our clothes, attendants brought long napkins, of the softest and whitest linen, which were wreathed into turbans and togas round us: then, placing our feet in wooden pattens, inlaid with mother-of-pearl, we walked on marble floors through several chambers and passages of gradually increasing heat, until we reached a vaulted apartment, from whose marbled sides gushed four fountains of hot water. Here cushions were laid for us, and we were served with pipes, and nargilehs, and iced sherbets: thence we were conducted into the inner-most and warmest apartment, where we sat down on marbled stools, close to fountains of almost boiling water. This was poured over us from silver cups; we were then covered with a rich foam of scented soap, applied with the silken fibres of the palm, then bathed again with the warm water and shampooed, in which process the whole skin seemed to peel off, and every joint was made to crack. Then we were again lathered, and again soused, and found our skins as flower-soft as that of a little child. We now left the warmest room, and were met at the door by slaves, with bundles of exquisitely soft, warm linen, in which we were again shawled, turbaned, and kilted; and so we passed out into the cool fountain chamber, where another change of linen awaited us.

It was a sudden and pleasant alternation, from burning suns, and craggy roads, and sweltering horses, to find ourselves reclining on silken cushions, in the shaded niche of an arched window; through which cool breezes, filled with orange perfumes, breathed gently over us. The sensation of repose after a Turkish bath is at all times delicious; but here it was heightened by every appliance that could win the tranced senses to enjoyment, without disturbing their repose. The bubbling of fountains, the singing of birds, the whispering of trees, were the only sounds that reached the ear. The slaves glided about silently and somnambulistically, or stood with folded arms watching for a sign. If the languid eye was lifted to the window, it found a prospect of unequalled splendour over the mountains to the sea; and nearer were rich gardens, and basins full of gold fishes, swimming about with such luxurious motion that it rested the sight to follow them. There were amber-mouthed pipes of delicious Latakeea, and fragrant coffee, and sherbet cooled in the fountain; and black slaves, with gold-embroidered napkins to wipe our hands.

This was too pleasant to last long; the soft slippers gave way to the heavy boot, the light turban of the serai to that of the mountain; a shower of rose-water was sprinkled over us; we took a last view of the spacious courts, with their long array of cloisters, built lightly and gracefully, as if in bowers; the princely pile of Saracenic elegance that surmounted these, and the vaulted stables that supported them; and then we dashed away at a gallop.[14]

Among the Western nations, baths of any kind were a good deal harder to come by. In his *Gatherings from Spain* (published in 1861) Richard Ford tells us that, although the Spaniards insist on prodigious quantities of water to drink,

it must be remembered that this fluid is applied with greater prodigality in washing their inside than their outside. Indeed, a classical author remarks that the Spaniards only learnt the use of *hot* water, as applicable to the toilette, from the Romans after the second Punic war. Their baths and *thermæ* were destroyed by the Goths, because they tended to encourage effeminacy; and those of the Moors were prohibited by the Gotho-Spaniards partly from similar reasons, but more from a religious hydrophobia. Ablutions and lustral purifications formed an article of faith with the Jew and Moslem, with whom 'cleanliness is godliness.' The mendicant Spanish monks, according to their practice of setting up a directly antagonist principle, considered physical dirt as the test of moral purity and true faith; and by dining and sleeping from year's end to year's end in the same unchanged woollen frock, arrived at the height of their ambition, according to their view of the odour of sanctity, insomuch that Ximenez, who was himself a shirtless Franciscan, induced Ferdinand and Isabella, at the conquest of Granada, to close and abolish the Moorish baths. They forbade not only the Christians but the Moors from using anything but holy water. Fire, not water, became the grand element of inquisitorial purification.

The fair sex was warned by monks, who practised what they preached, that they should remember the cases of Susanna, Bathsheba, and La Cava, whose fatal bathing under the royal palace at Toledo led to the downfall of the Gothic monarchy. Their aqueous anathemas extended not only to public, but to minutely private washings, regarding which Sanchez instructs the Spanish confessor to question his fair penitents, and not to absolve the over-washed. Many instances could be produced of the practical working of this enjoined rule; for instance, Isabella, the favourite daughter of Philip II., his eye, as he called her, made a solemn vow never to change her shift until Ostend was taken. The siege lasted three years, three months, and thirteen days. The royal garment acquired a tawny colour, which was called *Isabel* by the courtiers, in compliment to the pious princess.[15]

Nor, alas, is this deep-rooted monastic suspicion of washing confined to the Roman Catholic Church. I myself remember as if it were yesterday an incident in 1963, which I recorded in my book on *Mount Athos*:

Some monasteries tend to be more broadminded than others, but in all of them it is as well to be on one's guard lest monkish susceptibilities be offended. Washing, for example, is always a problem. 'He who is once washed in Christ,' wrote St Jerome, 'needs not to wash again.' This fearful dictum accurately summarizes the general monastic attitude to soap and water. They are not considered sinful, merely unnecessary; and though one or two monasteries have installed guest bathrooms of a kind, in most houses the visitors' efforts in the cause of hygiene are regarded with an amused and faintly patronising forbearance as he crouches with sponge and toothbrush beneath the single spluttering tap at the foot of the main staircase. The same is true of his laundry. On Athos, where mules are nowadays less plentiful than they were, it is unwise to travel with more clothes or equipment than can conveniently be carried on the back; and, as the sun is hot and the paths dusty, a few minutes each day at the wash-tub are rarely ill-spent. Seldom on the Mountain have I ever seen monks' garments hanging out to dry; but nevertheless most monasteries provide some rudimentary clothes-line to accommodate the whims of the passing traveller.

The Grand Lavra possesses both a clothes-line and a wash-house. Being also the largest and among the most frequently visited of Athonite foundations, it might have been supposed to be relatively enlightened in these matters. Alas, it is not – as I learnt within a few hours of my arrival. My first shock came when I was requested, politely but firmly, by the guest-master to remove a pair of underpants then fluttering happily from the line. This, he pointed out, was a monastery; shirts, socks, handkerchiefs, even vests, might be dried with propriety within its walls. But underpants were a shameful abomination and could on no account be permitted. Meekly, I obeyed; but worse was to come. I woke the following morning at dawn. The monks were, as usual, in church; my fellow-guests were still asleep;

the whole monastery lay in silence. I had unfortunately ignored the advice of the Rev. Athelstan Riley, who recommends all travellers to Athos to provide themselves with a 'portable india-rubber bath', but this seemed the perfect opportunity to do the best I could without one; and I made quietly for the wash-house. Its principal furnishing was a huge stone trough; and into this I now clambered, turning on all four of the taps set at regular intervals along its length and covering myself from head to foot in a deep and luxurious lather. At this point the guest-master appeared. He was a youngish man and, clearly, a fanatic; he took one look at me and exploded. Never have I seen anyone so angry. The flood of hysterical Greek that poured from the depths of that enormous beard was largely incomprehensible to me, but his message was plain. For the second time in twelve hours I had desecrated his monastery. Having already offended God and the Mother of God with the spectacle of my underpants I was now compounding the sacrilege by standing stark naked under the very roof of the Grand Lavra. I was the Whore of Babylon, I was Sodom and Gomorrah, I was a minion of Satan sent to corrupt the Holy Mountain. I was to put on my scabrous clothes at once and return with all speed to the foul pit whence I had come.

This time I felt genuinely aggrieved. There were several questions I should have liked to ask. How could one wash properly with one's clothes on? Might one never wash the lower half of the body at all? Did monks never do so? Come to that, did they ever wash the upper half? Was nudity never permitted? Was it a sin? If one could not strip when alone in a wash-room, where could one strip? And whom was I shocking? God? But had not God designed me in the first place? Him, the guest-master? Then why didn't he go away? And incidentally, why wasn't he in Church where he belonged?

But language failed, and without language how can resolution remain firm? Hastily pulling trousers back over still-soapy legs, I retreated to the dormitory, wondering only how this outraged vigilante would have reacted to the vision of Mr Athelstan Riley in all that india-rubber.[16]

CHAPTER FIFTEEN

Animals

There was once a scholarly Dane named Niels Horrebow who, in 1758, published a book of encyclopaedic learning entitled *The Natural History of Iceland*. My favourite chapter is Chapter XLII, the title of which is 'Concerning Owls'. I shall quote it in its entirety:

There are no owls of any kind in the whole island.[1]

Iceland, for all its other attractions, is – apart of course from fish – not rich in fauna. (Indeed, I am told that Icelandic is almost the only language of the civilised world into which the works of Beatrix Potter have never been translated – small, furry animals being unknown to the local children and consequently of no conceivable interest to them.) As a country, therefore, it is quite inappropriate to this chapter: I shall pass on at once to Egypt.

And in particular to Herodotus, who has some very interesting things to say about cats and dogs:

The number, already large, of domestic animals would have been greatly increased, were it not for an odd thing that happens to the cats. The females, when they have kittens, avoid the toms; but the toms, thus deprived of their satisfaction, get over the difficulty very ingeniously, for they either openly seize, or secretly steal, the kittens and kill them – but without eating them – and the result is that the females, deprived of their kittens and wanting more (for their maternal instinct is very strong), go off to look for mates again. What happens when a house catches fire is most extraordinary: nobody takes the least trouble to put it out, for it is only the cats that matter: everyone stands in a row, a little distance from his neighbour, trying to protect the cats, who nevertheless slip through the line, or jump over it, and hurl themselves into the flames. This causes the Egyptians deep distress. All the inmates of a house where a cat has died a natural death shave their eyebrows, and when a dog dies they shave the whole body including the head. Cats which have died are taken to Bubastis, where they are embalmed and buried in sacred receptacles; dogs are buried, also in sacred burial-places, in the towns where they belong. Weasels are buried in the same way as dogs; field-mice and hawks are taken to Buto, ibises to Hermopolis. Bears, which are scarce, and wolves (which in Egypt are not much bigger than jackals) are buried wherever they happen to be found lying dead.[2]

At least so far as cats are concerned, some curious mystique seems to have survived right up to modern times. Some twenty- three centuries after Herodotus we find Lady Duff Gordon writing from Luxor:

A few evenings ago, I was sitting here quietly drinking tea, and four or five men were present, when a cat came to the door. I called 'biss, biss', and offered milk, but pussy, after looking at us, ran away. 'Well dost thou, oh Lady', said a quiet, sensible man, a merchant here, 'to be kind to the cat, for I dare say he gets little enough at home; *his* father, poor man, cannot cook for his children every day.' And then in an explanatory tone to the company, 'That is Alee Nasseeree's boy Yussuf – it must be Yussuf, because his fellow twin Ismaeen is with his mule at Negadeh.' I shivered, I confess, not but what I have heard things almost as absurd from gentlemen and ladies in Europe; but an 'extravagance' in a *kuftan* has quite a different effect from one in a tail coat. 'What! My butcher's boy who brings the meat – a cat?' I gasped. 'To be sure, and he knows well where to look for a bit of good cookery, you see. All twins go out as cats at night if they go to sleep hungry; and their own bodies lie at home like dead meanwhile, but no one must touch them, or they would die. When they grow up to ten or twelve they leave it off. Why your boy Ahmad does it. Oh Ahmad! do you go out as a cat at night?' 'No,' said Ahmad tranquilly, 'I am not a twin – my sister's sons do.' I inquired if people were not afraid of such cats. 'No, there is no fear, they only eat a little of the cookery, but if you beat them they will tell their parents next day, "So-and-so beat me in his house last night", and show their bruises. No, they are not Afreets, they are *beni Adami* (sons of Adam), only twins do it, and if you give them a sort of onion broth and camel's milk the first thing when they are born, they don't do it at all.' Omar professed never to have heard of it, but I am sure he had, only he dreads being laughed at.[3]

Herodotus is interesting about other animals too: notably the crocodile, which he appears to know so much about that one feels he must have seen some for himself:

It is a four-footed, amphibious creature, lays and hatches its eggs on land, where it spends the greater part of the day, and stays all night in the river, where the water is warmer than the night-air and the dew. The difference in size between the young and the full-grown crocodile is greater than in any other known creature; for a crocodile's egg is hardly bigger than a goose's, and the young when hatched is small in proportion, yet it grows to a size of some twenty-three feet long or even more. It has eyes like a pig's but great fang-like teeth in proportion to its body, and is the only animal to have no tongue and a stationary lower jaw; for when it eats it brings the upper jaw down upon the under. It has powerful claws and a scaly hide, which on its back is impenetrable. It cannot see under water, though on land its sight is remarkably quick. One result of its spending so much time in the water is that the inside of its mouth gets covered with leeches. Other animals avoid the crocodile, as do all birds too with one exception – the sandpiper, or Egyptian plover; this bird is of service to the crocodile and lives, in consequence, in the greatest amity with him; for when the crocodile comes ashore and lies with his mouth wide open (which he generally does facing towards the west), the bird hops in and swallows the leeches. The crocodile enjoys this, and never, in consequence, hurts the bird. Some Egyptians reverence the crocodile as a sacred beast; others do not, but treat it as an enemy. The strongest belief in its sanctity is to be found in Thebes and round about Lake Moeris; in these places they keep one particular crocodile, which they tame, putting rings made of glass or gold into its ears and bracelets round its front feet, and giving it special food and ceremonial offerings. In fact, while these creatures are alive they treat them with every kindness, and, when they die, embalm them and bury them in sacred tombs. On the other hand, in the neighbourhood of Elephantine crocodiles are not considered sacred animals at all, but are eaten. In the Egyptian language these creatures are called *champsae*. The name crocodile – or 'lizard' – was given them by the Ionians, who saw they resembled the lizards commonly found on stone walls in their own country.

Of the numerous different ways of catching crocodiles I will describe the one which seems to me the most interesting. They bait a hook with a chine of pork and let it float out into midstream, and at the same time, standing on the bank, take a live pig and beat it. The crocodile, hearing its squeals, makes a rush towards it, encounters the bait, gulps it down, and is hauled out of the water. The first thing the huntsman does when he has got the beast on land is to plaster its eyes with mud; this done, it is dispatched easily enough – but without this precaution it will give a lot of trouble.[4]

A lot of trouble – that must rate as the understatement of the fifth century B.C. (Going up the Nile in 1960 with an international group of journalists to look at the temples about to be engulfed by the new Aswan dam, I well remember our official bear-leader warning us on no account to bathe over the side since the water was '70 per cent crocodiles'. We never discovered what he meant.) Herodotus, oddly enough, fails to mention the beast's man-eating tendencies; but they are presumably not unlike those of its near relative, the cayman or alligator, of which a graphic instance is given in *The Naturalist on the River Amazons*, by Henry Walter Bates, FRS, published in 1892:

He never attacks man when his intended victim is on his guard; but he is cunning enough to know when he may do this with impunity: of this we had proof at Caiçara ... The river had sunk to a very low point, so that the port and bathing-place of the village now lay at the foot of a long sloping bank, and a large cayman made his appearance in the shallow and muddy water. We were all obliged to be very careful in taking our bath; most of the people simply using a calabash, pouring the water over themselves while standing on the brink. A large trading canoe, belonging to a Barra merchant named Soares, arrived at this time, and the Indian crew, as usual, spent the first day or two after their coming into port in drunkenness and debauchery ashore. One of the men, during the greatest heat of the day, when almost every one was enjoying his afternoon's nap, took it into his head, whilst in a tipsy state, to go down alone to bathe. He was seen only by the Juiz de Paz, a feeble old man who was lying in his hammock, in the open verandah at the rear of his house on the top of the bank, and who shouted to the besotted Indian to beware of the alligator. Before he could repeat his warning the man stumbled, and a pair of gaping jaws, appearing suddenly above the surface, seized him round the waist, and drew him under the water. A cry of agony, 'Ai Jesús!' was the last sign made by the wretched victim. The village was aroused: the young men with praiseworthy readiness seized their harpoons and hurried down to the bank: but of course it was too late; a winding track of blood on the surface of the water was all that could be seen. They embarked, however, in montarias, determined on vengeance: the monster was traced, and when, after a short lapse of time, he came up to breathe – one leg of the man sticking out from his jaws – was despatched with bitter curses.[5]

If we all had to vote for our favourite animal, the dolphin – or porpoise – would, I feel sure, come high on the list; and the most dazzling description ever penned of dolphins at play is by Patrick Leigh Fermor, in his book *Mani*. Here it is:

soon the delighted cry of '*Delphinia!*' went up: a school of dolphins was gambolling half a mile further out to sea. They seemed to have spotted us at the same moment, for in a second half a dozen were tearing their way towards us, all surfacing in the same parabola and plunging together as though they were in some invisible harness. Soon they were careering alongside and round the bows and under the bowsprit, glittering mussel-blue on top, fading at the sides through gun-metal dune-like markings to pure white, streamlined and gleaming from their elegant beaks to the clean-cut flukes of their tails. They were beautiful abstractions of speed, energy, power and ecstasy leaping out of the water and plunging and spiralling and vanishing like swift shadows, each soon to materialize again and sail into the air in another great loop so fast that they seemed to draw the sea after them and shake it off in mid-air, to plunge forward again tearing two great frothing bow-waves with their beaks; diving down again, falling behind and criss-crossing under the keel and deviating and returning. Sometimes they flung themselves out of the sea with the insane abandon, in reverse, of a suicide from a skyscraper; up, up, until they hung poised in mid-air shaking in a muscular convulsion from beak to tail as though resolved to abandon their element for ever. But gravity, as though hauling on an oblique fishing-line, dragged them forward and down again into their rifled and bubbling green tunnels. The headlong speed through the water filled the air with a noise of rending and searing. Each leap into the air called forth a chorus of gasps, each plunge a sigh.

These creatures bring a blessing with them. No day in which they have played a part is like other days. I first saw them at dusk, many years ago, on the way to Mount Athos. A whole troop appeared alongside the steamer, racing her and keeping us company for three-quarters of an hour. Slowly it grew darker and as night fell the phosphorescent water turned them into fishes of pale fire. White-hot flames whirled from them. When they leapt from the water they shook off a million fiery diamonds, and when they plunged, it was a fall of comets spinning down fathom after fathom – league upon league of dark sky, it seemed – in whirling incandescent vortices, always to rise again; till at last, streaming down all together as though the heavens were falling and each trailing a ribbon of blazing and feathery wake they became a far-away constellation on the sea's floor. They suddenly turned and vanished, dying away along the abyss like ghosts. Again, four years ago, when I was sailing in a yacht with six friends through the Outer Cyclades in the late afternoon of a long and dreamlike day, there was another visitation. The music from the deck floated over the water and the first champagne cork had fired its sighting-shot over the side. The steep flank of Sikinos, tinkling with goat bells and aflutter with birds, rose up to starboard, and, close to port, the sheer cliffs of nereid-haunted Pholegandros. Islands enclosed the still sea like a lake at the end of the world. A few bars of unlikely mid-summer cloud lay across the west. All at once the sun's rim appeared blood red under the lowest bar, hemming the clouds with gold wire and sending a Japanese flag of widening sunbeams alternating with expanding spokes of deeper sky into the air for miles and spreading rose petals and sulphur green across this silk lake. Then, some distance off, a dolphin sailed into the air, summoned from the depths, perhaps, by the strains of *Water Music*, then another and yet another, until a small company were flying and diving and chasing each other and hovering in mid-air in static semicircles, gambolling and curvetting and almost playing leapfrog, trying to stand on tip-toe, pirouetting and jumping over the sinking sun. All we could hear was an occasional splash, and so smooth was the water that one could see spreading rings when they swooped below the surface. The sea became a meadow and these antics like the last game of children on a lawn before going to bed. Leaning spellbound over the bulwarks and in the rigging we watched them in silence. All at once, on a sudden decision, they vanished; just as they vanish from the side of the *Aphrodite* in this chapter, off the stern and shadowless rocks of the Mani.

'*Kala einai ta delphinia,*' the captain said when they had gone. 'They're good.'[6]

Porpoise-calling: I had never heard of it until I read Sir Arthur Grimble's book *A Pattern of Islands*. Even now, I hardly know what to think – except about the last two paragraphs, where I know all too well.

It was common rumour in the Gilbert Islands that certain local clans had the power of porpoise-calling; but it was rather like the Indian rope-trick; you never met anyone who had actually witnessed the thing. If I had been a reasonably plump young man, I might never have come to see what I did see on the beach of Butaritari lagoon. But I was skinny. It was out of sheer pity for my poor thin frame that old Kitiona set his family porpoise-caller working. We were sitting together one evening in his canoe-shed by the beach, and he was delivering a kind of discourse on the beauty of human fatness.

... 'You should eat porpoise-flesh,' he said simply, 'then you too would swell in the proper places.' That led me to inquire how I might come by a regular supply of the rare meat. The long and the short of his reply was that his own kinsmen in Kuma village, seventeen miles up-lagoon, were the hereditary porpoise-callers of the High Chiefs of Butaritari and Makin-Meang. His first cousin was a leading expert at the game; he could put himself into the right kind of dream on demand. His spirit went out of his body in such a dream; it sought out the porpoise-folk in their home under the western horizon and invited them to a dance, with feasting, in Kuma village. If he spoke the words of the invitation aright (and very few had the secret of them) the porpoise would follow him with cries of joy to the surface.

Having led them to the lagoon entrance, he would fly forward to rejoin his body and warn the people of their coming. It was quite easy for one who knew the way of it. The porpoise never failed to arrive. Would I like some called for me? After some rather idle shilly-shallying, I admitted that I would ... We fixed on a day early in January, some weeks ahead, before I left him.

No further word came from Kitiona until his big canoe arrived one morning to collect me. There was not a breath of wind, so sailing was out of the question. The sun was white-hot. It took over six hours of grim paddling to reach our destination. By the time we got there, I was cooked like a prawn and wrapped in gloom. When the fat, friendly man who styled himself the High Chief's hereditary porpoise-caller came waddling down the beach to greet me, I asked irritably when the porpoise would arrive. He said he would have to go into his dream first, but thought he could have them there for me by three or four o'clock. Please, though, he added firmly, would I be careful to call them, from now on, *only* 'our friends from the west'. The other name was tabu. They might not come at all if I said it aloud. He led me as he spoke to a little hut screened with newly plaited coconut leaves, which stood beside his ordinary dwelling. Alone in there, he explained, he would do his part of the business. Would I honour his house by resting in it while he dreamed? 'Wait in peace now,' he said when I was installed, 'I go on my journey,' and disappeared into the screened hut.

Kuma was a big village in those days: its houses stretched for half a mile or more above the lagoon beach. The dreamer's hut lay somewhere near the centre of the line. The place was dead quiet that afternoon under its swooning palms. The children had been gathered in under the thatches. The women were absorbed in plaiting garlands and wreaths of flowers. The men were silently polishing their ceremonial ornaments of shell. Their friends from the west were being invited to a dance, and everything they did in the village that day was done to maintain the illusion.

Even the makings of a feast lay ready piled in baskets beside the houses. I could not bring myself to believe that the people expected just nothing to come of all this careful business.

But the hours dragged by, and nothing happened. Four o'clock passed. My faith was beginning to sag under the strain when a strangled howl burst from the dreamer's hut. I jumped round to see his cumbrous body come hurtling head first through the torn screens. He sprawled on his face, struggled up, and staggered into the open, a slobber of saliva shining on his chin. He stood awhile clawing at the air and whining on a queer high note like a puppy's. Then words came gulping out of him: '*Teirake! Teirake!* (Arise! Arise! ...) They come! Let us go ... Our friends from the west ... They come! ... Let us go down and greet them.' He started at a lumbering gallop down the beach.

A roar went up from the village, 'They come, they come!' I found myself rushing helter-skelter with a thousand others into the shallows, bawling at the top of my voice that our friends from the west were coming. I ran behind the dreamer; the rest converged on him from north and south. We strung ourselves out, line abreast, as we stormed through the shallows. Everyone was wearing the garlands woven that afternoon. The farther out we got, the less the clamour grew. When we stopped, breast deep, fifty yards from the reef's edge, a deep silence was upon us; and so we waited.

I had just dipped my head to cool it when a man near me yelped and stood pointing; others took up his cry, but I could make out nothing for myself at first in the splintering glare of the sun on the water. When at last I did see them, everyone was screaming hard; they were pretty near by then, gambolling towards us at a fine clip. When they came to the edge of the blue water by the reef, they slackened speed, spread themselves out and started cruising back and forth in front of our line. Then, suddenly, there was no more of them.

In the strained silence that followed, I thought they were gone. The disappointment was so sharp, I did not stop to think then that, even so, I had seen a very strange thing. I was in the act of touching the dreamer's shoulder to take my leave when he turned his still face to me: 'The king out of the west comes to meet me,' he murmured, pointing downwards. My eyes followed his hand. There, not ten yards away, was the great shape of a porpoise poised like a glimmering shadow in the glass-green water. Behind it followed a whole dusky flotilla of them.

They were moving towards us in extended order with spaces of two or three yards between them, as far as my eye could reach. So slowly they came, they seemed to be hung in a trance. Their leader drifted in hard by the dreamer's leg. He turned without a word to walk beside it as it idled towards the shallows. I followed a foot or two behind its almost motionless tail. I saw other groups to right and left of us turn shorewards one by one, arms lifted, faces bent upon the water.

A babble of quiet talk sprang up; I dropped behind to take in the whole scene. The villagers were welcoming their guests ashore with crooning words. Only men were walking beside them; the women and children followed in their wake, clapping their hands softly in the rhythm of a dance. As we approached the emerald shallows, the keels of the creatures began to take the sand; they flapped gently as if asking for help. The men leaned down to throw their arms around the great barrels and ease them over the ridges. They showed no least sign of alarm. It was as if their single wish was to get to the beach.

When the water stood only thigh deep, the dreamer flung his arms high and called. Men from either flank came crowding in to surround the visitors, ten or more to each beast. Then, 'Lift!' shouted the dreamer, and the ponderous black shapes were half-dragged, half-carried, unresisting, to the lip of the tide. There they settled down, those beautiful, dignified shapes, utterly at peace, while all hell broke loose around them. Men, women and children, leaping and posturing with shrieks that tore the sky, stripped off their garlands and flung them around the still bodies, in a sudden dreadful fury of boastfulness and derision. My mind still shrinks from the last scene – the raving humans, the beasts so triumphantly at rest.

We left them garlanded where they lay and returned to our houses. Later, when the falling tide had stranded them high and dry, men went down with knives to cut them up. There was feasting and dancing in Kuma that night. A chief's portion of the meat was set aside for me. I was expected to have it cured as a diet for my thinness. It was duly salted, but I could not bring myself to eat it. I never did grow fat in the Gilbert Islands.[7]

To China now, and the nightmare journey of Martha Gellhorn and her 'Unwilling Companion' (see Chapter Six). Mr Ma was their official interpreter:

I noticed that some of the unending hills were black stubble and asked Mr Ma, probably testing whether I could still speak, 'Why do they burn off the hills, Mr Ma?'

'To get rid of the tigers.'

'*Tigers*, Mr Ma?'

'Yes, many, more or less. You see, tigers eat some kind of tender little roots and sweet grasses, and when it is all burned, they get hungry and go away.'

U.C. lay back on the stony ground and raised his face to heaven with the radiant smile of one who has heard angels singing. Mr Ma's vegetarian tigers have taken on a complex and changing symbolism over the years, and always rejoin me in the blackest hours of other horror journeys.

Before the day was over, my notes state: 'U.C.'s horse fell on him.' U.C. stretched his arm over the saddle and under the horse's belly and picked it up, muttering about cruelty to animals, and started to walk with it. I said sharply, 'Put that horse down.' He said, 'I will not, poor bloody horse.' I said, 'You're insulting the Chinese. Put it down!' He said, 'My first loyalty is to this horse.' I said, '*You must drop that horse! Please!*' 'Okay, poor old horse, walk by yourself if you can.' All afternoon the stable coolie behind me held his stomach and groaned.[8]

A similar incident to this last was, incidentally, recorded by Lady Duff Gordon in a letter from Luxor in the 1860s:

I went a few days ago out to Medamoot, and lunched in Mustapha's tent, among his bean harvest. I was immensely amused by the man who went with me on to Medamoot, one Sheriff, formerly an illustrious robber, now a watchman and very honest man. He rode a donkey, about the size of Stirling's wee pony, and I laughed, and said, 'The man should carry the ass'. No sooner said than done, Sheriff dismounted, or rather let his beast down from between his legs, shouldered the donkey, and ran on.[9]

So much for donkeys; now for a word or two on mules, and in particular the mules of Spain. Our authority is that well-known Hispanophile Richard Ford:

Spaniards in general prefer mules and asses to the horse, which is more delicate, requires greater attention, and is less sure-footed over broken and precipitous ground. The mule performs in Spain the functions of the camel in the East, and has something in his morale (besides his physical suitableness to the country) which is congenial to the character of his masters; he has the same self-willed obstinacy, the same resignation under burdens, the same singular capability of endurance of labour, fatigue, and privation. The mule has always been much used in Spain, and the demand for them very great; yet, from some mistaken crotchet of Spanish political economy (which is very Spanish), the breeding of the mule has long been attempted to be prevented, in order to encourage that of the horse. One of the reasons alleged was, that the mule was a non-reproductive animal; an argument which might or ought to apply equally to the monk; a breed for which Spain could have shown for the first prize, both as to number and size, against any other country in all Christendom.[10]

As for horses, the choice of items for inclusion in a book like this one is obviously endless; but here is a pleasant little conversation recorded by Evelyn Waugh in *Ninety-two Days*, sub-titled *The Account of a Tropical Journey Through British Guiana and Part of Brazil*. At this particular moment the author is on a river-steamer in Guiana:

Our only companions on the top deck were a Belgian rancher, his Indian wife, some of their children, and his wife's sister. They were the first Indians I had seen. Since they had taken up with a European they wore hats and stockings and high-heeled shoes, but they were very shy, guarding their eyes like nuns, and giggling foolishly when spoken to; they had squat little figures and blank, Mongol faces. They had bought a gramophone and a few records in town, which kept them happy for the twelve hours we were together. Conversation was all between Mr Bain and the rancher, and mostly about horses. Quite different standards of quality seemed to be observed here from those I used to learn from Captain Hance.

'I tell you, Mr Bain, that buckskin of mine was the finest mare bred in this district. You didn't have to use no spur or whip to her. Why before you was on her back, almost, she was off like the wind and *nothing* would stop her. And if she didn't want to go any particular way *nothing* would make her. Why I've been carried six miles out of my course many a time, pulling at her with all my strength. *And* how she could rear.'

'Yes, she *could rear*,' said Mr Bain in wistful admiration. 'It was lovely to see her.'

'And if she got you down she'd roll on you. She wouldn't get up till she'd broken every bone in your body. She killed one of my boys that way.'

'But what about my Tiger?'

'Ah, he was a good horse. You could see by the way he rolled his eyes.'

'Did you ever see him *buck*? Why he'd buck all over the corral. And he was wicked too. He struck out at you if he got a chance.'

'That was a *good* horse, Tiger. What became of him?'

'Broke his back. He bolted over some rocks into a creek with one of the boys riding him.'

'Still you know I think that for *bucking* my Shark ...'

And so it went on. Presently I asked in some apprehension, 'And the horse I am to ride tomorrow. Is he a *good* horse too?'

'One of the strongest in the country,' said Mr Bain. 'It will be just like the English Grand National for you.'[11]

I have already introduced – in Chapter Three – Colonel Angus Buchanan, who dedicated his book *Sahara* to his camel. In fact he went even further, and in his own third chapter transcribed what must surely be the only *autobiography* of a camel ever written. I append a sample – with its master's epilogue:

'At first my master did not ride so easily as the camel-men of our land, being more stiff and ungiving of poise; but, as he became familiar with my gait, that alien insensibility passed and we travelled as one.

'I found I had one fault that annoyed my master. Through being badly frightened, when young, by an evil-smelling animal that pounced at me, I could not refrain from being startled whenever I saw any black object close to me on the sand. . . .

'It was chiefly on account of this trait that I was given the name by which my master called me: *Feri n'Gashi*, which, I believe, meant "White Feather" in native tongue, and this, in his language, was a term applied to anyone showing signs of cowardice. But the name also referred to my white coat of hair. My master often spoke in a curious tongue that was foreign to me, but, as time went on, I came to understand that he gradually lost all thought of associating my name with any insinuation of fear. . . .

'It was during this period of ever-increasing strain that my master met with a distressing accident. To carry the loads of my dead or exhausted comrades, some fresh camels were collected from men-people of a rocky land of name I did not comprehend. They were animals of a wild region, and had been long free on the ranges, so that they greatly feared the hand of men-people. When they first felt the weight of my master's boxes on their backs they plunged wildly in all directions, and everything was scattered to the ground. Yet patiently the men-people worked with them, coaxing and replacing the fallen loads; until, finally, we were all led into line ready to start. But just at that moment there was further disaster and a wild stampede, and my master, holding hard to the head of the maddest brute of all, was suddenly kicked to the ground as the animal plunged free. And there he lay, while others rushed blindly over him in their consternation, trampling him underfoot, until a quick-witted camel-man rushed in and dragged him clear; which, mayhap, saved his life. Then it was seen that he was bleeding profusely, and could no longer walk.

'For some days afterwards he lay and could not move, and I wondered what would become of my master.

'When next I saw him he had long sticks below his arms and walked strangely and slowly. On recommencing travel he could no longer ride in the saddle, because of a helpless leg, and was placed, with soft clothing, on the top of the boxes carried by one of my old comrades. For the first time since the start I was without my master. But he did not give me a load to carry, nor let another take his place, and I was allowed to walk behind him with the empty saddle.

'So soon as he could manage, he came to ride me again, and I was glad. I knew he was not strong then, for I could feel a strangeness in his seat, and was therefore gentle on the trail, so that I might not jar or hurt him. . . .

'It was about two months after this that the desert ended, and the remnants of my master's caravan crawled into a strange town where the people were foreign to me, as was the scent in the air. I was alone, except for my master, for none of my comrades of Katsina were left; and I had a heavy heart. I could see my master was happy, yet strangely sad. He stroked me often while the loads were being taken away and stacked in a pile, and I felt he would have liked to break down the barriers of dumbness and articulated words in my own language. And I understood, and rubbed my soft nose against him.

'After a time the men-people gathered us all together and led us away down the street of the strange town. We had gone but half-way when my master's servant came running after us, and I was taken back to him.

'He stood beside me and stroked me ever so gently, and I knew, then, that his heart was heavy as mine. And then I was led away down the strange, unfriendly street again.

'I was terribly tired: I knew, somehow, that I would never see my master again – and that is all I remembered.'

Feri n'Gashi died, without the slightest sign of illness or pain, about one hour after our parting, marking one of the saddest experiences in my life and the passing of one of the noblest animals that ever lived.[12]

Now here is a piece of fine observation and beautiful writing combined. (Would that it happened more often!) The author is Peter Fleming, the book *Brazilian Adventure*:

On a branch hanging low over the water sat a kingfisher, a tiny kingfisher, a bird so small that it seemed impossible that it should exercise the functions of a king-fisher. It was smaller than a sparrow. It had a sharp black beak and sharp black eyes, surely too small to be of any service. Its markings were gay, distinct, and contrast-ing, like the colours of a toy. An orange chest: dark-green back and wings, very lustrous: a black head and a neat white ring round its neck. It looked very compact and proud, and at the same time rather absurd: like a medieval page in a new and splendid livery.

As I watched, it plunged suddenly, wounding the surface of the water hardly more than a falling leaf. Then it went back to the branch, having missed its prey, and sat glaring and fussing the water out of its feathers. Failure rankled. It registered a microscopic indignation.

At this rate, I thought, we shall have the butterflies hawking for fish.

And indeed the only butterfly in sight, which was electric blue and had wings four inches wide, seemed to have much more substance, to be much more capable of wresting a living from the river, than this puny upstart creature. The butterfly, which was of the sort called morpho, came slowly past me from upstream, loitering resplendent, aimlessly quartering the channel, as though in vanity desiring to keep as close as it might to its image in the water. When it left the river it floated through the trees close to the ground, like a delicate sliver flaked from the blue roof of the world, unable to rest on earth: an unreal homeless thing, disowned by all the elements.[13]

In *Escape with Me!* Osbert Sitwell attempts much the same thing, per-haps a shade less successfully. He is at Angkor Wat, shortly before the Second World War:

All varieties of water-birds are now plentiful enough here, more numerous than men: the forests, you would say, are divided between them and the monkeys. . . . One morning I was standing by the deserted moat of the Gate of the Dead. In front of the entrance, some of the stone giants still remain in place, but the water of the moat has moved away, though there is still, on either side, a smaller, flat pool of shallow water. It was very pleasant there, for it was about ten in the morning and, at this particular point, enormous and impenetrable barriers of leaves and branches protected one from the sun, and even a little damped down the heat, although the huge masks over the gate, in themselves so cold and meditative, were bathed in a fierce light that made every grain of their stone glitter. . . . This, I reflected, must have been one of the busiest places in the ancient city, and I tried to imagine the sentries and groups of soldiers, the horses and elephants, the palanquins and parasols of the grandees, the yellow-robed priests, the chattering throngs, with their chignons and bracelets, coming and going, rich men with their retainers following them, and the naked beggars with clawing hands outthrust toward them, the lepers collecting alms outside the gate. . . . At the present moment, however, the peace of the scene, and the beauty of it, were prodigious. Kingfishers clapped their wings over the water, and large tropical butterflies floated and glided and leapt on the hot, honey-sweet air; faint, contented purrings and cracklings issued from the jungle within the walls. A tall, wide-winged water-bird, a creation in salmon-pink and white and flame colour, with a touch of magenta and Parma-violet here and there, but, in spite of this outward ostentation, very dignified and like a policeman in mien and gait, stood, ankle-deep, in the pool; fishing, I supposed, for he kept thrusting his neck down into the reeds. He stalked slowly, and with what Americans term 'poise.' . . . It seemed as though an almost sinister silence had descended, there was no longer a sound, not a movement from the trees. Then, suddenly, while the bird's head was immersed in the water, a shriek of gutter-snipe laughter broke out from the branches, and a hundred or so very hard and pointed nuts, propelled by a hundred little hairy arms, cunning in their aim, shot out from the foliage at its superbly feathered rump. . . . The stately bird withdrew his head from the water as swiftly as he could without in any way impairing his self-respect, and uttered a sound that, though low in tone and couched, as it were, in diplomatic terms, distinctly signified protest and reproval, at the same time opening and shutting his broad and lovely wings. He made several menacing but rather pompous gestures, and looked as though, if this sort of hooliganism continued, he would bring the matter up before the League Assembly. . . . The monkeys, meanwhile, were indulging in joy-flights in the branches, which rustled and swept low as they swung backward and forward, silently but in 2–3 time, from bough to bough. Then, their amusement exhausted, they became still and hid once more. . . . After a moment of tense, breathless excitement, they repeated their manœuvre; and, on this occasion, the bird, since he was on the watch and peering about him, was hit on the neck. He made an audible remonstrance, referring to Clause XVI, and uttered a further warning sound. He began to open his wings, but they were more for show, I apprehend, than for use, and the unfolding of these rather obsolete, if fantastic, pinions, required time and effort. Beautiful as they looked, the amount of business, the creaking and fluttering and beating the air, that were required in order to prepare them for flight, seemed, in truth, somewhat antiquated and absurd. The monkeys could no longer contain their delight; they swung and turned somersaults and shrieked in the trees in an ecstasy, and aimed now quite openly and singly. . . . Slowly, a diminishing rocket of flame and rosy feathers, the vast bird made its spiral ascent, sailing away and up, high above the giant masks of gate and temple, over the most distant trees. His dignity was safe now. Stillness once more brooded upon the water.[14]

And so to the elephant. Hakluyt's *Voyages* contains an account of a journey by one Ralph Fitch to Goa and Siam, which took place between 1583 and 1591. At this point in his narrative, the author is speaking of Pegu, in Burma:

Within the first gate of the king's house is a great large room, on both sides whereof are houses made for the king's elephants, which be marvellous great and fair, and are brought up to wars and in service of the king. And among the rest he hath four white elephants, which are very strange and rare: for there is none other king which hath them but he: if any other king hath one, he will send unto him for it. When any of these white elephants is brought unto the king, all the merchants in the city are commanded to see them, and to give him a present of half a ducat, which doth come to a great sum: for that there are many merchants in the city. After that you have given your present you may come and see them at your pleasure, although they stand in the king's house. This king in his title is called the king of the white elephants. If any other king hath one, and will not send it him, he will make war with him for it: for he had rather lose a great part of his kingdom, than not to conquer him. They do very great service unto these white elephants; every one of them standeth in an house gilded with gold, and they do feed in vessels of silver and gilt. One of them when he doth go to the river to be washed, as every day they do, goes under a canopy of cloth of gold or of silk carried over him by six or eight men, and eight or ten men go before him playing on drums, shawms, or other instruments: and when he is washed and cometh out of the river, there is a gentleman which doth wash his feet in a silver basin: which is his office given him by the king. There is no such account made of any black elephant, be he never so great. The king hath above five thousand elephants of war. There be many huntsmen, which go into the wilderness with she elephants: for without the she they are not to be taken. And they be taught for that purpose: and every hunter hath five or six of them: and they say that they anoint the she elephants with a certain ointment, which when the wild elephant doth smell, he will not leave her. When they have brought the wild elephant near unto the place, they send word unto the town, and many horsemen and footmen come out and cause the she elephant to enter into a strait way which doth go to the palace, and the she and the he do run in: for it is like a wood: and when they be in, the gate doth shut. Afterward they get out the female: and when the male seeth that he is left alone, he weepeth and crieth, and runneth against the walls, which be made of so strong trees, that some of them do break their teeth with running against them. Then they prick him with sharp canes, and cause him to go into a strait house, and there they put a rope about his middle and about his feet, and let him stand there three or four days without eating or drinking: and then they bring the female to him, with meat and drink, and within few days he becometh tame. The chief force of the king is in these elephants. And when they go into the wars they set a frame of wood upon their backs, bound with great cords, wherein sit four or six men, which fight with guns, bows and arrows, darts and other weapons. And they say that their skins are so thick that a pellet of an arquebus will scarce pierce them, except it be in some tender place.[15]

Another even earlier voyager, also included in Hakluyt, is John Lok, who sailed to Guinea in 1554. He too wrote of elephants – though this time of the African variety – and noted an interesting piece of additional information:

They have continual war against dragons, which desire their blood because it is very cold: and therefore the dragon lieth in wait as the elephant passeth by.[16]

In 1878, Mrs Isabella Bird was staying at the British Residency at Kwala Kangsa in the Malay Peninsula. When she arrived, the Resident was absent – probably 'away up-country', as Residents tended to be – but she didn't mind that:

I was received by a magnificent Oriental butler, and after I had had a delicious bath, dinner, or what Assam was pleased to call breakfast, was 'served.' The word 'served' was strictly applicable, for linen, china, crystal, flowers, cooking, were all alike exquisite. Assam, the Madrassee, is handsomer and statelier than Babu at Malacca; a smart Malay lad helps him, and a Chinaman sits on the steps and pulls the punkah. All things were harmonious, the glorious coco-palms, the bright green slopes, the sunset gold on the lake-like river, the ranges of forest-covered mountains etherealising in the purple light, the swarthy faces and scarlet uniforms of the Sikh guard, and rich and luscious odours, floated in on balmy airs, glories of the burning tropics, untellable and incommunicable!

My valise had not arrived, and I had been obliged to re-dress myself in my mud-splashed tweed dress, therefore I was much annoyed to find the table set for three, and I hung about unwillingly in the verandah, fully expecting two Government clerks in faultless evening dress to appear, and I was vexed to think that my dream of solitude was not to be realised, when Assam more emphatically assured me that the meal was 'served,' and I sat down, much mystified, at the well-appointed table, when he led in a large ape, and the Malay servant brought in a small one, and a Sikh brought in a large retriever and tied him to my chair! This was all done with the most profound solemnity. The circle being then complete, dinner proceeded with great stateliness. The apes had their curry, chutney, pine-apple, eggs, and bananas on porcelain plates, and so had I. The chief difference was that, whereas I waited to be helped, the big ape was impolite enough occasionally to snatch something from a dish as the butler passed round the table, and that the small one before very long migrated from his chair to the table, and, sitting by my plate, helped himself daintily from it. What a grotesque dinner party! What a delightful one! My 'next of kin' were so reasonably silent; they required no conversational efforts; they were most interesting companions. 'Silence is golden,' I felt; shall I ever enjoy a dinner party so much again?[17]

Not surprisingly, perhaps, we have not yet said much about frogs. They do not normally impinge too much on the travel writer's consciousness; but in *A Reed Shaken by the Wind* Gavin Maxwell gives us a piece of brilliantly sustained description which earns them a place here:

As the sun began to set the wind dropped to a breath, and the confined water became glass calm, a mirror reflecting a sky from which all colour had ebbed, and even the sun sinking behind the sharply etched *cheval de frise* of reed tops was a blanched glare of light without hue. The great wilderness of water and reeds became pressing and mysterious as does a forest when the darkness comes, and with the hush of evening came the voices of the frogs.

Of all the strange sounds and sights of the marshes I think that I shall remember longest the tumultuous voices of the frogs, those million million voices that could turn the great marsh desert into a cauldron of sound seeming more limitless even than the falling horizons themselves. Later during our journey, when we were crossing the open water of some great lake and the giant reed-beds were a low golden wall in the distance there would be a temporary silence, a silence that seemed somehow uneasy because of the absence of a thing familiar; then, when the *tarada* was still half a mile from the reed-beds, it would creep back into the air like the distant murmur of a great concourse of men. At a quarter of a mile the tone would change to the jabbering of tens of thousands of monkeys; then, as the reeds closed round the canoe, it became a jagged wall of sound that cut one off from the open world outside.

There are several individual types of voice that fuse to compose that mad babel; and on that first evening, as the white sun sank and silhouetted the reed tops, the voices began individually before they gathered sweep and volume to engulf the night, so that for a minute or two it was possible to isolate the notes and search for comparison. The first voice of which I was conscious was loud and staccato and near at hand, a quick chatter indistinguishable from that of a magpie, ragged teeth of sound cutting into the gleaming bubble of low sun and water and the small liquid noises of the paddles. A second voice answered, a rhythmic double note exactly like a man sawing wood, harsh and rasping; a third was boisterous and expansive and could be mistaken for the quacking of a farmyard drake; a fourth would have passed in any Kensington drawing-room for the yapping of a hoarse Pekinese dog. Inherent in each of these voices, despite their differences, is some quality suggestive of remarkable enthusiasm, as though their owners were engaged upon some pleasurable and essentially exhilarating task. These diverse sounds fuse into a continuous and confused uproar, until only the very nearest have any recognisable form.

One seldom sees the owners of these voices except as a quick retiring ripple in the water; and I think the majority, anyway, are of no great size. Once, walking over partially flooded land near the perimeter of the permanent marshes, I picked up one of the many empty terrapin shells that lay on the short green turf. I was turning it over in my hands, when, from the hole where the living tortoise's neck should be, a small grey-green face emerged sharply. It gave a gruff and startled exclamation, regarded me glassily with the far-seeing and imperious eyes of a senior naval officer, and withdrew. I was peering after it when a second head, greener and larger than the first, popped out from the other end, emitted a single outraged gasp, and remained staring for a moment or two with a pulse beating angrily in its cheek. Nothing that I could do could persuade either of the occupants to show themselves again; I dropped the shell in a puddle and turned away. I had not taken more than two or three paces when I heard a chatter of insane laughter behind me, and whirled round in time to see a frog shoot out from each end of the terrapin and land with a plop in the shallow water. That was as near as I ever got to examining any member of the fabulous orchestra.[18]

I must now commend to you a book entitled *Life in Mexico*, by Madame Calderón de la Barca. Her maiden name was Frances Inglis, and she was an Englishwoman who went first to America – where she was a friend of Prescott and Longfellow – and there, in 1838, married the Spanish Minister Don Angel Calderón de la Barca, who was almost immediately transferred to Mexico. There she remained for the next two years, and the book is a collection of her letters home. She loved the country, but was not entirely enamoured of its fauna:

For four months in the year, *tierra caliente* must be a paradise, and it has the advantage over the coasts, in being quite free from yellow fever. But the heat in summer, and the number of poisonous insects, are great drawbacks. Of these, the *alacrans*, or scorpions, which haunt all the houses, are amongst the worst. Their bite is poisonous, and, to a child, deadly, which is one of the many reasons why these estates are left entirely to the charge of an agent, and though visited occasionally by the proprietor, rarely lived in by the family. The effects are more or less violent in different constitutions. Some persons will remain for eight days in convulsions, foaming at the mouth, and the stomach swelled, as if by dropsy; others, by immediate remedies, do not suffer much. The chief cures are brandy, taken in sufficient quantities to stupefy the patient, guyacum and boiled milk, which last is considered most efficacious. In Durango they are particularly numerous and venomous, so that a reward is given for so many *head* of scorpions to the boys there, to encourage them to destroy them. The Señora ——, who lives there, feels no inconvenience from their bite, but the scorpion who bites her immediately dies! It is pretended that they prefer dark people to fair, which is to suppose them very discriminating. Though as yet there have been few seen in the houses, I must confess that we feel rather uneasy at night, and scrupulously examine our beds and their environs before venturing to go to sleep. The walls being purposely whitewashed, it is not difficult to detect them; but where the roofs are formed of beams, they are very apt to drop through.

There are other venomous reptiles, for whose sting there is no remedy, and if you would like to have a list of these interesting creatures, according to the names by which they are known in these parts, I can furnish you with one from the best authority. These, however, are generally to be found about outhouses, and only occasionally visit your apartments. There is the *chicaclina*, a striped viper, of beautiful colours – the *coralillo*, a viper of a coral colour, with a black head – the *vinagrillo*, an animal like a large cricket. You can discover it, when in the room, by its strong smell of vinegar. It is orange-coloured, and taps upon the person whom it crawls over, without giving any pain, but leaving a long train of deadly poison – I have fancied that I smelt vinegar in every room since hearing this – the *salamanquesa*, whose bite is fatal: it is shaped like a lizard – the *eslaboncillo*, which throws itself upon you, and if prevented from biting you, dies of spite – the *cencoatl*, which has five feet, and shines in the dark; so that fortunately a warning is given of the vicinity of these animals in different ways; in some by the odour they exhale, in some by the light they emit, and in others, like the rattlesnake, by the sound they give out.

Then there is a beautiful black and red spider, called the *chinclaquili*, whose sting sends a pain through all your bones; the only cure for which is to be shut up for several days in a room thick with smoke. There are also the *tarantula* and *casampulga* spiders. Of the first, which is a shocking-looking soft fat creature, covered with dark hair, it is said that the horse which treads on it instantly loses its hoof – but this wants confirmation. Of the scorpions, the small yellowish coloured ones are the most dangerous, and it is pretended that their bite is most to be apprehended at midday. The workmen occasionally eat them, after pulling out the sting. The flesh of the viper is also eaten roasted, as a remedy against eruptions of the skin. Methinks the remedy is worse than the disease. . . .[19]

But some tropical insects actually had their uses, as Captain John Stedman discovered in Surinam:

On the 16th I was visited by a neighbouring gentleman, whom I conducted up my ladder; but he had no sooner entered my aerial dwelling, than he leapt down from the top to the ground, roaring like a madman with agony and pain, after which he instantly plunged his head into the river. Looking up, I soon discovered the cause of his distress to be an enormous nest of wild bees in the thatch, directly above my head as I stood within my door. I immediately took to my heels as he had done, and ordered them to be demolished by my slaves without delay. A tar mop was now brought, and the devastation just going to commence, when an old negro stepped up, and offered to receive any punishment I should decree if ever one of these bees should sting *me in person*. '*Masera*,' said he, 'they would have stung you long ere now had you been a stranger to them; but they being your tenants, and having been gradually allowed to build upon your premises, they assuredly know both you and yours, and will never hurt either you or them.' I instantly assented to the proposition, and tying the old black man to a tree, ordered my boy Quaco to ascend the ladder quite naked, which he did and was not stung. I then ventured to follow, and I declare upon my honour that, even after shaking the nest which made its inhabitants buzz about my ears, not a single bee attempted to sting me. I next released the old negro, and rewarded him with a gallon of rum and five shillings for the discovery. This swarm of bees I since kept unhurt as my bodyguards, and they have made many overseers take a desperate leap for my amusement, as I generally sent them up my ladder upon some frivolous message, when I wished to punish them for injustice and cruelty.[20]

I am going to end this chapter with two of my favourite passages in all travel literature. The first is from James Morris's glorious book *Venice*:

I cannot help thinking that the old Venetians went a little queer about lions, for the profusion of stone specimens in Venice is almost unbelievable. The city crawls with lions, winged lions and ordinary lions, great lions and petty lions, lions on doorways, lions supporting windows, lions on corbels, self-satisfied lions in gardens, lions rampant, lions soporific, amiable lions, ferocious lions, rickety lions, vivacious lions, dead lions, rotting lions, lions on chimneys, on flower-pots, on garden gates, on crests, on medallions, lurking among foliage, blatant on pillars, lions on flags, lions on tombs, lions in pictures, lions at the feet of statues, lions realistic, lions symbolic, lions heraldic, lions archaic, mutilated lions, chimerical lions, semi-lions, super-lions, lions with elongated tails, feathered lions, lions with jewelled eyes, marble lions, porphyry lions, and one real lion, drawn from the life, as the artist proudly says, by the indefatigable Longhi, and hung among the rest of his *genre* pictures in the Querini-Stampalia gallery. There are Greek lions, Gothic lions, Byzantine lions, even Hittite lions. There are seventy-five lions on the Porta della Carta, the main entrance to the Doge's Palace. There is a winged lion on every iron insurance plate. There is even a sorrowing lion at the foot of the Cross itself, in a picture in the Scuola di San Marco.

The most imperial lion in Venice is the winged beast painted by Carpaccio in the Doge's Palace, with a moon-lily beside his front paw, and a tail four or five feet long. The ugliest pair of lions lie at the feet of a French Ambassador's tomb in the church of San Giobbe, and were carved, with crowns on their heads and tongues slightly protruding, by the French sculptor Perreau. The silliest lion stands in the Public Gardens, removed there from the façade of the Accademia: Minerva is riding this footling beast side-saddle, and on her helmet is perched another anatomical curiosity – an owl with knees. The eeriest lion is the so-called crab-lion, which you may find in a dark archway near the church of Sant' Aponal, and which looks less like a crab than a kind of feathered ghoul. The most unassuming stands on a pillar outside San Nicolò dei Mendicoli; he holds the book of St. Mark in his paws, but has never presumed to apply for the wings. The most froward stands on a bridge near Santa Chiara, behind the car park, where a flight of steps runs fustily down to the canal like a Dickensian staircase in the shadows of London Bridge, and this unlikeable beast glowers at you like Mrs. Grundy.

The most pathetic lion is an elderly animal that stands on the palisade of the Palazzo Franchetti, beside the Accademia bridge, bearing listlessly in his mouth a label inscribed *Labore*. The most undernourished is a long lion on the south façade of the Basilica, three or four of whose ribs protrude cruelly through his hide. The most glamorous is the winged lion on his column in the Piazzetta, whose eyes are made of agate, whose legs were damaged when Napoleon removed him to Paris, and whose Holy Book was inserted neatly under his paws when he was first brought to Venice from the pagan East, converted from a savage basilisk to a saint's companion.

The most indecisive lion is the creature at the foot of the Manin statue, in the Campo Manin, whose creator was evidently uncertain whether such carnivores had hair under their wings, or feathers (as Ruskin said of another pug-like example, which has fur wings, 'in several other points the manner of his sculpture is not uninteresting'). The most senile lions are the ones on the Dogana, which are losing their teeth pitifully, and look badly in need of a pension. The most long-suffering are the porphyry lions in the Piazzetta dei Leoncini, north of the Basilica, which have been used by generations of little Venetians as substitutes for rocking horses. The frankest lions, the ones most likely to succeed, are the pair that crouch, one dauntless but in chains, the other free and awfully noble, beneath the fine equestrian statue of Victor Emmanuel on the Riva degli Schiavoni.

The most enigmatical is the gaunt bald lion, outside the gates of the Arsenal, whose rump is carved with nordic runes. The most confident is the new lion that stands outside the naval school at Sant' Elena, forbidding entry to all without special permission from the commandant. The most athletic looks sinuously past the Doge Foscari on the Porta della Carta. The most threatening crouches on the façade of the Scuola di San Marco, his paws protruding, ready to leap through the surrounding marble. The most reproachful looks down from the Clock Tower in the Piazza, more in sorrow than in anger, as though he has just seen you do something not altogether creditable beneath the arcade. The jolliest – but there, none of the lions of Venice are really very unpleasant, and comparisons are invidious.

They provide an essential element in the Venetian atmosphere, an element of cracked but affectionate obsession. It is no accident that in the very centre of Tintoretto's vast Paradise, in the Doge's Palace, the lion of St. Mark sits in unobtrusive comfort, nestling beside his master amid the surrounding frenzy, and disputing with that saintly scribe, so Mark Twain thought, the correct spelling of an adjective.[21]

My concluding favourite needs a little introduction, which takes the form of an extract from a letter written on 10 August 1940 by Lawrence Durrell to Henry Miller. Miller reproduces it in the appendix to *The Colosssus of Maroussi*, a portrait of his friend and the subject of this story, George Katsimbalis:

We all went up to the Acropolis the other evening very drunk and exalted by wine and poetry; it was a hot black night and our blood was roaring with cognac. We sat on the steps outside the big gate, passing the bottle, Katsimbalis reciting and G— weeping a little, when all of a sudden K. was seized with a kind of fit. Leaping to his feet he yelled out – 'Do you want to hear the cocks of Attica, you damned moderns?' His voice had a hysterical edge to it. We didn't answer and he wasn't waiting for one. He took a little run to the edge of the precipice, like a faery queen, a heavy black faery queen, in his black clothes, threw back his head, clapped the crook of his stock into his wounded arm, and sent out the most blood-curdling clarion I have ever heard. Cock-a-doodle-doo. It echoed all over the city – a sort of dark bowl dotted with lights like cherries. It ricochetted from hillock to hillock and wheeled up under the walls of the Parthenon. . . . We were so shocked that we were struck dumb. And while we were still looking at each other in the darkness, lo, from the distance silvery clear in the darkness a cock drowsily answered – then another, then another. This drove K. wild. Squaring himself, like a bird about to fly into space, and flapping his coat tails, he set up a terrific scream – and the echoes multiplied. He screamed until the veins stood out all over him, looking like a battered and ravaged rooster in profile, flapping on his own dunghill. He screamed himself hysterical and his audience in the valley increased until all over Athens like bugles they were calling and calling, answering him. Finally between laughter and hysteria we had to ask him to stop. The whole night was alive with cockcrows – all Athens, all Attica, all Greece, it seemed, until I almost imagined you being woken at your desk late in New York to hear these terrific silver peals: Katsimbaline cockcrow in Attica.[22]

In another extract from *Mani*, Paddy Leigh Fermor recalls how, one summer night, he and some friends were sitting in a quiet garden talking of this incident, and of how the phantom cockcrows had reverberated across all Attica and perhaps all Greece. At this point his own imagination takes over:

Perhaps all Greece. The distance between Cythera and Cape Matapan on the tattered map in my pocket, was somewhere between twenty and thirty miles. This enormously extended the possible ambit of George's initial cockcrow. If the Maniots, with a helping wind, could hear the cocks of Cythera, the traffic, with a different wind, could be reversed, and leap from the Mani (or better still, Cape Malea) to Cythera, from Cythera to Anticythera, and from Anticythera to the piratical peninsulas of western Crete; only to die out south of the great island in a last lonely crow on the islet of Gavdos, in the Libyan Sea. ... But a timely west wind could carry it to the eastern capes of Crete, over the Cassos straits, through the islands of the Dodecanese, and thence to the Halicarnassus peninsula and the Taurus mountains. ... The possibilities became suddenly tremendous and in our mind's ear the ghostly clarion travelled south-west into Egypt, south-east to the Persian Gulf; up the Nile, past the villages of the stork-like Dinkas, through the great forests, from kraal to kraal of the Zulus, waking the drowsy Boers of the Transvaal and expiring from a chicken-run on Table Mountain over the Cape of Good Hope. North of Athens, all was plain sailing; it would be through the Iron Curtain, over the Great Balkan range and across the Danube within the hour, with nothing to hinder its spread across the Ukraine and Great Russia – the sudden hubbub in a hundred collective farms alerting the N.K.V.D. and causing a number of arrests on suspicion – until it reached the reindeer-haunted forests of Lapland, and called across the ice towards Nova Zembla to languish among igloos. How far north could poultry thrive? We didn't know, but every moment the wind was becoming a more reliable carrier and further-flung and the cocks robuster. Thus, as the northern call fell silent among the tongue-tied penguins of the Arctic floes, the westward sweep, after startling the solitary Magyar herdsman with the untimely uproar and alarming the night-capped Normans with thoughts of theft, was culminating in ultimate unanswered challenges from John o' Groats and the Blasket Islands, Finisterre and Cape Trafalgar, and a regimental mascot in Gibraltar was already rousing the Berbers of Tangier. ... Due to the new impetus of Leghorn – enough to send a tremor through the doffed headgear of Bersagliere in many a draughty barrack-room – the Sicilian barnyards had long been astir.

The south-eastern tributary meanwhile, after sailing across Baluchistan, was initiating a fuse of clamour across the Deccan, and, reaching Cape Cormorin, leaping the straits, like the magic bridge of Hanuman, to set the roof-tops of Kandy ringing; travelling east to Burma and raising winged mutinies in the Celebes and the Malaccas. There was no problem here. Thanks to swarms of the far-wandering junks of the bird-loving Chinese, shrill calls were soon sounding across the gunfire of Malaya: fumbling for their blowpipes, head-hunters rubbed their eyes in Borneo; Samoans were stretching and yawning on the split bamboo of their stilt-borne floors and hieratic and glittering birds, poised on branches heavy with almond blossom, were swelling their bright throats above the distant triangle of Fujiyama. . . . And what of the long eastern journey from the Asia Minor? Those solitary cries across the Oxus, those noisy resurrections among the black yurts of the Khirgiz and the Karakalpacks? The contagious din of nomad poultry ringing across steppe and tundra, waking the wiry Mongol fowl and sailing forlornly over the Great Wall of China; turning north to Kamschatka and straining for the Aleutians? What of the shivering, ruffled frustration of the Behring Straits?

Yes, what indeed?

Hearing us talking with some excitement, the moonlit figure of our hostess had appeared at the top of the ladder with another blue enamel half-*oka* can; and before we were a third of the way down it, we were across: a whale-fishing fleet materialized in the mists, each vessel captained by an eccentric Ahab engaged on a poultry-fancying competition with his colleagues, and it was entirely due to their hardy pets, beating their icicle-weighted wings and calling over the dark sea, that their Athenian message ever reached Alaska and the new world, crossed the Rockies and rang forth across the Hudson Bay towards Baffin Land. Without them, the Mormon roosters of Utah would have slept on; it would never have needed the sudden boost of Rhode Island which was to waft it safely across the mangrove swamps of Louisiana and through the Maya temples and the nightmares of Nicaraguan revolutionaries and across the Panama Canal. Now it spread like a jungle-fire through the southern hemisphere and a strident spark of sound leapt the swift-flowing narrows of Trinidad to ignite the whole Caribbean chain, jolting the rum-sodden slumbers of the Barbadians and touching off, in the throats of sacrificial birds in Haiti that the dark fingers of Voodoo priests were soon to silence, a defiant *morituri te salutamus*. In the dank unexplored recesses of the Amazonian hinterland, aboriginal and unclassified poultry were sending up shrill and uncouth cries and high in the cold Andean starlight gleaming birds were spreading their wings and filling their breasts on the great tumbled blocks of Inca palaces. The volume of the call was swelling now, sweeping south across the pampas, the Gran Chaco, the Rio Grande; and then dwindling as the two great oceans inexorably closed in, causing the superstitious giants of Patagonia to leap from their rough couches and peer into their wattle hen-coops wild-eyed. Now the dread moment came, the final staging-point and terminus of those great Katsimbalis lungs; the last desperate conflagration of sound in Tierra del Fuego with the ultimate chanticleer calling and calling and calling, unanswered but undaunted, to the maelstroms and the tempests, the hail and the darkness and the battering waves of Cape Horn. . . .

For there was no hope here. It was the end. We thought with sorrow of the silent poles and the huge bereaved antipodes, of the scattered islets and archipelagos that were out of range; of combed heads tucked in sleep under many a speckled wing that no salutation from the Parthenon would ever wake: the beautiful cocks of the Easter and Ellis and the Gilbert islanders, of the Marquesas, the Melanesians and the Trobrianders, of Tristan da Cunha and St. Helena. This gentle melancholy was diffidently interrupted by our hostess: she was going to bed, but if we would like to sit on and enjoy the moonlight, she would leave the street door open, if we would lock up and slip the key under the door. Remembering our early start next day, we rose and asked for the bill. She smiled and said there was nothing to pay. Covert benefactors, the sailors had paid it on the way out and turned us into their guests.[23]

CHAPTER SIXTEEN

Customs of the Country

My favourite sentence of Herodotus:

Apart from the fact that they prostitute their daughters, the Lydian way of life is not unlike our own.[1]

If I say no more about the Lydians in this – or indeed in any other – chapter, it is because what we all really enjoy in travel literature is to read about ways of life which differ from our own in the greatest imaginable degree. Of such life-styles, fortunately, there is an endless variety even today, and in the course of history there must have been infinitely more; once again, therefore, I am confronted with an *embarras de richesse*, finding myself obliged to compress into one short chapter a subject for which an entire book would hardly suffice. The simplest way of dealing with the problem seems to be to adopt, so far as is possible, a universal approach, covering as many different places and periods as I can.

Let us begin with France, and with that most entertaining of observers, Horace Walpole. Here he is, writing to his friend John Chute from Paris on 3 October 1765:

What strikes me the most upon the whole is, the total difference of manners between them and us, from the greatest object to the least. There is not the smallest similitude in the twenty-four hours. It is obvious in every trifle. Servants carry their lady's train, and put her into her coach with their hat on. They walk about the streets in the rain with umbrellas to avoid putting on their hats; driving themselves in open chaises in the country without hats, in the rain too, and yet often wear them in a chariot in Paris when it does not rain. The very footmen are powdered from the break of day, and yet wait behind their master, as I saw the Duc of Praslin's do, with a red pocket-handkerchief about their necks. Versailles, like everything else, is a mixture of parade and poverty, and in every instance exhibits something most dissonant from our manners. In the colonnades, upon the staircases, nay in the antechambers of the royal family, there are people selling all sorts of wares. While we were waiting in the Dauphin's sumptuous bedchamber, till his dressing-room door should be opened, two fellows were sweeping it, and dancing about in sabots to rub the floor.

You perceive that I have been presented. The Queen took great notice of me;

none of the rest said a syllable. You are let into the King's bedchamber just as he has put on his shirt; he dresses and talks good-humouredly to a few, glares at strangers, goes to mass, to dinner, and a-hunting. The good old Queen, who is like Lady Primrose in the face, and Queen Caroline in the immensity of her cap, is at her dressing-table, attended by two or three old ladies, who are languishing to be in Abraham's bosom, as the only man's bosom to whom they can hope for admittance. Thence you go to the Dauphin, for all is done in an hour. He scarce stays a minute; indeed, poor creature, he is a ghost, and cannot possibly last three months. The Dauphiness is in her bedchamber, but dressed and standing; looks cross, is not civil, and has the true Westphalian grace and accents. The four Mesdames, who are clumsy plump old wenches, with a bad likeness to their father, stand in a bedchamber in a row, with black cloaks and knotting-bags, looking good-humoured, not knowing what to say, and wriggling as if they wanted to make water. This ceremony too is very short; then you are carried to the Dauphin's three boys, who you may be sure only bow and stare. The Duke of Berry looks weak and weak-eyed: the Count de Provence is a fine boy; the Count d'Artois well enough. The whole concludes with seeing the Dauphin's little girl dine, who is as round and as fat as a pudding.[2]

In Spain, according to Richard Ford, much thought has always been given to the manner of concealing scars on the face, especially those resulting from wounds inflicted by jealous husbands. During the reign of Philip IV, he tells us, the sovereign panacea was cat's grease,

which then removed such superfluous marks; while Don Quixote considered the oil of Apariccio to be the only cure for scratches inflicted by female or feline claws.

In process of time, as science advanced, this was superseded by *Unto del hombre*, or man's grease. Our estimable friend Don Nicolas Molero, a surgeon in high practice at Seville, assured us that previously to the French invasion he had often prepared this cataleptic specific, which used to be sold for its weight in gold, until, having been adulterated by unprincipled empirics, it fell into disrepute. The receipt of the balsam of Fierabras has puzzled the modern commentators of Don Quixote, but the kindness of Don Nicolas furnished us with the ingredients of this *pommade divine*, or rather *mortale*. 'Take a man in full health who has been just killed, the fresher the better, pare off the fat round the heart, melt it over a slow fire, clarify, and put it away in a cool place for use.' The multitudinous church ceremonies and holidays in Spain, which bring crowds together, combined with the sun, wine, and women, have always ensured a supply of fine subjects.[3]

And so to Germany, where I have two extracts. The first is from *A Tramp Abroad*, by Mark Twain. What sparks him off is the sight of a rich farmhouse in the Black Forest:

The house was big enough for an hotel. ... The eaves projected far down, like sheltering, hospitable wings. ... Before the ground-floor door was a huge pile of manure. The door of a second-story room on the side of the house was open, and occupied by the rear elevation of a cow. Was this probably the drawing-room? All of the front half of the house from the ground up seemed to be occupied by the people, the cows, and the chickens, and all the rear half by draught animals and hay. But the chief feature all around this house was the big heaps of manure. . . .

The importance of this feature has not been properly magnified in the Black Forest stories. Manure is evidently the Black Forester's main treasure – his coin, his jewel, his pride, his Old Master, his keramics, his bric-à-brac, his darling, his title to public consideration, envy, veneration, and his first solicitude when he gets ready to make his will. The true Black Forest novel, if it is ever written, will be skeletoned somewhat in this way:

SKELETON FOR BLACK FOREST NOVEL

Rich old farmer, named Huss. Has inherited great wealth of manure, and by diligence has added to it. It is double-starred in 'Baedeker.'* The Black Forest artist paints it – his masterpiece. The King comes to see it. Gretchen Huss, daughter and heiress. Paul Hoch, young neighbour, suitor for Gretchen's hand – ostensibly; he really wants the manure. Hoch has a good many cartloads of the Black Forest currency himself, and therefore is a good catch; but he is sordid, mean, and without sentiment, whereas Gretchen is all sentiment and poetry. Hans Schmidt, young neighbour, full of sentiment, full of poetry, loves Gretchen; Gretchen loves him. But he has no manure. Old Huss forbids him the house. His heart breaks, he goes away to die in the woods, far from the cruel world – for he says, bitterly, 'What is man, without manure?'

[Interval of six months.]

Paul Hoch comes to old Huss and says, 'I am at last as rich as you required – come and view the pile.' Old Huss views it, and says, 'It is sufficient – take her and be happy' – meaning Gretchen.

[Interval of two weeks.]

Wedding party assembled in old Huss's drawing-room; Hoch placid and content, Gretchen weeping over her hard fate. Enter old Huss's head book-keeper. Huss says fiercely, 'I gave you three weeks to find out why your books don't balance, and to prove that you are not a defaulter; the time is up – find me the missing property or you go to prison as a thief.' Book-keeper: 'I have found it.' 'Where?' Book-keeper (sternly – tragically): 'In the bridegroom's pile! – behold the thief – see him blench and tremble!' [Sensation.] Paul Hoch: 'Lost, lost!' – falls over the cow in a swoon and is handcuffed. Gretchen: 'Saved!' – falls over the calf in a swoon of joy, but is caught in the arms of Hans Schmidt, who springs in at that moment. Old Huss: 'What, you here, varlet? Unhand the maid and quit the place.' Hans (still supporting the insensible girl): 'Never! Cruel old man, know that I come with claims which even you cannot despise.'

Huss: 'What, *you*? Name them.'

Hans: 'Then listen. The world had forsaken me, I forsook the world. I wandered in the solitude of the forest, longing for death, but finding none. I fed upon roots, and in my bitterness I dug for the bitterest, loathing the sweeter kind. Digging, three days agone, I struck a manure mine! – a Golconda, a limitless Bonanza of solid

---

* When Baedeker's guide-books mention a thing and put two stars ** after it, it means 'well worth visiting.' – M.T.

manure! I can buy you *all*, and have mountain ranges of manure left! Ha, ha! *now* thou smilest a smile!' [Immense sensation.] Exhibition of specimens from the mine. Old Huss, enthusiastically: 'Wake her up, shake her up, noble young man, she is yours!' Wedding takes place on the spot; book-keeper restored to his office and emoluments; Paul Hoch led off to gaol. The Bonanza King of the Black Forest lives to a good old age, blessed with the love of his wife and of his twenty-seven children, and the still sweeter envy of everybody around.[4]

The second is by Patrick Leigh Fermor, describing in *A Time of Gifts* his first visit, in the 1930s, to a Munich beer-cellar:

The trunks of these feasting burghers were as wide as casks. The spread of their buttocks over the oak benches was not far short of a yard. They branched at the loins into thighs as thick as the torsos of ten-year-olds and arms on the same scale strained like bolsters at the confining serge. Chin and chest formed a single column, and each close-packed nape was creased with its three deceptive smiles. Every bristle had been cropped and shaven from their knobbly scalps. Except when five o'clock veiled them with shadow, surfaces as polished as ostriches' eggs reflected the lamplight. The frizzy hair of their wives was wrenched up from scarlet necks and pinned under slides and then hatted with green Bavarian trilbys and round one pair of elephantine shoulders a little fox stole was clasped. The youngest of this group, resembling a matinée idol under some cruel spell, was the bulkiest. Under tumbling blond curls his china blue eyes protruded from cheeks that might have been blown up with a bicycle pump, and cherry lips laid bare the sort of teeth that make children squeal. There was nothing bleary or stunned about their eyes. The setting may have reduced their size, but it keyed their glances to a sharper focus. Hands like bundles of sausages flew nimbly, packing in forkload on forkload of ham, salami, frankfurter, krenwurst and blutwurst and stone tankards were lifted for long swallows of liquid which sprang out again instantaneously on cheek and brow. They might have been competing with stop-watches, and their voices, only partly gagged by the cheekfuls of good things they were grinding down, grew louder while their unmodulated laughter jarred the air in frequent claps. Pumpernickel and aniseed rolls and bretzels bridged all the slack moments but supplies always came through before a true lull threatened. Huge oval dishes, laden with schweinebraten, potatoes, sauerkraut, red cabbage and dumplings were laid in front of each diner. They were followed by colossal joints of meat – unclassifiable helpings which, when they were picked clean, shone on the scoured chargers like calves' pelvises or the bones of elephants. Waitresses with the build of weight-lifters and all-in wrestlers whirled this provender along and features dripped and glittered like faces at an ogre's banquet. But all too soon the table was an empty bone-yard once more, sound faltered, a look of bereavement clouded those small eyes and there was a brief hint of sorrow in the air. But succour was always at hand; beldames barged to the rescue at full gallop with new clutches of mugs and fresh plate-loads of consumer goods; and the damp Laestrygonian brows unpuckered again in a happy renewal of clamour and intake.

I strayed by mistake into a room full of S.S. officers, Gruppen- and Sturm-bannführers, black from their lightning-flash-collars to the forest of tall boots underneath the table. The window embrasure was piled high with their skull-and-crossbones caps. I still hadn't found the part of this Bastille I was seeking, but at last a noise like the rush of a river guided me downstairs again to my journey's end.

The vaults of the great chamber faded into infinity through blue strata of smoke. Hobnails grated, mugs clashed and the combined smell of beer and bodies and old clothes and farmyards sprang at the newcomer. I squeezed in at a table full of peasants, and was soon lifting one of those masskrugs to my lips. It was heavier than a brace of iron dumb-bells, but the blond beer inside was cool and marvellous, a brooding, cylindrical litre of Teutonic myth. This was the fuel that had turned the berserk feeders upstairs into Zeppelins and floated them so far from heart's desire. The gunmetal-coloured cylinders were stamped with a blue HB conjoined under the Bavarian crown, like the foundry-mark on cannon. The tables, in my mind's eye, were becoming batteries where each gunner served a silent and recoil-less piece of ordnance which, trained on himself, pounded away in steady siege. *Mass*-gunfire! Here and there on the tables, with their heads in puddles of beer, isolated bombardiers had been mown down in their emplacements. The vaults reverberated with the thunder of a creeping barrage. There must have been over a thousand pieces engaged! – Big Berthas, Krupp's pale brood, battery on battery crashing at random or in salvoes as hands adjusted the elevation and traverse and then tightened on the stone trigger-guard. Supported by comrades, the walking wounded reeled through the battle smoke and a fresh gunner leaped into each place as it fell empty.

My own gun had fired its last shot, and I wanted to change to a darker-hued explosive. A new *Mass* was soon banged down on the board. In harmony with its colour, it struck a darker note at once, a long Wagnerian chord of black-letter semibreves: *Nacht und Nebel!* Rolling Bavarian acres formed in the inscape of the mind, fanning out in vistas of poles planted pyramidally with the hops gadding over them heavy with poppy-sombre flowers.

The peasants and farmers and the Munich artisans that filled the tables were much nicer than the civic swallowers overhead. Compared to the trim, drilled figures of the few soldiers there, the Storm Troopers looked like brown-paper parcels badly tied with string. There was even a sailor with two black silk streamers falling over his collar from the back of his cap, round the front of which, in gold letters, was written *Unterseeboot*. What was this Hanseatic submariner doing here, so far inland from Kiel and the Baltic? My tablemates were from the country, big, horny-handed men, with a wife or two among them. Some of the older men wore green and grey loden jackets with bone buttons and badgers' brushes or blackcocks' feathers in the back of their hatbands. The bone mouthpieces of long cherrywood pipes were lost in their whiskers and on their glazed china bowls, painted castles and pine-glades and chamois glowed cheerfully while shag-smoke poured through the perforations of their metal lids. Some of them, gnarled and mummified, puffed at cheroots through which straws were threaded to make them draw better. They gave me one and I added a choking tribute to the enveloping cloud. The accent had changed again, and I could only grasp the meaning of the simplest sentences. Many words were docked of their final consonants; '*Bursch*' – 'a chap' – for instance, became 'bua'; 'A' was rolled over into 'O', 'Ö' became 'E', and every O and U seemed to have a final A appended, turning it into a disyllable. All this set up a universal moo-ing note, wildly distorted by resonance and echo; for these millions of vowels, prolonged and bent into boomerangs, sailed ricochetting up through the fog to swell the tidal thunder. This echoing and fluid feeling, the bouncing of sounds and syllables and the hogsheads of pungent liquid that sloshed about the tables and blotted the sawdust underfoot, must have been responsible for the name of this enormous hall. It was called the *Schwemme*, or horse-pond. The hollowness of those tall mugs augmented the volume of noise like the amphorae which the Greeks embedded in masonry to add resonance to their chants. My own note, as the mug emptied, was sliding down to middle C.

Mammoth columns were rooted in the flagstones and the sawdust. Arches flew in broad hoops from capital to capital; crossing in diagonals, they groined the barrel-vaults that hung dimly above the smoke. The place should have been lit by pine-torches in stanchions. It was beginning to change, turning now, under my clouding glance, into the scenery for some terrible Germanic saga, where snow vanished under the breath of dragons whose red-hot blood thawed sword-blades like icicles. It was a place for battle-axes and bloodshed and the last pages of the *Nibelungenlied* when the capital of Hunland is in flames and everybody in the castle is hacked to bits. Things grew quickly darker and more fluid; the echo, the splash, the boom and the roar of fast currents sunk this beer-hall under the Rhine-bed; it became a cavern full of more dragons, misshapen guardians of gross treasure; or the fearful abode, perhaps, where Beowulf, after tearing the Grendel's arm out of its socket, tracked him over the snow by the bloodstains and, reaching the mere's edge, dived in to swim many fathoms down and slay his loathsome water-hag of a mother in darkening spirals of gore.

Or so it seemed, when the third mug arrived.[5]

For Italy, here is Catherine Wilmot, in March 1803, on the subject of the San Carlo Opera House in Naples:

This being the King's birthday, it was an Universal gala, and in the evening all the world went to the Theatre of St. Carlos, which is reckon'd the most beautiful one in the world; we went to the Princess Charace's Box, in which were the two reigning Belles of Naples. . . . A succession of brocaded Princes during the entire evening frequented the Box, dress'd in cut velvet embroider'd suits, swords and Bags &c. The display of diamonds among the Ladies surpassed everything I cou'd have imagin'd, everyone blazed like a constellation! The seams of their gowns even were studded with diamonds, and what with diamond chains, Necklaces, sprays of brilliants, towering on the head like feathers, diamond nets, combs, head-dresses, and fringes to the gowns &c., really our eyes ached at looking at all we saw. Everyone was the same, and my fancy would have made me believe myself in the country of Golconda, had I not been inform'd that amongst the nobility all the women were Princesses or Duchesses and that if twenty daughters were in a family, all the accomplishments, money and diamonds are given to one, and the rest shut up in Convents for Life. . . . Scarcely any attention was paid to the performance excepting when the principal vocal musick began, and then they deign'd to look sometimes on the stage and were moved to the most animated expressions of delight. As during the time we were at Naples we went for an hour almost every evening to this or one of the other Theatres, I observ'd very frequently the curtains of the Boxes scarcely undrawn and, but that we heard voices, and saw their moving shadows, we should have been totally unconscious whether they were inhabited or not. I liked exceedingly the fashion of paying visits about the House, instead of getting the cramp from the stagnation of an entire night. You are conducted about by a gallant Cavalliere, first to one Box, then to another, upstairs and down stairs, until you come puffing and blowing back again to the Box you left, where you find in general quite a fresh assortment of company from those you had quitted. And now while visiting is on the carpet, the style of salutation naturally occurs to one's mind which is in the fashion of the French, but that instead of being kiss'd peacably and quietly, the smack of the Neapolitans resounds throughout the room; the ladies kiss or rather smack one another on both cheeks, the gentlemen ditto; the ladies' hands are kiss'd by the gentlemen, but our English trick of shaking hands, they look upon as the most hoity toity impudent custom in the world and cannot reconcile it with the vestal demeanor of the English Ladies.[6]

Eastward we go to the dominions of the Ottoman Sultan; but before we get to the Sublime Porte itself, let us pause briefly in Thrace with Lady Mary Wortley Montagu:

The summer is already far advanced, in this part of the world; and, for some miles round Adrianople, the whole ground is laid out in gardens, and the banks of the rivers are set with rows of fruit-trees, under which all the most considerable Turks divert themselves every evening, not with walking, that is not one of their pleasures; but a set party of them chuse out a green spot, where the shade is very thick, and there they spread a carpet, on which they sit drinking their coffee, and are generally attended by some slave with a fine voice, or that plays on some instrument. Every twenty paces you may see one of these little companies listening to the dashing of the river; and this taste is so universal, that the very gardeners are not without it. I have often seen them and their children sitting on the banks of the river, and playing on a rural instrument, perfectly answering the description of the antient *fistula*, being composed of unequal reeds, with a simple, but agreeable softness in the sound.

Mr. Addison might here make the experiment he speaks of in his travels; there not being one instrument of music among the Greek or Roman statues, that is not to be found in the hands of the people of this country. The young lads generally divert themselves with making garlands for their favourite lambs, which I have often seen painted and adorned with flowers, lying at their feet, while they sung or played. It is not that they ever read romances. But these are the antient amusements here, and as natural to them as cudgel-playing and foot-ball to our British swain; the softness and warmth of the climate forbidding all rough exercises, which were never so much as heard of amongst them, and naturally inspiring a laziness and aversion to labour, which the great plenty indulges. These gardeners are the only happy race of country people in Turkey. They furnish all the city with fruits and herbs, and seem to live very easily. They are most of them Greeks, and have little houses in the midst of their gardens, where their wives and daughters take a liberty, not permitted in the town, I mean, to go unveiled. These wenches are very neat and handsome, and pass their time at their looms, under the shade of the trees.[7]

In Chapter Eleven I quoted another letter from the same source about a visit to a Turkish lady; here, by contrast, is an account of a visit to a real harem – or hareem, as Harriet Martineau preferred to call it in *Eastern Life, Present and Past*. How strange, one feels, that it should be so exactly as one had imagined . . .

A party of eunuchs stood before a faded curtain, which they held aside when the gentlemen of our party and the dragomen had gone forward. Retired some way behind the curtain stood, in a half circle, eight or ten slave girls, in an attitude of deep obeisance. Two of them then took charge of each of us, holding us by the arms above the elbows, to help us upstairs. – After crossing a lobby at the top of the stairs, we entered a handsome apartment, where lay the chief wife, – at that time an invalid. – The ceiling was gaily painted; and so were the walls, the latter with curiously bad attempts at domestic perspective. There were four handsome mirrors; and the curtains in the doorway were of a beautiful shawl fabric, fringed and tasselled. A Turkey carpet not only covered the whole floor, but was turned up at the corners. Deewáns extended round nearly the whole room, – a lower one for ordinary use, and a high one for the seat of honour. The windows, which had a sufficient fence of blinds, looked upon a pretty garden, where I saw orange trees and many others, and the fences were hung with rich creepers.

On cushions on the floor lay the chief lady, ill and miserable-looking. She rose as we entered; but we made her lie down again: and she was then covered with a silk counterpane. Her dress was, as we saw when she rose, loose trowsers of blue striped cotton under her black silk jacket: and the same blue cotton appeared at the wrists, under her black sleeves. Her head-dress was of black net, bunched out curiously behind. Her hair was braided down the sides of this head-dress behind, and the ends were pinned over her forehead. Some of the black net was brought round her face, and under the chin, showing the outline of a face which had no beauty in it, nor traces of former beauty, but which was interesting to-day from her manifest illness and unhappiness. There was a strong expression of waywardness and peevishness about the mouth, however. She wore two handsome diamond rings; and she and one other lady had watches and gold chains. She complained of her head; and her left hand was bound up: she made signs, by pressing her bosom, and imitating the dandling of a baby, which, with her occasional tears, persuaded my companions that she had met with some accident and had lost her infant. On leaving the hareem, we found that it was not a child of her own that she was mourning, but that of a white girl in the hareem: and that the wife's illness was wholly from grief for the loss of this baby; – a curious illustration of the feelings and manners of the place! The children born in large hareems are extremely few: and they are usually idolised, and sometimes murdered. . . .

We saw, I think, about twenty more women, – some slaves, – most or all young – some good-looking, but none handsome. Some few were black; and the rest very light: – Nubians or Abyssinians and Circassians, no doubt. One of the best figures, as a picture, in the hareem, was a Nubian girl, in an amber-coloured watered silk, embroidered with black, looped up in festoons, and finished with a black bodice. The richness of the gay printed cotton skirts and sleeves surprised us: the finest shawls could hardly have looked better. One graceful girl had her pretty figure well shown by a tight-fitting black dress. Their heads were dressed much like the chief lady's. Two, who must have been sisters, if not twins, had patches between the eyes. One handmaid was barefoot, and several were without shoes. Though there were none of the whole large number who could be called particularly pretty individually, the scene was, on the whole, exceedingly striking, as the realisation of what one knew before, but as in a dream. The girls went and came in, but, for the most part, stood in a half circle. Two sat on their heels for a time: and some went to play in the neighbouring apartments.

Coffee was handed to us twice, with all the well-known apparatus of jewelled cups, embroidered tray cover, and gold-flowered napkins. There were chibouques, of course: and sherbets in cut glass cups. The time was passed in attempts to have conversation by signs; attempts which are fruitless among people of the different ideas which belong to different races. . . . They pitied us European women heartily, that we had to go about travelling, and appearing in the streets without being properly taken care of – that is, watched. They think us strangely neglected in being left so free, and boast of their spy system and imprisonment as tokens of the value in which they are held. . . .

The difficulty is to get away, when one is visiting a hareem. The poor ladies cannot conceive of one's having anything to do; and the only reason they can understand for the interview coming to an end is the arrival of sunset, after which it would, they think, be improper for any woman to be abroad. And the amusement to them of such a visit is so great that they protract it to the utmost, even in such a case as ours to-day, when all intercourse was conducted by dumb show. It is certainly very tiresome; and the only wonder is that the hostesses can like it. To sit hour after hour on the deewán, without any exchange of ideas, having our clothes examined, and being plied with successive cups of coffee and sherbet, and pipes, and being gazed at by a half-circle of girls in brocade and shawls, and made to sit down again as soon as one attempts to rise, is as wearisome an experience as one meets with in foreign lands. . . .

At the third move, and when it was by some means understood that we were waited for, we were permitted to go, – after a visit of above two hours. The sick lady rose from her cushions, notwithstanding our opposition, and we were conducted forth with much observance. On each side of the curtain which overhung the outer entrance stood a girl with a bottle of rose-water, some of which was splashed in our faces as we passed out.[8]

There were, however, other less agreeable sights to meet the eye of the unsuspecting visitor. The following is an extract from the *Letters from the East* of John Carne, who published them in 1826:

As I sat one afternoon beneath the portico of the Palace of the Janizaries in Constantinople, two Greeks, of a superior class, were brought in under a guard. It was impossible not to be moved at such a scene. They were both elderly men; and as they walked with a firm step, their looks were placid and resigned. Their fate was inevitable; their retreat had been discovered, and they were torn from their families to die. Indeed, it was singular to observe the resignation, approaching to apathy, with which the Greeks in general met their fate. One unfortunate man had made his escape; but so strong was his desire after a few weeks to see his family again, that he ventured back. The very evening of his return he was discovered in Galata, and dragged forth. The Greek knelt down, folded his arms on his breast tranquilly, without any change of feature, and was instantly slain. I passed by the body of this man twice afterwards: the Turks, as was their frequent practice after beheading, had fixed the head between the knees in an upright position, so that its ghastly aspect was sure to meet the eye of the passenger. The Musulmen certainly excel all other people in their dexterity in taking off the head at one blow. Afterwards, at Smyrna, I went early one morning to the execution of twenty-three Greeks, who were put to death in this way with little pain. But the scene was closed before I arrived at the spot, where the bodies were then lying in a heap. It was truly shocking to see how cheap human life was held.[9]

Actually, he seems oddly matter-of-fact about it all himself; a few pages later he writes:

At the foot of the gate lay a number of heads of the wretched Greeks, and the boys were tumbling them about like footballs.[10]

The Turks were succinctly summed up by Lord Baltimore, who visited Constantinople in 1767:

The religion, laws, and customs of the *Turks* are, as much as they can make them, in direct opposition to ours; they eat, write, sleep, and sit low, we high; their dead they carry out head, we feet, foremost; their cloaths are long, ours short; they have many wives and mistresses allowed by law, we only one; they have few wh---s, we a multitude; they believe in One God, we in the Trinity; they believe in predestination, we do not; our potentates send embassadors to each other, the Grand Signior sends none; they say on this head, that embassadors rather create than remedy disputes.
The *Turks* make great use of baths, we do not.[11]

But to return to the subject of women, and their place in the world of Islam. The next extract, from Eliot Warburton's *The Crescent and the Cross*, concerns those of Egypt, though there is no doubt that the stories he tells could have been easily paralleled in Constantinople itself:

Let them laugh on, in their happy ignorance of a better lot, while around them is gathered all that their lord can command of luxury and pleasantness: his wealth is hoarded for them alone; and the time is weary that he passes away from his home and his hareem. The sternest tyrants are gentle there: Mehemet Ali never refused a woman's prayer; and even Ali Pasha was partly humanized by his love for Emineh. In the time of the Mamelukes, criminals were led to execution blindfolded, because, if they met a woman and could touch her garment, they were saved, as by a sanctuary, whatever was their crime. Thus idolized, watched, and guarded, the Egyptian woman's life is, nevertheless, entirely in the power of her lord, and her death is the inevitable penalty of his dishonour. No piquant case of *crim. con.* ever amuses the Egyptian public: the injured husband is his own judge and jury; his only 'gentlemen of the long robe' are his eunuchs; and the knife or the Nile the only damages. The law never interferes in these little domestic arrangements. . . .

Poor Fatima! shrined as she was in the palace of a tyrant, the fame of her beauty stole abroad through Cairo. She was one amongst a hundred in the hareem of Abbas Pasha, a man stained with every foul and loathsome vice; and who can wonder, though many may condemn, if she listened to a daring young Albanian, who risked his life to obtain but a sight of her! Whether she *did* listen or not, none can ever know; but the eunuchs saw the glitter of the Arnaut's arms, as he leaped from the terrace into the Nile and vanished in the darkness. . . . The following night, a merry English party dined together on board Lord Exmouth's boat, as it lay moored off the Isle of Rhoda; conversation had sunk into silence, as the calm night came on; a faint breeze floated perfumes from the gardens over the star-lit Nile, and scarcely moved the clouds that rose from the chibouque; a dreamy languor seemed to pervade all nature, and even the city lay hushed in deep repose – when suddenly a boat, crowded with dark figures among which arms gleamed, shot out from one of the arches of the palace; it paused under the opposite bank, where the water rushed deep and gloomily along, and for a moment a white figure glimmered along the boat's dark crew; there was a slight movement and a faint splash – and then – the river flowed on as merrily as if poor Fatima still sang her Georgian song to the murmur of its waters. . . .

I was riding one evening along the banks of the Mareotis; the low lands, half swamp, half desert, was level as the lake: there was no sound, except the ripple of the waves along the far extended shore, and the heavy flapping of the pelican's wings as she rose from the water's edge. Not a palm-tree raised its plumy head, not a shrub crept along the ground; the sun was low, but there was nothing to cast a shadow over the monotonous waste, except a few Moslem tombs with their sculptured turbans: these stood apart from every sign of life, and even of their kindred dead, like those upon the Lido at Venice. As I paused to contemplate this scene of desolation, an Egyptian hurried past me with a bloody knife in his hand; his dress was mean and ragged, but his countenance was one that the father of Don Carlos might have worn; he never raised his eyes as he rushed by: – my groom, who just then came up, told me he had slain his wife, and was going to her father's village to denounce her. . . .

My boat was moored in the little harbour of Assouan, the old Syene, the boundary between Egypt and Ethiopia; opposite, lies Elephantina, the 'Isle of Flowers,' strewed with ruins, and shaded by magnificent palm-trees; the last eddies of the cataract of the Nile foam round dark red granite cliffs, which rise precipitously from the river, and are piled into a mountain crowned by a ruined Saracenic castle. A forest of palm-trees divides the village from the quiet shore on whose silvery sands my tent was pitched. A man in an Egyptian dress saluted me in Italian, and in a few moments was smoking my chibouque, by invitation, and sipping coffee by my side: he was very handsome; but his faded cheek and sunken eye showed hardship and suffering, and he spoke in a low and humble voice. In reply to my question, as to how a person of his appearance came into this remote region, he told me that he had been lately practising as a surgeon in Alexandria; he had married a Levantine girl, whose beauty was to him as 'la faccia del cielo:' he had been absent from his home, and she had betrayed him. On his return, he met her with a smiling countenance; in the evening, he accompanied her to a deep well, whither she went to draw water, and, as she leant over it, he threw her in. As he said this, he paused, and placed his hands upon his ears, as if he still heard her dying shriek. He then continued: 'I have fled from Alexandria till the affair is blown over: I was robbed near Siout, and have supported myself miserably ever since, by giving medical advice to the poor country people: I shall soon return, and all will be forgotten. If I had not avenged myself, her own family, you know, must have done so.' And so this woman-murderer smoked on, and continued talking in a low and gentle voice till the moon was high; then he went his way, and I saw him no more.[12]

A happier Egyptian tale is that told by Sir Ronald Storrs in *Orientations*:

Sometime in 1906 I was walking in the heat of the day through the Bazaars. As I passed an Arab Café an idle wit, in no hostility to my straw hat but desiring to shine before his friends, called out in Arabic, 'God curse your father, O Englishman'. I was young then and quicker tempered, and foolishly could not refrain from answering in his own language that I would also curse his father if he were in a position to inform me which of his mother's two and ninety admirers his father had been. I heard footsteps behind me and slightly picked up the pace, angry with myself for committing the sin Lord Cromer would not pardon – a row with Egyptians. In a few seconds I felt a hand on each arm. 'My brother', said the original humorist, 'return, I pray you, and drink with us coffee and smoke (In Arabic one speaks of 'drinking' smoke.) I did not think that Your Worship knew Arabic, still less the correct Arabic abuse, and we would fain benefit further by your important thoughts.'[13]

When we last met Catherine Wilmot, she was at the Opera in Naples; seven months later she was in Russia, staying with the Princess Daschkaw at Troitskoe, and writing to her mother:

Think of our weather being fine enough for the Princess and me to drive out in a *Droshka*, a sort of Jaunting Car quite expos'd to the air, and I have just left her overseeing her labourers who are sinking a Pond. Her servants are building a Wall, and no Masons could perform better. . . . I believe I have before now spoke of the Versatility of the Russians. It is really astonishing, but the number of servants is dreadful. Think of 2, 3 and often 400 servants to attend a small family. A Russian Lady scorns to use her own feet to go up stairs, and I do not Romance when I assure you that two powder'd footmen support her lily white elbows and nearly lift her from the ground, while a couple more follow with all manner of Shawls, Pelises, &c. &c. &c. There is not a Bell in Russia except to the Churches, but if a fair one gently calls four or five footmen are ready in an antechamber to obey her summons. Princess D. however has no reproach to make to herself on this subject – her servants work like Labourers. Order them to sing, and five or six will sing the airs of the country in different parts with a concord and melody that is delightful –

others will play on a variety of instruments with equal taste, indebted only to Nature. I have never yet seen a Russ Man dance. The women are very fond of dancing, and do so in a stile quite peculiar. We have a little Theatre here, and our labourers, our Cooks, our footmen, and *femmes de Chambres* turn into Princes, Princesses, Shepherds and Shepherdesses &c. &c. and perform with a degree of spirit that is astonishing. 'tis droll enough to be attended at Supper by the Herd of the piece who has been strutting before your Eyes in Gilded robes &c. &c. for half the Evening.[14]

Miss Wilmot did not, alas, visit the steppes of Central Asia; had she done so, she would have found its customs a good deal less domestic. The Hungarian Arminius Vámbéry was there in 1863, travelling across the Turcoman Desert to Khiva, Bokhara and Samarkand. Here he is in Khiva:

I had almost forgotten to mention that the Yasaul led me to the treasurer to receive the sum for my daily board. My claim was soon settled; but this personage was engaged in so singular an occupation that I must not omit to particularise it. He was assorting the Khilat (robes of honour) which were to be sent to the camp, to reward those who had distinguished themselves. They consisted of about four kinds of silken coats with staring colours, and large flowers worked in them in gold. I heard them styled four-headed, twelve-headed, twenty-headed, and forty-headed coats. As I could see upon them no heads at all in painting or embroidery, I demanded the reason of the appellation, and I was told that the most simple coats were a reward for having cut off four heads of enemies, and the most beautiful a recompense for forty heads, and that they were now being forwarded to the camp. Some one proceeded to tell me 'that if this was not an usage in Roum, I ought to go next morning to the principal square, where I should be a witness of this distribution.' Accordingly, the next morning I did really see about a hundred horsemen arrive from the camp covered with dust. Each of them brought at least one prisoner with him, and amongst the number, children and women, also bound either to the tail of the horse or to the pommel of the saddle; besides all which, he had buckled behind him a large sack containing the heads of his enemies, the evidence of his heroic exploits. On coming up he handed over the prisoners as presents to the Khan, or some other great personage, then loosened his sack, seized it by the two lower corners, as if he were about to empty potatoes, and there rolled the bearded or beardless heads before the accountant, who kicked them together with his feet until a large heap was composed, consisting of several hundreds. Each hero had a receipt given to him for the number of heads delivered, and a few days later came the day of payment.[15]

The unwary visitor, arriving for the first time in the Yemen, is immediately struck by the curious fact that every male over the age of twelve appears to be lodging a tennis ball in his cheek. This is soon unattractively revealed to be a mouthful of *qat*, a plant of mildly narcotic properties that is as universal there as is tobacco elsewhere in the Arab world. For me, as for most Westerners, the unpleasantness of chewing what seemed indistinguishable from a mouthful of privet hedge easily outweighed the putative rewards; and I quickly gave up at my first attempt. Jonathan Raban, however, in *Arabia Through the Looking Glass*, showed that he was made of sterner stuff:

Hamud and I were invited to go to Ali's house that afternoon, to chew *qat* with the family. Quite suddenly, the Yemen had come to seem an easy hospitable place to get around in. . . .

Ali's house was in the centre of a warren of junk, sleeping dogs and crumbling mud bungalows. Everything had gone to the colour of piecrust in the sun: burnt dogs, burnt clay, the burnt-out chassis of wrecked cars from which every last nut and bolt had been assiduously beachcombed. Hamud, worried for his springs, inched the car down a street of boulders and pot-holes. A lame dog lurched ahead of us. Too torpid to bother to stop and cock its leg, it leaked as it walked. Its thin trickle of urine dried the instant that it hit the dust. Hamud blew his horn at it, but the dog ignored him. It looked as if it didn't greatly care whether it lived or died. I made some spinsterly English noises about the miserable state of the animals in the city.

'The government likes to shoot dogs. That is good, I think, to shoot dogs.'

We took our bundle of *qat* and crossed the street to Ali's house. A front door opened on a tiny courtyard where the family kept their two goats and half-dozen chickens. A further door led to the room in which the men lived.

After the desolation of the street outside, the room seemed palatial in its comforts. It was warm and rainbow-coloured. Squares of brightly-patterned dress material had been tacked over the windows to filter the sunlight, which fell in splashes of lemon, red and purple on the carpets and cushions. A cluster of tall brass hubble-bubbles occupied the centre of the room, and there were silver trays with Thermos flasks of coffee and iced water, fingerbowls, ears of sweetcorn and packs of cigarettes. Beside everyone's cushion was a brass spittoon and a goblet of burning incense. The *qat* lay in a communal heap. We added our sprigs to this green Guy Fawkes bonfire, and I was formally introduced to the family.

The bearded grandfather made a little speech of welcome; brothers and cousins bowed and shook hands. I was shown to my cushion, and the *qat*-session began.

The solemnity of it, the coloured light, the churchy gleam of hammered brass and silver, reminded me of a communion service. Hamud taught me how to nip off the topmost leaves from each stalk, chew them, then store them in the pouch of my cheek. Gradually one builds up a fibrous wad of crushed leaves from which one sucks the juice through one's teeth. *Qat*-chewing parches one's throat; one needs draughts of coffee and water every few minutes, and I found that managing this acidic mouthful of dry hedge was difficult enough, without having to undertake the further rigours of making conversation.

Qat is the kind of drug which creeps slowly up on you from behind. I had just decided that it was having no effect on me whatsoever when I heard a shrill schoolgirl giggle and realized that I was the one who was giggling. There seemed, in fact, to be two of me. One fellow was crouched in a recess, soberly recording the details of the *qat*-session for his notebook; the other was skittish and voluble. This second man was trying to make a joke in Arabic – an enterprise which struck the first man as so vain and foolhardy that he felt mortified at having to listen to the attempt. The second man's main trouble was that he found it impossible to remember words that he had spoken only a second or two before. He found himself in the middle of a sentence without having the least idea of how he had arrived there or in which direction he was supposed to be going. This did not seem to matter very much, since he appeared to be getting on extremely well with a cousin who was studying 'the telegraph'.

'You like the *qat*?' Hamud asked.

'It doesn't have any effect on me,' I said, exchanging clothes with the cousin. He put on my jacket, I put on his tunic. He gave me his belt and dagger. When I tried to fasten the belt around my waist, the two ends were six inches short of each other.

'I am too fat,' I said.

'All Englishmen are fat,' said the cousin, whose own waist cannot have been more than eighteen inches in circumference. He unclipped a small holster from his belt and gave it to me: it contained a Czech automatic pistol with a full clip of slugs and the safety-catch off.

'We could go and shoot some dogs,' I said. The cousin laughed and put the safety-catch on before handing the pistol back to me.

'Let's go and shoot a dog – '

'You see, you like the *qat*. This is the best *qat* in Yemen.'

'There's a dog outside. We could shoot that.'

'This is the first time you eat *qat*?'

'It doesn't do anything for me. Why don't we shoot some dogs?'

The other me skulked in a corner, watching these goings-on with an expression of detached scepticism. He noted the new telephone installed in a whitewashed alcove. He observed that the flex of the instrument was tied up in a neat loop; it was attached to nothing. If you picked up the receiver, it would be like putting a shell to your ear: you might, with luck, be able to hear the sound of the sea. Some shaky black-and-white pictures were flickering on the portable TV, and a cousin was putting a tape of Arab music into a Hitachi radio-recorder.

I had emptied a whole Thermosful of coffee. The grandfather called to the women's quarters for more, and offered me a turn on the hubble-bubble. Sucking, chewing, giggling, idly watching the feet of the women passing behind the half-open door which led to their kitchen, I was reduced to a state of contented infantilism. Another Thermos of coffee was brought in by a tiny, scrawny child of three or four. No woman would enter the male quarters when guests were being entertained there, and small children were necessary go-betweens. The little girl went to her grandfather to be cuddled. She had a skin-disease of some kind on her face, and looked as if she was on the verge of malnutrition.

My more active self had forgotten his enthusiasm for shooting dogs and was planning a European tour for the cousin. The cousin had the chance of pursuing his study of the telegraph in Paris: nothing was actually fixed; as yet he was only a candidate for a scholarship, but on *qat* he was already there, and we were busy with sights and itineraries. He was going to be away for three years, and we were fixing trips to London, Florence, Monte Carlo and the Scottish Highlands. I felt someone jogging my elbow, and found it was me again; the sceptic in the corner had detected a flaw in the arrangements.

'What about your wife and your child? Will they go too?'

'No, they stay in Sana'a.'

'But won't you miss them? Is it good to go away for so long when you have a wife and a young child growing up?'

'My mother will look after my wife. She will be quite safe.'

'But won't you miss her?'

'Why? I am only going away for three years.' He shrugged. 'It is no time.'

'When do you leave?'

He looked suddenly vague. He tore off another handful of leaves from his branch of *qat* and sat chewing them for a few moments. 'Next month,' he said. 'Yes. I think I will go to Paris next month.'

Ali said: 'Perhaps I will go to Paris too. I would like to see the Folies Bergères. In Paris there are many things to do in the nights.'

'If you want a night out in Sana'a, what do you do?'

'Nothing. There is nothing to do. You cannot go out after ten o'clock. That is the law. There is one cinema. The seats are cracked, they show the same old film always. Two years ago, I go. Then one month ago I go again. The people were the same people, they sit in the same seats, the film is the same film. In Sana'a, they are narrow-minded, you see. It is not like Paris.' ...

Hamud and I left. It was already dark, and I felt jittery and on edge. *Qat* produces a hangover which makes one feel altogether too alert for one's own good. Hamud's unusually careful driving struck me as dangerously fast and wild. When we reached the Dar Al-Hamd Palace, I got out my wallet to pay him.

'Please,' Hamud said. 'Yesterday, we were not friends. Today you are my friend.'

'Hamud, really, I would like to pay –'

'You are my friend, now, yes?'

'Yes –'

'Because you are my friend, you give me fifty rials more than what you say yesterday. I think that is right. For friendship.'[16]

Qat has always seemed to me quite disagreeable enough; but there are plenty of other local customs that leave it standing. Take, for example, that encountered by Mary Kingsley at Efoua, in what is now the Gabon:

One of the chiefs had his house cleared out for me. It consisted of two apartments almost bare of everything save a pile of boxes, and a small fire on the floor, some little bags hanging from the roof poles, and a general supply of insects. The inner room contained nothing save a hard plank, raised on four short pegs from the earth floor. ...

Every hole in the side walls had a human eye in it, and I heard new holes being bored in all directions; so I deeply fear the chief, my host, must have found his palace sadly draughty. I felt perfectly safe and content, however, although Ngouta suggested the charming idea that 'P'r'aps them M'fetta Fan done sell we.' The only grave question I had to face was whether I should take off my boots or not; they were wet through, from wading swamps, &c., and my feet were very sore; but on the other hand, if I took those boots off, I felt confident that I should not be able to get them on again next morning, so I decided to lef 'em.

As soon as all my men had come in, and established themselves in the inner room for the night, I curled up among the boxes, with my head on the tobacco sack, and dozed. Waking up I noticed the smell in the hut was violent, from being shut up I suppose, and it had an unmistakably organic origin. Knocking the ash end off the smouldering bush-light that lay burning on the floor, I investigated, and tracked it to those bags, so I took down the biggest one, and carefully noted exactly how the tie-tie had been put round its mouth; for these things are important and often mean a lot. I then shook its contents out in my hat, for fear of losing anything of value. They were a human hand, three big toes, four eyes, two ears, and other portions of the human frame. The hand was fresh, the others only so so, and shrivelled.

Replacing them I tied the bag up, and hung it up again. I subsequently learnt that although the Fans will eat their fellow friendly tribesfolk, yet they like to keep a little something belonging to them as a memento. This touching trait in their character I learnt from Wiki; and, though it's to their credit, under the circumstances, still it's an unpleasant practice when they hang the remains in the bedroom you occupy, particularly if the bereavement in your host's family has been recent. I did not venture to prowl round Efoua; but slid the bark door aside and looked out to get a breath of fresh air.[17]

Before we leave Africa, I cannot resist including here a piece of information imparted, by an apparently authoritative source, to Robert Byron at a dinner party in Darjeeling:

I sat next a bishop, robed in purple, who kindly quieted my doubts as to whether the Abyssinian Church really had canonized Pontius Pilate. 'Another curious feature of their observance', he continued, 'is their consecration of bishops by breathing instead of the laying-on of hands. As the Abyssinian bishops-elect often find it difficult to come to Alexandria, where the Coptic Patriarch resides, a paper bag is employed as intermediary. The Patriarch breathes into it. It is sealed, transported to Abyssinia, and there exploded over the bishop-elect's head with a loud POP!!' – and he burst into a thunderous guffaw which astonished the whole table.[18]

Much as I love the novels of E. M. Forster, I have enjoyed none of them so much as *The Hill of Devi*, the account of his life in India as Private Secretary to the Maharajah of Dewas. Here is a description of the Gokul Ashtami, an eight-day feast in honour of Krishna, who was born at Gokul. The date is 28 August 1921:

For four hours yesterday evening I walked barefoot in petticoats through the streets with black and red powders smeared over my forehead, cheeks, and nose.

Things began to warm up at 11.30 p.m. on the 26th when, dressed in our best, we sat cross-legged in the temple aisles, awaiting the Birth. The altar was as usual smothered in mess, and the gold and silver and rich silks that make up its equipment were so disposed as to produce no effect. Choked somewhere in rose leaves lay chief Dolly, but I could not locate him. Why, since he had been listening to hymns for eight days, he was now to be born was a puzzle to me; but no one else asked the question, and of course the Festival is no more illogical than Christmas, though it seemed so owing to its realism. My memory is so bad and the muddle so great that I forget the details of the Birth already, but the Maharajah announced it from his end of the carpet and then went to the altar and buried his face in the rose leaves, much moved. Next, a miniature cradle was set up in the aisle, and a piece of crimson silk, folded so that it looked like an old woman over whom a traction engine has passed, was laid in it and rocked by him, Bhau Sahib, the Dewan, the Finance Member, and other leading officials of the state. Noise, I need hardly add, never stopped – the great horn brayed, the cymbals clashed, the harmonium and drums did their best, while in the outer courtyard the three elephants were set to bellow and the band played 'Nights of Gladness' as loudly as possible. Under these circumstances the child was named 'Krishna' by H.H. I was now nearly dead with the heat. What I thought were little animals running down my legs proved to be streams of sweat. But I sat while the chief personages revisited the altar and were concealed by a pink and green curtain from our gaze, behind which they ate. – I forgot to say that we were each given a paper tray of red powder and that when the Birth was announced we threw it in the air so that the whole aisle was filled with crimson smoke. Or that H.H. carried the folded silk (which did *not* contain the image, who mustn't be moved) in his arms among the people who squatted row behind row far into the distance. And I must not waste time telling of my troubles with the decorations, of the mottoes from English Poetry that wouldn't stick up, or of the glass battery-cases that I filled with water and live fish and into which some humanitarian idiot dropped handfuls of flour so that the fish should not starve. You couldn't have seen a whale. Oh such an emptying and slopping to get it right, and two of the fish died, through over-eating, and had to be buried in a flowerpot in case H.H. should see them.

I must get on to the final day – the most queer and also the most enjoyable day of the series. There was a sermon in the morning, but after it we began to play games before the altar in a ceremonial fashion; there were games of this sort in the Christian Middle Ages and they still survive in the Cathedral of Seville at Easter. With a long stick in his hand H.H. churned imaginary milk and threshed imaginary wheat and hit (I suppose) imaginary enemies and then each took a pair of little sticks, painted to match the turban, and whacked them together. (You must never forget that cymbals never cease, nor does a harmonium.) Real butter came next and was stuck on the forehead of a noble in a big lump and when he tried to lick it off another noble snatched it from behind. (Very deep meaning in all this, says H.H., though few know it.) I had a little butter too. Then we went under a large black vessel, rather handsome, that was hung up in the aisle, and we banged it with our painted sticks, and the vessel broke and a mass of grain soaked in milk fell down on our heads. We fed each other with it. This was the last of the games, and the mess was now awful and swarms of flies came.

Still holding our painted sticks we went into the court and began to form the procession. There was a palanquin, large and gorgeous, and shaped like a gondola with silver dragons at each end. Dolly got in with his rose leaves and tea services and a chromo picture of Tukaram, the Maratha Saint, and banana leaves and fans and the Village of Gokul and I don't know what else. Still I couldn't see him. But H.H., determined I should, broke off his hymns, and brought me quite close. I saw the thing at last – face like an ill-tempered pea: curious little lump for so much to centre round.

The procession started with an elephant – no one on its back to indicate humility – then all of the army that possess uniforms or musical instruments, then the twelve bands of singers who had been at it all the week, but they showed no signs of feebleness, H.H., leading the last band, just in front of the palanquin, which another elephant followed. The view, looking back, after we had passed through the outer palace gateway, was really fine. The 18th-century architecture, though not splendid, is better than anything Dewas has produced since – blue birds over the arch and elephants tussling on the cornice – and the rich round banners that accompanied the palanquin (shaped like magnifying-glasses) and the pennons, and the fans of peacock's feather – all under a pink evening sky. Timed for 3.0, the start was at 6.0, and the pace so slow that darkness fell before the palace went out of sight. The route was kept fairly well by lines of schoolboys, who joined hands. Being barefoot, I was allowed to walk inside the lines, indeed close to the palanquin if I chose. The preacher of the sermon and another very pious man walked with me, indeed we were hand in hand, and the predominant sanctity of our group brought offerings of sugar candy and coconut in large quantities and smears of red and black powder for our foreheads and noses. I was very glad of them, the offerings I mean, as the night wore on, and the other holy men gave me theirs as well, and when I began to feel sickish we gave to children instead, and thus acquired the merit of being saints. I enjoyed the walk, for the preacher (an Indore man) was well educated and explained what the various groups were singing – some praised God without attributes, others with attributes: the same mixture of fatuity and philosophy that ran through the whole festival. A lady fanatic was in the Dewans' group. She was gaudily yet neatly dressed in purple and yellow, a circlet of jasmine flowers was round her chignon and in her hands were a pair of tongs with which she accompanied herself. We could not discover whether she was praising God with or without attributes. Her voice was too loud. She nodded and smiled in a very pleasant way.

My feet held out well – I had hardened them purposely in the previous days until I could run over heaps of coal. But my back – I thought it would break. 'We are pained to see your pain,' remarked the Indore preacher, 'but we are greatly pleased by your so good nature. We have not met an Englishman like you previously.' At the Jail there was a great crush, for a prisoner was released – a lady who had murdered her husband, and has been pulling up weeds in the Palace Garden for me in consequence. Her expression was beautiful as she flung herself before H.H. and the Dewan. The expressions of most people were beautiful that day.

By 10.0 we reached the Tank and the queer impressive ceremony of drowning the Town of Gokul was performed. The town – about a yard square – was stripped of its flagstaffs and, after prayers and meals, was handed to a man whose hereditary duty it is to drown the Town of Gokul. He was half naked and waded into the water and the darkness, pushing the city before him on a floating tray. When he was far out he upset it, all the dolls fell into the water and were seen no more and the town, being of mud, dissolved immediately. The tray was brought back and worshipped slightly, while elephants trumpeted and cannon were fired. I limped to a Victoria which I had waiting and drove straight to the Guest House at the other side of the Tank, there to wash my face, drink sherry, eat sardines, sausages, and stewed fruit, and reel to my bed. The others had two more hours of it, getting back to the Old Palace at midnight.

As to the explanation of this, as apart from what one was told by the pious, I know too little to conjecture, but was reminded of the Adonis festival, where the God is born, dies, and is carried to the water, all in a short time. H.H. says the Town of Gokul is meant to represent Krishna who cannot of course be drowned. *His* end came next morning, but my own end was too near for me to go down to the Old Palace to witness it. At midday the purple and green curtain was drawn before the altar and all the prominent officials burst into tears.

Festivals are endless. Today Ganpati (the Elephant God) has a little show, the day before yesterday the bullocks were worshipped, tomorrow ladies may eat practically nothing but vegetable marrows.[19]

One of the most readable of the early travellers is an Arab, Ibn Battuta. Born in Tangier in 1304, he travelled widely in Africa, India and Central Asia, faithfully describing all he saw. The following is a good example of his style – never striving after effect, but quite extraordinarily vivid none the less:

Once in the town of Amjari [Amjhera, near Dhar] I saw three women whose husbands had been killed in battle and who had agreed to burn themselves. Each one had a horse brought to her and mounted it, richly dressed and perfumed. In her right hand she held a coconut, with which she played, and in her left a mirror, in which she looked at her face. They were surrounded by Brahmans and their own relatives, and were preceded by drums, trumpets and bugles. Everyone of the infidels said to them 'Take greetings from me to my father, or brother or mother, or friend' and they would say 'Yes' and smile at them. I rode out with my companions to see the way in which the burning was carried out. After three miles we came to a dark place with much water and shady trees, amongst which there were four pavilions, each containing a stone idol. Between the pavilions there was a basin of water over which a dense shade was cast by trees so thickly set that the sun could not penetrate them. The place looked like a spot in hell – God preserve us from it! On reaching these pavilions they descended to the pool, plunged into it and divested themselves of their clothes and ornaments, which they distributed as alms. Each one was then given an unsewn garment of coarse cotton and tied part of it round her waist and part over her head and shoulders. The fires had been lit near this basin in a low lying spot, and oil of sesame poured over them, so that the flames were increased. There were about fifteen men there with faggots of thin wood and about ten others with heavy pieces of wood, and the drummers and trumpeters were standing by waiting for the woman's coming. The fire was screened off by a blanket held by some men, so that she should not be frightened by the sight of it. I saw one of them, on coming to the blanket, pull it violently out of the men's hands, saying to them with a smile 'Do you frighten me with the fire? I know that it is a fire, so let me alone.' Thereupon she joined her hands above her head in salutation to the fire and cast herself into it. At the same moment the drums, trumpets and bugles were sounded, the men threw their firewood on her and the others put the heavy wood on top of her to prevent her moving, cries were raised and there was a loud clamour. When I saw this I had all but fallen off my horse, if my companions had not quickly brought water to me and laved my face, after which I withdrew.[20]

Now on to Burma and the kingdom of Pegu. We have been there before, looking at the royal white elephants as described by Ralph Fitch, the London merchant. But while he was in Pegu, Mr Fitch noticed several other still more remarkable peculiarities of the country:

In Pegu, the men wear bunches or little round balls in their privy members: some of them wear two and some three. They cut the skin and so put them in, one into one side and another into the other side: which they do when they be 25 or 30 years old, and at their pleasure they take one or more of them out as they think good. When they be married the husband is for every child which his wife has, to put in one until he comes to three and then no more: for they say the women do desire them. They were invented because they should not abuse the male sex. For in times past all those countries were so given to that villainy, that they were very scarce of people. The bunches be of divers sorts: the least be as big as a little walnut, and very round: the greatest are as big as a little hen's egg: some are of brass and some of silver: but those of silver be for the king and his noble men. These are gilded and made with great cunning, and ring like a little bell. The king sometimes taketh his out, and giveth them to his noblemen as a great gift: and because he hath used them, they esteem them greatly. They will put one in, and heal up the place in seven or eight days.[21]

Few women of our age had a more extraordinary life than Alexandra David-Neel, described in a recent reprint of *My Journey to Lhasa* as 'indomitable traveller, opera singer and anchorite, a one-time director of the Tunis Casino and the first Western woman to be granted an audience with the Dalai Lama'. By the time that book was first published in 1927, she had herself been a lama for sixteen years, travelling for most of them with her boy companion Yongden. She died as recently as 1969, just before her 101st birthday. The following story may make some people wonder a little: all I can say is that you don't get the *Grande Médaille d'Or de la Société de Géographie* for nothing:

I called the young man back, gathered as much fuel as I could, and, certain that nobody was wandering in that wilderness, we decided to pitch our tent in a low place among a few bushes. The flint and steel which, according to Thibetan custom, Yongden carried attached to his belt in a pouch, had become wet during our passage across the snow fields, and now it did not work at all. This was a serious matter. Of course we were no longer on the top of the range and we had only a few hours to wait before the sun would rise; but even if we escaped being frozen, we were not at all certain that we should not catch pneumonia or some other serious disease.

'Jetsunma,'* said Yongden, 'you are, I know, initiated in the *thumo reskiang* practice. Warm yourself and do not bother about me. I shall jump and move to keep my blood moving.'

True, I had studied under two Thibetan *gompchens* the strange art of increasing the internal heat. For long I had been puzzled by the stories I had heard and read on the subject and as I am of a somewhat scientific turn of mind I wanted to make the experiment myself. With great difficulties, showing an extreme perseverance in my desire to be initiated into the secret, and after a number of ordeals, I succeeded in reaching my aim. I saw some hermits seated night after night, motionless on the snow, entirely naked, sunk in meditation, while the terrible winter blizzard whirled and hissed around them! I saw under the bright full moon the test given to their disciples who, on the shore of a lake or a river in the heart of the winter, dried on their bodies, as on a stove, a number of sheets dipped in the icy water! And I learned the means of performing these feats. I had inured myself, during five months of the cold season, to wearing the single thin cotton garment of the students at a 13,000-foot level. But the experience once over, I felt that a further training would have been a waste of time for me, who, as a rule, could choose my dwelling in less severe climates or provide myself with heating apparatus. I had, therefore, returned to fires and warm clothes, and thus could not be taken for an adept in the *thumo reskiang*, as my companion believed! Nevertheless, I liked at times to remember the lesson I had learned and to sit on some snowy summit in my thin dress of *reskiang*. But the present was not the time to look selfishly after my own comfort. I wanted to try to kindle a fire that had nothing miraculous about it, but which could warm my adopted son as well as myself.

'Go!' said I to Yongden, 'collect as much dry cow dung and dry twigs as you can; the exertion will prevent you from getting cold. I will see after the fire business.'

He went, convinced that the fuel was useless; but I had got an idea. After all, the flint and steel were wet and cold. What if I warmed them on me, as I had dried dripping sheets when a student of *thumo reskiang*? *Thumo reskiang* is but a way devised by the Thibetan hermits of enabling themselves to live without endangering their health on the high hills. It has nothing to do with religion, and so it can be used for ordinary purposes without lack of reverence.

I put the flint and steel and a pinch of the moss under my clothes, sat down, and began the ritualistic practice. I mentioned that I felt sleepy on the road; the exertion while collecting fuel and pitching the tent, the effort to kindle the fire, had shaken my torpor, but now, being seated, I began to doze. Yet my mind continued to be concentrated on the object of the *thumo* rite. Soon I saw flames arising around me; they grew higher and higher; they enveloped me, curling their tongues above my head. I felt deliciously comfortable.

A loud report awakened me. The ice on the river was rending. The flames suddenly died down as if entering the ground. I opened my eyes. The wind was blowing hard and my body burned. I made haste. The flint and steel and moss would work this time; I was convinced of it. I was still half dreaming, although I had got up and walked toward the tent. I felt fire bursting out of my head, of my fingers.

---

*'Jetsunma' or 'Jetsun Kusho': 'Reverend lady' or 'your reverend ladyship,' is the highest honourific title of address for a woman belonging to the religious order.

I placed on the ground a little dry grass, a small piece of very dry cow dung, and I knocked the stone. A spark sprang out of it. I knocked again; another sprang out . . . another . . . another . . . a miniature fireworks. . . . The fire was lighted; it was a little baby flame which wanted to grow, to eat, to live. I fed it and it leaped higher and higher. When Yongden arrived with a quantity of dry cow dung in the lap of his dress and some branches between his arms, he was joyfully astonished.

'How have you done it?' he asked.

'Well, it is the fire of *thumo*,' I answered, smiling.[22]

By far the best book I have ever read about Indo-China is *A Dragon Apparent*, by Norman Lewis, who made an extended tour through Laos, Cambodia and Vietnam in 1951. Here he tells of an incident which occurred among the Moï tribe – an attractive if somewhat alcoholic people of whom I had never before heard:

It was at a village in the vicinity of Buon Dieo, where two years previously an extraordinary affair had taken place. A family of eight persons were suspected of magic practices to the detriment of the village. According to local custom a representative was chosen as accuser and a trial by ordeal arranged. This consisted of the villagers' champion and the head of the accused family plunging their heads under water, the first to withdraw his head, in this case the accused, being held to have lost the day. According to the rulings of customary law governing this rather unusual case the charged persons were found to be possessed by certain minor demons, located in each case in a bodily organ. The general attitude thus was a sympathetic one. The prisoners were regarded as dangerously sick and only curable by the removal of the affected organ. After this was done they would be once more regarded as entirely normal members of society. The fact that death quickly followed the operations was entirely incidental and most sincerely regretted by all concerned. This was all the more so since the eight were regarded as having, quite accidentally, died the 'bad' death and therefore certain to be converted into revengeful ghouls unless propitiated by the most costly sacrifices, spread over a period of two years. In conformity with this obligation every animal in the village was soon slaughtered and the rice reserves converted into alcohol. The villagers then borrowed from neighbouring communities until their credit was completely exhausted, after which they settled down to starve.

It was at this point that the affair reached the administrator's ears. As a result eight of the principals in the case were tried in the French court and received thirty years apiece. No Moï, of course, could ever understand the justice of this, and it would be impossible to convince him that the appalling fate of the prisoners, all praiseworthy men in their eyes, is anything more than the revenge of the spirits of the eight who died. It is because their sacrifices were insufficient. If only their resources hadn't given out, all would have been well. And there is something in the last suggestion, because it was only the exhaustion of the food supplies that caused the administrator to hear about the affair.[23]

William Dampier was born in 1652. His early life was spent as a buccaneer and pirate, but he lived to write one of the great bestsellers of its time, *A New Voyage Round the World*. Not only is it a fascinating piece of travel literature in its own right; it is also a work of encyclopaedic scholarship, with information about the botany, anthropology and natural history of various remote corners of the earth which was not to be superseded for another century or more. Here is his description of the Chinese:

They are of an ashy Complexion; their Hair is black, and their Beards thin and long, for they pluck the Hair out by the Roots, suffering only some few very long straggling Hairs to grow about their Chin, in which they take great Pride, often combing them, and sometimes tying them up in a knot, and they have such Hairs too growing down from each side of their upper-Lip like Whiskers. The ancient *Chinese* were very proud of the Hair of their Heads, letting it grow very long, and stroking it back with their Hands curiously, and then winding the Plats all together round a Bodkin, thrust through it at the hinder-part of the Head; and both Men and Women did thus. But when the *Tartars* conquered them, they broke them of this Custom they were so fond of by main Force . . . and to this Day they follow the Fashion of their Masters the *Tartars*, and shave all their Heads, only reserving one Lock, which some tye up, others let it hang down to a great or small length as they please. The *Chinese* in other Countries still keep their old Custom, but if any of the *Chinese* is found wearing long Hair in *China*, he forfeits his Head; and many of them have abandoned their Country to preserve their Liberty of wearing their Hair, as I have been told by themselves.

The *Chinese* have no Hats, Caps, or Turbans; but when they walk abroad, they carry a small Umbrello in their Hands, wherewith they fence their Head from the Sun or the Rain, by holding it over their Heads. If they walk but a little way, they carry only a large Fan made of Paper, or Silk, of the same Fashion as those our Ladies have, and many of them are brought over hither; one of these every Man carried in his Hand if he do but cross the Street, skreening his Head with it, if he hath not an Umbrello with him.

The common Apparel of the Men, is a loose Frock and Breeches. They seldom wear Stockings, but they have Shoes, or a sort of Slippers rather. The Men's Shoes are made diversly. The Women have very small Feet, and consequently but little Shoes; for from their Infancy their Feet are kept swathed up with Bands, as hard as they can possibly endure them; and from the time they can go till they have done growing they bind them up every Night. This they do purposely to hinder them from growing, esteeming little Feet to be a great Beauty. But by this unreasonable Custom they do in a manner lose the use of their Feet, and instead of going they only stumble about their Houses, and presently squat down on their Breeches again, being as it were confined to sitting all Days of their Lives. They seldom stir abroad, and one would be apt to think, that as some have conjectured, their keeping up their fondness for this Fashion were a Stratagem of the Mens, to keep them from gadding and gossipping about, and confine them at home. They are kept constantly to their Work, being fine Needle Women, and making many curious Embroideries, and they make their own Shoes; but if any Stranger be desirous to bring away any for Novelty's sake, he must be a great Favourite to get a pair of Shoes of them, though he give twice their Value. The poorer sort of Women trudge about Streets, and to the Market, without Shoes or Stockings; and these cannot afford to have little Feet, being to get their living with them. . . .

The *Chinese* are very great Gamesters, and they will never be tired with it, playing Night and Day, till they have lost all their Estates; then it is usual with them to hang themselves. This was frequently done by the *Chinese* Factors at *Manila*, as I was told by *Spaniards* that lived there. The *Spaniards* themselves are much addicted to Gaming, and are very expert at it; but the *Chinese* are too subtle for them, being in general a very cunning People.[24]

On now, and across the Pacific to the New World. I have already on more than one occasion quoted Captain John Stedman on the subject of Surinam (or, if you prefer it, Dutch Guiana); if I do so again, it is because he seems to me such a first-class reporter. Take, for example, his account of a day in the life of a typical Dutch planter:

A planter in Surinam, when he lives on his estate (which is but seldom, as they mostly prefer the society of Paramaribo) gets out of his hammock with the rising sun, about six o'clock in the morning, and makes his appearance under the piazza of his house, where his coffee is ready waiting for him. This he generally takes with his pipe instead of toast and butter, and there he is attended by half a dozen of the finest young slaves, both male and female, to serve him. At this *sanctum-sanctorum* he is next accosted by his overseer, who regularly every morning attends at his levee, and having made his bows at several yards distance, with the most profound respect informs his greatness what work was done the day before, what negroes deserted, died, fell sick, recovered, were bought or born, and, above all things, which of them neglected their work, affected sickness, or had been drunk or absent. The prisoners are generally present, being secured by the negro-drivers, and are instantly tied up to the beams of the piazza or a tree without so much as being heard in their own defence, and the flogging begins, with men, women, or children, without exception. The instruments of torture on these occasions are long hempen whips, that cut round at every lash and crack like pistol-shot, during which they alternately repeat, '*Dankee, masera*' (Thank you, master). In the meantime he stalks up and down with his overseer, affecting not so much as to hear their cries, till they are sufficiently mangled, when they are untied and ordered to return to their work without so much as a dressing.

This ceremony being over, the dressy negro (a black surgeon) comes to make his report. After he has been dismissed with a hearty curse for *allowing* any slaves to be sick, a superannuated matron next makes her appearance with all the young negro children of the estate, over whom she is governess. These, being clean washed in the river, clap their hands and cheer in chorus, when they are sent away to breakfast on a large platter of rice and plantains, and the levee ends with a low bow from the overseer, as it begun.

His worship now saunters out in his morning dress, which consists of a pair of the finest Holland trousers, white silk stockings, and red or yellow Morocco slippers, the neck of his shirt open and nothing over it, a loose flowing nightgown of the finest India chintz excepted. On his head is a cotton nightcap, as thin as a cobweb, and over that an enormous beaver hat that protects his meagre visage from the sun. This is already the colour of mahogany, while his whole carcase seldom weighs above eight or ten stone, being generally exhausted by the climate and dissipation.

Having loitered about his estate, or sometimes ridden on horseback to his fields to view his increasing stores, he returns about eight o'clock when, if he goes abroad, he dresses, but if not, remains just as he is. Should the first take place, having only exchanged his trousers for a pair of thin linen or silk breeches, he sits down and holding out one foot after the other, like a horse going to be shod, a negro boy puts on his stockings and shoes, which he also buckles, while another dresses his hair, his wig, or shaves his chin, and a third is fanning him to keep off the mosquitoes. Having now shifted, he puts on a thin coat and waistcoat, all white; then, under an umbrella, carried by a black boy, he is conducted to his barge, which is in waiting for him with six or eight oars, well provided with fruit, wine, water and tobacco by his overseer, who no sooner has seen him depart, than he resumes the command with all the usual insolence of office. But should this prince not mean to stir from his estate, he goes to breakfast about ten o'clock, for which a table is spread in the large hall, provided with a bacon ham, hung-beef, fowls, or pigeons broiled; plantains and sweet cassavas roasted; bread, butter, cheese, etc. with which he drinks strong beer, and a glass of Madeira, Rhenish, or Moselle wine, while the cringing overseer sits at the farther end, keeping his proper distance, both being served by the most beautiful slaves that can be selected.

After this he takes a book, plays at chess or billiards, entertains himself with music, etc. till the heat of the day forces him to return into his cotton hammock to enjoy his meridian nap, which he could no more dispense with than a Spaniard with his *siesta*, and in which he rocks to and fro, like a performer on the slack-rope, till he falls asleep without either bed or covering. During this time he is fanned by a couple of his black attendants, to keep him cool.

About three o'clock he awakes by natural instinct when, having washed and perfumed himself, he sits down to dinner, attended as at breakfast by his deputy governor and sable pages. Here nothing is wanting that the world can afford in a western climate, of meat, fowls, venison, fish, vegetables and fruits, and the most exquisite wines are often squandered in profusion; after this a cup of strong coffee and a liqueur finish the repast. At six o'clock he is again waited on by his overseer, attended as in the morning by negro-drivers and prisoners, when the flogging once more having continued for some time, and the necessary orders being given for the next day's work, the assembly is dismissed, and the evening spent with weak punch, sangaree, cards and tobacco. His worship generally begins to yawn about ten or eleven o'clock, when he withdraws and is undressed by his sooty pages. He then retires to rest, where he passes the night in the arms of one or other of his sable sultanas (for he always keeps a seraglio) till about six in the morning, when he again repairs to his piazza walk, where his pipe and coffee are waiting for him, and where, with the rising sun, he begins his round of dissipation, like a petty monarch, as capricious as he is despotic and despisable.

Such absolute power indeed, cannot fail to be peculiarly delightful to a man who, in all probability, was in his own country, Europe, a – nothing. Exceptions, however, take place in every circumstance of life; and I have known many planters in

Surinam as good men as I ever would desire to be acquainted with, which I have already mentioned.

As for the ladies, they indulge themselves just as much, by giving way to their unbounded passions and especially to the most relentless barbarity. But while I can bear witness to the exalted virtues of a few women whose characters shine with treble lustre, I shall draw a veil over all the imperfections too common to their sex in this climate. Before I drop this subject, however, I must attest that hospitality is in no country practised with greater cordiality or with less ceremony, a stranger being everywhere at home, and finding his table and his bed at whatever estate necessity or choice may occasion him to visit.[25]

Of all the customs of all the peoples of the world, few can be more unpleasant than the human sacrifices of the Aztecs of Mexico. When they went to war, they did so not for territorial gain but solely to take prisoners, in enormous quantities, for sacrifice. While inaugurating their new temple shortly before the arrival of the Spaniards under Hernán Cortés, they slaughtered no less than 20,000 a day for four days. And their method of killing was, if anything, even more terrible than the killing itself. Here is an eye-witness description of it by Bernal Díaz del Castillo. By the time of which he is writing, the conquest has entered on its final phase: an uneasy peace has given way to out-and-out war, and the Spaniards are beating a temporary retreat from the Aztec capital, Tenochtitlán:

When we had retired almost to our quarters, across a great opening full of water, their arrows, darts, and stones could no longer reach us. Sandoval, Francisco de Lugo, and Andrés de Tapia were standing with Pedro de Alvarado, each one telling his story and discussing Cortés' orders, when the dismal drum of Huichilobos sounded again, accompanied by conches, horns, and trumpet-like instruments. It was a terrifying sound, and when we looked at the tall *cue* from which it came we saw our comrades who had been captured in Cortés' defeat being dragged up the steps to be sacrificed. When they had hauled them up to a small platform in front of the shrine where they kept their accursed idols we saw them put plumes on the heads of many of them; and then they made them dance with a sort of fan in front of Huichilobos. Then after they had danced the *papas* laid them down on their backs on some narrow stones of sacrifice and, cutting open their chests, drew out their palpitating hearts which they offered to the idols before them. Then they kicked the bodies down the steps, and the Indian butchers who were waiting below cut off their arms and legs and flayed their faces, which they afterwards prepared like glove leather, with their beards on, and kept for their drunken festivals. Then they ate their flesh with a sauce of peppers and tomatoes. They sacrificed all our men in this way, eating their legs and arms, offering their hearts and blood to their idols as I have said, and throwing their trunks and entrails to the lions and tigers and serpents and snakes that they kept in the wild-beast houses I have described in an earlier chapter.[26]

When I first went to Mexico in 1968, I well remember the embarrassment of the Mexican Tourist Office when the question of human sacrifices came up; in one of their brochures they got around the problem magnificently by referring to the ruins of the temple 'where the cardiectomies were performed'. But now the Aztecs are gone and the cardiectomies with them; and the country is, for me, one of the most enchanting in the world. Charles Macomb Flandrau thought so too; and in another extract from *Viva Mexico!* he suggests why:

One afternoon in a small Mexican town I kept tab from my balcony on what, for about eight minutes, took place in the street below. Although the town was small and the day an unusually quiet one, owing to a fiesta in the neighborhood to which many of the inhabitants had gone, there was no dearth of incident against the usual background of big-hatted cargadores waiting for employment in the middle of the street; of burros, each with four large cobblestones in a box on its back; of biblical-looking girls (an endless stream of them) bearing huge water-jars to and from a circular fountain lined with pale-blue tiles; of old men who wail at intervals that they are selling pineapple ice cream; of old women with handfuls of white and yellow and green lottery tickets; of basket sellers and sellers of flowers (the kind of adorable bouquets that haven't been seen anywhere else since the early seventies; composed of damp moss, tinfoil, toothpicks, a lace petticoat, a wooden handle, and, yes, some flowers arranged in circles according to color); of mozos who you feel sure have been sent on an errand and told to 'come right back,' but who have apparently no intention of returning for several hours; of ladies draped in black lace on their way to meditate in church; of hundreds of other leisurely moving figures that were as a bright-colored, shifting chorus to the more striking episodes.

Item one (so runs my page of hasty notes): Three rather fragile-looking young men swinging along with a grand piano on their heads. Under my window they all stop a moment to let one of them ask a passerby to stick a cigarette in his mouth and light it, which is duly done.

Item two: A flock of sheep followed by a shepherd in clean white cotton with a crimson sarape around his shoulders. He looks like Vedder's Lazarus. The sheep have just piled into the open door of the hotel and are trying to come upstairs. In the excitement a new-born lamb has its leg hurt. The shepherd gathers it in his arms, wraps it in the sarape, thoughtfully kisses it twice on the head and proceeds.

Item three: A funeral. As there are only three streets in this place that aren't built up and down a mountain side, there are no vehicles, and coffins, like everything else, are carried on men's backs. This is an unusually expensive coffin, but then of course the silver handles are only hired for the occasion. They'll be removed at the grave, as otherwise they would be dug up and stolen. I wonder why women so rarely go to funerals here? There is a string of men a block long, but no women. Some of them (probably relatives) have in their hands lighted candles tied with crape. They are nice, fat candles and don't blow out. Everybody in the street takes his hat off as the cortège passes.

Item four: The daily pack train of mules from the Concepción sugar hacienda. There must be two hundred and fifty of them, and their hoofs clatter on the cobblestones like magnified hail. The street is jammed with them, and where the sidewalk narrows to almost nothing, people are trying to efface themselves against the wall. A wonderful exhibition of movement and color in the blazing sunlight: the warm seal-brown of the mules, the paler yellow-brown of the burlap in which are wrapped the conical sugar loaves (eight to a mule), with the arrieros in yellow straw hats, brilliant blue shirts and scarlet waist bandas bringing up the rear.

Item five: A dog fight.

Item six: Another and much worse dog fight.

Item seven: An Indian woman with apparently a whole poultry farm half concealed upon her person. She calls up to ask if I would like to buy a chicken. Why on earth should a young man on a balcony of a hotel bedroom like to buy a chicken?

Item eight: An acquaintance makes a megaphone of his hands and inquires if I am very busy. I reply, 'Yes, frightfully,' and we adjourn to the plaza for the afternoon.[27]

And so north to the United States. I hope my American friends will forgive me if the extract I quote here is not entirely flattering; but if all the passages included in this book were complimentary, what a boring volume it would be. The reporter on this occasion is Charles Dickens, writing his *American Notes*:

The Senate is a dignified and decorous body, and its proceedings are conducted with much gravity and order. Both houses are handsomely carpeted; but the state to which these carpets are reduced by the universal disregard of the spittoon with which every honourable member is accommodated, and the extraordinary improvements on the pattern which are squirted and dabbled upon it in every direction, do not admit of being described. I will merely observe, that I strongly recommend all strangers not to look at the floor; and if they happen to drop anything, though it be their purse, not to pick it up with an ungloved hand on any account.

It is somewhat remarkable too, at first, to say the least, to see so many honourable members with swelled faces; and it is scarcely less remarkable to discover that this appearance is caused by the quantity of tobacco they contrive to stow within the hollow of the cheek. It is strange enough too, to see an honourable gentleman leaning back in his tilted chair with his legs on the desk before him, shaping a convenient 'plug' with his penknife, and when it is quite ready for use, shooting the old one from his mouth, as from a pop-gun, and clapping the new one in its place.

I was surprised to observe that even steady old chewers of great experience, are not always good marksmen, which has rather inclined me to doubt that general proficiency with the rifle, of which we have heard so much in England. Several gentlemen called upon me who, in the course of conversation, frequently missed the spittoon at five paces; and one (but he was certainly short-sighted) mistook the closed sash for the open window, at three. On another occasion, when I dined out, and was sitting with two ladies and some gentlemen round a fire before dinner, one of the company fell short of the fireplace, six distinct times. I am disposed to think, however, that this was occasioned by his not aiming at that object; as there was a white marble hearth before the fender, which was more convenient, and may have suited his purpose better.[28]

Finally, back across the Atlantic to England, where we have some pretty rum customs ourselves. A perceptive observer of them was Daniel Defoe, who had some curious things to say about life in Essex:

I have one remark more, before I leave this damp part of the world, and which I cannot omit on the womens account; namely, that I took notice of a strange decay of the sex here; insomuch, that all along this county it was very frequent to meet with men that had had from five or six, to fourteen or fifteen wives; nay, and some more; and I was inform'd that in the marshes on the other side the river over-against Candy Island, there was a farmer, who was then living with the five and twentieth wife, and that his son who was but about 35 years old, had already had about fourteen; indeed this part of the story, I only had by report, tho' from good hands too; but the other is well known, and easie to be inquired in to, about Fobbing, Curringham, Thundersly, Benfleet, Prittlewell, Wakering, Great Stambridge, Cricksea, Burnham, Dengy, and other towns of the like situation: The reason, as a merry fellow told me, who said he had had about a dozen and half of wives, (tho' I found afterwards he fibb'd a little) was this; That they being bred in the marshes themselves, and season'd to the place, did pretty well with it; but that they always went up into the hilly country, or to speak their own language into the uplands for a wife: That when they took the young lasses out of the wholesome and fresh air, they were healthy, fresh and clear, and well; but when they came out of their native air into the marshes among the fogs and damps, there they presently chang'd their complexion, got an ague or two, and seldom held it above half a year, or a year at most; and then, said he, we go to the uplands again, and fetch another; so that marrying of wives was reckon'd a kind of good farm to them: It is true, the fellow told this in a kind of drollery, and mirth; but the fact, for all that, is certainly true; and that they have abundance of wives by that very means.[29]

CHAPTER SEVENTEEN

Dress

One of the sadder casualties of the ease and speed of modern travel has been the slow disappearance of national dress. I am not talking about folkloric costumes; they are dying out too, but for other reasons. What I mean is the natural variation in everyday clothing from one country to another. When I was a child before the Second World War, one had only to cross the Channel to be immediately aware of how differently the French and the English dressed. Oddly enough, the contrast was considerably greater between the men than between the women. Englishwomen wore the same *sort* of clothes as Frenchwomen, only dowdier; Frenchmen, on the other hand, had a radically different repertoire. The beret was in those days – at least in my childhood memory – almost *de rigueur*; only slightly less common were the flowing cravat, the pepper-and-salt tweed Norfolk jacket with the belt let into the back, and the plus-fours – the latter popular enough among adults but universal among teen-age schoolboys, a large number of whom, in summer, affected to wear them without socks.

Nowadays all that has gone, and it has become increasingly difficult to tell one Western European from another until he opens his mouth. (I make an honourable exception for the Austrians and, to a lesser extent, the Germans, who have doggedly preserved their *Tracht* – the lodens, dirndls and the rest – and thereby made, it seems to me, no small contribution to the gaiety of nations.) But if the gulf has narrowed so dramatically in the past half-century, how much wider yet it must have been 200 years ago! Just listen to that crusty old crosspatch Tobias Smollett, writing from Paris in October 1763 – no wonder Laurence Sterne nicknamed him 'Smelfungus':

The French, however, with all their absurdities, preserve a certain ascendency over us, which is very disgraceful to our nation; and this appears in nothing more than in the article of dress. We are contented to be thought their apes in fashion; but, in fact, we are slaves to their tailors, mantua-makers, barbers, and other tradesmen. One would be apt to imagine that our own tradesmen had joined them in a combination against us. When the natives of France come to London, they appear, in all public places, with clothes made according to the fashion of their own country, and this fashion is generally admired by the English. Why, therefore, don't we follow it implicitly? No, we pique ourselves upon a most ridiculous deviation from the very modes we admire, and please ourselves with thinking this deviation is a mark of our spirit and liberty. But we have not spirit enough to persist in this deviation when we visit their country; otherwise, perhaps, they would come to admire and follow our example; for, certainly, in point of true taste, the fashions of both countries are equally absurd. At present, the skirts of the English descend from the fifth rib to the calf of the leg, and give the coat the form of a Jewish gaberdine; and our hats seem to be modelled after that which *Pistol* wears upon the stage. In France, the haunch buttons and pocket-holes are within half a foot of the coat's extremity; their hats look as if they had been pared round the brims, and the crown is covered with a kind of cordage, which in my opinion produces a very beggarly effect. In every other circumstance of dress, male and female, the contrast between the two nations appears equally glaring. What is the consequence? when an Englishman comes to Paris, he cannot appear until he has undergone a total metamorphosis. At his first arrival he finds it necessary to send for the tailor, *perruquier*, hatter, shoemaker, and every other tradesman concerned in the equipment of the human body. He must even change his buckles, and the form of his ruffles; and, though at the risk of his life, suit his clothes to the mode of the season. For example, though the weather should be never so cold, he must wear his *habit d'été*, or *demi-saison*, without presuming to put on a warm dress before the day which fashion has fixed for that purpose; and neither old age nor infirmity will excuse a man for wearing his hat upon his head, either at home or abroad. Females are, if possible, still more subject to the caprices of fashion; and as the articles of their dress are more manifold, it is enough to make a man's heart ache to see his wife surrounded by a multitude of *cotturieres*, milliners, and tire-women. All her sacks and negligees must be altered and new-trimmed. She must have new caps, new laces, new shoes, and her hair new cut. She must have their taffaties for the summer, her flowered silks for the spring and autumn, her satins and damasks for winter. The good man, who used to wear the *beau drap d'Angleterre* quite plain all the year round, with a long bob, or tie-periwig, must here provide himself with a camblet suit trimmed with silver for spring and autumn, with silk clothes for summer, and cloth laced with gold, or velvet, for winter; and he must wear his bag-wig *à la pigeon*. This variety of dress is absolutely indispensable for all those who pretend to any rank above the mere *bourgeois*. On his return to his own country, all this frippery is useless. He cannot appear in London until he has undergone another thorough metamorphosis; so that he will have some reason to think that the tradesmen of Paris and London have combined to lay him under contribution; and they, no doubt, are the directors who regulate the fashions in both capitals; the English, however, in a subordinate capacity; for the puppets of their making will not pass at Paris, nor indeed in any other part of Europe; whereas a French *petit maître* is reckoned a complete figure everywhere, London not excepted.[1]

There was another, though admittedly smaller, danger which also beset English travellers in France in the eighteenth century – Captain Philip Thicknesse issued a dire warning:

When fine cambrick handkerchiefs, &c. are given to be washed, take care they are not trimmed round two inches narrower, to make borders to *Madame la*

Blanchisseuse's night caps: this is a little *douceur* which they think themselves entitled to, from my Lord *Anglois*, whom they are sure is *tres riche*, and consequently ought to be plundered by the poor.[2]

Let us now turn our attention to Spain – although in 1949, the date of her book *Fabled Shore*, Rose Macaulay might just as easily have been writing about any of the Roman Catholic countries of Europe. Her theme is that age-old problem which must exist all over Christendom – and, I suspect, the Jewish world as well, though not I think the Islamic or the Buddhist – what to wear for worship; she is speaking of the little town of Cadaques:

The church, Santa Maria (undamaged both by republicans and rebels), has a fine Romanesque-looking exterior, but inside is dated 1662, and is a gorgeous riot of baroque. It was in the porch of this church that I first read the placards which, all over Spain, warn señoras and señoritas what they must wear in church. 'Señora! Señorita! You present yourself without stockings? In a short dress? With short sleeves? You go into church? Stop! Stop! If you go thus into church, you will be turned out. If you go thus indecorously to confession, you will not be given absolution. If you have the audacity to approach the Blessed Sacrament, you will be refused in the presence of all.'

Apart from the sex unfairness of this (for it seems that señores may wear what they like) what strikes one is the profound difference of attitude between the Roman and the Anglican Churches, the one making church-going an occasion, a mystery, to be approached *en grande tenue*, in especial clothes, the other easy, casual, laissez-faire, go-as-you-please, come-as-you-are, come in your working and playing clothes, bare headed, bare armed, bare legged, just as you happen to be. (Vain hope, for how seldom do we come at all!) To surround religious devotion with pomp and ceremony, awe, stockings, voluminous ceremonial clothes, has much to be said for it, though the stocking requirement must keep many women from church; in these fishing ports stockings are seldom seen; the women mending nets on the beach and marketing in the town never wear them; they may keep a pair for church, but to go home and put them on when the bell clangs for a service must be difficult. On the other hand, those who do go to church thus decorously attired, thus set apart from their secular workaday selves, must, I suppose, feel very blest and spiritually prepared. As, no doubt, church-goers in Victorian England used to feel, processing churchward on Sunday mornings in top-hats and Sunday frocks. The Anglicans, who have dropped so much, have dropped all that; 'come as you are, my dear people,' is now the vicar's vain and coaxing plea. What English vicar would dare to placard his church door with 'Ladies! Stop! Stop! Change your clothes or you will be turned away!' The same difference in attitude lies, I think, behind the so careful guarding of Spanish churches, so that between one and four, when caretakers and sacristans are having their midday meal and their siesta, you will find every church and cathedral locked against visitors; very disappointing for those who are passing through in the afternoon and cannot wait. In England, cathedrals and churches stand casually and negligently open to all comers all day until dark; you may wander about them, stockingless, in mid-afternoon. The difference may, in part, be due to fear of the ancient Spanish tradition of ecclesioclasm, which has done in the past such irretrievable hurt to churches. But there is, I think, also a difference in attitude; the Holy Mysteries, the Heavenly Sanctuary, too hallowed for unguarded approach, as against come-and-go-as-you-please.[3]

I have several times quoted the letters of Lady Mary Wortley Montagu – and with good reason, for no traveller wrote better about life in the Near East in her day. She writes, however, as an outside observer, so it comes as something of a surprise to discover that she habitually wore Turkish dress. Here – after a rather crotchety start – she describes it to her sister, writing in 1717 from Adrianople:

I wish to God, dear sister, that you were as regular in letting me know what passes on your side of the globe, as I am careful in endeavouring to amuse you by the account of all I see here, that I think worth your notice. . . . Pray let me into more particulars, and I will try to awaken your gratitude by giving you a full and true relation of the novelties of this place, none of which would surprise you more than a sight of my person, as I am now in my Turkish habit, though I believe you would be of my opinion, that 'tis admirably becoming. – I intend to send you my picture; in the mean time accept of it here.

The first part of my dress is a pair of drawers, very full, that reach to my shoes, and conceal the legs more modestly than your petticoats. They are of a thin rose-coloured damask, brocaded with silver flowers. My shoes are of a white kid leather, embroidered with gold. Over this hangs my smock, of a fine white silk gauze, edged with embroidery. This smock has wide sleeves hanging half-way down the arm, and is closed at the neck with a diamond button, but the shape and colour of the bosom is very well to be distinguished through it. – The Antery is a waistcoat, made close to the shape, of white and gold damask, with very long sleeves falling back, and fringed with deep gold fringe, and should have diamond or pearl buttons. My Caftan, of the same stuff with my drawers, is a robe exactly fitted to my shape and reaching to my feet, with very long strait falling sleeves. Over this is the girdle, of about four fingers broad, which all that can afford it, have entirely of diamonds or other precious stones; those, who will not be at that expence, have it of exquisite embroidery on sattin; but it must be fastened before with a clasp of diamonds. – The *Curdée* is a loose robe they throw off, or put on, according to the weather, being of a rich brocade (mine is green and gold) either lined with ermine or sables; the sleeves reach very little below the shoulders. The head-dress is composed of a cap called Talpock, which is, in winter, of fine velvet embroidered with pearls or diamonds, and, in summer, of a light shining silver stuff. This is fixed on one side of the head, hanging a little way down with a gold tassel, and bound on, either with a circle of diamonds (as I have seen several) or a rich embroidered handkerchief. On the other side of the head the hair is laid flat; and here the ladies are at liberty to shew their fancies; some putting flowers, others a plume of heron's feathers, and, in short, what they please; but the most general fashion is, a large Bouquet of jewels, made like natural flowers, that is, the buds of pearl; the roses of different coloured rubies; the jessamines of diamonds; the jonquils of topazes, &c. so well set and enamelled, 'tis hard to imagine any thing of that kind so beautiful. The hair hangs at its full length behind, divided into tresses braided with pearl or ribbon, which is always in great quantity. I never saw in my life, so many fine heads of hair. In one lady's I have counted a hundred and ten of the tresses, all natural; but it must be owned that every kind of beauty is more common here than with us. 'Tis surprising to see a young woman that is not very handsome. They have naturally the most beautiful complexion in the world, and generally large black eyes. . . . They generally shape their eye-brows, and, both Greeks and Turks have this custom of putting round their eyes a black tincture, that, at a distance, or by candle-light, adds very much to the blackness of them. I fancy many of our ladies would be overjoyed to know this secret; but 'tis too visible by day. They dye their nails a rose colour; but I own I cannot enough accustom myself to this fashion, to find any beauty in it.

As to their morality or good conduct, I can say, like Harlequin, that 'tis just as 'tis with you; and the Turkish ladies don't commit one sin the less for not being Christians. Now that I am a little acquainted with their ways, I cannot forbear admiring, either exemplary discretion, or extreme stupidity of all the writers that have given accounts of them. 'Tis very easy to see, they have in reality more liberty than we have. No woman, of what rank soever, is permitted to go into the streets without two *Murlins*, one that covers her face, all but her eyes; and another, that hides the whole dress of her head, and hangs halfway down her back. Their shapes are also wholly concealed by a thing they call a *Ferigée*, which no woman of any sort appears without; this has strait sleeves, that reach to their fingers ends, and it laps all round them, not unlike a riding-hood. In winter, 'tis of cloth; and in summer, of plain stuff or silk. You may guess then how effectually this disguises them, so that there is no distinguishing the great lady from her slave. 'Tis impossible for the most jealous husband to know his wife, when he meets her, and no man dare touch or follow a woman in the street.[4]

There was no doubt about it: all the loveliest clothes – as well as the most ragged and tattered ones – were to be found in the East. Mrs Amelia B. Edwards called her book *A Thousand Miles Up the Nile*; but she had to go no further than Cairo to write this description:

Meanwhile, the crowd ebbs and flows unceasingly – a noisy, changing, restless, parti-coloured tide, half European, half Oriental, on foot, on horseback, and in carriages. Here are Syrian dragomans in baggy trousers and braided jackets; barefooted Egyptian fellaheen in ragged blue shirts and felt skull-caps; Greeks in absurdly stiff white tunics, like walking penwipers; Persians with high mitre-like caps of dark woven stuff; swarthy Bedouins in flowing garments, creamy-white with chocolate stripes a foot wide, and head-shawl of the same bound about the brow with a fillet of twisted camel's hair; Englishmen in palm-leaf hats and knicker-bockers, dangling their long legs across almost invisible donkeys; native women of the poorer class, in black veils that leave only the eyes uncovered, and long trailing garments of dark blue and black striped cotton; dervishes in patchwork coats, their matted hair streaming from under fantastic head-dresses; blue-black Abyssinians with incredibly slender, bowed legs, like attenuated ebony balustrades; Armenian priests, looking exactly like Portia as the Doctor, in long black gowns and high square caps; majestic ghosts of Algerine Arabs, all in white; mounted Janissaries with jingling sabres and gold-embroidered jackets; merchants, beggars, soldiers, boatmen, labourers, workmen, in every variety of costume, and of every shade of complexion from fair to dark, from tawny to copper-colour, from deepest bronze to bluest black.

Now a water-carrier goes by, bending under the weight of his newly-replenished goatskin, the legs of which being tied up, the neck fitted with a brass cock, and the hair left on, looks horribly bloated and life-like. Now comes a sweetmeat-vendor with a tray of that gummy compound known to English children as 'Lumps of Delight'; and now an Egyptian lady on a large grey donkey led by a servant with a showy sabre at his side. The lady wears a rose-coloured silk dress and white veil, besides a black silk outer garment, which, being cloak, hood, and veil all in one, fills out with the wind as she rides, like a balloon. She sits astride; her naked feet, in their violet velvet slippers, just resting on the stirrups. She takes care to display a plump brown arm laden with massive gold bracelets, and, to judge by the way in which she uses a pair of liquid black eyes, would not be sorry to let her face be seen also. Nor is the steed less well dressed than his mistress. His close-shaven legs and hindquarters are painted in blue and white zigzags picked out with bands of pale yellow; his high-pommelled saddle is resplendent with velvet and embroidery; and his headgear is all tags, tassels, and fringes. Such a donkey as this is worth from sixty to a hundred pounds sterling. Next passes an open barouche full of laughing Englishwomen; or a grave provincial sheykh all in black, riding a handsome bay Arab, *demi-sang;* or an Egyptian gentleman in European dress and Turkish fez, driven by an English groom in an English phaeton. Before him, wand in hand, bare-legged, eager-eyed, in Greek skull-cap and gorgeous gold-embroidered waistcoat and fluttering white tunic, flies a native Saïs, or running footman. No person of position drives in Cairo without one or two of these attendants. The Saïs (strong, light, and beautiful, like John of Bologna's Mercury) are said to die young. The pace kills them. Next passes a lemonade-seller, with his tin jar in one hand, and his decanter and brass cups in the other; or an itinerant slipper-vendor with a bunch of red and yellow morocco shoes dangling at the end of a long pole; or a London-built miniature brougham containing two ladies in transparent Turkish veils, preceded by a Nubian outrider in semi-military livery; or, perhaps, a train of camels, ill-tempered and supercilious, craning their scrannel necks above the crowd, and laden with canvas bales scrawled over with Arabic addresses.[5]

Buying clothes for a long and arduous journey can often be something of a problem; for few of us, however, has the task been so unpleasant – and the results so ultimately unsatisfactory – as it was for the Abbés Huc and Gabet (we first met them in Chapter Six) on their way across Tartary in the 1840s:

Upon receiving our sapeks, we proceeded to buy the winter clothing we needed. Upon a consideration of the meagreness of our exchequer, we came to the resolution that it would be better to purchase what we required at some secondhand shop. In China and Tartary no one has the smallest repugnance to wear other people's clothes; he who has not himself the attire wherein to pay a visit or make a holiday, goes without ceremony to a neighbour and borrows a hat, or a pair of trousers, or boots, or shoes, or whatever else he wants, and nobody is at all surprised at these borrowings, which are quite a custom. The only hesitation any one has in lending his clothes to a neighbour, is, lest the borrower should sell them in payment of some debt, or, after using them, pawn them. People who buy clothes buy them indifferently, new or secondhand. The question of price is alone taken into consideration, for there is no more delicacy felt about putting on another man's hat or trousers, than there is about living in a house that some one else has occupied before you.

This custom of wearing other people's things was by no means to our taste, and all the less so, that, ever since our arrival at the mission of Si-Wang, we had not been under the necessity of departing from our old habits in this respect. Now, however, the slenderness of our purse compelled us to waive our repugnance. We went out, therefore, in search of a secondhand clothes shop, of which, in every town here, there are a greater or less number, for the most part in connection with pawnshops, called in these countries Tang-Pou. Those who borrow upon pledges, are seldom able to redeem the articles they have deposited, which they accordingly leave to die, as the Tartars and Chinese express it; or in other words, they allow the period of redemption to pass, and the articles pass altogether from them. The old clothes shops of the Blue Town were filled in this way with Tartar spoils, so that we had the opportunity of selecting exactly the sort of things we required, to suit the new costume we had adopted.

At the first shop we visited they showed us a quantity of wretched garments turned up with sheep-skin; but though these rags were exceedingly old, and so covered with grease that it was impossible to guess at their original colour, the price asked for them was exorbitant. After a protracted haggling, we found it impossible to come to terms, and we gave up this first attempt; and we gave it up, be it added, with a certain degree of satisfaction, for our self-respect was somewhat wounded at finding ourselves reduced even to the proposition of wearing such filthy rags. We visited another shop, and another, a third, and a fourth, and still several more. We were shown magnificent garments, handsome garments, fair garments, endurable garments, but the consideration of expense was, in each instance, an impracticable stumbling-block. The journey we had undertaken might endure for several years, and extreme economy, at all events in the outset, was indispensable. After going about the whole day, after making the acquaintance of all the rag-merchants in the Blue Town, after turning over and over all their old clothes, we were fain to return to the secondhand dealer whom we had first visited, and to make the best bargain we could with him. We purchased from him, at last, two ancient robes of sheep-skin, covered with some material, the nature of which it was impossible to identify, and the original colour of which we suspected to have been yellow. We proceeded to try them on, and it was at once evident that the tailor in making them had by no means had us in his eye. M. Gabet's robe was too short, M. Huc's too long; but a friendly exchange was impracticable, the difference in height between the two missionaries being altogether too disproportionate. We at first thought of cutting the excess from the one, in order to make up the deficiency of the other; but then we should have had to call in the aid of a tailor, and this would have involved another drain upon our purse; the pecuniary consideration decided the question, and we determined to wear the clothes as they were, M. Huc adopting the expedient of holding up, by means of a girdle, the surplus of his robe, and M. Gabet resigning himself to the exposure to the public gaze of a portion of his legs; the main inconvenience, after all, being the manifestation to all who saw us that we could not attire ourselves in exact proportion to our size.[6]

For Henry Walter Bates, FRS, author of *The Naturalist on the River Amazons*, cold was not normally a problem; but he too dressed practically, for the job on hand:

Between 9 and 10 a.m. I prepare for the woods: a coloured shirt, pair of trousers, pair of common boots, and an old hat, are all my clothing; over my left shoulder slings my double-barrelled gun, loaded, one with No. 10, one with No. 4 shot. In my right hand I take my net; on my left side is suspended a leathern bag with two pockets, one for my insect box, the other for powder and two sorts of shot; on my right side hangs my 'game bag,' an ornamental affair, with red leather trappings and thongs to hang lizards, snakes, frogs, or large birds; one small pocket in this bag contains my caps; another, papers for wrapping up the delicate birds; others for wads, cotton, box of powdered plaister, and a box with damped cork for the microlepidoptera; to my shirt is pinned my pincushion, with six sizes of pins.[7]

Mrs Isabella Bird is another familiar figure in these pages. She went just about everywhere sooner or later; we find her here in Malacca in 1878, describing a Chinese child most unusually – one would have thought – attired for a morning call:

During the morning four children of a rich Chinese merchant, attended by a train of Chinese and Malay servants, came to see Mrs. Shaw. There were a boy and girl of five and six years old, and two younger children. A literal description of their appearance reads like fiction. The girl wore a yellow petticoat of treble satin (mandarin yellow) with broad box pleats in front and behind, exquisitely embroidered with flowers in shades of blue silk, with narrow box pleats between, with a trail of blue silk flowers on each. Over this there was a short robe of crimson brocaded silk, with a broad border of cream-white satin, with the same exquisite floral embroidery in shades of blue silk. Above this was a tippet of three rows of embroidered lozenge-shaped 'tabs' of satin. The child wore a crown on her head, the basis of which was black velvet. At the top was an aigrette of diamonds of the purest water, the centre one as large as a six-penny-piece. Solitaires flashing blue flames blazed all over the cap, and the front was ornamented with a dragon in fine filigree work in red Malay gold set with diamonds. I fear to be thought guilty of exaggeration when I write that this child wore seven necklaces, all of gorgeous beauty. The stones were all cut in facets at the back, and highly polished, and their beauty was enhanced by the good taste and skilful workmanship of the setting. The first necklace was of diamonds set as roses and crescents, some of them very large, and all of great brilliancy; the second of emeralds, a few of which were as large as acorns, but spoilt by being pierced; the third of pearls set whole; the fourth of hollow filigree beads in red, burned gold; the fifth of sapphires and diamonds; the sixth a number of finely worked chains of gold with a pendant of a gold filigree fish set with diamonds; the seventh, what they all wear, a massive gold chain, which looked heavy enough even by itself to weigh down the fragile little wearer, from which depended a gold shield, on which the Chinese characters forming the child's name were raised in rubies, with fishes and flowers in diamonds round it, and at the back a god in rubies similarly surrounded. Magnificent diamond earrings and heavy gold bracelets completed the display.

And all this weight of splendour, valued at the very least at $40,000, was carried by a frail human mite barely four feet high, with a powdered face, gentle, pensive expression, and quiet grace of manner, who came forward and most winsomely shook hands with us, as did all the other grave gentle mites. They were also loaded with gold and diamonds. Some sugar-plums fell on the floor, and as the eldest girl stooped to pick them up, diamond solitaires fell out of her hair, which were gathered up by her attendants as if they were used to such occurrences. Whenever she moved her diamonds flashed, scintillated, and gave forth their blue light.[8]

Finally, a letter from E. M. Forster, written while staying in the Palace of the Rajah of Dewas and reproduced in *The Hill of Devi*:

On 29 Dec [1912] the Rajah gave an Indian banquet to the newly married pair. I have both forgotten the time it was meant to be and the time it was. As usual they differed widely, but at all events, as darkness fell, the garden and road by the Guest House filled up with soldiers, policemen, horses, children, torch bearers, and a most gorgeous elephant. (There are two state elephants but the other did not feel quite well.) Goodall was to wear Indian dress, and I retired to my tent to put on my English evening things. Baldeo, much excited by the splendour that surrounded us, was making the best of my simple wardrobe and helping to snip my shirt cuffs where they were frayed, when there was a cry of 'may I come in', and enter the Rajah, bearing Indian raiment for me also. A Sirdar (courtier) came with him, a very charming boy, and they two aided Baldeo to undress me and re-dress me. It was a very funny scene. At first nothing fitted, but the Rajah sent for other garments off people's backs until I was suited. Let me describe myself. Shoes – I had to take them off when the Palace was reached, so they don't count. My legs were clad in Jodpores made of white muslin. Hanging outside these was the youthful Sirdar's white shirt, but it was concealed by a waistcoat the colours of a Neapolitan ice – red, white, and green, and this was almost concealed by my chief garment – a magnificent coat of claret-coloured silk, trimmed with gold. I never found out to whom this belonged. It came to below my knees and fitted round my wrists closely and very well, and closely to my body. Cocked rakishly over one ear was a Maratha Turban of scarlet and gold – not to be confused with the ordinary turban; it is a made-up affair, more like a cocked hat. Nor was this all. I carried in my left hand a scarf of orange-coloured silk with gold ends, and before the evening ended a mark like a loaf of bread was stamped on my forehead in crimson, meaning that I was of the sect of Shiva. Meanwhile the others too had been surprised with Indian costumes, Malcolm looking very fine in pink with a sword, and the other man in purple. The ladies went as themselves. At last we were ready, and really it was a glorious sight when the Goodalls were perched on the elephant, sitting on real cloth of gold, with torches around them and above splendid starlight. The band played, the children cheered, and the Darlings' nice old Ayah stood in the veranda invoking blessings from Heaven. We went each in a carriage with Sirdars: I had two old men and one fat one, all gorgeous, but conversation not as good as our clothes. An elephant being pensive in its walk, we didn't reach the New Palace for a long time, though it is close to the Guest House. Hideous building! But it was too dark to see it. After the Rajah had welcomed us we went to the Banquet Room.[9]

CHAPTER EIGHTEEN

Cuisine

We finished the previous chapter with an account of E. M. Forster being dressed for a wedding banquet; we start this one by continuing the story where we left off – at the beginning of the banquet itself:

We all sat on the floor, cross-legged, round the edge of a great hall, the servants running about in the middle. Each was on a legless chair and had in front a tray like a bed tray on which was a metal tray, on which the foods were ranged. The Brahmins ate no meat, and were waited on by special attendants, naked to the waist. The rest of us had meat as well as the other dishes. Round each man's little domain an ornamental pattern was stencilled in chalk on the floor. My tray was arranged somewhat as follows, but 'Jane, Jane, however shall we recollect the dishes?', as Miss Bates remarked.

1. A mound of delicious rice – a great standby.
2. Brown tennis balls of sugar – not bad.
3. Golden curlicues – sweet to sickliness.
4. Little spicy rissoles.
5. Second mound of rice, mixed with spices and lentils.
6. Third mound of rice, full of sugar and sultanas – very nice.
7. Curry in metal saucer – to be mixed with rice no. 1.
8. Sauce, as if made from apples that felt poorly. Also to be mixed with rice, but only once by me.
9. Another sauce, chooey-booey and brown.
10, 11, 12. Three dreadful little dishes that tasted of nothing till they were well in your mouth, when your whole tongue suddenly burst into flame. I got to hate this side of the tray.
13. Long thin cake, like a brandy snap but salt.

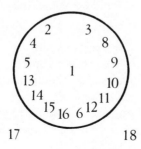

14. It may have been vermicelli.
15. As for canaries.
16. Fourth mound of rice to which I never came.
17. Water.
18. Native bread – thin oat-cake type.

Some of these dishes had been cooked on the supposition that an elephant arrives punctually, and lay cooling on our trays when we joined them. Others were brought round hot by the servants who took a fistful and laid it down wherever there was room. Sometimes this was difficult, and the elder dishes had to be rearranged, and accommodate themselves. When my sweet rice arrived a great pushing and squeezing and patting took place, which I rather resented, not knowing how attached I should become to the new comer. Everything had to be eaten with the hand and with one hand – it is bad manners to use the left – and I was in terror of spoiling my borrowed plumes. Much fell, but mostly into the napkin, and the handkerchief that I had brought with me. I also feared to kneel in the sauces or to trail my orange scarf in the ornamental chalk border, which came off at the slightest touch and actually did get on to the Jodpores. The cramp too was now and then awful. The courtiers saw that I was in pain, and told the servants to move the tray that I might stretch, but I refused, nor would I touch the entire English dinner that was handed round during the meal – roast chicken, vegetables, blancmange &c. As each guest finished, he sang a little song from the Vedas in praise of some god, and the Rajah was, as usual, charming. He made the Goodalls feed each other five times and pronounce each other's name aloud. These are among their marriage customs. Afterwards he, his brother, the Dewan, and all of us went on to the Palace roof, where was champagne and betel nut, and we danced in our grand clothes and our socks to the music of the band which was playing down in the square. This suited me very well. We were interrupted by a message from the Rani – she desired to see us. This was a great surprise to me. The two ladies went first, and then we, and had a lovely vision. She was extraordinarily beautiful, with dark 'gazelle' eyes. Having shaken hands all round, she leant against the door-post and said nothing. There was an awkward if respectful pause, and after Malcolm had talked a little Urdu and received no answer, we went. Her dress was on the negligée side, but she had not been intending to receive. The Rajah was pleased she had sent for us. He longs to modernize her, but she remains a lovely wild creature. We returned to the hall below, sitting on the floor again and hearing a little singing from nautch girls. We drove back to the Guest House to find Mrs D. and Mrs G. in the most magnificent Indian dresses: the Rani had dressed them and sent them back in a Purdah carriage. – So ended a very charming evening, full of splendour yet free of formality.[1]

Now back to Europe, and a reminder that the French have not always had the same reputation for superb food and drink that they enjoy today. Again and again, in their letters and memoirs, English travellers of former centuries describe the gastronomic nightmares that they have suffered across the Channel; and though one could, I suppose, argue that it was their palates that were at fault rather than their hosts' cuisine, such a thesis is hard to maintain in the face of reports like this one, from Philip Thicknesse:

I am particular in dating this letter, in hopes that every English traveller may avoid the place I write from [the Post-House, St George, six leagues from Lyon], by either stopping short, or going beyond it, as it is the only house of reception for travellers in the village, and the worst I have met with in my whole journey. We had been scurvily treated here as we went; but having arrived at it after dark, and leaving it early, I did not recollect it again, till the mistress by her sour face and sorry fare betrayed it; for she well remembered *us*. As a specimen of French auberge cookery, I cannot help serving up a dish of spinnage to you, as it was served to me at this house. We came in early in the afternoon, and while I was in the court-yard, I saw a flat basket stand upon the ground, the bottom of which was covered with boiled spinnage; and as my dog, and several others in the yard, had often put their noses into it, I concluded it was put down for *their* food, not *mine*, till I saw a dirty girl patting it up into round balls, and two children, the eldest of them not above three years old, slavering in and playing with it, one of whom, *to lose no time*, was performing *an office* that none could *do for her*. I asked the maid what she was about, and what it was she was so preparing? for I began to think I had been mistaken, till she told me it was spinnage; – not for me, I hope, said I, – 'oui, *pour vous et le monde*.' I then forbad her bringing any to my table, and putting the little girl *off her center*, by an angry push, made her almost as dirty as the spinnage; and I could perceive her mother, the hostess, and some French travellers who were near, looked upon me as a brute, for *disturbing la pauvre enfant;* nevertheless, with my *entree* came up a dish of this *delicate spinnage*, with which I made the girl a very pretty *Chapeau Anglois*; for I turned it, dish and all, upon her head; this set the house in such an uproar, that, if there had not come in an old gentleman-like *Bourgeois* of *Paris*, at that instant, I verily believe I should have been turned out; but he engaged warmly in my defence, and insisted upon it that I had treated the girl just as he would have done, had she brought such a dirty dish to him after being cautioned not to do so; nor should I have got any supper, had I not prevailed on this good-natured man, who never eat any, to order a supper for himself, and transfer it to me.[2]

Rather than risk this sort of thing more often than was absolutely necessary, Tobias Smollett preferred to prepare a daily picnic:

The people of this country dine at noon, and travellers always find an ordinary prepared at every *auberge*, or public-house, on the road. Here they sit down promiscuously, and dine at so much a head. The usual price is thirty sols for dinner, and forty for supper, including lodging; for this moderate expense they have two courses and a dessert. If you eat in your own apartment, you pay, instead of forty sols, three, and in some places four livres a head. I and my family could not well dispense with our tea and toast in the morning, and had no stomach to eat at noon. For my part, I hate the French cookery, and abominate garlic, with which all their ragouts in this part of the country are highly seasoned; we therefore formed a different plan of living upon the road. Before we left Paris we laid in a stock of tea, chocolate, cured neats tongues and *saucissons*, or Bologna sausages, both of which we found in great perfection in that capital, where, indeed, there are excellent provisions of all sorts. About ten in the morning we stopped to breakfast at some *auberge*, where we always found bread, butter, and milk. In the mean time, we ordered a *poulard* or two to be roasted, and these wrapped in a napkin were put into the boot of the coach, together with bread, wine, and water. About two or three in the afternoon, while the horses were changing, we laid a cloth upon our knees, and producing our store, with a few earthen plates, discussed our short meal without further ceremony. This was followed by a dessert of grapes and other fruit, which we had also provided. I must own, I found these transient refreshments much more agreeable than any regular meal I ate upon the road. The wine commonly used in Burgundy is so weak and thin, that you would not drink it in England. The very best which they sell at Dijon, the capital of the province, for three livres a bottle, is, in strength, and even in flavour, greatly inferior to what I have drank in London. I believe all the first growth is either consumed in the houses of the *noblesse*, or sent abroad to foreign markets.[3]

Even in Henry James's day you could not be certain of what the fates had in store. In *A Little Tour in France*, he tells of an unhappy visit to Narbonne. It started badly enough when he failed to find a hotel room, but it got far worse:

Finally, at an advanced hour, one of the servants of the Hôtel de France, where I had attempted to dine, came to me in triumph to proclaim that he had secured for me a charming apartment in a *maison bourgeoise*. I took possession of it gratefully, in spite of its having an entrance like a stable and being pervaded by an odour compared with which that of a stable would have been delicious. As I have mentioned, my landlord was a locksmith, and he had strange machines which rumbled and whirred in the rooms below my own. Nevertheless I slept. . . .

I was obliged to cultivate relations with the cuisine of this establishment. Nothing could have been more *méridional*; indeed, both the dirty little inn and Narbonne at large seemed to me to have the infirmities of the south without its usual graces. Narrow, noisy, shabby, belittered and encumbered, filled with clatter and chatter, the Hôtel de France would have been described in perfection by Alphonse Daudet. For what struck me above all in it was the note of the Midi as he has represented it – the sound of universal talk. The landlord sat at supper with sundry friends in a kind of glass cage, with a genial indifference to arriving guests; the waiters tumbled over the loose luggage in the hall; the travellers who had been turned away leaned gloomily against door-posts; and the landlady, surrounded by confusion, unconscious of responsibility, and animated only by the spirit of conversation, bandied high-voiced compliments with the *voyageurs de commerce*. At ten o'clock in the morning there was a table d'hôte for breakfast – a wonderful repast, which overflowed into every room and pervaded the whole establishment. I sat down with a hundred hungry marketers, fat, brown, greasy men, with a good deal of the rich soil of Languedoc adhering to their hands and their boots. I mention the latter articles because they almost put them on the table. It was very hot, and there were swarms of flies; the viands had the strongest odour; there was in particular a horrible mixture known as *gras-double*, a light grey, glutinous, nauseating mess, which my companions devoured in large quantities. A man opposite to me had the dirtiest fingers I ever saw; a collection of fingers which in England would have excluded him from a farmers' ordinary. The conversation was mainly bucolic; though a part of it, I remember, at the table at which I sat, consisted of a discussion as to whether or no the maid-servant were *sage* – a discussion which went on under the nose of this young lady, as she carried about the dreadful *gras-double*, and to which she contributed the most convincing blushes. It was thoroughly *méridional.*[4]

Poor Henry James – for anyone as fastidious as he was, foreign travel must have been almost continual purgatory; one admires him less for writing about it than for doing it in the first place. The time has now come to read of people actually enjoying themselves – and who better than Sybille Bedford, leaving New York by train with a friend, on her way to Mexico. One of the many things I especially enjoy about Mrs. Bedford is her obvious interest in – and profound knowledge of – food and drink; in *A Visit to Don Otavio*, she describes one of the most delicious-sounding train meals on record:

Off at last. I got out a pint of gin, a Thermos with ice-cubes, some Angostura and from a leather case the Woolworth glasses that had long replaced the silver-bound, cut-glass mugs with which our elders travelled about a better world, and made two large pink-gins.

'Did someone tip the boy from Bellows?' said E.

'I didn't. Did you return the book to Mr. Holliday?'

'I forgot. How awful.'

'There is nothing we can do about it now.' What respite, what freedom! We were in someone's anonymous and by assumption capable hands, the Great Eastern and Missouri Railroad's. There'd be four nights of it and almost four days. Four hours upright on a seat are a bore; eight damned long, twelve frightful. A difference in degree is a difference in kind: four days on a train are an armistice with life. And there is always food. I had packed a hamper and a cardboard box. Whenever I can I bring my own provisions; it keeps one independent and agreeably employed, it is cheaper and usually much better. I had got us some tins of tunny fish, a jar of smoked roe, a hunk of salami and a hunk of provolone; some rye bread, and some black bread in Cellophane that keeps. That first night we had fresh food. A chicken, roasted that afternoon at a friend's house, still gently warm; a few slices of that American wonder, Virginia ham; marble-sized, dark red tomatoes from the market stands on Second Avenue; watercress, a flute of bread, a square of cream cheese, a bag of cherries and a bottle of pink wine. It was called Lancer's Sparkling Rosé, and one ought not to be put off by the name. The wine is Portuguese and delicious. A shining, limpid wine, full almost, not growing thin and mean on one in the way of many rosés. It has the further charm of being bottled in an earthenware jug, so that once cooled it stays nicely chilled for hours. I drew the cork with my French Zigzag. The neatest sound on earth.

'Have an olive,' I said.

With a silver clasp-knife I halved the tomatoes. A thread of oil from a phial, two crushed leaves of basil. 'Have you seen the pepper?'

I took the wooden mill from its case. It was filled with truffle-black grains of Tellichery. I snuffed them. That pepper-mill must be the last straw. The gods could not smile on it. A friend once told me about a dachshund who used to be led about the streets of Paris on a red leash. He wore a trim red coat and in the coat was a pocket and out of the pocket peeped a handkerchief with the dachshund's initials. It proved more than canine flesh and blood could stand. He was set upon by a dog without a collar and bitten through the neck. I often felt for that dachshund.[5]

Consider now the cookery of Spain. It too seems to have improved out of all recognition in the past century. Here is Richard Ford, whose *Gatherings from Spain* was published in 1861:

The national cookery of Spain is for the most part Oriental; and the ruling principle of its preparation is *stewing;* for, from a scarcity of fuel, roasting is almost unknown; their notion of which is putting meat into a pan, setting it in hot ashes, and then covering the lid with burning embers. The pot, or *olla,* has accordingly become a synonyme for the dinner of Spaniards, just as beefsteaks or frogs are vulgarly supposed to constitute the whole bill of fare of two other mighty nations. Wherever meats are bad and thin, the sauce is very important; it is based in Spain on oil, garlic, saffron, and red peppers. In hot countries, where beasts are lean, oil supplies the place of fat, as garlic does the want of flavour, while a stimulating condiment excites or curries up the coats of a languid stomach. It has been said of our heretical countrymen that we have but one form of sauce – melted butter – and a hundred different forms of religion, whereas in orthodox Spain there is but one of each, and, as with religion, so to change this sauce would be little short of heresy. As to colour, it carries that rich burnt umber, raw sienna tint, which Murillo imitated so well; and no wonder, since he made his particular brown from baked olla bones, whence it was extracted, as is done to this day by those Spanish painters who indulge in meat. This brown *negro de hueso* colour is the livery of tawny Spain, where all is brown from the *Sierra Morena* to duskier man. Of such hue is his cloak, his terra-cotta house, his wife, his ox, his ass, and everything that is his. This sauce has not only the same colour, but the same flavour everywhere; hence the difficulty of making out the material of which any dish is composed. Not Mrs. Glass herself could tell, by taste at least, whether the ingredients of the cauldron be hare or cat, cow or calf, the aforesaid ox or ass. It puzzles even the acumen of a Frenchman; for it is still the great boast of the town of Olvera that they served up some donkeys as rations to a Buonapartist detachment. All this is very Oriental. Isaac could not distinguish tame kid from wild venison, so perplexing was the disguise of the savoury sauce; and yet his senses of smell and touch were keen, and his suspicions of unfair cooking were awakened. A prudent diner, therefore, except when forced to become his own cook, will never look too closely into the things of the kitchen if he wishes to live a quiet life; for *quien las cosas mucho apura, no vive vida segura.*[6]

And now compare James Morris, who published *The Presence of Spain* in 1964:

This is still a country of local specialities. Wines vary widely from town to town, and so do foods. In San Sebastián they make small pastries designed to look like ham and eggs. In Toledo they make marzipan. Oviedo is famous for its stews, richly compounded of vegetable broth and black pudding, and Vigo for its eel-pies. Segovia is the place for suckling pigs, their forlorn little carcases spread-eagled pink and spongy in the restaurant windows. Seville is the home of *gazpacho*, a delicious cold soup of cucumber, tomato, and miscellaneous garnishings. In Estremadura they feed their pigs on snake-flesh, to improve the quality of the ham. In Aranjuez, near Madrid, they will offer you the best strawberries in Europe, served with a little orange juice and ripe in early March. Only in Catalonia can you eat a proper *zarzuela*, a gargantuan fish soup; only in Valencia will they make you a really superlative *paella*; in only one Spanish town – Soria – have I ever been given fresh-water crayfish.[7]

As a general rule, of course, it can be stated that the more primitive the country, the worse the food – inevitable in a way but unfortunate too, since the greater the hardships that the traveller is called upon to suffer, the more he needs that particular form of sustenance, mental as well as physical, that only a good, palatable square meal – washed down, ideally, by a comforting bottle of wine – can afford. Let me quote once more Belloc's 'The Modern Traveller':

> To turn to more congenial topics,
>   I said a little while ago
>   The food was very much below
> The standard needed to prepare
> Explorers for the special fare
> Which all authorities declare
>   Is needful in the tropics.
> A Frenchman sitting next to us
> Rejected the asparagus;
> The turtle soup was often cold,
> The ices hot, the omelettes old,
> The coffee worse than I can tell;
> And Sin (who had a happy knack
> Of rhyming rapidly and well
> Like Cyrano de Bergerac)
>   Said 'Quant à moi, je n'aime pas
>   Du tout ce pâté de foie gras!'
> But this fastidious taste
> Succeeded in a startling way;
> At Dinner on the following day
>   They gave us Bloater Paste. . . .
>
> And yet I really must complain
> About the Company's Champagne!
>   This most expensive kind of wine
> In England is a matter

Of pride or habit when we dine
    (Presumably the latter).
Beneath an equatorial sky
You *must* consume it or you die;
And stern indomitable men
Have told me, time and time again,
'The nuisance of the tropics is
The sheer necessity of fizz.'[8]

For Fynes Moryson, who never reached the tropics, champagne was fortunately not essential. When travelling between Crete and Constantinople in 1597, however, he managed to do very nicely on Muscadet:

This voyage was more tedious to us, in that howsoever landing we had somtimes good dyet, yet while we were at Sea, we had no good victuals in the ship. For the Greeke Marriners feede of Onions, Garlike, and dried fishes, (one kinde whereof they call Palamides, and the Italians call Palamito) and in stead of a banket, they will give you a head of Garlick rosted in the ashes, and pleasantly call it a pigeon. With this and Bisket they content themselves, and these we were forced to eate, having omitted to provide any dried or salt meates at Candia, because wee hoped to find those in our Barke, and knowing that it was in vaine to provide any fresh meates, because they would not suffer a fier to be made in so small a Barke, wherewith we might dresse them. But after we had eaten Bisket and dried fishes, we had an unknowne comfort or helpe to disgest them. For in our privat cabbin, we had the head of a tun of Muskedine lying under our heads when we slept, in stead of a bolster, and our ship being bound on the upper part of the sides with bundles of Reedes, to beate off the force of the waves, we taking one of the long Reedes, found meanes to pierce the vessell, and get good Wine to our ill fare, and drunke so merrily, that before wee came to our journies end, our former Reede became too short, so as we were faine to piece it with another.[9]

One is not entirely surprised by Moryson's description of the food on board his vessel: the Greeks have never been celebrated for the excellence of their cuisine. On the other hand they can produce several supremely good dishes, and I can remember many a Greek meal which I would not have exchanged for any other in the world. The following passage from my book on *Mount Athos* quotes, in the words of a seventeenth-century English traveller, a description of the best fare that he – or, I suspect, anyone else – ever got on the Holy Mountain; and, in my own, an account of the more usual provender:

The great annual feasts of the Church are punctiliously observed with such ceremony as tradition may dictate. Once a year, too, each monastery celebrates its own individual feast when, after several days of frenzied preparation, official guests from neighbouring houses and any other travellers who may be passing are bidden to join the brothers in the refectory for a meal – an experience from which, if they are strangers to the Mountain, they will not immediately recover.

But feasts on Mount Athos are much less frequent than fasts; and the amount of food consumed per head must be the lowest in Europe. For a start, all the monasteries fast for two months before Easter, a month following Whitsun, a fortnight before the Dormition, another fortnight before the feast of St Peter and St Paul, and forty days before Christmas. To these prolonged periods must be added a considerable number of day-long fasts in honour of various saints; and we are left with the sobering conclusion that Athonite monks subsist, for at least five months a year, at little above starvation level. Moreover, even during the remainder of the year in the cenobitic monasteries, one meal only is provided on Mondays, Wednesdays and Fridays. It is served at noon, and may contain no cheese, butter or oil. In these monasteries eggs and fresh fish (apart from shell-fish and octopus) are reserved for feast-days only; meat is never seen at all. The idiorrhythmics do slightly better, for here the monks eat in their own quarters and can therefore do so as frequently as they wish; but they, too, keep Wednesdays and Fridays as lean days. At other times they may eat meat, but they do so very rarely; it is expensive (since hunting on the Mountain is forbidden by Canon Law), invariably tough, and – in theory at any rate – may not be prepared in monastic kitchens.

Such austerity has not been an invariable rule. The first known English visitor to Mount Athos, Dr John Covel, later Master of Christ's College, Cambridge, wrote rapturously of the delicacies offered to him at the Lavra in 1677: '. . . the best monkish fare that could be gotten was provided, excellent fish (severall ways), oyl, salet, beanes, hortechokes, beets, chees, onions, garlick, olives, caveor, Pyes of herbs, φακαίς, κτωπόδι, pepper, salt and saffron in all. At last conserved little oranges, most exquisite, good wine (a sort of small claret) and we alwayes drank most plentifully. . . . He is no Greek that cannot drink twenty or thirty plump glasses at a setting.' Covel, be it said, was a man of adventurous palate, a fact which he proved at Vatopedi where 'they gave us Limpets thrice as big as oures in England and yellow, all cover'd with a fat yellow mosse which they eat either alone or with oil; and tast well'. A Dr Hunt, who early in the last century was invited to dine with Gregorios V, the exiled Patriarch of Constantinople, fared better still. 'The hour of dinner was 9 o'clock in the morning; we found his table furnished in a style quite unconventual, with lamb, sausages, hams and French wines. His dispensing power seems to remain although he is dethroned; and seven or eight of the salad-fed monks who dined with us appeared to be much pleased with their change of diet. . . . His conversation seemed to indicate that he looked forward to be reinstated in his honours.'

Gregorios did in fact return soon afterwards to Constantinople – but not for long. In the spring of 1821 news of the Greek rising reached the Porte; on Easter morning, by order of the Sultan, he was publicly hanged over the main gate of his Patriarchate and a massacre of thirty thousand Greeks followed. But that is a story that does not concern us here. Rather let us return to Athonite food, a subject of inexhaustible fascination on which scarcely any writer with first-hand experience of the Holy Mountain has forborne to comment. Few of these comments, it must be said, have been as favourable as those quoted above; and today there can be no question about it – any visit to Athos spells gastronomic martyrdom. For the first few meals, while courage and self-discipline remain steady, a person of normal digestive sensibility may be able to contemplate – and even, in part, consume – the interminable platefuls of beans, spasmodically enlivened by a single slice of anchovy or a slab of briny cheese, which, if the monasteries had their way, would stand alone between himself and starvation. But on such a diet the spirit soon flags. Within a day or two those liverish-white lumps, glaring remorselessly up at him from their puddle of stone-cold grease, take on a new expression, hostile and challenging. 'Bet you can't,' they seem to say. And they are right.

Thus, even more than its inexpressible nastiness, it is the uniformity of the monastic menu that wears one down. The memory gratefully cherishes an omelette at Karakallou; Lavra noodles; and once, at Chilandar, a perfectly splendid fish. It also returns to an evening at Dionysiou on my first visit, when we caught an octopus and were promised it for breakfast. Alas, we were disappointed; it was hung up for the night, like an apron, behind the kitchen door and the cat had got most of it by morning. But these occasions are exceptional. Over all normal meals those unrelenting beans will continue to cast their baleful spell; and the visitor will feel more and more like a refractory child who, having refused its lunch, finds itself confronted with the same grim offering, congealed, at supper. Now at last he will fully appreciate the old custom of cenobitic monasteries according to which, as the monks pass out of the refectory, the cooks ask pardon on their knees for the atrociousness of the meal; now, too, he will begin to understand why, among all the ascetic disciplines of the Mountain, that of almost continuous fasting is so insistently stressed.[10]

Even then, I have to admit that the Hon. Robert Curzon, visiting Athos in 1834, had a harder time of it than I ever did:

I was informed that no female animal of any sort or kind is admitted on any part of the peninsula of Mount Athos; and that since the days of Constantine the soil of the Holy Mountain had never been contaminated by the tread of a woman's foot. That this rigid law is infringed by certain small and active creatures who have the audacity to bring their wives and large families within the very precincts of the monastery I soon discovered to my sorrow, and heartily regretted that the stern monastic law was not more rigidly enforced; nevertheless, I slept well on my divan, and the next morning at sunrise received a visit from the agoumenos, who came to wish me good-day. After some conversation on other matters, I inquired about the library, and asked permission to view its contents. The agoumenos declared his willingness to show me everything that the monastery contained. 'But first,' said he, 'I wish to present you with something excellent for your breakfast; and from the special goodwill that I bear towards so distinguished a guest I shall prepare it with my own hands, and will stay to see you eat it; for it is really an admirable dish, and one not presented to all persons.' 'Well,' thought I, 'a good breakfast is not a bad thing;' and the fresh mountain-air and the good night's rest had given me an appetite; so I expressed my thanks for the kind hospitality of my lord abbot, and he, sitting down opposite to me on the divan, proceeded to prepare his dish. 'This,' said he, producing a shallow basin half-full of a white paste, 'is the principal and most savoury part of this famous dish; it is composed of cloves of garlic, pounded down, with a certain quantity of sugar. With it I will now mix the oil in just proportions, some shreds of fine cheese (it seemed to be of the white acid kind, which resembles what is called caccia cavallo in the south of Italy, and which almost takes the skin off your fingers, I believe), and sundry other nice little condiments, and now it is completed!' He stirred the savoury mess round and round with a large wooden spoon until it sent forth over room and passage and cell, over hill and valley, an aroma which is not to be described. 'Now,' said the agoumenos, crumbling some bread into it with his large and somewhat dirty hands, 'this is a dish for an emperor! Eat, my friend, my much-respected guest; do not be shy. Eat; and when you have finished the bowl you shall go into the library and anywhere else you like; but you shall go nowhere till I have had the pleasure of seeing you do justice to this delicious food, which, I can assure you, you will not meet with everywhere.'

I was sorely troubled in spirit. Who could have expected so dreadful a martyrdom as this? The sour apple of the hermit down below was nothing – a trifle in comparison! Was ever an unfortunate bibliomaniac dosed with such a medicine before? It would have been enough to have cured the whole Roxburghe Club from meddling with libraries and books for ever and ever. I made every endeavour to escape this honour. 'My Lord,' said I, 'it is a fast; I cannot this morning do justice to this delicious viand; it is a fast; and I am under a vow. Englishmen must not eat that dish in this month. It would be wrong; my conscience won't permit it, though the odour certainly is most wonderful! Truly an astonishing savour! Let me see you eat it, O agoumenos!' continued I; 'for behold, I am unworthy of anything so good!' 'Excellent and virtuous young man!' said the agoumenos, 'no, I will not eat it. I will not deprive you of this treat. Eat it in peace; for know, that to travellers all such vows are set aside. On a journey it is permitted to eat all that is set before you, unless it is meat that is offered to idols. I admire your scruples: but be not afraid, it is lawful. Take it, my honoured friend, and eat it: eat it all, and then we will go into the library.' He put the bowl into one of my hands and the great wooden spoon into the other: and in desperation I took a gulp, the recollection of which still makes me tremble. What was to be done? Another mouthful was an impossibility: not all my ardour in the pursuit of manuscripts could give me the necessary courage. I was overcome with sorrow and despair. My servant saved me at last; he said 'that English gentlemen never ate such rich dishes for breakfast, from religious feelings, he believed; but he requested that it might be put by, and he was sure I should like it very much later in the day.' The agoumenos looked vexed, but he applauded my principles; and just then the board sounded for church. 'I must be off, excellent and worthy English lord,' said he; 'I will take you to the library, and leave you the key. Excuse my attendance on you there, for my presence is required in the church.' So I got off better than I expected; but the taste of that ladleful stuck to me for days.[11]

From Greece it is but a short step to Turkey, where the food is in my experience much the same only rather better. Mark Twain, if we are to judge from what he wrote in *The Innocents Abroad*, was somewhat less impressed:

I never shall want another Turkish lunch. The cooking apparatus was in the little lunch room, near the bazaar, and it was all open to the street. The cook was slovenly, and so was the table, and it had no cloth on it. The fellow took a mass of sausage-meat and coated it round a wire and laid it on a charcoal fire to cook. When it was done, he laid it aside and a dog walked sadly in and nipped it. He smelt it first, and probably recognised the remains of a friend. The cook took it away from him and laid it before us. Jack said, 'I pass' – he plays euchre sometimes – and we all passed in turn. Then the cook baked a broad, flat, wheaten cake, greased it well with the sausage, and started towards us with it. It dropped in the dirt, and he picked it up and polished it on his breeches, and laid it before us. Jack said, 'I pass.' We all passed. He put some eggs in a frying-pan, and stood pensively prying slabs of meat from between his teeth with a fork. Then he used the fork to turn the eggs with – and brought them along. Jack said 'Pass again.' All followed suit. We did not know what to do, and so we ordered a new ration of sausage. The cook got out his wire, apportioned a proper amount of sausage-meat, spat it on his hands and fell to work! This time, with one accord, we all passed out. We paid and left. That is all I learned about Turkish lunches. A Turkish lunch is good, no doubt, but it has its little drawbacks.[12]

In 1846, Messrs Chapman & Hall published a volume entitled *Notes of a Journey from Cornhill to Grand Cairo, By Way of Lisbon, Athens, Constantinople and Jerusalem*. The author was one 'M. A. Titmarsh', who was later revealed to be none other than William Makepeace Thackeray. The tone is for the most part quite embarrassingly facetious, and Thackeray's pawky brand of humour nowadays strikes one as being about as funny as an old *Punch* cartoon; but his description of his visit to the great kitchens in the Palace of Topkapi is worth including none the less:

The kitchens are the most sublime part of the seraglio. There are nine of these great halls, for all ranks, from his highness downwards; where many hecatombs are roasted daily, according to the accounts; and where cooking goes on with a savage Homeric grandeur. Chimneys are despised in these primitive halls; so that the roofs are black with the smoke of hundreds of furnaces, which escapes through apertures in the domes above. These, too, give the chief light in the rooms, which streams downwards, and thickens and mingles with the smoke, and so murkily lights up hundreds of swarthy figures busy about the spits and the cauldrons. Close to the door by which we entered, they were making pastry for the sultanas; and the chief pastrycook, who knew my guide, invited us courteously to see the process, and partake of the delicacies prepared for those charming lips. How those sweet lips must shine after eating these puffs! First, huge sheets of dough are rolled out till the paste is about as thin as silver paper: then an artist forms the dough-muslin into a sort of drapery, curling it round and round in many fanciful and pretty shapes, until it is all got into the circumference of a round metal tray in which it is baked. Then the cake is drenched in grease most profusely; and, finally, a quantity of syrup is poured over it, when the delectable mixture is complete. The moon-faced ones are said to devour immense quantities of this wholesome food; and, in fact, are eating grease and sweetmeats from morning till night. I don't like to think what the consequences may be, or allude to the agonies which the delicate creatures must inevitably suffer.

The good-natured chief pastrycook filled a copper basin with greasy puffs; and, dipping a dubious ladle into a large cauldron, containing several gallons of syrup, poured a liberal portion over the cakes, and invited us to eat. One of the tarts was quite enough for me; and I excused myself on the plea of ill health from imbibing any more grease and sugar. But my companion, the dragoman, finished some forty puffs in a twinkling. They slipped down his opened jaws as the sausages do down Clown's throat in a pantomime. His moustachios shone with grease, and it dripped down his beard and fingers. We thanked the smiling chief pastrycook, and rewarded him handsomely for the tarts. It is something to have eaten of the dainties prepared for the ladies of the harem; but I think Mr. Cockle ought to get the names of the chief sultanas among the exalted patrons of his Antibilious Pills.[13]

At this point in the book, some readers may be conscious of a mild but increasing feeling of surprise at the continued non-appearance of that prince of oriental travellers, Sir Richard Burton. (Even in his life-time he was renowned for his unpunctuality.) Let me now belatedly introduce him, the first British non-Muslim ever to visit Mecca, dining in the Holy City in 1853:

Before leaving Meccah I was urgently invited to dine by old Ali bin Ya Sin, the Zemzemi; a proof that he entertained inordinate expectations, excited, it appeared, by the boy Mohammed, for the simple purpose of exalting his own dignity. One day we were hurriedly summoned about three p.m. to the senior's house, a large building in the Zukak al-Hajar. We found it full of pilgrims, amongst whom we had no trouble to recognise our fellow-travellers, the quarrelsome old Arnaut and his impudent slave-boy. Ali met us upon the staircase, and conducted us into an upper room, where we sat upon diwans, and with pipes and coffee prepared for dinner. Presently the semicircle arose to receive a eunuch, who lodged somewhere in the house. He was a person of importance, being the guardian of some dames of high degree at Cairo and Constantinople: the highest place and the best pipe were unhesitatingly offered to and accepted by him. He sat down with dignity, answered diplomatically certain mysterious questions about the dames, and applied his blubber lips to a handsome mouthpiece of lemon-coloured amber. It was a fair lesson of humility for a man to find himself ranked beneath this high-shouldered, spindle-shanked, beardless bit of neutrality; and as such I took it duly to heart.

The dinner was served up in a *Sini*, a plated copper tray about six feet in circumference, and handsomely ornamented with arabesques and inscriptions. Under this was the usual *Kursi*, or stool, composed of mother-o'-pearl facets set in sandalwood; and upon it a well-tinned and clean-looking service of the same material as the *Sini*. We began with a variety of stews – stews with spinach, stews with *Bamiyah* (hibiscus), and rich vegetable stews. These being removed, we dipped hands in *Biryani*, a meat pillaw, abounding in clarified butter; *Kimah*, finely chopped meat; *Warak Mahshi*, vine leaves filled with chopped and spiced mutton, and folded into small triangles; *Kabab*, or bits of rôti spitted in mouthfuls upon a splinter of wood; together with a *Salatah* of the crispest cucumber, and various dishes of water-melon cut up into squares.

Bread was represented by the Eastern scone, but it was of superior flavour, and far better than the ill-famed Chapati of India. Our drink was water perfumed with mastic. After the meat came a *Kunafah*, fine vermicelli sweetened with honey, and sprinkled with powdered white sugar; several stews of apples and quinces; *Muhallibah*, a thin jelly made of rice, flour, milk, starch, and a little perfume; together with squares of *Rahah*,* a confiture highly prized in these regions, because it comes from Constantinople. Fruits were then placed upon the table; plates full of pomegranate grains and dates of the finest flavour. The dinner concluded with a pillaw of rice and butter, for the easier discussion of which we were provided with carved wooden spoons.

Arabs ignore the delightful French art of prolonging a dinner. After washing your hands, you sit down, throw an embroidered napkin over your knees, and with a 'Bismillah,' by way of grace, plunge your hand into the attractive dish, changing *ad libitum*, occasionally sucking your fingertips as boys do lollipops, and varying that diversion by cramming a chosen morsel into a friend's mouth. When your hunger is satisfied, you do not sit for your companions; you exclaim 'Al Hamd!' edge away from the tray, wash your hands and mouth with soap, display signs of repletion, otherwise you will be pressed to eat more, seize your pipe, sip your coffee, and take your 'Kayf.' Nor is it customary, in these lands, to sit together after dinner – the evening prayer cuts short the *séance*.[14]

Beduin food is, naturally, a good deal less sophisticated, though the manner of tackling it has always been much the same. Here Gavin Maxwell, in *A Reed Shaken by the Wind*, describes what can normally be expected:

Eating in the Arab manner requires to be learnt, and at the beginning I found it humiliatingly impossible. The *pièce de résistance* of all meals is the same, a conical mountain of rice which is often two feet across and a foot high, and its manipulation is not easily mastered. The guests sit cross-legged on the floor before one or more of these mountains, round which, in a sheikh's *mudhif*, are usually ranged bowls of gravy, mutton, whole small chickens, and plates of a thin greyish gelatinous substance tasting like the smell of scented soap. All this is to be eaten with the hand, and the right hand only, though the left may be used to hold a chicken while the right pulls the carcase apart. Any Arab host worthy of the name will kill chickens – worth about four shillings each – for his guests, and a hospitable sheikh will sometimes kill a sheep, whose boiled and nauseous head is placed among the other dishes to announce the fact. Pieces of flesh from the ears, the hair still attached, are esteemed as a delicacy, and hospitable fingers explore for a guest the gums and palate, producing strips and morsels which would be appetising if the head were not staring at the eater with those dreadful boiled eyes.

I have found in Desmond Stewart's *New Babylon* an Arab proverb which I did not know when I was in Iraq, and which would have explained a great deal to me

---

* Familiar for 'Rahat al-Hulkum,' – the pleasure of the throat, – a name which has sorely puzzled our tourists [who nowadays know it better as Turkish Delight (J.J.N.)]. This sweetmeat would be pleasant did it not smell so strongly of the perruquier's shop. Rosewater tempts to many culinary sins in the East; and Europeans cannot dissociate it from the idea of a lotion. However, if a guest is to be honoured, rosewater must often take the place of the pure element, even in tea.

if I had: 'Eat like a camel and be the first to finish.' Every meal is, indeed, a sort of eating race, and each man crams himself feverishly, in a silence unbroken but for champing jaws and an occasional belch. Whatever the embellishments, the rice is the main meal. One pours a little gravy over the claim one has staked on the mountain slope, and digs in a fist. This should be done with the back of the hand uppermost and the thumb on the palm; the fingers enclose the rice, and when the hand reaches the mouth the thumb pushes the rice up into it – if, that is to say, there is any rice left to push.

That first evening, I found, there rarely was. The mere fact of being cross-legged made the rice a disconcertingly long way off, and no matter how large a handful I set out with, so to speak, it had dwindled to a few grains by the time the hand reached the mouth. Such of the intervening space as was not occupied by my lap was covered by a section of the gigantic waterproof floor-cloth that the servants had spread before laying the meal; on to this resonant surface the rice from my hand pattered and plopped like a hail shower. I began to cheat wildly, pouring on more gravy and squeezing the rice into adhesive balls in my palm; for the first week this, though an acknowledgment of defeat, was the only method I found possible.

When the eating race was over – and Thesiger, who had introduced among his own men the Bedouin custom of rising simultaneously, was an easy winner – it became clear that, however efficient were the other contestants, there were many messy feeders among them, for on the great cloth lay several pounds of scattered rice among the bones and other discarded litter.

Eventually I became able to eat rice quickly and efficiently, without spilling a grain; but to the end, though I could detect no difference between my handling of it and theirs, the Arabs insisted that I was somehow doing it wrong.

When one has eaten, one's right hand is necessarily covered in rice and dripping oily gravy, and it is quite in order to clean the hand by licking it. If, however, a chicken has been part of the menu, the left hand, which has been allowed to hold while the right hand mauls, is equally covered with gravy and fragments; and to me it proved practically impossible to remember that if one is licking one food-covered hand one may not lick the other.[15]

Even Wilfred Thesiger himself, toughest of the tough and with a lifetime of experience of the East, admits (in *The Marsh Arabs*) to an occasional twinge of misgiving:

It was useless to worry about the diseases I might catch, but sometimes it was more difficult not to feel squeamish about the food and water. Two occasions in particular upset me, both in the middle of summer when I was travelling on horseback among the cultivators north of the Marshes. On the first I had followed a shallow irrigation ditch for several miles towards the village that was my destination. The ditch contained a foot or two of water flowing sluggishly in the same direction. I passed a dead dog lying in it and farther on a dead buffalo calf; the skin had soaked off its ribs. Both smelt horribly. Near the village, the edge of the ditch was foul, since Arabs always try to defecate near water so as to be able to wash afterwards. The *mudhif* was on the edge of the ditch, and the water there was almost stagnant under a covering of green slime. Even they won't drink that, I thought.

I arrived in the middle of a grilling afternoon. They brought me a drink from the pitcher at the end of the room and it tasted cold and fresh. Hearing I was there, many people came to the *mudhif*, some just sociably inclined, others wanting treatment. After the usual courtesies, I moved outside into the shadow of the building, where I operated, injected and distributed medicines. There was a slight breeze but it was still unbearably hot, for in summer the temperature on these plains rises to over 120° in the shade. Needing more water, I gave a bowl to a boy to fetch some. Seeing him go to the ditch I called impatiently, 'No, not that filthy stuff, bring me some clean water from the *mudhif*,' which he did, after giving me a surprised look. Later, I watched the pitcher being filled again from the ditch and reflected unhappily that I had agreed to remain another day.

On the second occasion, I was staying with a sheikh who was a friend of mine. I had arrived at his village the evening before and the usual crowd of patients turned up early next morning. It was stiflingly hot and humid, with never a breath of air. Even sitting still, the sweat trickled down my face and body. The sheikh, a hospitable old man, killed a sheep to feed his guests who by now were a hundred or more. Four men, one of them a large black slave, staggered into the room, bent double with the weight of a copper dish, four feet across and heaped with rice, on top of which was a boiled sheep, with lolling tongue and soggy eyes. As they carried the dish in, the sweat was dripping off their noses and chins on to the rice, and I knew they must have carried it like that a distance of a hundred yards or more. Pouring a bowl of liquid butter over the rice, the sheikh turned to us. 'Welcome, welcome to my guests. Today is a blessed day.'

As I sat down to the dish he said, 'Now, Sahib, the more you like me, the more you will eat!'[16]

In the Arab world, class scarcely exists; a very different system, however, is – or was – to be found in Abyssinia, when Mansfield Parkyns was there in the middle of the last century. There, questions of precedence were all-important; and where precedence stopped, favouritism took over. The unhappy traveller could only pray that he would be neither preferred nor favoured:

The nobler guests are first seated and eat of the finest bread; then those of humbler rank take their places and partake of the second class of bread; and so on in succession till the coarsest is eaten by the servants and poor friends. The cakes supply the place of napkins, as the fingers of the guests are frequently wiped on them after being dipped in the dish or rendered bloody by the raw meat. This, however, does not in the least affect the appetites of those who, coming after, have to eat them. The company being assembled, the most distinguished personages are requested to be seated, and are placed according to their rank by the 'Shelika zifàn beyt' or 'Agafàri Adderash,' two dignitaries of whose duties, &c., we will more fully speak in the proper place. A good deal of politeness sometimes ensues as to precedence, but, all being at last settled down in their places, the 'soub-hè' or cooked dishes are brought in by the cook women, each of whom receives a piece of bread dipped in the dish she has carried. These are placed on the table according to their quality, the best nearest the top; and the 'asalafy,' or waiters, take a piece of bread from before each person, and, sopping it in the sauce, return it to him. They also serve the guests with meat from the dishes, cutting, or with their fingers tearing it into pieces of a convenient size; and in doing this they frequently show great favouritism, giving the kidneys and tit-bits to one, and the gristle and bones to another. They are very attentive, never allowing any one to be a moment unsupplied. The guests take their bread and sauce and mix them together into a sort of paste, of which they make balls, long and rounded like small black puddings: these they consider it polite to poke into the mouths of their neighbours; so that, if you happen to be a distinguished character, or a stranger to whom they wish to pay attention, which often was my case, you are in a very disagreeable position; for your two neighbours, one on each side, cram into your mouth these large and peppery proofs of their esteem so quickly one after the other, that, long before you can chew and swallow the one, you are obliged to make room for the next. They generally succeed in half choking you; and if you feel you are losing the skin of your mouth, lips, and throat from the fiery effects of the pepper, you dare not ask for water, as that would be considered rude; and the mead is seldom served till the dinner is over. While these dishes, which are generally made of mutton, are on the table, the cow is killed and flayed outside; and immediately on their removal the 'broundo' is brought in, each servant carrying a yet quivering lump in his hands. The choicest pieces are carried to the highest tables, where are seated the master of the feast and the most distinguished guests. There is usually a piece of meat to every five or six persons, among whom arises some show of ceremony as to which of them shall first help himself; this being at length decided, the person chosen takes hold of the meat with his left hand, and with his sword or knife cuts a strip a foot or fifteen inches long from the part which appears the nicest and tenderest. The others then help themselves in like manner.[17]

No wonder that after three years of this sort of thing Mr Parkyns allowed himself his little fantasies:

When you have been for years in a strange land, where you scarcely ever see a white face, and never perhaps meet a single fellow-countryman, with whom to hold sweet converse in your mother-tongue, will not the thoughts of home – of those you have left behind, fond scenes, friends, and relatives – sometimes present themselves? Who can doubt it? Surely, then, I may be excused for entertaining fond wishes and recollections of the past. Often, very often, in those dreary solitudes, have I wished for oysters and porter. After much experimenting, I discovered that a raw sheep's liver, if cut up in small pieces and nicely arranged in a spoon, and well peppered and vinegared, with a little salt, was by no means a bad substitute for an oyster; and while eating this preparation I have sometimes shut my eyes, and almost cheated myself into the belief that I was again in England.[18]

And now, two tales from Tartary. The first is told by our old friend the Abbé Huc, on his way with his fellow-Lazarist M. Gabet from China to Tibet:

After a brief silence, the old man went on: 'Holy personages, whatever may be the associations of this day, in other respects it is truly a festival for us, since you have deigned to enter our poor habitation. Let us not further occupy our breasts with sad thoughts. Child,' said he to a young man seated on the threshold of the tent, 'if the mutton is boiled enough, clear away these things.' This command having been executed, the eldest son of the family entered, bearing in both hands a small oblong table, on which was a boiled sheep, cut into four quarters, heaped one on the other. The family being assembled round the table, the chief drew a knife from his girdle, severed the sheep's tail, and divided it into two equal pieces, which he placed before us.

With the Tartars, the tail is considered the most delicious portion of their sheep, and accordingly the most honourable. These tails of the Tartarian sheep are of immense size and weight, the fat upon them alone weighing from six to eight pounds.

The fat and juicy tail having thus been offered a homage to the two stranger guests, the rest of the company, knife in hand, attacked the four quarters of the animal, and had speedily, each man, a huge piece before him. Plate or fork there was none, the knees supplied the absence of the one, the hands of the other, the flowing grease being wiped off, from time to time, upon the front of the jacket. Our own embarrassment was extreme. That great white mass of fat had been given to us with the best intentions, but, not quite clear of European prejudices, we could not make up our stomachs to venture, without bread or salt, upon the lumps of tallow that quivered in our hands. We briefly consulted, in our native tongue, as to what on earth was to be done under these distressing circumstances. Furtively, to replace the horrible masses upon the table would be imprudent; openly to express to our Amphytrion our repugnance to this *par excellence* Tartarian delicacy, was impossible, as wholly opposed to Tartar etiquette. We devised this plan: we cut the villanous tail into numerous pieces, and insisted, in that day of general rejoicing, upon the company's partaking with us of this precious dish. There was infinite reluctance to deprive us of the treat; but we persisted, and by degrees got entirely clear of the abominable mess, ourselves rejoicing, instead, in a cut from the leg, the savour of which was more agreeable to our early training.[19]

The second is from *My Journey to Lhasa* by Alexandra David-Neel. She and Yongden, her companion and adopted son, are disguised as poor pilgrims:

The thing which proved most tiresome, and even at times became excessively difficult in the life I was now leading, was the part that I was always obliged to play in order to preserve my incognito. In a country where everything is done in public, down to the most intimate personal acts, I was forced to affect peculiar local customs which embarrassed me terribly. Happily, our way lay at times through large tracts of uninhabited land, and the greater freedom which I enjoyed there somewhat relieved my painful nervous tension. There, especially, I was able to avoid the indescribable soups which the kindly but poverty-stricken fellows, our hosts, bestowed upon us, and which we had to swallow down with a smile, for fear of suspicious comments. Once only did I depart from my accustomed attitude of the beggar to whom everything tastes good, but that day! . . .

We have arrived toward nightfall in a little village. It was very cold and the stark surroundings afforded no shelter. We had already been refused hospitality at several houses, when a woman opened her door to us – the rickety door of an exceedingly miserable dwelling. We entered; a fire burned on the hearth, and in this frosty weather this in itself afforded comfort. The husband of the woman came back shortly afterwards, bringing out some handfuls of *tsampa* from the bottom of a beggar's wallet, and we realised that no supper could be expected from people who had nothing to eat themselves. After a few words of praise for the generosity of an imaginary thief who has given him a rupee, Yongden declares that he will buy some meat, if there is any to be had in the village.

'I know of a good place,' said our host at once, scenting a windfall. From the corner where I was crouching, I insisted that it should be of good quality. Most Thibetans eat without any repugnance the putrefied flesh of animals which have died of disease.

'Do not bring back the flesh of an animal which has died, nor a piece which is decayed,' I said.

'No, no,' said the man. 'I know what I am about. You shall have something good.'

About ten minutes passed. The village is not large, and the peasant soon returned.

'There,' he said, triumphantly, drawing a large parcel of some kind from beneath his sheepskin robe.

What can this be? . . . The room is lighted only by the embers of the fire, and I cannot clearly distinguish anything. . . . The man seems to be opening something, probably a cloth which he has wrapped round his purchase.

Ugh! . . . A most fearsome odour suddenly fills the room, the smell of a charnel-house. It is sickening.

'Oh,' says Yongden, in a voice that trembles slightly, concealing the nausea that he is obliged to repress. 'Oh, it is a stomach!'

I understand now. The Thibetans, when they kill a beast, have a horrible habit of enclosing in the stomach, the kidneys, heart, liver, and entrails of the animal. They then sew up this kind of bag, and its contents go on decaying inside for days, weeks, and even longer.

'Yes, it is a stomach,' repeats its purchaser, whose voice also trembles somewhat, but with joy, seeing the mass of foodstuff falling out of the now opened bag. 'It is full,' he exclaims, 'quite full! Oh, what a lot!'

He has placed the horror on the floor, is plunging his hands into it, taking out the gelatinous entrails. Three children who were asleep on a heap of tatters have awakened, and are now squatting in front of their father, watching him eagerly with covetous eyes.

'Yes . . . yes, a stomach!' repeats Yongden, in consternation.

'Here, mother, here is a saucepan,' says the woman, kindly, addressing me: 'You can prepare your supper.'

What! Am I to handle this filth? I whisper hastily to my son, 'Tell them that I am ill.'

'It always seems your turn to be ill when something unpleasant befalls us,' Yongden growls, under his breath. But the boy is resourceful; he has already regained his self-possession.

'The old mother is ill,' he announces. 'Why do you not make the *tupa* [thick soup] yourselves? I want everybody to have a share.'

The two peasants do not wait to be invited a second time, and the youngsters, realizing that a feast is in course of preparation, stay quietly by the fire, having no desire to go to sleep again. The mother takes up a chopper and a rustic chopping-block made out of a log, on which she cuts the carrion into small pieces. From time to time one of these drops upon the floor, and then the children fall upon it like young puppies and devour it raw.

Now this foul soup is boiling, and a little barley meal is added. Finally the supper is ready.

'Take some, mother; it will do you good,' say the husband and wife. I confine myself to groaning, in the corner where I have stretched myself.

'Let her sleep,' says Yongden.

He cannot himself be excused. *Arjopas* who spend a rupee on meat and do not touch it do not exist. To-morrow the whole village would be taking about it. He has to swallow down a full bowl of the evil-smelling liquid, but beyond that he cannot go, and he declares that he, too, is not feeling very well. I do not wonder at it. The others feast long and gluttonously upon the broth, smacking their lips in silence, overcome with joy at this unexpected *bonne bouche*, and I am overtaken by sleep whilst the family is still masticating noisily.[20]

Peter Fleming has a nasty little story, too, which he tells in *One's Company*. The scene is the village of Pingshek in South China, a little way up the Pei river from Canton:

We got a room opening on to the stone roof of the inn, on which I slept under an enormous moon; the small white forts stood up out of a nacreous haze which hung low above the river and shone as if they had been made of silver. Although the local wine was good, the dinner was the worst of the journey – so bad, indeed, that it took me half a minute's mastication to discover that a morsel, selected with chop-sticks in an uncertain light, was in fact the left claw of a chicken. At this we lodged a complaint and the proprietress, a woman of spirit, beat her cook over the head with a stool. The dish was sent down again to the kitchen. On its return it was found to contain, among other things, the chicken's beak. After that we gave it up.[21]

My penultimate offering is an extract from *Letters from Iceland*, a curious mish-mash of a book, compiled rather than written, by W. H. Auden and Louis MacNeice after a visit there in the 1930s. In a chapter entitled 'For Tourists' we read:

Soups: Many of these are sweet and very unfortunate. I remember three with particular horror, one of sweet milk and hard macaroni, one tasting of hot marzipan, and one of scented hair oil. (But there is a good sweet soup, raspberry coloured, made of bilberry. L. M.)

Fish: Dried fish is a staple food in Iceland. This should be shredded with the fingers and eaten with butter. It varies in toughness. The tougher kind tastes like toe-nails, and the softer kind like the skin off the soles of one's feet.

In districts where salmon are caught, or round the coast, you get excellent fish, the grilled salmon particularly.

Meat: This is practically confined to mutton in various forms. The Danes have influenced Icelandic cooking, and to no advantage. Meat is liable to be served up in glutinous and half-cold lumps, covered with tasteless gravy. At the poorer farms you will only get Hángikyrl, *i.e.* smoked mutton. This is comparatively harmless when cold as it only tastes like soot, but it would take a very hungry man indeed to eat it hot. . . .

Oddities

For the curious there are two Icelandic foods which should certainly be tried. One is Hákarl, which is half-dry, half-rotten shark. This is white inside with a prickly horn rind outside, as tough as an old boot. Owing to the smell it has to be eaten out of doors. It is shaved off with a knife and eaten with brandy. It tastes more like boot-polish than anything else I can think of. The other is Reyngi. This is the tail of the whale, which is pickled in sour milk for a year or so. If you intend to try it, do not visit a whaling station first. Incidentally, talking about pickling in sour milk, the Icelanders also do this to sheeps' udders, and the result is surprisingly very nice.[22]

No pair of countries in the world could be more dissimilar than Iceland and Burma. And yet that intrepid cyclist John Foster Fraser, author of *Round the World on a Wheel*, found not far from Mandalay a dish that would, one imagines, have made any wandering Icelander feel very much at home:

In time we got to Fyaukmyaung, or Kyoukmoung, or anything you care to call it, but notorious a year or two back for being looted by the dacoits. We were a little tired of a rice diet, and Lowe in his innocence suggested a fish dinner. The idea was brilliant, but it nearly killed the three of us. We had eaten frogs' legs in France, and regarded with equanimity the consumption of spring puppies in China. Therefore a feed of Burmese *nga-pee* was appropriate.

When we had recovered from our illness we investigated how the food was prepared. First of all the fish were caught and laid in the sun for three days to dry. The fish being then dead, though moving, were pounded in plenty of salt. Then they were put into a jar, and when the mouth was opened people five miles away knew all about it. *Nga-pee*, I soon saw, was a delicacy that could only be appreciated by cultured palates. The taste is original; it is salt, rather like rancid butter flavoured with Limburger cheese, garlic, and paraffin oil. The odour is more interesting than the taste. It is more conspicuous.[23]

CHAPTER NINETEEN

Bad Moments

On 13 February 1599 Master Thomas Dallam, a London organ-builder, set
sail on board the *Hector* from Gravesend. He was bound for Constantinople,
and was taking with him a magnificent instrument of his own construction as
a present from Queen Elizabeth to Sultan Mehmet III. The ship did not make
very good time: on 9 August it was still beating up the northern coast of the
Sea of Marmara when rough weather forced it to take shelter, and its passengers found themselves in the little Greek village of Ganos, obliged to seek a
night's lodging as best they could. Deciding, as Dallam puts it in his account
of the journey, that 'the condetion[*sic*] of the people was not to our lykinge',
they eventually found a house outside the village, 'upon the verrie brinke
or end of the hill, beinge the heighte of St Paules Churche a bove [*sic*] the
sea; and we weare to go up a ladder into a gallarie . . . and thare was a little
dowre to go into the roume wheare we shoulde lodge upon the bare bordes.'
    Only in the middle of the night did the trouble start:

Growinge towards nyghte, and rememberinge whate hard lodginge we should
have in our new In, findinge a thicke softe weed, that growed by the wood sid,
everrie one of us that was thare gathered a bundle of it to laye under our heades,
when we should sleepe.
    Nyghte beinge come, and our supper ended, everie man chalked out his ristinge
place upon the bare bordes; our jenisarie placed him selfe upon a borde that laye
louse upon the joistes. Everie man had his Sorde reddie Drawne lyinge by his side;
tow of our company had musketes. When we had layne about halfe an houre, we
that had our weeden pillowes weare sodonly wonderfully tormented with a varmen
that was in our pillowes, the which did bite farr worss than fleaes, so that we weare
glad to throw awaye our pillowes, and swepe the house cleane; but we could not
clense our selves so sowne. Thus as we laye wakinge in a Darke uncomfortable
house, Mr. Glover tould us what strainge varmen and beastes he had sene in that
contrie, for he had lived longe thare. He spoake verrie muche of Aderes, snaykes,
and sarpentes, the defferance and the bignes of som which he had sene.
    Passinge awaye the time with such lyke talke, the moste parte of us fell a sleepe,
and som that could not sleepe laye still and sayd nothinge for disquietinge of the
reste, all beinge whyshte. Mr. Baylye had occasion to goe to the dore to make
water, the dore was verrie litle, and opened very straitly into the gallarie, the wynde
blowed marvalus strongly, and made a greate noyse, for the house lay verrie open

340

to the sea and wether. Mr. Baylle, when he lay downe to sleepe, had untied his garters a litle, so that when he came into the gallarie, the wynde blew his garter, that was louse and trayled after him, rounde aboute the other legge; it was a greate silke garter, and by the force of the wynde it fettered his legges bothe faste together. Our talk a litle before, of Aders, snakes, and sarpentes, was yeat in his rememberance, and the place was neare wheare muche varmen was. He thoughte they had swarmed aboute him, but aboute his legges he Thought he was sur of a sarpente, so that soddonly he cried oute with all the voyce he hade: A sarpente! a sarpente! a sarpente! and was so frighted that he could not finde the doore to gitt in, but made a great buslinge and noyse in the gallarie. On the other side, we that weare in the house, did thinke that he had saide: Assalted! assalted! for before nyghte we doubted that some tritcherie would hapen unto us in that towne, so that we thoughte the house had bene besett with people to cutt our Throtes. Thare was 15 of us in the house, and it was bute a litle house; everie man touke his sorde in hande, one reddie to spoyle another, not any one knowinge the Cause. One that could not finde his sorde, goot to the Chimnay, and offeringe to climbe up, Downe fell a parte of the chimnaye tope upon his heade, and hurte him a litle; another, that was sodonly awakede, strouke aboute him with his sorde, and beate downe the shelfe and broke the pitcheres and plateres which stood thar on; the roume being verrie darke, for it was a boute mydnyghte. Otheres did thinke that they weare pullinge downe the house over our heades. Our janisarie, who should have bene our garde, and have protecked us from all Daingeres, he lykwyse doubtinge the people of the towne, and hearinge suche a noyse sodonly, he touke up the louse borde wheare on he laye, and sliped Downe into the valte. As we weare thus all amayzed, at the laste Mr. Bayllye founde the waye in at the doore. When Mr. Glover saw him com in, he sayd unto him: How now, man, what is the matter, who do you se? Mr. Baylle was even bretheless with feare, cryinge out, and with struglinge to gitt in at the doore, so thet he could not answer him at the first; at last he sayd: A sarpente! a sarpente! had trubled him. When Mr. Glover harde him say so, than feare was gone, and he wente to the Dore, and thare he founde Mr. Bayllis' garter reddie to be carried away with the wynde. After we a litle wondered at our great amayz-mente for so smale a cause, Mr. Glover caled everie man by his name, to se yf any man weare slayne or wounded; for thare was sixtene of us in all, our weaperns all drawne, and the roume was but litle. Everie man beinge caled, we weare all alive, and but smale hurtes done. At laste we founde our janisarie wanting; who myghte well be ashamed to make it knowne wheare he was; but Mr. Glover callinge him verrie earnestly, he answered in the valte. He could not git out any way, but Mr. Gonzale Touke up the borde that laye wheare he wente downe, and lyinge a longe upon the floure, he could but hardly reatche him, to take him by the hande; without muche adew theye puled him up. When he leaped into the valte, beinge verrie sore frighted, he caste of his uper garmente, and lefte it behind him in the valte, but no man could perswade him to goo downe againe and fetche it, for the place was lothesom, and it should seme that he was thare frighted with somthinge, in that kinde Mr. Baylye was; so his garmente remayned there till the morninge, that he who oued the house did fetche it.[1]

Nine years after this somewhat farcical incident, Thomas Coryat had a distinctly bad moment when walking through Germany:

There hapned unto me a certaine disaster about the middest of my journey betwixt Franckendall and Wormes, the like whereof I did not sustaine in my whole journey out of England. Which was this. I stept aside into a vineyard in the open field that was but a litle distant from the high waie, to the end to taste of their grapes wherewith I might something asswage my thirst: hoping that I might as freely have done it there, as I did often times before in many places of Lombardie without any controulement. There I pulled two little clusters of them, and so returned into my way againe travelling securely and joviaslly towards Wormes, whose lofty Towers I saw neere at hand. But there came a German Boore upon me (for so are the clownes of the country commonly called) with a halbert in his hand, & in a great fury pulled off very violently my hat from my head . . . looked very fiercely upon me with eyes sparkling fire in a manner, and with his Almanne wordes which I understood not, swaggered most insolently with me, holding up his halbert in that threatning manner at me, that I continually expected a blow, and was in deadly feare lest he would have made me a prey for the wormes before I should ever put my foote in the gallant City of Wormes. For it was in vaine for me to make any violent resistance, because I had no more weapon then a weake staffe, that I brought with me out of Italy. Although I understood not his speeches, yet I gathered by his angry gestures that the onely cause of his quarrel was for that he saw me come forth of a vineyard (which belike was his maisters) with a bunch of grapes in my hand. All this while that he threatned me with these menacing termes I stood before him almost as mute as a Seriphian frogge, or an Acanthian grashopper, scarce opening my mouth once unto him, because I thought that as I did not understand him, so likewise on the other side he did not understand me. At length with my tongue I began to reencounter him, tooke heart a grace, and so discharged a whole volley of Greeke and Latin shot upon him, supposing that it would bee an occasion to pacifie him somewhat if he did but onely thereby conceive that I had a little learning. But the implacable Clowne . . . was so farre from being mitigated with my strange Rhetoricke, that he was rather much the more exasperated against me. In the end after many bickerings had passed betwixt us, three or foure good fellowes that came from Wormes, glaunced by, and inquired of me what the quarrell was. I being not able to speake Dutch asked them whether any of the company could speake Latin. Then immediately one replyed unto me that he could. Whereupon I discovered unto him the whole circumstance of the matter, and desired him to appease the rage of that inexorable and unpleasant peasant, that he might restore my hat againe to me. Then he like a very sociable companion interposed himselfe betwixt us as a mediator. But first he told me that I had committed a penal trespasse in presuming to gather grapes in a vineyard without leave, affirming that the Germanes are so exceeding sparing of their grapes, that they are wont to fine any of their owne countreymen that they catch in their vineyards without leave, either with purse or body; much more a stranger. Notwithstanding he promised to do his endevour to get my hat againe, because this should be a warning for me, and for that he conceived that opinion of me that I was a good fellow. And so at last with much adoe this controversie was compounded betwixt the cullian and my selfe, my hat being restored unto me for a small price of redemption, which was twelve of their little coynes called fennies, which countervaile twenty pence of our English money. But I would counsel thee gentle reader whatsoever thou art that meanest to travell into Germany, to beware by my example of going into any of their vineyardes without leave. For if thou shalt happen to be apprehended in ipso facto (as I was) by some rustical and barbarous Corydon of the country, thou mayest perhaps pay a farre deerer price for thy grapes then I did, even thy dearest blood.[2]

You have been warned. While we are still in the seventeenth century, here are two passages from *The Rare Adventures and Painfull Peregrinations* of William Lithgow – a book that deserves a modern reprint as much as any I know. For the first extract, we find Lithgow on the bank of the river Jordan with a company of friars and pilgrims:

Approaching to the banke-side, we dismounted, and uncloathed our selves, going in naked to the River, we washed us to refresh our bodies; our Souldiers lying a little off from us, as pledges of our lives, and their owne safegards, stayed as Bulwarks for our protection.

The water of Jordan hath beene transported to Venice in barrels, for that purity it hath; which will reserve unspoiled, both moneths and yeares, and the longer it is kept, it is the more fresher; and to drinke it, is an excellent remedy for the fever quartan or quotidian, being neare in vertue to the Wine of Lebanon.

Considering the auncient reputation of this famous river, and the rare sight of such an unfrequented place, I climbed up to the top of a Turpentine tree, which grew within the limited flood, a little above where I left my company even naked, as I came from swimming, and cut downe a faire hunting rod of the heavy and sad Turpentine tree, being three yards long, wondrous straight, full of small knots, and of a yellowish colour; which afterward, with great paines, I brought to England, and did present it (as the rarest gemme of a Pilgrimes treasure) to his Majesty. But I remember in the choosing thereof an unexpected accident fell out: For I being sequestrat from the sight of the company, upon this solitary tree, with broad obscuring leaves, the Friers and Souldiers removed; keeping their course towards Jericho: but within two furlongs from Jordan, they were beset with the former Nocturnall enemies [Arabs], who assailed them with a hard conflict: For I hearing the Harquebuse go off, was straight in admiration, and looking downe to the place where I left my associates, they were gone; so bending my eyes a little further in the Plaine, I saw them at a martiall combate: which sight gave me suddenly, the threatning of despaire: not knowing whether to stay intrenched, within the circundating leaves, to approve the events of my auspicuous fortunes: Or in prosecuting a reliefe, to be participant of their doubtfull deliverance.

In the end pondering, I could hardly, or never escape their hands, either there, or by the way going up to Jerusalem, leapt downe from the tree, leaving my Turkish cloathes lying upon the ground, tooke onely in my hand the rod & Shasse which I wore on my head: and ranne starke naked above a quarter of a mile amongst thistles, and sharpe pointed grasse, which pittifully pricked the soles of my feete, but the feare of death for the present, expel'd the griefe of that unlooked for paine. Approaching on the safe side of my company, one of our Souldiers broke forth on horsebacke, being determined to kill mee for my staying behinde: Yea, and three times stroke at me with his halfe-pike; but his horse being at his speed, I prevented his cruelty, first by falling downe, next by running in amongst the thickest of the Pilgrimes, recovering the Guardians face, which when the Guardian espied, and saw my naked body, hee presently pulled off his gray gowne, and threw it to me, whereby I might hide the secrets of nature: By which meanes, (in the space of an houre) I was cloathed three manner of wayes: First, like a Turke: Secondly, like a wild Arabian: And thirdly, like a grey Frier, which was a barbarous, a savage, and a religious habit.[3]

The second piece is a good deal more harrowing. While in Malaga, Lithgow is suddenly apprehended on suspicion of being a British agent. I have abridged his account of his subsequent sufferings as much out of respect for the feelings of my more sensitive readers as for any reasons of space:

The day following the Governour entered my Prison alone, intreating me to confesse that I was a spy, and he would be my friend, and procure my pardon, neither should I lacke (interim) any needfull thing: But I still attesting my innocency, hee wrathfully swore I should see his face no more, till grievous torments should make me doe it.

But withall in my audience, he commanded Areta, that none should come neare mee except the slave, nor no food should be given mee but three ounces of moosted browne bread, every second day, and a Fuleto or English Pint of water, neither any bed, pillow, or coverlet to be allowed mee: And close up sayd he, this window in his roome, with lyme and stone, stop the holes of the doore with double Matts, hanging another locking to it; and to withdraw all visible and sensible comfort from him, let no tongue, nor feet be heard neare him, till I have my designes accomplished: And thou Hazier I charge thee, at thy incommings to have no conference with him, nor at thy out-goings abroad to discover him to the English Factors, as thou wilt answer upon thy life, and the highest torments can be devised.

These directions delivered, my roome was made a darke-drawn Dungeon, my belly the anatomy of mercilesse hunger, my comfortlesse hearing, the receptacle of sounding Bells, my eye wanting light, a loathsome languishing in despaire, and my ground lying body, the woefull mirrour of misfortunes: every houre wishing anothers comming, every day the night, and every night the morning.

And now being every second or third day attended with the twinckling of an eye, and my sustenance agreeable to my attendance, my body grew exceeding debile and infirme; insomuch that the Governour (after his answers receaved from Madrid) made haste to put in execution, his bloody and mercilesse purpose before Christmas Holydayes: least ere the expiring of the twelfth day, I should be utterly famished, and unable to undergoe my triall, without present perishing, yet unknowne to me, save onely in this knowledge, that I was confident to dye a fearefull and unacquainted death: for it is a current custome with the Spaniard, that if a stranger be apprehended upon any suspicion, he is never brought to open tryall, and common Jayle, but clapd up in a Dungeon, and there tortured, impoysoned, or starved to death . . .

In end, by Gods permission, the scourge of my fiery tryall approaching; upon the forty seventh day after my first imprisonment, and five dayes before Christmas; about two a clocke in the morning, I heard the noyse of a Coach in the fore-street, marvelling much what it might meane.

The former nine Sergeants, accompanied with the Scrivan, entered the roome without word speaking, and carrying mee thence, with irons and all, on their armes through the house, to the street, they layd mee on my backe in the Coach: where two of them sat up beside mee, (the rest using great silence) went softly along by the Coach side. Then Baptista the Coach-man, an Indian Negro droving out at the Sea-gate, the way of the shoare-side, I was brought Westward almost a league from the Towne, to a Vine-presse house, standing alone amongst Vineyards, where they inclosed mee in a roome till day light, for hither was the Racke brought the night before, and privately placed in the ende of a Trance.

And all this secresie was used, that neyther English, French, or Flemings, should see or get any knowledge of my Tryall, my grievous Tortures, and dreadfull dispatch, because of their treacherous and cruel proceedings. . . .

Well, the Governours interrogation and my Confession being mutually subscribed: He and Don Francesco besought me earnestly to acknowledge and confesse my guiltinesse in time: if not, he would deliver me in the Alcaldes hands there present.

But finding mee stand fast to the marke of my spotlesse innocency, he, invective, and malicious hee, after many tremendous threatnings, commanded the Scrivan to draw up a Warrant for the chiefe Justice: And done, he set his hand to it, and taking me by the hand, delivered me and the Warrant in the Alcalde Majors hands, to cause mee bee Tortured, broken, and cruelly Tormented.

Whence being carried along on the Sergeants armes, to the end of a Trance or stone Gallery, where the Pottaro or Racke was placed: The Encarnador or Tormentor, begunne to disburden me of my irons, which beeing very hard inbolted he could not Ram-verse the Wedges for a long time: Whereat the Chiefe Justice being offended, the malicious Villaine with the Hammer which he had in his hand, stroake away above an inch of my left heele with the Bolt. Whereupon I grievously groaning, beeing exceeding faint, and without my three ounces of bread, and a little Water for three dayes together: The Alcalde sayd, O Traytor all this is nothing, but the earnest of a greater bargaine you have in hand. . . .

After this, the Alcalde, and Scrivan, being both chaire-set, the one to examine, the other to write downe my Confession and Tortures: I was by the Executioner stripped to the skin, brought to the Racke, and then mounted by him on the top of it: Where eftsoones I was hung by the bare shoulders, with two small Cords, which went under both mine armes, running on two Rings of iron that were fixed in the Wall above my head.

Thus being hoysed, to the appoynted height, the Tormentor discended below, and drawing downe my Legs, through the two sides of the three-planked Racke, hee tyed a Cord about each of my ancles: And then ascending upon the Racke, hee drew the Cords upward, and bending forward with maine force, my two knees, against the two plankes; the sinewes of my hammes burst a sunder, and the lids of my knees beeing crushed, and the Cords made fast, I hung so demayned, for a large houre. . . .

Now mine eyes begun to startle, my mouth to foame and froath, and my teeth to chatter like to the doubling of Drummers stickes. O strange inhumanity of Men-monster Manglers! surpassing the limits of their nationall Law; three score Tortures beeing the tryall of Treason, which I had, and was to indure: yet thus to inflict a seaven-fold surplussage of more intollerable cruelties: And notwithstanding of my shivering lippes, in this fiery passion my vehement groaning, and blood-springing fonts, from armes, broake sinewes, hammes, and knees; yea, and my depending weight on flesh-cutting Cords; yet they stroke mee on the face with Cudgels, to abate and cease the thundring noyse of my wrestling voyce.

At last being loosed from these Pinnacles of paine, I was hand-fast set on the floore, with this their incessant imploration: Confesse, confesse, confesse in time, for thine inevitable torments ensue: where finding nothing from me, but still innocent, O I am innocent, O Jesus! the Lambe of God have mercy upon mee, and strengthen mee with patience, to undergoe this barbarous murder.

Then by command of the Justice, was my trembling body layd above, and along upon the face of the Racke, with my head downe-ward, inclosed within a circled hole, my belly upmost, and my heeles upward toward the top of the Racke: my legs and armes being drawne a sunder, were fastned with pinnes and Cords, to both sides of the outward plankes; for now was I to receive my maine torments. . . .

Then the Tormentor having charged the first passage about my body (making fast by a device each torture as they were multiplied) he went to an earthen Jarre standing full of water, a little beneath my head: from whence carrying a pot full of water; in the bottome whereof, there was in incised hole, which being stopd by his thumb, till it came to my mouth, hee did powre it in my bellie; the measure being a Spanish Sombre, which is an English Potle: The first and second services I gladly receaved, such was the scorching drouth of my tormenting payne, and likewise I had drunke none for three dayes before.

But afterward, at the third charge, perceiving these measures of water to be inflicted upon me as tortures, O strangling tortures! I closed my lips, gaine-standing that eager crudelity.

Whereat the Alcalde inraging, set my teeth asunder with a payre of iron cadges, detayning them there, at every severall turne, both mainely and manually; whereupon my hunger-clungd bellie waxing great, grew Drumm-like imbolstered: for it being a suffocating payne, in regard of my head hanging downeward, and the water reingorging it selfe in my throat with a strugling force; it strangled and swallowed up my breath from youling and groaning. . . .

Thus lay I sixe houres upon the Racke, betweene foure a clocke afternoone, and ten a clocke at night, having had inflicted upon me three score seven torments: Neverthelesse they continued me a large halfe houre (after all my tortures) at the full bending; where my body being all begored with blood, and cut through in every part, to the crushed and bruised bones, I pittifully remayned, still roaring, howling, foaming, bellowing, and gnashing my teeth, with insupportable cryes, before the pinnes were undone, and my body loosed. At last my head being by their armes advanced, and my body taken from the Rack, the water regushed abundantly from my mouth; then they recloathing my broken, bloody, and cold trembling body, being all this time starke naked, I fell twice in a sounding trance: which they againe refreshed with a little Wine, and two warme Egges, not for charity done, but that I should be reserved to further punishment.

And now at last they charged my broken legs, with my former eye-frighting irons, and done, I was lamentably carryed on their armes to the Coach, being after midnight, and secretly transported to my former Dungeon without any knowledge of the Towne, save onely these my lawlesse, and mercilesse Tormentors: where, when come, I was layd with my head and my heeles alike high, on my former stones. . . .

Upon Christmas day Mariana the Ladies Gentlewoman got permission to visit me, and with her licence, she brought abundance of teares presenting me also with a dish of Honey and sugar, some confections, and Rasins in a great plenty to my no small comfort, besides using many sweet speeches for consolations sake.

Shee gone, and the next morning of Saint Johns day come, long ere day the Towne was in Armes, the Bells ringing backward, the people shouting, and Drummes beating; whereat my soule was over-joyed, thinking that the Moores had seased upon all: And in the after noone the Turke comming to me with bread and water, being by chance the second day, I asked him what the fray was? who replyed, be of good courage, I hope in God and Mahomet, that you and I ere long shall be set at liberty; for your Countrey-men, the English Armado, and mine the Moores, are joyned together, and comming to sacke Malaga: And this morning Post came from Alicante to premonish the Governour thereof; whereupon he and the Towne have instantly pulled downe, all the Cowper shops, and dwelling houses that were builded without by the shoare side, adjoyning to the Townes Wall: But yet sayd he it is no matter, the Towne may easily be surprised, and I hope we shall be merry in Algiers, for there is above a hundred sayle seene comming hither; and therewith kissing my cheeke, hee kindly left mee.[4]

To this day, in many parts of the world, the traveller finds it impossible to indulge in the most innocent sightseeing without arousing the suspicions of the local authorities; though few, thank heavens, have been made to suffer as much as the unfortunate Lithgow. Even the great and famous have their occasional moments of misunderstanding – like Goethe, for example, when on 14 September 1786 he visited Malcesine on the shores of Lake Garda:

As I had planned, early in the morning I walked to the old castle, which, since it is without gates, locks or sentries, is accessible to anyone. I sat down in the courtyard facing the old tower, which is built upon and into the rock. I had found an ideal spot for drawing, at the top of three or four steps that led to a locked door. In the frame of this door stood a little carved stone seat of the kind one can still come across in old buildings in our country.

I had not been sitting there long before several persons entered the courtyard, looked me over and walked up and down. Quite a crowd gathered. Then they came to a stop and I found myself surrounded. I realized that my drawing had created a sensation, but I did not let this disturb me and went calmly on with my work. At last a somewhat unprepossessing-looking man pushed himself forward, came up close to me and asked what I was doing there. I replied that I was drawing the old tower so as to have a memento of Malcesine. This was not allowed, he said, and I must stop at once. Since he spoke in Venetian dialect, which I hardly understand, I retorted that I didn't know what he was saying. At this, with typical Italian nonchalance he tore the page up, though he left it on the pad. When this happened I noticed that some of the bystanders showed signs of indignation, especially one old woman who said this wasn't right. They should call the *podestà*, who was the proper judge of such matters. I stood on the step with my back against the door and took in the faces of the crowd, which still kept growing. The eager stares, the good-natured expression on most of them and all the other characteristics of a crowd of strange people afforded me much amusement. I fancied I saw before me the chorus of 'Birds', whom, as the 'True Friend', I had so often made fun of on the stage of the Ettersburg theatre. By the time the *podestà* arrived on the scene with his actuary, I was in the highest spirits and greeted him without reserve. When he asked me why I had made a drawing of their fortress, I said modestly that I had not realized that these ruins were a fortress. I pointed to the ruinous state of the tower and the walls, the lack of gates, in short, to the general defenceless condition of the whole place, and assured him it had never crossed my mind that I was drawing anything but a ruin. He answered: If it were only a ruin, why was it worth noticing? Wishing to gain time and his good will, I went into a detailed exposition; they probably knew, I said, that a great many travellers came to Italy only to see ruins, that Rome, the capital of the world, had been devastated by the Barbarians and was now full of ruins which people had drawn hundreds of times, that not everything from antiquity had been as well preserved as the amphitheatre in Verona, which I hoped to see soon.

The *podestà* stood facing me, but on a lower step. He was a tall, though hardly a lanky, man of about thirty. The dull features of his stupid face were in perfect accord with the slow and obtuse way in which he put his questions. The actuary, though smaller and smarter, also did not seem to know how to handle such a novel and unusual case. I kept on talking about this and that. The people seemed to enjoy listening, and when I directed my words at some kindly-looking women, I thought I could read assent and approval in their faces.

But when I mentioned the amphitheatre in Verona, which is known here by the name 'arena', the actuary, who had been collecting his wits in the meantime, broke in: that might be all very well, he said, in the case of a world-famous Roman monument, but there was nothing noteworthy about these towers except that they marked the frontier between Venetia and the Austrian Empire, for which reason they were not to be spied upon. I parried this by explaining at some length that the buildings of the Middle Ages were just as worthy of attention as those of Greek and Roman times, though they could not be expected to recognize, as I did, the picturesque beauty of buildings which had been familiar to them since childhood. By good luck, the morning sun at this point flooded the tower, rocks and walls with a lovely light and I began describing the beauty of the scene with great enthusiasm. Since my audience was standing with their backs to it and did not want to withdraw their attention from me completely, they kept screwing their heads round, like wrynecks, in order to see with their eyes what I was praising to their ears. Even the *podestà* turned round, though with greater dignity; they looked so absurd that I became quite hilarious and spared them nothing, least of all the ivy which had luxuriantly covered the rocks and walls for so many centuries.

The actuary returned to his argument: this was all very well, but the Emperor Joseph was a troublesome *signore* who certainly had evil designs on the republic of Venice. I might well be a subject of his, sent to spy on the frontier.

'Far from being a subject of the Emperor,' I exclaimed, 'I can boast of being, like yourselves, the citizen of a republic which, though it cannot compare in power and greatness with the illustrious state of Venice, nevertheless also governs itself and, in its commercial activity, its wealth and the wisdom of its councillors, is inferior to no city in Germany. I am, that is to say, a native of Frankfurt-am-Main, a city of whose name and renown you must certainly have heard.'

'From Frankfurt-am-Main!' cried a pretty young woman. 'Now you will be able to find out at once, Signor Podestà, the kind of man this stranger is. I am certain he is honest. Send for Gregorio – he was in service there for a long time – he is the best person to clear up the whole matter.'

The number of kindly-disposed faces around me had increased, the original troublemaker had disappeared, and when Gregorio arrived, the tide turned definitely in my favour. Gregorio was a man in his fifties with one of those familiar olive-skinned Italian faces. He spoke and behaved like someone to whom anything strange is not strange at all. He at once told me that he had been in service with Bolongaro and would be happy to hear news from me about this family and about the city which he remembered with great pleasure. Fortunately, he had resided there when I was a young man, so that I had the double advantage of being able to tell him exactly what had happened in his day and what changes had taken place later. I had been acquainted with all the Italian families, so I gave him news of them all and he was delighted to hear many facts: that Signor Alessina, for instance, had celebrated his golden wedding in 1774, and that a medal, struck on that occasion, was in my possession. He remembered that the maiden name of this wealthy merchant's wife had been Brentano. I was also able to tell him many things about the children and grandchildren – how they had grown up, been provided for, married and had children in their turn.

While I gave him the most accurate information I could about everything, his features grew jovial and solemn by turns. He was moved and happy. The bystanders got more and more excited and hung on every word of our conversation, though he had to translate some of it into their dialect.

At the end he said: 'Signor Podestà, I am convinced that this man is an honest and educated gentleman who is travelling to enlarge his knowledge. We should treat him as a friend and set him at liberty, so that he may speak well of us to his countrymen and encourage them to visit Malcesine, the beautiful situation of which so well deserves the admiration of foreigners.'

I gave added force to these friendly words by praising the countryside, the town and its inhabitants, nor did I forget to mention the prudence and wisdom of its authorities.

All this was well received and I was given permission to look at anything in the neighbourhood I liked, in the company of Master Gregorio.[5]

Goethe's *Italian Journey* makes instructive reading, above all for the astonishing differences between his reactions and what ours would have been in similar circumstances. Seven months after the Malcesine incident he was in Sicily:

This afternoon we visited the pleasant valley in the mountains to the south of Palermo, along which meanders the river Oreto. . . .

The fair spring weather and the luxuriant vegetation lent an air of grace and peace to the whole valley, which our stupid guide proceeded to ruin with his erudition, for he started telling us in great detail how, long ago, Hannibal had given battle here and what stupendous feats of valour had taken place on this very spot. I angrily rebuked him for such an odious evocation of defunct ghosts. It was bad enough, I said, that from time to time crops have to be trampled down, if not always by elephants, still by horses and men, but at least one need not shock the imagination out of its peaceful dreams by recalling scenes of savage violence from the past.

He was very astonished that I, on such a spot, should not want to hear anything about classical times, and, of course, I could not make him understand my objections to this mixing-up of the past and the present.

He must have thought me still more of an eccentric when he saw me searching for pebbles in the shoals which the river had left high and dry, especially when I pocketed several specimens. Again, I could not explain to him that the quickest way to get an idea of any mountainous region is to examine the types of rock fragments washed down by its streams, or that there was any point in studying rubble to get the idea of these eternal classical heights of the prehistoric earth.[6]

What Goethe seems to lack here above all is a sense of humour; it is therefore with something like relief that one turns back to travellers like Robert Curzon, who never hesitates to tell a story against himself. At Thebes in Upper Egypt, Curzon meets a Coptic carpenter, who tells him of a library from a ruined monastery, now lying hidden in a Pharaonic tomb; the carpenter offers to take him there, but insists that they go at dead of night, to avoid being seen by prying, and perhaps predatory, Muslims. They enter the tomb – a vast and echoing one – accompanied only by the carpenter's small son; and there, sure enough, are the Coptic manuscripts. Now let Curzon take up the story:

Having found these ancient books, we proceeded to examine their contents, and, to accomplish this at our ease, we stuck the candles on the ground, and the carpenter and I sat down before them, while his son brought us the volumes from the steps of the altar, one by one.

. . . While we were poring over them, we thought we heard a noise. 'O father of hammers,' said I to the carpenter, 'I think I heard a noise: what could it be? – I thought I heard something move.' 'Did you, hawaja?' (O merchant), said the carpenter; 'it must have been my son moving the books, for what else could there be here? – No one knows of this tomb or of the holy manuscripts which it contains. Surely there can be nothing here to make a noise, for are we not here alone, a hundred feet under the earth, in a place where no one comes? – It is nothing; certainly it is nothing.' And so saying, he lifted up one of the candles, and peered about in the darkness; but as there was nothing to be seen, and all was silent as the grave, he sat down again, and at our leisure we completed our examination of all the books which lay upon the steps.

They proved to be all church books, liturgies for different seasons, or homilies; and not historical, nor of any particular interest, either from their age or subject. There now remained only the great book upon the altar, a ponderous quarto, bound either in brown leather or wooden boards; and this the carpenter's son with difficulty lifted from its place, and laid it down before us on the ground; but, as he did so, we heard the noise again. The carpenter and I looked at each other: he turned pale – perhaps I did so too; and we looked over our shoulders in a sort of anxious, nervous kind of way, expecting to see something – we did not know what. However we saw nothing; and feeling a little ashamed, I again settled myself before the three candle-ends, and opened the book, which was written in large black characters of unusual size. As I bent over the huge volume, to see what it was about, suddenly there arose a sound somewhere in the cavern, but from whence it came I could not comprehend; it seemed all round us at the same moment. There was no room for doubt now: it was a fearful howling, like the roar of a hundred wild beasts. The carpenter looked aghast; the tall and grisly figures of the Egyptian gods seemed to stare at us from the walls. I thought of Cornelius Agrippa, and felt a gentle perspiration coming on which would have betokened a favourable crisis in a fever. Suddenly the dreadful roar ceased, and as its echoes died away in the tomb we felt considerably relieved, and were beginning to try and put a good face upon the matter, when, to our unutterable horror, it began again, and waxed louder and louder as if legions of infernal spirits were let loose upon us. We could stand this no longer; the carpenter and I jumped up from the ground, and his son in his terror stumbled over the great Coptic manuscript, and fell upon the candles, which were all put out in a moment; his screams were now added to the uproar which resounded in the cave: seeing the twinkling of a star through the vista of the two outer chambers, we all set off as hard as we could run, our feelings of alarm being increased to desperation when we perceived that something was chasing us in the darkness, while the roar seemed to increase every moment. How we did tear along! The devil take the hindmost seemed about to be literally fulfilled; and we raised stifling clouds of dust, as we scrambled up the steep slope which led to the outer door. 'So then,' thought I, 'the stories of gins, and ghouls, and goblins, that I have read of and never believed, must be true after all, and in this city of the dead it has been our evil lot to fall upon a haunted tomb!'

Breathless and bewildered, the carpenter and I bolted out of this infernal palace into the open air, mightily relieved at our escape from the darkness and the terrors of the subterranean vaults. We had not been out a moment, and had by no means collected our ideas, before our alarm was again excited to its utmost pitch.

The evil one came forth in bodily shape, and stood revealed to our eyes distinctly in the pale light of the moon.

While we were gazing upon the appearance, the carpenter's son, whom we had quite forgotten in our hurry, came creeping out of the doorway of the tomb upon his hands and knees.

'Why, father!' said he, after a moment's silence, 'if that is not old Fatima's donkey, which has been lost these two days! It is lucky that we have found it, for it must have wandered into this tomb, and it might have been starved if we had not met with it to-night.'

The carpenter looked rather ashamed of the adventure; and as for myself, though I was glad that nothing worse had come of it, I took comfort in the reflection that I was not the first person who had been alarmed by the proceedings of an ass.[7]

Visits to Monasteries of the Levant is unquestionably Curzon's best book; but I am still awaiting a reprint of his other publication, *Armenia*, sub-titled *A Year at Erzeroom, and on the Frontiers of Russia, Turkey, and Persia.* In it he tells of the sudden illness that overtook him at Erzerum, and the curious circumstances of his recovery:

I felt perfectly well when we went to dinner, when suddenly it appeared to me that what I was eating was burning hot, and had a strange odd taste. I believe I got up and staggered across the room, but here my senses failed me, and I remained insensible for twenty-seven days. An attack of brain-fever had come upon me like a blow, as sudden and overwhelming as a flash of lightning.

On the 27th of October I awoke in the morning, but, as I suppose, went to sleep for a while; in the afternoon I fairly came to my senses, and saw my servant sitting on the scarlet-cloth divan under the window looking at me. I felt something strange and still and gloomy in the air, and was rather bewildered with the sensation. This was soon to be accounted for: the servant, seeing that I was alive, came forward towards the bed, while a low rumbling noise made itself heard. This noise became louder: flakes of plaster fell from the ceiling; the room trembled, and was filled with a fine dust, with which I was nearly choked. My man exclaimed, 'The earth moves – are you not afraid?' As he spoke the noise which we had heard increased, and an immense beam, made of the trunk of a whole tree, which was immediately above my bed, split, with a report like a cannon. The earthquake shook the house terribly; it creaked and trembled like a ship in a heavy gale of wind; the noise increased to a roar, not like thunder, but howling and bellowing, with a low rumbling sound, while the air was as still as if nature was paralysed with dread; every now and then a tremendous crash gave notice of a falling house. The one opposite our house, belonging to a poor widow, was entirely destroyed; and, in the midst of a most fearful uproar, the two rooms, one on each side of my bedroom, fell in; while the air was darkened altogether, as in an eclipse, with clouds of dust. So great was the noise of the earthquake all around, that neither my attendant nor I distinguished the particular crash when the two rooms adjoining us fell in. Some of the minarets, and many of the houses of the city, were demolished: parts of the ancient castellated walls fell down. The top of one of the two beautiful minarets of the old medressé, the glory of Erzeroom, called usually Eki Chifteh, disappeared. Those who were out, and able to witness the devastation, and to hear the awful roaring noise, said they had never seen or heard anything more tremendous than the scene before their eyes. It is difficult to express in words the strange, awful sensation produced by the seeming impossible contradiction of a dead stilness in the midst of the crash of falling buildings, the sullen, low bellowing, which perhaps sounded from beneath the ground, and the tremendous uproar that arose on all sides during the earthquake. I have not met with an account of this strange phenomenon in the descriptions of other earthquakes, and do not know whether it is a usual accompaniment to these terrible convulsions of nature.

The earthquake accomplished its mission: in the midst of terror and destruction, it restored one poor creature to life. I regained my senses and my faculties on the 27th, as suddenly as I had lost them on the 1st day of this month. God give me grace to make a good use of the life which was restored to me under such awful circumstances![8]

Alexander Kinglake is even more entertaining. The following anecdote, from *Eothen*, is perhaps my favourite in all travel literature. In it Kinglake tells of the terrible moment when, riding across the Sinai desert to Cairo, he suddenly spots an Englishman, in an English shooting-jacket, bearing down on him from the opposite direction:

At first there was a mere moving speck in the horizon; my party, of course, became all alive with excitement, and there were many surmises; soon it appeared that three laden camels were approaching, and that two of them carried riders; in a little while we saw that one of the riders wore the European dress, and at last the travellers were pronounced to be an English gentleman and his servant; by their side there were a couple of Arabs on foot; and this, if I rightly remember, was the whole party. . . .

This Englishman, as I afterwards found, was a military man returning to his country from India, and crossing the Desert at this part in order to go through Palestine. As for me, I had come pretty straight from England, and so here we met in the wilderness at about half way from our respective starting points. As we approached each other, it became with me a question whether we should speak. I thought it likely that the stranger would accost me, and in the event of his doing so, I was quite ready to be as sociable and chatty as I could be according to my nature; but still I could not think of anything particular that I had to say to him. Of course among civilized people, the not having anything to say is no excuse at all for not speaking; but I was shy, and indolent, and I felt no great wish to stop, and talk like a morning visitor, in the midst of those broad solitudes. The traveller, perhaps, felt as I did, for, except that we lifted our hands to our caps, and waved our arms in courtesy, we passed each other quite as distantly as if we had passed in Pall Mall. Our attendants, however, were not to be cheated of the delight that they felt in speaking to new listeners, and hearing fresh voices once more. The masters, therefore, had no sooner passed each other, than their respective servants quietly stopped and entered into conversation. As soon as my camel found that her companions were not following her, she caught the social feeling and refused to go on. I felt the absurdity of the situation, and determined to accost the stranger, if only to avoid the awkwardness of remaining stuck fast in the Desert whilst our servants were amusing themselves. When with this intent I turned round my camel, I found that the gallant officer had passed me by about thirty or forty yards, and was exactly in the same predicament as myself. I put my now willing camel in motion and rode up towards the stranger: seeing this he followed my example, and came forward to meet me. He was the first to speak: too courteous to address me as if he admitted the possibility of my wishing to accost him from any feeling of mere sociability or civilian-like love of vain talk, he at once attributed my advances to a laudable wish of acquiring statistical information, and accordingly when we got within speaking distance, he said, 'I dare say you wish to know how the Plague is going on at Cairo?' and then he went on to say he regretted that his information did not enable him to give me in numbers a perfectly accurate statement of the daily deaths. He afterwards talked pleasantly enough upon other and less ghastly subjects. I thought him manly and intelligent – a worthy one of the few thousand strong Englishmen to whom the Empire of India is committed.[9]

The progress of the Plague was doubtless a useful opening gambit for conversation; but to Kinglake, bound as he was for Cairo, it must also have been a subject of considerable interest. He follows, a few pages later, with an admirable description of the stricken city, and an account of yet another incident of the kind that always seemed to happen to him:

Although the Plague was now spreading quick ... I did not see very plainly any corresponding change in the looks of the streets until the seventh day after my arrival: I then first observed that the city was *silenced*. There were no outward signs of despair nor of violent terror, but many of the voices that had swelled the busy hum of men were already hushed in death, and the survivors, so used to scream and screech in their earnestness whenever they bought or sold, now showed an unwonted indifference about the affairs of this world: it was less worth while for men to haggle and haggle, and crack the sky with noisy bargains, when the Great Commander was there, who could 'pay all their debts with the roll of his drum'.

At this time I was informed that of 25,000 people at Alexandria, 12,000 had died already, the Destroyer had come rather later to Cairo, but there was nothing of weariness in his strides. The deaths came faster than ever they befell in the Plague of London; but the calmness of Orientals under such visitations, and their habit of using biers for interment instead of burying coffins along with the bodies, rendered it practicable to dispose of the dead in the usual way, without shocking the people by any unaccustomed spectacle of horror. There was no tumbling of bodies into carts, as in the Plague of Florence, and the Plague of London; every man, according to his station, was properly buried, and that in the accustomed way, except that he went to his grave at a pace more than usually rapid.

The funerals pouring through the streets were not the only public evidence of deaths. In Cairo this custom prevails: – at the instant of a man's death (if his property is sufficient to justify the expense) professional howlers are employed. I believe that these persons are brought near to the dying man, when his end appears to be approaching, and the moment that life is gone, they lift up their voices, and send forth a loud wail from the chamber of Death. Thus I knew when my near neighbours died: sometimes the howls were near; sometimes more distant. Once I was awakened in the night by the wail of death in the next house, and another time by a like howl from the house opposite; and there were two or three minutes, I recollect, during which the howl seemed to be actually *running* along the street.

I happened to be rather teazed at this time by a sore throat, and I thought it would be well to get it cured, if I could, before I again started on my travels. I therefore inquired for a Frank doctor, and was informed that the only one then at Cairo was a Bolognese Refugee, a very young practitioner, and so poor that he had not been able to take flight, as the other medical men had done. At such a time as this it was out of the question to *send* for an European physician; a person thus summoned would be sure to suppose that the patient was ill of the Plague, and would decline to come. I therefore rode to the young Doctor's residence, ascended a flight or two of stairs, and knocked at his door. No one came immediately, but after some little delay the Medico himself opened the door and admitted me. I, of course, made him understand that I had come to consult him, but before entering upon my throat grievance, I accepted a chair, and exchanged a sentence or two of common-place conversation. Now, the natural common-place of the city at this season was of a gloomy sort – 'Come va la peste?' (how goes the plague?), and this was precisely the question I put. A deep sigh, and the words 'Sette cento per giorno, Signor' (seven hundred a day), pronounced in a tone of the deepest sadness and dejection, were the answer I received. The day was not oppressively hot, yet I saw that the Doctor was transpiring profusely, and even the outside surface of the thick shawl dressing-gown in which he had wrapped himself appeared to be moist. He was a handsome, pleasant-looking young fellow, but the deep melancholy of his tone did not tempt me to prolong the conversation, and without farther delay, I requested that my throat might be looked at. The Medico held my chin in the usual way, and examined my throat; he then wrote me a prescription, and almost immediately afterwards I bid him farewell; but as he conducted me towards the door, I observed an expression of strange and unhappy watchfulness in his rolling eyes. It was not the next day, but the next day but one, if I rightly remember, that I sent to request another interview with my Doctor. In due time Dthemetri, my messenger, returned, looking sadly aghast. He had '*met* the Medico', for so he phrased it, 'coming out from his house – in a bier!'

It was, of course, plain that when the poor Bolognese stood looking down my throat and almost mingling his breath with mine, he was already stricken of the Plague.[10]

Another sad little Egyptian tale, awakening all the right reflections in the mind of a Victorian reader, is told by Eliot Warburton in *The Crescent and the Cross*:

About two o'clock our party broke up; and, notwithstanding threats of *coup de soleil* and brain-fever, we set out once more on our adventures across the mountains: the sun was scorching hot, and his rays, reflected from the calcareous cliffs, poured down as in a focus upon our heads, while the hills excluded every breath of air. Nothing but the turban can stand this sort of sun-artillery with impunity; and to the defence which this afforded, our guides added cloaks, carpets, and whatever they could wrap round them.

As we descended a steep path that would have puzzled a European goat, my horse put his foot on the breast of a mummy king,* not recognising its humanity; and this once reverenced corpse was trodden into fragments by the rest of the party. What a story that ghastly royal village told of ambition and fallen power, and its vanity! A Pharaoh affording footing to an Arab horse, and trampled on by a

---

* These are royal cemeteries.

stranger from the far north! 'Is this the man that made the earth tremble, that did shake kingdoms; – that made the world as a wilderness, and destroyed the cities thereof; that opened not the house of his prisoners?'[11]

A happier moral, however, is drawn by Edward Lear from an unfortunate occurrence which befell him in Albania:

While taking a parting cup of coffee with the postmaster I unluckily set my foot on a handsome pipe-bowl (pipe-bowls are always snares to near-sighted people moving over Turkish floors, as they are scattered in places quite remote from the smokers, who live at the farther end of the prodigiously long pipe-sticks) – crash; but nobody moved; only on apologizing through Giorgio, the polite Mohammedan said: 'The breaking of such a pipe-bowl would indeed, under ordinary circumstances, be disagreeable; but in a friend every action has its charm!'[12]

Let us now turn to West Africa, and that area just north of the river Niger which now forms part of the Republic of Mali. Here it was that Mungo Park, while a prisoner of the Moors – not those of Morocco, but a negroid tribe of the deep Sahara – avoided what might have been a moment of supreme embarrassment with a presence of mind of which any traveller might have been proud:

The curiosity of the Moorish ladies had been very troublesome to me ever since my arrival at Benowm; and on the evening of the 25th (whether from the instigation of others, or impelled by their own ungovernable curiosity, or merely out of frolic, I cannot affirm), a party of them came into my hut, and gave me plainly to understand that the object of their visit was to ascertain, by actual inspection, whether the rite of circumcision extended to the Nazarenes (Christians), as well as to the followers of Mahomet. The reader will easily judge of my surprise at this unexpected declaration; and in order to avoid the proposed scrutiny, I thought it best to treat the business jocularly. I observed to them, that it was not customary in my country to give ocular demonstration in such cases, before so many beautiful women; but that if all of them would retire, except the young lady to whom I pointed (selecting the youngest and handsomest), I would satisfy her curiosity. The ladies enjoyed the jest, and went away laughing heartily, and the young damsel herself to whom I had given the preference (though she did not avail herself of the privilege of inspection), seemed no way displeased at the compliment, for she soon afterwards sent me some meal and milk for my supper.[13]

Mary Kingsley, while exploring the lower reaches of the Ogowe river, also had a lucky escape – though of a rather different kind:

About five o'clock I was off ahead and noticed a path which I had been told I should meet with, and, when met with, I must follow. The path was slightly indistinct, but by keeping my eye on it I could see it. Presently I came to a place where it went out, but appeared again on the other side of a clump of underbush fairly distinctly. I made a short cut for it and the next news was I was in a heap, on a lot of spikes, some fifteen feet or so below ground level, at the bottom of a bag-shaped game pit.

It is at these times you realise the blessing of a good thick skirt. Had I paid heed to the advice of many people in England, who ought to have known better, and did not do it themselves, and adopted masculine garments, I should have been spiked to the bone, and done for. Whereas, save for a good many bruises, here I was with the fulness of my skirt tucked under me, sitting on nine ebony spikes some twelve inches long, in comparative comfort, howling lustily to be hauled out. The Duke came along first, and looked down at me. I said, 'Get a bush-rope, and haul me out.' He grunted and sat down on a log. The Passenger came next, and he looked down. 'You kill?' says he. 'Not much,' say I; 'get a bush-rope and haul me out.' 'No fit', says he, and sat down on the log. Presently, however, Kiva and Wiki came up, and Wiki went and selected the one and only bush-rope suitable to haul an English lady, of my exact complexion, age, and size, out of that one particular pit.

They seemed rare round there from the time he took; and I was just casting about in my mind as to what method would be best to employ in getting up the smooth, yellow, sandy-clay, incurved walls, when he arrived with it, and I was out in a twinkling, and very much ashamed of myself, until Silence, who was then leading, disappeared through the path before us with a despairing yell. Each man then pulled the skin cover off his gun lock, carefully looked to see if things there were all right and ready loosened his knife in its snake-skin sheath; and then we set about hauling poor Silence out, binding him up where necessary with cool green leaves; for he, not having a skirt, had got a good deal frayed at the edges on those spikes. Then we closed up, for the Fans said these pits were symptomatic of the immediate neighbourhood of Efoua.[14]

Dear Miss Kingsley: like Curzon and Kinglake, she always sees the joke. This time she is travelling up the Ogowe by canoe:

We hadn't gone 200 yards before we met a current coming round the end of a rock reef that was too strong for us to hold our own in, let alone progress. On to the bank I was ordered and went; it was a low slip of rugged confused boulders and fragments of rocks, carelessly arranged, and evidently under water in the wet season. I scrambled along, the men yelled and shouted and hauled the canoe, and the inhabitants of the village, seeing we were becoming amusing again, came, legging it like lamp-lighters, after us, young and old, male and female, to say nothing of the dogs. Some good souls helped the men haul, while I did my best to amuse the others by diving headlong from a large rock on to which I had elaborately climbed, into a thick clump of willow-leaved shrubs. They applauded my performance vociferously, and then assisted my efforts to extricate myself, and during the rest of my scramble they kept close to me, with keen competition for the front row, in hopes that I would do something like it again. But I refused the *encore*, because, bashful as I am, I could not but feel that my last performance was carried out with all the superb reckless *abandon* of a Sarah Bernhardt, and a display of art of this order should satisfy any African village for a year at least. At last I got across the rocks on to a lovely little beach of white sand, and stood there talking, surrounded by my audience, until the canoe got over its difficulties and arrived almost as scratched as I; and then we again said farewell and paddled away, to the great grief of the natives, for they don't get a circus up above Njole every week, poor dears.[15]

That other fearless lady traveller, Mrs Amelia B. Edwards – who, it will be remembered, journeyed *A Thousand Miles Up the Nile* for the sole purpose of getting out of the rain – experienced a particularly bad moment a mile or two south of Philae, when on a brief shore excursion with a few of her fellow-passengers from the Nile steamer:

The Painter pitches his tent at the top of the sand-drift; and the Writer sketches the ruined convent opposite; and L. and the Little Lady write no end of letters; and the Idle Man, with Mehemet Ali for a retriever, shoots quail; and everybody is satisfied.

Hapless Idle Man! – hapless, but homicidal. If he had been content to shoot only quail, and had not taken to shooting babies! What possessed him to do it? Not – not, let us hope – an ill-directed ambition, foiled of crocodiles! He went serene and smiling, with his gun under his arm, and Mehemet Ali in his wake. Who so light of heart as that Idle Man? Who so light of heel as that turbaned retriever? We heard our sportsman popping away presently in the barley. It was a pleasant sound, for we knew his aim was true. 'Every shot,' said we, 'means a bird.' We little dreamed that one of those shots meant a baby.

All at once, a woman screamed. It was a sharp, sudden scream, following a shot – a scream with a ring of horror in it. Instantly it was caught up from point to point, growing in volume and seeming to be echoed from every direction at once. At the same moment, the bank became alive with human beings. They seemed to spring from the soil – women shrieking and waving their arms; men running; all making for the same goal. The Writer heard the scream, saw the rush, and knew at once that a gun accident had happened.

A few minutes of painful suspense followed. Then Mehemet Ali appeared, tearing back at the top of his speed; and presently – perhaps five minutes later, though it seemed like twenty – came the Idle Man; walking very slowly and defiantly, with his head up, his arms folded, his gun gone, and an immense rabble at his heels.

Our scanty crew, armed with sticks, flew at once to the rescue, and brought him off in safety. We then learned what had happened.

A flight of quail had risen; and as quail fly low, skimming the surface of the grain and diving down again almost immediately, he had taken a level aim. At the instant that he fired, and in the very path of the quail, a woman and child who had been squatting in the barley, sprang up screaming. He at once saw the coming danger; and, with admirable presence of mind, drew the charge of his second barrel. He then hid his cartridge-box and hugged his gun, determined to hold it as long as possible. The next moment he was surrounded, overpowered, had the gun wrenched from his grasp, and received a blow on the back with a stone. Having captured the gun, one or two of the men let go. It was then that he shook off the rest, and came back to the boat. Mehemet Ali at the same time flew to call a rescue. He, too, came in for some hard knocks, besides having his shirt rent and his turban torn off his head.

Here were we, meanwhile, with less than half our crew, a private war on our hands, no captain, and one of our three guns in the hands of the enemy. What a scene it was! A whole village, apparently a very considerable village, swarming on the bank; all hurrying to and fro; all raving, shouting, gesticulating. If we had been on the verge of a fracas in Tafah, here we were threatened with a siege.

Drawing in the plank between the boat and the shore, we held a hasty council of war.

The woman being unhurt, and the child, if hurt at all, hurt very slightly, we felt justified in assuming an injured tone calling the village to account for a case of cowardly assault and demanding instant restitution of the gun. We accordingly sent Talhamy to parley with the head-man of the place and peremptorily demand the gun. We also bade him add – and this we regarded as a master-stroke of policy – that if due submission was immediately made, the Howadji, one of whom was a Hakeem, would permit the father to bring his child on board to have its hurts attended to.

Outwardly indifferent, inwardly not a little anxious, we waited the event. Talhamy's back being towards the river, we had the whole semicircle of swarthy faces full in view – bent brows, flashing eyes, glittering teeth; all anger, all scorn, all defiance. Suddenly the expression of the faces changed – the change beginning with those nearest the speaker, and spreading gradually outwards. It was as if a wave had passed over them. We knew then that our *coup* was made. Talhamy returned. The villagers crowded round their leaders, deliberating. Numbers now began to sit down; and when a Nubian sits down, you may be sure that he is no longer dangerous.

Presently – after perhaps a quarter of an hour – the gun was brought back uninjured, and an elderly man carrying a blue bundle appeared on the bank. The plank was now put across; the crowd was kept off; and the man with the bundle, and three or four others, were allowed to pass.

The bundle being undone, a little brown imp of about four years of age, with shaven head and shaggy scalp-lock, was produced. He whimpered at first, seeing the strange white faces; but when offered a fig, forgot his terrors, and sat munching it like a monkey. As for his wounds, they were literally skin-deep, the shot having but slightly grazed his shoulders in four or five places. The Idle Man, however, solemnly sponged the scratches with warm water, and L. covered them with patches of sticking-plaister. Finally, the father was presented with a Napoleon; the patient was wrapped in one of his murderer's shirts; and the first act of the tragedy ended.[16]

Particularly in the travel books of the nineteenth century, stories abound of highway robberies and brigandage. Normally, there is not much that the unfortunate victim can do; but Augustus Hare, travelling in Naples in 1881–2, managed to mitigate the inconvenience by a most unusual method – appealing not to the better nature of the brigands but to their *snobbery*:

At Naples, returning at night from the hotels in the lower town to those on the ridge of the hill, a gentleman engaged me in conversation and strolled along by my side. Suddenly, in the most desolate part of the road, he blew a whistle, and another man leapt out of the bushes, and both rushing upon me demanded '*L'orológio e la bórsa* [Your watch and purse].' I declared that I had neither watch nor purse. They insisted on my turning out all my pockets, which contained only three francs in paper and sixteen soldi in copper. Then they demanded my ring. I refused, and said it was no use for them to try to get it; it had not been off my finger for more than thirty years: it would not come off. They struggled to get it off, but could not. Then they whispered together. I said, 'I see what you mean to do: you mean to cut off my finger and then drop me into the sea (which there – opposite the Boschetto – is deep water); but remember, I shall be missed and looked for.' – 'No, we took good care to ascertain that first,' said my first acquaintance; 'you said you had only been two days in Naples (and so I had): people who have been only two days in Naples are never missed.' – 'But I do know Naples well – *bisogna esaminarmi sopra Napoli* [you must ask me about Naples],' I protested. '*Dunque chi fu la Principessa Altamonti* [Then who is the Princess Altamonti]?' – '*Fu figlia del Conte Cini di Roma, sorella della Duchessa Cirella* [She is the daughter of Count Cini of Rome and sister of the Duchess Cirella].' – '*E chi è il Principe S. Teodoro* [And who is Prince S. Teodoro].' – '*Fu Duca di S. Arpino, se maritava con una signora Inglese, Lady Burghersh, chi sta adesso Lady Walsingham* [He is Duke of S. Arpino, who married an English lady, Lady Burghersh, who is now Lady Walsingham].' After this they decided to let me go! But the strangest part of all was that the first brigand said, 'After this scene you will not be able to walk home, and a carriage from the *guardia* costs sixty centesimi; therefore that sum I shall give you back,' and they counted twelve soldi from the sum they had taken. It is this fact which makes me speak of the men who attacked me at Naples as brigands, not as robbers.[17]

Another problem was piracy. The stock picture of the pirate that we all have in our minds – the one-eyed, one-legged buccaneer wearing a three-cornered hat over a bandana handkerchief, a cutlass and a couple of pistols stuck into his sash and the skull and crossbones a-flutter above his head, was firmly established by a single book, *A General History of the Robberies and Murders of the Most Notorious Pyrates*, first published in 1724. The name of the author was given as a certain Captain Charles Johnson, about whom some mystery attaches: he may have been a contemporary playwright of that name, who actually wrote a tragi-comedy called *The Successful Pyrate*; nowadays, however, he is more usually identified with Daniel Defoe. (See the fascinating introduction, by Christopher Lloyd, to the Folio Society edition.)

Whoever was responsible for it, the book contains plenty of splendid stories, including that of the capture off the Carolinas of a Boston sloop commanded by a Captain Beer. The pirate concerned was the notorious Captain Bellamy, who sounds as if he must have come straight from Central Casting – almost too good to be true. Here, for example, is his speech to his luckless victim:

'D—n my b—d,' says he, 'I am sorry they won't let you have your sloop again, for I scorn to do anyone a mischief, when it is not for my advantage; damn the sloop we must sink her, and she might be of use to you. Though, damn ye, you are a sneaking puppy, and so are all those who will submit to be governed by Laws which rich men have made for their own security, for the cowardly whelps have not the courage otherwise to defend what they get by their knavery. But damn ye altogether. Damn them for a pack of crazy rascals, and you, who serve them, for a parcel of hen-hearted numskulls. They villify us, the scoundrels do, when there is only this difference, they rob the poor under the cover of Law, forsooth, and we plunder the rich under the protection of our own courage. Had you not better make one of us, than sneak after the a—s of those villains for Employment?' Capt. Beer told him that his conscience would not allow him to break through the Laws of God and man. 'You are a devillish conscientious rascal, d—n ye,' replied Bellamy. 'I am a free prince, and I have as much authority to make war on the whole world as he who has a hundred sail of ships at sea, and an army of 100,000 men in the field, and this my conscience tells me. But there is no arguing with such snivelling puppies, who allow superiors to kick them about deck at pleasure and pin their faith upon a pimp of a parson, a squab, who neither practises nor believes what he puts upon the chuckle-headed fools he preaches to.'[18]

But Captain Bellamy was by no means the last of his line: contrary to public belief, pirates did not die out in the eighteenth century. Captain Joshua Slocum had a narrow escape from them as recently as 1895:

Monday, August 25, the *Spray* sailed from Gibraltar, well repaid for whatever deviation she had made from a direct course to reach the place. A tug belonging to her Majesty towed the sloop into the steady breeze clear of the mount, where her sails caught a volant wind, which carried her once more to the Atlantic, where it rose rapidly to a furious gale. My plan was, in going down this coast, to haul offshore, well clear of the land, which hereabouts is the home of pirates; but I had hardly accomplished this when I perceived a felucca making out of the nearest port, and finally following in the wake of the *Spray*. Now, my course to Gibraltar had been taken with a view to proceed up the Mediterranean Sea, through the Suez Canal, down the Red Sea, and east about, instead of a western route, which I finally adopted. By officers of vast experience in navigating these seas, I was influenced to make the change. Longshore pirates on both coasts being numerous, I could not afford to make light of the advice. But here I was, after all, evidently in the midst of pirates and thieves! I changed my course; the felucca did the same, both vessels sailing very fast, but the distance growing less and less between us. The *Spray* was doing nobly; she was even more than at her best; but, in spite of all I could do, she would broach now and then. She was carrying too much sail for safety. I must reef or be dismasted and lose all, pirate or no pirate. I must reef, even if I had to grapple with him for my life.

I was not long in reefing the mainsail and sweating it up – probably not more than fifteen minutes; but the felucca had in the meantime so shortened the distance between us that I now saw the tuft of hair on the heads of the crew – by which, it is said, Mohammed will pull the villains up into heaven, – and they were coming on like the wind. From what I could clearly make out now, I felt them to be the sons of generations of pirates, and I saw by their movements that they were now preparing to strike a blow. The exultation on their faces, however, was changed in an instant to a look of fear and rage. Their craft, with too much sail on, broached to on the crest of a great wave. This one great sea changed the aspect of affairs suddenly as the flash of a gun. Three minutes later the same wave overtook the *Spray* and shook her in every timber. At the same moment the sheet-strop parted, and away went the main-boom, broken short at the rigging. Impulsively I sprang to the jib-halyards and down-haul, and instantly downed the jib. The head-sail being off, and the helm put hard down, the sloop came in the wind with a bound. While shivering there, but a moment though it was, I got the mainsail down and secured inboard, broken boom and all. How I got the boom in before the sail was torn I hardly know; but not a stitch of it was broken. The mainsail being secured, I hoisted away the jib, and, without looking round, stepped quickly to the cabin and snatched down my loaded rifle and cartridges at hand; for I made mental calculations that the pirate would by this time have recovered his course and be close aboard, and that when I saw him it would be better for me to be looking at him along the barrel of a gun. The piece was at my shoulder when I peered into the mist, but there was no pirate within a mile. The wave and squall that carried away my boom dismasted the felucca outright. I perceived his thieving crew, some dozen or more of them, struggling to recover their rigging from the sea. Allah blacken their faces![19]

There are, I suspect, several traditional dangers to travellers that are assumed no longer to exist, but which one still ignores at one's peril. In South America, we have read of quite recent instances of explorers being eaten by cannibals; and though there must nowadays be few European women who can claim to have been set upon by wolves, this is exactly what happened to Dervla Murphy on her bicycle journey to India, when she had got no further than Yugoslavia:

On the following morning, with the optimism of impatience, I started to cycle towards Niš; but it had frozen again during the night and though the cold was no longer intolerable I had to admit defeat by black ice once more.

Before mid-day a Montenegrin driver had taken Roz [her bicycle] and me up ten miles outside Belgrade, but at dusk we were still trying, by one road or another, to reach Niš. In despair my companion finally decided to try a détour via a third-class mountain road of which he knew nothing. So, as darkness gathered in the deep valleys, and spread upwards to cover the wooded mountains, we slowly ascended a twisting track, its ridged surface made all the more dangerous by the beginnings of the thaw. My companion had been driving all through the night from Zagreb, his mate having been taken ill there, so I felt the greatest sympathy for him, and I attribute our next misfortune to his extreme fatigue.

At one of the bends, before I could realize what was happening, the truck had skidded off the road and was leaning at a slight angle against a sturdy and very fortunately placed tree, which probably saved us from death at the foot of the precipice.

Having reassured each other that we had received no more than minor injuries, we got out the map, which told us that a village lay about two miles away through the forest on our left. It seemed unlikely that any other traffic would appear and my companion was obviously too exhausted, and too shaken by the crash, to undertake the walk himself, so I suggested that he should write a note for me to deliver to the village policeman, explaining the situation.

It was soon after 6 p.m. when, leaving Roz on the truck, I set off along a convenient cart-track through the trees, where the snow had been packed down by sleighs collecting fire-wood. It was some fifteen minutes later when a heavy weight hurled itself at me without warning.

I stumbled, dropping the torch that I had been carrying, then recovered my balance, and found one animal hanging by its teeth from the left shoulder of my wind-cheater, another worrying at the trousers around my right ankle, and a third standing about two yards away, looking on, only its eyes visible in the starlight.

Ironically enough, I had always thought that there was something faintly comical in the idea of being devoured by wolves. It had seemed to me the sort of thing that doesn't *really* happen . . . So now, as I braced my body against the hanging weight, slipped off my glove, pulled my .25 out of my pocket, flicked up the safety-catch and shot the first animal through the skull, I was possessed by the curious conviction that none of this was true, while at the same time all my actions were governed by sheer panic.

At the sound of the report, and as the first animal dropped to the ground, the second one released my ankle and was about to make off when I fired at him. Meanwhile the third member of the pack (if three can be said to constitute a pack) had tactfully disappeared. Retrieving the torch, I found that one bullet had got the second animal in the ribs – a fantastic fluke shot. Both animals (some authorities think they may have been wild dogs) were males, hardly as big as the average Irish sheepdog, with dreadfully emaciated bodies.

It was when I had left the scene that the reaction set in. Also, forgetting that there was another mile and a half between me and the village, I had lavishly, and quite unnecessarily, emptied my gun, so that every real or imaginary sound made me tremble with apprehension. Walking rapidly, I dwelt with morbid fascination on the part that luck had played in my escape, and the longer I thought about this the more terrified I became, until at last the conviction that I must have gone astray prompted me to take out my compass to confirm the fact that I was still going towards the village.

When I arrived there, the policeman and his wife were having their supper of cold garlic sausage and pickled cucumbers. While the policeman was driving by sleigh to the truck his wife bathed the scalp-wound I had suffered in the crash and gave me hot rum. I slept soundly that night; only during the following week did I start having nightmares about wolves.[20]

Bad moments, however, are not inseparable from extreme physical danger. For Martha Gellhorn, her trip to China in 1941 seems to have consisted of very little else. Here is just one instance:

We were quartered in a stone house in a stone room on a stone floor. It was very cold. The door opened on to the street and the smell thereof. The mosquitoes were competing with the flies and losing. The whisky, our only source of warmth, had run out owing to Generals' enthusiasm for it. I lay on my boards, a foot off the floor, and said in the darkness, 'I wish to die.'

'Too late,' answered U.C. from across the room. 'Who wanted to come to China?'

Why this village presented a particular problem I no longer know. In the cold grey morning I was faced with the unfair fact that a female cannot modestly relieve herself, and no place to retire in a landscape of bare rice paddies, a sea of mud. The village latrine was a public monument, a bamboo tower, reached by a fragile bamboo ladder, the top screened in mats. Beneath, a five foot tall Ali Baba jar stood on the ground to collect valuable human manure.

'I can't do it,' I said, staring at the tower.

'Nobody asks you to,' said U.C. 'You haven't seen any Chinese women fooling around with modesty, have you? I recommend the duck pond, it's the popular spot here.'

'No.'

'Put up or shut up, M., we have to start for the next speeches.'

Cautiously, I climbed the ladder, nervous about the bamboo structure but comforted by the mat screens. At this moment, someone hammered on the nose cap from a Japanese bomb, which served in these villages as air raid siren. I looked down to see the peasants evaporating; the village was empty, even the pigs had departed. Far below, in the street, U.C. grinned up at me.

'What now, M.? What now?'

'Nothing!' I shouted, enraged by my ridiculous situation. 'Here I am and here I stay!'

'The best of Chinese luck to you,' U.C. called and withdrew to a doorway. A squadron of Japanese planes passed, very high and very fast. It must have been the regular run to Kunming. I had an excellent view. I picked my way carefully down the ladder where U.C. met me, laughing heartily.

'Oh poor M., what an inglorious death it would have been. M., the intrepid war correspondent, knocked off in the line of duty. But where? But how, the press of the world inquires.'[21]

In Mexico, too, they are not unknown. In *A Visit to Don Otavio*, Sybille Bedford tells of a lovely bad moment in Guadalajara:

We pulled up in front of a large and beautiful sixteenth-century palace. 'Hotel Guzman,' said Anthony. 'Don't worry, it's all fixed up new inside. You've never seen such bathrooms. Solid black marble.'

We all shot up in a small, fast lift. The manager flung open a door and ushered us into a splendid apartment full of divan beds and somebody's clothes.

'Why that's *my* room,' said Anthony.

'Yes, Sir. I had beds for the ladies moved in while you were absent.'

'Now, see here ...' said Anthony.

E. took over. 'We do not want to be three in a room,' she said gently.

'No room for three? But the gentleman said he was expecting two ladies.'

'Yes, and here we are. But you see we don't want all three to share one room.'

'That is all right, Señora. It is a large room. In Holy Week when there are many travellers we would have a family of seven, nine persons in such a room. And their servants in the bathroom.'

'But this isn't Holy Week.'

'It is not, Señora. In Holy Week there would be a family and servants in every room, now it is only one gentleman and two ladies. It costs more in Holy Week, too.'

'Look here,' I said, 'we have strange habits and we want two, or at least one other room. Have you got them?'

'Yes, yes, many rooms. We are the newest hotel in Guadalajara.'

'Well, can we see them?'

'They are very new, Señora. More new than this room. We are still working on the newness.'

After a good deal more of this, a bed for Anthony was moved into a cupboard leading out of our room. The cupboard had a window, but it opened into a corridor. Ours had an open view over red-tiled roof tops and a brilliant nocturnal sky. The night was warmer than it had been in Morelia. We were very hungry.

A cry of distress from E. in the bathroom. 'My dear, I can't make the water run. Do try.'

Indeed: hot tap, cold tap, tub and basin, not a drop. There was a telephone on the wall, I picked it up.

'There doesn't seem to be any water in our bathroom.'

'Of course not, Señora. It has not been laid on. One thing after another. Perhaps next year? Yes, certainly next year. If we do well. You will recommend us?'

Ready first, I proceeded to go downstairs. I walked up the corridor, none too well-lit, then saw, caught myself, and knees buckling reeled a step backward, collapsed against a wall and howled for Anthony.

He came running. 'What's the matter?'

'THERE ARE NO STAIRS.'

'Well, what d'you want stairs for?'

'I was about to go down.'

'What's wrong with the elevator?'

'Oh God, Anthony, don't be so yourself. And don't let's have a Mexican conversation. Go and see . . . No, don't go! Be careful!'

Anthony went a few steps up the corridor. 'Jesus Christ,' he said.

The corridor ended in space. Seventy feet below, at the bottom of the crater left by flights of marble recently ripped out, lay invisible in a dim pool of light the reception desk, the leather armchairs and the spittoons of the entrance hall. Between, a void. They had begun working on the newness on the top floor. Anthony and I fetched E. from the room and we all went down in the lift.[22]

Let me end this chapter with an extract from Evelyn Waugh's *Remote People*, reprinted in *When the Going Was Good*. Waugh is in Aden, the guest of 'a general merchant, commercial agent, and ship-owner of importance, the only European magnate in the Settlement'. He calls him Mr Leblanc, but the character is clearly modelled on M. Antonin Besse, later to be the founder of St Anthony's College, Oxford. During dinner, Mr

Leblanc tells Waugh of how he takes his clerks on 'little walks over the rocks together':

'To walk in the hills is free. They get up out of the town into the cool air, the views are magnificent, the gentle exercise keeps them in condition for their work. It takes their minds, for a little, off business. You must come with us one day on one of our walks.'

I agreed readily. After the torpid atmosphere of Aden it would be delightful to take some gentle exercise in the cool air. And so it was arranged for the following Saturday afternoon. . . .

I was to lunch first with the young men at their 'mess' – as all communal *ménages* appear to be called in the East. I presented myself dressed as I had seen photographs of 'hikers', with shorts, open shirt, stout shoes, woollen stockings, and large walking-stick. We had an excellent luncheon, during which they told me how, one evening, they had climbed into the Parsees' death-house, and what a row there had been about it. Presently one of them said, 'Well, it's about time to change. We promised to be round at the old man's at half past.'

'Change?'

'Well, it's just as you like, but I think you'll find those things rather hot. We usually wear nothing except shoes and shorts. We leave our shirts in the cars. They meet us on the bathing-beach. And if you've got any rubber-soled shoes I should wear them. Some of the rocks are pretty slippery.' Luckily I happened to have some rubber shoes. I went back to the chaplain's house where I was then living, and changed. I was beginning to be slightly apprehensive.

Mr Leblanc looked magnificent. He wore newly creased white shorts, a silk openwork vest, and white *espadrilles* laced like a ballet dancer's round his ankles. He held a tuberose, sniffing it delicately. 'They call it an Aden lily sometimes,' he said. 'I can't think why.'

There was with him another stranger, a guest of Mr Leblanc's on a commercial embassy from an oil firm. 'I say, you know,' he confided in me, 'I think this is going to be a bit stiff. I'm scarcely in training for anything very energetic.'

We set out in the cars and drove to a dead end at the face of the cliffs near the ancient reservoirs. I thought we must have taken the wrong road, but everyone got out and began stripping off his shirt. The Leblanc party went hatless; the stranger and I retained our topees.

'I should leave those sticks in the car,' said Mr Leblanc.

'But shan't we find them useful?' (I still nursed memories of happy scrambles in the Wicklow hills.)

'You will find them a great nuisance,' said Mr Leblanc.

We did as we were advised.

Then the little walk started. Mr Leblanc led the way with light, springing steps. He went right up to the face of the cliff, gaily but purposefully as Moses may have approached the rocks from which he was about to strike water. There was a little crack running like fork-lightning down the blank wall of stone. Mr Leblanc stood below it, gave one little skip, and suddenly, with great rapidity and no apparent effort, proceeded to ascend the precipice. He did not climb; he rose. It was as if someone were hoisting him up from above and he had merely to prevent himself from swinging out of the perpendicular, by keeping contact with rocks in a few light touches of foot and hand.

In just the same way, one after another, the Leblanc party were whisked away out of sight. The stranger and I looked at each other. 'Are you all right?' came reverberating down from very far ahead. We began to climb. We climbed for about half an hour up the cleft in the rock. Not once during that time did we find a place where it was possible to rest or even to stand still in any normal attitude. We just went on from foothold to foothold; our topees made it impossible to see more than a foot or two above our heads. Suddenly we came to the Leblanc party sitting on a ledge.

'You look hot,' said Mr Leblanc. 'I see you are not in training. You will find this most beneficial.'

As soon as we stopped climbing, our knees began to tremble. We sat down. When the time came to start again, it was quite difficult to stand up. Our knees seemed to be behaving as they sometimes do in dreams, when they suddenly refuse support in moments of pursuit by bearded women broadcasters.

'We thought it best to wait for you,' continued Mr Leblanc, 'because there is rather a tricky bit here. It is easy enough when you know the way, but you need someone to show you. I discovered it myself. I often go out alone in the evenings finding tricky bits. Once I was out all night, quite stuck. I thought I should be able to find a way when the moon rose. Then I remembered there was no moon that night. It was a very cramped position.'

The tricky bit was a huge overhanging rock with a crumbling, flaky surface.

'It is really quite simple. Watch me and then follow. You put your right foot here ...' – a perfectly blank, highly polished surface of stone – '... then rather slowly you reach up with your left hand until you find a hold. You have to stretch rather far ... so. Then you cross your right leg under your left – this is the difficult part – and feel for a footing on the other side ... With your right hand you just steady yourself ... so.' Mr Leblanc hung over the abyss partly out of sight. His whole body seemed prehensile. He *stood* there like a fly on the ceiling. 'That is the position. It is best to trust more to the feet than the hands – push up rather than pull down ... you see the stone here is not always secure.' By way of demonstration he splintered off a handful of apparently solid rock from above his head and sent it tinkling down to the road below. 'Now all you do is to shift the weight from your left foot to your right, and swing yourself round ... so.' And Mr Leblanc disappeared from view.

Every detail of that expedition is kept fresh in my mind by recurrent nightmares. Eventually after about one hour's fearful climb we reached the rim of the crater. The next stage was a tramp across the great pit of loose cinders; then the ascent of the other rim to the highest point of the peninsula. Here we paused to admire the view, which was indeed most remarkable; then we climbed down to the sea. Variety was added to this last phase by the fact that we were now in the full glare of the sun, which had been beating on the cliffs from noon until they were blistering hot.

'It will hurt the hands if you hang on too long,' said Mr Leblanc. 'One must jump on the foot from rock to rock like the little goats.'

At last, after about three hours of it, we reached the beach. Cars and servants were waiting. Tea was already spread; bathing-dresses and towels laid out.

'We always bathe here, not at the club,' said Mr Leblanc. 'They have a screen there to keep out the sharks – while in this bay, only last month, two boys were devoured.'

We swam out into the warm sea. An Arab fisherman, hopeful of a tip, ran to the edge of the sea and began shouting to us that it was dangerous. Mr Leblanc laughed happily and, with easy, powerful strokes, made for the deep waters. We returned to shore and dressed. My shoes were completely worn through, and there was a large tear in my shorts where I had slipped among the cinders and slid some yards. Mr Leblanc had laid out for him in the car a clean white suit, a shirt of green crêpe-de-Chine, a bow tie, silk socks, buckskin shoes, ivory hairbrushes, scent spray, and hair lotion. We ate banana sandwiches and drank very rich China tea.

For a little additional thrill on the way back, Mr Leblanc took the wheel of his car. I am not sure that that was not the most hair-raising experience of all.[23]

CHAPTER TWENTY

Events and Entertainments

In our last chapter we left Thomas Dallam, organ-maker extraordinary but traveller somewhat timorous, on his way to Constantinople. Let us now return to find him safely arrived at the Sublime Porte, and preparing to present his magnificent contrivance to the Sultan. Despite another bad moment at the outset, the whole operation proves a terrific success:

The 17th [August] we wente aborde our ship for the presente, and carried it to our imbassaders house in the Cittie of Gallata, in the vines of Peara; and because there was no roome heie enoughe to sett it up in his house, he caused a roome to be made with all speed withoute the house in the courte, to sett it up in, that it myghte there be made perfitt before it should be carried to the surralia.

The twentethe daye, beinge Mondaye, we begane to louke into our worke; but when we opened our chistes we founde that all glewinge worke was clene Decayed, by reason that it hade layne above six monthes in the hould of our ship, whicte was but newly bulte, so that the extremetie of the heete in the hould of the shipe, with the workinge of the sea and the hootnes of the cuntrie, was the cause that all glewinge fayled; lyke wyse divers of my mettle pipes weare brused and broken.

When our Imbassader, Mr. Wyllyam Aldridge, and other jentlmen, se in what case it was in, theye weare all amayzed, and sayde that it was not worthe iid. My answeare unto our Imbassader and to Mr. Aldridge, at this time I will omitt; but when Mr. Aldridge harde what I sayede, he tould me that yf I did make it perfitt he would give me, of his owne purss, 15li., so aboute my worke I wente.

The 30th daye my worke was finished, and made perfitt at the imbassaderes house. . . .

The 11th Daye [September], beinge Tusdaye, we Carried our instramente over the water to the Grand Sinyors Courte, Called the surralya, and thare in his moste statlyeste house I began to sett it up. . . .

The 24, at nyghte our ambassodor Caled me into his Chamber and gave me a greate Charge to goo the next morninge betimes to the surralia and make the instrumente as perfitt as possibly I could, for that daye, before noune, the Grand Sinyor would se it, and he was to Deliver his imbassage to the Grand Sinyor. . . .

The nexte morninge, being the 25, I wente to the Surralia, and with me my mate Harvie, who was the ingener, Mr. Rowland Buckett the paynter, and Myghell Watson the joyner.

Aboute an houre or tow after my lorde was reddie, and sett forwarde towardes the surralya, he did ride lyke unto a kinge, onlye that he wanted a crowne. Thare roode with him 22 jentlmen and martchantes, all in clothe of goulde . . . thare wente on foute 28 more in blew gounes made after the Turkie fation, and everie man a silke grogren [coarse] cape, after the Itiallian fation. My Livery was a faire clooke of a Franche greene, etc.

Now when I had sett all my worke in good order, the jemyglanes which kepte that house espied the Grand Sinyor cominge upon the water in his goulden Chieke [caïque], or boate, for he cam that morning six myles by water; whear I stoode I saw when he sett foote on the shore.

Than the jemyglanes told me that I muste avoyd the house, for the Grand Sinyor would be thare presently. It was almoste halfe a myle betwyxte the water and that house; but the Grand Sinyor, haveinge a desier to se his presente, came thether wythe marvalus greate speed. . . .

The Grand Sinyor, beinge seated in his Chaire of estate, commanded silence. All being quiett, and no noyes at all, the presente began to salute the Grand Sinyor; for when I lefte it I did alow a quarter of an houre for his cominge thether. Firste the clocke strouke 22; than The chime of 16 bels went of, and played a songe of 4 partes. That beinge done, tow personagis which stood upon to corners of the seconde storie, houldinge tow silver trumpetes in there handes, did lifte them to theire heades, and sounded a tantarra. Than the muzicke went of, and the orgon played a song of 5 partes twyse over. In the tope of the orgon, being 16 foute hie, did stande a holly bushe full of blacke birds and thrushis, which at the end of the musick did singe and shake theire wynges. Divers other motions thare was which the Grand Sinyor wondered at. Than the Grand Sinyor asked the Coppagawe [gatekeeper] yf it would ever doo the lyke againe. He answered that it would doo the lyke againe at the next houre. Cothe he: I will se that. In the meane time, the Coppagaw, being a wyse man, and doubted whether I hade so appoynted it or no, for he knew that it would goo of it selfe but 4 times in 24 houres, so he cam unto me, for I did stand under the house sid, wheare I myghte heare the orgon goo, and he asked me yf it would goo againe at the end of the nexte houre; but I tould him that it would not, for I did thinke the Grand Sinyor would not have stayed so longe by it; but yf it would please him, that when the clocke had strouk he would tuche a litle pin with his finger, which before I had shewed him, it would goo at any time. Than he sayde that he would be as good as his worde to the Grand Sinyor. When the clocke began to strick againe, the Coppagaw went and stood by it; and when the clocke had strouke 23, he tuched that pinn, and it did the lyke as it did before. Than the Grand Sinyor sayed it was good. He satt verrie neare vnto it, ryghte before the Keaes [keys], wheare a man should playe on it by hande. He asked whye those keaes did move when the orgon wente and nothinge did tuche them. He Tould him that by those thinges it myghte be played on at any time. Than the Grande Sinyor asked him yf he did know any man that could playe on it. He sayd no, but he that came with it coulde, and he is heare without the dore. Fetche him hether, cothe the Grand Sinyor, and lett me se how he dothe it. Than the Coppagaw opemed that Dore which I wente out at, for I stoode neare unto it. He came and touke me by the hande, smylinge upon me; but I bid my drugaman aske him what I should dow, or whither I shoulde goo. He answered that it was the Grand Sinyore's pleasur that

I should lett him se me playe on the orgon. So I wente with him. When I came within the Dore, That which I did se was verrie wonderfull unto me. I cam in direcktly upon the Grand Sinyore's ryghte hande, som 16 of my passis [paces] from him, but he would not turne his head to louke upon me. He satt in greate state, yeat the sighte of him was nothinge in Comparrison of the traine that stood behinde him, the sighte whearof did make me almoste to thinke that I was in another worlde. The Grand Sinyor satt still, behouldinge the presente which was befor him, and I stood daslinge my eyes with loukinge upon his people that stood behinde him, the which was four hundrethe persons in number. Tow hundrethe of them weare his princepall padgis, the yongest of them 16 yeares of age, som 20, and som 30. They weare apparled in ritche clothe of goulde made in gowns to the mydlegge; upon theire heades litle caps of clothe of goulde, and som clothe of Tissue [inter-woven]; great peecis of silke abowte theire wastes instead of girdls; upon their leges Cordivan buskins, reede. Theire heades wear all shaven, savinge that behinde Their ears did hange a locke of hare like a squirel's taile; theire beardes shaven, all savinge theire uper lips. Those 200 weare all verrie proper men, and Christians borne.

The thirde hundrethe weare Dum men, that could nether heare nor speake, and theye weare likwyse in gouns of riche Clothe of gould and Cordivan buskins; bute theire Caps weare of violett velvett, the croune of them made like a lether bottell, the brims devided into five picked [peaked] corneres. Som of them had haukes in theire fistes.

The fourthe hundrethe weare all dwarffs, bige-bodied men, but verrie low of stature. Everie Dwarfe did weare a simmeterrie [scimitar] by his side, and they weare also apareled in gowns of Clothe of gould.

I did moste of all wonder at those dumb men, for they lett me understande by theire perfitt sins [signs] all thinges that they had sene the presente dow by its motions.

When I had stode almost one quarter of an houre behouldinge this wonder full sighte, I harde the Grande Sinyore speake unto the Coppagaw, who stood near unto him. Than the Coppagaw cam unto me, and touke my cloake from aboute me, and laye it Doune upon the Carpites, and bid me go and playe on the organ; but I refused to do so, because the Grand Sinyor satt so neare the place wheare I should playe that I could not com at it, but I muste needes turne my backe Towardes him and touche his Kne with my britchis, which no man, in paine of deathe, myghte dow, savinge only the Coppagaw. So he smyled, and lett me stande a litle. Than the Grand Sinyor spoake againe, and the Coppagaw, with a merrie countenance, bid me go with a good curridge, and thruste me on. When I cam verrie neare the Grand Sinyor, I bowed my heade as low as my kne, not movinge my cape, and turned my backe righte towardes him, and touched his kne with my britchis.

He satt in a verrie ritche Chaire of estate, upon his thumbe a ringe with a diamon in it halfe an inche square, a faire simeterie by his side, a bow, and a quiver of Arros.

He satt so righte behinde me that he could not se what I did; tharfore he stood up, and his Coppagaw removed his Chaire to one side, wher he myghte se my handes; but, in his risinge from his chaire, he gave me a thruste forwardes, which he could not otherwyse dow, he satt so neare me; but I thought he had bene drawinge his sorde to cut of my heade.

I stood thar playinge suche thinge as I coulde untill the cloke stroucke, and than I boued my heade as low as I coulde, and wente from him with my backe towardes him. As I was taking of my cloake, the Coppagaw came unto me and bid me stand still and lett my cloake lye; when I had stood a litle whyle, the Coppagaw bid me goo and cover the Keaes of the organ; then I wente Close to the Grand Sinyor againe, and bowed myselfe, and then I wente backewardes to my Cloake. When the Company saw me do so theye semed to be glad, and laughed. Than I saw the Grand Sinyor put his hande behind him full of goulde, which the Coppagaw Receved, and broughte unto me fortie and five peecis of gould called chickers [sequins], and than was I put out againe wheare I came in, beinge not a little joyfull of my good suckses.

Beinge gotten oute of the surralia, I made all the spede I could to that gate where the imbassador wente in, for he and all his Company stode all these tow houres expecktinge the Grand Sinyors cominge to another place whear he should deliver his imbassege and Letteres.

When I came to that greate gate I sawe our Imbassador takeinge horse to begone. As I was making haste towardes him, he saw me, and came to me, Askinge me yf the Grand Sinyor had sene the presente. I tould him yeas, and that I had sene the Grand Sinyor, and that I had gould out of his pockett; whearat he semed to be verrie glade.[1]

Not, perhaps, one of the greatest of travellers, but certainly one of the greatest eccentrics in the whole history of travel, was the celebrated Lady Hester Stanhope. The niece of William Pitt and his hostess during the last years of his premiership, she became progressively disenchanted with English society and in 1810 left the country, never to return. The next twenty-nine years she spent in the East, living for the latter part of them in a deserted monastery near Djoun in the mountains of Lebanon, among whose ruins we used to picnic in the 1950s. Among the Beduin tribes, however, she quickly acquired an extraordinary reputation as a prophetess – which accounts for the ceremonial welcome they gave her on her first entrance into Palmyra in March 1813. The following account of it is by her medical attendant and travelling companion Dr Charles Meryon, who subsequently published no less than six volumes about his life with her:

The inhabitants had resolved on welcoming Lady Hester in the best manner they could, and had gone out in a body to meet her. There might be altogether fifty men on foot, who, naked down to the waist, without shoes or stockings, and covered with a sort of antique petticoat, ran by the side of as many horsemen, galloping in all directions, with rude kettle-drums beating and colours flying. The tanned skins of the men on foot formed a curious contrast with the cowry shells, or blackamoor's teeth, studded on the two belts which crossed their shoulders, and to which were suspended their powder-flasks and cartouch-boxes. These Palmyrenes carry matchlocks, slung across their backs, and are very skilful in the use of them. They are huntsmen by profession, and they are often engaged in petty warfare with the Bedouins, for the protection of their caravans.

For the amusement of Lady Hester and Mr. B., they displayed before them a mock attack and defence of a caravan. Each party, anxious to distinguish itself in the eyes of the English lady, fought with a pretended fury that once or twice might almost have been thought real. The men on foot exhibited on the person of a horseman the mode of stripping for plunder, and no valet de chambre could undress his master more expeditiously.

On entering the Valley of the Tombs, Lady Hester's attention was absorbed in viewing the wonders around her, and the combatants desisted. But another sight, prepared by the Palmyrenes, here awaited her. In order to increase the effect which ruins cause on those who enter them for the first time, the guides led us up through the long colonnade, which extends four thousand feet in length from north-west to south-east, in a line with the gate of the temple. This colonnade is terminated by a triumphal arch. The shaft of each pillar, to the right and left, at about the height of six feet from the ground, has a projecting pedestal, called in architecture a console, under several of which is a Greek or Palmyrene inscription; and upon each there once stood a statue, of which at present no vestige remains excepting the marks of the cramp-iron for the feet. What was our surprise to see, as we rode up the avenue, and just as the triumphal arch came in sight, that several beautiful girls (selected, as we afterwards learned, from the age of twelve to sixteen) had been placed on these very pedestals, in the most graceful postures, and with garlands in their hands; their elegant shapes being but slightly concealed by a single loose robe, girded at the waist with a zone, and a white crape veil covering their heads. On each side of the arch other girls, no less lovely, stood by threes, whilst a row of six was ranged across the gate of the arch, with thyrsi in their hands. Whilst Lady Hester advanced, these living statues remained immoveable on their pedestals; but when she had passed they leaped on the ground, and joined in a dance by her side. On reaching the triumphal arch, the whole in groups, together with men and girls intermixed, danced around her. Here some bearded elders chanted verses in her praise, and all the spectators joined in chorus. The sight was truly interesting, and I have seldom seen one that moved my feelings more. Lady Hester herself seemed to partake of the emotions to which her presence in this remote spot had given rise. Nor was the wonder of the Palmyrenes less than our own. They beheld with amazement a woman, who had ventured thousands of miles from her own country, and had now crossed a waste where hunger and thirst were only a part of the evils to be dreaded. The procession advanced, after a pause, to the gate of the Temple, being by this time increased by the addition of every man, woman, and child, in the village.[2]

And so to Paris, where we find Horace Walpole on 21 April 1739, writing to his friend Richard West:

You figure us in a set of pleasures, which, believe me, we do not find; cards and eating are so universal, that they absorb all variation of pleasures. The operas, indeed, are much frequented three times a week; but to me they would be a greater penance than eating maigre: their music resembles a gooseberry tart as much as it does harmony. We have not yet been at the Italian playhouse; scarce any one goes there. Their best amusement, and which, in some parts, beats ours, is the comedy;

three or four of the actors excel any we have: but then to this nobody goes, if it is not one of the fashionable nights; and then they go, be the play good or bad – except on Molière's nights, whose pieces they are quite weary of. Gray and I have been at the Avare to-night; I cannot at all commend their performance of it. Last night I was in the Place de Louis le Grand (a regular octagon, uniform, and the houses handsome, though not so large as Golden Square), to see what they reckoned one of the finest burials that ever was in France. It was the Duke de Tresmes, governor of Paris and marshal of France. It began on foot from his palace to his parish-church, and from thence in coaches to the opposite end of Paris, to be interred in the church of the Celestins, where is his family-vault. ... A long procession of flambeaux and friars; no plumes, trophies, banners, led horses, scutcheons, or open chariots; nothing but

> friars,
> White, black, and grey, with all their trumpery.

This godly ceremony began at nine at night, and did not finish till three this morning; for, each church they passed, they stopped for a hymn and holy water. By the bye, some of these choice monks, who watched the body while it lay in state, fell asleep one night, and let the tapers catch fire of the rich velvet mantle lined with ermine and powdered with gold flower-de-luces, which melted the lead coffin, and burnt off the feet of the deceased before it awakened them. The French love show; but there is a meanness reigns through it all. ...

The weather is still so bad, that we have not made any excursions to see Versailles and the environs, not even walked in the Tuileries; but we have seen almost every thing else that is worth seeing in Paris, though that is very considerable. They beat us vastly in buildings, both in number and magnificence. The tombs of Richelieu and Mazarin at the Sorbonne and the College de Quatre Nations are wonderfully fine, especially the former. We have seen very little of the people themselves, who are not inclined to be propitious to strangers, especially if they do not play and speak the language readily. ... If we did not remember there was such a place as England, we should know nothing of it: the French never mention it, unless it happens to be in one of their proverbs![3]

But what about the entertainments at home? Nearly half a century later, on 13 June 1782, the German Carl Philip Moritz writes a letter in his turn:

Although I had so often heard of Ranelagh I had no very clear idea of it. I knew it was a garden, somewhat differently arranged than Vauxhall, but exactly how I did not know.

Yesterday I started out on foot to visit this resort of pleasure; I missed my way, however, and eventually found myself in Chelsea. There I met a man pushing a wheelbarrow, who not only directed me very politely but also spoke with me during the time he went with me. He asked me from which country I came, and when I told him I was from Prussia, he inquired very eagerly about our King of Prussia and listened to many stories I told him about that monarch.

So at last I came to Ranelagh, and, after paying my half-crown at the entrance, asked the way to the garden door. This was pointed out to me and then, to my great astonishment, I found myself in a garden rather large but sickly in its aspect, unseemly, ill lit and sparsely inhabited. I had not been there long before a young lady who was likewise strolling about offered me her arm without introduction and asked me why I was going about all alone. It struck me at that moment that this could not possibly be the magnificent and much recommended Ranelagh! So, as I saw several people go through a door, I followed, hoping by that way to come out into the fresh air or at least to a change of scene.

But what a sight I saw as I came from the darkness of that garden into the glare of a round building lit with hundreds of lamps, surpassing in splendour and beauty any I had ever seen before! Everything here was circular. Above stood a gallery with private boxes; in one part of this gallery stood an organ and a well-built choir apse, from which poured forth music both vocal and instrumental. Round the building were set richly painted alcoves for those who wished to take refreshments. On the floor lay carpets surrounding four high black pillars containing ornate fireplaces where coffee, tea and punch were being prepared, and round all the circle tables were set with refreshments. Around these four high pillars all of fashionable London revolved like a gaily coloured distaff, sauntering in a compact throng.

On my entry I mixed with this crowd, and what with the constant changing of the faces around me (most of them strikingly beautiful), the illuminations, the majesty and splendour of the place, and the ever-present strains of music, I felt for a moment as a child would on first looking into a fairy-tale.

When I became tired of the crowd and of strolling round in a circle I sat down in one of the alcoves in order to take some refreshment, and from this vantage-point watched with ease the play and gathering of this happy carefree world. A waiter politely asked me what I should like and in a few minutes brought me my order. To my astonishment he would take no payment for the refreshments he had brought, and this I failed to understand until he explained that these had already been paid for with my half-crown entrance-fee and that I had only to say if I wanted more. If I wished, however, I might give him a small tip. This I did with great pleasure, since my half-crown could hardly pay for so much courtesy and entertainment.

I then went into the gallery and sat in one of the boxes, from which, like a solemn watcher of the world, I looked down on the concourse still turning round and round in circles. Some wore stars and symbols of noble orders, French hairdressing or official wigs. Old and young, nobility and commoners, I saw them all crossing and recrossing in a motley swarm. At my request an Englishman who had joined me pointed out the princes and peers who, with their huge stars, eclipsed the remainder of the company.

In one direction, some who wished to see and to be seen were going round in an everlasting circle, in another, a group of music-lovers had gathered to delight their ears in front of the orchestra; others were delighting their palates in a more substantial manner at the well-served tables. More, like myself, sat alone in the corner of a box in the gallery contemplating all these from above.

Every now and then I would compare for my own satisfaction the glitter of this scene with the darkness in the garden outside, in order to recapture some of the thrill I had enjoyed when I first entered the building. Well into the night I amused myself thus, until the throng began to thin out. Then I took a coach and drove home.

The company at Ranelagh looked superior to that at Vauxhall, for none of the lower class go there unless dressed in their best, so seeking to accommodate themselves to the prevailing social tone of the place. At least, I saw no one in all that throng who did not wear silk stockings. The poorest families make an effort to go to Ranelagh at least once a year, my landlady assures me; she herself always fixes a day in the year when without fail she will be ferried to Ranelagh. Moreover, the expense is not so great in Ranelagh as in Vauxhall if you take into account the cost of refreshments. Anyone who wants to dine in Vauxhall – as most of them do – can be charged half a guinea for a very sparing meal.[4]

In St Petersburg, on the other hand, the public entertainment – though agreeable and amusing enough – was somewhat less sophisticated. Our old friend Miss Catherine Wilmot wrote to her father on 7 March 1804:

I was a few days ago for the first time on the Mountains of Ice which you may have read of in the history of the amusements of St Petersburg. It was extremely amusing. We were mounted on a staircase of at least eighty feet, at the top of which we found a charming arbour ornamented with green branches of Fir, from that an Ally of Wood which was elevated to the summit of the height and descended gradually to the ground. It was perfectly smooth for Water had been thrown on it which froze instantly. Well let us mount once more into the Arbour and sit down in an Arm Chair with one companion. The Chair has Skates instead of feet. A man who is behind you pushes you. He is provided with Skates. He directs the chair, and there you are without the least possibility of stopping till you arrive at the end of your journey. I should think the sensation must resemble the flight of a Bird. I found it very agreeable, as you may believe when I went seven times.[5]

Just over a hundred years after that – in 1907 to be precise – Maurice Baring found himself at the annual Fair of Nijni-Novgorod. He describes it in *The Puppet Show of Memory*:

What surprised and struck me most about the Fair was the great size of it. I had not guessed that the Fair was a large town consisting entirely of shops, hotels, and restaurants. The most important merchandise that passed hands at the Fair was furs. But there were goods of every variety: second-hand books, tea, and silks from China, gems from the Urals, and *art nouveau* furniture. There were also old curiosity shops rich in church vestments, stiff copes and jewelled chasubles, which would be found most useful by those people who like to furnish their drawing-rooms entirely with objects diverted from their proper use; that is to say, teapots made out of musical instruments and old book bindings. Nijni, during the Fair, was almost entirely inhabited by merchants – merchants of every kind and description. The majority of them wore loose Russian shirts and top-boots. I noticed that at Nijni it did not in the least signify how untidily one was dressed; however untidy one looked, one was sure of being treated with respect, because slovenliness at Nijni did not necessarily imply poverty, and the people of the place justly reasoned that however sordid our exterior appearance might be, there was no knowing but it might clothe a millionaire. Another thing which struck me here, a thing which has struck me in several other places, was the way in which people determined your nationality by your clothes. While they paid no attention to *degree* in the matter of clothes at Nijni, as to whether they were shabby or new, they paid a great deal of attention to kind. For instance, the day I arrived I was wearing an ordinary English straw hat. This headgear caused quite a sensation amongst the sellers of Astrakan fur. They crowded round me, crying out: 'Vairy nice, vairy cheap, Eng-leesh.' I bought a different kind of hat, a white yachting cap, and loose silk Russian shirt, such as the merchants wore.

That evening I went to a restaurant at which there was a musical performance. I fell into conversation with a young merchant sitting at the next table, and he said to me after we had had some conversation: 'You are, I suppose, from the Caucasus.' I said 'No.' We talked of other things, the Far East among other topics. He then exclaimed: 'You are, I suppose, from the Far East.' I again said 'No,' and we again talked of other things. He had some friends with him who joined in the conversation, and they were consumed with curiosity as to whence I had come, and I told them they could guess. They guessed various places, such as Archangel, Irkutsk, Warsaw, and Saghalien, and at last one of them cried out with joy: 'I know what place you belong to; you are a native of Nijni.' They went away triumphant. Their place was taken by a very old merchant, a rugged, grey-haired, bearded peasant. He looked on at the singing and dancing which was taking place on the stage for some time, and then he said to me: 'Don't you wish you were twenty years younger?' I said I did, but I did not think that I should in that case be better equipped for this particular kind of entertainment, as I should be only twelve years old. 'Impossible!' said the old man indignantly. 'You are quite bald, and bear every sign of old age.'[6]

A form of entertainment that is to be found, in one manifestation or another, in every country in the world is the dance – intended sometimes as a spectacle for the delectation of others; sometimes as a satisfaction in itself, giving pleasure only to the dancers; and sometimes as a religious ritual. The Dance of the Sprouting Corn, as reported by D. H. Lawrence in *Mornings in Mexico*, falls into this last category – although it must have given a considerable thrill to Lawrence when he witnessed it. As a piece of sustained descriptive writing, I suppose that this passage must rank pretty high; and yet, and yet ... somehow, it reads more like a parody of Lawrence's style than the real thing. In the original, moreover, it goes on for pages and pages, all of the same remorseless intensity; here I have cut it down to little more than half its length. How one longs for a touch of humour now and then:

Roughly the low, square, mud-pie houses make a wide street where all is naked earth save a doorway or a window with a pale-blue sash. At the end of the street, turn again into a parallel wide, dry street. And there, in the dry, oblong aridity, there tosses a small forest that is alive: and thud – thud – thud goes the drum, and the deep sound of men singing is like the deep soughing of the wind, in the depths of a wood.

You realize that you had heard the drum from the distance, also the deep, distant roar and boom of the singing, but that you had not heeded, as you don't heed the wind.

It all tosses like young, agile trees in a wind. This is the dance of the sprouting corn, and everybody holds a little, beating branch of green pine. Thud – thud – thud – thud – thud! goes the drum, heavily the men hop and hop and hop, sway, sway, sway, sway go the little branches of green pine. It tosses like a little forest, and the deep sound of men's singing is like the booming and tearing of a wind deep inside a forest. They are dancing the Spring Corn Dance.

This is the Wednesday after Easter, after Christ Risen and the corn germinated. They dance on Monday and on Tuesday. Wednesday is the third and last dance of this green resurrection.

You realize the long line of dancers, and a solid cluster of men singing near the drum. You realize the intermittent black-and-white fantasy of the hopping Koshare, the jesters, the Delight-Makers. You become aware of the ripple of bells on the knee-garters of the dancers, a continual pulsing ripple of little bells; and of the sudden wild, whooping yells from near the drum. Then you become aware of the seed-like shudder of the gourd-rattles, as the dance changes, and the swaying of the tufts of green pine-twigs stuck behind the arms of all the dancing men, in the broad green arm-bands.

Gradually come through to you the black, stable solidity of the dancing women, who poise like solid shadow, one woman behind each rippling, leaping male. The long, silky black hair of the women streaming down their backs, and the equally long, streaming, gleaming hair of the males, loose over broad, naked, orange-brown shoulders. . . .

When you look at the women, you forget the men. The bare-armed, bare-legged, barefoot women with streaming hair and lofty green tiaras, impassive, downward-looking faces, twigs swaying outwards from subtle, rhythmic wrists; women clad in the black, prehistoric short gown fastened over one shoulder, leaving the other shoulder bare, and showing at the arm-place a bit of pink or white undershirt; belted also round the waist with a woven woollen sash, scarlet and green on the hand-woven black cassock. The noble, slightly submissive bending of the tiara-ed head. The subtle measure of the bare, breathing, bird-like feet, that are flat, and seem to cleave to earth softly, and softly lift away. The continuous outward swaying of the pine-sprays.

But when you look at the men, you forget the women. The men are naked to the waist, and ruddy-golden, and in the rhythmic hopping leap of the dance their breasts shake downwards, as the strong, heavy body comes down, down, down, down, in the downward plunge of the dance. The black hair streams loose and living down their backs, the black brows are level, the black eyes look out unchanging from under the silky lashes. They are handsome, and absorbed with a deep rhythmic absorption, which still leaves them awake and aware. Down, down, down they drop, on the heavy, ceaseless leap of the dance, and the great necklaces of shell-cores spring on the naked breasts, the neck-shell flaps up and down, the short white kilt of woven stuff, with the heavy woollen embroidery, green and red and black, opens and shuts slightly to the strong lifting of the knees: the heavy whitish cords that hang from the kilt-band at the side sway and coil for ever down the side of the right leg, down to the ankle, the bells on the red-woven garters under the knees ripple without end, and the feet, in buckskin boots furred round the ankle with a beautiful band of skunk fur, black with a white tip, come down with a lovely, heavy, soft precision, first one, then the other, dropping always plumb to earth. Slightly bending forward, a black gourd rattle in the right hand, a small green bough in the left, the dancer dances the eternal drooping leap, that brings his life down, down, down, down from the mind, down from the broad beautiful shaking breast, down to the powerful pivot of the knees, then to the ankles, and plunges deep from the ball of the foot into the earth, towards the earth's red centre, where these men belong, as is signified by the red earth with which they are smeared.

And meanwhile, the shell-cores from the Pacific sway up and down, ceaselessly on their breasts. ...

Suddenly the solitary man pounding the drum swings his drum round, and begins to pound on the other end, on a higher note, pang – pang – pang! instead of the previous brumm! brumm! brumm! of the bass note. The watchful man next the drummer yells and waves lightly, dancing on bird-feet. The Koshare make strange, eloquent gestures to the sky.

And again the gleaming bronze-and-dark men dancing in the rows shudder their rattles, break the rhythm, change into a queer, beautiful two-step, the long lines suddenly curl into rings, four rings of dancers, the leaping, gleaming-seeming men between the solid, subtle, submissive blackness of the women who are crowned with emerald-green tiaras, all going subtly round in rings. Then slowly they change again, and form a star. Then again, unmingling, they come back into rows. ...

And all the time, running like queer spotted dogs, they weave nakedly, through the unheeding dance, comical, weird, dancing the dance-step naked and fine, prancing through the lines, up and down the lines, and making fine gestures with their flexible hands, calling something down from the sky, calling something up from the earth, and dancing forward all the time. Suddenly as they catch a word from the singers, name of a star, of a wind, a name for the sun, for a cloud, their hands soar up and gather in the air, soar down with a slow motion. And again, as they catch a word that means earth, earth deeps, water within the earth, or red-earth-quickening, the hands flutter softly down, and draw up the water, draw up the earth-quickening, earth to sky, sky to earth, influences above to influences below, to meet in the germ-quick of corn, where life is. ...

And the mystery of germination, not procreation, but *putting forth*, resurrection, life springing within the seed, is accomplished. The sky has its fire, its waters, its stars, its wandering electricity, its winds, its fingers of cold. The earth has its reddened body, its invisible hot heart, its inner waters and many juices and un-accountable stuffs. Between them all, the little seed: and also man, like a seed that is busy and aware. And from the heights and from the depths man, the caller, calls: man, the knower, brings down the influences and brings up the influences, with his knowledge: man, so vulnerable, so subject, and yet even in his vulnerability and subjection, a master, commands the invisible influences and is obeyed. Commands in that song, in that rhythmic energy of dance, in that still-submissive mockery of the Koshare. And he accomplishes his end, as master. He partakes in the springing of the corn, in the rising and budding and earing of the corn. And when he eats his bread at last, he recovers all he once sent forth, and partakes again of the energies he called to the corn, from out of the wide universe.[7]

Well, yes. Personally, I prefer Norman Lewis's description of a popular celebration in Northern Guatemala. It comes from an essay called 'A Quiet Evening in Huehuetenango', included in his book *The Changing Sky*:

The sleepiness of the place was beginning to paralyse us. Nothing stirred but the vultures waving their scarves of shadow over the flower beds. Calmo said, 'Yesterday a market-day, tomorrow a procession; so that today we have no prospect but an early night. There is really nothing to do.' As he spoke, a man came riding into the plaza on a tall, bony horse. The man looked like an Englishman on his way to a fancy-dress ball: he was lean, pink-cheeked, mildly aloof of expression, and his improbable costume of black leather with silver facings had clearly been hired out too often and was on the loose side for its present wearer. He was carrying a bundle of what looked like yard-brooms wrapped up in coloured paper. Calmo explained that these would be rockets for use in the next day's celebrations. The clip-clop of the hooves died away, and the silence came down like a drop-curtain. . . .

After dinner I resigned myself to an early evening, and went to bed under a religious picture consisting of an eye projecting rays in all directions, and beneath it the question: 'What is a moment of pleasure weighed in the scales against an eternity of punishment?' I had hardly dozed off when I was awakened by an explosion. I got up and opened the window. The street had filled up with people who were all going in the same direction and chattering excitedly. A siren wailed and a motorcycle policeman went past deafeningly, snaking in and out of the crowd. There was another explosion, and as this was the homeland of revolutions it was natural to assume that one had started. I dressed and went out into the courtyard, where the hotel boy was throwing a bayonet at an anatomical chart given away with a Mexican journal devoted to home medicine. The boy said that so far as he knew there had been no *pronunciamento*, and the bangs were probably someone celebrating his saint's day. I then remembered the lean horseman.

As the tumult showed no signs of abating I walked down to the plaza, which had filled up with blank-faced Indians moving slowly round in an anti-clockwise direction as if stirred up by some gigantic invisible spoon. There were frequent scuffles and outcries as young men singled out girls from the promenading groups and broke coloured eggs on their heads, rubbing the contents well into the thick black hair. The eggs were being sold by the basketful all over the plaza, and they turned out to have been emptied, refilled with some brittle, wafer-like substance, repaired and then painted. When a girl sometimes returned the compliment, the gallant thus favoured stopped to bow, and said: 'Muchas gracias.'

Calmo, whom I soon ran into, his jacket pockets bulging with eggs, said it looked as if there were going to be a fiesta after all. He couldn't think why. There was really no excuse for it. The fashionable town-Indians, most of them shopkeepers, had turned out in all their finery, headed by the 'Queen of Huehuetenango' herself – a splendidly beflounced creature with ribbon-entwined pigtails down to her thighs, who was said to draw her revenues from a *maison de rendezvous* possessing radioactive baths. There was a sedate sprinkling of whites, hatted and begloved for the occasion.

Merchants had put up their stalls and were offering sugar skulls, holy pictures, plastic space-guns, and a remedy for heart-sickness which is a speciality of Huehuetenango and tastes like inferior port. We found the lean horseman launching his rockets in military fashion from a wooden rack-like contraption. They were aimed so as to hiss as alarmingly low as possible over the heads of the crowds, showering them with sparks, and sometimes they cleared the building opposite and sometimes they did not. Other enthusiasts were discharging *mortaretes*, miniature flying bombs, which leaped two or three hundred feet straight up into the air before exploding with an ear-stunning crack. The motor-cycle policeman on his scarlet Harley-Davidson with wide-open exhaust, and eight front and six rear lights, came weaving and bellowing round the plaza at intervals of about a minute, and a travelling movie-show was using part of the cathedral's baroque façade as the screen for a venerable Mexican film called *Ay mi Jalisco* featuring a great deal of gun-play.

A curious hollow structure looking like a cupola sliced in half had been built on the top of the town hall, and about this time powerful lights came on in its interior and nine sad-faced men in dark suits entered it by an invisible door, carrying what looked like several grand pianos. A moment later these pieces of furniture had been placed end to end to form an enormous marimba, under an illuminated sign that said 'Musica Civica'. A cosmic voice coughed electrically and then announced that in response to the esteemed public's many requests the municipal orchestra would have pleasure in rendering a selection of notable composers' works. Eighteen hammers then came down on the keys with a resounding opening flourish, and the giant marimba raced into an athletic version of 'If You Were the Only Girl in the World'.

Calmo and I took refuge from the torrent of sound in a tavern called The Little Chain of Gold. It was a place of great charm containing a shrine and a newly installed juke-box in addition to the usual accessories, and was decorated with beautiful calendars given away by Guatemalan bus companies and a couple of propaganda pictures of mutilated corpses put out by the new government after the last revolution. The Little Chain advertised the excellence of its 'hots-doogs'. Most of its customers were *preparados* Indians who had done military service and had rejected their tribal costumes in favour of brightly coloured imitations of American army uniforms. Some of them added a slightly sinister touch to their gay ensembles of reds and blues by covering the lower part of their faces with black cloths, a harmless freak of fashion which I was told had originated in a desire to breathe in as little dust as possible when foot-slogging along the country roads.

Calmo said that the main difference between a preparado and a tribal Indian was that the preparado, who had acquired a civilized taste for whisky, couldn't afford to get drunk so often as an uncivilized drinker of aguardiente.

We drank the aguardiente.[8]

My next offering fits a little uncertainly into this chapter, but I have nowhere else to put it; I am determined to get it in somewhere, because it has stuck in my mind ever since I first read it, over twenty years ago, when travelling in the country it describes. It is by Geoffrey Gorer, and comes from a most remarkable book called *Africa Dances*:

A man called Epiphane had had a silver bracelet stolen. Instead of going to the police about his loss he called in a fetisher. The fetisher took up a position just off the main road a little way out of Abomey (where the bracelet had been stolen) and had a chicken brought to him. He held the chicken by the claws in his left hand above his head, so that the bird's beak was level with his mouth, and started talking to it quietly. He was telling it about the theft, repeating the same words over and over again. After some little time the chicken began to bleed from the mouth, a drop every few minutes. The fetisher went on talking quietly. This had been going on for more than half an hour when a man suddenly arrived desperately out of breath and with his pagne torn; he fell panting on the ground by the fetisher. The fetisher went on talking to the bird, which suddenly gave a sort of strangled squawk, at which the exhausted man confessed that he had stolen the bracelet and explained how he had taken it and where it was. The fetisher put the chicken on the ground; it started pecking rather uncertainly.

Prince Aho explained that this was the usual method of dealing with stolen property. When the chicken started to bleed the thief was forced to come to where the fetisher was, wherever he might be and whatever he was doing. Only certain fetishers knew how to do this. I wanted to see it repeated, but never had another opportunity.

Benga and I were made, as it were, honorary members of the Agassou (panther) fetish, on the ground that I was certainly and he probably harbouring the spirit of a dead fetisher. But before our initiation we were made to swear that we would neither write nor speak about anything we might see or experience, and we had to leave cameras, pencils and notebooks behind. For the greater part I was going rather regretfully to keep my word – regretfully, for a number of very curious things occurred. I realize that this sounds rather like Herodotus with the Egyptian mysteries, and I think we may both be in the same position; after all, we are both of us pretty good liars, and could make up perfectly satisfying marvels if we wanted to. Concerning three incidents, however, I am going to break my vow; they are none of them fundamental but all to my mind interesting.

The first occurred before we were admitted into the convent. A sacrifice was being made at which we could not be present, and we both stood outside the courtyard on the grass in the moonlight holding a piece of dried grass in our left hands (this grass played a considerable rôle later), probably looking ridiculous and feeling very silly and rather alarmed. Our sponsor and interpreter was with the priest. After a time he came out and said to me, 'You live in a white house on a hill surrounded by trees; you have a mother and two brothers who are walking under the trees' (a quite adequate description of my home and family; and it was very probable that on 25 June they would have been walking in the garden in the evening). Then he turned to Benga and said, 'You have no home. In the place you think of as home there are many people. Your two sisters are well, but your dead mother's husband was taken very ill two days ago; he will recover, however, before you see him again.' This was exact in every particular; on 23 June Benga's stepfather had had a severe attack, as we verified on our return to Dakar, and he was quite convalescent before we returned. We were more than a thousand miles from Dakar at the time, and had received no communications from there for the better part of a month.

After a night spent in the convent we were considered to be fetishers. Fairly early in the morning we went with the priest and the other fetishers into the open country, among maize fields. A chicken was killed – the number of animals which were killed that night, and I presume every night in Dahomey, is astounding – and the priest started to sing in a low voice. The rest of us stood about, smoking or chewing cola. After about half an hour a full-grown panther walked out of the maize and started moving among the people; it was quickly followed by another, and in a short time there were fifteen panthers among us. They arrived from every direction. We had been told most earnestly on no account to touch them, and not to be afraid of them, for they would only harm wicked men (i.e. sorcerers). I was scared so that I felt my legs shaking, but I was able to keep quiet. When the fetisher stopped singing they went away again. The first animal had eaten the chicken. This was the only time in Africa that I saw any of the fiercer mammals alive and in freedom. There were a number of villages within an hour's walk. It was about fifteen miles from Abomey.

It was a particularly fine and cloudless afternoon when we visited the convent of the worshippers of Héviosso, the thunder fetish. After the usual sacrifice three men went into a trance inside the hut, while we stood in what shade we could find in the courtyard. Suddenly against the blue sky there was a flash of lightning, followed shortly by a loud peal of thunder. The flashes and thunder got more frequent and louder, till they seemed simultaneous, and the thunder gave that particularly unpleasant crack which it does in the tropics when the storm is nearly directly overhead. Gradually the thunder and lightning got fainter and finally died in a rumble. It had been exactly like a quick tropical thunderstorm, except that there had been no rain and no clouds; the sun was shining all the time.[9]

And now, for a little light relief, is Evelyn Waugh describing – in *Labels* – a circus in Port Said:

We were the only Europeans in the tent. The chairs were ranged on rather unstable wooden steps ascending from the ring to a considerable height at the back. Behind the back row were a few heavily curtained boxes for the women; there were very few there; most of the large audience consisted of young men, a few of them in ready-made suits of European pattern, but all wearing the red *taboosh*. A number of small boys were huddled between the front row and the ringside, and a policeman was employing his time in whisking these off the parapet with a cane. The seats seemed all to be the same price; we paid 5 piastres each and chose places near the back. Attendants were going about between the rows selling nuts, mineral waters, coffee, and hubble-bubbles. These were of the simplest pattern, consisting simply of a coconut half full of water, a little tin brazier of tobacco, and a long bamboo mouthpiece. The doctor warned me that if I smoked one of these I was bound to catch some frightful disease; I did so, however, without ill effect. The vendor keeps several alight at a time by sucking at each in turn. We all drank coffee, which was very thick and sweet and gritty.

The show had begun before we arrived, and we found ourselves in the middle of a hugely popular comic turn; two Egyptians in European costume were doing cross-talk. It was, of course, wholly unintelligible to us; now and then they smacked or kicked each other, so I have no doubt it was much the same as an English music-hall turn. After what seemed an unconscionable time the comedians went away amid thunderous applause, and their place was taken by a very pretty little white girl in a ballet dress; she cannot have been more than ten or twelve years old; she danced a Charleston. Later she came round and sold picture postcards of herself. She turned out to be French. To those that enjoy moralizing about such things there is food for reflection in the idea of this African dance, travelling across two continents from slave to gigolo, and gradually moving south again towards the land of its origin.

Then there were some Japanese jugglers, and then an interminable comic turn performance by the whole company. They sang a kind of doleful folk song and then, one at a time, with enormous elaboration of 'business', came in and lay down on the ground; after all the grown-ups were settled the little girl came in and lay down too; finally a tiny child of two or three tottered in and lay down. All this took at least a quarter of an hour. Then they all got up again, still singing, one at a time in the same order, and went out. After that there was an interval, during which everyone left his place and strolled about in the ring as people do at Lord's between the innings. After this a negro of magnificent physique appeared. First he thrust a dozen or so knitting-needles through his cheeks, so that they protruded on either side of his head; he walked about among the audience bristling in this way and thrusting his face into ours with a fixed and rather frightful grin. Then he took some nails and hammered them into his thighs. Then he stripped off everything except a pair of diamanté drawers, and rolled about without apparent discomfort on a board stuck with sharp carving-knives.

It was while he was doing this that a fight began. It raged chiefly round the exit, which was immediately below our seats. The heads of the combatants were on a level with our feet, so that we were in a wholly advantageous position to see everything without serious danger. It was difficult to realize quite what was happening; more and more of the audience joined in. The negro got up from his board of knives, feeling thoroughly neglected and slighted, and began addressing the crowd, slapping his bare chest and calling their attention to the tortures he was suffering for them. The man on my right, a grave Egyptian with a knowledge of English, with whom I had had some conversation, suddenly stood up, and leaning across all three of us struck down with his umbrella a resounding blow on the top of one of the fighting heads; then he sat down again with unruffled gravity and devoted himself to his hubble-bubble.

'What is the fight about?' I asked him.

'Fight?' he said. 'Who has been fighting? I saw no fight.'

'There.' I pointed to the seething riot in the doorway which seemed to threaten the collapse of the entire tent.

'Oh, that!' he said. 'Forgive me, I thought you said "fight". That is only the police.'

And sure enough, when the crowd eventually parted some minutes later, there emerged from its depths two uncontrollably angry police constables whom the onlookers had been attempting to separate. They were ejected at last to settle their quarrel outside; the crowd began sorting out and dusting their fallen fezes; everything became quiet again, and the big negro resumed his self-lacerations in an appreciative calm.[10]

We have not yet said anything about sport. Let me therefore now quote Dervla Murphy's account, in *Full Tilt*, of a polo match in Sher Quila, Gilgit:

Last night while we were having dinner wonderful music (very Afghan-like) began to play near by and when I asked why, I was told that it was the traditional way of announcing that an important polo-match would be played on the following day. Afterwards we went to look at the band. One old, bearded man was playing on a sort of primitive flute and two drummers were beating with their bare hands on the tight-skin ends of earthen-ware pitchers, which seemed similar to Afghan instruments. Polo is the national game here and the children begin to practise as tots by running around hitting stones with polo sticks; the result is astonishingly like our national game of hurling. Of course the sticks are home-made – branches of trees cut so cleverly at inter-sections that they look exactly like the real thing – but the balls used in matches are orthodox, made of bamboo root and imported from East Pakistan.

At 4.30 this afternoon the band began to play again. Then, at 5, I threw in the ball and, as Michael O'Hehir would say, the game was on! What a game to watch! Never anywhere have I seen such a thrilling spectacle. Of course it was totally unlike polo as we know it; there are *no* rules in this version and every sort of attack and defence is allowed. Blood was soon streaming from over half the twelve players' heads and hands and backs but they carried on regardless. The pace was tremendously fast and the horses streaked up and down the pitch foaming with sweat. Polo sticks were broken and replaced by the minute and the ball flew all over the place like a meteor – as often in the air as on the ground. The band played non-stop in time to the thudding hoofs and wild, whirling, clashing sticks and the faster the game the faster the music, till the three musicians were in almost as much of a lather as the horses.

One thing I noticed was the complete absence of fouls as distinct from accidents. Though this was a tremendously important championship game no tempers were lost and no one deliberately went for an opponent – the injuries were as often as not received from a member of the same team during what I can only describe as one of the scrums, when the ball got stuck beside a stone wall and all twelve horses 'packed down' with every man leaning from his saddle and poking towards it through the frantic jumble of horses' legs – anything less scientific it would be difficult to imagine. The only law concerned time; after thirty minutes there was a ten-minute interval (but no change of horses – they were simply walked about by little boys while their riders mopped up each other's blood) and then the teams changed sides and I threw in the ball again and off they went. At this stage it was Sher Quila: 1–Gulapur: 5, and the crowds sitting all around on the stone walls were silent and depressed. Then Sher Quila got going and scored four goals in rapid succession, which feat caused frenzied cheering. However, Gulapur soon came back with two, leaving it 7–5 and eight minutes to go – by now I was hoarse from yelling for Sher Quila! For those minutes the pace was incredible – the horses flashed up and down the field wheeling at each end like ballet dancers and the air was full of the noise of cracked sticks, new ones being flung out for the riders to catch in mid-air as they galloped by. With half a minute to go Sher Quila equalized, and the villagers nearly fell off the walls in their delight. At full time it was decided to play an extra ten minutes, and Sher Quila scored again, to win. I was quite exhausted by excitement and suspense as I scrambled off the wall: it took a full bottle of Punial Water to revive me! The visiting team spend the night here after these games as both men and horses are too tired to go home and I'm now being entertained by the band still playing vigorously for their benefit, on the other side of the compound.[11]

There is a perfectly splendid book by Patrick Balfour – later, as Lord Kinross, the author of a number of other first-rate travel books – called *Grand Tour*. It is the diary of a journey in the 1930s, that began with a drive from London to Delhi in two Rolls-Royces and continued through Siam to Indo-China and Malaya. (I use, with relief, the place names current at the time.) In Malaya, one gathers, sport and culture are both strongly represented among the local entertainments – although neither, perhaps, takes quite the same form as we are accustomed to in the West:

Animal fights are popular with the Kelantan Malay. Tumpat has a regular season of bullfights. These are between bull and bull, or more often between two water buffaloes. The fight does not usually last more than four or five minutes because one of the animals always (and with admirable sense) runs away. But fights have been known to last an hour. The bulls rarely gore each other: they wrestle and butt and one will sometimes throw the other right over his back, as in jiu-jitsu. Sometimes they charge straight for one another from the start and their heads meet with a report like a cannon. Once, after such a charge, a bull ran wild round the town for an hour, chased by its adversary, and when it finally collapsed its head was found to be smashed to pulp. Sometimes, if the bull does not at first catch sight of his opponent, he singles out someone in the crowd instead and chases him round and round the ring.

Once a fight was staged between a water buffalo and a black panther. But on seeing the buffalo the panther turned and fled. It then looked around, caught sight of its keeper, and killed him. The general European opinion (which is against such gladiatorial shows) held that it served him right.

Fish-fights, where the fishes tear one another to pieces in bottles are popular, though forbidden by law. But the favourite sport of the Kelantan Malay is cock-fighting, at which he gambles frenziedly and enormous sums change hands. Though it was not yet the season a special cockfight was staged for us for a purse of $1.50. The birds fought as scientifically as two boxers, with none of the wild disorder that one might expect from animals. Heads down, they watched each other warily, then closed; broke apart, watched, closed again. Most of the hitting was done with the feet, the beak being used primarily to get a purchase on the other cock's neck. When tired one would put its head under the other's wing and take a rest – like boxers clinching. The rounds lasted twenty minutes each. In the interval the owners bathed their combatants like seconds do, put feathers down their throats to clear them, sewed up their wounds, lifted their eyelids and so forth. One, obviously the weaker, was a sorry spectacle, much exhausted, but fought gamely when the next round began, resting a good deal beneath its adversary's wing, but scoring a few shrewd hits. Finally it ran away: the greater stamina of the other cock had told. A fight nearly always ends in this way and cocks are rarely killed.

Another Tumpat amusement was the opera. It was given in a kind of tent by a touring-company from Malacca. The orchestra was a family affair, composed almost entirely of children. A very small boy beat away at the drums and cymbals when he felt inclined, but got a bit listless at times. Another small boy, whose feet hardly touched the ground, played a violin almost as big as himself with remarkable confidence and skill. He looked as a grown man would look if he played the 'cello like a violin, holding it to his neck. He too stopped whenever he felt like it. Two other children played the saxophone and the second violin respectively, and the father of the party thumped what notes he could persuade to sound on the piano. Perhaps because it was tuned a semitone higher than the other instruments, he played it quite independently of them, as though in a different orchestra altogether. Between them they produced an astonishing and cacophonous mixture of American hot jazz and Oriental wailings; a singularly infelicitous union of East and West.

The show was a melodrama interspersed with musical turns. It seemed to be largely impromptu, like a children's charade, the actors talking whenever they felt like it and losing all interest when they did not. Like a children's performance, too, it lacked all sense of time or dramatic effect. A bewildering series of languid abductions, secret assignations, clandestine marriages and revolutions followed one another in lethargic and desultory sequence, the big revolutionary scene being performed to a speeded-up and almost unrecognizable version of *The Man Who Broke the Bank at Monte Carlo*. The cast was all female except for the comedian. His principal joke was to have a football for a tummy, to which the ladies of the chorus pointed now and then, giving it an occasional tap. He had various English phrases which he interchanged indiscriminately: 'I say!' 'My God!' 'All right!' became 'I right!' 'All God!' 'My say!' 'I God!' 'My right!' 'All say!'; and sometimes he strung them all together.

There was a chorus of houris, made up pink and white in European style, who sang in shrill, monotonous voices like schoolchildren chanting a 'piece'. Each number was interminable, as every member of the chorus had a verse to sing, and it was a long verse. The leitmotiv was a dreary tune, half Eastern, half Western, whose name, apparently, was *Amy Johnson*. There was no attempt at dancing: the chorus shuffled back and forward in listless steps, continuously, with an occasional apology for a chassé. Two of their numbers were more sophisticated, the ladies appearing dressed in turn as sailors and as jockeys, and wailing in Malay to the tune of *He's a Jolly Good Fellow! I'm For Ever Blowing Bubbles* was another success, but the principal boy could not quite manage the top notes and descended to a lower register when they came.

We left after the first two hours. The show was then half-way through. The audience displayed as little enthusiasm over it as the actors, but still it went on and still they sat.[12]

But, where entertainments are concerned, the worst problem that can beset the traveller is being called upon to provide one himself. It was all right for Laurie Lee: when he walked out that midsummer morning (as we read in Chapter Four) he took his violin with him; and when, a month or two later, he found himself staying the night with a peasant family in a small Spanish village – its name now forgotten – and they asked him to play, he must have been delighted to oblige:

The evening now was close and smoky. The lamp was lit, and the great doors shut. I was getting used to this pattern of Spanish life, which could have been that of England two centuries earlier. This house, like so many others I'd seen already, held nothing more than was useful for living – no fuss of furniture and unnecessary decoration – being as self-contained as the ark. Pots, pans, the chairs and tables, the manger and drinking-trough, all were of wood, stone or potter's clay, simply shaped and polished like tools. At the end of the day, the doors and windows admitted all the creatures of the family: father, son, daughter, cousin, the donkey, the pig, the hen, even the harvest mouse and the nesting swallow, bedded together at the fall of darkness.

So it was with us in this nameless village; night found us wrapped in this glowing barn, family and stranger gathered round the long bare table to a smell of wood-smoke, food and animals. Across the whitewashed walls the shadows of man and beast flickered huge like ancestral ghosts, which since the days of the caves have haunted the corners of fantasy, but which the electric light has killed.

We sat close together, the men drinking and smoking, elbows at rest among the empty plates. It was the short drowsy space between work and sleep, with nothing left of the day but gossip. Doña Maria, who was cobbling a piece of tattered harness, dominated the table with her thick warm voice, telling tales which to me were inscrutable, alas, but which to the others seemed vaguely familiar. The old man was a motionless mask in the shadows, though he showed a tooth in an occasional cackle. The sons sat near me, nudging me politely in the ribs and nodding their heads whenever the mother made a joke. The daughter, sitting close to the only lamp, buried her fingers in her sewing and listened, raising her huge Arab eyes every moment or so, to meet my glance of dumb conjecture.

I was half drunk now; in fact I felt like a bonfire, full of dull smoke and hot congestion. My eyes were hopelessly moored to those small neat breasts, rocking sadly to their rise and fall, till she seemed to be floating before me on waves of breath, naked as a negress in her tight black dress.

But the brothers surrounded me, and Doña Maria crouched near, watching me with warm but suspicious indulgence. So I sat and swayed in my drowsy conflagration, fitting sentences together in my mind, then producing them slowly, like a string of ill-knotted flags, for the family's polite astonishment.

Suddenly, one of the sons spotted my rolled-up blanket with the violin sticking out of it. 'Musica!' he cried, and went and fetched the bundle and laid it gingerly on the table before me.

'Yes, man,' said the mother. 'Come, divert us a little. Touch us a little tune.' The old man woke up, and the daughter put down her sewing, lifted her head, and even smiled.

There was nothing else for it. I sat down on the ground and tore drunkenly into an Irish reel. They listened, open-mouthed, unable to make head or tail of it; I might have been playing a Tibetan prayer-wheel. Then I tried a woozy fandango which I'd picked up in Zamora, and comprehension jerked them to life. The girl stiffened her body, the boys grabbed a handful of spoons and began slapping them across their knees, and the woman leapt to her feet and started stamping the ground, raising great clouds of dust around me. Not to be outdone, the old man left the shadows, struck a posture, and faced the woman. Doña Maria all flesh, he thin as a straw, together they began a dance of merciless contest, while the boys thumped their spoons, the woman shouted 'Ha!' and the hens flew squawking under the table.

It was no longer just a moment of middle-aged horseplay. The old man danced as if his life was at stake. While the woman was suddenly transformed, her great lumpen body becoming a thing of controlled and savage power. Moving with majestic assurance, her head thrown back, her feet pawing the ground like an animal, she stamped and postured round her small hopping husband as if she would tread him into oblivion. The dance was soon over, but while it lasted she was a woman unsheathed and terrible. Then the old man fell back, threw up his hands in defeat, and retired gasping to the safety of the walls.

The woman was left alone, and the mantle fell from her, and she stood like a girl, mopping her face and giggling, deprecating her performance with little hen-like cluckings and surprised shakings of her head.

'This is not for an old woman. My bones ache,' she said.

'Egyptian!' hissed the man from the shadows.

The sons asked me for another tune, and this time they danced together, with linked arms, rather sedate and formal. The daughter came quietly and sat on the floor beside me, watching my fingers as I played. The scent of her nearness swam troublesomely around me with a mixture of pig's lard and sharp clean lavender.

The evening's routine had been broken, and no one seemed eager to sleep. So some further celebration was possible. The girl was asked to sing, and she did as she was told, in a flat unaffected voice. The songs were simple and moving, and probably local; anyway, I've never heard them since. She sang them innocently, without art, taking breath like a child, often in the middle of a word. Staring blankly before her, without movement or expression, she simply went through each one, then stopped – as though she'd really no idea what the songs were about, only that they were using her to be heard.

With the singing over, we sat in silence for a while, hearing only the trembling sound of the lamp. Then the woman grunted and spoke, and the boys got up from the table and fetched the mattresses and laid them down by the wall.

'You sleep there,' said the mother. 'My sons will watch you.' She pulled knowingly at one of her eyelids. 'Come then,' she added, and the girl rose from her knees and followed her quickly to another part of the house, while the husband's crinkled old face simply disappeared from the air, soundlessly, like a snuffed-out candle.[13]

A less successful evening's entertainment was one of which I still retain all too vivid a picture. It took place at Aozou, in the Tibesti mountains of Northern Chad, early in 1966; thinking of it, I am reminded of Belloc's immortal couplet in 'The Moral Alphabet':

> Decisive action in the hour of need
> Denotes the hero, but does not succeed.[14]

The hero in this case was my old friend and travelling-companion Costa; and I have never admired him more than I did that evening. This is how I recorded it at the time:

From the start Aozou struck us as being a happy sort of place. . . . It hardly ever sees a foreigner, and our appearance threw it into a state of excitement far greater than that which we normally expected to arouse. As usual we drove straight to the fort to notify the authorities of our arrival; and when we emerged a few minutes later we found every child in the village, male and female, and a fair admixture of the adult population as well, gathered round the Land Rovers. Every face was quick with expectation, determined not to miss an instant of the free entertainment we were offering. To begin with this entertainment must have struck many of them as a bit of a let-down; it certainly seemed one to me when the lieutenant in charge . . . insisted on taking us on a conducted tour of his vegetable garden. By this time we had all of us inspected a good many Sahara vegetable gardens of one kind or another, and the novelty of picking our way between soggy irrigation ditches, murmuring, 'Ah, les belles tomates' at regular intervals, had begun to pall; we bore up as best we could, but it was a relief to us all when our guide returned us to the starting-point and said, 'Maintenant il faut chercher un beau site pour votre camp.' This, in fact, seemed to be the moment the crowd had been waiting for. With much laughter, occasionally interspersed with loud falsetto whoops of joy, they surrounded the lieutenant and ourselves and accompanied us to a spot on the edge of the palm-grove, beside a little running stream, where it was generally agreed that we should be most comfortable. Then, forming themselves into as tight a circle as our own activities permitted, they settled down to watch.

Sooner or later on our travels, we nearly all of us run up against the problem of the uninhibited onlookers – usually in the form of a group of peasants who appear from nowhere at the start of a picnic, take up a position a yard or two away and then, refusing all offers of food themselves, follow every mouthful with their eyes until the meal is over. Even at picnics this technique can be unnerving enough; but at a night camp, where there are no tents to afford the minimum of privacy and not even any bushes for cover, it can become a serious matter, and never have I known it to attain such formidable proportions as that evening at Aozou. The crowd at the start must have numbered at least forty – forty pairs of staring, unblinking eyes, missing nothing, examining every item we drew from our kitbags, taking in our every move. As we worked on and their fascination increased, they became more serious; slowly their laughter died, then even their conversation. Never, I should emphasise, was there anything remotely hostile about them; they were perfectly friendly – just very, very curious.

Our own reactions varied between agonised embarrassment and stoic fortitude. None of us felt like asking them, in so many words, to go away; such a request would, we feared, be thought exceedingly impolite, and the last thing we wanted was to cause offence. I argued furthermore that inconveniences of this kind were part and parcel of travelling – that the further afield one ranged the greater the attention one was bound to attract, and that one must simply resign oneself to it just as one did to any other discomfort. All that was needed, anyway, was patience. Sooner or later our audience was bound to get bored and wander off. No, I was told, this was insensate optimism. Were not the Toubou famous for their staying power? If strong action were not taken nobody would be able to undress at all; meanwhile there were other needs that were even more pressing. I looked round; they were quite right. One or two of the older spectators had indeed slipped away; but the hard core that remained, consisting almost entirely of children and adolescents, clearly had no thought of departure. They had on the contrary decided that a long vigil lay ahead, and they were even now digging themselves in for the night.

At last Costa took the matter in hand. 'Then,' he said, 'if they are looking for entertainment, that is what we must give them. Then they will be satisfied and go away.' We looked doubtful. Would not any form of entertainment we could offer simply whet their appetite for more? Besides, what could we possibly do to amuse them? But Costa, delighted at his idea and by now looking forward hugely to his own performance, was not to be shaken. Delving into his kitbag, he extracted some colourful garment, twisted it expertly into a funny hat and put it on. Then, trousers rolled up to the knee, he began to dance; and as he danced he sang:

> Y avait dix filles dans un pré,
> Toutes les dix à marier,
> Y avait Line, y avait Chine,
> Y avait Claudine et Martine,
> Ha, ha, Cat'rinette et Cat'rina;
> Y avait la belle Suzon,
> La duchess' de Montbazon,
> Y avait Célimène,
> Et y avait la du Maine.

Costa is not, perhaps, outstandingly gifted for the dance; his grasp of melody is also at moments uncertain. But he made up amply in verve what he lacked in technique, and he certainly deserved a greater success than he achieved. His audience was baffled. They had not bargained for this. It was quite unlike anything they had ever seen or heard before and, having no idea how they were meant to respond, they wisely chose not to respond at all. Visibly shaken, Costa tried again:

> Le fils du Roi vint a passer,
> Toutes les dix les fit coucher;
> Paille à Line, Paille à Chine,

Paille à Claudine et Martine,
Ha, ha, Cat'rinette et Cat'rina;
Paille à la belle Suzon,
La duchess' de Montbazon,
Paille à Célimène,
Mais beau lit à la du Maine.

The line of little dark faces still stared stonily back at him. There was not a word, not a whisper, far less a smile. The flop was total. Now genuinely sad, poor Costa took off his funny hat, unrolled his trousers and returned to the rest of us, shaking his head, '*En effet*,' he murmured, '*c'est un public très difficile.*'

Then, to our astonishment, we saw that it had worked. Within minutes of the song's end, the entire audience had faded away into the darkness. Just what prompted them to leave remains a mystery. Perhaps they had enjoyed it all far more than their faces had revealed and had accepted it as we had hoped they would, as the grand finale to a memorable evening. Perhaps, on the other hand, they had hated it and had been impelled to flee from the dreadful possibility of an encore. My own theory is that by directing his energies so squarely towards them Costa had somehow made them feel involved, saddled with responsibilities which they did not clearly understand. The whole thing had suddenly become too complicated; they preferred to go.[15]

But let us finish on an up-beat. Redmond O'Hanlon and James Fenton, to whom generous hospitality is being shown in a Kenyah longhouse somewhere in the wilds of Borneo, also find themselves called upon to perform. In their two different ways, each proves a thundering success:

The musicians sat in front of us. An old man held a keluri, a dried gourd shaped like a chemical retort but held upwards, and with six bamboo pipes projecting in a bundle from its bulb; a group of young men sat ready with a bamboo harp (a tube of bamboo with raised strips cut from its surface), a bamboo xylophone, a bamboo flute, and a single stringed instrument, a dugout-canoe-like sounding box carved from a single block of wood, the string so heavy it had to be pulled with an iron hook.

The chief's son entered, transformed. On his head he wore a war-helmet, a woven rattan cap set with black and yellow and crimson beads, topped with six long black and white plumes from the tail of the Helmeted hornbill. He was dressed in a war-coat, made from the skin of the largest cat in Borneo, the Clouded leopard. His head placed through an opening at the front of the skin, the bulk stretched down his back, and on to it were fastened row upon row of Rhinoceros hornbill feathers. Around his waist, slung on a silver belt and sheathed in a silver scabbard, was a parang to outshine all other parangs, its hilt intricately carved in horn from the antler of the kijang, the big Borneo deer. In his left hand, his arm crooked behind it, he carried a long shield, pointed at both ends, and from the centre of which a huge mask regarded us implacably, its eyes red, its teeth the painted tusks of the wild boar. Thick black tufts of hair hung in neat lines down either edge and across the top and bottom, tufts of hair which, we were led to believe, had long ago been taken from the scalps of heads cut off in battle.

Laying the ancient, and presumably fragile, shield carefully against the wall, the warrior took up his position at the centre of the floor. He crouched down and, at a nod from the man on the base string, a hollow, complicated, urgent, rhythmic music began. With exaggerated movements, his thigh muscles bunching and loosening, his tendons taut, a fierce concentration on his face, the chief's son turned slowly in time with the music, first on one foot and then on another, rising, inch by inch, to his own height, apparently peering over some imaginary cover. Sighting the enemy, he crouched again, and then, as the music quickened, he drew his bright parang and leapt violently forward, weaving and dodging, with immense exertion, cutting and striking, parrying unseen blows with his mimed shield. For a small second, his ghostly foe was off-guard, tripped on the shingle, and the heir to the Lordship of all the Kenyah of Nanga Sinyut claimed his victory with one malicious blow.

Everyone clapped and cheered, and so did I. Five young girls rushed forward to take off the hero's hornbill helmet, and war-coat, and parang. It was wonderful. The girls were very beautiful. All was right with the world. And then I realised, as a Rajah Brooke's birdwing took a flap around my duodenum, that the beautiful girls, in a troop, were coming, watched by all the longhouse, for me.

'You'll be all right,' said James, full of tuak. 'Just do your thing. Whatever it is.'

Strapped into the war-coat and the parang, the hornbill feathers on my head, I had a good idea. It would be a simple procedure to copy the basic steps that the chief's son had just shown us. There really was not much to it, after all. The music struck up, sounding just a little bit stranger than it had before.

I began the slow crouch on one leg, turning slightly. Perhaps, actually, this was a mistake, I decided. Ghastly pains ran up my thighs. Terminal cramp hit both buttocks at once. Some silly girl began to titter. A paraplegic wobble spread down my back. The silly girl began to laugh. Very slowly, the floor came up to say hello, and I lay down on it. There was uproar in the longhouse. How very funny, indeed.

Standing up, I reasoned that phase two would be easier. Peering over the imaginary boulder, I found myself looking straight into the eyes of an old man on the far side of the verandah. The old fool was crying with laughter, his ridiculous long ears waggling about. Drawing the parang, which was so badly aligned that it stuck in the belt and nearly took my fingers off, I advanced upon the foe, jumping this way and that, feeling dangerous. The old man fell off his seat. There was so much misplaced mirth, so much plain howling, that I could not hear the music, and so perhaps my rhythm was not quite right.

'Redsi!' came an unmistakable shout, 'why don't you improvise?'

Stabbed in the back just as I was about to take my very first head, I spun round violently to glare at the Fenton. I never actually saw him, because the cord of the war-helmet, not used to such movements, slipped up over the back of my head, and the helmet itself, flying forward, jammed fast over my face. Involuntarily, I took a deep gasp of its sweat-smooth rattan interior, of the hair of generations of Kenyah warriors who had each been desperate to impress the girls of their choice. It was an old and acrid smell.

The boards were shaking. The audience was out of control. And then, just in time, before suffocation set in, the five girls, grossly amused, set me free.

'Go and get James,' I spluttered, 'you go and get James.'

'Now you sing song,' shouted Leon.

'No, no – James sing songs.'

'Jams!' shouted Leon, remembering his mission.

'Jams!' The longhouse reverberated. 'Jams! Jams!' Leon had done his work well.

With great theatrical presence, offering almost no resistance to the five young girls, James processed on to the stage. The Kenyah fell silent. T. D. Freeman, in his work on Iban augury, tells us that the King of the Gods, Singalang Burong, may well be encountered in dreams. There is no mistaking him. He is almost as old as the trees, awe-inspiring, massive of body, and, a characteristic which puts his identity beyond doubt, completely bald. Judging by the slightly uneasy, deferential, expectant faces around me, Bali Penyalong, the High God of the Kenyah, was but a different name for the same deity.

The attendants withdrew. James, resplendent in leopard skin and hornbill feathers, looked even more solemn than is his habit. With the accumulated experience of many thousands of evenings at the theatre, of years of drama criticism, he regarded his audience; his huge brown eyes appeared to fix on everyone in turn. There was some backward shuffling in the front row. A dog whimpered.

The music began, a little shakily. James, in time with the music, began to mime. He was hunting something, in a perfunctory way; he made rootling movements with his head, and grunted. He was hunting a pig. Evidently successful, he butchered his quarry, selected the joint he had in mind, hung the carcase from a hook in the roof and betook himself to his ideal kitchen. Passion entered the show; James began to concentrate; his gestures quickened and the mesmerised musicians increased their tempo. He scored the pork; he basted it; he tied it with string; he made extraordinarily complex sauces; he cooked potatoes and sprouts and peas and beans and broccoli and *zucchini*, I think, until they were *fritti*. After many a tasting and many an alchemical manoeuvre with a *batterie de cuisine* decidedly better than Magny's, James deemed the gravy to be perfect. The apple sauce was plentiful. The decanted Burgundy was poured into a glass. James looked fondly at his creation and began to eat. The crackling crackled between his teeth. The warriors of the Kenyah, as if they had been present at a feast of the Gods, rose to their feet and burped. Everybody cheered.

'Jams very hungry,' said Leon to me confidentially, 'he must eat more rices.'

James held up a hand. Everyone sat down again, cross-legged.

'And now,' he announced, 'we will have a sing-song.'

'Inglang song! Inglang song!' shouted Inghai, wildly excited, and full of arak.

And then James really did astonish me. To the beat of the big string he launched into a rhyming ballad, a long spontaneous poem about our coming from a far country, entering the Rajang from the sea, about the pleasures of the Baleh and the danger of the rapids and the hospitality of the strongest, the most beautiful people in all the world, the Kenyah of Nanga Sinyut.

I clapped as wildly as Inghai. 'Bravo Jams!' I shouted; 'Bravo Jams!' mimicked Inghai; 'Bravo! Bravo!' sang the Kenyah.

James indicated that he was tired; he pillowed his black-and-white-plumed head on his hands. But it was no use. We wanted more songs. We wanted so many, in fact, that I discovered, to my amazement, that he knew almost every popular and music-hall song back to about 1910 and that he could adapt their tunes to the vagaries of the bamboo gourd-pipes with professional ease.

James was saved, just before he collapsed from exhaustion, when the longhouse clown stood up, jealous of his great success. The helmet and coat were laid aside, and James sat down.[16]

CHAPTER TWENTY-ONE

Euphoria

A good traveller does not much mind the uninteresting places. He is there to be inside them, as a thread is inside the necklace it strings. The world, with unknown and unexpected variety, is a part of his own Leisure; and this living participation is, I think, what separates the traveller and the tourist, who remains separate, as if he were at a theatre, and not himself a part of whatever the show may be.

A certain amount of trouble is required before one can enter into such unity, since every country, and every society inside it, has developed its own ritual of living, as well as its own language. Some knowledge of both is essential, and – just as our circumambient air contains melody but cannot express it until a voice is given – so a technique or voice is needed for human, or indeed for all intercourse. To find this unity makes me happy: its discovery comes unexpectedly upon me, not only with people, but with animals, or trees or rocks, or days and nights in their mere progress. A sudden childish delight envelops me and the frontiers of myself disappear.[1]

'A sudden childish delight' – every traveller has known it sooner or later, and not always because he necessarily feels that identification with his surroundings that Freya Stark describes in *Alexander's Path*. It can spring from any one of a dozen other causes: from the beauty of the landscape, from the kindness or the hospitality of the local people, from pride of achievement, or even simply from that gentle, trance-like state born of long hours of slow and regular motion – on horse or mule or camel, or (best of all, perhaps) on foot. Sometimes, as far as one can judge, it springs from nothing at all. To Peter Fleming, for example, it suddenly came in the middle of the Amazonian jungle, among surroundings very different from those which had awakened it in the past:

For some reason, I remember that hot bright noon as being full of a curious delight. I was in that psychological state always described by the characters in Mr. Ernest Hemingway's novels as 'feeling good'. My perceptions were sharper than usual, my power to appreciate had suddenly expanded. All the things I saw seemed to me exactly right; I read their meaning so easily, so instinctively, that there was for once no need to try and define it. I had that uncritical exhilaration, that clear conviction that this was a good day in a good world, which one has known so seldom since childhood, when snow overnight would evoke it, or permission to bathe before breakfast, or the crackle of brown paper on a Christmas morning.[2]

Graham Greene, by contrast, describes it (in *Journey Without Maps*) as a sort of reaction after extreme exhaustion and a bad bout of fever in the hinterland of Liberia:

I remember nothing of the trek to Zigi's Town and very little of the succeeding days. I was so exhausted that I couldn't write more than a few lines in my diary; I hope never to be so tired again. I retain an impression of continuous forest, occasional hills emerging above the bush so that we could catch a glimpse on either side of the great whalebacked forests driving to the sea. Outside Zigi's Town there was a stream trickling down the slope and a few ducks with a curiously English air about them. I remember trying to sit down, but immediately having to deal with the town chief over food for the carriers, trying to sit down again and rising to look for threepenny-bits the cook needed for buying a chicken, trying to sit down and being forced up again to dress a carrier's sores. I couldn't stand any more of it; I swallowed two tablespoonfuls of Epsom in a cup of strong tea (we had finished our tinned milk long ago) and left my cousin to deal with anything else that turned up. My temperature was high. I swallowed twenty grains of quinine with a glass of whisky, took off my clothes, wrapped myself in blankets under the mosquito-net and tried to sleep.

A thunderstorm came up. It was the third storm we'd had in a few days; there wasn't any time to lose if we were to reach the Coast, and I lay in the dark as scared as I have ever been. There were no rats, at any rate, but I caught a jigger under my toe when I crawled out to dry myself. I was sweating as if I had influenza; I couldn't keep dry for more than fifteen seconds. The hurricane lamp I left burning low on an up-ended chop box and beside it an old whisky bottle full of warm filtered water. I kept remembering Van Gogh at Bolahun burnt out with fever. He said you had to lie up for at least a week: there wasn't any danger in malaria if you lay up long enough; but I couldn't bear the thought of staying a week here, another seven days away from Grand Bassa. Malaria or not, I'd got to go on next day and I was afraid.

The fever would not let me sleep at all, but by the early morning it was sweated out of me. My temperature was a long way below normal, but the worst boredom of the trek for the time being was over. I had made a discovery during the night which interested me. I had discovered in myself a passionate interest in living. I had always assumed before, as a matter of course, that death was desirable.

It seemed that night an important discovery. It was like a conversion, and I had never experienced a conversion before. (I had not been converted to a religious faith. I had been convinced by specific arguments in the probability of its creed.) If the experience had not been so new to me, it would have seemed less important, I should have known that conversions don't last, or if they last at all it is only as a little sediment at the bottom of the brain. Perhaps the sediment has value, the memory of a conversion may have some force in an emergency; I may be able to strengthen myself with the intellectual idea that once in Zigi's Town I had been completely convinced of the beauty and desirability of the mere act of living.[3]

That very particular form of euphoria that springs from pride of achievement is above all, I suppose, the prerogative of mountain climbers; for Sir

Richard Burton, on the other hand, it came – not surprisingly – with his first sight of Mecca. Virtually every other visitor to the city, gazing on it for the first time, must feel what any pilgrim feels when he catches sight of the end of his pilgrimage; but for Burton, as one of the small handful of non-Muslims ever to have penetrated its formidable defences, there was a very different emotion – the identity of which, to his credit, he makes no attempt to conceal:

Scarcely had the first smile of morning beamed upon the rugged head of the eastern hill, Abu Kubays, when we arose, bathed, and proceeded in our pilgrim-garb to the Sanctuary. We entered by the Bab al-Ziyadah, or principal northern door, descended two long flights of steps, traversed the cloister, and stood in sight of the Bayt Allah.

There at last it lay, the bourn of my long and weary Pilgrimage, realising the plans and hopes of many and many a year. The mirage medium of Fancy invested the huge catafalque and its gloomy pall with peculiar charms. There were no giant fragments of hoar antiquity as in Egypt, no remains of graceful and harmonious beauty as in Greece and Italy, no barbarous gorgeousness as in the buildings of India; yet the view was strange, unique – and how few have looked upon the celebrated shrine! I may truly say that, of all the worshippers who clung weeping to the curtain, or who pressed their beating hearts to the stone, none felt for the moment a deeper emotion than did the Haji from the far-north. It was as if the poetical legends of the Arab spoke truth, and that the waving wings of angels, not the sweet breeze of morning, were agitating and swelling the black covering of the shrine. But, to confess humbling truth, theirs was the high feeling of religious enthusiasm, mine was the ecstasy of gratified pride.[4]

I am not moralist enough to know how elevated that particular emotion may be; but there were other occasions when Burton was able to sublimate even his enormous egotism, and riding in the desert was one of them:

Let the traveller who suspects exaggeration leave the Suez road for an hour or two, and gallop northwards over the sands: in the drear silence, the solitude, and the fantastic desolation of the place, he will feel what the Desert may be.

And then the Oases, and little lines of fertility – how soft and how beautiful! – even though the Wady al-Ward (the Vale of Flowers) be the name of some stern flat upon which a handful of wild shrubs blossom while struggling through a cold season's ephemeral existence. In such circumstances the mind is influenced through the body. Though your mouth glows, and your skin is parched, yet you feel no languor, the effect of humid heat; your lungs are lightened, your sight brightens, your memory recovers its tone, and your spirits become exuberant; your fancy and imagination are powerfully aroused, and the wildness and sublimity of the scenes around you stir up all the energies of your soul – whether for exertion, danger, or strife. Your *morale* improves; you become frank and cordial, hospitable and single-minded: the hypocritical politeness and the slavery of civilisation are left behind you in the city. Your senses are quickened: they require no stimulants but air and exercise, – in the Desert spirituous liquors excite only disgust. There is a keen enjoyment in mere animal existence. The sharp appetite disposes of the most indigestible food; the sand is softer than a bed of down, and the purity of the air suddenly puts to flight a dire cohort of diseases. Hence it is that both sexes, and every age, the most material as well as the most imaginative of minds, the tamest citizen, the parson, the old maid, the peaceful student, the spoiled child of civilisation, all feel their hearts dilate, and their pulses beat strong, as they look down from their dromedaries upon the glorious Desert. Where do we hear of a traveller being disappointed by it? It is another illustration of the ancient truth that Nature returns to man, however unworthily he has treated her. And believe me, when once your tastes have conformed to the tranquillity of such travel, you will suffer real pain in returning to the turmoil of civilisation. You will anticipate the bustle and the confusion of artificial life, its luxury and its false pleasures, with repugnance. Depressed in spirits, you will for a time after your return feel incapable of mental or bodily exertion. The air of cities will suffocate you, and the care-worn and cadaverous countenances of citizens will haunt you like a vision of judgment.[5]

The desert has always exerted a strange power over the minds and imaginations of travellers. There is the sheer vastness of it for one thing, the immense distances which are themselves immeasurably increased by the dryness, and hence the almost unearthly clarity, of the atmosphere. Then there is the silence, of a depth virtually unknown in the civilised world, broken only by the sound of the relentless wind. Finally there is the cleanness of everything, the complete absence of dust or decay, so that sand and rock together shine and sparkle in the sun. No other landscape, in my experience at least, so potently affects the spirit. But nature, unspoilt and untrammelled, nearly always arouses strong emotions of one kind or another, and if these are of intense and undefinable happiness – rather than of depression or even of fear – well, so much the better. Here is Mrs. Isabella Bird, writing this time of *A Lady's Life in the Rocky Mountains*:

I rode towards the head of the lake, which became every moment grander and more unutterably lovely. The sun was setting fast, and against his golden light green promontories, wooded with stately pines, stood out one beyond another in a medium of dark rich blue, while grey bleached summits, peaked, turreted, and snow-slashed, were piled above them, gleaming with amber light. Darker grew the blue gloom, the dew fell heavily, aromatic odours floated on the air, and still the lofty peaks glowed with living light, till in one second it died off from them, leaving them with the ashy paleness of a dead face. It was dark and cold under the mountain shadows, the frosty chill of the high altitude wrapped me round, the solitude was overwhelming, and I reluctantly turned my horse's head towards Truckee, often looking back to the ashy summits in their unearthly fascination. Eastwards the look of the scenery was changing every moment, while the lake for long remained 'one burnished sheet of living gold,' and Truckee lay utterly out of sight in a hollow filled with lake and cobalt. Before long a carnival of colour began which I can only describe as delirious, intoxicating, a hardly bearable joy, a tender anguish, an indescribable yearning, an unearthly music, rich in love and worship. It lasted considerably more than an hour, and though the road was growing very dark, and the train which was to take me thence was fast climbing the Sierras, I could not ride faster than a walk.

The eastward mountains, which had been grey, blushed pale pink, the pink deepened into rose, and the rose into crimson, and then all solidity etherealised away and became clear and pure as an amethyst, while all the waving ranges and the broken pine-clothed ridges below etherealised too, but into a dark rich blue, and a strange effect of atmosphere blended the whole into one perfect picture. It changed, deepened, reddened, melted, growing more and more wonderful, while under the pines it was night, till, having displayed itself for an hour, the jewelled peaks suddenly became like those of the sierras, wan as the face of death. Far later the cold golden light lingered in the west, with pines in relief against its purity, and where the rose light had glowed in the east, a huge moon upheaved itself, and the red flicker of forest fires luridly streaked the mountain sides near and far off. I realised that night had come with its *eeriness*, and putting my great horse into a gallop I clung on to him till I pulled him up in Truckee, which was at the height of its evening revelries – fires blazing out of doors, bar-rooms and saloons crammed, lights glaring, gaming-tables thronged, fiddle and banjo in frightful discord, and the air ringing with ribaldry and profanity.[6]

Suppressing as best we can the unworthy thought that Truckee sounds rather fun, let us now pass to that sure-fire euphoria inducer, the island of Samoa – here celebrated not by Joseph Conrad or by Robert Louis Stevenson but by the unlikelier pen of Rupert Brooke. The volume from which the passage is taken bears the misleading title of *Letters from America*, but the picture is no less brilliant for that:

The South Sea Islands have an invincible glamour. Any bar in 'Frisco or Sydney will give you tales of seamen who slipped ashore in Samoa or Tahiti or the Marquesas for a month's holiday, five, ten, or twenty years ago. Their wives and families await them yet. They are compound, these islands, of all legendary heavens. They are Calypso's and Prospero's isle, and the Hesperides, and Paradise, and every timeless and untroubled spot. Such tales have been made of them by men who have been there, and gone away, and have been haunted by the smell of the bush and the lagoons, and faint thunder on the distant reef, and the colours of sky and sea and coral, and the beauty and grace of the islanders. And the queer thing is that it's all, almost tiresomely, true. In the South Seas the Creator seems to have laid Himself out to show what He *can* do. Imagine an island with the most perfect climate in the world, tropical, yet almost always cooled by a breeze from the sea. No malaria or other fevers. No dangerous beasts, snakes, or insects. Fish for the catching, and fruits for the plucking. And an earth and sky and sea of immortal loveliness. What more could civilisation give? Umbrellas? Rope? Gladstone bags? ... Any one of the vast leaves of the banana is more waterproof than the most expensive woven stuff. And from the first tree you can tear off a long strip of fibre that holds better than any rope. And thirty seconds' work on a great palm-leaf produces a basket-bag which will carry incredible weights all day, and can be thrown away in the evening. A world of conveniences. And the things which civilisation has left behind or missed by the way are there, too, among the Polynesians: beauty and courtesy and mirth. I think there is no gift of mind or body that the wise value which these people lack. A man I met in some other islands, who had travelled much all over the world, said to me, 'I have found no man, in or out of Europe, with the good manners and dignity of the Samoan, with the possible exception of the Irish peasant.' A people among whom an Italian would be uncouth, and a high-caste Hindu vulgar, and Karsavina would seem clumsy, and Helen of Troy a frump.

. . . It is a magic of a different way of life. In the South Seas, if you live the South Sea life, the intellect soon lapses into quiescence. The body becomes more active, the senses and perceptions more lordly and acute. It is a life of swimming and climbing and resting after exertion. The skin seems to grow more sensitive to light and air, and the feel of water and the earth and leaves. Hour after hour one may float in the warm lagoons, conscious, in the whole body, of every shred and current of the multitudinous water, or diving under in a vain attempt to catch the radiant butterfly-coloured fish that flit in and out of the thousand windows of their gorgeous coral palaces. Or go up, one of a singing flower-garlanded crowd, to a shaded pool of a river in the bush, cool from the mountains. The blossom-hung darkness is streaked with the bodies that fling themselves, head or feet first, from the cliffs around the water, and the haunted forest-silence is broken by laughter. It is part of the charm of these people that, while they are not so foolish as to 'think,' their intelligence is incredibly lively and subtle, their sense of humour and their intuitions of other people's feelings are very keen and living. They have built up, in the long centuries of their civilisation, a delicate and noble complexity of behaviour and of personal relationships. A white man living with them soon feels his mind as deplorably dull as his skin is pale and unhealthy among those glorious golden-brown bodies. But even he soon learns to be his body (and so his true mind), instead of using it as a stupid convenience for his personality, a moment's umbrella against this world. He is perpetually and intensely aware of the subtleties of taste in food, of every tint and line of the incomparable glories of those dawns and evenings, of each shade of intercourse in fishing or swimming or dancing with the best companions in the world. That alone is life; all else is death. And after dark, the black palms against a tropic night, the smell of the wind, the tangible moonlight like a white, dry, translucent mist, the lights in the huts, the murmur and laughter of passing figures, the passionate, queer thrill of the rhythm of some hidden dance – all this will seem to him, inexplicably and almost unbearably, a scene his heart has known long ago, and forgotten, and yet always looked for.[7]

What, I wonder, would be the Orient's answer to Samoa? If we are to believe Robert Byron, the Persian hill-town of Mahun might be a serious contender for the title. Byron makes no direct mention of his own feelings; but there can be no doubt that the writer of these words was, at the moment when he wrote them, a supremely happy man:

Mahun (6300 ft.), March 25th. – Travellers from the Indian frontier, Christopher among them, have thought they were in paradise when they arrived at Mahun after crossing the Baluchistan sand-desert. Even on the way from Kirman, this desert impinges a sinister presence. There are sand-drifts on the road, and these must mean the end of Persia, since Persian deserts are stony.

The Shrine of Niamatullah brings a sudden reprieve, a blessing of water and rustle of leaves. The purple cushions on the judas trees and a confetti of early fruit-blossom are reflected in a long pool. In the next court is another pool, shaped like a cross and surrounded by formal beds newly planted with irises. It is cooler here. Straight black cypresses, overtopped by the waving umbrellas of quicker-growing pines, throw a deep, woody shade. Between them shines a blue dome crossed with black and white spiders' webs, and a couple of blue minarets. A dervish totters out, wearing a conical hat and an embroidered yellow sheepskin. He leads the way past the tomb of the saint below the dome, through a spacious white-washed hall, to a third and larger court, which has a second and larger pair of minarets at the far end. A last formal pool, and a mighty plane tree gleaming with new sap, stand outside the last gate. The country round is covered with vineyards, fields of ninepins full of clay cones to support the vines, as mulberries support them on the Lombardy Plain. A high range of mountains in a dress of snow and violet mist bounds the horizon.

While the cadent sun throws lurid copper streaks across the sand-blown sky, all the birds in Persia have gathered for a last chorus. Slowly, the darkness brings silence, and they settle themselves to sleep with diminishing flutterings, as of a child arranging its bedclothes. And then another note begins, a hot metallic blue note, timidly at first, gaining courage, throbbing without cease, until, as if the second violins had crept into action, it becomes two notes, now this, now that, and is answered from the other side of the pool by a third. Mahun is famous for its nightingales. But for my part I celebrate the frogs. I am out in the court by now, in the blackness beneath the trees. Suddenly the sky clears, and the moon is reflected three times, once on the dome and twice on the minarets. In sympathy, a circle of amber light breaks from the balcony over the entrance, and a pilgrim begins to chant. The noise of water trickling into the new-dug flower-beds succeeds him. I am in bed at last.[8]

John Carne, writing in his *Letters from the East* of Damascus in the 1820s, seems to have preferred less complicated pleasures:

The greatest luxuries the city contains are the coffee-houses; many of these are built on the bosom of the river, and supported by piles. The platform of the coffee-house is raised only a few inches above the level of the stream; the roof is supported by slender rows of pillars, and it is quite open on every side; innumerable small seats cover the floor, and you take one of these and place it in the position you like best; the river, whose surrounding banks are covered with wood, rushes rapidly by close to your feet. Near the coffee-houses are one or two cataracts several feet high, with a few trees growing out of the river beside them; and the perpetual sound of their fall, and the coolness they spread around, are exquisite luxuries in the sultry heat of day. At night, when the lamps, suspended from the slender pillars, are lighted, and Turks, of different ranks, in all the varieties of their rich costume, cover the platform, just above the surface of the river, on which, and on its foaming waterfalls, the moonlight rests, and the sound of music is heard, you fancy that if ever the Arabian Nights' enchantments are to be realized, it is here.

These cool and delightful places were our daily and favourite lounge: they are resorted to at all hours of the day. There are two or three coffee-houses constructed somewhat differently from the one just described. A low gallery divides the platform from the tide; fountains play on the floor, which is furnished with sofas and cushions; and music and dancing always abound. Together with a pipe and coffee, they bring you two or three delicious sherbets, and fruit of some kind is also put into the vase presented you. In the middle of the river that rushed round one of these latter cafés, was a little island covered with verdure and trees, where you might go and sit for hours without once desiring a change of place.[9]

Sylvia Plath, the American poetess, knew what euphoria was – just as she was later, alas, to know despair. Here is an extract from a postcard she sent to her mother on 7 January 1956. I repeat, an *extract* – she still had room for another nine and a half lines and the address. Writing from Nice, she tells of the afternoon when she took a motor-scooter inland to Vence (for 'cathedral' read 'chapel'):

How can I describe the beauty of the country? Everything is so small, close, exquisite and fertile. Terraced gardens on steep slopes of rich, red earth, orange and lemon trees, olive orchards, tiny pink and peach houses. To Vence – small, on a sun-warmed hill, uncommercial, slow, peaceful. Walked to Matisse cathedral – small, pure, clean-cut. White, with blue-tile roof sparkling in the sun. But shut! Only open to public two days a week. A kindly talkative peasant told me stories of how rich people came daily in large cars from Italy, Germany, Sweden, etc., and were not admitted, even for large sums of money. I was desolate and wandered to the back of the walled nunnery, where I could see a corner of the chapel and sketched it, feeling like Alice outside the garden, watching the white doves and orange trees. Then I went back to the front and stared with my face through the barred gate. I began to cry. I knew it was so lovely inside, pure white with the sun through blue, yellow and green stained windows.

Then I heard a voice. 'Ne pleurez plus, entrez,' and the Mother Superior let me in, after denying all the wealthy people in cars.

I just knelt in the heart of the sun and the colours of sky, sea and sun, in the pure white heart of the chapel. 'Vous êtes si gentille,' I stammered. The nun smiled. 'C'est la miséricorde de Dieu.' It was.[10]

For our last two passages, we must return to the East. First, a romantic – but not, I think, an inaccurate – description of oriental travel during the greater part of the nineteenth century. It comes from Eliot Warburton's *The Crescent and the Cross*:

Towns in the East are so disagreeable, and have so few resources, the country is so beautiful and full of interest, that I always felt a lively pleasure in passing out from the guarded gates of some old city to return to the tent and the wild pathway of the plain or mountain. Travel in the East is the occupation of your whole time, not a mere passage from one place of residence to another; the haunts of men soon become distasteful, and their habits irksome, to one accustomed to the wild freedom and perfect independence of an Eastern wanderer's life: the very hardships of the latter have a charm, and its dangers an excitement, all unknown to the European traveller.

You are wakened in the morning by the song of birds, which the sleeping ear, all regardless of the jackall's howl or the ocean's roar throughout the night, yet recognises as its expected summons. You fling off the rough capote, your only covering – start from the carpet, your only couch – and, with a plunge into the river or the sea, your toilet is made at once. The rainbow mists of morning are still heavy on the landscape while you sip your coffee; but by the time you spring into the saddle all is clear and bright, and you feel, while you press the sides of your eager horse, and the stirring influence of morning buoys you up, as if fatigue could never come. The breeze, full of Nature's perfume and Nature's music, blusters merrily round your turban as you gallop to the summit of some hill to watch the Syrian sunrise spread in glory over Lebanon, Hermon, or Mount Carmel. Meanwhile, your tent is struck; your various luggage packed upon the horses, with a complete-ness and celerity that only the wandering Arab can attain to, and a heap of ashes alone remains to mark the site of your transient home. Your cavalcade winds slowly along the beaten path, but you have many a castled crag, or woody glen, or lonely ruin to explore: and your untiring Arab courser seems ever fresh and vigorous as when he started. Occasionally you meet some traveller armed to the teeth, who inquires news of the road you have come, and perhaps relates some marvellous adventure from which he has just escaped. He bristles like a porcupine, with a whole armoury of pistols, daggers, and yataghans, but his first and parting saluta-tion is that of 'Peace!' – in no country of the world is that gentle word so often used, or so little felt.

Some khan, or convent, or bubbling spring marks your resting-place during the burning noon: and you are soon again in motion, with all the exhilaration of a second morning. Your path is as varied as your thoughts; now over slippery crags, upon some view-commanding mountain's brow; now, along verdant valleys, or through some ravine, where the winter torrent was the last passenger. Oleanders in rich bloom are scattered over the green turf; your horse treads odours out of a carpet of wild flowers; strange birds of brilliant plumage are darting from bough to bough of the wild myrtle and the lemon-tree; lizards are gleaming among the rocks; and the wide sea is so calm, and bright, and mirror-like, that the solitary ship upon its bosom seems suspended, like Mahomet's coffin, between two skies.

All this time you are travelling in the steps of prophets, conquerors, and apostles; perhaps along the very path which the Saviour trod. 'What is yonder village?' 'Nazareth.' 'What yonder lake?' 'The sea of Galilee.' Only he who has heard these answers from a native of Palestine can understand their thrilling sound.

But evening approaches; your horse's step is as free, but less elastic than fourteen hours ago. Some wayside khan or village presents itself for the night's encampment; but, more frequently, a fountain or a river's bank is the only inducement that decides you to hold up your hand: suddenly, at that sign, the horses stop; down comes the luggage; and, by the time you have unbridled and watered your horse, a carpet is spread on the green turf, and a fire is already blazing. As you fling yourself on the hard couch of earth with a sensation of luxury, one of your attendants presents you with the soothing chibouque, while another hands a tiny cup of coffee; this at once restores tone to your system, and enables you to look out upon the lovely sunset with absorbing satisfaction. Meanwhile, your tent has risen silently over you; the baggage is arranged in a crescent form round the door; the horses are picketted in front. Your simple meal is soon despatched, and a quiet stroll by moonlight concludes the day. Then, wrapped in your capote, you fling yourself once more upon your carpet, place your pistols under your saddle pillow, and are soon lost in such sleep as only the care-free traveller knows.[11]

Once again, if this is not euphoria, it seems to me to be something very like it. And so we end, as we began, with Freya Stark – telling us, in *The Southern Gates of Arabia*, of a night in Mukalla and what was, unquestionably, the real thing:

When the evening came, and the sweet shrill cry of the kites, that fills the daylight, stopped, 'Awiz appeared with three paraffin lanterns, which he dotted about the floor in various places, and, having given me my supper, departed to his home. The compound with its dim walls, its squares of moist earth planted with vegetables and few trees, grew infinite and lovely under the silence of the moon. The gate of the city was closed now; a dim glow showed where the sentries beguiled their watch with a hookah in the guard house; at more or less hourly intervals they struck a gong suspended between poles, and so proclaimed the hour. And when I felt tired, I would withdraw from my veranda, collect and blow out the superfluous lanterns, and retire to my room. None of the doors shut easily, so I did not bother to lock them; I had refused the offer of a guard to sleep at my threshold, the precaution was so obviously unnecessary. As I closed my eyes in this security and silence, I thought of the Arabian coasts stretching on either hand – three hundred miles to Aden; how many hundred to Muscat in the other direction? the Indian Ocean in front of me, the inland deserts behind: within these titanic barriers I was the only European at that moment. A dim little feeling came curling up through my sleepy senses; I wondered for a second what it might be before I recognized it: it was Happiness, pure and immaterial; independent of affections and emotions, the aetherial essence of happiness, a delight so rare and so impersonal that it seems scarcely terrestrial when it comes.[12]

CHAPTER TWENTY-TWO

Homecomings

This last chapter is the shortest, for just as all departures are different, all homecomings are in a sense the same: there is the same relief that the journey has been satisfactorily and successfully completed – for, after all, one has at least got back alive; the same feeling of achievement, great or small; the same element of regret at the end of an adventure, carrying as it does the knowledge that one has said goodbye to people and places never, perhaps, to be seen again; and the same curiosity about what lies in store at home – the pile of waiting letters, the news of family and friends, the gossip, the scandals, the obituaries.

The first great homecoming in travel literature – for if *The Odyssey* is not a travel book, I don't know what is – is that of Odysseus' return to Ithaca, where for ten years his wife Penelope has been faithfully waiting:

Then to his wife said Odysseus of many wiles: 'Wife, we have not yet come to the end of all our trials, but still hereafter there is to be measureless toil, long and hard, which I must fulfil to the end. . . . But come, wife, let us to bed, that lulled now by sweet slumber we may take our joy of rest.'

Then wise Penelope answered him: 'Thy bed shall be ready for thee whensoever thy heart shall desire it, since the gods have indeed caused thee to come back to thy well-built house and thy native land. . . .'

Thus they spoke to one another; and meanwhile Eurynome and the nurse made ready the bed of soft coverlets by the light of blazing torches. But when they had busily spread the stout-built bedstead, the old nurse went back to her chamber to lie down, and Eurynome, the maiden of the bedchamber, led them on their way to the couch with a torch in her hands; and when she had led them to the bridal chamber, she went back. And they then gladly came to the place of the couch that was theirs of old. But Telemachus and the neatherd and the swineherd stayed their feet from dancing, and stayed the women, and themselves lay down to sleep throughout the shadowy halls.

But when the two had had their fill of the joy of love, they took delight in tales, speaking each to the other. She, the fair lady, told of all that she had endured in the halls, looking upon the destructive throng of the wooers, who for her sake slew many beasts, cattle and goodly sheep; and great store of wine was drawn from the jars. But Zeus-born Odysseus recounted all the woes that he had brought on men, and all the toil that in his sorrow he had himself endured, and she was glad to listen, nor did sweet sleep fall upon her eyelids, till he had told all the tale.

He began by telling how at the first he overcame the Cicones, and then came to the rich land of the Lotus-eaters, and all that the Cyclops wrought, and how he made him pay the price for his mighty comrades, whom the Cyclops had eaten, and had shown no pity. Then how he came to Aeolus, who received him with a ready heart, and sent him on his way; but it was not yet his fate to come to his dear native land, nay, the storm-wind caught him up again, and bore him over the teeming deep, groaning heavily. Next how he came to Telepylus of the Laestrygonians, who destroyed his ships and his well-greaved comrades one and all, and Odysseus alone escaped in his black ship. Then he told of all the wiles and craftiness of Circe, and how in his benched ship he had gone to the dank house of Hades to consult the spirit of Theban Teiresias, and had seen all his comrades and the mother who bore him and nursed him, when a child. And how he heard the voice of the Sirens, who sing unceasingly, and had come to the Wandering Rocks, and to dread Charybdis, and to Scylla, from whom never yet had men escaped unscathed. Then how his comrades slew the kine of Helios, and how Zeus, who thunders on high, smote his swift ship with a flaming thunderbolt, and his goodly comrades perished all together, while he alone escaped the evil fates. And how he came to the isle Ogygia and to the nymph Calypso, who kept him there in her hollow caves, yearning that he should be her husband, and tended him, and said that she would make him immortal and ageless all his days; yet she could never persuade the heart in his breast. Then how he came after many toils to the Phaeacians, who heartily showed him all honour, as if he were a god, and sent him in a ship to his dear native land, after giving him stores of bronze and gold and raiment. This was the end of the tale he told, when sweet sleep, that loosens the limbs of men, leapt upon him, loosening the cares of his heart.[1]

A classic of a different kind – and I suspect, incidentally, the greatest passage of English prose ever written by a foreigner – is from Joseph Conrad's *The Nigger of the 'Narcissus'*:

A week afterwards the *Narcissus* entered the chops of the Channel.

Under white wings she skimmed low over the blue sea like a great tired bird speeding to its nest. The clouds raced with her mastheads; they rose astern enormous and white, soared to the zenith, flew past, and, falling down the wide curve of the sky, seemed to dash headlong into the sea – the clouds swifter than the ship, more free, but without a home. The coast to welcome her stepped out of space into the sunshine. The lofty headlands trod masterfully into the sea; the wide bays smiled in the light; the shadows of homeless clouds ran along the sunny plains, leaped over valleys, without a check darted up the hills, rolled down the slopes; and the sunshine pursued them with patches of running brightness. On the brows of dark cliffs white lighthouses shone in pillars of light. The Channel glittered like a blue mantle shot with gold and starred by the silver of the capping seas. The *Narcissus* rushed past the headlands and the bays. Outward-bound vessels crossed her track, lying over, and with their masts stripped for a slogging fight with the hard sou'wester. And, inshore, a string of smoking steamboats waddled, hugging the coast, like migrating and amphibious monsters, distrustful of the restless waves.

At night the headlands retreated, the bays advanced into one unbroken line of gloom. The lights of the earth mingled with the lights of heaven; and above the tossing lanterns of a trawling fleet a great lighthouse shone steadily, like an enormous riding light burning above a vessel of fabulous dimensions. Below its steady glow, the coast, stretching away straight and black, resembled the high side of an indestructible craft riding motionless upon the immortal and unresting sea. The dark land lay alone in the midst of waters, like a mighty ship bestarred with vigilant lights – a ship carrying the burden of millions of lives – a ship freighted with dross and with jewels, with gold and with steel. She towered up immense and strong, guarding priceless traditions and untold suffering, sheltering glorious memories and base forgetfulness, ignoble virtues and splendid transgressions. A great ship! For ages had the ocean battered in vain her enduring sides; she was there when the world was vaster and darker, when the sea was great and mysterious, and ready to surrender the prize of fame to audacious men. A ship mother of fleets and nations! The great flagship of the race; stronger than the storms! and anchored in the open sea.

The *Narcissus*, heeling over to off-shore gusts, rounded the South Foreland, passed through the Downs, and, in tow, entered the river. Shorn of the glory of her white wings, she wound obediently after the tug through the maze of invisible channels. As she passed them the red-painted light-vessels, swung at their moorings, seemed for an instant to sail with great speed in the rush of tide, and the next moment were left hopelessly behind. The big buoys on the tails of banks slipped past her sides very low, and, dropping in her wake, tugged at their chains like fierce watchdogs. The reach narrowed; from both sides the land approached the ship. She went steadily up the river. On the riverside slopes the houses appeared in groups – seemed to stream down the declivities at a run to see her pass, and, checked by the mud of the foreshore, crowded on the banks. Farther on, the tall factory chimneys appeared in insolent bands and watched her go by, like a straggling crowd of slim giants, swaggering and upright under the black plummets of smoke, cavalierly aslant. She swept round the bends; an impure breeze shrieked a welcome between her stripped spars; and the land, closing in, stepped between the ship and the sea.

A low cloud hung before her – a great opalescent and tremulous cloud, that seemed to rise from the steaming brows of millions of men. Long drifts of smoky vapours soiled it with livid trails; it throbbed to the beat of millions of hearts, and from it came an immense and lamentable murmur – the murmur of millions of lips praying, cursing, sighing, jeering – the undying murmur of folly, regret, and hope exhaled by the crowds of the anxious earth. The *Narcissus* entered the cloud; the shadows deepened; on all sides there was the clang of iron, the sound of mighty blows, shrieks, yells. Black barges drifted stealthily on the murky stream. A mad jumble of begrimed walls loomed up vaguely in the smoke, bewildering and mournful, like a vision of disaster. The tugs backed and filled in the stream, to hold the ship steady at the dock gates; from her bows two lines went through the air whistling, and struck at the land viciously, like a pair of snakes. A bridge broke in two before her, as if by enchantment; big hydraulic capstans began to turn all by themselves, as though animated by a mysterious and unholy spell. She moved through a narrow lane of water between two low walls of granite, and men with check-ropes in their hands kept pace with her, walking on the broad flagstones. A group waited impatiently on each side of the vanished bridge: rough heavy men in caps; sallow-faced men in high hats; two bareheaded women; ragged children, fascinated, and with wide eyes. A cart coming at a jerky trot pulled up sharply. One of the women screamed at the silent ship – 'Hallo, Jack!' without looking at any one in particular, and all hands looked at her from the forecastle head. – 'Stand clear! Stand clear of that rope!' cried the dockmen, bending over stone posts. The crowd murmured, stamped where they stood. – 'Let go your quarter-checks! Let go!' sang out a ruddy-faced old man on the quay. The ropes splashed heavily falling in the water, and the *Narcissus* entered the dock.

The stony shores ran away right and left in straight lines, enclosing a sombre and rectangular pool. Brick walls rose high above the water – soulless walls, staring through hundreds of windows as troubled and dull as the eyes of over-fed brutes. At their base monstrous iron cranes crouched, with chains hanging from their long necks, balancing cruel-looking hooks over the decks of lifeless ships. A noise of wheels rolling over stones, the thump of heavy things falling, the racket of feverish winches, the grinding of strained chains, floated on the air. Between high buildings the dust of all the continents soared in short flights; and a penetrating smell of per-fumes and dirt, of spices and hides, of things costly and of things filthy, pervaded the space, made for it an atmosphere precious and disgusting. The *Narcissus* came gently into her berth; the shadows of soulless walls fell upon her, the dust of all the continents leaped upon her deck, and a swarm of strange men, clambering up her sides, took possession of her in the name of the sordid earth. She had ceased to live.[2]

As a sort of epilogue, let me quote the ending of the *Rare Adventures and Painfull Peregrinations* of our old friend William Lithgow – retaining, of course, the original layout:

And now to conclude, as a Painter, may spoyle a Picture, but not the face; so may some Reader misconceave
some parts of this eye-set History, though not able to
marre the trueth of it: yet howsoever, here is the just
relation of nineteene yeares travells, perfited in three
deare-bought voyages: The general computation of which
spaces, in my goings, traversings, and returnings,
through Kingdomes, Continents, and Ilands, which
my paynefull feet traced over (besides my passages of Seas and Rivers) amounteth to
thirty six thousand and odde miles,
which draweth neare to twice
the circumference of the
whole Earth. And so
farewell.[3]

FINIS

Bibliography

Chapter One: Advice to Travellers

1 Francis Bacon, 'Of Travel', in *Essays or Counsels Civill and Morall*,1625.
2 Eric Newby, *Slowly Down the Ganges*, Hodder & Stoughton, 1966.
3 Isabella Bird, *Unbeaten Tracks in Japan*, John Murray, 1880.
4 Freya Stark, *Hints for Travellers*, Royal Geographical Society, 1938.
5 *Murray's Handbook for Northern Europe*, John Murray, 1849.
6 Francis Galton, *The Art of Travel; or, Shifts and Contrivances Available in Wild Countries*, 1872.
7 Freya Stark, *Baghdad Sketches*, The Times Press, 1932.
8 Dr K. Baedeker, *Switzerland*, 1899.
9 Redmond O'Hanlon, *Into the Heart of Borneo*, The Salamander Press, 1984.
10 Ibid.
11 Baedeker, *Switzerland*.
12 Dr K. Baedeker, *Palestine and Syria*, 1906.
13 Ibid.
14 Ibid.
15 Ibid.
16 Dr K. Baedeker, *Egypt*, 1878.
17 J. G. Hava, *Arabic–English Dictionary*, Kegan Paul, 1962.
18 Noël Coward, *Collected Lyrics*, William Heinemann, 1965.
19 *Conversational Italian*, G. Alfano.
20 *Hossfeld's New Practical Method for Learning the Spanish Language*, 1885.
21 *Hossfeld's New Practical Method for Learning the Russian Language*, 1903.
22 A Gentleman of Experience, *A Guide to the Native Languages of Africa*, 1890.
23 A Gentleman of Quality, *French for the English*, 1894.
24 Coward, *Collected Lyrics*.
25 Mansfield Parkyns, *Life in Abyssinia*, John Murray, 1868.
26 Charles Waterton, *Wanderings in South America*, Macmillan, 1878.
27 Leaflet enclosed with Dr J. Collis Browne's Chlorodyne.
28 William Dampier, *A New Voyage Round the World*, 1697.
29 Galton, *The Art of Travel*.
30 Freya Stark, *A Winter in Arabia, 1937–8*, John Murray, 1949.
31 C. M. Doughty, *Travels in Arabia Deserta*, 1888.
32 *Información Guadalajara: aeropuerto internacional* (leaflet; no date).
33 Osbert Lancaster, *Classical Landscape with Figures*, John Murray, 1947.
34 William Kitchiner, MD, *The Traveller's Oracle, or Maxims for Locomotion*, 1827.

Chapter Two: Motivations

1 C. M. Doughty, *Travels in Arabia Deserta*, 1888.

2 Noël Coward, *Collected Lyrics*, William Heinemann, 1965.
3 *An Itinerary Written by Fynes Moryson, Gent.*, 1617 (1907 edn, James Maclehose & Sons).
4 Mungo Park, *Travels in the Interior Districts of Africa*, 1799.
5 Mary Kingsley, *Travels in West Africa*, Macmillan & Co., 1897.
6 Freya Stark, *The Coast of Incense*, John Murray, 1953.
7 Peter Levi, *The Light Garden of the Angel King*, William Collins, 1972.
8 Bruce Chatwin, *In Patagonia*, Jonathan Cape, 1977.
9 Eric Newby, *Slowly Down the Ganges*, Hodder & Stoughton, 1966.
10 Wilfred Thesiger, *Arabian Sands*, Longmans, Green, 1959.
11 Ibid.
12 Hilaire Belloc, *The Path to Rome*, Thomas Nelson, 1902.
13 Fred Burnaby, *A Ride to Khiva*, Cassell, Petter & Galpin, 1877.
14 Amelia B. Edwards, *A Thousand Miles Up the Nile*, Longmans, 1877.
15 John Foster Fraser, *Round the World on a Wheel*, Methuen, 1899.
16 J. R. Ackerley, *Hindoo Holiday*, Chatto & Windus, 1932.
17 Peter Fleming, *Brazilian Adventure*, Jonathan Cape, 1933.
18 *Rudyard Kipling's Verse, The Definitive Edition*, Hodder & Stoughton, 1940.

Chapter Three: Beginnings

1 *The Gentleman's Guide in his Tour through France*, 1770, title listed in the second volume of S. Halkett and J. Laing, *Dictionary of Anonymous and Pseudonymous English Literature*, 3rd rev. edn, ed. J. Horden, Longman, 1980.
2 Colonel Angus Buchanan, *Sahara*, John Murray, 1926.
3 Geoffrey Chaucer, *The Canterbury Tales*, tr. Nevill Coghill, Penguin Books, 1951.
4 Marco Polo, *The Travels of Marco Polo*, ed. and tr. R. E. Latham, Penguin Books, 1982.
5 Victoria Sackville-West, *Twelve Days*, Hogarth Press, 1928.
6 James Morris, *The Presence of Spain*, Faber & Faber, 1964.
7 Jonathan Raban, *Old Glory*, William Collins, 1981.
8 Charles Dickens, *American Notes*, Chapman & Hall, 1898.
9 Sybille Bedford, *A Visit to Don Otavio*, William Collins, 1960 (first published as *The Sudden View*, Victor Gollancz, 1953).
10 Gavin Maxwell, *A Reed Shaken by the Wind*, Longmans, Green, 1957.
11 Evelyn Waugh, *Waugh in Abyssinia*, Longmans, Green, 1935 (partially reprinted in *When the Going Was Good*, Duckworth, 1946).
12 Patrick Leigh Fermor, *A Time of Gifts*, John Murray, 1977.

Chapter Four: Departures

1 Dr K. Baedeker, *Traveller's Manual*, 1886.
2 Fred Burnaby, *A Ride to Khiva*, Cassell, Petter & Galpin, 1877.
3 Evelyn Waugh, *Scoop*, Chapman & Hall, 1938.
4 Joshua Slocum, *Sailing Alone Around the World*, 1900.
5 Peter Fleming, *One's Company*, Jonathan Cape, 1934.
6 Robert Byron, *The Station*, Duckworth, 1931.
7 Robert Byron, *The Road to Oxiana*, Macmillan, 1937.
8 Alexander Kinglake, *Eothen*, 1844.
9 Eliot Warburton, *The Crescent and the Cross*, Henry Colburn, 1845.

10 Edward Lear, *Journal of a Landscape Painter in Corsica*, 1851 (1965 edn, Kimber).
11 John Foster Fraser, *Round the World on a Wheel*, Methuen, 1899.
12 Robert Louis Stevenson, *Across the Plains*, 1892.
13 *Flaubert in Egypt*, selected and tr. Francis Steegmuller, The Bodley Head, 1972.
14 Lawrence Durrell, *Bitter Lemons*, Faber & Faber, 1957.
15 Laurie Lee, *As I Walked Out One Midsummer Morning*, André Deutsch, 1969.
16 James Elroy Flecker, *Hassan*, 1922 (1951 edn, William Heinemann).
17 Flecker, *Hassan* manuscript, Fitzwilliam Museum, Cambridge.

Chapter Five: First Impressions

1 Henry James, *English Hours*, 1888.
2 Catherine Wilmot, *An Irish Peer on the Continent, 1801–1803*, Williams & Norgate, 1920.
3 Hilaire Belloc, *The Path to Rome*, Thomas Nelson, 1902.
4 Evelyn Waugh, *Labels*, Duckworth, 1929 (partially reprinted in *When the Going Was Good*, Duckworth, 1946).
5 Patty Wilkinson's diary, quoted in Thomas Campbell, *The Life of Mrs Siddons*, Vol. II, 1834.
6 Charles Dickens, *Pictures from Italy*, 1846.
7 Ibid.
8 Anon, 'A Fashionable New Yorker Abroad', in *Nothing To Do: A Tilt at Our Best Society*, Boston, 1857 (quoted in *A Literary Companion to Travel in Greece*, ed. Richard Stoneman, Penguin Books, 1984).
9 Mark Twain, *A Tramp Abroad*, 1880.
10 Graham Greene, *Journey Without Maps*, The Bodley Head, 1936.
11 Ibid.
12 Eliot Warburton, *The Crescent and the Cross*, Henry Colburn, 1845.
13 Sir Richard F. Burton, *Personal Narrative of a Pilgrimage to Al-Madinah and Meccah*, Longman & Co., 1855–6.
14 Harriet Martineau, *Eastern Life, Present and Past*, 1848.
15 Freya Stark, *Letters from Syria, 1927–8*, John Murray, 1942.
16 Robert Curzon, *Visits to Monasteries in the Levant*, John Murray, 1849.
17 Robert Byron, *The Road to Oxiana*, Macmillan, 1937.
18 Robert Byron, *First Russia Then Tibet*, Macmillan, 1933.
19 Anne, Lady Wilson, *Letters from India*, William Blackwood, 1911.
20 Lafcadio Hearn, *Glimpses of Unfamiliar Japan*, 1894 (partially reprinted in *Writings from Japan*, selected by Francis King, Penguin Books, 1984).
21 Bernal Díaz del Castillo, *The True History of the Conquest of New Spain*, 1632 (1963 edn, Penguin Books).
22 Sir Charles Johnston, 'Air Travel in Arabia', in *Poems and Journeys*, The Bodley Head for Sir Charles Johnston, 1979.

Chapter Six: Modes of Travel

1 Carl Philip Moritz, *Travels, Chiefly on Foot, Through Several Parts of England in 1782, Described in Letters to a Friend*, 1795.
2 Frances Ann Kemble, *Record of a Girlhood*, Vol. II, 1878.
3 Hamilton Ellis, *Nineteenth Century Railway Carriages*, Transport Publishing Co., 1949.

4 Robert Louis Stevenson, *Across the Plains*, 1892.
5 Peter Fleming, *One's Company*, Jonathan Cape, 1934.
6 Fred Burnaby, *A Ride to Khiva*, Cassell, Petter & Galpin, 1877.
7 *Murray's Handbook for Northern Europe*, John Murray, 1849.
8 M. Huc, *Travels in Tartary, Thibet and China*, tr. William Hazlitt, 1852.
9 *The Letters of Horace Walpole*, ed. Peter Cunningham, 1891.
10 Eliza Fay, *Original Letters from India, 1779–1815*, Hogarth Press, 1925.
11 Amelia B. Edwards, *A Thousand Miles Up the Nile*, Longmans, 1877.
12 Alexander Kinglake, *Eothen*, 1844.
13 Isabella Bird, *The Golden Chersonese*, John Murray, 1883.
14 Freya Stark, *Beyond Euphrates*, John Murray, 1951.
15 Peter Fleming, *Brazilian Adventure*, Jonathan Cape, 1933.
16 Robert Curzon, *Visits to Monasteries in the Levant*, John Murray, 1849.
17 Ibid.
18 Sir Henry Layard, *Early Adventures in Persia, Susiana and Babylon*, John Murray, 1887.
19 Martha Gellhorn, *Travels with Myself and Another*, Allen Lane, 1978.
20 Mark Twain, *A Tramp Abroad*, 1880.
21 Gavin Young, *Slow Boats to China*, Hutchinson, 1981.
22 Dr K. Baedeker, *Traveller's Manual*, 1886.
23 Philip Magnus, *King Edward the Seventh*, John Murray, 1964.

Chapter Seven: Journeys

1 Palinurus (Cyril Connolly), *The Unquiet Grave*, The Curwen Press, for *Horizon*, 1944.
2 Lady Diana Cooper, *The Light of Common Day*, Rupert Hart-Davis, 1959.
3 William Morris, *Journals of Travel in Iceland*, Clarendon Press, 1969.
4 Sir Ronald Storrs, *Orientations*, Nicholson & Watson, 1937.
5 *The Letters of Oscar Wilde*, ed. Rupert Hart-Davis, Rupert Hart-Davis, 1962.

Chapter Eight: Architecture

1 *The Illustrated Journeys of Celia Fiennes, 1685–1703*, ed. Christopher Morris, Macdonald, 1982.
2 Charles Macomb Flandrau, *Viva Mexico!*, D. Appleton, 1908 (1982 edn, Eland Books).
3 John Ruskin, *The Stones of Venice*, 1851–3.
4 *The Letters of Horace Walpole*, ed. Peter Cunningham, 1891.
5 J. W. von Goethe, *Italian Journey*, tr. W. H. Auden and Elizabeth Mayer, William Collins, 1962.
6 Ibid.
7 Patrick Leigh Fermor, *The Traveller's Tree*, John Murray, 1951.
8 Robert Byron, *The Road to Oxiana*, Macmillan, 1937.
9 Maurice Rowdon, *The Companion Guide to Umbria*, William Collins, 1969.
10 Lady Diana Cooper, *Trumpets from the Steep*, Rupert Hart-Davis, 1960.

Chapter Nine: Nature

1 *The Letters of Horace Walpole*, ed. Peter Cunningham, 1891.
2 Lafcadio Hearn, *Glimpses of Unfamiliar Japan*, 1894 (partially reprinted in *Writings from Japan*, selected by Francis King, Penguin Books, 1984).

3 Robert Byron, *The Station*, Duckworth, 1931.
4 Charles Dickens, *Pictures from Italy*, 1846.
5 Edward Lear, *A Leaf from the Journals of a Landscape Painter*, Arthur Barker, 1952.
6 Rupert Brooke, *Letters from America*, Sidgwick & Jackson, 1916.
7 Catherine Wilmot, *The Russian Journals of Martha and Catherine Wilmot, 1803–1808*, ed. Marchioness of Londonderry and H. M. Hyde, Macmillan, 1934.
8 John Ruskin, *Praeterita*, George Allen, 1885–9.
9 *Flaubert in Egypt*, selected and tr. Francis Steegmuller, The Bodley Head, 1972.
10 Mary Kingsley, *Travels in West Africa*, Macmillan & Co., 1897.
11 Mildred Cable and Francesca French, *The Gobi Desert*, Hodder & Stoughton, 1943.

Chapter Ten: Towns, Islands and Other Places

1 *An Itinerary Written by Fynes Moryson, Gent.*, 1617 (1907 edn, James Maclehose & Sons).
2 Ibid.
3 Thomas Coryat, *Coryat's Crudities*, 1611 (1905 edn, James Maclehose & Sons).
4 Freya Stark, *Ionia*, John Murray, 1954.
5 Evelyn Waugh, *Labels*, Duckworth, 1929 (partially reprinted in *When the Going Was Good*, Duckworth, 1946).
6 Peter Fleming, *One's Company*, Jonathan Cape, 1934.
7 Mildred Cable and Francesca French, *The Gobi Desert*, Hodder & Stoughton, 1943.
8 Henry James, *A Little Tour in France*, 1884.
9 Mary McCarthy, *Venice Observed*, Zwemmer, 1956.
10 John Ruskin, *The Stones of Venice*, 1851–3.
11 Lawrence Durrell, *Reflections on a Marine Venus*, Faber & Faber, 1953.
12 Henry Miller, *The Colossus of Maroussi*, William Heinemann, 1941 (1950 edn, Penguin Books).
13 Mark Twain, *The Innocents Abroad*, 1869.
14 Peter Fleming, *Brazilian Adventure*, Jonathan Cape, 1933.
15 Georg Christoph Lichtenberg, *Lichtenberg's Visits to England*, tr. and annotated by Margaret L. Mare and W. H. Quarrell, Clarendon Press, 1938.

Chapter Eleven: Characters and Social Intercourse

1 Charles Macomb Flandrau, *Viva Mexico!*, D. Appleton, 1908 (1982 edn, Eland Books).
2 Bruce Chatwin, *In Patagonia*, Jonathan Cape, 1977.
3 Peter Fleming, *One's Company*, Jonathan Cape, 1934.
4 John Julius Norwich, *Sahara*, Longman, 1968.
5 Colin Thubron, *Jerusalem*, William Heinemann, 1969.
6 Robert Byron, *The Station*, Duckworth, 1931.
7 John Carne, *Letters from the East*, Henry Colburn, 1826.
8 Hilaire Belloc, 'The Modern Traveller', in *Collected Poems*, ed. W. N. Roughead, Nonsuch Press, 1954.
9 Mildred Cable and Francesca French, *The Gobi Desert*, Hodder & Stoughton, 1943.
10 Lady Mary Wortley Montagu, *Letters*, 1763.
11 Lucie Duff Gordon, *Letters from the Cape*, 1864 and 1875.
12 Peter Mayne, *A Year in Marrakesh*, John Murray, 1953.
13 Alexander Kinglake, *Eothen*, 1844.
14 Norman Lewis, *A Dragon Apparent*, Jonathan Cape, 1951.

Chapter Twelve: Travelling Companions

1 Geoffrey Chaucer, *The Canterbury Tales*, tr. Nevill Coghill, Penguin Books, 1951.
2 William Lithgow, *Rare Adventures and Painfull Peregrinations*, 1632.
3 Eliza Fay, *Original Letters from India, 1779–1815*, Hogarth Press, 1925.
4 Rev. Francis Kilvert, *Kilvert's Diary*, ed. William Plomer, Jonathan Cape, 1938–40.
5 Maurice Baring, *What I Saw in Russia*, William Heinemann, 1927.
6 Paul Theroux, *The Great Railway Bazaar*, Hamish Hamilton, 1975.
7 Eric Newby, *Slowly Down the Ganges*, Hodder & Stoughton, 1966.
8 Martha Gellhorn, *Travels with Myself and Another*, Allen Lane, 1978.
9 Captain Philip Thicknesse, *A Year's Journey Through France and Part of Spain*, 1777.
10 Eric Newby, *A Short Walk in the Hindu Kush*, Martin Secker & Warburg, 1958.

Chapter Thirteen: Hardships

1 William Lithgow, *Rare Adventures and Painfull Peregrinations*, 1632.
2 Thomas Coryat, *Coryat's Crudities*, 1611 (1905 edn, James Maclehose & Sons).
3 Captain John Stedman, *Expedition to Surinam*, J. Johnson, 1796.
4 Ibid.
5 Alexander Kinglake, *Eothen*, 1844.
6 Robert Curzon, *Visits to Monasteries in the Levant*, John Murray, 1849.
7 Isabella Bird, *Unbeaten Tracks in Japan*, John Murray, 1880.
8 Mungo Park, *Journal*, published posthumously.
9 Dervla Murphy, *Full Tilt*, John Murray, 1965.
10 Wilfred Thesiger, *Arabian Sands*, Longmans, Green, 1959.
11 Fred Burnaby, *A Ride to Khiva*, Cassell, Petter & Galpin, 1877.
12 Thesiger, *Arabian Sands*.
13 Nigel Ryan, *A Hitch or Two in Afghanistan*, Weidenfeld & Nicolson, 1983.
14 Robert Byron, *The Road to Oxiana*, Macmillan, 1937.

Chapter Fourteen: Health and Hygiene

1 Queen Victoria, *Leaves from the Journal of Our Life in the Highlands*, Smith, Elder, 1868.
2 Tobias Smollett, *Travels Through France and Italy*, 1766.
3 *Murray's Handbook*, John Murray, 1847.
4 *Murray's Handbook for Northern Europe*, John Murray, 1849.
5 Lady Mary Wortley Montagu, *Letters*, 1763.
6 Hilaire Belloc, 'The Modern Traveller', in *Collected Poems*, ed. W. N. Roughead, Nonsuch Press, 1954.
7 Freya Stark, *The Southern Gates of Arabia*, John Murray, 1936.
8 *An Itinerary Written by Fynes Moryson, Gent.*, 1617 (1907 edn, James Maclehose & Sons).
9 Charles Waterton, *Wanderings in South America*, Macmillan, 1878.
10 Freya Stark, *A Winter in Arabia, 1937–8*, John Murray, 1949.
11 Penelope Chetwode, *Two Middle-Aged Ladies in Andalusia*, John Murray, 1963.
12 Mary Kingsley, *Travels in West Africa*, Macmillan & Co., 1897.

13 Montagu, *Letters.*
14 Eliot Warburton, *The Crescent and the Cross*, Henry Colburn, 1845.
15 Richard Ford, *Gatherings from Spain*, John Murray, 1861.
16 John Julius Norwich, *Mount Athos*, Hutchinson, 1966.

Chapter Fifteen: Animals

1 Niels Horrebow, *The Natural History of Iceland*, 1758.
2 Herodotus, *History*, Book Two.
3 Lucie Duff Gordon, *Letters from Egypt*, 1865.
4 Herodotus, Book Two.
5 Henry Walter Bates, *The Naturalist on the River Amazons*, John Murray, 1892.
6 Patrick Leigh Fermor, *Mani*, John Murray, 1958.
7 Arthur Grimble, *A Pattern of Islands*, John Murray, 1952.
8 Martha Gellhorn, *Travels with Myself and Another*, Allen Lane, 1978.
9 Duff Gordon, *Letters from Egypt.*
10 Richard Ford, *Gatherings from Spain*, John Murray, 1861.
11 Evelyn Waugh, *Ninety-two Days*, Duckworth, 1934 (partially reprinted in *When the Going Was Good*, Duckworth, 1946).
12 Colonel Angus Buchanan, *Sahara*, John Murray, 1926.
13 Peter Fleming, *Brazilian Adventure*, Jonathan Cape, 1933.
14 Osbert Sitwell, *Escape with Me!*, Macmillan, 1939.
15 Richard Hakluyt, *The Principal Navigations, Voyages, Traffiques and Discoveries of the English Nation*, 1589, ed. Jack Beeching, Penguin Books, 1982.
16 Ibid.
17 Isabella Bird, *The Golden Chersonese*, John Murray, 1883.
18 Gavin Maxwell, *A Reed Shaken by the Wind*, Longmans, Green, 1957.
19 Madame Calderón de la Barca, *Life in Mexico*, Chapman & Hall, 1843.
20 Captain John Stedman, *Expedition to Surinam*, 1796.
21 James Morris, *Venice*, Faber & Faber, 1960.
22 Henry Miller, *The Colossus of Maroussi*, William Heinemann, 1941 (1950 edn, Penguin Books).
23 Leigh Fermor, *Mani.*

Chapter Sixteen: Customs of the Country

1 Herodotus, Book Two.
2 *The Letters of Horace Walpole*, ed. Peter Cunningham, 1891.
3 Richard Ford, *Gatherings from Spain*, John Murray, 1861.
4 Mark Twain, *A Tramp Abroad*, 1880.
5 Patrick Leigh Fermor, *A Time of Gifts*, John Murray, 1977.
6 Catherine Wilmot, *An Irish Peer on the Continent, 1801–1803*, Williams & Norgate, 1920.
7 Lady Mary Wortley Montagu, *Letters*, 1763.
8 Harriet Martineau, *Eastern Life, Present and Past*, 1848.
9 John Carne, *Letters from the East*, Henry Colburn, 1826.
10 Ibid.
11 Lord Baltimore, *A Tour to the East*, 1767.
12 Eliot Warburton, *The Crescent and the Cross*, Henry Colburn, 1845.
13 Sir Ronald Storrs, *Orientations*, Nicholson & Watson, 1937.

14 Catherine Wilmot, *The Russian Journals of Martha and Catherine Wilmot, 1803–1808*, ed. Marchioness of Londonderry and H. M. Hyde, Macmillan, 1934.

15 Arminius Vámbéry, *Travels in Central Asia*, John Murray, 1865.

16 Jonathan Raban, *Arabia Through the Looking Glass*, William Collins, 1979.

17 Mary Kingsley, *Travels in West Africa*, Macmillan & Co., 1897.

18 Robert Byron, *First Russia Then Tibet*, Macmillan, 1933.

19 E. M. Forster, *The Hill of Devi*, Edward Arnold, 1953.

20 Ibn Battuta, *Travels in Asia and Africa, 1325–54*, tr. and selected by H.A.R. Gibb, George Routledge & Sons, 1929.

21 Richard Hakluyt, *The Principal Navigations, Voyages, Traffiques and Discoveries of the English Nation*, 1589, ed. Jack Beeching, Penguin Books, 1982.

22 Alexandra David-Neel, *My Journey to Lhasa*, William Heinemann, 1927.

23 Norman Lewis, *A Dragon Apparent*, Jonathan Cape, 1951.

24 William Dampier, *A New Voyage Round the World*, 1697.

25 Captain John Stedman, *Expedition to Surinam*, J. Johnson, 1796.

26 Bernal Díaz de Castillo, *History of the Conquest of New Spain*, 1842 (1963 edn, Penguin Books).

27 Charles Macomb Flandrau, *Viva Mexico!*, D. Appleton, 1908 (1982 edn, Eland Books).

28 Charles Dickens, *American Notes*, 1842.

29 Daniel Defoe, *Tour Thro' the Whole Island of Great Britain*, 3 vols, 1724–6.

Chapter Seventeen: Dress

1 Tobias Smollett, *Travels Through France and Italy*, 1766.

2 Captain Philip Thicknesse, *A Year's Journey Through France and Part of Spain*, 1777.

3 Rose Macaulay, *Fabled Shore*, Hamish Hamilton, 1949.

4 Lady Mary Wortley Montagu, *Letters*, 1763.

5 Amelia B. Edwards, *A Thousand Miles Up the Nile*, Longmans, 1877.

6 M. Huc, *Travels in Tartary, Thibet and China*, tr. William Hazlitt, 1852.

7 Henry Walter Bates, *The Naturalist on the River Amazons*, John Murray, 1892.

8 Isabella Bird, *The Golden Chersonese*, John Murray, 1883.

9 E. M. Forster, *The Hill of Devi*, Edward Arnold, 1953.

Chapter Eighteen: Cuisine

1 E. M. Forster, *The Hill of Devi*, Edward Arnold, 1953.

2 Captain Philip Thicknesse, *A Year's Journey Through France and Part of Spain*, 1777.

3 Tobias Smollett, *Travels Through France and Italy*, 1766.

4 Henry James, *A Little Tour in France*, 1884.

5 Sybille Bedford, *A Visit to Don Otavio*, William Collins, 1960 (first published as *The Sudden View*, Victor Gollancz, 1953).

6 Richard Ford, *Gatherings from Spain*, John Murray, 1861.

7 James Morris, *The Presence of Spain*, Faber & Faber, 1964.

8 Hilaire Belloc, 'The Modern Traveller', in *Collected Poems*, ed. W. N. Roughead, Nonsuch Press, 1954.

9 *An Itinerary Written by Fynes Moryson, Gent.*, 1617 (1907 edn, James Maclehose & Sons).

10 John Julius Norwich, *Mount Athos*, Hutchinson, 1966.

11 Robert Curzon, *Visits to Monasteries in the Levant*, John Murray, 1849.

12 Mark Twain, *The Innocents Abroad*, 1869.

13 M. A. Titmarsh (W. M. Thackeray), *Notes of a Journey from Cornhill to Grand Cairo*, Chapman & Hall, 1846.

14 Sir Richard F. Burton, *Personal Narrative of a Pilgrimage to Al-Madinah and Meccah*, Longman & Co., 1855–6.

15 Gavin Maxwell, *A Reed Shaken by the Wind*, Longmans, Green, 1957.

16 Wilfred Thesiger, *The Marsh Arabs*, Longmans, Greens, 1964.

17 Mansfield Parkyns, *Life in Abyssinia*, John Murray, 1868.

18 Ibid.

19 M. Huc, *Travels in Tartary, Thibet and China*, tr. William Hazlitt, 1852.

20 Alexandra David-Neel, *My Journey to Lhasa*, William Heinemann, 1927.

21 Peter Fleming, *One's Company*, Jonathan Cape, 1934.

22 W. H. Auden and Louis MacNeice, *Letters from Iceland*, Faber & Faber, 1937.

23 John Foster Fraser, *Round the World on a Wheel*, Methuen, 1899.

Chapter Nineteen: Bad Moments

1 *The Diary of Master Thomas Dallam, 1599-1600*, ed. J. Theodore Bent, Hakluyt Society, 1893.

2 Thomas Coryat, *Coryat's Crudities*, 1611 (1905 edn, James Maclehose & Sons).

3 William Lithgow, *Rare Adventures and Painfull Peregrinations*, 1632.

4 Ibid.

5 J. W. von Goethe, *Italian Journey*, tr. W. H. Auden and Elizabeth Mayer, William Collins, 1962.

6 Ibid.

7 Robert Curzon, *Visits to Monasteries in the Levant*, John Murray, 1849.

8 Robert Curzon, *Armenia*, John Murray, 1854.

9 Alexander Kinglake, *Eothen*, 1844.

10 Ibid.

11 Eliot Warburton, *The Crescent and the Cross*, Henry Colburn, 1845.

12 Edward Lear, *Journal of a Landscape Painter in Corsica*, 1851 (1965 edn, Kimber).

13 Mungo Park, *Travels in the Interior Districts of Africa*, 1799.

14 Mary Kingsley, *Travels in West Africa*, Macmillan & Co., 1897.

15 Ibid.

16 Amelia B. Edwards, *A Thousand Miles Up the Nile*, Longmans, 1877.

17 Augustus Hare, *The Story of My Life*, George Allen, 1900.

18 Captain Charles Johnson (Daniel Defoe?), *A General History of the Robberies and Murders of the Most Notorious Pyrates*, 1724.

19 Joshua Slocum, *Sailing Alone Around the World*, 1900.

20 Dervla Murphy, *Full Tilt*, John Murray, 1965.

21 Martha Gellhorn, *Travels with Myself and Another*, Allen Lane, 1978.

22 Sybille Bedford, *A Visit to Don Otavio*, William Collins, 1960 (first published as *The Sudden View*, Victor Gollancz, 1953).

23 Evelyn Waugh, *Remote People*, Duckworth, 1931 (partially reprinted in *When the Going Was Good*, Duckworth, 1946).

Chapter Twenty: Events and Entertainments

1 *The Diary of Master Thomas Dallam, 1599–1600*, ed. J. Theodore Bent, Hakluyt Society, 1893.
2 Charles Meryon, *Memoirs of the Lady Hester Stanhope*, 1845.
3 *The Letters of Horace Walpole*, ed. Peter Cunningham, 1891.
4 Carl Philip Moritz, *Journeys of a German in England*, 1795.
5 Catherine Wilmot, *The Russian Journals of Martha and Catherine Wilmot, 1803–1808*, ed. Marchioness of Londonderry and H. M. Hyde, Macmillan, 1934.
6 Maurice Baring, *The Puppet Show of Memory*, William Heinemann, 1922.
7 D. H. Lawrence, *Mornings in Mexico*, Martin Secker, 1927.
8 Norman Lewis, *The Changing Sky*, Jonathan Cape, 1959.
9 Geoffrey Gorer, *Africa Dances*, Faber & Faber, 1935.
10 Evelyn Waugh, *Labels*, Duckworth, 1929 (partially reprinted in *When the Going Was Good*, Duckworth, 1946).
11 Dervla Murphy, *Full Tilt*, John Murray, 1965.
12 Patrick Balfour, *Grand Tour*, John Long, 1934.
13 Laurie Lee, *As I Walked Out One Midsummer Morning*, André Deutsch, 1969.
14 Hilaire Belloc, 'The Moral Alphabet', in *Collected Poems*, ed. W. N. Roughead, Nonsuch Press, 1954.
15 John Julius Norwich, *Sahara*, Longman, 1968.
16 Redmond O'Hanlon, *Into the Heart of Borneo*, The Salamander Press, 1984.

Chapter Twenty-One: Euphoria

1 Freya Stark, *Alexander's Path*, John Murray, 1958.
2 Peter Fleming, *Brazilian Adventure*, Jonathan Cape, 1933.
3 Graham Greene, *Journey Without Maps*, The Bodley Head, 1936.
4 Sir Richard F. Burton, *Personal Narrative of a Pilgrimage to Al-Madinah and Meccah*, Longman & Co., 1855–6.
5 Ibid.
6 Isabella Bird, *A Lady's Life in the Rocky Mountains*, John Murray, 1879.
7 Rupert Brooke, *Letters from America*, Sidgwick & Jackson, 1916.
8 Robert Byron, *The Road to Oxiana*, Macmillan, 1937.
9 John Carne, *Letters from the East*, Henry Colburn, 1826.
10 Sylvia Plath, *Letters Home: Correspondence, 1950–63*, ed. Aurelia Schober Plath, Faber & Faber, 1976.
11 Eliot Warburton, *The Crescent and the Cross*, Henry Colburn, 1845.
12 Freya Stark, *The Southern Gates of Arabia*, John Murray, 1936.

Chapter Twenty-Two: Homecomings

1 Homer, *The Odyssey*, tr. A. T. Murray, William Heinemann, 1919.
2 Joseph Conrad, *The Nigger of the 'Narcissus'*, 1898.
3 William Lithgow, *Rare Adventures and Painfull Peregrinations*, 1632.

Index

Index

INDEX

A NOTE ON THE TYPE

The text of this book was set on the Linotron in a type face known as Stemple Garamond. The design is based on letter forms originally created by Claude Garamond (c.1480-1561). Garamond was a pupil of Geoffroy Tory and may have patterned his letter forms on Venetian models. To this day, the type face that bears his name is one of the most attractive used in book composition, and the intervening years have caused it to lose little of its freshness or beauty.

Composed by Filmtype Services, Limited,
Scarborough, North Yorkshire, England.
Printed and bound by Fairfield Graphics,
Fairfield, Pennsylvania.